becoming2008

THE COMPLETE NEW TESTAMENT

THOMAS NELSON
Since 1798

NASHVILLE DALLAS MEXICO CITY RIO DE JANEIRO BEIJING

www.thomasnelson.com

becoming2008

THE COMPLETE NEW TESTAMENT

Published in Nashville, TN, by Thomas Nelson. Thomas Nelson is a trademark of Thomas Nelson, Inc.

The preliminary research and development of the *New Century Version* was done by the World Bible Translation Center, Inc., Fort Worth, TX 76182.

Managing Editor: Margaret Oines

Cover Design: Emily Keafer, Anderson Thomas Design

Interior Design: Emily Keafer and Kristi Smith, Anderson Thomas Design

Cover Photography: Dean Dixon

Cover Model: Amber Lehman

Contributors: Valerie Gibbs, Janella Griggs, Whitney Hopler, Carrie Marrs, Erin Marshall, Margaret Oines, and Jennifer Hesse

Photos: Some interior photos ©2007 JupiterImages Corporation

Printed in The United States of America.
2 3 4 5 6 7 8 9 10 — 11 10 09 08

Letter from the Editors

SUNRISE IS ONE OF THE TENDEREST TIMES OF THE DAY.

Those who wake up early enough to experience it find both comfort and beauty as the first soft lights of day illuminate the horizon.

Sunrise is a welcome reminder of new beginnings. Even while we're sleeping, it echoes a message that God wants all of us to grasp: through him, all things can be made new. Nothing is beyond his redemption. He can illuminate the darkest of situations with his power, set us free from sin, and empower us to be the women he created us to be.

Becoming is about helping women experience a spiritual dawn. It's about taking a fresh look at God's Word and discovering how it instructs us to become more intimate followers of Jesus (God's Son).

Throughout the pages of *Becoming*, you'll find the entire New Testament in an easy-to-read version known as the New Century Version (NCV). As you read, you'll discover stories of Jesus and the way he lived, loved, and led others, and you'll learn of Jesus' followers who carried a life-changing message to the world.

Along the way, you'll find lots of articles, insights, and notes to help you understand more about God and the life he's calling you to live. Each book of the Bible opens with an **Introduction** that helps you understand the background, purpose, and intended audience, and **The Big Picture** closes each book, helping you to digest and dig deeper into what you've read.

In each book, you'll find helpful insights on scriptures known as **What's the Point?**, and you'll also find **Worldviews** sprinkled throughout to help you figure out how the Bible should shape the way you think about the world around you.

Life Issues and **Q&A** tackle some of the tough issues that women have to deal with, while **Health** and **Beauty Becomes Her** explore different aspects of both spiritual and physical beauty. **All About Men** helps you know what he's *really* thinking, and **Balancing Act** helps you discover how to hold it all together—mentally, emotionally, professionally, and spiritually.

Along the way, you'll find fun cooking tips in **Savvy Chef** and some reflective moments in our creative **Quizzes**. And you'll be challenged to try something new with our monthly **Calendars**!

The beauty of reading the Bible is that it reminds us of our need for God. Our hope and our prayer for you is that *Becoming* will make you want to know God better. As you read through the following pages, may the light of God arise on your heart and illuminate your path as you draw closer to him and his ways.

— THE EDITORS OF *BECOMING*

Table of Contents

The New Testament

Bible Reading Plan

All About Men

Balancing Act

Be Still & Know

Beauty Becomes Her

Become Involved

Big Picture

Book Reviews

Health

Life Issues

Modern Worship

Overcoming Fear

Q&A

Quizzes

Relationships

Savvy Chef

Virtue Building

Women & Men of the Bible

Worldviews

Calendars

A Note About the New Century Version

God never intended the Bible to be too difficult for his people. To make sure God's message was clear, the authors of the Bible recorded God's Word in familiar everyday language. These books brought a message that the original readers could understand. These first readers knew that God spoke through these books. Down through the centuries, many people wanted a Bible so badly that they copied different Bible books by hand!

Today, now that the Bible readily available, many Christians do not regularly read it. Many feel that the Bible is too hard to understand or irrelevant to life.

The New Century Version captures the clear and simple message that the very first readers understood. This version presents the Bible as God intended it: clear and dynamic.

A team of scholars from the World Bible Translation Center worked together with twenty-one other experienced Bible scholars from all over the world to translate the text directly from the best available Greek and Hebrew texts. You can trust that this Bible accurately presents God's Word as it came to us in the original languages.

Translators kept sentences short and simple. They avoided difficult words and worked to make the text easier to read. They used modern terms for places and measurements. And they put figures of speech and idiomatic expressions ("he was gathered to his people") in language that even children understand ("he died").

Following the tradition of other English versions, the New Century Version indicates the divine name, Yahweh, by putting LORD, and sometimes GOD, in capital letters. This distinguishes it from Adonai, another Hebrew word that is translated Lord.

We acknowledge the infallibility of God's Word and yet our own frailty. We pray that God will use this Bible to help you understand his rich truth for yourself. To God be the glory.

—THE PUBLISHER

THE NEW TESTAMENT

matthew

Most people who've ever had the opportunity to meet a movie star or professional athlete can't help but tell everyone about the experience. Matthew was no different! But instead of touting an autograph or sports jersey, he wrote about his experiences and encounters with Jesus.

And we're glad he did!

Matthew provides a rich account of the life of Jesus. While all the Gospels deal with the life of Christ, Matthew focuses on particular aspects of Jesus' mission and ministry. Entire chapters are devoted to the life-giving words that Jesus spoke during his time on earth. In addition, Matthew goes out of his way to prove that Jesus is the long-awaited Messiah described by the Jewish prophets in the Old Testament. He repeatedly points out how Jesus' life—from his humble birth in Bethlehem to his brutal crucifixion and subsequent resurrection—fulfilled Old Testament prophecy. To the original readers (who likely had Jewish backgrounds), Matthew shows that Jesus was the Messiah they were waiting for.

Matthew skillfully bridges the Old and New Testaments, showing that Christ truly fulfills the Law and the prophets. Yet in spite of its grand scope, Matthew's Gospel satisfies the simple desire to know Jesus.

The Family History of Jesus

1 This is the family history of Jesus Christ. He came from the family of David, and David came from the family of Abraham.

[2]Abraham was the father[n] of Isaac.
Isaac was the father of Jacob.
Jacob was the father of Judah and his brothers.
[3]Judah was the father of Perez and Zerah.
(Their mother was Tamar.)
Perez was the father of Hezron.
Hezron was the father of Ram.
[4]Ram was the father of Amminadab.
Amminadab was the father of Nahshon.
Nahshon was the father of Salmon.
[5]Salmon was the father of Boaz.
(Boaz's mother was Rahab.)
Boaz was the father of Obed.
(Obed's mother was Ruth.)
Obed was the father of Jesse.
[6]Jesse was the father of King David.
David was the father of Solomon.
(Solomon's mother had been Uriah's wife.)
[7]Solomon was the father of Rehoboam.
Rehoboam was the father of Abijah.
Abijah was the father of Asa.[n]
[8]Asa was the father of Jehoshaphat.
Jehoshaphat was the father of Jehoram.
Jehoram was the ancestor of Uzziah.
[9]Uzziah was the father of Jotham.
Jotham was the father of Ahaz.
Ahaz was the father of Hezekiah.
[10]Hezekiah was the father of Manasseh.
Manasseh was the father of Amon.
Amon was the father of Josiah.
[11]Josiah was the grandfather of Jehoiachin[n] and his brothers.
(This was at the time that the people were taken to Babylon.)

1:2 father "Father" in Jewish lists of ancestors can sometimes mean grandfather or more distant relative. **1:7 Asa** Some Greek copies read "Asaph," another name for Asa (see 1 Chronicles 3:10). **1:11 Jehoiachin** The Greek reads "Jeconiah," another name for Jehoiachin (see 2 Kings 24:6 and 1 Chronicles 3:16).

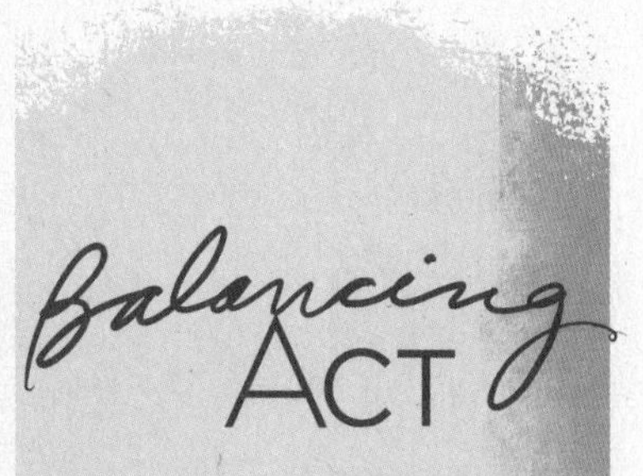

Rx: Take a Vacation

It starts with that feeling of dread as your alarm clock sounds. You're snappy with your friends and curt with co-workers. Maybe you're tired for no apparent reason. It's a classic case of burnout. The cure? A vacation! All work and no play is not what God had in mind for us. (See Matthew 11:28.) You may be refreshed with a few days of vegging on the couch, or you might prefer hiking in the mountains. Perhaps a fantasy sports camp or a short-term outreach is right for you. Do whatever restores your joy. A vacation is also the perfect time to take stock of your life. Are you burnt out because you've simply been working too hard—or are you unhappy with your career path? The answer to that question could be the key to preventing future burnout.

[12]After they were taken to Babylon:
Jehoiachin was the father of
Shealtiel.
Shealtiel was the grandfather of
Zerubbabel.
[13]Zerubbabel was the father of Abiud.
Abiud was the father of Eliakim.
Eliakim was the father of Azor.
[14]Azor was the father of Zadok.
Zadok was the father of Akim.
Akim was the father of Eliud.
[15]Eliud was the father of Eleazar.
Eleazar was the father of Matthan.
Matthan was the father of Jacob.
[16]Jacob was the father of Joseph.
Joseph was the husband of Mary,
and Mary was the mother of Jesus.
Jesus is called the Christ.

[17]So there were fourteen generations from Abraham to David. And there were fourteen generations from David until the people were taken to Babylon. And there were fourteen generations from the time when the people were taken to Babylon until Christ was born.

The Birth of Jesus Christ

[18]This is how the birth of Jesus Christ came about. His mother Mary was engaged[n] to marry Joseph, but before they married, she learned she was pregnant by the power of the Holy Spirit. [19]Because Mary's husband, Joseph, was a good man, he did not want to disgrace her in public, so he planned to divorce her secretly.

[20]While Joseph thought about these things, an angel of the Lord came to him in a dream. The angel said, "Joseph, descendant of David, don't be afraid to take Mary as your wife, because the baby in her is from the Holy Spirit. [21]She will give birth to a son, and you will name him Jesus,[n] because he will save his people from their sins."

[22]All this happened to bring about what the Lord had said through the prophet: [23]"The virgin will be pregnant. She will have a son, and they will name him Immanuel,"[n] which means "God is with us."

[24]When Joseph woke up, he did what the Lord's angel had told him to do. Joseph took Mary as his wife, [25]but he did not have sexual relations with her until she gave birth to the son. And Joseph named him Jesus.

Wise Men Come to Visit Jesus

2 Jesus was born in the town of Bethlehem in Judea during the time when Herod was king. When Jesus was born, some wise men from the east came to Jerusalem. [2]They asked, "Where is the baby who was born to be the king of the Jews? We saw his star in the east and have come to worship him."

[3]When King Herod heard this, he was troubled, as were all the people in Jerusalem. [4]Herod called a meeting of all the leading priests and teachers of the law and asked them where the Christ would be born. [5]They answered, "In the town of Bethlehem in Judea. The prophet wrote about this in the Scriptures:

[6]'But you, Bethlehem, in the land of
Judah,
are not just an insignificant
village in Judah.
A ruler will come from you
who will be like a shepherd for
my people Israel.' " *Micah 5:2*

[7]Then Herod had a secret meeting with the wise men and learned from them the exact time they first saw the star. [8]He sent the wise men to Bethlehem, saying, "Look carefully for the child. When you find him, come tell me so I can worship him too."

[9]After the wise men heard the king, they left. The star that they had seen in the east went before them until it stopped above the place where the child was. [10]When the wise men saw the star, they were filled with joy. [11]They came to the house where the child was and saw him with his mother, Mary, and they bowed down and worshiped him. They opened their gifts and gave him treasures of gold, frankincense, and myrrh. [12]But God warned the wise men in a dream not to go back to Herod, so they returned to their own country by a different way.

Jesus' Parents Take Him to Egypt

[13]After they left, an angel of the Lord came to Joseph in a dream and said, "Get up! Take the child and his mother and escape to Egypt, because Herod is starting to look for the child so he can kill him. Stay in Egypt until I tell you to return."

[14]So Joseph got up and left for Egypt

1:18 engaged For the Jewish people an engagement was a lasting agreement, which could only be broken by a divorce. If a bride-to-be was unfaithful, it was considered adultery, and she could be put to death. **1:21 Jesus** The name "Jesus" means "salvation." **1:23 "The virgin . . . Immanuel"** Quotation from Isaiah 7:14.

during the night with the child and his mother. [15]And Joseph stayed in Egypt until Herod died. This happened to bring about what the Lord had said through the prophet: "I called my son out of Egypt."[n]

Herod Kills the Baby Boys

[16]When Herod saw that the wise men had tricked him, he was furious. So he gave an order to kill all the baby boys in Bethlehem and in the surrounding area who were two years old or younger. This was in keeping with the time he learned from the wise men. [17]So what God had said through the prophet Jeremiah came true:

[18]"A voice was heard in Ramah
of painful crying and deep sadness:
Rachel crying for her children.
She refused to be comforted,
because her children are dead."
Jeremiah 31:15

Joseph and Mary Return

[19]After Herod died, an angel of the Lord spoke to Joseph in a dream while he was in Egypt. [20]The angel said, "Get up! Take the child and his mother and go to the land of Israel, because the people who were trying to kill the child are now dead."

[21]So Joseph took the child and his mother and went to Israel. [22]But he heard that Archelaus was now king in Judea since his father Herod had died. So Joseph was afraid to go there. After being warned in a dream, he went to the area of Galilee, [23]to a town called Nazareth, and lived there. And so what God had said through the prophets came true: "He will be called a Nazarene."[n]

The Work of John the Baptist

3 About that time John the Baptist began preaching in the desert area of Judea. [2]John said, "Change your hearts and lives because the kingdom of heaven is near." [3]John the Baptist is the one Isaiah the prophet was talking about when he said:

"This is a voice of one
who calls out in the desert:
'Prepare the way for the Lord.
Make the road straight for him.' "
Isaiah 40:3

[4]John's clothes were made from camel's hair, and he wore a leather belt around his waist. For food, he ate locusts and wild honey. [5]Many people came from Jerusalem and Judea and all the area around the Jordan River to hear John. [6]They confessed their sins, and he baptized them in the Jordan River.

[7]Many of the Pharisees and Sadducees came to the place where John was baptizing people. When John saw them, he said, "You are snakes! Who warned you to run away from God's coming punishment? [8]Do the things that show you really have changed your hearts and lives. [9]And don't think you can say to yourselves, 'Abraham is our father.' I tell you that God could make children for Abraham from these rocks. [10]The ax is now ready to cut down the trees, and every tree that does not produce good fruit will be cut down and thrown into the fire.[n]

[11]"I baptize you with water to show that your hearts and lives have changed. But there is one coming after me who is greater than I am, whose sandals I am not good enough to carry. He will baptize you with the Holy Spirit and fire. [12]He will come ready to clean the grain, separating the good grain from the chaff. He will put

Matthew 3:8–12

Just because your friend has a gym membership doesn't mean you have one, too, right? And if you want one, you don't just hang around the gym lobby, trying to look and act like a gym member. Of course not! You'd inquire about getting a membership yourself. The same idea goes for people coming to Christ. We don't become part of God's family because we have Christian parents or have some godly behaviors down pat.

Even so, that's exactly the kind of thing Jewish religious leaders were banking on back in John the Baptist's day. They thought being Abraham's descendants, God's "chosen people," guaranteed they were okay in God's book. But John taught that ancestry doesn't affect whether people belong to God. When we're truly God's chosen people, our lives will reflect it. That's why John told religious leaders to change their hearts and lives. He was saying that just being related to Abraham doesn't mean much if your life doesn't show true obedience to God. Of course, our actions don't save us—Jesus' sacrifice does. But his presence in our lives changes our hearts *and* our actions!

Relying on anything other than Jesus is pointless. Put all your faith in God's grace, and completely depend on a personal relationship with Jesus.

2:15 "I called . . . Egypt." Quotation from Hosea 11:1. **2:23 Nazarene** A person from the town of Nazareth. Matthew may be referring to Isaiah 11:1, where the Hebrew word translated "branch" sounds like "Nazarene." **3:10 The ax . . . fire.** This means that God is ready to punish his people who do not obey him.

Women & Men of the BIBLE

Vashti: A Woman of Dignity

Queen Vashti might have been on the cover of fashion magazines if she were alive today. Her husband, King Xerxes, was all about beautiful women, and she was drop-dead gorgeous. But he generally wanted his queen to be seen and not heard. One day as he was enjoying a nice, long ego trip with his buddies, he called for her to come and prance around for them. She refused to act in such an unbecoming, unladylike manner. This stand for moral purity ended up costing her dearly. She was stripped of her title and crown—but not her dignity! (Esther 1)

the good part of the grain into his barn, but he will burn the chaff with a fire that cannot be put out."[n]

Jesus Is Baptized by John

[13]At that time Jesus came from Galilee to the Jordan River and wanted John to baptize him. [14]But John tried to stop him, saying, "Why do you come to me to be baptized? I need to be baptized by you!"

[15]Jesus answered, "Let it be this way for now. We should do all things that are God's will." So John agreed to baptize Jesus.

[16]As soon as Jesus was baptized, he came up out of the water. Then heaven opened, and he saw God's Spirit coming down on him like a dove. [17]And a voice from heaven said, "This is my Son, whom I love, and I am very pleased with him."

The Temptation of Jesus

4 Then the Spirit led Jesus into the desert to be tempted by the devil. [2]Jesus fasted for forty days and nights. After this, he was very hungry. [3]The devil came to Jesus to tempt him, saying, "If you are the Son of God, tell these rocks to become bread."

[4]Jesus answered, "It is written in the Scriptures, 'A person lives not on bread alone, but by everything God says.' "[n]

[5]Then the devil led Jesus to the holy city of Jerusalem and put him on a high place of the Temple. [6]The devil said, "If you are the Son of God, jump down, because it is written in the Scriptures:

'He has put his angels in charge of
you.
They will catch you in their hands
so that you will not hit your foot on a
rock.' " *Psalm 91:11–12*

[7]Jesus answered him, "It also says in the Scriptures, 'Do not test the Lord your God.' "[n]

[8]Then the devil led Jesus to the top of a very high mountain and showed him all the kingdoms of the world and all their splendor. [9]The devil said, "If you will bow down and worship me, I will give you all these things."

[10]Jesus said to the devil, "Go away from me, Satan! It is written in the Scriptures, 'You must worship the Lord your God and serve only him.' "[n]

[11]So the devil left Jesus, and angels came and took care of him.

Jesus Begins Work in Galilee

[12]When Jesus heard that John had been put in prison, he went back to Galilee. [13]He left Nazareth and went to live in Capernaum, a town near Lake Galilee, in the area near Zebulun and Naphtali. [14]Jesus did this to bring about what the prophet Isaiah had said:

[15]"Land of Zebulun and land of
Naphtali
along the sea,
beyond the Jordan River.
This is Galilee where the
non-Jewish people live.
[16]These people who live in darkness
will see a great light.
They live in a place covered with the
shadows of death,
but a light will shine on them."
Isaiah 9:1–2

Jesus Chooses Some Followers

[17]From that time Jesus began to preach, saying, "Change your hearts and lives, because the kingdom of heaven is near."

[18]As Jesus was walking by Lake Galilee, he saw two brothers, Simon (called Peter) and his brother Andrew. They were throwing a net into the lake because they were fishermen. [19]Jesus said, "Come follow me, and I will make you fish for people." [20]So Simon and Andrew immediately left their nets and followed him.

[21]As Jesus continued walking by Lake Galilee, he saw two other brothers, James and John, the sons of Zebedee. They were in a boat with their father Zebedee, mending their nets. Jesus told them to come with him. [22]Immediately they left the boat and their father, and they followed Jesus.

Jesus Teaches and Heals People

[23]Jesus went everywhere in Galilee, teaching in the synagogues, preaching the Good News about the kingdom of heaven, and healing all the people's diseases and sicknesses. [24]The news about Jesus spread all over Syria, and people brought all the sick to him. They were suffering from different kinds of diseases. Some were in great pain, some had demons, some were epileptics,[n] and some were paralyzed. Jesus healed all of them. [25]Many people from Galilee, the Ten Towns,[n] Jerusalem, Judea, and the land across the Jordan River followed him.

Jesus Teaches the People

5 When Jesus saw the crowds, he went up on a hill and sat down. His followers came to him, [2]and he began to teach them, saying:

[3]"They are blessed who realize their
spiritual poverty,
for the kingdom of heaven
belongs to them.

3:12 He will . . . out. This means that Jesus will come to separate good people from bad people, saving the good and punishing the bad. **4:4 'A person . . . says.'** Quotation from Deuteronomy 8:3. **4:7 'Do . . . God.'** Quotation from Deuteronomy 6:16. **4:10 'You . . . him.'** Quotation from Deuteronomy 6:13. **4:24 epileptics** People with a disease that causes them sometimes to lose control of their bodies and maybe faint, shake strongly, or not be able to move. **4:25 Ten Towns** In Greek, called "Decapolis." It was an area east of Lake Galilee that once had ten main towns.

[4]They are blessed who grieve,
for God will comfort them.
[5]They are blessed who are humble,
for the whole earth will be theirs.
[6]They are blessed who hunger and
thirst after justice,
for they will be satisfied.
[7]They are blessed who show mercy to
others,
for God will show mercy to them.
[8]They are blessed whose thoughts are
pure,
for they will see God.
[9]They are blessed who work for peace,
for they will be called God's
children.
[10]They are blessed who are persecuted
for doing good,
for the kingdom of heaven
belongs to them.

[11]"People will insult you and hurt you. They will lie and say all kinds of evil things about you because you follow me. But when they do, you will be blessed. [12]Rejoice and be glad, because you have a great reward waiting for you in heaven. People did the same evil things to the prophets who lived before you.

You Are Like Salt and Light

[13]"You are the salt of the earth. But if the salt loses its salty taste, it cannot be made salty again. It is good for nothing, except to be thrown out and walked on.

[14]"You are the light that gives light to the world. A city that is built on a hill cannot be hidden. [15]And people don't hide a light under a bowl. They put it on a lampstand so the light shines for all the people in the house. [16]In the same way, you should be a light for other people. Live so that they will see the good things you do and will praise your Father in heaven.

The Importance of the Law

[17]"Don't think that I have come to destroy the law of Moses or the teaching of the prophets. I have not come to destroy them but to bring about what they said. [18]I tell you the truth, nothing will disappear from the law until heaven and earth are gone. Not even the smallest letter or the smallest part of a letter will be lost until everything has happened. [19]Whoever refuses to obey any command and teaches other people not to obey that command will be the least important in the kingdom of heaven. But whoever obeys the commands and teaches other people to obey them will be great in the kingdom of heaven. [20]I tell you that if you are no more obedient than the teachers of the law and the Pharisees, you will never enter the kingdom of heaven.

Jesus Teaches About Anger

[21]"You have heard that it was said to our people long ago, 'You must not murder anyone.'[n] Anyone who murders another will be judged.' [22]But I tell you, if you are angry with a brother or sister,[n] you will be judged. If you say bad things to a brother or sister, you will be judged by the council. And if you call someone a fool, you will be in danger of the fire of hell.

[23]"So when you offer your gift to God at the altar, and you remember that your brother or sister has something against you, [24]leave your gift there at the altar. Go and make peace with that person, and then come and offer your gift.

[25]"If your enemy is taking you to court, become friends quickly, before you go to court. Otherwise, your enemy might turn

Matthew 5:3–12

"Bless you!" "We're so blessed . . . " "What a blessing that was!" People sometimes use the word "bless" a lot. But what does it really mean to be blessed? Matthew 5:3–12, a passage called The Beatitudes, provides some answers. It specifically names those who are blessed. But it's not just a random list of fortunate people groups. It describes a transformation from prideful independence to the true blessing of knowing God.

Descriptive phrases like "great spiritual needs" and "those who are sad" can remind us how poor we are, spiritually speaking, without God. It's about knowing in our hearts we have nothing to offer God; we're destitute. One critical step in drawing near to God is recognizing and rejecting our sin. We all start out broken before receiving God's grace. The next step, Jesus says, is becoming people who love righteousness, show mercy, and work for peace.

We start out spiritual beggars and are transformed into heirs of the kingdom of heaven . . . talk about being blessed! In God's kingdom, we don't fight for personal gain. Instead, we just humble ourselves before God so we can experience his grace, closeness, and good plans for our lives.

Measure your life by Jesus' words. Are you blessed?

5:21 'You . . . anyone.' Quotation from Exodus 20:13; Deuteronomy 5:17. **5:22 sister** Some Greek copies continue, "without a reason."

Tune It Out

Have you ever considered all the ways we get information? With data coming at us from every direction—television, radio, newspapers, magazines, the Internet, e-mail—it can be a little overwhelming. Being informed about current events is definitely important, and it can encourage us to pray for the world around us and those in need. But if TMI (too much information) is making you fearful, it may be time to make some lifestyle changes. Philippians 4:8 reminds us to think about the things that are good, worthy of praise, true, honorable, right, pure, beautiful, and respected. So instead of catching the news on TV or the web right before bed, try reading Scripture. Or try replacing talk radio on your commute with soothing jazz or your favorite worship tunes. Little changes can make a big difference!

you over to the judge, and the judge might give you to a guard to put you in jail. 26I tell you the truth, you will not leave there until you have paid everything you owe.

Jesus Teaches About Sexual Sin

27“You have heard that it was said, ‘You must not be guilty of adultery.’[n] 28But I tell you that if anyone looks at a woman and wants to sin sexually with her, in his mind he has already done that sin with the woman. 29If your right eye causes you to sin, take it out and throw it away. It is better to lose one part of your body than to have your whole body thrown into hell. 30If your right hand causes you to sin, cut it off and throw it away. It is better to lose one part of your body than for your whole body to go into hell.

Jesus Teaches About Divorce

31“It was also said, ‘Anyone who divorces his wife must give her a written divorce paper.’[n] 32But I tell you that anyone who divorces his wife forces her to be guilty of adultery. The only reason for a man to divorce his wife is if she has sexual relations with another man. And anyone who marries that divorced woman is guilty of adultery.

Make Promises Carefully

33“You have heard that it was said to our people long ago, ‘Don’t break your promises, but keep the promises you make to the Lord.’[n] 34But I tell you, never swear an oath. Don’t swear an oath using the name of heaven, because heaven is God’s throne. 35Don’t swear an oath using the name of the earth, because the earth belongs to God. Don’t swear an oath using the name of Jerusalem, because that is the city of the great King. 36Don’t even swear by your own head, because you cannot make one hair on your head become white or black. 37Say only yes if you mean yes, and no if you mean no. If you say more than yes or no, it is from the Evil One.

Don’t Fight Back

38“You have heard that it was said, ‘An eye for an eye, and a tooth for a tooth.’[n] 39But I tell you, don’t stand up against an evil person. If someone slaps you on the right cheek, turn to him the other cheek also. 40If someone wants to sue you in court and take your shirt, let him have your coat also. 41If someone forces you to go with him one mile, go with him two miles. 42If a person asks you for something, give it to him. Don’t refuse to give to someone who wants to borrow from you.

Love All People

43“You have heard that it was said, ‘Love your neighbor[n] and hate your enemies.’ 44But I say to you, love your enemies. Pray for those who hurt you.[n] 45If you do this, you will be true children of your Father in heaven. He causes the sun to rise on good people and on evil people, and he sends rain to those who do right and to those who do wrong. 46If you love only the people who love you, you will get no reward. Even the tax collectors do that. 47And if you are nice only to your friends, you are no better than other people. Even those who don’t know God are nice to their friends. 48So you must be perfect, just as your Father in heaven is perfect.

Jesus Teaches About Giving

6 “Be careful! When you do good things, don’t do them in front of people to be seen by them. If you do that, you will have no reward from your Father in heaven.

2“When you give to the poor, don’t be like the hypocrites. They blow trumpets in the synagogues and on the streets so that people will see them and honor them. I tell you the truth, those hypocrites already have their full reward. 3So when you give to the poor, don’t let anyone know what you are doing. 4Your giving should be done in secret. Your Father can see what is done in secret, and he will reward you.

Jesus Teaches About Prayer

5“When you pray, don’t be like the hypocrites. They love to stand in the synagogues and on the street corners and pray so people will see them. I tell you the truth, they already have their full reward. 6When you pray, you should go into your room and close the door and pray to your Father who cannot be seen. Your Father can see what is done in secret, and he will reward you.

5:27 ‘You . . . adultery.’ Quotation from Exodus 20:14; Deuteronomy 5:18. **5:31 ‘Anyone . . . divorce paper.’** Quotation from Deuteronomy 24:1. **5:33 ‘Don’t . . . Lord.’** This refers to Leviticus 19:12; Numbers 30:2; Deuteronomy 23:21. **5:38 ‘An eye . . . tooth.’** Quotation from Exodus 21:24; Leviticus 24:20; Deuteronomy 19:21. **5:43 ‘Love your neighbor’** Quotation from Leviticus 19:18. **5:44 you** Some Greek copies continue, “Bless those who curse you, do good to those who hate you.” Compare Luke 6:28.

[7]"And when you pray, don't be like those people who don't know God. They continue saying things that mean nothing, thinking that God will hear them because of their many words. [8]Don't be like them, because your Father knows the things you need before you ask him. [9]So when you pray, you should pray like this:

'Our Father in heaven,
may your name always be kept holy.
[10]May your kingdom come
and what you want be done,
here on earth as it is in heaven.
[11]Give us the food we need for each day.
[12]Forgive us for our sins,
just as we have forgiven those
who sinned against us.
[13]And do not cause us to be tempted,
but save us from the Evil One.' [The
kingdom, the power, and the
glory are yours forever. Amen.][n]

[14]Yes, if you forgive others for their sins, your Father in heaven will also forgive you for your sins. [15]But if you don't forgive others, your Father in heaven will not forgive your sins.

Jesus Teaches About Worship

[16]"When you fast,[n] don't put on a sad face like the hypocrites. They make their faces look sad to show people they are fasting. I tell you the truth, those hypocrites already have their full reward. [17]So when you fast, comb your hair and wash your face. [18]Then people will not know that you are fasting, but your Father, whom you cannot see, will see you. Your Father sees what is done in secret, and he will reward you.

God Is More Important than Money

[19]"Don't store treasures for yourselves here on earth where moths and rust will destroy them and thieves can break in and steal them. [20]But store your treasures in heaven where they cannot be destroyed by moths or rust and where thieves cannot break in and steal them. [21]Your heart will be where your treasure is.

[22]"The eye is a light for the body. If your eyes are good, your whole body will be full of light. [23]But if your eyes are evil, your whole body will be full of darkness. And if the only light you have is really darkness, then you have the worst darkness.

[24]"No one can serve two masters. The person will hate one master and love the other, or will follow one master and refuse to follow the other. You cannot serve both God and worldly riches.

Don't Worry

[25]"So I tell you, don't worry about the food or drink you need to live, or about the clothes you need for your body. Life is more than food, and the body is more than clothes. [26]Look at the birds in the air. They don't plant or harvest or store food in barns, but your heavenly Father feeds them. And you know that you are worth much more than the birds. [27]You cannot add any time to your life by worrying about it.

[28]"And why do you worry about clothes? Look at how the lilies in the field grow. They don't work or make clothes for themselves. [29]But I tell you that even Solomon with his riches was not dressed as beautifully as one of these flowers. [30]God clothes the grass in the field, which is alive today but tomorrow is thrown into the fire. So you can be even more sure that God will clothe you. Don't have so little faith! [31]Don't worry and say, 'What will we eat?' or 'What will we drink?' or 'What will we wear?' [32]The people who don't know God keep trying to get these things, and your Father in heaven knows you need them. [33]Seek first God's kingdom and what God wants. Then all your other needs will be met as well. [34]So don't worry about tomorrow, because tomorrow will have its own worries. Each day has enough trouble of its own.

HE SAID ↙ ↗ SHE SAID

What does it mean to love?

He: To aim your entire life toward God

She: To lay down your life for someone else

Be Careful About Judging Others

7 "Don't judge others, or you will be judged. [2]You will be judged in the same way that you judge others, and the amount you give to others will be given to you.

[3]"Why do you notice the little piece of dust in your friend's eye, but you don't notice the big piece of wood in your own eye? [4]How can you say to your friend, 'Let me take that little piece of dust out of your eye'? Look at yourself! You still have that big piece of wood in your own eye. [5]You hypocrite! First, take the wood out of your own eye. Then you will see clearly to take the dust out of your friend's eye.

[6]"Don't give holy things to dogs, and don't throw your pearls before pigs. Pigs will only trample on them, and dogs will turn to attack you.

Ask God for What You Need

[7]"Ask, and God will give to you. Search, and you will find. Knock, and the door will open for you. [8]Yes, everyone who asks will receive. Everyone who searches will find. And everyone who knocks will have the door opened.

[9]"If your children ask for bread, which of you would give them a stone? [10]Or if your children ask for a fish, would you give them a snake? [11]Even though you are bad, you know how to give good gifts to

6:13 The . . . Amen. Some Greek copies do not contain the bracketed text. **6:16 fast** The people would give up eating for a special time of prayer and worship to God. It was also done to show sadness and disappointment.

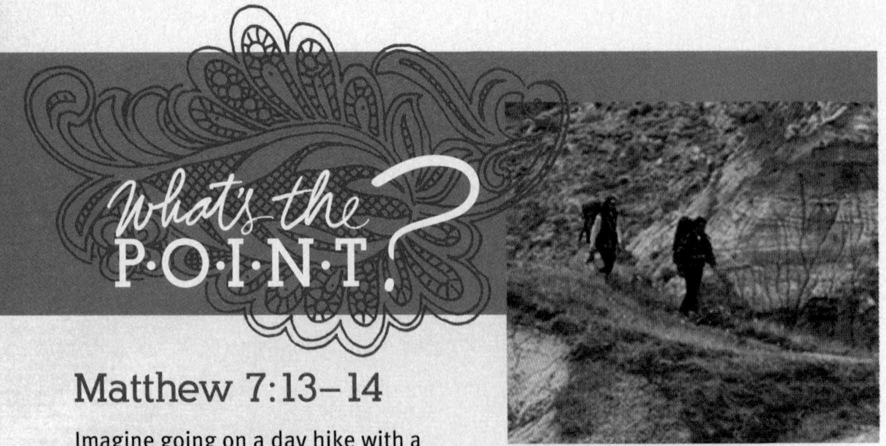

Matthew 7:13–14

Imagine going on a day hike with a friend. After hours of winding along mountain paths, completely engrossed in great conversations, you find yourselves deep in the wilderness. There's a fork in the path, and you realize you're not exactly sure where you are. Dusk is fast approaching, and you feel the pressure to choose correctly. The right path will lead safely home. But if you take the wrong path, you could end up wandering through the dark wilderness for hours with no flashlight or cell phone reception!

Spiritually speaking, there are basically two paths available. Option one is a wide path with a wide gate. It's a superhighway with enough space for all kinds of religions, philosophies, and lifestyles. But even though it's nice and roomy, this path leads away from God. The other path is completely different. It's straight and narrow, and the gate is tiny—no room for sin or indecision. But this is the path that leads to true life.

The Bible offers a map revealing which path leads to which destination. Jesus said he's the small gate and the narrow road; people can reach heaven only through *him* (John 14:6). Listen to his eternal wisdom and carefully choose his path daily.

your children. How much more your heavenly Father will give good things to those who ask him!

The Most Important Rule

12"Do to others what you want them to do to you. This is the meaning of the law of Moses and the teaching of the prophets.

The Way to Heaven Is Hard

13"Enter through the narrow gate. The gate is wide and the road is wide that leads to hell, and many people enter through that gate. 14But the gate is small and the road is narrow that leads to true life. Only a few people find that road.

People Know You by Your Actions

15"Be careful of false prophets. They come to you looking gentle like sheep, but they are really dangerous like wolves. 16You will know these people by what they do. Grapes don't come from thornbushes, and figs don't come from thorny weeds. 17In the same way, every good tree produces good fruit, but a bad tree produces bad fruit. 18A good tree cannot produce bad fruit, and a bad tree cannot produce good fruit. 19Every tree that does not produce good fruit is cut down and thrown into the fire. 20In the same way, you will know these false prophets by what they do.

21"Not all those who say 'You are our Lord' will enter the kingdom of heaven. The only people who will enter the kingdom of heaven are those who do what my Father in heaven wants. 22On the last day many people will say to me, 'Lord, Lord, we spoke for you, and through you we forced out demons and did many miracles.' 23Then I will tell them clearly, 'Get away from me, you who do evil. I never knew you.'

Two Kinds of People

24"Everyone who hears my words and obeys them is like a wise man who built his house on rock. 25It rained hard, the floods came, and the winds blew and hit that house. But it did not fall, because it was built on rock. 26Everyone who hears my words and does not obey them is like a foolish man who built his house on sand. 27It rained hard, the floods came, and the winds blew and hit that house, and it fell with a big crash."

28When Jesus finished saying these things, the people were amazed at his teaching, 29because he did not teach like their teachers of the law. He taught like a person who had authority.

Jesus Heals a Sick Man

8 When Jesus came down from the hill, great crowds followed him. 2Then a man with a skin disease came to Jesus. The man bowed down before him and said, "Lord, you can heal me if you will."

3Jesus reached out his hand and touched the man and said, "I will. Be healed!" And immediately the man was healed from his disease. 4Then Jesus said to him, "Don't tell anyone about this. But go and show yourself to the priest[n] and offer the gift Moses commanded[n] for people who are made well. This will show the people what I have done."

Jesus Heals a Soldier's Servant

5When Jesus entered the city of Capernaum, an army officer came to him, begging for help. 6The officer said, "Lord, my servant is at home in bed. He can't move his body and is in much pain."

7Jesus said to the officer, "I will go and heal him."

8The officer answered, "Lord, I am not worthy for you to come into my house. You

8:4 show . . . priest The Law of Moses said a priest must say when a Jewish person with a skin disease was well. **8:4 Moses commanded** Read about this in Leviticus 14:1–32.

only need to command it, and my servant will be healed. [9]I, too, am a man under the authority of others, and I have soldiers under my command. I tell one soldier, 'Go,' and he goes. I tell another soldier, 'Come,' and he comes. I say to my servant, 'Do this,' and my servant does it.

[10]When Jesus heard this, he was amazed. He said to those who were following him, "I tell you the truth, this is the greatest faith I have found, even in Israel. [11]Many people will come from the east and from the west and will sit and eat with Abraham, Isaac, and Jacob in the kingdom of heaven. [12]But those people who should be in the kingdom will be thrown outside into the darkness, where people will cry and grind their teeth with pain."

[13]Then Jesus said to the officer, "Go home. Your servant will be healed just as you believed he would." And his servant was healed that same hour.

Jesus Heals Many People

[14]When Jesus went to Peter's house, he saw that Peter's mother-in-law was sick in bed with a fever. [15]Jesus touched her hand, and the fever left her. Then she stood up and began to serve Jesus.

[16]That evening people brought to Jesus many who had demons. Jesus spoke and the demons left them, and he healed all the sick. [17]He did these things to bring about what Isaiah the prophet had said:

"He took our suffering on him
and carried our diseases."
Isaiah 53:4

People Want to Follow Jesus

[18]When Jesus saw the crowd around him, he told his followers to go to the other side of the lake. [19]Then a teacher of the law came to Jesus and said, "Teacher, I will follow you any place you go."

[20]Jesus said to him, "The foxes have holes to live in, and the birds have nests, but the Son of Man has no place to rest his head."

[21]Another man, one of Jesus' followers, said to him, "Lord, first let me go and bury my father."

[22]But Jesus told him, "Follow me, and let the people who are dead bury their own dead."

Jesus Calms a Storm

[23]Jesus got into a boat, and his followers went with him. [24]A great storm arose on the lake so that waves covered the boat, but Jesus was sleeping. [25]His followers went to him and woke him, saying, "Lord, save us! We will drown!"

[26]Jesus answered, "Why are you afraid? You don't have enough faith." Then Jesus got up and gave a command to the wind and the waves, and it became completely calm.

[27]The men were amazed and said, "What kind of man is this? Even the wind and the waves obey him!"

Jesus Heals Two Men with Demons

[28]When Jesus arrived at the other side of the lake in the area of the Gadarene[n] people, two men who had demons in them met him. These men lived in the burial caves and were so dangerous that people could not use the road by those caves. [29]They shouted, "What do you want with us, Son of God? Did you come here to torture us before the right time?"

[30]Near that place there was a large herd of pigs feeding. [31]The demons begged Jesus, "If you make us leave these men, please send us into that herd of pigs."

[32]Jesus said to them, "Go!" So the demons left the men and went into the pigs. Then the whole herd rushed down the hill into the lake and were drowned. [33]The herdsmen ran away and went into town, where they told about all of this and what had happened to the men who had demons. [34]Then the whole town went out to see Jesus. When they saw him, they begged him to leave their area.

Jesus Heals a Paralyzed Man

9 Jesus got into a boat and went back across the lake to his own town. [2]Some people brought to Jesus a man who was paralyzed and lying on a mat. When Jesus saw the faith of these people, he said to the paralyzed man, "Be encouraged, young man. Your sins are forgiven."

[3]Some of the teachers of the law said to themselves, "This man speaks as if he were God. That is blasphemy!"[n]

[4]Knowing their thoughts, Jesus said, "Why are you thinking evil thoughts? [5]Which is easier: to say, 'Your sins are forgiven,' or to tell him, 'Stand up and walk'? [6]But I will prove to you that the Son of Man has authority on earth

all about MEN

About His Family . . .

Like it or not, in many ways your guy is a product of his heritage. Whether he's an everyday Joe or borderline quirky, he's been influenced by the fruits and nuts on his family tree! Kidding aside, his family relationships (their existence or absence) impact your relationship. His relatives deserve your respect—even if their actions don't earn your admiration. Talk to him about any issues you have with them, but pray first and tread carefully. Those folks are a part of him, and their influence helped form the boy they knew into the man you love. Ask God for help embracing your differences while keeping healthy boundaries, and search for ways to support your honey when it comes to his family.

8:28 Gadarene From Gadara, an area southeast of Lake Galilee. The exact location is uncertain and some Greek copies read "Gergesene"; others read "Gerasene." **9:3 blasphemy** Saying things against God or not showing respect for God.

to forgive sins." Then Jesus said to the paralyzed man, "Stand up, take your mat, and go home." [7]And the man stood up and went home. [8]When the people saw this, they were amazed and praised God for giving power like this to human beings.

Jesus Chooses Matthew

[9]When Jesus was leaving, he saw a man named Matthew sitting in the tax collector's booth. Jesus said to him, "Follow me," and he stood up and followed Jesus.

[10]As Jesus was having dinner at Matthew's house, many tax collectors and "sinners" came and ate with Jesus and his followers. [11]When the Pharisees saw this, they asked Jesus' followers, "Why does your teacher eat with tax collectors and sinners?"

[12]When Jesus heard them, he said, "It is not the healthy people who need a doctor, but the sick. [13]Go and learn what this means: 'I want kindness more than I want animal sacrifices.'[n] I did not come to invite good people but to invite sinners."

Jesus' Followers Are Criticized

[14]Then the followers of John[n] came to Jesus and said, "Why do we and the Pharisees often fast[n] for a certain time, but your followers don't?"

[15]Jesus answered, "The friends of the bridegroom are not sad while he is with them. But the time will come when the bridegroom will be taken from them, and then they will fast.

[16]"No one sews a patch of unshrunk cloth over a hole in an old coat. If he does, the patch will shrink and pull away from the coat, making the hole worse. [17]Also, people never pour new wine into old leather bags. Otherwise, the bags will break, the wine will spill, and the wine bags will be ruined. But people always pour new wine into new wine bags. Then both will continue to be good."

Jesus Gives Life to a Dead Girl and Heals a Sick Woman

[18]While Jesus was saying these things, a leader of the synagogue came to him. He bowed down before Jesus and said, "My daughter has just died. But if you come and lay your hand on her, she will live again." [19]So Jesus and his followers stood up and went with the leader.

[20]Then a woman who had been bleeding for twelve years came behind Jesus and touched the edge of his coat. [21]She was thinking, "If I can just touch his clothes, I will be healed."

[22]Jesus turned and saw the woman and said, "Be encouraged, dear woman. You are made well because you believed." And the woman was healed from that moment on.

[23]Jesus continued along with the leader and went into his house. There he saw the funeral musicians and many people crying. [24]Jesus said, "Go away. The girl is not dead, only asleep." But the people laughed at him. [25]After the crowd had been thrown out of the house, Jesus went into the girl's room and took hold of her hand, and she stood up. [26]The news about this spread all around the area.

Jesus Heals More People

[27]When Jesus was leaving there, two blind men followed him. They cried out, "Have mercy on us, Son of David!"

[28]After Jesus went inside, the blind men went with him. He asked the men, "Do you believe that I can make you see again?"

They answered, "Yes, Lord."

[29]Then Jesus touched their eyes and said, "Because you believe I can make

BECOME *Involved*

Heifer International

If ever there was a unique ministry, this is it! Heifer International (www.heifer.org) is a practical yet extraordinary solution to ending poverty in the United States and around the world. Families who are living in extreme poverty are given live animals to help nourish their children and produce a sustainable income.

One of the fantastic things about the program is that the recipients receive a sense of dignity and self-reliance as they're trained to care for their animals. They are no longer depending on temporary gifts from others because they actually have something they can keep and grow. Best of all, it is standard practice that recipients give some of the offspring from their gift to others in need. The giving cycle keeps going, blessing more and more families.

You can support Heifer International by giving a donation to their work or by volunteering at one of their ranches or on a trip. A fun way to support them is to literally purchase animals for a family in need. When you choose to buy in someone else's honor, that person receives a certificate that tells about the live animal that was donated in his/her name. It's a great program!

9:13 'I want . . . sacrifices.' Quotation from Hosea 6:6. **9:14 John** John the Baptist, who preached to people about Christ's coming (Matthew 3, Luke 3). **9:14 fast** The people would give up eating for a special time of prayer and worship to God. It was also done to show sadness and disappointment.

RELATIONSHIPS

Sarcasm's Poison

Know anyone who thrives on sarcasm—someone who loves tossing out "joking" remarks, often as a way of hiding uglier statements? Joking is one thing, but it can really hurt when it's at someone else's expense. Instead of letting the sarcasm eat at a relationship's health, trade the negative words for encouraging ones. There are lots of good, kind words to choose from! Words that show grace and love honor God and others—*and* grow great relationships. Proverbs 18:19–21 and James 3:2–10 warn about speech. Before it affects your relationships, restrain the sarcasm and opt for words that give life.

you see again, it will happen." [30]Then the men were able to see. But Jesus warned them strongly, saying, "Don't tell anyone about this." [31]But the blind men left and spread the news about Jesus all around that area.

[32]When the two men were leaving, some people brought another man to Jesus. This man could not talk because he had a demon in him. [33]After Jesus forced the demon to leave the man, he was able to speak. The crowd was amazed and said, "We have never seen anything like this in Israel."

[34]But the Pharisees said, "The prince of demons is the one that gives him power to force demons out."

[35]Jesus traveled through all the towns and villages, teaching in their synagogues, preaching the Good News about the kingdom, and healing all kinds of diseases and sicknesses. [36]When he saw the crowds, he felt sorry for them because they were hurting and helpless, like sheep without a shepherd. [37]Jesus said to his followers, "There are many people to harvest but only a few workers to help harvest them. [38]Pray to the Lord, who owns the harvest, that he will send more workers to gather his harvest."[n]

Jesus Sends Out His Apostles

10 Jesus called his twelve followers together and gave them authority to drive out evil spirits and to heal every kind of disease and sickness. [2]These are the names of the twelve apostles: Simon (also called Peter) and his brother Andrew; James son of Zebedee, and his brother John; [3]Philip and Bartholomew; Thomas and Matthew, the tax collector; James son of Alphaeus, and Thaddaeus; [4]Simon the Zealot and Judas Iscariot, who turned against Jesus.

[5]Jesus sent out these twelve men with the following order: "Don't go to the non-Jewish people or to any town where the Samaritans live. [6]But go to the people of Israel, who are like lost sheep. [7]When you go, preach this: 'The kingdom of heaven is near.' [8]Heal the sick, raise the dead to life again, heal those who have skin diseases, and force demons out of people. I give you these powers freely, so help other people freely. [9]Don't carry any money with you—gold or silver or copper. [10]Don't carry a bag or extra clothes or sandals or a walking stick. Workers should be given what they need.

[11]"When you enter a city or town, find some worthy person there and stay in that home until you leave. [12]When you enter that home, say, 'Peace be with you.' [13]If the people there welcome you, let your peace stay there. But if they don't welcome you, take back the peace you wished for them. [14]And if a home or town refuses to welcome you or listen to you, leave that place and shake its dust off your feet.[n] [15]I tell you the truth, on the Judgment Day it will be better for the towns of Sodom and Gomorrah[n] than for the people of that town.

Jesus Warns His Apostles

[16]"Listen, I am sending you out like sheep among wolves. So be as clever as snakes and as innocent as doves. [17]Be careful of people, because they will arrest you and take you to court and whip you in their synagogues. [18]Because of me you will be taken to stand before governors and kings, and you will tell them and the non-Jewish people about me. [19]When you are arrested, don't worry about what to say or how to say it. At that time you will be given the things to say. [20]It will not really be you speaking but the Spirit of your Father speaking through you.

9:37–38 "There are . . . harvest." As a farmer sends workers to harvest the grain, Jesus sends his followers to bring people to God. **10:14 shake . . . feet** A warning. It showed that they had rejected these people. **10:15 Sodom and Gomorrah** Two cities that God destroyed because the people were so evil.

Matthew 11:26–30

Picture yourself running in a marathon. (If you really have to *imagine* here, it's okay.) Now imagine hefting a piece of oversized, packed-to-the-brim luggage over your shoulder and trying to keep up the pace. You might chug along for a while on sheer determination. But eventually you'd hit a breaking point and shut down, collapsing in utter exhaustion. Your body just wasn't built to carry that load!

The people Jesus was speaking to in these verses were weary, not from physical loads but from the weight of their sin. They were absolutely overloaded by the requirements of the Law. They'd reached a point of spiritual exhaustion, and that's when Jesus offered them real rest. He took the weight of their sin and carried it for them . . . all the way to the Cross. He took the burden of perfection off every human being and lived a completely sin-free life. And more than that, he still offers to carry those heavy loads today.

Are you worn out from trying to be perfect? Is there sin in your heart that's weighing you down? Go to Jesus. Acknowledge the truth he's spoken, the saving work he's completed, and your deep need for him. Then lay down your load at his feet—and rest.

[21]"Brothers will give their own brothers to be killed, and fathers will give their own children to be killed. Children will fight against their own parents and have them put to death. [22]All people will hate you because you follow me, but those people who keep their faith until the end will be saved. [23]When you are treated badly in one city, run to another city. I tell you the truth, you will not finish going through all the cities of Israel before the Son of Man comes.

[24]"A student is not better than his teacher, and a servant is not better than his master. [25]A student should be satisfied to become like his teacher; a servant should be satisfied to become like his master. If the head of the family is called Beelzebul, then the other members of the family will be called worse names!

Fear God, Not People

[26]"So don't be afraid of those people, because everything that is hidden will be shown. Everything that is secret will be made known. [27]I tell you these things in the dark, but I want you to tell them in the light. What you hear whispered in your ear you should shout from the housetops. [28]Don't be afraid of people, who can kill the body but cannot kill the soul. The only one you should fear is the one who can destroy the soul and the body in hell. [29]Two sparrows cost only a penny, but not even one of them can die without your Father's knowing it. [30]God even knows how many hairs are on your head. [31]So don't be afraid. You are worth much more than many sparrows.

Tell People About Your Faith

[32]"All those who stand before others and say they believe in me, I will say before my Father in heaven that they belong to me. [33]But all who stand before others and say they do not believe in me, I will say before my Father in heaven that they do not belong to me.

[34]"Don't think that I came to bring peace to the earth. I did not come to bring peace, but a sword. [35]I have come so that

'a son will be against his father,
a daughter will be against her mother,
a daughter-in-law will be against her mother-in-law.
[36] A person's enemies will be members of his own family.'
Micah 7:6

[37]"Those who love their father or mother more than they love me are not worthy to be my followers. Those who love their son or daughter more than they love me are not worthy to be my followers. [38]Whoever is not willing to carry the cross and follow me is not worthy of me. [39]Those who try to hold on to their lives will give up true life. Those who give up their lives for me will hold on to true life. [40]Whoever accepts you also accepts me, and whoever accepts me also accepts the One who sent me. [41]Whoever meets a prophet and accepts him will receive the reward of a prophet. And whoever accepts a good person because that person is good will receive the reward of a good person. [42]Those who give one of these little ones a cup of cold water because they are my followers will truly get their reward."

Jesus and John the Baptist

11 After Jesus finished telling these things to his twelve followers, he left there and went to the towns in Galilee to teach and preach.

[2]John the Baptist was in prison, but he heard about what the Christ was doing. So John sent some of his followers to Jesus.

[3]They asked him, "Are you the One who is to come, or should we wait for someone else?"

[4]Jesus answered them, "Go tell John what you hear and see: [5]The blind can see, the crippled can walk, and people with skin diseases are healed. The deaf can hear, the dead are raised to life, and the Good News is preached to the poor. [6]Those who do not stumble in their faith because of me are blessed."

[7]As John's followers were leaving, Jesus began talking to the people about John. Jesus said, "What did you go out into the desert to see? A reed[n] blown by the wind? [8]What did you go out to see? A man dressed in fine clothes? No, those who wear fine clothes live in kings' palaces. [9]So why did you go out? To see a prophet? Yes, and I tell you, John is more than a prophet. [10]This was written about him:

'I will send my messenger ahead of you,
who will prepare the way for you.' *Malachi 3:1*

[11]I tell you the truth, John the Baptist is greater than any other person ever born, but even the least important person in the kingdom of heaven is greater than John. [12]Since the time John the Baptist came until now, the kingdom of heaven has been going forward in strength, and people have been trying to take it by force. [13]All the prophets and the law of Moses told about what would happen until the time John came. [14]And if you will believe what they said, you will believe that John is Elijah, whom they said would come. [15]Let those with ears use them and listen!

[16]"What can I say about the people of this time? What are they like? They are like children sitting in the marketplace, who call out to each other,

[17]'We played music for you, but you did not dance;
we sang a sad song, but you did not cry.'

[18]John came and did not eat or drink like other people. So people say, 'He has a demon.' [19]The Son of Man came, eating and drinking, and people say, 'Look at him! He eats too much and drinks too much wine, and he is a friend of tax collectors and sinners.' But wisdom is proved to be right by what she does."

Jesus Warns Unbelievers

[20]Then Jesus criticized the cities where he did most of his miracles, because the people did not change their lives and stop sinning. [21]He said, "How terrible for you, Korazin! How terrible for you, Bethsaida! If the same miracles I did in you had happened in Tyre and Sidon,[n] those people would have changed their lives a long time ago. They would have worn rough cloth and put ashes on themselves to show they had changed. [22]But I tell you, on the Judgment Day it will be better for Tyre and Sidon than for you. [23]And you, Capernaum,[n] will you be lifted up to heaven? No, you will be thrown down to the depths. If the miracles I did in you had happened in Sodom,[n] its people would have stopped sinning, and it would still be a city today. [24]But I tell you, on the Judgment Day it will be better for Sodom than for you."

Jesus Offers Rest to People

[25]At that time Jesus said, "I praise you, Father, Lord of heaven and earth, because you have hidden these things from the people who are wise and smart. But you have shown them to those who are like little children. [26]Yes, Father, this is what you really wanted.

[27]"My Father has given me all things. No one knows the Son, except the Father. And no one knows the Father, except the Son and those whom the Son chooses to tell.

[28]"Come to me, all of you who are tired and have heavy loads, and I will give you rest. [29]Accept my teachings and learn from me, because I am gentle and humble in spirit, and you will find rest for your lives. [30]The burden that I ask you to accept is easy; the load I give you to carry is light."

Jesus Is Lord of the Sabbath

12 At that time Jesus was walking through some fields of grain on a Sabbath day. His followers were hungry, so they began to pick the grain and eat it. [2]When the Pharisees saw this, they said to Jesus, "Look! Your followers are doing what is unlawful to do on the Sabbath day."

[3]Jesus answered, "Have you not read

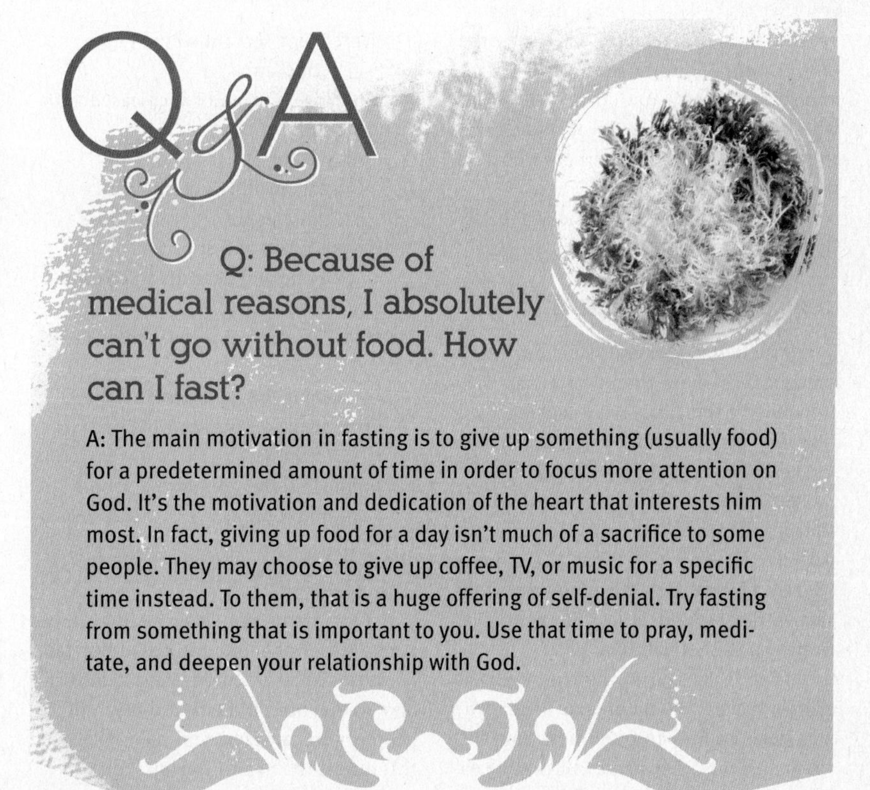

Q&A

Q: Because of medical reasons, I absolutely can't go without food. How can I fast?

A: The main motivation in fasting is to give up something (usually food) for a predetermined amount of time in order to focus more attention on God. It's the motivation and dedication of the heart that interests him most. In fact, giving up food for a day isn't much of a sacrifice to some people. They may choose to give up coffee, TV, or music for a specific time instead. To them, that is a huge offering of self-denial. Try fasting from something that is important to you. Use that time to pray, meditate, and deepen your relationship with God.

11:7 reed It means that John was not ordinary or weak like grass blown by the wind. **11:21 Tyre and Sidon** Towns where wicked people lived. **11:21, 23 Korazin . . . Bethsaida . . . Capernaum** Towns by Lake Galilee where Jesus preached to the people. **11:23 Sodom** A city that God destroyed because the people were so evil.

LIFEISSUES

When a Colleague Steals the Credit

You pitch a great idea to your boss but watch someone else get the credit for it in the next company meeting. While your co-workers applaud, you are secretly hurt and wonder what to do. You may feel angry, but Ephesians 4:26 still applies: "When you are angry, do not sin." Study Scripture for wisdom, and pray to be sure your motives aren't for revenge. Ask God for a right spirit before approaching your boss, and seek godly counsel if you don't get an appropriate response. And remember: your career is still in God's hands.

what David did when he and the people with him were hungry? [4]He went into God's house, and he and those with him ate the holy bread, which was lawful only for priests to eat. [5]And have you not read in the law of Moses that on every Sabbath day the priests in the Temple break this law about the Sabbath day? But the priests are not wrong for doing that. [6]I tell you that there is something here that is greater than the Temple. [7]The Scripture says, 'I want kindness more than I want animal sacrifices.'[n] You don't really know what those words mean. If you understood them, you would not judge those who have done nothing wrong.

[8]"So the Son of Man is Lord of the Sabbath day."

Jesus Heals a Man's Hand

[9]Jesus left there and went into their synagogue, [10]where there was a man with a crippled hand. They were looking for a reason to accuse Jesus, so they asked him, "Is it right to heal on the Sabbath day?"[n]

[11]Jesus answered, "If any of you has a sheep, and it falls into a ditch on the Sabbath day, you will help it out of the ditch. [12]Surely a human being is more important than a sheep. So it is lawful to do good things on the Sabbath day."

[13]Then Jesus said to the man with the crippled hand, "Hold out your hand." The man held out his hand, and it became well again, like the other hand. [14]But the Pharisees left and made plans to kill Jesus.

Jesus Is God's Chosen Servant

[15]Jesus knew what the Pharisees were doing, so he left that place. Many people followed him, and he healed all who were sick. [16]But Jesus warned the people not to tell who he was. [17]He did these things to bring about what Isaiah the prophet had said:

[18]"Here is my servant whom I have
chosen.
I love him, and I am pleased with
him.
I will put my Spirit upon him,
and he will tell of my justice to
all people.
[19]He will not argue or cry out;
no one will hear his voice in the
streets.
[20]He will not break a crushed blade of
grass
or put out even a weak flame
until he makes justice win the
victory.
[21]In him will the non-Jewish people
find hope." *Isaiah 42:1–4*

Jesus' Power Is from God

[22]Then some people brought to Jesus a man who was blind and could not talk, because he had a demon. Jesus healed the man so that he could talk and see. [23]All the people were amazed and said, "Perhaps this man is the Son of David!"

[24]When the Pharisees heard this, they said, "Jesus uses the power of Beelzebul, the ruler of demons, to force demons out of people."

[25]Jesus knew what the Pharisees were thinking, so he said to them, "Every kingdom that is divided against itself will be destroyed. And any city or family that is divided against itself will not continue. [26]And if Satan forces out himself, then Satan is divided against himself, and his kingdom will not continue. [27]You say that I use the power of Beelzebul to force out demons. If that is true, then what power do your people use to force out demons? So they will be your judges. [28]But if I use the power of God's Spirit to force out demons, then the kingdom of God has come to you.

[29]"If anyone wants to enter a strong person's house and steal his things, he must first tie up the strong person. Then he can steal the things from the house.

[30]"Whoever is not with me is against me. Whoever does not work with me is working against me. [31]So I tell you, people can be forgiven for every sin and everything they say against God. But whoever speaks against the Holy Spirit will not be forgiven. [32]Anyone who speaks against the Son of Man can be forgiven, but anyone who speaks against the Holy Spirit will not be forgiven, now or in the future.

People Know You by Your Words

[33]"If you want good fruit, you must make the tree good. If your tree is not good, it will have bad fruit. A tree is known by the kind of fruit it produces. [34]You snakes! You are evil people, so how can you say anything good? The mouth speaks the things that are in the heart. [35]Good people have good things in their hearts, and so they say good things. But evil people have evil in their hearts, so they say evil things. [36]And I tell you that on the Judgment Day people will be responsible for every careless thing they have said. [37]The words you have said will be used to judge you. Some of your words will prove you right, but some of your words will prove you guilty."

The People Ask for a Miracle

[38]Then some of the Pharisees and teachers of the law answered Jesus, say-

12:7 'I . . . sacrifices.' Quotation from Hosea 6:6. **12:10 Is it right . . . day?** It was against Jewish Law to work on the Sabbath day.

ing, "Teacher, we want to see you work a miracle as a sign."

[39]Jesus answered, "Evil and sinful people are the ones who want to see a miracle for a sign. But no sign will be given to them, except the sign of the prophet Jonah. [40]Jonah was in the stomach of the big fish for three days and three nights. In the same way, the Son of Man will be in the grave three days and three nights. [41]On the Judgment Day the people from Nineveh[n] will stand up with you people who live now, and they will show that you are guilty. When Jonah preached to them, they were sorry and changed their lives. And I tell you that someone greater than Jonah is here. [42]On the Judgment Day, the Queen of the South[n] will stand up with you people who live today. She will show that you are guilty, because she came from far away to listen to Solomon's wise teaching. And I tell you that someone greater than Solomon is here.

People Today Are Full of Evil

[43]"When an evil spirit comes out of a person, it travels through dry places, looking for a place to rest, but it doesn't find it. [44]So the spirit says, 'I will go back to the house I left.' When the spirit comes back, it finds the house still empty, swept clean, and made neat. [45]Then the evil spirit goes out and brings seven other spirits even more evil than it is, and they go in and live there. So the person has even more trouble than before. It is the same way with the evil people who live today."

Jesus' True Family

[46]While Jesus was talking to the people, his mother and brothers stood outside, trying to find a way to talk to him. [47]Someone told Jesus, "Your mother and brothers are standing outside, and they want to talk to you."[n]

[48]He answered, "Who is my mother? Who are my brothers?" [49]Then he pointed to his followers and said, "Here are my mother and my brothers. [50]My true brother and sister and mother are those who do what my Father in heaven wants."

A Story About Planting Seed

13 That same day Jesus went out of the house and sat by the lake. [2]Large crowds gathered around him, so he got into a boat and sat down, while the people stood on the shore. [3]Then Jesus used stories to teach them many things. He said: "A farmer went out to plant his seed. [4]While he was planting, some seed fell by the road, and the birds came and ate it all up. [5]Some seed fell on rocky ground, where there wasn't much dirt. That seed grew very fast, because the ground was not deep. [6]But when the sun rose, the plants dried up, because they did not have deep roots. [7]Some other seed fell among thorny weeds, which grew and choked the good plants. [8]Some other seed fell on good ground where it grew and produced a crop. Some plants made a hundred times more, some made sixty times more, and some made thirty times more. [9]Let those with ears use them and listen."

Why Jesus Used Stories to Teach

[10]The followers came to Jesus and asked, "Why do you use stories to teach the people?"

[11]Jesus answered, "You have been chosen to know the secrets about the kingdom of heaven, but others cannot know these secrets. [12]Those who have understanding will be given more, and they will have all they need. But those who do not have understanding, even what they have will be taken away from them. [13]This is why I use stories to teach the people: They see, but they don't really see. They hear, but they don't really hear or understand. [14]So they show that the things Isaiah said about them are true:

'You will listen and listen, but you
 will not understand.
You will look and look, but you
 will not learn.
[15]For the minds of these people have
 become stubborn.
They do not hear with their ears,
 and they have closed their eyes.
Otherwise they might really
 understand
what they see with their eyes
 and hear with their ears.
They might really understand in
 their minds
and come back to me and be
 healed.' *Isaiah 6:9–10*

[16]But you are blessed, because you see with your eyes and hear with your ears. [17]I tell you the truth, many prophets and good people wanted to see the things that you now see, but they did not see them. And they wanted to hear the things that you now hear, but they did not hear them.

All That Glitters Is Not Gold

What woman wouldn't want to have all the brand-name designer clothes, accessories, and hair products the magazines advertise? Hollywood stars spend millions each year just to keep up with the trends. But the truth is that God says all that stuff is irrelevant to real beauty. First Peter 3:3 says, "It is not fancy hair, gold jewelry, or fine clothes that should make you beautiful." It's what's on the inside that counts. So next time you're shopping, give thanks to the Lord that your beauty comes from your heart—not your wallet.

12:41 Nineveh The city where Jonah preached to warn the people. Read Jonah 3. **12:42 Queen of the South** The Queen of Sheba. She traveled a thousand miles to learn God's wisdom from Solomon. Read 1 Kings 10:1–13. **12:47 Someone . . . you.** Some Greek copies do not have verse 47.

Jesus Explains the Seed Story

[18]"So listen to the meaning of that story about the farmer. [19]What is the seed that fell by the road? That seed is like the person who hears the message about the kingdom but does not understand it. The Evil One comes and takes away what was planted in that person's heart. [20]And what is the seed that fell on rocky ground? That seed is like the person who hears the teaching and quickly accepts it with joy. [21]But he does not let the teaching go deep into his life, so he keeps it only a short time. When trouble or persecution comes because of the teaching he accepted, he quickly gives up. [22]And what is the seed that fell among the thorny weeds? That seed is like the person who hears the teaching but lets worries about this life and the temptation of wealth stop that teaching from growing. So the teaching does not produce fruit[n] in that person's life. [23]But what is the seed that fell on the good ground? That seed is like the person who hears the teaching and understands it. That person grows and produces fruit, sometimes a hundred times more, sometimes sixty times more, and sometimes thirty times more."

A Story About Wheat and Weeds

[24]Then Jesus told them another story: "The kingdom of heaven is like a man who planted good seed in his field. [25]That night, when everyone was asleep, his enemy came and planted weeds among the wheat and then left. [26]Later, the wheat sprouted and the heads of grain grew, but the weeds also grew. [27]Then the man's servants came to him and said, 'You planted good seed in your field. Where did the weeds come from?' [28]The man answered, 'An enemy planted weeds.' The servants asked, 'Do you want us to pull up the weeds?' [29]The man answered, 'No, because when you pull up the weeds, you might also pull up the wheat. [30]Let the weeds and the wheat grow together until the harvest time. At harvest time I will tell the workers, "First gather the weeds and tie them together to be burned. Then gather the wheat and bring it to my barn." ' "

Stories of Mustard Seed and Yeast

[31]Then Jesus told another story: "The kingdom of heaven is like a mustard seed that a man planted in his field. [32]That seed is the smallest of all seeds, but when it grows, it is one of the largest garden plants. It becomes big enough for the wild birds to come and build nests in its branches."

[33]Then Jesus told another story: "The kingdom of heaven is like yeast that a woman took and hid in a large tub of flour until it made all the dough rise."

[34]Jesus used stories to tell all these things to the people; he always used stories to teach them. [35]This is as the prophet said:

> "I will speak using stories;
> I will tell things that have been secret since the world was made." *Psalm 78:2*

Jesus Explains About the Weeds

[36]Then Jesus left the crowd and went into the house. His followers came to him and said, "Explain to us the meaning of the story about the weeds in the field."

[37]Jesus answered, "The man who planted the good seed in the field is the Son of Man. [38]The field is the world, and the good seed are all of God's children who belong to the kingdom. The weeds are those people who belong to the Evil One. [39]And the enemy who planted the bad seed is the devil. The harvest time is the end of the age, and the workers who gather are God's angels.

[40]"Just as the weeds are pulled up and burned in the fire, so it will be at the end of the age. [41]The Son of Man will send out his angels, and they will gather out of his kingdom all who cause sin and all who do evil. [42]The angels will throw them into the blazing furnace, where the people will cry and grind their teeth with pain. [43]Then the good people will shine like the sun in the kingdom of their Father. Let those with ears use them and listen.

Be Still & Know

Honesty Is the Best Policy

Did you know that God already knows what you think before you even tell him? He knows your heart intimately (2 Chronicles 6:30). There is nowhere you can go to hide from him (Psalm 139:7–10). Sometimes that can be a scary thought. But it doesn't have to be. Since the Father already knows our doubts and fears, there is no need to pretend they're not there. You can (and should!) be open and honest with him about every struggle. Pray to him with reverence, but be up front about how you feel. He is full of mercy. His Holy Spirit will gladly help guide you through every doubt, fear, and struggle!

13:22 produce fruit To produce fruit means to have in your life the good things God wants.

Stories of a Treasure and a Pearl

[44]"The kingdom of heaven is like a treasure hidden in a field. One day a man found the treasure, and then he hid it in the field again. He was so happy that he went and sold everything he owned to buy that field.

[45]"Also, the kingdom of heaven is like a man looking for fine pearls. [46]When he found a very valuable pearl, he went and sold everything he had and bought it.

A Story of a Fishing Net

[47]"Also, the kingdom of heaven is like a net that was put into the lake and caught many different kinds of fish. [48]When it was full, the fishermen pulled the net to the shore. They sat down and put all the good fish in baskets and threw away the bad fish. [49]It will be this way at the end of the age. The angels will come and separate the evil people from the good people. [50]The angels will throw the evil people into the blazing furnace, where people will cry and grind their teeth with pain."

[51]Jesus asked his followers, "Do you understand all these things?"

They answered, "Yes, we understand."

[52]Then Jesus said to them, "So every teacher of the law who has been taught about the kingdom of heaven is like the owner of a house. He brings out both new things and old things he has saved."

Jesus Goes to His Hometown

[53]When Jesus finished teaching with these stories, he left there. [54]He went to his hometown and taught the people in the synagogue, and they were amazed. They said, "Where did this man get this wisdom and this power to do miracles? [55]He is just the son of a carpenter. His mother is Mary, and his brothers are James, Joseph, Simon, and Judas. [56]And all his sisters are here with us. Where then does this man get all these things?" [57]So the people were upset with Jesus.

But Jesus said to them, "A prophet is honored everywhere except in his hometown and in his own home."

[58]So he did not do many miracles there because they had no faith.

74% of adults like the photo on their driver's license.

(Reader's Digest)

How John the Baptist Was Killed

14 At that time Herod, the ruler of Galilee, heard the reports about Jesus. [2]So he said to his servants, "Jesus is John the Baptist, who has risen from the dead. That is why he can work these miracles."

[3]Sometime before this, Herod had arrested John, tied him up, and put him into prison. Herod did this because of Herodias, who had been the wife of Philip, Herod's brother. [4]John had been telling Herod, "It is not lawful for you to be married to Herodias." [5]Herod wanted to kill John, but he was afraid of the people, because they believed John was a prophet.

[6]On Herod's birthday, the daughter of Herodias danced for Herod and his guests, and she pleased him. [7]So he promised with an oath to give her anything she wanted. [8]Herodias told her daughter what to ask for, so she said to Herod, "Give me the head of John the Baptist here on a platter." [9]Although King Herod was very sad, he had made a promise, and his dinner guests had heard him. So Herod ordered that what she asked for be done. [10]He sent soldiers to the prison to cut

Crunchy Whole-Grain French Toast

Put a healthy spin on an old breakfast favorite. In a shallow dish, whisk an egg with a touch of milk. In another dish, combine crushed cereal (such as Golden Grahams or another favorite) with chopped pecans. Dip 2 slices of whole-grain bread in the egg mixture, and then coat the slices with the cereal-nut mixture. Reduce your calories by using nonstick spray on the griddle. Variety is the spice of life, so experiment with different cereals and nuts or try adding vanilla, cinnamon, or nutmeg to the egg mixture.

WORLDVIEWS

Know Your Worldview

People everywhere have these basic questions about the world and about life. *Where did this world come from? Why am I here? Does my life have a purpose?* Maybe you haven't asked those exact questions, but haven't you ever had a deep desire to know for sure that you *matter* . . . that there's a point to your life?

A system for answering those questions is called a worldview. It's a way of viewing the world and everything in it, including how we're supposed to live. What do you believe? What defines how you think, act, and live?

Some people say there is no God—they believe this whole world just happened by itself. This worldview leads to some dark places, and a world without God has no real meaning. If this world is just a big accident, how can there be any point? And how do we know what's right or wrong if there's no one around to tell us? We'd basically have to make up our own values and rules. All we'd have left is ourselves: our selfish desires and empty hearts. You probably know people with this worldview. They might be confused about what's right, they may live selfishly, and they can easily become disheartened about life because it seems meaningless.

Well, here's a tip: life *is* meaningless without God. That's where Christianity comes in. Christianity is so much more than religious activities you do on Sundays. The Bible is the key to knowing God, knowing who you are, and learning how you should live. The truth is that God made you for a purpose, and he wants you to know him. If the Bible explains how you can know him, isn't it clear what you should do? Make it your priority to let God (and his Word) be the foundation of your worldview.

[10]After Jesus called the crowd to him, he said, "Listen and understand what I am saying. [11]It is not what people put into their mouths that makes them unclean. It is what comes out of their mouths that makes them unclean."

[12]Then his followers came to him and asked, "Do you know that the Pharisees are angry because of what you said?"

[13]Jesus answered, "Every plant that my Father in heaven has not planted himself will be pulled up by the roots. [14]Stay away from the Pharisees; they are blind leaders.[n] And if a blind person leads a blind person, both will fall into a ditch."

[15]Peter said, "Explain the example to us."

[16]Jesus said, "Do you still not understand? [17]Surely you know that all the food that enters the mouth goes into the stomach and then goes out of the body. [18]But what people say with their mouths comes from the way they think; these are the things that make people unclean. [19]Out of the mind come evil thoughts, murder, adultery, sexual sins, stealing, lying, and speaking evil of others. [20]These things make people unclean; eating with unwashed hands does not make them unclean."

Jesus Helps a Non-Jewish Woman

[21]Jesus left that place and went to the area of Tyre and Sidon. [22]A Canaanite woman from that area came to Jesus and cried out, "Lord, Son of David, have mercy on me! My daughter has a demon, and she is suffering very much."

[23]But Jesus did not answer the woman. So his followers came to Jesus and begged him, "Tell the woman to go away. She is following us and shouting."

[24]Jesus answered, "God sent me only to the lost sheep, the people of Israel."

[25]Then the woman came to Jesus again and bowed before him and said, "Lord, help me!"

[26]Jesus answered, "It is not right to take the children's bread and give it to the dogs."

[27]The woman said, "Yes, Lord, but even the dogs eat the crumbs that fall from their masters' table."

[28]Then Jesus answered, "Woman, you have great faith! I will do what you asked." And at that moment the woman's daughter was healed.

Jesus Heals Many People

[29]After leaving there, Jesus went along the shore of Lake Galilee. He went up on a hill and sat there.

[30]Great crowds came to Jesus, bringing with them the lame, the blind, the crippled, those who could not speak, and many others. They put them at Jesus' feet, and he healed them. [31]The crowd was amazed when they saw that people who could not speak before were now able to speak. The crippled were made strong. The lame could walk, and the blind could see. And they praised the God of Israel for this.

More than Four Thousand Fed

[32]Jesus called his followers to him and said, "I feel sorry for these people, because

15:14 leaders Some Greek copies continue, "of blind people."

they have already been with me three days, and they have nothing to eat. I don't want to send them away hungry. They might faint while going home."

[33]His followers asked him, "How can we get enough bread to feed all these people? We are far away from any town."

[34]Jesus asked, "How many loaves of bread do you have?"

They answered, "Seven, and a few small fish."

[35]Jesus told the people to sit on the ground. [36]He took the seven loaves of bread and the fish and gave thanks to God. Then he divided the food and gave it to his followers, and they gave it to the people. [37]All the people ate and were satisfied. Then his followers filled seven baskets with the leftover pieces of food. [38]There were about four thousand men there who ate, besides women and children. [39]After sending the people home, Jesus got into the boat and went to the area of Magadan.

The Leaders Ask for a Miracle

16 The Pharisees and Sadducees came to Jesus, wanting to trick him. So they asked him to show them a miracle from God.

[2]Jesus answered,[n] "At sunset you say we will have good weather, because the sky is red. [3]And in the morning you say that it will be a rainy day, because the sky is dark and red. You see these signs in the sky and know what they mean. In the same way, you see the things that I am doing now, but you don't know their meaning. [4]Evil and sinful people ask for a miracle as a sign, but they will not be given any sign, except the sign of Jonah."[n] Then Jesus left them and went away.

Guard Against Wrong Teachings

[5]Jesus' followers went across the lake, but they had forgotten to bring bread. [6]Jesus said to them, "Be careful! Beware of the yeast of the Pharisees and the Sadducees."

[7]His followers discussed the meaning of this, saying, "He said this because we forgot to bring bread."

[8]Knowing what they were talking about, Jesus asked them, "Why are you talking about not having bread? Your faith is small. [9]Do you still not understand? Remember the five loaves of bread that fed the five thousand? And remember that you filled many baskets with the leftovers? [10]Or the seven loaves of bread that fed the four thousand and the many baskets you filled then also? [11]I was not talking to you about bread. Why don't you understand that? I am telling you to beware of the yeast of the Pharisees and the Sadducees." [12]Then the followers understood that Jesus was not telling them to beware of the yeast used in bread but to beware of the teaching of the Pharisees and the Sadducees.

Peter Says Jesus Is the Christ

[13]When Jesus came to the area of Caesarea Philippi, he asked his followers, "Who do people say the Son of Man is?"

[14]They answered, "Some say you are John the Baptist. Others say you are Elijah, and still others say you are Jeremiah or one of the prophets."

[15]Then Jesus asked them, "And who do you say I am?"

[16]Simon Peter answered, "You are the Christ, the Son of the living God."

[17]Jesus answered, "You are blessed, Simon son of Jonah, because no person taught

Matthew 16:13–17

As you grow closer to someone—whether it's a friendship or a romantic relationship—your love comes out in what you say and do. When you say, "He's my best friend" or "This is my fiancé," you're speaking volumes about this person's place in your heart. And when you invest your energy in that person, you show that your love is real.

The same principle goes for your relationship with God. When Jesus asked his followers who they believed he was, Peter acknowledged Jesus as the Son of God. He saw this as a life-altering truth and displayed his devotion clearly in his words and actions.

If we say to Jesus, "You are the Christ, the Son of the living God," but then hold back in living for his glory, how can that truth be alive in our hearts? If we believe he's our Savior and Lord, our entire lives will be fully submitted to him.

If you've identified Christ as your Lord but shy away from talking about the Bible or obeying him in every area of your life, consider why your public life doesn't line up with what you've acknowledged to Christ privately. Picture Jesus asking you, "Who do you say I am?" And then answer him from your heart—*and* with your words and actions.

16:2–3 answered Some Greek copies do not have the rest of verse 2 and verse 3. **16:4 sign of Jonah** Jonah's three days in the fish are like Jesus' three days in the tomb. The story about Jonah is in the Book of Jonah.

HE SAID ↙ ↗ SHE SAID

What's the most important thing your dad taught you?

He: Love and serve your wife.

She: Never run for a bus—there will always be another.

you that. My Father in heaven showed you who I am. [18]So I tell you, you are Peter.[n] On this rock I will build my church, and the power of death will not be able to defeat it. [19]I will give you the keys of the kingdom of heaven; the things you don't allow on earth will be the things that God does not allow, and the things you allow on earth will be the things that God allows." [20]Then Jesus warned his followers not to tell anyone he was the Christ.

Jesus Says that He Must Die

[21]From that time on Jesus began telling his followers that he must go to Jerusalem, where the Jewish elders, the leading priests, and the teachers of the law would make him suffer many things. He told them he must be killed and then be raised from the dead on the third day.

[22]Peter took Jesus aside and told him not to talk like that. He said, "God save you from those things, Lord! Those things will never happen to you!"

[23]Then Jesus said to Peter, "Go away from me, Satan![n] You are not helping me! You don't care about the things of God, but only about the things people think are important."

[24]Then Jesus said to his followers, "If people want to follow me, they must give up the things they want. They must be willing even to give up their lives to follow me. [25]Those who want to save their lives will give up true life, and those who give up their lives for me will have true life. [26]It is worthless to have the whole world if they lose their souls. They could never pay enough to buy back their souls. [27]The Son of Man will come again with his Father's glory and with his angels. At that time, he will reward them for what they have done. [28]I tell you the truth, some people standing here will see the Son of Man coming with his kingdom before they die."

Jesus Talks with Moses and Elijah

17 Six days later, Jesus took Peter, James, and John, the brother of James, up on a high mountain by themselves. [2]While they watched, Jesus' appearance was changed; his face became bright like the sun, and his clothes became white as light. [3]Then Moses and Elijah[n] appeared to them, talking with Jesus.

[4]Peter said to Jesus, "Lord, it is good that we are here. If you want, I will put up three tents here—one for you, one for Moses, and one for Elijah."

[5]While Peter was talking, a bright cloud covered them. A voice came from the cloud and said, "This is my Son, whom I love, and I am very pleased with him. Listen to him!"

[6]When his followers heard the voice, they were so frightened they fell to the ground. [7]But Jesus went to them and touched them and said, "Stand up. Don't be afraid." [8]When they looked up, they saw Jesus was now alone.

[9]As they were coming down the mountain, Jesus commanded them not to tell anyone about what they had seen until the Son of Man had risen from the dead.

[10]Then his followers asked him, "Why do the teachers of the law say that Elijah must come first?"

[11]Jesus answered, "They are right to say that Elijah is coming and that he will make everything the way it should be. [12]But I tell you that Elijah has already come, and they did not recognize him. They did to him whatever they wanted to do. It will be the same with the Son of Man; those same people will make the Son of Man suffer." [13]Then the followers understood that Jesus was talking about John the Baptist.

Jesus Heals a Sick Boy

[14]When Jesus and his followers came back to the crowd, a man came to Jesus and bowed before him. [15]The man said, "Lord, have mercy on my son. He has epilepsy[n] and is suffering very much, because he often falls into the fire or into the water. [16]I brought him to your followers, but they could not cure him."

[17]Jesus answered, "You people have no faith, and your lives are all wrong. How long must I put up with you? How long must I continue to be patient with you? Bring the boy here." [18]Jesus commanded the demon inside the boy. Then the demon came out, and the boy was healed from that time on.

fun facts

In a recent survey, 84% of women said they like to dress down on weekends.

(Self.com)

16:18 Peter The Greek name "Peter," like the Aramaic name "Cephas," means "rock." **16:23 Satan** Name for the devil, meaning "the enemy." Jesus means that Peter was talking like Satan. **17:3 Moses and Elijah** Two of the most important Jewish leaders in the past. God had given Moses the Law, and Elijah was an important prophet. **17:15 epilepsy** A disease that causes a person sometimes to lose control of his body and maybe faint, shake strongly, or not be able to move.

[19]The followers came to Jesus when he was alone and asked, "Why couldn't we force the demon out?"

[20]Jesus answered, "Because your faith is too small. I tell you the truth, if your faith is as big as a mustard seed, you can say to this mountain, 'Move from here to there,' and it will move. All things will be possible for you. [[21]That kind of spirit comes out only if you use prayer and fasting.]"[n]

Jesus Talks About His Death

[22]While Jesus' followers were gathering in Galilee, he said to them, "The Son of Man will be handed over to people, [23]and they will kill him. But on the third day he will be raised from the dead." And the followers were filled with sadness.

Jesus Talks About Paying Taxes

[24]When Jesus and his followers came to Capernaum, the men who collected the Temple tax came to Peter. They asked, "Does your teacher pay the Temple tax?"

[25]Peter answered, "Yes, Jesus pays the tax."

Peter went into the house, but before he could speak, Jesus said to him, "What do you think? The kings of the earth collect different kinds of taxes. But who pays the taxes—the king's children or others?"

[26]Peter answered, "Other people pay the taxes."

Jesus said to Peter, "Then the children of the king don't have to pay taxes. [27]But we don't want to upset these tax collectors. So go to the lake and fish. After you catch the first fish, open its mouth and you will find a coin. Take that coin and give it to the tax collectors for you and me."

Who Is the Greatest?

18 At that time the followers came to Jesus and asked, "Who is greatest in the kingdom of heaven?"

[2]Jesus called a little child to him and stood the child before his followers. [3]Then he said, "I tell you the truth, you must change and become like little children. Otherwise, you will never enter the kingdom of heaven. [4]The greatest person in the kingdom of heaven is the one who makes himself humble like this child.

[5]"Whoever accepts a child in my name accepts me. [6]If one of these little children believes in me, and someone causes that child to sin, it would be better for that person to have a large stone tied around the neck and be drowned in the sea. [7]How terrible for the people of the world because of the things that cause them to sin. Such things will happen, but how terrible for the one who causes them to happen! [8]If your hand or your foot causes you to sin, cut it off and throw it away. It is better for you to lose part of your body and live forever than to have two hands and two feet and be thrown into the fire that burns forever. [9]If your eye causes you to sin, take it out and throw it away. It is better for you to have only one eye and live forever than to have two eyes and be thrown into the fire of hell.

A Lost Sheep

[10]"Be careful. Don't think these little children are worth nothing. I tell you that they have angels in heaven who are always with my Father in heaven. [[11]The Son of Man came to save lost people.][n]

[12]"If a man has a hundred sheep but one of the sheep gets lost, he will leave the other ninety-nine on the hill and go to look for the lost sheep. [13]I tell you the truth, if he finds it he is happier about that one sheep than about the ninety-nine that were never lost. [14]In the same way, your Father in heaven does not want any of these little children to be lost.

When a Person Sins Against You

[15]"If your fellow believer sins against you,[n] go and tell him in private what he did wrong. If he listens to you, you have helped that person to be your brother or sister again. [16]But if he refuses to listen, go to him again and take one or two other people with you. 'Every case may be proved by two or three witnesses.'[n] [17]If he refuses to listen to them, tell the church. If he refuses to listen to the church, then treat him like a person who does not believe in God or like a tax collector.

[18]"I tell you the truth, the things you don't allow on earth will be the things God does not allow. And the things you allow on earth will be the things that God allows.

[19]"Also, I tell you that if two of you on earth agree about something and pray for it, it will be done for you by my Father in heaven. [20]This is true because if two or three people come together in my name, I am there with them."

Health

Super Foods

You are what you eat, and your body *is* a temple (1 Corinthians 6:19–20), so drop the cheese doodles! It's time to stock up on "super foods"—nutritional powerhouses packed with disease-fighting compounds. Here are the basics to eating like a hero: *Stick with whole foods*—raw vegetables, lean meats, whole grains, etc.—as opposed to their processed counterparts. (Tomatoes are the exception. Compared to raw tomatoes, canned tomatoes contain more lycopene, which wards off cancer.) *Eat the rainbow.* Blueberries, spinach, pumpkin, and other foods rich in color are bursting with antioxidants and beta-carotene. *Not all fat is bad.* Salmon, olive oil, and walnuts contain omega-3 fatty acids that actually help lower blood cholesterol. Finally, *take time for tea.* Green and black varieties (not instant or bottled) are believed to fight cardiovascular disease and may even treat depression.

17:21 That . . . fasting. Some Greek copies do not contain the bracketed text. **18:11 The . . . people.** Some Greek copies do not contain the bracketed text. **18:15 against you** Some Greek copies do not have "against you." **18:16 'Every . . . witnesses.'** Quotation from Deuteronomy 19:15.

RELATIONSHIPS

Little Acts of Service

When you hear the word "servant," do butlers in tuxedos and maids waving feather dusters come to mind? True service goes far beyond hired help! Christians are called to serve one another with love. A serving attitude in a relationship creates an environment of love and encouragement. When you help a busy loved one with household chores or spend time doing what someone else enjoys, you're showing that you care enough to put that person's needs first. How much better when both people serve each other! Little acts of service build rewarding relationships.

An Unforgiving Servant

[21]Then Peter came to Jesus and asked, "Lord, when my fellow believer sins against me, how many times must I forgive him? Should I forgive him as many as seven times?"

[22]Jesus answered, "I tell you, you must forgive him more than seven times. You must forgive him even if he wrongs you seventy times seven.

[23]"The kingdom of heaven is like a king who decided to collect the money his servants owed him. [24]When the king began to collect his money, a servant who owed him several million dollars was brought to him. [25]But the servant did not have enough money to pay his master, the king. So the master ordered that everything the servant owned should be sold, even the servant's wife and children. Then the money would be used to pay the king what the servant owed.

[26]"But the servant fell on his knees and begged, 'Be patient with me, and I will pay you everything I owe.' [27]The master felt sorry for his servant and told him he did not have to pay it back. Then he let the servant go free.

[28]"Later, that same servant found another servant who owed him a few dollars. The servant grabbed him around the neck and said, 'Pay me the money you owe me!'

[29]"The other servant fell on his knees and begged him, 'Be patient with me, and I will pay you everything I owe.'

[30]"But the first servant refused to be patient. He threw the other servant into prison until he could pay everything he owed. [31]When the other servants saw what had happened, they were very sorry. So they went and told their master all that had happened.

[32]"Then the master called his servant in and said, 'You evil servant! Because you begged me to forget what you owed, I told you that you did not have to pay anything. [33]You should have showed mercy to that other servant, just as I showed mercy to you.' [34]The master was very angry and put the servant in prison to be punished until he could pay everything he owed.

[35]"This king did what my heavenly Father will do to you if you do not forgive your brother or sister from your heart."

Jesus Teaches About Divorce

19 After Jesus said all these things, he left Galilee and went into the area of Judea on the other side of the Jordan River. [2]Large crowds followed him, and he healed them there.

[3]Some Pharisees came to Jesus and tried to trick him. They asked, "Is it right for a man to divorce his wife for any reason he chooses?"

[4]Jesus answered, "Surely you have read in the Scriptures: When God made the world, 'he made them male and female.'[n] [5]And God said, 'So a man will leave his father and mother and be united with his wife, and the two will become one body.'[n] [6]So there are not two, but one. God has joined the two together, so no one should separate them."

[7]The Pharisees asked, "Why then did Moses give a command for a man to divorce his wife by giving her divorce papers?"

[8]Jesus answered, "Moses allowed you to divorce your wives because you refused to accept God's teaching, but divorce was not allowed in the beginning. [9]I tell you that anyone who divorces his wife and marries another woman is guilty of adultery.[n] The only reason for a man to divorce his wife is if his wife has sexual relations with another man."

[10]The followers said to him, "If that

19:4 'he made . . . female' Quotation from Genesis 1:27 or 5:2. **19:5 'So . . . body.'** Quotation from Genesis 2:24. **19:9 adultery** Some Greek copies continue, "And anyone who marries a divorced woman is guilty of adultery." Compare Matthew 5:32.

is the only reason a man can divorce his wife, it is better not to marry."

[11]Jesus answered, "Not everyone can accept this teaching, but God has made some able to accept it. [12]There are different reasons why some men cannot marry. Some men were born without the ability to become fathers. Others were made that way later in life by other people. And some men have given up marriage because of the kingdom of heaven. But the person who can marry should accept this teaching about marriage."[n]

Jesus Welcomes Children

[13]Then the people brought their little children to Jesus so he could put his hands on them[n] and pray for them. His followers told them to stop, [14]but Jesus said, "Let the little children come to me. Don't stop them, because the kingdom of heaven belongs to people who are like these children." [15]After Jesus put his hands on the children, he left there.

A Rich Young Man's Question

[16]A man came to Jesus and asked, "Teacher, what good thing must I do to have life forever?"

[17]Jesus answered, "Why do you ask me about what is good? Only God is good. But if you want to have life forever, obey the commands."

[18]The man asked, "Which commands?"

Jesus answered, " 'You must not murder anyone; you must not be guilty of adultery; you must not steal; you must not tell lies about your neighbor; [19]honor your father and mother;[n] and love your neighbor as you love yourself.' "[n]

[20]The young man said, "I have obeyed all these things. What else do I need to do?"

[21]Jesus answered, "If you want to be perfect, then go and sell your possessions and give the money to the poor. If you do this, you will have treasure in heaven. Then come and follow me."

[22]But when the young man heard this, he left sorrowfully, because he was rich.

[23]Then Jesus said to his followers, "I tell you the truth, it will be hard for a rich person to enter the kingdom of heaven. [24]Yes, I tell you that it is easier for a camel to go through the eye of a needle than for a rich person to enter the kingdom of God."

[25]When Jesus' followers heard this, they were very surprised and asked, "Then who can be saved?"

[26]Jesus looked at them and said, "For people this is impossible, but for God all things are possible."

[27]Peter said to Jesus, "Look, we have left everything and followed you. So what will we have?"

[28]Jesus said to them, "I tell you the truth, when the age to come has arrived, the Son of Man will sit on his great throne. All of you who followed me will also sit on twelve thrones, judging the twelve tribes of Israel. [29]And all those who have left houses, brothers, sisters, father, mother,[n] children, or farms to follow me will get much more than they left, and they will have life forever. [30]Many who are first now will be last in the future. And many who are last now will be first in the future.

A Story About Workers

20 "The kingdom of heaven is like a person who owned some land. One morning, he went out very early to hire some people to work in his vineyard. [2]The man agreed to pay the workers one coin[n] for working that day. Then he sent them into the vineyard to work. [3]About nine o'clock the man went

Matthew 19:16–30

When something you want is beyond your price range, what do you do? If it's truly valuable to you, there's a good chance you'd revise your spending habits to come up with enough cash. Normal budget constraints weaken when you're faced with your heart's desire! But what could be so valuable that you'd trade everything you possess for it?

Jesus made some pretty tough statements in this conversation with the rich young man. How could Jesus demand that he give up everything he owned?

The young man's questions revealed his pride—he thought he could please God on his own. So Jesus went beyond the surface "goodness" of this man's actions and showed what the young man really valued most. In this case, Jesus exposed the man's materialism.

Absolute perfection is necessary to get into heaven. And that, of course, is just as impossible as threading a camel through the eye of a needle. People can't achieve salvation! But God can do the impossible.

This story ends tragically. Unwilling to admit his spiritual poverty, this man clung to earthly wealth and walked away from Jesus, the only hope of salvation. We all have to ask ourselves: *Will I hold on to worthless "treasures" of this world or drop everything and follow Jesus?*

19:12 But . . . marriage. This may also mean, "The person who can accept this teaching about not marrying should accept it." **19:13 put his hands on them** Showing that Jesus gave special blessings to these children. **19:19 'You . . . mother.'** Quotation from Exodus 20:12–16; Deuteronomy 5:16–20. **19:19 'love . . . yourself.'** Quotation from Leviticus 19:18. **19:29 mother** Some Greek copies continue, "or wife." **20:2 coin** A Roman denarius. One coin was the average pay for one day's work.

to the marketplace and saw some other people standing there, doing nothing. [4]So he said to them, 'If you go and work in my vineyard, I will pay you what your work is worth.' [5]So they went to work in the vineyard. The man went out again about twelve o'clock and three o'clock and did the same thing. [6]About five o'clock the man went to the marketplace again and saw others standing there. He asked them, 'Why did you stand here all day doing nothing?' [7]They answered, 'No one gave us a job.' The man said to them, 'Then you can go and work in my vineyard.'

[8]"At the end of the day, the owner of the vineyard said to the boss of all the workers, 'Call the workers and pay them. Start with the last people I hired and end with those I hired first.'

[9]"When the workers who were hired at five o'clock came to get their pay, each received one coin. [10]When the workers who were hired first came to get their pay, they thought they would be paid more than the others. But each one of them also received one coin. [11]When they got their coin, they complained to the man who owned the land. [12]They said, 'Those people were hired last and worked only one hour. But you paid them the same as you paid us who worked hard all day in the hot sun.' [13]But the man who owned the vineyard said to one of those workers, 'Friend, I am being fair to you. You agreed to work for one coin. [14]So take your pay and go. I want to give the man who was hired last the same pay that I gave you. [15]I can do what I want with my own money. Are you jealous because I am good to those people?'

[16]"So those who are last now will someday be first, and those who are first now will someday be last."

Jesus Talks About His Own Death

[17]While Jesus was going to Jerusalem, he took his twelve followers aside privately and said to them, [18]"Look, we are going to Jerusalem. The Son of Man will be turned over to the leading priests and the teachers of the law, and they will say that he must die. [19]They will give the Son of Man to the non-Jewish people to laugh at him and beat him with whips and crucify him. But on the third day, he will be raised to life again."

A Mother Asks Jesus a Favor

[20]Then the wife of Zebedee came to Jesus with her sons. She bowed before him and asked him to do something for her.

[21]Jesus asked, "What do you want?"

She said, "Promise that one of my sons will sit at your right side and the other will sit at your left side in your kingdom."

[22]But Jesus said, "You don't understand what you are asking. Can you drink the cup that I am about to drink?"[n]

The sons answered, "Yes, we can."

[23]Jesus said to them, "You will drink from my cup. But I cannot choose who will sit at my right or my left; those places belong to those for whom my Father has prepared them."

[24]When the other ten followers heard this, they were angry with the two brothers.

[25]Jesus called all the followers together and said, "You know that the rulers of the non-Jewish people love to show their power over the people. And their important leaders love to use all their authority. [26]But it should not be that way among you. Whoever wants to become great among you must serve the rest of you like a servant. [27]Whoever wants to become first among you must serve the rest of you like a slave. [28]In the same way, the Son of Man did not come to be served. He came to serve others and to give his life as a ransom for many people."

Jesus Heals Two Blind Men

[29]When Jesus and his followers were leaving Jericho, a great many people followed him. [30]Two blind men sitting by the road heard that Jesus was going by, so they shouted, "Lord, Son of David, have mercy on us!"

[31]The people warned the blind men to be quiet, but they shouted even more, "Lord, Son of David, have mercy on us!"

[32]Jesus stopped and said to the blind men, "What do you want me to do for you?"

[33]They answered, "Lord, we want to see."

[34]Jesus felt sorry for the blind men and touched their eyes, and at once they could see. Then they followed Jesus.

Jesus Enters Jerusalem as a King

21 As Jesus and his followers were coming closer to Jerusalem, they stopped at Bethphage at the hill called the Mount of Olives. From there Jesus sent two of his followers [2]and said to them, "Go to the town you can see there. When you enter it, you will quickly find a donkey tied there with its colt. Untie them and bring them to me. [3]If anyone

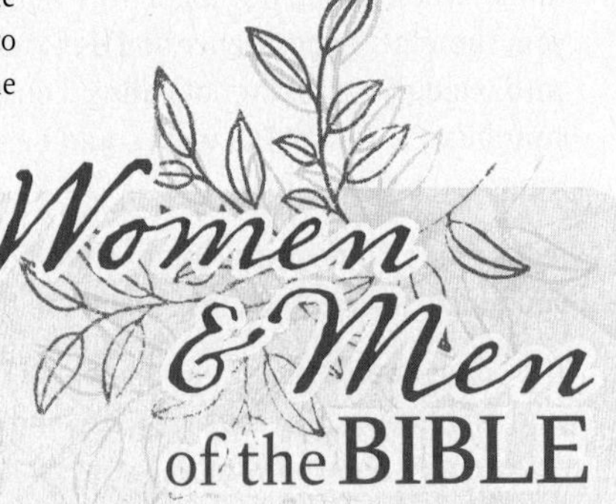

Timothy: The Original Apprentice

Timothy might have been young, but he was passionate about God. His mother and grandmother had modeled the importance of having a personal relationship with Christ. So it's no wonder Paul recognized a special spark in the young man. As they traveled the world, Paul gave him valuable on-the-job training and helped to develop his leadership qualities. Later, he even sent him out as his own personal representative to different churches. Paul wrote Timothy two letters encouraging him in the faith and reminding him that his mentor was always thankful for him. (1 and 2 Timothy)

20:22 drink . . . drink Jesus used the idea of drinking from a cup to ask if they could accept the same terrible things that would happen to him.

january

New Year's Day. Buy yourself a journal and start writing. 1	Reflect on your spiritual and personal goals for the year. 2	3	Celebrate National Spaghetti Day with a big plate of pasta and veggies. 4	Schedule birthday reminders for loved ones www.birthdayalarm.com 5
Learn how to recycle your Christmas tree www.christmastree.org 6	Make sure your gym membership is current. 7	8	Plan a winter adventure! Go skiing or sledding with friends. 9	10
11	12	Read a book that's reviewed in *Becoming 2008.* 13	14	It's *Martin Luther King, Jr.'s birthday.* Research his faith online. 15
16	Read Matthew 6—8. Share what you learn with a friend. 17	18	19	Keep a food diary for 3 days. Commit to healthy eating choices. 20
Celebrate Volunteer Blood Donor Month with a donation. 21	22	Pray for a person of influence: it's Mariska Hargitay's birthday. 23	Reflect on your New Year's resolutions. Are you still keeping them? 24	25
26	Review your finances and develop a plan to pay off any debt. 27	28	Pray for a person of influence: it's Oprah Winfrey's birthday. 29	30
As you receive them, file your W-2 tax forms in a safe place. 31				

The Beauty of Good Sense

Developing beauty of the body without developing beauty of the mind is useless. You could be the most beautiful woman in the world, but if you're not using the pretty head on your shoulders, you might as well be putting jewelry on a filthy animal. It's out of place and of no use. Proverbs 11:22 says, "A beautiful woman without good sense is like a gold ring in a pig's snout." A godly woman is as dedicated to her mind as she is to her spirit and body. Being smart, alert, aware, and informed—now *that's* beautiful!

asks you why you are taking the donkeys, say that the Master needs them, and he will send them at once."

[4]This was to bring about what the prophet had said:

[5]"Tell the people of Jerusalem,
'Your king is coming to you.
He is gentle and riding on a donkey,
on the colt of a donkey.' "
Isaiah 62:11; Zechariah 9:9

[6]The followers went and did what Jesus told them to do. [7]They brought the donkey and the colt to Jesus and laid their coats on them, and Jesus sat on them. [8]Many people spread their coats on the road. Others cut branches from the trees and spread them on the road. [9]The people were walking ahead of Jesus and behind him, shouting,

"Praise[n] to the Son of David!
God bless the One who comes in the name of the Lord! *Psalm 118:26*
Praise to God in heaven!"

[10]When Jesus entered Jerusalem, all the city was filled with excitement. The people asked, "Who is this man?"

[11]The crowd said, "This man is Jesus, the prophet from the town of Nazareth in Galilee."

Jesus Goes to the Temple

[12]Jesus went into the Temple and threw out all the people who were buying and selling there. He turned over the tables of those who were exchanging different kinds of money, and he upset the benches of those who were selling doves. [13]Jesus said to all the people there, "It is written in the Scriptures, 'My Temple will be called a house for prayer.'[n] But you are changing it into a 'hideout for robbers.' "[n]

[14]The blind and crippled people came to Jesus in the Temple, and he healed them. [15]The leading priests and the teachers of the law saw that Jesus was doing wonderful things and that the children were praising him in the Temple, saying, "Praise[n] to the Son of David." All these things made the priests and the teachers of the law very angry.

[16]They asked Jesus, "Do you hear the things these children are saying?"

Jesus answered, "Yes. Haven't you read in the Scriptures, 'You have taught children and babies to sing praises'?"[n]

[17]Then Jesus left and went out of the city to Bethany, where he spent the night.

The Power of Faith

[18]Early the next morning, as Jesus was going back to the city, he became hungry. [19]Seeing a fig tree beside the road, Jesus went to it, but there were no figs on the tree, only leaves. So Jesus said to the tree, "You will never again have fruit." The tree immediately dried up.

[20]When his followers saw this, they were amazed. They asked, "How did the fig tree dry up so quickly?"

[21]Jesus answered, "I tell you the truth, if you have faith and do not doubt, you will be able to do what I did to this tree and even more. You will be able to say to this mountain, 'Go, fall into the sea.' And if you have faith, it will happen. [22]If you believe, you will get anything you ask for in prayer."

Leaders Doubt Jesus' Authority

[23]Jesus went to the Temple, and while he was teaching there, the leading priests and the elders of the people came to him. They said, "What authority do you have to do these things? Who gave you this authority?"

[24]Jesus answered, "I also will ask you a question. If you answer me, then I will tell you what authority I have to do these things. [25]Tell me: When John baptized people, did that come from God or just from other people?"

They argued about Jesus' question, saying, "If we answer, 'John's baptism was from God,' Jesus will say, 'Then why didn't you believe him?' [26]But if we say, 'It was from people,' we are afraid of what the crowd will do because they all believe that John was a prophet."

fun facts

Between 1970 and 2000, the number of women attending college increased by 136%.

(The Atlantic.com)

21:9, 15 Praise Literally, "Hosanna," a Hebrew word used at first in praying to God for help. At this time it was probably a shout of joy used in praising God or his Messiah. **21:13 'My Temple . . . prayer.'** Quotation from Isaiah 56:7. **21:13 'hideout for robbers'** Quotation from Jeremiah 7:11. **21:16 'You . . . praises.'** Quotation from the Septuagint (Greek) version of Psalm 8:2.

[27]"So they answered Jesus, "We don't know."

Jesus said to them, "Then I won't tell you what authority I have to do these things.

A Story About Two Sons

[28]"Tell me what you think about this: A man had two sons. He went to the first son and said, 'Son, go and work today in my vineyard.' [29]The son answered, 'I will not go.' But later the son changed his mind and went. [30]Then the father went to the other son and said, 'Son, go and work today in my vineyard.' The son answered, 'Yes, sir, I will go and work,' but he did not go. [31]Which of the two sons obeyed his father?"

The priests and leaders answered, "The first son."

Jesus said to them, "I tell you the truth, the tax collectors and the prostitutes will enter the kingdom of God before you do. [32]John came to show you the right way to live. You did not believe him, but the tax collectors and prostitutes believed him. Even after seeing this, you still refused to change your ways and believe him.

A Story About God's Son

[33]"Listen to this story: There was a man who owned a vineyard. He put a wall around it and dug a hole for a winepress and built a tower. Then he leased the land to some farmers and left for a trip. [34]When it was time for the grapes to be picked, he sent his servants to the farmers to get his share of the grapes. [35]But the farmers grabbed the servants, beat one, killed another, and then killed a third servant with stones. [36]So the man sent some other servants to the farmers, even more than he sent the first time. But the farmers did the same thing to the servants that they had done before. [37]So the man decided to send his son to the farmers. He said, 'They will respect my son.' [38]But when the farmers saw the son, they said to each other, 'This son will inherit the vineyard. If we kill him, it will be ours!' [39]Then the farmers grabbed the son, threw him out of the vineyard, and killed him. [40]So what will the owner of the vineyard do to these farmers when he comes?"

[41]The priests and leaders said, "He will surely kill those evil men. Then he will lease the vineyard to some other farmers who will give him his share of the crop at harvest time."

[42]Jesus said to them, "Surely you have read this in the Scriptures:

'The stone that the builders
rejected
became the cornerstone.
The Lord did this,
and it is wonderful to us.'
Psalm 118:22-23

[43]"So I tell you that the kingdom of God will be taken away from you and given to people who do the things God wants in his kingdom. [44]The person who falls on this stone will be broken, and on whomever that stone falls, that person will be crushed."[n]

[45]When the leading priests and the Pharisees heard these stories, they knew Jesus was talking about them. [46]They wanted to arrest him, but they were afraid of the people, because the people believed that Jesus was a prophet.

A Story About a Wedding Feast

22 Jesus again used stories to teach them. He said, [2]"The kingdom of heaven is like a king who prepared a wedding feast for his son. [3]The king

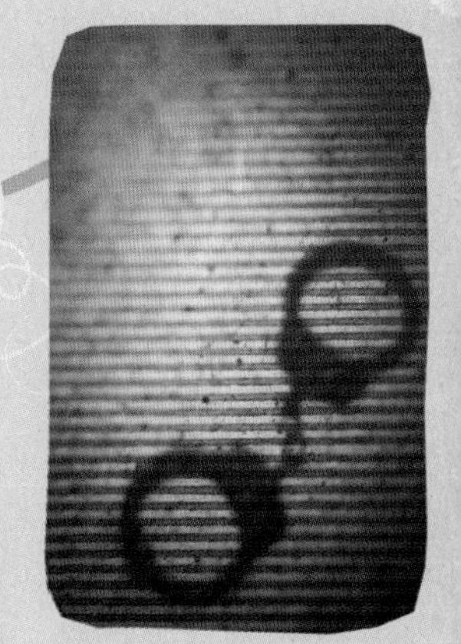

Voice of the Martyrs

As you might guess, the Voice of the Martyrs (VOM) is all about giving voice to the persecuted church. Every day, all around the world, countless men and women are tortured and/or killed simply because of their faith in Jesus. Despite the risk to their lives, they keep sharing the Good News with others. It's like something straight out of the Book of Acts!

You can subscribe to VOM's free newsletter for timely information and incredible stories of courage and sacrifice. Your faith will be inspired as you learn of your brothers and sisters in Christ who are suffering intense persecution. Through the newsletter and their online community (www.persecution.com), VOM not only raises awareness but also generates prayer support.

If the Lord places this ministry on your heart, you may want to donate to their ongoing programs of outreach and evangelism. And they're always looking for people who will help by being an advocate to raise more awareness among Christians in the United States. But more than anything, VOM begs you to pray for your fellow believers. That's something everyone can do!

21:44 The . . . crushed. Some Greek copies do not have verse 44.

invited some people to the feast. When the feast was ready, the king sent his servants to tell the people, but they refused to come.

4"Then the king sent other servants, saying, 'Tell those who have been invited that my feast is ready. I have killed my best bulls and calves for the dinner, and everything is ready. Come to the wedding feast.'

5"But the people refused to listen to the servants and left to do other things. One went to work in his field, and another went to his business. 6Some of the other people grabbed the servants, beat them, and killed them. 7The king was furious and sent his army to kill the murderers and burn their city.

8"After that, the king said to his servants, 'The wedding feast is ready. I invited those people, but they were not worthy to come. 9So go to the street corners and invite everyone you find to come to my feast.' 10So the servants went into the streets and gathered all the people they could find, both good and bad. And the wedding hall was filled with guests.

11"When the king came in to see the guests, he saw a man who was not dressed for a wedding. 12The king said, 'Friend, how were

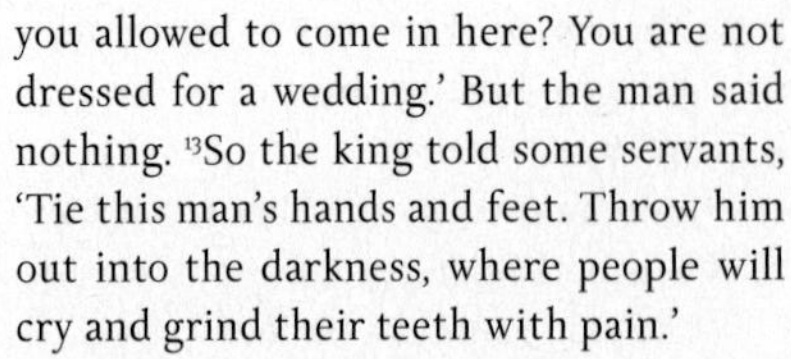

you allowed to come in here? You are not dressed for a wedding.' But the man said nothing. 13So the king told some servants, 'Tie this man's hands and feet. Throw him out into the darkness, where people will cry and grind their teeth with pain.'

14"Yes, many are invited, but only a few are chosen."

Is It Right to Pay Taxes or Not?

15Then the Pharisees left that place and made plans to trap Jesus in saying something wrong. 16They sent some of their own followers and some people from the group called Herodians.[n] They said, "Teacher, we know that you are an honest man and that you teach the truth about God's way. You are not afraid of what other people think about you, because you pay no attention to who they are. 17So tell us what you think. Is it right to pay taxes to Caesar or not?"

18But knowing that these leaders were trying to trick him, Jesus said, "You hypocrites! Why are you trying to trap me? 19Show me a coin used for paying the tax." So the men showed him a coin.[n] 20Then Jesus asked, "Whose image and name are on the coin?"

21The men answered, "Caesar's."

Then Jesus said to them, "Give to Caesar the things that are Caesar's, and give to God the things that are God's."

22When the men heard what Jesus said, they were amazed and left him and went away.

Some Sadducees Try to Trick Jesus

23That same day some Sadducees came to Jesus and asked him a question. (Sadducees believed that people would not rise from the dead.) 24They said, "Teacher, Moses said if a married man dies without having children, his brother must marry the widow and have children for him. 25Once there were seven brothers among us. The first one married and died. Since he had no children, his brother married the widow. 26Then the second brother also died. The same thing happened to the third brother and all the other brothers. 27Finally, the woman died. 28Since all seven men had married her, when people rise from the dead, whose wife will she be?"

29Jesus answered, "You don't understand, because you don't know what the Scriptures say, and you don't know about the power of God. 30When people rise from the dead, they will not marry, nor will they be given to someone to marry. They will be like the angels in heaven. 31Surely you have read what God said to you about rising from the dead. 32God said, 'I am the God of Abraham, the God of Isaac, and the God of Jacob.'[n] God is the God of the living, not the dead."

33When the people heard this, they were amazed at Jesus' teaching.

The Most Important Command

34When the Pharisees learned that the Sadducees could not argue with Jesus' answers to them, the Pharisees met together. 35One Pharisee, who was an expert on the law of Moses, asked Jesus this question to test him: 36"Teacher, which command in the law is the most important?"

37Jesus answered, " 'Love the Lord your God with all your heart, all your soul, and all your mind.'[n] 38This is the first and most important command. 39And the second command is like the first: 'Love your neighbor as you love yourself.'[n] 40All the law and the writings of the prophets depend on these two commands."

all about MEN

The Girlfriend or the Girl Friend?

Your guy loves God and treats you like gold. But there's one problem . . . his girl friend. They go way back. She doesn't seem to be a romantic threat, but your relationship with him feels crowded. As your commitment grows, opposite-sex friendships need to adjust, but handle this situation gently. Your concerns are valid, but so is their history. You're now enjoying time with him that she used to have, so be sensitive to the fact that they both may feel a loss. Study Proverbs 25:11–12, 15 for wisdom in approaching the subject with him. Pray for balanced emotions, choose your words carefully, and listen to his feelings. As your relationship deepens, theirs likely will modify itself on its own.

22:16 Herodians A political group that followed Herod and his family. **22:19 coin** A Roman denarius. One coin was the average pay for one day's work. **22:32 'I am . . . Jacob.'** Quotation from Exodus 3:6. **22:37 'Love . . . mind.'** Quotation from Deuteronomy 6:5. **22:39 'Love . . . yourself.'** Quotation from Leviticus 19:18.

Jesus Questions the Pharisees

[41]While the Pharisees were together, Jesus asked them, [42]"What do you think about the Christ? Whose son is he?"

They answered, "The Christ is the Son of David."

[43]Then Jesus said to them, "Then why did David call him 'Lord'? David, speaking by the power of the Holy Spirit, said,

[44]'The Lord said to my Lord,
"Sit by me at my right side,
until I put your enemies under
your control." ' *Psalm 110:1*

[45]David calls the Christ 'Lord,' so how can the Christ be his son?"

[46]None of the Pharisees could answer Jesus' question, and after that day no one was brave enough to ask him any more questions.

Jesus Accuses Some Leaders

23 Then Jesus said to the crowds and to his followers, [2]"The teachers of the law and the Pharisees have the authority to tell you what the law of Moses says. [3]So you should obey and follow whatever they tell you, but their lives are not good examples for you to follow. They tell you to do things, but they themselves don't do them. [4]They make strict rules and try to force people to obey them, but they are unwilling to help those who struggle under the weight of their rules.

[5]"They do good things so that other people will see them. They enlarge the little boxes[n] holding Scriptures that they wear, and they make their special prayer clothes very long. [6]Those Pharisees and teachers of the law love to have the most important seats at feasts and in the synagogues. [7]They love people to greet them with respect in the marketplaces, and they love to have people call them 'Teacher.'

[8]"But you must not be called 'Teacher,' because you have only one Teacher, and you are all brothers and sisters together. [9]And don't call any person on earth 'Father,' because you have one Father, who is in heaven. [10]And you should not be called 'Master,' because you have only one Master, the Christ. [11]Whoever is your servant is the greatest among you. [12]Whoever makes himself great will be made humble. Whoever makes himself humble will be made great.

[13]"How terrible for you, teachers of the law and Pharisees! You are hypocrites! You close the door for people to enter the kingdom of heaven. You yourselves don't enter, and you stop others who are trying to enter. [[14]How terrible for you, teachers of the law and Pharisees. You are hypocrites. You take away widows' houses, and you say long prayers so that people will notice you. So you will have a worse punishment.][n]

[15]"How terrible for you, teachers of the law and Pharisees! You are hypocrites! You travel across land and sea to find one person who will change to your ways. When you find that person, you make him more fit for hell than you are.

[16]"How terrible for you! You guide the

HE SAID ↙ ↗ SHE SAID

Which of Jesus' followers do you relate to best?

HE: Judas. Unfortunately, I have sold out too many times for selfish gain.

SHE: Peter. He made so many mistakes, but Jesus used him powerfully.

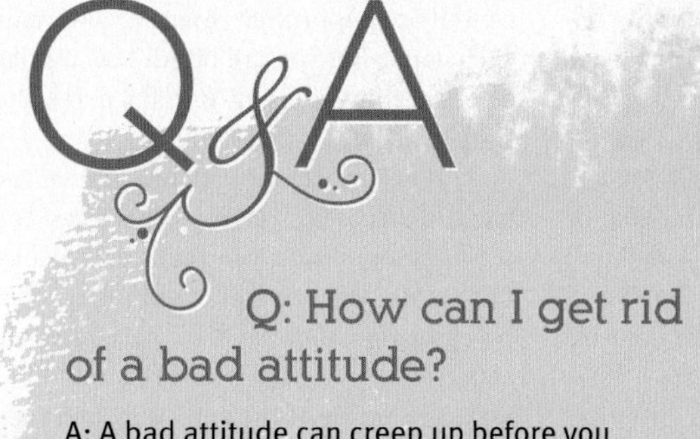

Q&A

Q: How can I get rid of a bad attitude?

A: A bad attitude can creep up before you know it. Your best bet is to nip it in the bud right away before it takes full root. As soon as you feel the 'tude approaching, make a purposeful choice not to give in. Take a moment to close your eyes, take a few deep breaths, and pray for the Holy Spirit to retake control of your heart. Confess your struggle to keep pure thoughts and ask the Lord to help you replace your attitude with one that glorifies him. The more you stop and do this, the easier it will become to battle the 'tude with grace!

23:5 boxes Small leather boxes containing four important Scriptures. Some Jews tied these to their foreheads and left arms, probably to show they were very religious. **23:14 How . . . punishment.** Some Greek copies do not contain the bracketed text.

Be Still & KNOW

No Time Like the Present

If you're a devoted Christ-follower, chances are the people around you know it. They will ask you to pray for them about different things, and even non-believers may ask for your prayers. When one of your friends shares a prayer request, do you ever

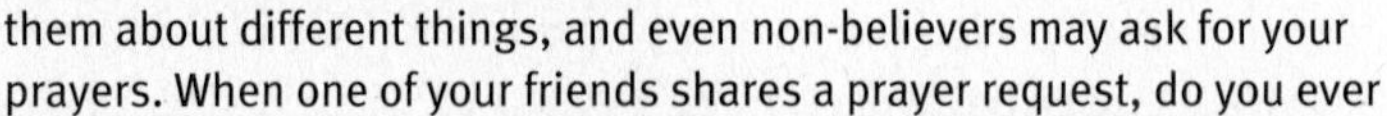

say you'll pray for them (with honest intentions) but occasionally forget to follow through? You're not alone! That's why it's a great practice to stop, focus, and pray *immediately* when you become aware of a need—even if you only have time for a quick prayer. If you're comfortable, consider praying with your friend aloud. That way you'll be sure to do what you promised. You can also pray on your own later on!

people, but you are blind. You say, 'If people swear by the Temple when they make a promise, that means nothing. But if they swear by the gold that is in the Temple, they must keep that promise.' [17]You are blind fools! Which is greater: the gold or the Temple that makes that gold holy? [18]And you say, 'If people swear by the altar when they make a promise, that means nothing. But if they swear by the gift on the altar, they must keep that promise.' [19]You are blind! Which is greater: the gift or the altar that makes the gift holy? [20]The person who swears by the altar is really using the altar and also everything on the altar. [21]And the person who swears by the Temple is really using the Temple and also everything in the Temple. [22]The person who swears by heaven is also using God's throne and the One who sits on that throne.

[23]"How terrible for you, teachers of the law and Pharisees! You are hypocrites! You give to God one-tenth of everything you earn—even your mint, dill, and cumin.[n] But you don't obey the really important teachings of the law—justice, mercy, and being loyal. These are the things you should do, as well as those other things. [24]You guide the people, but you are blind! You are like a person who picks a fly out of a drink and then swallows a camel![n]

[25]"How terrible for you, teachers of the law and Pharisees! You are hypocrites! You wash the outside of your cups and dishes, but inside they are full of things you got by cheating others and by pleasing only yourselves. [26]Pharisees, you are blind! First make the inside of the cup clean, and then the outside of the cup can be truly clean.

[27]"How terrible for you, teachers of the law and Pharisees! You are hypocrites! You are like tombs that are painted white. Outside, those tombs look fine, but inside, they are full of the bones of dead people and all kinds of unclean things. [28]It is the same with you. People look at you and think you are good, but on the inside you are full of hypocrisy and evil.

[29]"How terrible for you, teachers of the law and Pharisees! You are hypocrites! You build tombs for the prophets, and you show honor to the graves of those who lived good lives. [30]You say, 'If we had lived during the time of our ancestors, we would not have helped them kill the prophets.' [31]But you give proof that you are descendants of those who murdered the prophets. [32]And you will complete the sin that your ancestors started.

[33]"You are snakes! A family of poisonous snakes! How are you going to escape God's judgment? [34]So I tell you this: I am sending to you prophets and wise men and teachers. Some of them you will kill and crucify. Some of them you will beat in your synagogues and chase from town to town. [35]So you will be guilty for the death of all the good people who have been killed on earth—from the murder of that good man Abel to the murder of Zechariah[n] son of Berakiah, whom you murdered between the Temple and the altar. [36]I tell you the truth, all of these things will happen to you people who are living now.

Jesus Feels Sorry for Jerusalem

[37]"Jerusalem, Jerusalem! You kill the prophets and stone to death those who are sent to you. Many times I wanted to gather your people as a hen gathers her chicks under her wings, but you did not let me. [38]Now your house will be left completely empty. [39]I tell you, you will not see me again until that time when you will say, 'God bless the One who comes in the name of the Lord.' "[n]

The Temple Will Be Destroyed

24 As Jesus left the Temple and was walking away, his followers came up to show him the Temple's buildings. [2]Jesus asked, "Do you see all these buildings? I tell you the truth, not one stone will be left on another. Every stone will be thrown down to the ground."

[3]Later, as Jesus was sitting on the Mount of Olives, his followers came to be alone with him. They said, "Tell us, when will these things happen? And what will be the sign that it is time for you to come again and for this age to end?"

[4]Jesus answered, "Be careful that no one fools you. [5]Many will come in my name, saying, 'I am the Christ,' and they will fool many people. [6]You will hear about wars and stories of wars that are coming,

23:23 mint, dill, and cumin Small plants grown in gardens and used for spices. Only very religious people would be careful enough to give a tenth of these plants. **23:24 You . . . camel!** Meaning, "You worry about the smallest mistakes but commit the biggest sin." **23:35 Abel . . . Zechariah** In the order of the books of the Hebrew Old Testament, the first and last men to be murdered. **23:39 'God . . . Lord.'** Quotation from Psalm 118:26.

but don't be afraid. These things must happen before the end comes. [7]Nations will fight against other nations; kingdoms will fight against other kingdoms. There will be times when there is no food for people to eat, and there will be earthquakes in different places. [8]These things are like the first pains when something new is about to be born.

[9]"Then people will arrest you, hand you over to be hurt, and kill you. They will hate you because you believe in me. [10]At that time, many will lose their faith, and they will turn against each other and hate each other. [11]Many false prophets will come and cause many people to believe lies. [12]There will be more and more evil in the world, so most people will stop showing their love for each other. [13]But those people who keep their faith until the end will be saved. [14]The Good News about God's kingdom will be preached in all the world, to every nation. Then the end will come.

[15]"Daniel the prophet spoke about 'a blasphemous object that brings destruction.'[n] You will see this standing in the holy place." (You who read this should understand what it means.) [16]"At that time, the people in Judea should run away to the mountains. [17]If people are on the roofs[n] of their houses, they must not go down to get anything out of their houses. [18]If people are in the fields, they must not go back to get their coats. [19]At that time, how terrible it will be for women who are pregnant or have nursing babies! [20]Pray that it will not be winter or a Sabbath day when these things happen and you have to run away, [21]because at that time there will be much trouble. There will be more trouble than there has ever been since the beginning of the world until now, and nothing as bad will ever happen again. [22]God has decided to make that terrible time short. Otherwise, no one would go on living. But God will make that time short to help the people he has chosen. [23]At that time, someone might say to you, 'Look, there is the Christ!' Or another person might say, 'There he is!' But don't believe them. [24]False Christs and false prophets will come and perform great wonders and miracles. They will try to fool even the people God has chosen, if that is possible. [25]Now I have warned you about this before it happens.

[26]"If people tell you, 'The Christ is in the desert,' don't go there. If they say, 'The Christ is in the inner room,' don't believe it. [27]When the Son of Man comes, he will be seen by everyone, like lightning flashing from the east to the west. [28]Wherever the dead body is, there the vultures will gather.

[29]"Soon after the trouble of those days,
'the sun will grow dark,
and the moon will not give its light.
The stars will fall from the sky.
And the powers of the heavens
will be shaken.'

Isaiah 13:10; 34:4

[30]"At that time, the sign of the Son of Man will appear in the sky. Then all the peoples of the world will cry. They will see the Son of Man coming on clouds in the sky with great power and glory. [31]He will use a

virtue BUILDING: Love

What is true love? Maybe you're thinking of that sweet (and admittedly cheesy) romantic DVD you're tempted to watch on rainy days. Do you imagine that true love will happen when you meet the perfect guy? Those things might contain aspects of love, but the truth is that there is a lot more to real love.

Love isn't just those warm fuzzies you get when you're around someone you're interested in—it's about serious sacrifice. It's not just a token act of kindness here and there—it's a lifestyle of service.

Jesus' love led him to the Cross. He said that all of God's commands could be summed up in loving God and loving people. It sounds simple, but living it is impossible without divine assistance. Learning to truly love God and the people around us is what following Jesus is all about; it identifies us as Christians. Want to infuse your life with this virtue? Read on.

Scripture Breakdown

The best way to start understanding the virtue of love is by studying Jesus. He lived a perfect life of love, and you can read about it in the first four books of the New Testament. Then check out the short and profound Book of 1 John. The apostle John was described as "the follower Jesus loved" and definitely knew a thing or two about true love (John 13:23). And finally there is 1 Corinthians 13, the famous "Love Chapter." This handy list gives you all the vital info on what love is (and what it's not).

Build It into Your Life

- Consider what it means to live a life of love. Give love until it hurts, and then give some more.
- Love = Obedience to God. (John 14:15)
- Think of the most unlovable person you know, and come up with ways to act like Jesus toward him or her.
- What things in your life do you love more than God? Take steps to ensure that God is at the top of your love list.
- Reflect on how God shows his love for you, and take his love into every area of your life—how you think, speak, and act.

24:15 'a blasphemous object that brings destruction' Mentioned in Daniel 9:27; 12:11 (see also Daniel 11:31). **24:17 roofs** In Bible times houses were built with flat roofs. The roof was used for drying things such as flax and fruit. And it was used as an extra room, as a place for worship, and as a cool place to sleep in the summer.

RELATIONSHIPS

The Gossip Queen's Court

Most of us know a gossip queen, and most of us know gossip is wrong. But is it wrong to sit in her court of listeners . . . even for just a minute or two? Yes. Welcoming gossip isn't healthy for anyone. It reveals a lack of commitment to godly words and actions. While it may not feel easy or comfortable to walk away or say you'd rather not hear those stories, there's peace knowing you're pleasing God by avoiding gossip's destructive ways. Be a Proverbs 20:19 (not a Proverbs 26:22) person, and avoid the gossip queen's court.

loud trumpet to send his angels all around the earth, and they will gather his chosen people from every part of the world.

[32]"Learn a lesson from the fig tree: When its branches become green and soft and new leaves appear, you know summer is near. [33]In the same way, when you see all these things happening, you will know that the time is near, ready to come. [34]I tell you the truth, all these things will happen while the people of this time are still living. [35]Earth and sky will be destroyed, but the words I have said will never be destroyed.

When Will Jesus Come Again?

[36]"No one knows when that day or time will be, not the angels in heaven, not even the Son.[n] Only the Father knows. [37]When the Son of Man comes, it will be like what happened during Noah's time. [38]In those days before the flood, people were eating and drinking, marrying and giving their children to be married, until the day Noah entered the boat. [39]They knew nothing about what was happening until the flood came and destroyed them. It will be the same when the Son of Man comes. [40]Two men will be in the field. One will be taken, and the other will be left. [41]Two women will be grinding grain with a mill.[n] One will be taken, and the other will be left.

[42]"So always be ready, because you don't know the day your Lord will come. [43]Remember this: If the owner of the house knew what time of night a thief was coming, the owner would watch and not let the thief break in. [44]So you also must be ready, because the Son of Man will come at a time you don't expect him.

[45]"Who is the wise and loyal servant that the master trusts to give the other servants their food at the right time? [46]When the master comes and finds the servant doing his work, the servant will be blessed. [47]I tell you the truth, the master will choose that servant to take care of everything he owns. [48]But suppose that evil servant thinks to himself, 'My master will not come back soon,' [49]and he begins to beat the other servants and eat and get drunk with others like him? [50]The master will come when that servant is not ready and is not expecting him. [51]Then the master will cut him in pieces and send him away to be with the hypocrites, where people will cry and grind their teeth with pain.

According to a 14-year study, women who improved their endurance on treadmill tests halved their risk factors for heart disease.

(Self.com)

A Story About Ten Bridesmaids

25 "At that time the kingdom of heaven will be like ten bridesmaids who took their lamps and went to wait for the bridegroom. [2]Five

24:36 not even the Son Some Greek copies do not have this phrase. **24:41 mill** Two large, round, flat rocks used for grinding grain to make flour.

of them were foolish and five were wise. [3]The five foolish bridesmaids took their lamps, but they did not take more oil for the lamps to burn. [4]The wise bridesmaids took their lamps and more oil in jars. [5]Because the bridegroom was late, they became sleepy and went to sleep.

[6]"At midnight someone cried out, 'The bridegroom is coming! Come and meet him!' [7]Then all the bridesmaids woke up and got their lamps ready. [8]But the foolish ones said to the wise, 'Give us some of your oil, because our lamps are going out.' [9]The wise bridesmaids answered, 'No, the oil we have might not be enough for all of us. Go to the people who sell oil and buy some for yourselves.'

[10]"So while the five foolish bridesmaids went to buy oil, the bridegroom came. The bridesmaids who were ready went in with the bridegroom to the wedding feast. Then the door was closed and locked.

[11]"Later the others came back and said, 'Sir, sir, open the door to let us in.' [12]But the bridegroom answered, 'I tell you the truth, I don't want to know you.'

[13]"So always be ready, because you don't know the day or the hour the Son of Man will come.

A Story About Three Servants

[14]"The kingdom of heaven is like a man who was going to another place for a visit. Before he left, he called for his servants and told them to take care of his things while he was gone. [15]He gave one servant five bags of gold, another servant two bags of gold, and a third servant one bag of gold, to each one as much as he could handle. Then he left. [16]The servant who got five bags went quickly to invest the money and earned five more bags. [17]In the same way, the servant who had two bags invested them and earned two more. [18]But the servant who got one bag went out and dug a hole in the ground and hid the master's money.

[19]"After a long time the master came home and asked the servants what they did with his money. [20]The servant who was given five bags of gold brought five more bags to the master and said, 'Master, you trusted me to care for five bags of gold, so I used your five bags to earn five more.' [21]The master answered, 'You did well. You are a good and loyal servant. Because you were loyal with small things, I will let you care for much greater things. Come and share my joy with me.'

[22]"Then the servant who had been given two bags of gold came to the master and said, 'Master, you gave me two bags of gold to care for, so I used your two bags to earn two more.' [23]The master answered, 'You did well. You are a good and loyal servant. Because you were loyal with small things, I will let you care for much greater things. Come and share my joy with me.'

[24]"Then the servant who had been given one bag of gold came to the master and said, 'Master, I knew that you were a hard man. You harvest things you did not plant. You gather crops where you did not sow any seed. [25]So I was afraid and went and hid your money in the ground. Here is your bag of gold.' [26]The master answered, 'You are a wicked and lazy servant! You say you knew that I harvest things I did not plant and that I gather crops where I did not sow any seed. [27]So you should have put my gold in the bank. Then, when I came home, I would have received my gold back with interest.'

[28]"So the master told his other servants, 'Take the bag of gold from that servant and give it to the servant who has ten bags of gold. [29]Those who have much will get more, and they will have much more than they need. But those who do

Matthew 25:40

Think of the things that make up a meaningful relationship. What comes to mind? Communication, self-sacrifice, warmth, affection, closeness, quality time, and common experiences might make the list. If you want to begin and sustain a relationship, it's obvious that you'd need plenty of opportunities to connect with that person. It's no different in our relationship with God. To truly have a meaningful relationship with him, we need ways to communicate and express love.

God uses the Bible to clue us in on what makes him God—his love, his personality, the benefits he gives for free . . . not to mention that he paid for our sins before we ever knew he loved us. From his behavior, it's obvious that he is crazy about his people. So how can we show affection and thankfulness to *him*?

Scripture is full of ways to tell God how much we love him. Matthew 25:40 is a specific example: we love God in a tangible way by serving people that are ignored and rejected by society. God is near when we love the outcasts of the world.

Service is one of the many ways God provides for us to show love directly to him . . . don't miss these opportunities!

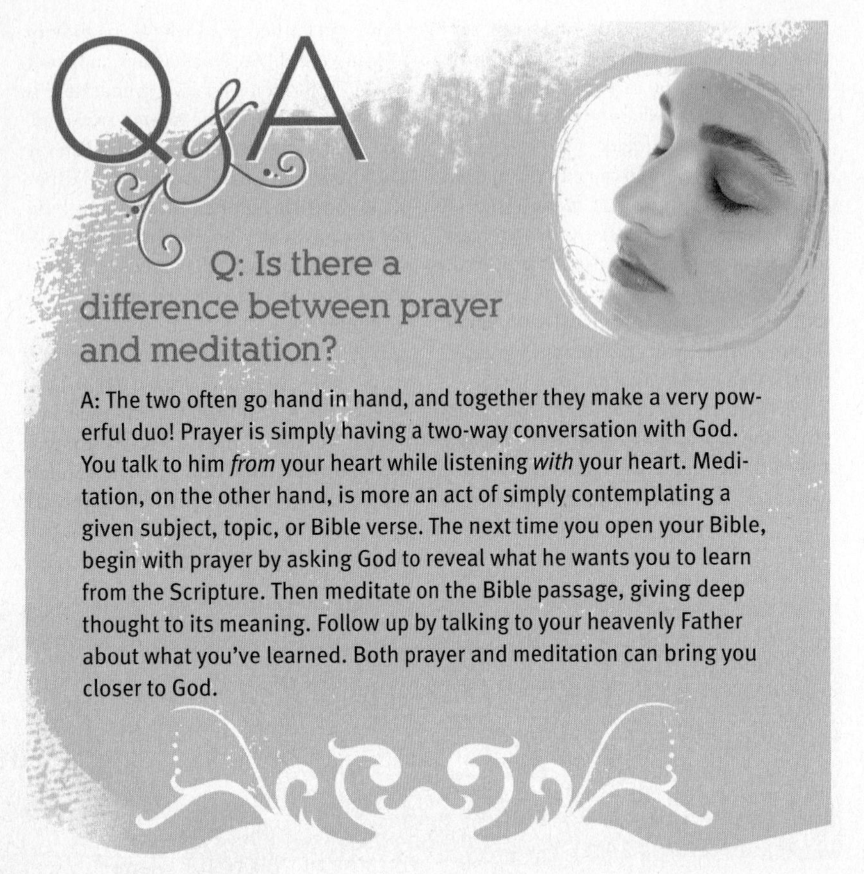

Q: Is there a difference between prayer and meditation?

A: The two often go hand in hand, and together they make a very powerful duo! Prayer is simply having a two-way conversation with God. You talk to him *from* your heart while listening *with* your heart. Meditation, on the other hand, is more an act of simply contemplating a given subject, topic, or Bible verse. The next time you open your Bible, begin with prayer by asking God to reveal what he wants you to learn from the Scripture. Then meditate on the Bible passage, giving deep thought to its meaning. Follow up by talking to your heavenly Father about what you've learned. Both prayer and meditation can bring you closer to God.

not have much will have everything taken away from them.' [30]Then the master said, 'Throw that useless servant outside, into the darkness where people will cry and grind their teeth with pain.'

The King Will Judge All People

[31]"The Son of Man will come again in his great glory, with all his angels. He will be King and sit on his great throne. [32]All the nations of the world will be gathered before him, and he will separate them into two groups as a shepherd separates the sheep from the goats. [33]The Son of Man will put the sheep on his right and the goats on his left.

[34]"Then the King will say to the people on his right, 'Come, my Father has given you his blessing. Receive the kingdom God has prepared for you since the world was made. [35]I was hungry, and you gave me food. I was thirsty, and you gave me something to drink. I was alone and away from home, and you invited me into your house. [36]I was without clothes, and you gave me something to wear. I was sick, and you cared for me. I was in prison, and you visited me.'

[37]"Then the good people will answer, 'Lord, when did we see you hungry and give you food, or thirsty and give you something to drink? [38]When did we see you alone and away from home and invite you into our house? When did we see you without clothes and give you something to wear? [39]When did we see you sick or in prison and care for you?'

[40]"Then the King will answer, 'I tell you the truth, anything you did for even the least of my people here, you also did for me.'

[41]"Then the King will say to those on his left, 'Go away from me. You will be punished. Go into the fire that burns forever that was prepared for the devil and his angels. [42]I was hungry, and you gave me nothing to eat. I was thirsty, and you gave me nothing to drink. [43]I was alone and away from home, and you did not invite me into your house. I was without clothes, and you gave me nothing to wear. I was sick and in prison, and you did not care for me.'

[44]"Then those people will answer, 'Lord, when did we see you hungry or thirsty or alone and away from home or without clothes or sick or in prison? When did we see these things and not help you?'

[45]"Then the King will answer, 'I tell you the truth, anything you refused to do for even the least of my people here, you refused to do for me.'

[46]"These people will go off to be punished forever, but the good people will go to live forever."

The Plan to Kill Jesus

26 After Jesus finished saying all these things, he told his followers, [2]"You know that the day after tomorrow is the day of the Passover Feast. On that day the Son of Man will be given to his enemies to be crucified."

[3]Then the leading priests and the elders had a meeting at the palace of the high priest, named Caiaphas. [4]At the meeting, they planned to set a trap to arrest Jesus and kill him. [5]But they said, "We must not do it during the feast, because the people might cause a riot."

Perfume for Jesus' Burial

[6]Jesus was in Bethany at the house of Simon, who had a skin disease. [7]While Jesus was there, a woman approached him with an alabaster jar filled with expensive perfume. She poured this perfume on Jesus' head while he was eating.

[8]His followers were upset when they saw the woman do this. They asked, "Why waste that perfume? [9]It could have been sold for a great deal of money and the money given to the poor."

[10]Knowing what had happened, Jesus said, "Why are you troubling this woman? She did an excellent thing for me. [11]You will always have the poor with you, but you will not always have me. [12]This woman poured perfume on my body to prepare me for burial. [13]I tell you the truth, wherever the Good News is preached in all the world, what this woman has done will be told, and people will remember her."

Judas Becomes an Enemy of Jesus

[14]Then one of the twelve apostles, Judas Iscariot, went to talk to the leading priests.

Guarding Worship

If we were created to worship God, why doesn't worship always come easily? Maybe you've sat in church trying to focus on God, only to leave wondering if you ever connected with him in the flurry of other thoughts. We can blame the busyness of our lifestyles, but we're really no different from other generations. Luke 10 tells of two sisters with different worship habits. Mary discovered true worship by trading her to-do list for time in Jesus' presence, while Martha grew discontent and distant from him in the rush of the moment. Like most of us, she needed to put aside her cares and practice focusing on the Lord. Someday we'll be free of this life's distractions. For now, we need to guard our worship time.

[15]He said, "What will you pay me for giving Jesus to you?" And they gave him thirty silver coins. [16]After that, Judas watched for the best time to turn Jesus in.

Jesus Eats the Passover Meal

[17]On the first day of the Feast of Unleavened Bread, the followers came to Jesus. They said, "Where do you want us to prepare for you to eat the Passover meal?"

[18]Jesus answered, "Go into the city to a certain man and tell him, 'The Teacher says: "The chosen time is near. I will have the Passover with my followers at your house." ' " [19]The followers did what Jesus told them to do, and they prepared the Passover meal.

[20]In the evening Jesus was sitting at the table with his twelve followers. [21]As they were eating, Jesus said, "I tell you the truth, one of you will turn against me."

[22]This made the followers very sad. Each one began to say to Jesus, "Surely, Lord, I am not the one who will turn against you, am I?"

[23]Jesus answered, "The man who has dipped his hand with me into the bowl is the one who will turn against me. [24]The Son of Man will die, just as the Scriptures say. But how terrible it will be for the person who hands the Son of Man over to be killed. It would be better for him if he had never been born."

[25]Then Judas, who would give Jesus to his enemies, said to Jesus, "Teacher, surely I am not the one, am I?"

Jesus answered, "Yes, it is you."

The Lord's Supper

[26]While they were eating, Jesus took some bread and thanked God for it and broke it. Then he gave it to his followers and said, "Take this bread and eat it; this is my body."

[27]Then Jesus took a cup and thanked God for it and gave it to the followers. He said, "Every one of you drink this. [28]This is my blood which is the new[n] agreement that God makes with his people. This blood is poured out for many to forgive their sins. [29]I tell you this: I will not drink of this fruit of the vine[n] again until that day when I drink it new with you in my Father's kingdom."

[30]After singing a hymn, they went out to the Mount of Olives.

Jesus' Followers Will Leave Him

[31]Jesus told his followers, "Tonight you will all stumble in your faith on account of me, because it is written in the Scriptures:

'I will kill the shepherd,
and the sheep will scatter.'

Zechariah 13:7

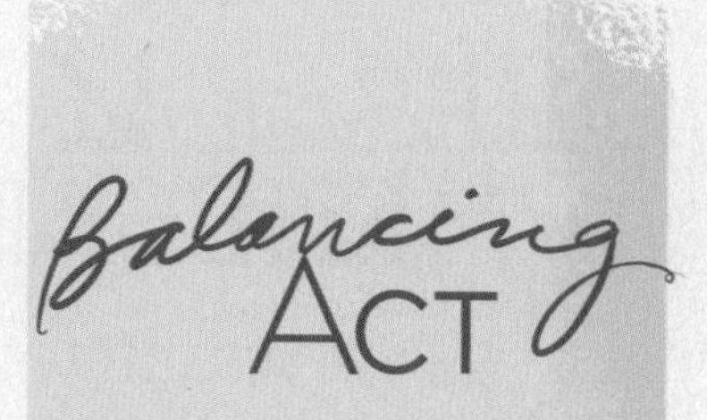

And Baby Makes Three

You met Mr. Right, got hitched, and spent the first year or so enjoying life as a newlywed. Now, you're entering phase two: parenthood. The arrival of a baby can send shockwaves through even the most solid marriage. The tendency to put your child's needs first is instinctual. But it's essential to remember you were a *wife* before you became a *mother*. Balancing dual roles is challenging, especially in the first few months. New responsibilities coupled with sleepless nights can cause tempers to flare and resentment to build. Still, the greatest gift you can give your child is the security of knowing she has two parents who love *her*, love *God*, and love *each other*. Alone time with your spouse allows you to relax, rejuvenate, and recharge—readying you to tackle parenting as a team! Remember, nurturing your marriage will ultimately benefit your child.

26:28 new Some Greek copies do not have this word. Compare Luke 22:20. **26:29 fruit of the vine** Product of the grapevine; this may also be translated "wine."

HE SAID ↙ ↗ SHE SAID

What country do you most want to visit as part of an outreach?

He: New Zealand

She: South Africa

[32]But after I rise from the dead, I will go ahead of you into Galilee."

[33]Peter said, "Everyone else may stumble in their faith because of you, but I will not."

[34]Jesus said, "I tell you the truth, tonight before the rooster crows you will say three times that you don't know me."

[35]But Peter said, "I will never say that I don't know you! I will even die with you!" And all the other followers said the same thing.

Jesus Prays Alone

[36]Then Jesus went with his followers to a place called Gethsemane. He said to them, "Sit here while I go over there and pray." [37]He took Peter and the two sons of Zebedee with him, and he began to be very sad and troubled. [38]He said to them, "My heart is full of sorrow, to the point of death. Stay here and watch with me."

[39]After walking a little farther away from them, Jesus fell to the ground and prayed, "My Father, if it is possible, do not give me this cup[n] of suffering. But do what you want, not what I want." [40]Then Jesus went back to his followers and found them asleep. He said to Peter, "You men could not stay awake with me for one hour? [41]Stay awake and pray for strength against temptation. The spirit wants to do what is right, but the body is weak."

[42]Then Jesus went away a second time and prayed, "My Father, if it is not possible for this painful thing to be taken from me, and if I must do it, I pray that what you want will be done."

[43]Then he went back to his followers, and again he found them asleep, because their eyes were heavy. [44]So Jesus left them and went away and prayed a third time, saying the same thing.

[45]Then Jesus went back to his followers and said, "Are you still sleeping and resting? The time has come for the Son of Man to be handed over to sinful people. [46]Get up, we must go. Look, here comes the man who has turned against me."

Jesus Is Arrested

[47]While Jesus was still speaking, Judas, one of the twelve apostles, came up. With him were many people carrying swords and clubs who had been sent from the leading priests and the Jewish elders of the people. [48]Judas had planned to give them a signal, saying, "The man I kiss is Jesus. Arrest him." [49]At once Judas went to Jesus and said, "Greetings, Teacher!" and kissed him.

[50]Jesus answered, "Friend, do what you came to do."

Then the people came and grabbed Jesus and arrested him. [51]When that happened, one of Jesus' followers reached for his sword and pulled it out. He struck the servant of the high priest and cut off his ear.

[52]Jesus said to the man, "Put your sword back in its place. All who use swords will be killed with swords. [53]Surely you know I could ask my Father, and he would give me more than twelve armies of angels. [54]But it must happen this way to bring about what the Scriptures say."

[55]Then Jesus said to the crowd, "You came to get me with swords and clubs as if I were a criminal. Every day I sat in the Temple teaching, and you did not arrest me there. [56]But all these things have happened so that it will come about as the prophets wrote." Then all of Jesus' followers left him and ran away.

Jesus Before the Leaders

[57]Those people who arrested Jesus led him to the house of Caiaphas, the high

Beauty Tricks

The quest for beauty can be tricky. It can trick you into thinking you have to look a certain way or act like you're a diva. Society's ever-changing definitions of it can drive you mad. Apparently, this very illusive desire for beauty has been tricking women for centuries because even King Solomon noticed it. In Proverbs 31:30 he says, "Charm can fool you, and beauty can trick you, but a woman who respects the Lord should be praised." Don't let the world fool you into seeking after something that is tricky and fleeting; seek after God instead.

26:39 cup Jesus is talking about the terrible things that will happen to him. Accepting these things will be very hard, like drinking a cup of something bitter.

priest, where the teachers of the law and the elders were gathered. [58]Peter followed far behind to the courtyard of the high priest's house, and he sat down with the guards to see what would happen to Jesus.

[59]The leading priests and the whole Jewish council tried to find something false against Jesus so they could kill him. [60]Many people came and told lies about him, but the council could find no real reason to kill him. Then two people came and said, [61]"This man said, 'I can destroy the Temple of God and build it again in three days.' "

[62]Then the high priest stood up and said to Jesus, "Aren't you going to answer? Don't you have something to say about their charges against you?" [63]But Jesus said nothing.

Again the high priest said to Jesus, "I command you by the power of the living God: Tell us if you are the Christ, the Son of God."

[64]Jesus answered, "Those are your words. But I tell you, in the future you will see the Son of Man sitting at the right hand of God, the Powerful One, and coming on clouds in the sky."

[65]When the high priest heard this, he tore his clothes and said, "This man has said things that are against God! We don't need any more witnesses; you all heard him say these things against God. [66]What do you think?"

The people answered, "He should die."

[67]Then the people there spat in Jesus' face and beat him with their fists. Others slapped him. [68]They said, "Prove to us that you are a prophet, you Christ! Tell us who hit you!"

Peter Says He Doesn't Know Jesus

[69]At that time, as Peter was sitting in the courtyard, a servant girl came to him and said, "You also were with Jesus of Galilee."

[70]But Peter said to all the people there that he was never with Jesus. He said, "I don't know what you are talking about."

[71]When he left the courtyard and was at the gate, another girl saw him. She said to the people there, "This man was with Jesus of Nazareth."

[72]Again, Peter said he was never with him, saying, "I swear I don't know this man Jesus!"

[73]A short time later, some people standing there went to Peter and said, "Surely you are one of those who followed Jesus. The way you talk shows it."

[74]Then Peter began to place a curse on himself and swear, "I don't know the man." At once, a rooster crowed. [75]And Peter remembered what Jesus had told him: "Before the rooster crows, you will say three times that you don't know me." Then Peter went outside and cried painfully.

Jesus Is Taken to Pilate

27 Early the next morning, all the leading priests and elders of the people decided that Jesus should die. [2]They tied him, led him away, and turned him over to Pilate, the governor.

Judas Kills Himself

[3]Judas, the one who had given Jesus to his enemies, saw that they had decided to kill Jesus. Then he was very sorry for what he had done. So he took the thirty silver coins back to the priests and the leaders, [4]saying, "I sinned; I handed over to you an innocent man."

The leaders answered, "What is that to us? That's your problem, not ours."

[5]So Judas threw the money into the Temple. Then he went off and hanged himself.

[6]The leading priests picked up the silver coins in the Temple and said, "Our law does not allow us to keep this money with the Temple money, because it has paid for a man's death." [7]So they decided to use the coins to buy Potter's Field as a place to bury strangers who died in Jerusalem. [8]That is why that field is still called the Field of Blood. [9]So what Jeremiah the prophet had said came true: "They took thirty silver coins. That is how little the Israelites thought he was worth. [10]They used those thirty silver coins to buy the potter's field, as the Lord commanded me."[n]

Pilate Questions Jesus

[11]Jesus stood before Pilate the governor, and Pilate asked him, "Are you the king of the Jews?"

Jesus answered, "Those are your words."

[12]When the leading priests and the elders accused Jesus, he said nothing.

[13]So Pilate said to Jesus, "Don't you hear them accusing you of all these things?"

Just Say the Name

Shakespeare asked, "What's in a name?" Power and authority, if you're talking about the name *Jesus*. In fact, the Bible says the name of Jesus is "greater than every other name" (Philippians 2:9–10). When you find yourself sinking in anxiety or worry, saying God's name out loud can comfort and empower you. Try speaking the name that fits your specific need. Do you have financial burdens? *Jehovah-jireh* means "the Lord who provides." Is there a medical crisis in your family? *Jehovah-rophe* means "the Lord who heals." Are you fighting a spiritual battle? *Jehovah-nissi* means "the Lord who reigns victorious." When you can't seem to put your finger on the root of your anxiety, *Jehovah-shalom* is a great encouragement: "the Lord of peace."

27:9–10 "They . . . commanded me." See Zechariah 11:12–13 and Jeremiah 32:6–9.

[14]But Jesus said nothing in answer to Pilate, and Pilate was very surprised at this.

Pilate Tries to Free Jesus

[15]Every year at the time of Passover the governor would free one prisoner whom the people chose. [16]At that time there was a man in prison, named Barabbas,[n] who was known to be very bad. [17]When the people gathered at Pilate's house, Pilate said, "Whom do you want me to set free: Barabbas[n] or Jesus who is called the Christ?" [18]Pilate knew that they turned Jesus in to him because they were jealous.

[19]While Pilate was sitting there on the judge's seat, his wife sent this message to him: "Don't do anything to that man, because he is innocent. Today I had a dream about him, and it troubled me very much."

[20]But the leading priests and elders convinced the crowd to ask for Barabbas to be freed and for Jesus to be killed.

[21]Pilate said, "I have Barabbas and Jesus. Which do you want me to set free for you?"

The people answered, "Barabbas."

[22]Pilate asked, "So what should I do with Jesus, the one called the Christ?"

They all answered, "Crucify him!"

[23]Pilate asked, "Why? What wrong has he done?"

But they shouted louder, "Crucify him!"

[24]When Pilate saw that he could do nothing about this and that a riot was starting, he took some water and washed his hands[n] in front of the crowd. Then he said, "I am not guilty of this man's death. You are the ones who are causing it!"

[25]All the people answered, "We and our children will be responsible for his death."

[26]Then he set Barabbas free. But Jesus was beaten with whips and handed over to the soldiers to be crucified.

[27]The governor's soldiers took Jesus into the governor's palace, and they all gathered around him. [28]They took off his clothes and put a red robe on him. [29]Using thorny branches, they made a crown, put it on his head, and put a stick in his right hand. Then the soldiers bowed before Jesus and made fun of him, saying, "Hail, King of the Jews!" [30]They spat on Jesus. Then they took his stick and began to beat him on the head. [31]After they finished, the soldiers took off the robe and put his own clothes on him again. Then they led him away to be crucified.

Jesus Is Crucified

[32]As the soldiers were going out of the city with Jesus, they forced a man from Cyrene, named Simon, to carry the cross for Jesus. [33]They all came to the place called Golgotha, which means the Place of the Skull. [34]The soldiers gave Jesus wine mixed with gall[n] to drink. He tasted the wine but refused to drink it. [35]When the soldiers had crucified him, they threw lots to decide who would get his clothes.[n] [36]The soldiers sat there and continued watching him. [37]They put a sign above Jesus' head with a charge against him. It said: THIS IS JESUS, THE KING OF THE JEWS. [38]Two robbers were crucified beside Jesus, one on the right and the other on the left. [39]People walked by and insulted Jesus and shook their heads, [40]saying, "You said you could destroy the Temple and build it again in three days. So save yourself! Come down from that cross if you are really the Son of God!"

Women & Men of the BIBLE

Queen of Sheba: Straight to the Source

The entire ancient world was buzzing about King Solomon's untold wisdom and wealth. But the queen of Sheba wondered if all the hype was for real. You can't believe everything you hear, after all. So she loaded up her servants and camels (and a spice rack to die for!) and set out to investigate for herself. She tested him with the deep questions of life and saw that his wisdom, fame, and fortune were not exaggerated. Afterward, she gave credit where credit was due and praised God for what she'd seen. (2 Chronicles 9:1–12)

War

There's nothing easy about war. It's heartbreaking to hear about the devastation. It's hard to say good-bye to loved ones leaving for combat. On the home front, debates heat up about whether we should be involved at all. But we can take positive action in the chaos. We can start by praying. Both sides need peace, leaders need godly wisdom, troops need courage over fear and loneliness, and civilians near the fighting need God's protection. We can also write letters to soldiers and lend a hand to their families. God can work mightily through every kindness you show.

27:16–17 Barabbas Some Greek copies read "Jesus Barabbas." **27:24 washed his hands** He did this as a sign to show that he wanted no part in what the people did. **27:34 gall** Probably a drink of wine mixed with drugs to help a person feel less pain. **27:35 clothes** Some Greek copies continue, "So what God said through the prophet came true, 'They divided my clothes among them, and they threw lots for my clothing.' " See Psalm 22:18.

[41]The leading priests, the teachers of the law, and the Jewish elders were also making fun of Jesus. [42]They said, "He saved others, but he can't save himself! He says he is the king of Israel! If he is the king, let him come down now from the cross. Then we will believe in him. [43]He trusts in God, so let God save him now, if God really wants him. He himself said, 'I am the Son of God.' " [44]And in the same way, the robbers who were being crucified beside Jesus also insulted him.

Jesus Dies

[45]At noon the whole country became dark, and the darkness lasted for three hours. [46]About three o'clock Jesus cried out in a loud voice, "Eli, Eli, lama sabachthani?" This means, "My God, my God, why have you abandoned me?"

[47]Some of the people standing there who heard this said, "He is calling Elijah."

[48]Quickly one of them ran and got a sponge and filled it with vinegar and tied it to a stick and gave it to Jesus to drink. [49]But the others said, "Don't bother him. We want to see if Elijah will come to save him."

[50]But Jesus cried out again in a loud voice and died.

[51]Then the curtain in the Temple[n] was torn into two pieces, from the top to the bottom. Also, the earth shook and rocks broke apart. [52]The graves opened, and many of God's people who had died were raised from the dead. [53]They came out of the graves after Jesus was raised from the dead and went into the holy city, where they appeared to many people.

[54]When the army officer and the soldiers guarding Jesus saw this earthquake and everything else that happened, they were very frightened and said, "He really was the Son of God!"

[55]Many women who had followed Jesus from Galilee to help him were standing at a distance from the cross, watching. [56]Mary Magdalene, and Mary the mother of James and Joseph, and the mother of James and John were there.

Jesus Is Buried

[57]That evening a rich man named Joseph, a follower of Jesus from the town of Arimathea, came to Jerusalem. [58]Joseph went to Pilate and asked to have Jesus' body. So Pilate gave orders for the soldiers to give it to Joseph. [59]Then Joseph took the body and wrapped it in a clean linen cloth. [60]He put Jesus' body in a new tomb that he had cut out of a wall of rock, and he rolled a very large stone to block the entrance of the tomb. Then Joseph went away. [61]Mary Magdalene and the other woman named Mary were sitting near the tomb.

The Tomb of Jesus Is Guarded

[62]The next day, the day after Preparation Day, the leading priests and the Pharisees went to Pilate. [63]They said, "Sir, we remember that while that liar was still alive he said, 'After three days I will rise from the dead.' [64]So give the order for the tomb to be guarded closely till the third day. Otherwise, his followers might come and steal the body and tell people that he has risen from the dead. That lie would be even worse than the first one."

[65]Pilate said, "Take some soldiers and go guard the tomb the best way you know." [66]So they all went to the tomb and made it safe from thieves by sealing the stone in the entrance and putting soldiers there to guard it.

Jesus Rises from the Dead

28 The day after the Sabbath day was the first day of the week.

Matthew 28:18

Nothing tears down someone's reputation faster than a nasty lie. If you haven't felt a personal blow from gossip yourself, you've surely seen it happen to other people. Jesus knows what that feels like! Within hours of his resurrection, Jewish religious leaders paid Roman soldiers who had been guarding his tomb to spread the rumor that Jesus' followers had stolen his body during the night. If Jesus' death was permanent, he couldn't have been God. But if his resurrection was real, he must have power over death—clear evidence that Jesus really is God.

People still try to avoid the truth about who Christ was and is. They twist Scripture and teach that Jesus never actually claimed he was God. Or they say he was just an influential teacher or a good person we should imitate. You might also hear people say Jesus was just a human, blessed with great wisdom and the ability to reveal God to other people.

But the bottom line is this: any view that denies Jesus is God *doesn't match Scripture*. His authority, his power, came directly from God. Stick with Scripture and don't buy into any lies . . . stand for the truth about who Jesus is.

27:51 curtain in the Temple A curtain divided the Most Holy Place from the other part of the Temple. That was the special building in Jerusalem where God commanded the Jewish people to worship him.

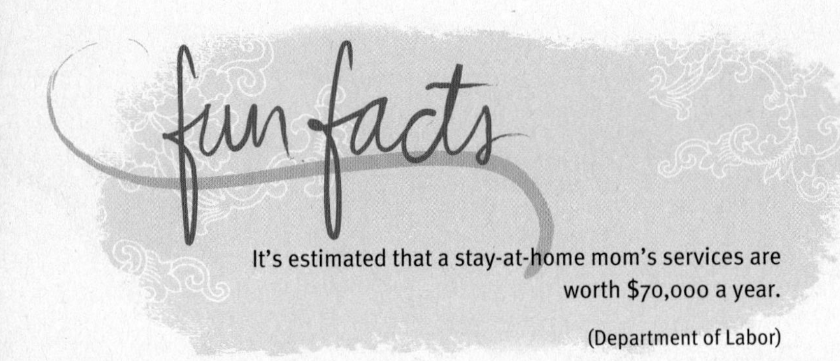

It's estimated that a stay-at-home mom's services are worth $70,000 a year.

(Department of Labor)

At dawn on the first day, Mary Magdalene and another woman named Mary went to look at the tomb.

[2]At that time there was a strong earthquake. An angel of the Lord came down from heaven, went to the tomb, and rolled the stone away from the entrance. Then he sat on the stone. [3]He was shining as bright as lightning, and his clothes were white as snow. [4]The soldiers guarding the tomb shook with fear because of the angel, and they became like dead men.

[5]The angel said to the women, "Don't be afraid. I know that you are looking for Jesus, who has been crucified. [6]He is not here. He has risen from the dead as he said he would. Come and see the place where his body was. [7]And go quickly and tell his followers, 'Jesus has risen from the dead. He is going into Galilee ahead of you, and you will see him there.' " Then the angel said, "Now I have told you."

[8]The women left the tomb quickly. They were afraid, but they were also very happy. They ran to tell Jesus' followers what had happened. [9]Suddenly, Jesus met them and said, "Greetings." The women came up to him, took hold of his feet, and worshiped him. [10]Then Jesus said to them, "Don't be afraid. Go and tell my followers to go on to Galilee, and they will see me there."

The Soldiers Report to the Leaders

[11]While the women went to tell Jesus' followers, some of the soldiers who had been guarding the tomb went into the city to tell the leading priests everything that had happened. [12]Then the priests met with the elders and made a plan. They paid the soldiers a large amount of money [13]and said to them, "Tell the people that Jesus' followers came during the night and stole the body while you were asleep. [14]If the governor hears about this, we will satisfy him and save you from trouble." [15]So the soldiers kept the money and did as they were told. And that story is still spread among the people even today.

Jesus Talks to His Followers

[16]The eleven followers went to Galilee to the mountain where Jesus had told them to go. [17]On the mountain they saw Jesus and worshiped him, but some of them did not believe it was really Jesus. [18]Then Jesus came to them and said, "All power in heaven and on earth is given to me. [19]So go and make followers of all people in the world. Baptize them in the name of the Father and the Son and the Holy Spirit. [20]Teach them to obey everything that I have taught you, and I will be with you always, even until the end of this age."

Jesus Is the Promised Messiah

Matthew's account of Jesus' life seems to be written with a Jewish audience in mind. He constantly refers back to the Old Testament, often bringing up Jewish customs without explaining them. Matthew's singular purpose is clear: to proclaim to the Jewish people that Jesus is the long-awaited Messiah!

The Book of Matthew provides a bridge between the Old and New Testaments, tying Jewish law with the new agreement Jesus provided for all believers (Matthew 26:28). Careful to show Jesus as both human (a son of Abraham) and divine (*the* Son of God), Matthew explains how Christ fulfilled prophecies from the Old Testament regarding the coming Messiah.

Matthew lets Jesus' own words do the teaching. Through Jesus' interaction with the Pharisees and Sadducees, we see how he sometimes disagreed with religious leaders of his day. We also witness Jesus' rejection by his own people. The fact that the tax collector, Matthew, was chosen as one of the first followers of Christ makes a statement about who Jesus came to save (Matthew 9:9–12). Jesus' sacrifice wasn't just for priests and kings—it was for every person who would call on his name and believe.

The climax of this book comes in its final verses as Jesus tells his followers to go spread his teachings throughout the world. This Great Commission is still the mission of Christians today!

So much of Scripture points to the events recorded in Matthew. Jesus the Messiah has come to rescue us from sin! This is the truth that defines us.

Get Real

What prophecies about Jesus' birth are fulfilled in Matthew? (Isaiah 7:14; 62:11; Micah 5:2; Zechariah 9:9)

Does God still heal and perform miracles today? (1 Corinthians 12:9–10; James 5:15–16)

Why did Jesus spend time with people of questionable character? (Mark 2:15–17; Luke 15:1–10)

What did Jesus' death and resurrection do for sinners? (Galatians 3:11–14)

How does Jesus' sacrifice make you want to live differently? (2 Corinthians 5:16–21)

mark

There's nothing like observing someone's actions to get a feel for who they are and what they stand for. Mark understood that concept. In this Gospel, Mark lets Jesus' actions speak for themselves.

While this book contains plenty of Old Testament prophecy references and examples of Jesus' teaching, Mark concentrates specifically on Jesus' actions. From the tiny fishing villages around Galilee to the Temple in Jerusalem, we get to see Jesus' love and power at work as he teaches challenging truths, heals hopelessly sick people, and performs phenomenal miracles. Everywhere Jesus went people got caught up in wondering just who this amazing man really was. He simply couldn't be ignored.

Eventually, his actions led to the Cross. Between his massive public following and his claims about being the Messiah, the religious and political officials had had enough. But Christ's death was not his final act. It was actually the very thing that set the stage for proving his eternal power over sin and death!

The things Jesus did during his time on earth leave no question about who he was. As you read this action-packed Gospel, consider your own life. What do your actions say about you?

John Prepares for Jesus

1 This is the beginning of the Good News about Jesus Christ, the Son of God,[n] [2]as the prophet Isaiah wrote:

"I will send my messenger ahead of you,
who will prepare your way."
Malachi 3:1

[3]"This is a voice of one
who calls out in the desert:
'Prepare the way for the Lord.
Make the road straight for him.' "
Isaiah 40:3

[4]John was baptizing people in the desert and preaching a baptism of changed hearts and lives for the forgiveness of sins. [5]All the people from Judea and Jerusalem were going out to him. They confessed their sins and were baptized by him in the Jordan River. [6]John wore clothes made from camel's hair, had a leather belt around his waist, and ate locusts and wild honey. [7]This is what John preached to the people: "There is one coming after me who is greater than I; I am not good enough even to kneel down and untie his sandals. [8]I baptize you with water, but he will baptize you with the Holy Spirit."

Jesus Is Baptized

[9]At that time Jesus came from the town of Nazareth in Galilee and was baptized by John in the Jordan River. [10]Immediately, as Jesus was coming up out of the water, he saw heaven open. The Holy Spirit came down on him like a dove, [11]and a voice came from heaven: "You are my Son, whom I love, and I am very pleased with you."

[12]Then the Spirit sent Jesus into the desert. [13]He was in the desert forty days and was tempted by Satan. He was with the wild animals, and the angels came and took care of him.

Jesus Chooses Some Followers

[14]After John was put in prison, Jesus went into Galilee, preaching the Good

1:1 the Son of God Some Greek copies do not have this phrase.

Be Still & KNOW

God First, Girlfriends Second

When troubles come, it's second nature to grab the cell phone and call your best friend. That's what she's there for after all! Her friendship is a true gift from God, and there's nothing like the encouraging connection that comes from godly friends. But should your friends be the first ones you run to? James 5:13 says, "Anyone who is having troubles should pray." Pray *first*. Run to Jesus *first*. He is the one who understands and loves you best. And he is the one who can give you peace in the middle of life's toughest storms. Pour out your heart to him. And then call your friends for encouragement and support.

News from God. [15]He said, "The right time has come. The kingdom of God is near. Change your hearts and lives and believe the Good News!"

[16]When Jesus was walking by Lake Galilee, he saw Simon[n] and his brother Andrew throwing a net into the lake because they were fishermen. [17]Jesus said to them, "Come follow me, and I will make you fish for people." [18]So Simon and Andrew immediately left their nets and followed him.

[19]Going a little farther, Jesus saw two more brothers, James and John, the sons of Zebedee. They were in a boat, mending their nets. [20]Jesus immediately called them, and they left their father in the boat with the hired workers and followed Jesus.

Jesus Forces Out an Evil Spirit

[21]Jesus and his followers went to Capernaum. On the Sabbath day he went to the synagogue and began to teach. [22]The people were amazed at his teaching, because he taught like a person who had authority, not like their teachers of the law. [23]Just then, a man was there in the synagogue who had an evil spirit in him. He shouted, [24]"Jesus of Nazareth! What do you want with us? Did you come to destroy us? I know who you are—God's Holy One!"

[25]Jesus commanded the evil spirit, "Be quiet! Come out of the man!" [26]The evil spirit shook the man violently, gave a loud cry, and then came out of him.

[27]The people were so amazed they asked each other, "What is happening here? This man is teaching something new, and with authority. He even gives commands to evil spirits, and they obey him." [28]And the news about Jesus spread quickly everywhere in the area of Galilee.

Jesus Heals Many People

[29]As soon as Jesus and his followers left the synagogue, they went with James and John to the home of Simon[n] and Andrew. [30]Simon's mother-in-law was sick in bed with a fever, and the people told Jesus about her. [31]So Jesus went to her bed, took her hand, and helped her up. The fever left her, and she began serving them.

[32]That evening, after the sun went down, the people brought to Jesus all who were sick and had demons in them. [33]The whole town gathered at the door. [34]Jesus healed many who had different kinds of sicknesses, and he forced many demons to leave people. But he would not allow the demons to speak, because they knew who he was.

[35]Early the next morning, while it was still dark, Jesus woke and left the house. He went to a lonely place, where he prayed. [36]Simon and his friends went to look for Jesus. [37]When they found him, they said, "Everyone is looking for you!"

[38]Jesus answered, "We should go to other towns around here so I can preach there too. That is the reason I came." [39]So he went everywhere in Galilee, preaching in the synagogues and forcing out demons.

Jesus Heals a Sick Man

[40]A man with a skin disease came to Jesus. He fell to his knees and begged Jesus, "You can heal me if you will."

[41]Jesus felt sorry for the man, so he reached out his hand and touched him and said, "I will. Be healed!" [42]Immediately the disease left the man, and he was healed.

[43]Jesus told the man to go away at once, but he warned him strongly, [44]"Don't tell anyone about this. But go and show yourself to the priest. And offer the gift Moses commanded for people who are made well.[n] This will show the people what I have done." [45]The man left there, but he began to tell everyone that Jesus had healed him, and so he spread the news about Jesus. As a result, Jesus could not enter a town if people saw him. He stayed in places where nobody lived, but people came to him from everywhere.

Jesus Heals a Paralyzed Man

2 A few days later, when Jesus came back to Capernaum, the news spread that he was at home. [2]Many people gathered together so that there was no room in the house, not even outside the door. And Jesus was teaching them God's message. [3]Four people came, carrying a paralyzed man. [4]Since they could not get to Jesus because of the crowd, they dug a hole in the roof right above where he was speaking. When they got through, they lowered the mat with the paralyzed man on it. [5]When Jesus saw the faith of these

1:16; 29 Simon Simon's other name was Peter. **1:44 Moses . . . well** Read about this in Leviticus 14:1–32.

people, he said to the paralyzed man, "Young man, your sins are forgiven."

[6]Some of the teachers of the law were sitting there, thinking to themselves, [7]"Why does this man say things like that? He is speaking as if he were God. Only God can forgive sins."

[8]Jesus knew immediately what these teachers of the law were thinking. So he said to them, "Why are you thinking these things? [9]Which is easier: to tell this paralyzed man, 'Your sins are forgiven,' or to tell him, 'Stand up. Take your mat and walk'? [10]But I will prove to you that the Son of Man has authority on earth to forgive sins." So Jesus said to the paralyzed man, [11]"I tell you, stand up, take your mat, and go home." [12]Immediately the paralyzed man stood up, took his mat, and walked out while everyone was watching him.

The people were amazed and praised God. They said, "We have never seen anything like this!"

[13]Jesus went to the lake again. The whole crowd followed him there, and he taught them. [14]While he was walking along, he saw a man named Levi son of Alphaeus, sitting in the tax collector's booth. Jesus said to him, "Follow me," and he stood up and followed Jesus.

[15]Later, as Jesus was having dinner at Levi's house, many tax collectors and "sinners" were eating there with Jesus and his followers. Many people like this followed Jesus. [16]When the teachers of the law who were Pharisees saw Jesus eating with the tax collectors and "sinners," they asked his followers, "Why does he eat with tax collectors and sinners?"

[17]Jesus heard this and said to them, "It is not the healthy people who need a doctor, but the sick. I did not come to invite good people but to invite sinners."

Jesus' Followers Are Criticized

[18]Now the followers of John[n] and the Pharisees often fasted[n] for a certain time. Some people came to Jesus and said, "Why do John's followers and the followers of the Pharisees often fast, but your followers don't?"

[19]Jesus answered, "The friends of the bridegroom do not fast while the bridegroom is still with them. As long as the bridegroom is with them, they cannot fast. [20]But the time will come when the bridegroom will be taken from them, and then they will fast.

[21]"No one sews a patch of unshrunk cloth over a hole in an old coat. Otherwise, the patch will shrink and pull away—the new patch will pull away from the old coat. Then the hole will be worse. [22]Also, no one ever pours new wine into old leather bags. Otherwise, the new wine will break the bags, and the wine will be ruined along with the bags. But new wine should be put into new leather bags."

Jesus Is Lord of the Sabbath

[23]One Sabbath day, as Jesus was walking through some fields of grain, his followers began to pick some grain to eat. [24]The Pharisees said to Jesus, "Why are your followers doing what is not lawful on the Sabbath day?"

[25]Jesus answered, "Have you never read what David did when he and those with him were hungry and needed food? [26]During the time of Abiathar the high priest, David went into God's house and ate the holy bread, which is lawful only for priests to eat. And David also gave some of the bread to those who were with him."

[27]Then Jesus said to the Pharisees, "The Sabbath day was made to help people; they were not made to be ruled by the Sabbath day. [28]So then, the Son of Man is Lord even of the Sabbath day."

BECOME Involved

See You at the Pole™

See You at the Pole™ is not just for kids anymore! What started with a small group of students praying for their school has turned into a nationwide movement for youth and adults alike. One morning every year at a specific date and time, millions of teenagers meet together to pray for their schools. The student-led prayer time is a powerful tool in reaching young people for Christ.

But what does that have to do with you, a full-grown adult who may barely remember the long-ago days of junior high? You may not be sporting your backpack or packing a lunch anymore, but you can still be involved in praying for local schools. One of the best things you can do is let young people know you support them. Lend your guidance as they publicize and plan the event.

Also, many churches have begun to come alongside their youth through sponsoring an adult version at church during the same time the students are praying at school. You may want to consider helping follow up on decisions made for Christ that day, too. Check out www.syatp.com for more ideas about becoming involved as an adult.

2:18 John John the Baptist, who preached to the Jewish people about Christ's coming (Mark 1:4-8). **2:18 fasted** The people would give up eating for a special time of prayer and worship to God. It was also done to show sadness and disappointment.

Mark 3:32–35

Have you ever known a family that's so special, you almost wish they could just informally "adopt" you? They have a sincere love for each other and a firm commitment to stick together. They're people you just want to be around!

Although it'd be interesting to learn more about Jesus' family life, Scripture doesn't give a lot of details about it. We do know that his younger brothers (well, half brothers, technically) didn't believe that Jesus was the Messiah until after the Resurrection.

But here's the really remarkable thing about Jesus' family. He said his true family members are those who "do what God wants" (Mark 3:35). So it's not a particular family tree, ethnicity, or birthplace that makes someone God's child. It's having a right relationship with God through the Cross and living like Jesus.

What a joy and honor that we're given the opportunity to be part of Jesus' family! Would you say you're living like Jesus' sister, like a child of God? If not, ask him to help you. He promises salvation to everyone who puts faith in Christ—and part of his saving grace includes giving you the ability to live like his daughter. Thank God each day for adopting you into his wonderful family.

Jesus Heals a Man's Hand

3 Another time when Jesus went into a synagogue, a man with a crippled hand was there. [2]Some people watched Jesus closely to see if he would heal the man on the Sabbath day so they could accuse him.

[3]Jesus said to the man with the crippled hand, "Stand up here in the middle of everyone."

[4]Then Jesus asked the people, "Which is lawful on the Sabbath day: to do good or to do evil, to save a life or to kill?" But they said nothing to answer him.

[5]Jesus was angry as he looked at the people, and he felt very sad because they were stubborn. Then he said to the man, "Hold out your hand." The man held out his hand and it was healed. [6]Then the Pharisees left and began making plans with the Herodians[n] about a way to kill Jesus.

Many People Follow Jesus

[7]Jesus left with his followers for the lake, and a large crowd from Galilee followed him. [8]Also many people came from Judea, from Jerusalem, from Idumea, from the lands across the Jordan River, and from the area of Tyre and Sidon. When they heard what Jesus was doing, many people came to him. [9]When Jesus saw the crowds, he told his followers to get a boat ready for him to keep people from crowding against him. [10]He had healed many people, so all the sick were pushing toward him to touch him. [11]When evil spirits saw Jesus, they fell down before him and shouted, "You are the Son of God!" [12]But Jesus strongly warned them not to tell who he was.

Jesus Chooses His Twelve Apostles

[13]Then Jesus went up on a mountain and called to him those he wanted, and they came to him. [14]Jesus chose twelve and called them apostles.[n] He wanted them to be with him, and he wanted to send them out to preach [15]and to have the authority to force demons out of people. [16]These are the twelve men he chose: Simon (Jesus named him Peter), [17]James and John, the sons of Zebedee (Jesus named them Boanerges, which means "Sons of Thunder"), [18]Andrew, Philip, Bartholomew, Matthew, Thomas, James the son of Alphaeus, Thaddaeus, Simon the Zealot, [19]and Judas Iscariot, who later turned against Jesus.

Some People Say Jesus Has a Devil

[20]Then Jesus went home, but again a crowd gathered. There were so many people that Jesus and his followers could not eat. [21]When his family heard this, they went to get him because they thought he was out of his mind. [22]But the teachers of the law from Jerusalem were saying, "Beelzebul is living inside him! He uses power from the ruler of demons to force demons out of people."

[23]So Jesus called the people together and taught them with stories. He said, "Satan will not force himself out of people. [24]A kingdom that is divided cannot continue, [25]and a family that is divided cannot continue. [26]And if Satan is against himself and fights against his own people, he cannot continue; that is the end of Satan. [27]No one can enter a strong person's house and steal his things unless he first ties up the strong person. Then he can steal things from the house. [28]I tell you the truth, all sins that people do and all the things people say against God can be forgiven. [29]But anyone who speaks against the Holy Spirit

3:6 Herodians A political group that followed Herod and his family. **3:14 and called them apostles** Some Greek copies do not have this phrase.

will never be forgiven; he is guilty of a sin that continues forever."

[30]Jesus said this because the teachers of the law said that he had an evil spirit inside him.

Jesus' True Family

[31]Then Jesus' mother and brothers arrived. Standing outside, they sent someone in to tell him to come out. [32]Many people were sitting around Jesus, and they said to him, "Your mother and brothers[n] are waiting for you outside."

[33]Jesus asked, "Who are my mother and my brothers?" [34]Then he looked at those sitting around him and said, "Here are my mother and my brothers! [35]My true brother and sister and mother are those who do what God wants."

A Story About Planting Seed

4 Again Jesus began teaching by the lake. A great crowd gathered around him, so he sat down in a boat near the shore. All the people stayed on the shore close to the water. [2]Jesus taught them many things, using stories. He said, [3]"Listen! A farmer went out to plant his seed. [4]While he was planting, some seed fell by the road, and the birds came and ate it up. [5]Some seed fell on rocky ground where there wasn't much dirt. That seed grew very fast, because the ground was not deep. [6]But when the sun rose, the plants dried up because they did not have deep roots. [7]Some other seed fell among thorny weeds, which grew and choked the good plants. So those plants did not produce a crop. [8]Some other seed fell on good ground and began to grow. It got taller and produced a crop. Some plants made thirty times more, some made sixty times more, and some made a hundred times more."

[9]Then Jesus said, "Let those with ears use them and listen!"

Jesus Tells Why He Used Stories

[10]Later, when Jesus was alone, the twelve apostles and others around him asked him about the stories.

[11]Jesus said, "You can know the secret about the kingdom of God. But to other people I tell everything by using stories [12]so that:

'They will look and look, but they will
not learn.
They will listen and listen, but
they will not understand.
If they did learn and understand,
they would come back to me and
be forgiven.' " *Isaiah 6:9–10*

Jesus Explains the Seed Story

[13]Then Jesus said to his followers, "Don't you understand this story? If you don't, how will you understand any story? [14]The farmer is like a person who plants God's message in people. [15]Sometimes the teaching falls on the road. This is like the people who hear the teaching of God, but Satan quickly comes and takes away the teaching that was planted in them. [16]Others are like the seed planted on rocky ground. They hear the teaching and quickly accept it with joy. [17]But since they don't allow the teaching to go deep into their lives, they keep it only a short time. When trouble or persecution comes because of the teaching they accepted, they quickly give up. [18]Others are like the seed planted among the thorny weeds. They hear the teaching, [19]but the worries of this life, the temptation of wealth, and many other evil desires keep the teaching from growing and producing fruit[n] in their lives. [20]Others are like the seed planted in the good ground. They hear the teaching and accept it. Then they grow and produce fruit—sometimes thirty times more, sometimes sixty times more, and sometimes a hundred times more."

Use What You Have

[21]Then Jesus said to them, "Do you hide a lamp under a bowl or under a bed? No! You put the lamp on a lampstand. [22]Everything that is hidden will be made clear and every secret thing will be made known. [23]Let those with ears use them and listen!

[24]"Think carefully about what you hear. The way you give to others is the way God will give to you, but God will give you even more. [25]Those who have understanding will be given more. But those who do not have understanding, even what they have will be taken away from them."

Health
Breast Cancer Update

There's new hope for the more than two hundred thousand women who will be diagnosed with breast cancer this year. Scientific advances are making early diagnosis—the most crucial element to survival—easier than ever before. Genetic screening tests allow women with a family history of breast cancer to be proactive in taking preventative measures and seeking treatment. With remarkable accuracy, these tests also predict how likely a cancer survivor is to have a recurrence, helping doctors tailor treatment plans to individual patients. Conventional mammograms are being replaced with more effective digital technology, which finds 15–25 percent more cancers. New generations of drugs are emerging, offering further treatment options. While God chooses to heal some people miraculously, he uses the skills of his children—through modern medicine—to heal others. Visit www.breastcancer.org for the latest on diagnosis and treatment.

Jesus Uses a Story About Seed

[26]Then Jesus said, "The kingdom of God is like someone who plants seed in the ground. [27]Night and day, whether the person is asleep or awake, the seed still grows, but the person does not

3:32 brothers Some Greek copies continue, "and sisters." **4:19 producing fruit** To produce fruit means to have in your life the good things God wants.

know how it grows. 28By itself the earth produces grain. First the plant grows, then the head, and then all the grain in the head. 29When the grain is ready, the farmer cuts it, because this is the harvest time."

A Story About Mustard Seed

30Then Jesus said, "How can I show you what the kingdom of God is like? What story can I use to explain it? 31The kingdom of God is like a mustard seed, the smallest seed you plant in the ground. 32But when planted, this seed grows and becomes the largest of all garden plants. It produces large branches, and the wild birds can make nests in its shade."

33Jesus used many stories like these to teach the crowd God's message—as much as they could understand. 34He always used stories to teach them. But when he and his followers were alone, Jesus explained everything to them.

Jesus Calms a Storm

35That evening, Jesus said to his followers, "Let's go across the lake." 36Leaving the crowd behind, they took him in the boat just as he was. There were also other boats with them. 37A very strong wind came up on the lake. The waves came over the sides and into the boat so that it was already full of water. 38Jesus was at the back of the boat, sleeping with his head on a cushion. His followers woke him and said, "Teacher, don't you care that we are drowning!"

39Jesus stood up and commanded the wind and said to the waves, "Quiet! Be still!" Then the wind stopped, and it became completely calm.

40Jesus said to his followers, "Why are you afraid? Do you still have no faith?"

41The followers were very afraid and asked each other, "Who is this? Even the wind and the waves obey him!"

A Man with Demons Inside Him

5 Jesus and his followers went to the other side of the lake to the area of the Gerasene[n] people. 2When Jesus got out of the boat, instantly a man with an evil spirit came to him from the burial caves. 3This man lived in the caves, and no one could tie him up, not even with a chain. 4Many times people had used chains to tie the man's hands and feet, but he always broke them off. No one was strong enough to control him. 5Day and night he would wander around the burial caves and on the hills, screaming and cutting himself with stones. 6While Jesus was still far away, the man saw him, ran to him, and fell down before him.

7The man shouted in a loud voice, "What do you want with me, Jesus, Son of the Most High God? I command you in God's name not to torture me!" 8He said this because Jesus was saying to him, "You evil spirit, come out of the man."

9Then Jesus asked him, "What is your name?"

He answered, "My name is Legion,[n] because we are many spirits." 10He begged Jesus again and again not to send them out of that area.

11A large herd of pigs was feeding on a hill near there. 12The demons begged Jesus, "Send us into the pigs; let us go into them." 13So Jesus allowed them to do this. The evil spirits left the man and went into the pigs. Then the herd of pigs—about two thousand of them—rushed down the hill into the lake and were drowned.

14The herdsmen ran away and went to the town and to the countryside, telling everyone about this. So people went out to see what had happened. 15They came to Jesus and saw the man who used to have the many evil spirits, sitting, clothed, and in his right mind. And they were frightened. 16The people who saw this told the others what had happened to the man who had the demons living in him, and they told about the pigs. 17Then the people began to beg Jesus to leave their area.

18As Jesus was getting back into the boat, the man who was freed from the demons begged to go with him.

19But Jesus would not let him. He said, "Go home to your family and tell them how much the Lord has done for you and how he has had mercy on you." 20So the man left and began to tell the people in the Ten Towns[n] about what Jesus had done for him. And everyone was amazed.

Real Sex
by Lauren F. Winner

Author Lauren F. Winner doesn't shy away from discussing the real issues involved with chastity. In *Real Sex*, Winner explores this virtue in depth, and her candid confessions and warm tone will pull you into the text. She acknowledges that pledging to avoid premarital sex might be easier if you're a teenager rather than a college graduate with no marriage prospects on the horizon, but it's worth the wait. If you're struggling to wait for God's best, this refreshing book will help you understand why chastity is so important and how you can practice it with confidence and peace.

5:1 Gerasene From Gerasa, an area southeast of Lake Galilee. The exact location is uncertain and some Greek copies read "Gergesene"; others read "Gadarene." **5:9 Legion** Means very many. A legion was about five thousand men in the Roman army. **5:20 Ten Towns** In Greek, called "Decapolis." It was an area east of Lake Galilee that once had ten main towns.

Jesus Gives Life to a Dead Girl and Heals a Sick Woman

[21]When Jesus went in the boat back to the other side of the lake, a large crowd gathered around him there. [22]A leader of the synagogue, named Jairus, came there, saw Jesus, and fell at his feet. [23]He begged Jesus, saying again and again, "My daughter is dying. Please come and put your hands on her so she will be healed and will live." [24]So Jesus went with him.

A large crowd followed Jesus and pushed very close around him. [25]Among them was a woman who had been bleeding for twelve years. [26]She had suffered very much from many doctors and had spent all the money she had, but instead of improving, she was getting worse. [27]When the woman heard about Jesus, she came up behind him in the crowd and touched his coat. [28]She thought, "If I can just touch his clothes, I will be healed." [29]Instantly her bleeding stopped, and she felt in her body that she was healed from her disease.

[30]At once Jesus felt power go out from him. So he turned around in the crowd and asked, "Who touched my clothes?"

[31]His followers said, "Look at how many people are pushing against you! And you ask, 'Who touched me?' "

[32]But Jesus continued looking around to see who had touched him. [33]The woman, knowing that she was healed, came and fell at Jesus' feet. Shaking with fear, she told him the whole truth. [34]Jesus said to her, "Dear woman, you are made well because you believed. Go in peace; be healed of your disease."

[35]While Jesus was still speaking, some people came from the house of the synagogue leader. They said, "Your daughter is dead. There is no need to bother the teacher anymore."

[36]But Jesus paid no attention to what they said. He told the synagogue leader, "Don't be afraid; just believe."

[37]Jesus let only Peter, James, and John the brother of James go with him. [38]When they came to the house of the synagogue leader, Jesus found many people there making lots of noise and crying loudly. [39]Jesus entered the house and said to them, "Why are you crying and making so much noise? The child is not dead, only asleep." [40]But they laughed at him. So, after throwing them out of the house, Jesus took the child's father and mother and his three followers into the room where the child was. [41]Taking hold of the girl's hand, he said to her, "Talitha, koum!" (This means, "Young girl, I tell you to stand up!") [42]At once the girl stood right up and began walking. (She was twelve years old.) Everyone was completely amazed. [43]Jesus gave them strict orders not to tell people about this. Then he told them to give the girl something to eat.

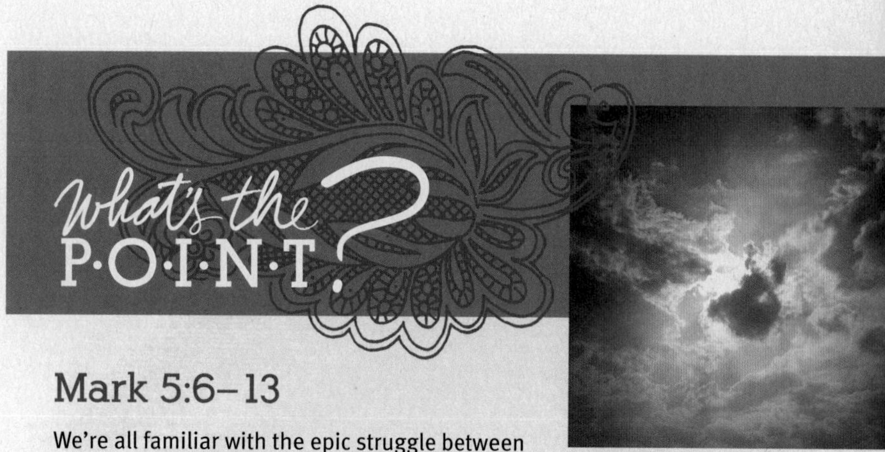

Mark 5:6–13

We're all familiar with the epic struggle between good and evil. It's the subject of countless movies and novels filled with dashing heroes who eventually defeat the villains. But real life doesn't always seem to reflect that. Sometimes evil can be so devastating that we wonder, *Where is God? Couldn't he have stopped this?*

Scripture leaves no room to question if God's power has limits. Christ defeated death itself, and he's above "all rulers, authorities, powers, and kings, not only in this world but also in the next" (Ephesians 1:21). The demons described in these verses cowered in Jesus' presence because they knew he was God. We're not talking about a power struggle here!

God will have the final word against evil—the Bible says Satan and his demons will be punished eternally for their rebellion. Everything will ultimately work out to give God the most glory and accomplish what's best for his people. So we cling to God's goodness, trust his wisdom, and patiently wait for the rest of the story. We have enough promises to steady our wondering hearts! Good will swallow up evil, and God will be praised for making everything right.

Jesus Goes to His Hometown

6 Jesus left there and went to his hometown, and his followers went with him. [2]On the Sabbath day he taught in the synagogue. Many people heard him and were amazed, saying, "Where did this man get these teachings? What is this wisdom that has been given to him? And where did he get the power to do miracles? [3]He is just the carpenter, the son of Mary and the brother of James, Joseph, Judas, and Simon. And his sisters are here with us." So the people were upset with Jesus.

[4]Jesus said to them, "A prophet is honored everywhere except in his hometown and with his own people and in his own home." [5]So Jesus was not able to work any miracles there except to heal a few sick people by putting his hands on them. [6]He was amazed at how many people had no faith.

Then Jesus went to other villages in that area and taught. [7]He called his twelve

Q&A

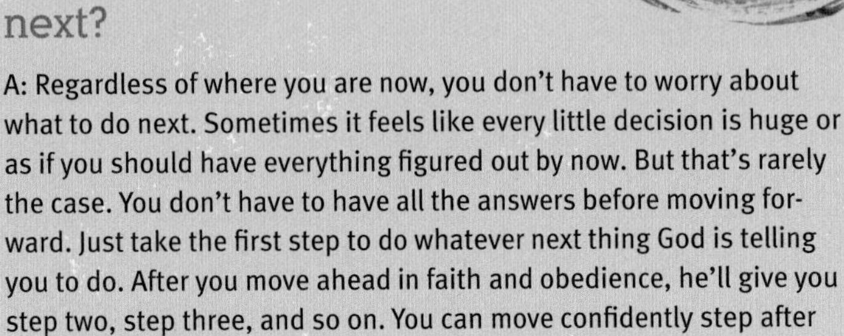

Q: How do I know what God wants me to do next?

A: Regardless of where you are now, you don't have to worry about what to do next. Sometimes it feels like every little decision is huge or as if you should have everything figured out by now. But that's rarely the case. You don't have to have all the answers before moving forward. Just take the first step to do whatever next thing God is telling you to do. After you move ahead in faith and obedience, he'll give you step two, step three, and so on. You can move confidently step after step knowing he already has the whole plan figured out.

followers together and got ready to send them out two by two and gave them authority over evil spirits. [8]This is what Jesus commanded them: "Take nothing for your trip except a walking stick. Take no bread, no bag, and no money in your pockets. [9]Wear sandals, but take only the clothes you are wearing. [10]When you enter a house, stay there until you leave that town. [11]If the people in a certain place refuse to welcome you or listen to you, leave that place. Shake its dust off your feet[n] as a warning to them."[n]

[12]So the followers went out and preached that people should change their hearts and lives. [13]They forced many demons out and put olive oil on many sick people and healed them.

How John the Baptist Was Killed

[14]King Herod heard about Jesus, because he was now well known. Some people said,[n] "He is John the Baptist, who has risen from the dead. That is why he can work these miracles."

[15]Others said, "He is Elijah."[n]

Other people said, "Jesus is a prophet, like the prophets who lived long ago."

[16]When Herod heard this, he said, "I killed John by cutting off his head. Now he has risen from the dead!"

[17]Herod himself had ordered his soldiers to arrest John and put him in prison in order to please his wife, Herodias. She had been the wife of Philip, Herod's brother, but then Herod had married her. [18]John had been telling Herod, "It is not lawful for you to be married to your brother's wife." [19]So Herodias hated John and wanted to kill him. But she couldn't, [20]because Herod was afraid of John and protected him. He knew John was a good and holy man. Also, though John's preaching always bothered him, he enjoyed listening to John.

[21]Then the perfect time came for Herodias to cause John's death. On Herod's birthday, he gave a dinner party for the most important government leaders, the commanders of his army, and the most important people in Galilee. [22]When the daughter of Herodias[n] came in and danced, she pleased Herod and the people eating with him.

So King Herod said to the girl, "Ask me for anything you want, and I will give it to you." [23]He promised her, "Anything you ask for I will give to you—up to half of my kingdom."

[24]The girl went to her mother and asked, "What should I ask for?"

Her mother answered, "Ask for the head of John the Baptist."

[25]At once the girl went back to the king and said to him, "I want the head of John the Baptist right now on a platter."

[26]Although the king was very sad, he had made a promise, and his dinner guests had heard it. So he did not want to refuse what she asked. [27]Immediately the king sent a soldier to bring John's head. The soldier went and cut off John's head in the prison [28]and brought it back on a platter. He gave it to the girl, and the girl gave it to her mother. [29]When John's followers heard this, they came and got John's body and put it in a tomb.

More than Five Thousand Fed

[30]The apostles gathered around Jesus and told him about all the things they had done and taught. [31]Crowds of people were coming and going so that Jesus and his followers did not even have time to eat. He said to them, "Come away by yourselves, and we will go to a lonely place to get some rest."

[32]So they went in a boat by themselves to a lonely place. [33]But many people saw them leave and recognized them. So from all the towns they ran to the place where Jesus was going, and they got there before him. [34]When he arrived, he saw a great crowd waiting. He felt sorry for them, because they were like sheep without a shepherd. So he began to teach them many things.

[35]When it was late in the day, his followers came to him and said, "No one lives in this place, and it is already very late. [36]Send the people away so they can go to the countryside and towns around here to buy themselves something to eat."

[37]But Jesus answered, "You give them something to eat."

They said to him, "We would all have to work a month to earn enough money to buy that much bread!"

6:11 Shake . . . feet A warning. It showed that they were rejecting these people. **6:11 them** Some Greek copies continue, "I tell you the truth, on the Judgment Day it will be better for the towns of Sodom and Gomorrah than for the people of that town." See Matthew 10:15. **6:14 Some people said** Some Greek copies read "He said." **6:15 Elijah** A great prophet who spoke for God and who lived hundreds of years before Christ. See 1 Kings 17. **6:22 When . . . Herodias** Some Greek copies read "When his daughter Herodias."

38Jesus asked them, "How many loaves of bread do you have? Go and see."

When they found out, they said, "Five loaves and two fish."

39Then Jesus told his followers to have the people sit in groups on the green grass. 40So they sat in groups of fifty or a hundred. 41Jesus took the five loaves and two fish and, looking up to heaven, he thanked God for the food. He divided the bread and gave it to his followers for them to give to the people. Then he divided the two fish among them all. 42All the people ate and were satisfied. 43The followers filled twelve baskets with the leftover pieces of bread and fish. 44There were five thousand men who ate.

Jesus Walks on the Water

45Immediately Jesus told his followers to get into the boat and go ahead of him to Bethsaida across the lake. He stayed there to send the people home. 46After sending them away, he went into the hills to pray.

47That night, the boat was in the middle of the lake, and Jesus was alone on the land. 48He saw his followers struggling hard to row the boat, because the wind was blowing against them. Between three and six o'clock in the morning, Jesus came to them, walking on the water, and he wanted to walk past the boat. 49But when they saw him walking on the water, they thought he was a ghost and cried out. 50They all saw him and were afraid. But quickly Jesus spoke to them and said, "Have courage! It is I. Do not be afraid." 51Then he got into the boat with them, and the wind became calm. The followers were greatly amazed. 52They did not understand about the miracle of the five loaves, because their minds were closed.

53When they had crossed the lake, they came to shore at Gennesaret and tied the boat there. 54When they got out of the boat, people immediately recognized Jesus. 55They ran everywhere in that area and began to bring sick people on mats wherever they heard he was. 56And everywhere he went—into towns, cities, or countryside—the people brought the sick to the marketplaces. They begged him to let them touch just the edge of his coat, and all who touched it were healed.

Obey God's Law

7 When some Pharisees and some teachers of the law came from Jerusalem, they gathered around Jesus. 2They saw that some of Jesus' followers ate food with hands that were not clean, that is, they hadn't washed them. 3(The Pharisees and all the Jews never eat before washing their hands in the way required by their unwritten laws. 4And when they buy something in the market, they never eat it until they wash themselves in a special way. They also follow many other unwritten laws, such as the washing of cups, pitchers, and pots.[n])

5The Pharisees and the teachers of the law said to Jesus, "Why don't your followers obey the unwritten laws which have been handed down to us? Why do your followers eat their food with hands that are not clean?"

6Jesus answered, "Isaiah was right when he spoke about you hypocrites. He wrote,

> 'These people show honor to me with words,
> but their hearts are far from me.
> 7Their worship of me is worthless.
> The things they teach are nothing but human rules.' *Isaiah 29:13*

8You have stopped following the commands of God, and you follow only human teachings."[n]

9Then Jesus said to them, "You cleverly ignore the commands of God so you can follow your own teachings. 10Moses said, 'Honor your father and your mother,'[n] and 'Anyone who says cruel things to his father or mother must be put to death.'[n] 11But you say a person can tell his father or mother, 'I have something I could use to help you, but it is Corban—a gift to God.' 12You no longer let that person use that money for his father or his mother. 13By your own rules, which you teach people, you are rejecting what God said. And you do many things like that."

14After Jesus called the crowd to him again, he said, "Every person should listen to me and understand what I am saying. 15There is nothing people put into their bodies that makes them unclean. People are made unclean by the things that come out of them. [16Let those with ears use them and listen.]"[n]

17When Jesus left the people and went into the house, his followers asked him about this story. 18Jesus said, "Do you still not understand? Surely you know that nothing that enters someone from the outside can make that person unclean. 19It does not go into the mind,

all about MEN

The Old Friend

You once turned to each other for a listening ear or to hang out on dateless Saturday nights—but not since he met his girlfriend. True, you were just friends and you're happy for them, but you feel a bit lost . . . replaced. But take heart! This new season for them is also an opportunity for you. Why not invite them to group stuff and include her in get-togethers with your other girlfriends? She may value the girl-time during these changes in her life. Claim Isaiah 43:19, and "look at the new thing [God is] going to do." Ask him to reveal the exciting new paths he's creating for you all. Instead of losing a friend, you just might gain one!

7:4 pots Some Greek copies continue, "and dining couches." **7:8 teachings** Some Greek copies continue, "You wash pitchers and jugs and do many other such things." **7:10 'Honor . . . mother.'** Quotation from Exodus 20:12; Deuteronomy 5:16. **7:10 'Anyone . . . death.'** Quotation from Exodus 21:17. **7:16 Let . . . listen.** Some Greek copies do not contain the bracketed text.

QUIZ

HOW WELL DO YOU KNOW THE WOMEN OF THE BIBLE?

1. SHE WON A BEAUTY PAGEANT AND BECAME THE NEW QUEEN.

- [ ] A. Esther
- [ ] B. Ruth
- [ ] C. Mary

2. SHE CHOSE TO MOVE FAR AWAY WITH HER MOTHER-IN-LAW EVEN THOUGH HER HUSBAND WAS DEAD.

- [ ] A. Elizabeth
- [ ] B. Martha
- [ ] C. Ruth

3. SHE AND HER SISTER HAD THE SAME HUSBAND AND WERE CONSTANTLY COMPETING WITH EACH OTHER TO HAVE THE MOST CHILDREN.

- [ ] A. Rebekah
- [ ] B. Eve
- [ ] C. Leah

4. SHE WAS THE MOST EVIL QUEEN EVER AND ENDED UP BEING EATEN BY WILD DOGS.

- [ ] A. Jezebel
- [ ] B. Lydia
- [ ] C. Sapphira

5. SHE HAD A BABY LONG AFTER NORMAL CHILDBEARING YEARS.

- [ ] A. Eve
- [ ] B. Deborah
- [ ] C. Sarah

6. SHE FIRST SAW HER HUSBAND FROM ACROSS THE FIELD; THEIR EYES MET AND IT WAS LOVE AT FIRST SIGHT!

- [ ] A. Mary
- [ ] B. Rebekah
- [ ] C. Esther

7. SHE ENCOURAGED JESUS TO PERFORM HIS FIRST MIRACLE AT A WEDDING FEAST.

- [ ] A. Mary
- [ ] B. Martha
- [ ] C. Lydia

8. SHE AND HER HUSBAND MADE CLOTHES OUT OF FIG LEAVES.

- [ ] A. Ruth
- [ ] B. Eve
- [ ] C. Rachel

9. SHE WAS A POWERFUL JUDGE IN ANCIENT ISRAEL.

- [ ] A. Deborah
- [ ] B. Jezebel
- [ ] C. Sapphira

10. SHE WAS THE MOTHER OF JOHN THE BAPTIST AND AUNT OF JESUS.

- [ ] A. Martha
- [ ] B. Elizabeth
- [ ] C. Priscilla

SCORING:

Give yourself one point for each question you answered correctly.

1.A 2.C 3.C 4.A 5.C 6.B 7.A 8.B 9.A 10.B

Regardless of how many points you racked up, you can be sure that learning more about the women of the Bible would greatly benefit your personal walk with Jesus. There are stories of amazing courage, love, and faith. And there are moments of incredible strength and heartbreaking desperation. You can learn from their behavior: the good, the bad, and the ugly. Reread the accounts of these famous women and be amazed all over again!

RELATIONSHIPS

The Hothead

Look out, she's gonna blow! Erupting volcano . . . or exploding temper? If you guessed the second, then you probably know a hothead. More than a tad temperamental, a bit impatient, or a smidge ornery, a hothead's fuse is always lit and ready to flare at the slightest provocation. Avoid a hothead's burn by remembering Proverbs 14:17: "Someone with a quick temper does foolish things, but someone with understanding remains calm." Douse the flame with a cool head and a calm approach. Don't give in to your own temper, and you'll show that you understand God's better way.

but into the stomach. Then it goes out of the body." (When Jesus said this, he meant that no longer was any food unclean for people to eat.)

[20]And Jesus said, "The things that come out of people are the things that make them unclean. [21]All these evil things begin inside people, in the mind: evil thoughts, sexual sins, stealing, murder, adultery, [22]greed, evil actions, lying, doing sinful things, jealousy, speaking evil of others, pride, and foolish living. [23]All these evil things come from inside and make people unclean."

Jesus Helps a Non-Jewish Woman

[24]Jesus left that place and went to the area around Tyre.[n] When he went into a house, he did not want anyone to know he was there, but he could not stay hidden. [25]A woman whose daughter had an evil spirit in her heard that he was there. So she quickly came to Jesus and fell at his feet. [26]She was Greek, born in Phoenicia, in Syria. She begged Jesus to force the demon out of her daughter.

[27]Jesus told the woman, "It is not right to take the children's bread and give it to the dogs. First let the children eat all they want."

[28]But she answered, "Yes, Lord, but even the dogs under the table can eat the children's crumbs."

[29]Then Jesus said, "Because of your answer, you may go. The demon has left your daughter."

[30]The woman went home and found her daughter lying in bed; the demon was gone.

Jesus Heals a Deaf Man

[31]Then Jesus left the area around Tyre and went through Sidon to Lake Galilee, to the area of the Ten Towns.[n] [32]While he was there, some people brought a man to him who was deaf and could not talk plainly. The people begged Jesus to put his hand on the man to heal him.

[33]Jesus led the man away from the crowd, by himself. He put his fingers in the man's ears and then spit and touched the man's tongue. [34]Looking up to heaven, he sighed and said to the man, "Ephphatha!" (This means, "Be opened.") [35]Instantly the man was able to hear and to use his tongue so that he spoke clearly.

[36]Jesus commanded the people not to tell anyone about what happened. But the more he commanded them, the more they told about it. [37]They were completely amazed and said, "Jesus does everything well. He makes the deaf hear! And those who can't talk he makes able to speak."

More than Four Thousand People Fed

8 Another time there was a great crowd with Jesus that had nothing to eat. So Jesus called his followers and said, [2]"I feel sorry for these people, because they have already been with me for three days, and they have nothing to eat. [3]If I send them home hungry, they will faint on the way. Some of them live a long way from here."

[4]Jesus' followers answered, "How can we get enough bread to feed all these people? We are far away from any town."

[5]Jesus asked, "How many loaves of bread do you have?"

They answered, "Seven."

[6]Jesus told the people to sit on the ground. Then he took the seven loaves, gave thanks to God, and divided the bread. He gave the pieces to his followers to give to the people, and they did so. [7]The followers also had a few small fish. After Jesus gave thanks for the fish, he told his followers to give them to the people also. [8]All the people ate and were satisfied. Then his followers filled seven baskets with the leftover pieces of food. [9]There were about four thousand people who ate. After they had eaten, Jesus sent them home. [10]Then right away he got into a boat with his followers and went to the area of Dalmanutha.

7:24 Tyre Some Greek copies continue, "and Sidon." **7:31 Ten Towns** In Greek, called "Decapolis." It was an area east of Lake Galilee that once had ten main towns.

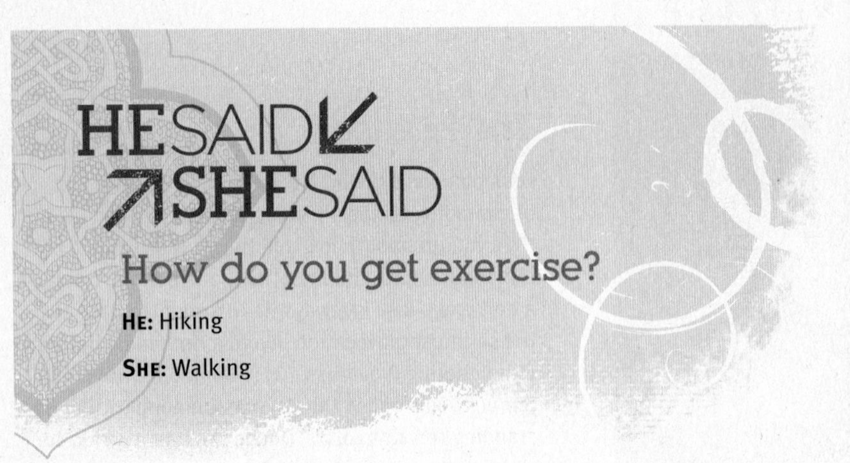

How do you get exercise?

He: Hiking

She: Walking

The Leaders Ask for a Miracle

11 The Pharisees came to Jesus and began to ask him questions. Hoping to trap him, they asked Jesus for a miracle from God. 12 Jesus sighed deeply and said, "Why do you people ask for a miracle as a sign? I tell you the truth, no sign will be given to you." 13 Then Jesus left the Pharisees and went in the boat to the other side of the lake.

Guard Against Wrong Teachings

14 His followers had only one loaf of bread with them in the boat; they had forgotten to bring more. 15 Jesus warned them, "Be careful! Beware of the yeast of the Pharisees and the yeast of Herod."

16 His followers discussed the meaning of this, saying, "He said this because we have no bread."

17 Knowing what they were talking about, Jesus asked them, "Why are you talking about not having bread? Do you still not see or understand? Are your minds closed? 18 You have eyes, but you don't really see. You have ears, but you don't really listen. Remember when 19 I divided five loaves of bread for the five thousand? How many baskets did you fill with leftover pieces of food?"

They answered, "Twelve."

20 "And when I divided seven loaves of bread for the four thousand, how many baskets did you fill with leftover pieces of food?"

They answered, "Seven."

21 Then Jesus said to them, "Don't you understand yet?"

Jesus Heals a Blind Man

22 Jesus and his followers came to Bethsaida. There some people brought a blind man to Jesus and begged him to touch the man. 23 So Jesus took the blind man's hand and led him out of the village. Then he spit on the man's eyes and put his hands on the man and asked, "Can you see now?"

24 The man looked up and said, "Yes, I see people, but they look like trees walking around."

25 Again Jesus put his hands on the man's eyes. Then the man opened his eyes wide and they were healed, and he was able to see everything clearly. 26 Jesus told him to go home, saying, "Don't go into the town."[n]

Peter Says Jesus Is the Christ

27 Jesus and his followers went to the towns around Caesarea Philippi. While they were traveling, Jesus asked them, "Who do people say I am?"

28 They answered, "Some say you are John the Baptist. Others say you are Elijah,[n] and others say you are one of the prophets."

29 Then Jesus asked, "But who do you say I am?"

Peter answered, "You are the Christ."

30 Jesus warned his followers not to tell anyone who he was.

31 Then Jesus began to teach them that the Son of Man must suffer many things and that he would be rejected by the Jewish elders, the leading priests, and the teachers of the law. He told them that the Son of Man must be killed and then rise from the dead after three days. 32 Jesus told them plainly what would happen. Then Peter took Jesus aside and began to tell him not to talk like that. 33 But Jesus turned and looked at his followers. Then he told Peter not to talk that way. He said, "Go away from me, Satan![n] You don't care about the things of God, but only about things people think are important."

Deep Cleansing

It's so refreshing and fun to give yourself a facial. You spread on the mud mask, look like a monster for a few minutes, rinse off, and . . . voilà! You are ready to go with fresh, beautiful, ultraclean skin. Did you know you can do that with your heart as well? Ask God to be your Soul Cleanser. The Bible says, "All who make themselves clean from evil will be used for special purposes" (2 Timothy 2:21). With your confession and repentance, mixed with God's grace and forgiveness, your heart will be clean and refreshed, ready to do any good work.

8:26 town Some Greek copies continue, "Don't even go and tell anyone in the town." **8:28 Elijah** A man who spoke for God and who lived hundreds of years before Christ. See 1 Kings 17. **8:33 Satan** Name for the devil meaning "the enemy." Jesus means that Peter was talking like Satan.

[34]Then Jesus called the crowd to him, along with his followers. He said, "If people want to follow me, they must give up the things they want. They must be willing even to give up their lives to follow me. [35]Those who want to save their lives will give up true life. But those who give up their lives for me and for the Good News will have true life. [36]It is worthless to have the whole world if they lose their souls. [37]They could never pay enough to buy back their souls. [38]The people who live now are living in a sinful and evil time. If people are ashamed of me and my teaching, the Son of Man will be ashamed of them when he comes with his Father's glory and with the holy angels."

9 Then Jesus said to the people, "I tell you the truth, some people standing here will see the kingdom of God come with power before they die."

Jesus Talks with Moses and Elijah

[2]Six days later, Jesus took Peter, James, and John up on a high mountain by themselves. While they watched, Jesus' appearance was changed. [3]His clothes became shining white, whiter than any person could make them. [4]Then Elijah and Moses[n] appeared to them, talking with Jesus.

[5]Peter said to Jesus, "Teacher, it is good that we are here. Let us make three tents—one for you, one for Moses, and one for Elijah." [6]Peter did not know what to say, because he and the others were so frightened.

[7]Then a cloud came and covered them, and a voice came from the cloud, saying, "This is my Son, whom I love. Listen to him!"

[8]Suddenly Peter, James, and John looked around, but they saw only Jesus there alone with them.

[9]As they were coming down the mountain, Jesus commanded them not to tell anyone about what they had seen until the Son of Man had risen from the dead.

[10]So the followers obeyed Jesus, but they discussed what he meant about rising from the dead.

[11]Then they asked Jesus, "Why do the teachers of the law say that Elijah must come first?"

[12]Jesus answered, "They are right to say that Elijah must come first and make everything the way it should be. But why does the Scripture say that the Son of Man will suffer much and that people will treat him as if he were nothing? [13]I tell you that Elijah has already come. And people did to him whatever they wanted to do, just as the Scriptures said it would happen."

Jesus Heals a Sick Boy

[14]When Jesus, Peter, James, and John came back to the other followers, they saw a great crowd around them and the teachers of the law arguing with them. [15]But as soon as the crowd saw Jesus, the people were surprised and ran to welcome him.

[16]Jesus asked, "What are you arguing about?"

[17]A man answered, "Teacher, I brought my son to you. He has an evil spirit in him that stops him from talking. [18]When the spirit attacks him, it throws him on the ground. Then my son foams at the mouth, grinds his teeth, and becomes very stiff. I asked your followers to force the evil spirit out, but they couldn't."

[19]Jesus answered, "You people have no faith. How long must I stay with you? How long must I put up with you? Bring the boy to me."

[20]So the followers brought him to Jesus. As soon as the evil spirit saw Jesus, it made the boy lose control of himself, and he fell down and rolled on the ground, foaming at the mouth.

[21]Jesus asked the boy's father, "How long has this been happening?"

The father answered, "Since he was very young. [22]The spirit often throws him into a fire or into water to kill him. If you can do anything for him, please have pity on us and help us."

[23]Jesus said to the father, "You said, 'If you can!' All things are possible for the one who believes."

[24]Immediately the father cried out, "I do believe! Help me to believe more!"

[25]When Jesus saw that a crowd was quickly gathering, he ordered the evil spirit, saying, "You spirit that makes people unable to hear or speak, I command you to come out of this boy and never enter him again!"

[26]The evil spirit screamed and caused the boy to fall on the ground again. Then the spirit came out. The boy looked as if he were dead, and many people said, "He is dead!" [27]But Jesus took hold of the boy's hand and helped him to stand up.

[28]When Jesus went into the house, his followers began asking him privately, "Why couldn't we force that evil spirit out?"

[29]Jesus answered, "That kind of spirit can only be forced out by prayer."[n]

Jesus Talks About His Death

[30]Then Jesus and his followers left that place and went through Galilee. He didn't want anyone to know where he was, [31]because he was teaching his followers. He

Fish Facts About Mercury

Do warnings about mercury in fish have you swimming upstream in your efforts to eat healthy? Vital fatty-acid-packed seafood is still an important part of a nutritious eating plan as long as you consume it in moderation. Shark, swordfish, king mackerel, and tilefish have high levels of mercury, but most other varieties contain some as well. Common recommendations include 12 ounces (or 2 average portions) per week of fish such as wild salmon, tuna (canned light is better than albacore), and shrimp, among others. It's worth researching, so fish for the truth about mercury consumption!

9:4 Elijah and Moses Two of the most important Jewish leaders in the past. God had given Moses the Law, and Elijah was an important prophet. **9:29 prayer** Some Greek copies continue, "and fasting."

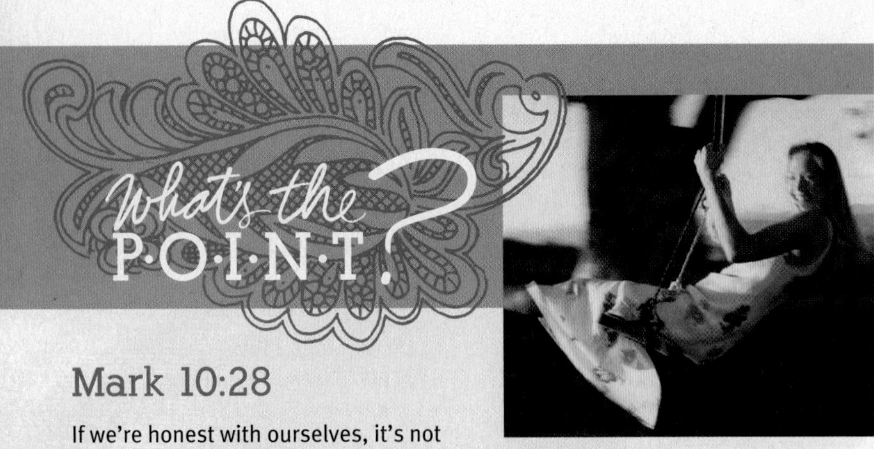

Mark 10:28

If we're honest with ourselves, it's not always easy to believe true satisfaction is found only in God. We have so many other things we're tempted to lean on: dependable cars, little black dresses, and friends with tons of good advice. While all of these are gifts from God, the only way to satisfy the deep rumbles of soul hunger is to trust the Giver more than the gifts.

Whenever we seek peace or joy apart from Christ, we essentially tell God, "I don't believe you're all I need." Jesus said, "Whoever drinks the water I give will never be thirsty" (John 4:14). If we really believe that knowing and loving Jesus is the ultimate satisfaction any human can experience, we should be overjoyed to give up everything (including our lives) just to be with him!

Jesus calls us to look beyond our personal dramas and see the needs of other people. But he promises heaven's reward will far outweigh all the empty things we sacrifice along the way. Whether you're blessed with comfort or called to suffering, learn to find all your satisfaction in Christ alone. As you grow in your faith and willingness to give up *everything* to follow Jesus, you'll find the best thing to experience has always been right there—a relationship with him.

said to them, "The Son of Man will be handed over to people, and they will kill him. After three days, he will rise from the dead." [32]But the followers did not understand what Jesus meant, and they were afraid to ask him.

Who Is the Greatest?

[33]Jesus and his followers went to Capernaum. When they went into a house there, he asked them, "What were you arguing about on the road?" [34]But the followers did not answer, because their argument on the road was about which one of them was the greatest.

[35]Jesus sat down and called the twelve apostles to him. He said, "Whoever wants to be the most important must be last of all and servant of all."

[36]Then Jesus took a small child and had him stand among them. Taking the child in his arms, he said, [37]"Whoever accepts a child like this in my name accepts me. And whoever accepts me accepts the One who sent me."

Anyone Not Against Us Is for Us

[38]Then John said, "Teacher, we saw someone using your name to force demons out of a person. We told him to stop, because he does not belong to our group."

[39]But Jesus said, "Don't stop him, because anyone who uses my name to do powerful things will not easily say evil things about me. [40]Whoever is not against us is with us. [41]I tell you the truth, whoever gives you a drink of water because you belong to the Christ will truly get his reward.

[42]"If one of these little children believes in me, and someone causes that child to sin, it would be better for that person to have a large stone tied around his neck and be drowned in the sea. [43]If your hand causes you to sin, cut it off. It is better for you to lose part of your body and live forever than to have two hands and go to hell, where the fire never goes out. [[44]In hell the worm does not die; the fire is never put out.][n] [45]If your foot causes you to sin, cut it off. It is better for you to lose part of your body and to live forever than to have two feet and be thrown into hell. [[46]In hell the worm does not die; the fire is never put out.][n] [47]If your eye causes you to sin, take it out. It is better for you to enter the kingdom of God with only one eye than to have two eyes and be thrown into hell. [48]In hell the worm does not die; the fire is never put out. [49]Every person will be salted with fire.

[50]"Salt is good, but if the salt loses its salty taste, you cannot make it salty again. So, be full of salt, and have peace with each other."

Jesus Teaches About Divorce

10 Then Jesus left that place and went into the area of Judea and across the Jordan River. Again, crowds came to him, and he taught them as he usually did.

[2]Some Pharisees came to Jesus and tried to trick him. They asked, "Is it right for a man to divorce his wife?"

[3]Jesus answered, "What did Moses command you to do?"

[4]They said, "Moses allowed a man to write out divorce papers and send her away."[n]

[5]Jesus said, "Moses wrote that command for you because you were stubborn. [6]But when God made the world, 'he made them male and female.'[n] [7]'So a man will leave his father and mother and be united with his wife,[n] [8]and the two will become one body.'[n] So there are not two, but one. [9]God has joined the two together, so no one should separate them."

[10]Later, in the house, his followers asked Jesus again about the question of divorce. [11]He answered, "Anyone who divorces his

9:44, 46 In . . . out. Some Greek copies do not contain the bracketed text. **10:4 "Moses . . . away."** Quotation from Deuteronomy 24:1. **10:6 'he made . . . female'** Quotation from Genesis 1:27. **10:7 and . . . wife** Some Greek copies do not have this phrase. **10:7–8 'So . . . body.'** Quotation from Genesis 2:24.

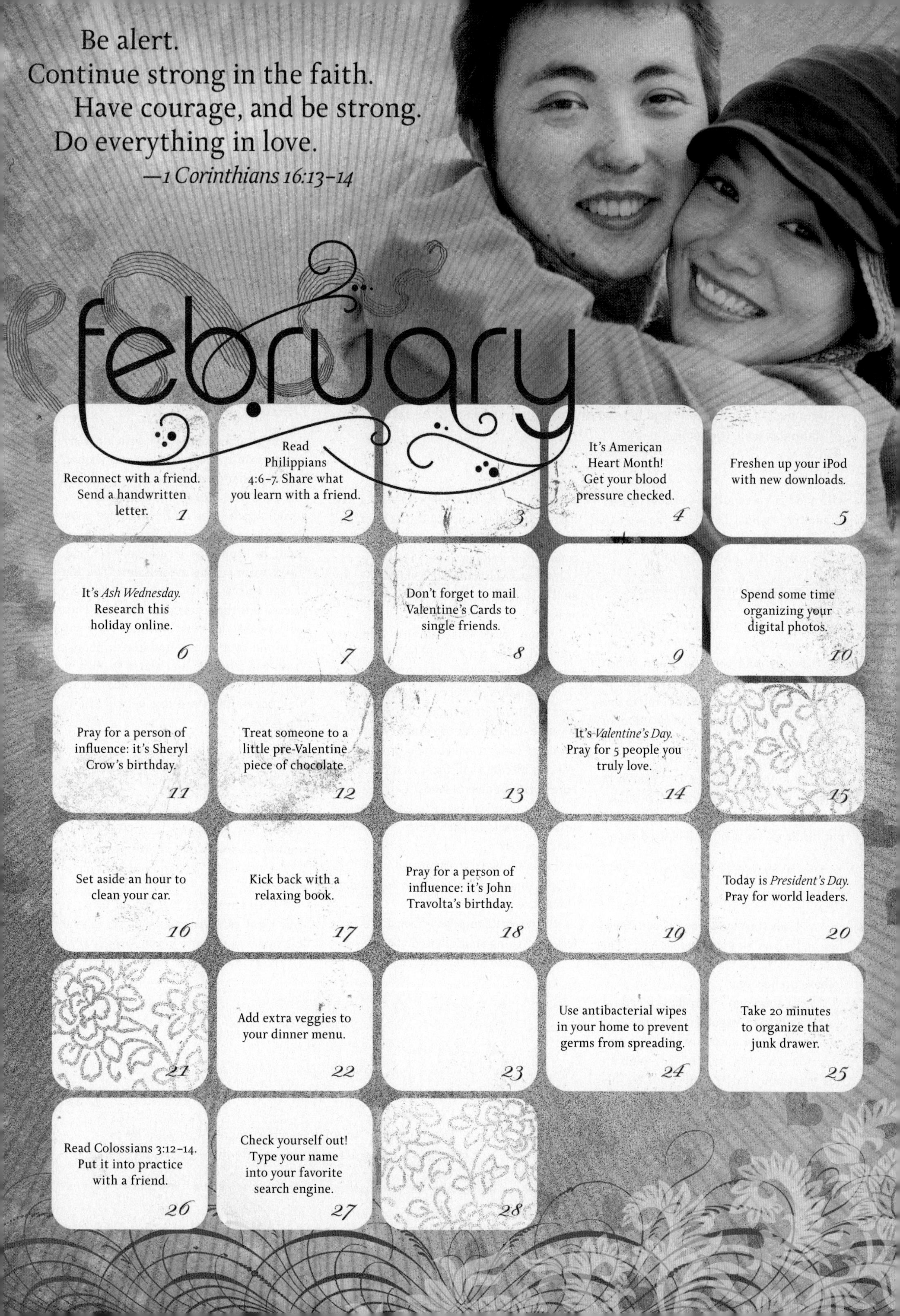

Be alert.
Continue strong in the faith.
Have courage, and be strong.
Do everything in love.
—1 Corinthians 16:13–14
february
Reconnect with a friend. Send a handwritten letter. 1
Read Philippians 4:6–7. Share what you learn with a friend. 2
3
It's American Heart Month! Get your blood pressure checked. 4
Freshen up your iPod with new downloads. 5
It's *Ash Wednesday.* Research this holiday online. 6
7
Don't forget to mail Valentine's Cards to single friends. 8
9
Spend some time organizing your digital photos. 10
Pray for a person of influence: it's Sheryl Crow's birthday. 11
Treat someone to a little pre-Valentine piece of chocolate. 12
13
It's *Valentine's Day.* Pray for 5 people you truly love. 14
15
Set aside an hour to clean your car. 16
Kick back with a relaxing book. 17
Pray for a person of influence: it's John Travolta's birthday. 18
19
Today is *President's Day.* Pray for world leaders. 20
21
Add extra veggies to your dinner menu. 22
23
Use antibacterial wipes in your home to prevent germs from spreading. 24
Take 20 minutes to organize that junk drawer. 25
Read Colossians 3:12–14. Put it into practice with a friend. 26
Check yourself out! Type your name into your favorite search engine. 27
28

Women & Men of the BIBLE

Nehemiah: Rebuilding Together

Nehemiah was one of the most remarkable leaders ever. His heart was broken because the city of his heritage lay in ruins. He courageously asked his boss (who happened to be a foreign king!) for a leave of absence and set out for his ancestors' homeland. When he got there, he looked everything over and made a workable plan. He motivated each family to pitch in and rebuild the part of the city wall that was in front of their own home. And best of all, he motivated his countrymen to rebuild their spiritual foundation as well. (Nehemiah 1–13)

wife and marries another woman is guilty of adultery against her. [12]And the woman who divorces her husband and marries another man is also guilty of adultery."

Jesus Accepts Children

[13]Some people brought their little children to Jesus so he could touch them, but his followers told them to stop. [14]When Jesus saw this, he was upset and said to them, "Let the little children come to me. Don't stop them, because the kingdom of God belongs to people who are like these children. [15]I tell you the truth, you must accept the kingdom of God as if you were a little child, or you will never enter it." [16]Then Jesus took the children in his arms, put his hands on them, and blessed them.

A Rich Young Man's Question

[17]As Jesus started to leave, a man ran to him and fell on his knees before Jesus. The man asked, "Good teacher, what must I do to have life forever?"

[18]Jesus answered, "Why do you call me good? Only God is good. [19]You know the commands: 'You must not murder anyone. You must not be guilty of adultery. You must not steal. You must not tell lies about your neighbor. You must not cheat. Honor your father and mother.' "[n]

[20]The man said, "Teacher, I have obeyed all these things since I was a boy."

[21]Jesus, looking at the man, loved him and said, "There is one more thing you need to do. Go and sell everything you have, and give the money to the poor, and you will have treasure in heaven. Then come and follow me."

[22]He was very sad to hear Jesus say this, and he left sorrowfully, because he was rich.

[23]Then Jesus looked at his followers and said, "How hard it will be for the rich to enter the kingdom of God!"

[24]The followers were amazed at what Jesus said. But he said again, "My children, it is very hard[n] to enter the kingdom of God! [25]It is easier for a camel to go through the eye of a needle than for a rich person to enter the kingdom of God."

[26]The followers were even more surprised and said to each other, "Then who can be saved?"

[27]Jesus looked at them and said, "For people this is impossible, but for God all things are possible."

[28]Peter said to Jesus, "Look, we have left everything and followed you."

[29]Jesus said, "I tell you the truth, all those who have left houses, brothers, sisters, mother, father, children, or farms for me and for the Good News [30]will get more than they left. Here in this world they will have a hundred times more homes, brothers, sisters, mothers, children, and fields. And with those things, they will also suffer for their belief. But in this age they will have life forever. [31]Many who are first now will be last in the future. And many who are last now will be first in the future."

Jesus Talks About His Death

[32]As Jesus and the people with him were on the road to Jerusalem, he was leading the way. His followers were amazed, but others in the crowd who followed were afraid. Again Jesus took the twelve apostles aside and began to tell them what was about to happen in Jerusalem. [33]He said, "Look, we are going to Jerusalem. The Son of Man will be turned over to the leading priests and the teachers of the law. They will say that he must die, and they will turn him over to the non-Jewish people, [34]who will laugh at him and spit on him. They will beat him with whips and crucify him. But on the third day, he will rise to life again."

Two Followers Ask Jesus a Favor

[35]Then James and John, sons of Zebedee, came to Jesus and said, "Teacher, we want to ask you to do something for us."

[36]Jesus asked, "What do you want me to do for you?"

[37]They answered, "Let one of us sit at your right side and one of us sit at your left side in your glory in your kingdom."

[38]Jesus said, "You don't understand

fun facts

The number of American women giving birth with the assistance of a midwife has more than doubled since 1990.

(Nursing)

10:19 'You . . . mother.' Quotation from Exodus 20:12-16; Deuteronomy 5:16–20. **10:24 hard** Some Greek copies continue, "for those who trust in riches."

what you are asking. Can you drink the cup that I must drink? And can you be baptized with the same kind of baptism that I must go through?"[n]

[39]They answered, "Yes, we can."

Jesus said to them, "You will drink the same cup that I will drink, and you will be baptized with the same baptism that I must go through. [40]But I cannot choose who will sit at my right or my left; those places belong to those for whom they have been prepared."

[41]When the other ten followers heard this, they began to be angry with James and John.

[42]Jesus called them together and said, "The other nations have rulers. You know that those rulers love to show their power over the people, and their important leaders love to use all their authority. [43]But it should not be that way among you. Whoever wants to become great among you must serve the rest of you like a servant. [44]Whoever wants to become the first among you must serve all of you like a slave. [45]In the same way, the Son of Man did not come to be served. He came to serve others and to give his life as a ransom for many people."

Jesus Heals a Blind Man

[46]Then they came to the town of Jericho. As Jesus was leaving there with his followers and a great many people, a blind beggar named Bartimaeus son of Timaeus was sitting by the road. [47]When he heard that Jesus from Nazareth was walking by, he began to shout, "Jesus, Son of David, have mercy on me!"

[48]Many people warned the blind man to be quiet, but he shouted even more, "Son of David, have mercy on me!"

[49]Jesus stopped and said, "Tell the man to come here."

So they called the blind man, saying, "Cheer up! Get to your feet. Jesus is calling you." [50]The blind man jumped up, left his coat there, and went to Jesus.

[51]Jesus asked him, "What do you want me to do for you?"

The blind man answered, "Teacher, I want to see."

[52]Jesus said, "Go, you are healed because you believed." At once the man could see, and he followed Jesus on the road.

Jesus Enters Jerusalem as a King

11 As Jesus and his followers were coming closer to Jerusalem, they came to the towns of Bethphage and Bethany near the Mount of Olives. From there Jesus sent two of his followers [2]and said to them, "Go to the town you can see there. When you enter it, you will quickly find a colt tied, which no one has ever ridden. Untie it and bring it here to me. [3]If anyone asks you why you are doing this, tell him its Master needs the colt, and he will send it at once."

[4]The followers went into the town, found a colt tied in the street near the door of a house, and untied it. [5]Some people were standing there and asked, "What are you doing? Why are you untying that colt?" [6]The followers answered the way Jesus told them to answer, and the people let them take the colt.

[7]They brought the colt to Jesus and put their coats on it, and Jesus sat on it. [8]Many people spread their coats on the road. Others cut branches in the fields and spread them on the road. [9]The people were walking ahead of Jesus and behind him, shouting,

"Praise God!
God bless the One who comes in the name of the Lord! *Psalm 118:26*
[10]God bless the kingdom of our father David!
That kingdom is coming!
Praise[n] to God in heaven!"

[11]Jesus entered Jerusalem and went into the Temple. After he had looked at everything, since it was already late, he went out to Bethany with the twelve apostles.

[12]The next day as Jesus was leaving Bethany, he became hungry. [13]Seeing a fig tree in leaf from far away, he went to see if it had any figs on it. But he found no figs, only leaves, because it was not the right season for figs. [14]So Jesus said to the tree, "May no one ever eat fruit from you again." And Jesus' followers heard him say this.

Be Still & KNOW

Imperfect but Forgiven

Isn't it comforting to know that God does not expect you to be perfect? You don't have to shoulder that burden. He knows you inside and out, and he has already provided a way to make things right when you do something wrong. First John 1:9 says that all you have to do is confess your sin, and he will forgive you from all the wrongs you have done. Let this confession of sin be a regular part of your prayer conversations. When you come to him with an honest and contrite heart, he promises to restore your relationship with him right away. Acknowledge your sin and imperfections, and then believe your Father when he says you are forgiven!

10:38 Can you . . . through? Jesus was asking if they could suffer the same terrible things that would happen to him. **11:10 Praise** Literally, "Hosanna," a Hebrew word used at first in praying to God for help, but at this time it was probably a shout of joy used in praising God or his Messiah.

Jesus Goes to the Temple

[15]When Jesus returned to Jerusalem, he went into the Temple and began to throw out those who were buying and selling there. He turned over the tables of those who were exchanging different kinds of money, and he upset the benches of those who were selling doves. [16]Jesus refused to allow anyone to carry goods through the Temple courts. [17]Then he taught the people, saying, "It is written in the Scriptures, 'My Temple will be called a house for prayer for people from all nations.'[n] But you are changing God's house into a 'hideout for robbers.' "[n]

[18]The leading priests and the teachers of the law heard all this and began trying to find a way to kill Jesus. They were afraid of him, because all the people were amazed at his teaching. [19]That evening, Jesus and his followers[n] left the city.

The Power of Faith

[20]The next morning as Jesus was passing by with his followers, they saw the fig tree dry and dead, even to the roots. [21]Peter remembered the tree and said to Jesus, "Teacher, look! The fig tree you cursed is dry and dead!"

[22]Jesus answered, "Have faith in God. [23]I tell you the truth, you can say to this mountain, 'Go, fall into the sea.' And if you have no doubts in your mind and believe that what you say will happen, God will do it for you. [24]So I tell you to believe that you have received the things you ask for in prayer, and God will give them to you. [25]When you are praying, if you are angry with someone, forgive him so that your Father in heaven will also forgive your sins. [[26]But if you don't forgive other people, then your Father in heaven will not forgive your sins.]"[n]

Leaders Doubt Jesus' Authority

[27]Jesus and his followers went again to Jerusalem. As Jesus was walking in the Temple, the leading priests, the teachers of the law, and the elders came to him. [28]They said to him, "What authority do you have to do these things? Who gave you this authority?"

[29]Jesus answered, "I will ask you one question. If you answer me, I will tell you what authority I have to do these things. [30]Tell me: When John baptized people, was that authority from God or just from other people?"

[31]They argued about Jesus' question, saying, "If we answer, 'John's baptism was from God,' Jesus will say, 'Then why didn't you believe him?' [32]But if we say, 'It was from other people,' the crowd will be against us." (These leaders were afraid of the people, because all the people believed that John was a prophet.)

[33]So they answered Jesus, "We don't know."

Jesus said to them, "Then I won't tell you what authority I have to do these things."

A Story About God's Son

12 Jesus began to use stories to teach the people. He said, "A man planted a vineyard. He put a wall around it and dug a hole for a winepress and built a tower. Then he leased the land to some farmers and left for a trip. [2]When it was time for the grapes to be picked, he sent a servant to the farmers to get his share of the grapes. [3]But the farmers grabbed the servant and beat him and sent him away empty-handed. [4]Then the man sent another servant. They hit him on the head and showed no respect for him. [5]So the man sent another servant, whom they killed. The man sent many other servants; the farmers beat some of them and killed others.

[6]"The man had one person left to send, his son whom he loved. He sent him last of all, saying, 'They will respect my son.'

[7]"But the farmers said to each other, 'This son will inherit the vineyard. If we kill him, it will be ours.' [8]So they took the son, killed him, and threw him out of the vineyard.

[9]"So what will the owner of the vineyard do? He will come and kill those farmers and will give the vineyard to other farmers. [10]Surely you have read this Scripture:

'The stone that the builders rejected
became the cornerstone.
[11]The Lord did this,
and it is wonderful to us.' "

Psalm 118:22–23

[12]The Jewish leaders knew that the story was about them. So they wanted to find a way to arrest Jesus, but they were afraid of the people. So the leaders left him and went away.

Is It Right to Pay Taxes or Not?

[13]Later, the Jewish leaders sent some Pharisees and Herodians[n] to Jesus to trap him in saying something wrong. [14]They came to him and said, "Teacher, we know that you are an honest man. You are not afraid of what other people think about you, because you pay no attention to who

LIFEISSUES

Caring for the Next Generation

Who made a difference in your life when you were a child? Parents? Relatives? Teachers? Neighbors? Today's younger generations need our time and care as well. You don't need to be a mother or an aunt to be a godly example to a child. Churches and community organizations need trustworthy, caring people to help with Sunday school and kids' programs. When you follow Jesus' example (Mark 10:13–16) and offer your heart, your time, and your resources to a child, you're giving a gift that will grow for generations to come. And you'll be blessed as well!

11:17 'My Temple . . . nations.' Quotation from Isaiah 56:7. **11:17 'hideout for robbers'** Quotation from Jeremiah 7:11. **11:19 his followers** Some Greek copies mention only Jesus here. **11:26 But . . . sins.** Some Greek copies do not contain the bracketed text. **12:13 Herodians** A political group that followed Herod and his family.

they are. And you teach the truth about God's way. Tell us: Is it right to pay taxes to Caesar or not? [15]Should we pay them, or not?"

But knowing what these men were really trying to do, Jesus said to them, "Why are you trying to trap me? Bring me a coin to look at." [16]They gave Jesus a coin, and he asked, "Whose image and name are on the coin?"

They answered, "Caesar's."

[17]Then Jesus said to them, "Give to Caesar the things that are Caesar's, and give to God the things that are God's." The men were amazed at what Jesus said.

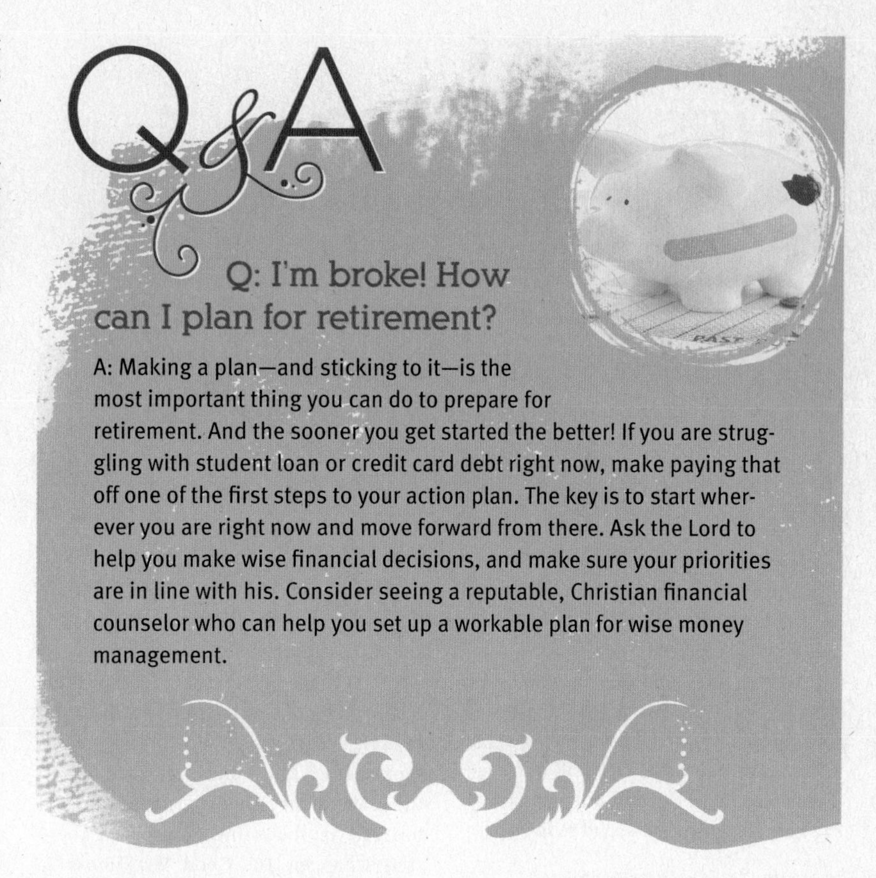

Some Sadducees Try to Trick Jesus

[18]Then some Sadducees came to Jesus and asked him a question. (Sadducees believed that people would not rise from the dead.) [19]They said, "Teacher, Moses wrote that if a man's brother dies, leaving a wife but no children, then that man must marry the widow and have children for his brother. [20]Once there were seven brothers. The first brother married and died, leaving no children. [21]So the second brother married the widow, but he also died and had no children. The same thing happened with the third brother. [22]All seven brothers married her and died, and none of the brothers had any children. Finally the woman died too. [23]Since all seven brothers had married her, when people rise from the dead, whose wife will she be?"

[24]Jesus answered, "Why don't you understand? Don't you know what the Scriptures say, and don't you know about the power of God? [25]When people rise from the dead, they will not marry, nor will they be given to someone to marry. They will be like the angels in heaven. [26]Surely you have read what God said about people rising from the dead. In the book in which Moses wrote about the burning bush,[n] it says that God told Moses, 'I am the God of Abraham, the God of Isaac, and the God of Jacob.'[n] [27]God is the God of the living, not the dead. You Sadducees are wrong!"

The Most Important Command

[28]One of the teachers of the law came and heard Jesus arguing with the Sadducees. Seeing that Jesus gave good answers to their questions, he asked Jesus, "Which of the commands is most important?"

[29]Jesus answered, "The most important command is this: 'Listen, people of Israel! The Lord our God is the only Lord. [30]Love the Lord your God with all your heart, all your soul, all your mind, and all your strength.'[n] [31]The second command is this: 'Love your neighbor as you love yourself.'[n] There are no commands more important than these."

[32]The man answered, "That was a good answer, Teacher. You were right when you said God is the only Lord and there is no other God besides him. [33]One must love God with all his heart, all his mind, and all his strength. And one must love his neighbor as he loves himself. These commands are more important than all the animals and sacrifices we offer to God."

[34]When Jesus saw that the man answered him wisely, Jesus said to him, "You are close to the kingdom of God." And after that, no one was brave enough to ask Jesus any more questions.

[35]As Jesus was teaching in the Temple, he asked, "Why do the teachers of the law say that the Christ is the son of David? [36]David himself, speaking by the Holy Spirit, said:

> 'The Lord said to my Lord,
> "Sit by me at my right side,
> until I put your enemies under your control."' *Psalm 110:1*

[37]David himself calls the Christ 'Lord,' so how can the Christ be his son?" The large crowd listened to Jesus with pleasure.

[38]Jesus continued teaching and said, "Beware of the teachers of the law. They like to walk around wearing fancy clothes, and they love for people to greet them with respect in the marketplaces. [39]They love to have the most important seats in the synagogues and at feasts. [40]But they cheat widows and steal their houses and then try to make themselves look good by saying long prayers. They will receive a greater punishment."

True Giving

[41]Jesus sat near the Temple money box and watched the people put in their money. Many rich people gave large sums

12:26 burning bush Read Exodus 3:1–12 in the Old Testament. **12:26 'I am . . . Jacob.'** Quotation from Exodus 3:6. **12:29–30 'Listen . . . strength.'** Quotation from Deuteronomy 6:4–5. **12:31 'Love . . . yourself.'** Quotation from Leviticus 19:18.

HE SAID ↙ ↗ SHE SAID

What's your favorite book in the Bible?

HE: Romans, because it explores our inheritance in Christ

SHE: Genesis, because it talks about the beginning of time

of money. [42]Then a poor widow came and put in two small copper coins, which were only worth a few cents.

[43]Calling his followers to him, Jesus said, "I tell you the truth, this poor widow gave more than all those rich people. [44]They gave only what they did not need. This woman is very poor, but she gave all she had; she gave all she had to live on."

The Temple Will Be Destroyed

13 As Jesus was leaving the Temple, one of his followers said to him, "Look, Teacher! How beautiful the buildings are! How big the stones are!"

[2]Jesus said, "Do you see all these great buildings? Not one stone will be left on another. Every stone will be thrown down to the ground."

[3]Later, as Jesus was sitting on the Mount of Olives, opposite the Temple, he was alone with Peter, James, John, and Andrew. They asked Jesus, [4]"Tell us, when will these things happen? And what will be the sign that they are going to happen?"

[5]Jesus began to answer them, "Be careful that no one fools you. [6]Many people will come in my name, saying, 'I am the One,' and they will fool many people. [7]When you hear about wars and stories of wars that are coming, don't be afraid. These things must happen before the end comes. [8]Nations will fight against other nations, and kingdoms against other kingdoms. There will be earthquakes in different places, and there will be times when there is no food for people to eat. These things are like the first pains when something new is about to be born.

[9]"You must be careful. People will arrest you and take you to court and beat you in their synagogues. You will be forced to stand before kings and governors, to tell them about me. This will happen to you because you follow me. [10]But before these things happen, the Good News must be told to all people. [11]When you are arrested and judged, don't worry ahead of time about what you should say. Say whatever is given you to say at that time, because it will not really be you speaking; it will be the Holy Spirit.

[12]"Brothers will give their own brothers to be killed, and fathers will give their own children to be killed. Children will fight against their own parents and cause them to be put to death. [13]All people will hate you because you follow me, but those people who keep their faith until the end will be saved.

[14]"You will see 'a blasphemous object that brings destruction'[n] standing where it should not be." (You who read this should understand what it means.) "At that time, the people in Judea should run away to the mountains. [15]If people are on the roofs[n] of their houses, they must not go down or go inside to get anything out of their houses. [16]If people are in the fields, they must not go back to get their coats. [17]At that time, how terrible it will be for women who are pregnant or have nursing babies! [18]Pray that these things will not happen in winter, [19]because those days will be full of trouble. There will be more trouble than there has ever been since the beginning, when God made the world, until now, and nothing as bad will ever happen again. [20]God has decided to make that terrible time short. Otherwise, no one would go on living. But God will make that time short to help the people he has chosen. [21]At that time, someone might say to you, 'Look, there is the Christ!' Or another person might say, 'There he is!' But don't believe them. [22]False Christs and false prophets will come and perform great wonders and miracles. They will try to fool even the people God has chosen, if that is possible. [23]So be careful. I have warned you about all this before it happens.

[24]"During the days after this trouble comes,

'the sun will grow dark,
  and the moon will not give its
    light.
[25]The stars will fall from the sky.
  And the powers of the heavens
    will be shaken.'

Isaiah 13:10; 34:4

[26]"Then people will see the Son of Man coming in clouds with great power and glory. [27]Then he will send his angels all around the earth to gather his chosen people from every part of the earth and from every part of heaven.

fun facts

35% of Americans say reading is their favorite leisure time activity.

(Harris Interactive)

13:14 'a blasphemous object that brings destruction' Mentioned in Daniel 9:27; 12:11 (cf. Daniel 11:31). **13:15 roofs** In Bible times houses were built with flat roofs. The roof was used for drying things such as flax and fruit. And it was used as an extra room, as a place for worship, and as a cool place to sleep in the summer.

[28]"Learn a lesson from the fig tree: When its branches become green and soft and new leaves appear, you know summer is near. [29]In the same way, when you see these things happening, you will know that the time is near, ready to come. [30]I tell you the truth, all these things will happen while the people of this time are still living. [31]Earth and sky will be destroyed, but the words I have said will never be destroyed.

[32]"No one knows when that day or time will be, not the angels in heaven, not even the Son. Only the Father knows. [33]Be careful! Always be ready,[n] because you don't know when that time will be. [34]It is like a man who goes on a trip. He leaves his house and lets his servants take care of it, giving each one a special job to do. The man tells the servant guarding the door always to be watchful. [35]So always be ready, because you don't know when the owner of the house will come back. It might be in the evening, or at midnight, or in the morning while it is still dark, or when the sun rises. [36]Always be ready. Otherwise he might come back suddenly and find you sleeping. [37]I tell you this, and I say this to everyone: 'Be ready!' "

The Plan to Kill Jesus

14 It was now only two days before the Passover and the Feast of Unleavened Bread. The leading priests and teachers of the law were trying to find a trick to arrest Jesus and kill him. [2]But they said, "We must not do it during the feast, because the people might cause a riot."

A Woman with Perfume for Jesus

[3]Jesus was in Bethany at the house of Simon, who had a skin disease. While Jesus was eating there, a woman approached him with an alabaster jar filled with very expensive perfume, made of pure nard. She opened the jar and poured the perfume on Jesus' head.

[4]Some who were there became upset and said to each other, "Why waste that perfume? [5]It was worth a full year's work. It could have been sold and the money given to the poor." And they got very angry with the woman.

Mark 14:38

If you're extremely drowsy but need to stay alert for a couple more hours to accomplish a few more tasks, how do you fight the urge to drift off? Would you snuggle up on your couch with a pillow? Probably not. Just like you'd use a smart strategy to fight the urge to sleep, followers of God need to use wise strategies to fight the temptation to sin! To guard yourself against sin, you must be intentional.

Even though Christians are new creations in Christ, our struggle with sin is still a reality. Our spirits may completely love Jesus, but they're still attached to the same sinful body we were born with. And until we get to heaven, we're called to put up a good fight with that sin! Jesus gave this practical advice to his followers about battling temptation: stay awake (keep on the alert) and pray for strength.

Do you ever find yourself "falling asleep" spiritually? Getting comfortable with sin is a serious danger, and we all need to guard against it. Watch carefully for sinful thoughts and attitudes that creep quietly into your heart, and kick them out immediately. Rely on God's strength to resist temptation; he's got more than enough power to help you. And be encouraged—the struggle with sin won't last forever. Christ will be victorious!

[6]Jesus said, "Leave her alone. Why are you troubling her? She did an excellent thing for me. [7]You will always have the poor with you, and you can help them anytime you want. But you will not always have me. [8]This woman did the only thing she could do for me; she poured perfume on my body to prepare me for burial. [9]I tell you the truth, wherever the Good News is preached in all the world, what this woman has done will be told, and people will remember her."

Judas Becomes an Enemy of Jesus

[10]One of the twelve apostles, Judas Iscariot, went to talk to the leading priests to offer to hand Jesus over to them. [11]These priests were pleased about this and promised to pay Judas money. So he watched for the best time to turn Jesus in.

Jesus Eats the Passover Meal

[12]It was now the first day of the Feast of Unleavened Bread when the Passover lamb was sacrificed. Jesus' followers said to him, "Where do you want us to go and prepare for you to eat the Passover meal?"

[13]Jesus sent two of his followers and said to them, "Go into the city and a man carrying a jar of water will meet you. Follow him. [14]When he goes into a house, tell the owner of the house, 'The Teacher says: "Where is

13:33 ready Some Greek copies continue, "and pray."

my guest room in which I can eat the Passover meal with my followers?"' [15]The owner will show you a large room upstairs that is furnished and ready. Prepare the food for us there."

[16]So the followers left and went into the city. Everything happened as Jesus had said, so they prepared the Passover meal.

[17]In the evening, Jesus went to that house with the twelve. [18]While they were all eating, Jesus said, "I tell you the truth, one of you will turn against me—one of you eating with me now."

[19]The followers were very sad to hear this. Each one began to say to Jesus, "I am not the one, am I?"

[20]Jesus answered, "It is one of the twelve—the one who dips his bread into the bowl with me. [21]The Son of Man will die, just as the Scriptures say. But how terrible it will be for the person who hands the Son of Man over to be killed. It would be better for him if he had never been born."

The Lord's Supper

[22]While they were eating, Jesus took some bread and thanked God for it and broke it. Then he gave it to his followers and said, "Take it; this is my body."

[23]Then Jesus took a cup and thanked God for it and gave it to the followers, and they all drank from the cup.

[24]Then Jesus said, "This is my blood which is the new[n] agreement that God makes with his people. This blood is poured out for many. [25]I tell you the truth, I will not drink of this fruit of the vine[n] again until that day when I drink it new in the kingdom of God."

[26]After singing a hymn, they went out to the Mount of Olives.

Jesus' Followers Will Leave Him

[27]Then Jesus told the followers, "You will all stumble in your faith, because it is written in the Scriptures:

'I will kill the shepherd,
and the sheep will scatter.'

Zechariah 13:7

[28]But after I rise from the dead, I will go ahead of you into Galilee."

[29]Peter said, "Everyone else may stumble in their faith, but I will not."

[30]Jesus answered, "I tell you the truth, tonight before the rooster crows twice you will say three times you don't know me."

[31]But Peter insisted, "I will never say that I don't know you! I will even die with you!" And all the other followers said the same thing.

Jesus Prays Alone

[32]Jesus and his followers went to a place called Gethsemane. He said to them, "Sit here while I pray." [33]Jesus took Peter, James, and John with him, and he began to be very sad and troubled. [34]He said to them, "My heart is full of sorrow, to the point of death. Stay here and watch."

[35]After walking a little farther away from them, Jesus fell to the ground and prayed that, if possible, he would not have this time of suffering. [36]He prayed, "Abba,[n] Father! You can do all things. Take away this cup[n] of suffering. But do what you want, not what I want."

[37]Then Jesus went back to his followers and found them asleep. He said to Peter, "Simon, are you sleeping? Couldn't you stay awake with me for one hour? [38]Stay awake and pray for strength against temptation. The spirit wants to do what is right, but the body is weak."

[39]Again Jesus went away and prayed the same thing. [40]Then he went back to his followers, and again he found them asleep, because their eyes were very heavy. And they did not know what to say to him.

BECOME *Involved*

The Glue Network

Imagine the impact an entire generation could make if they all stuck together to make a real difference. That's the idea behind thegluenetwork.com. Individuals, corporations, nonprofits, bands, athletes, artists, and musicians have all come together to form a unique avenue for connecting people and passions together in pursuit of changing the world. Whatever your passion is, they want you to pursue it with all you've got. And they want to help connect you with other people who share your purpose.

One of the most interesting things thegluenetwork.com is doing is building a virtual bridge around the globe, with each panel of the bridge representing one mile of the worldwide trek. As part of their online community, individuals, groups, and companies can build a mile of the bridge. They provide easy-to-follow instructions for designing your mile, and you can put it together based on your passion and purpose. Your creativity and involvement helps raise funds for a variety of different charities.

Check out www.thegluenetwork.com for more information about how individuals just like you are binding together to make a difference for others. Stick together—and change the world!

14:24 new Some Greek copies do not have this word. Compare Luke 22:20. **14:25 fruit of the vine** Product of the grapevine; this may also be translated "wine." **14:36 Abba** Name that a Jewish child called his father. **14:36 cup** Jesus is talking about the terrible things that will happen to him. Accepting these things will be very hard, like drinking a cup of something bitter.

RELATIONSHIPS

Minirelationships

Sometimes God sends us "minirelationships" that he uses for long-lasting purposes. When you help a frazzled mom on a plane or offer the elderly mail carrier a glass of water, your efforts might mean more than you can see. You never know what's going on in someone else's life, but God does. And he often puts his followers in the paths of hurting people to bring hope to their lives. Simple efforts can go a long way! Never underestimate any simple act of kindness. Watch for minirelationships—even though they're short-term, God might do long-term work through them.

[41]After Jesus prayed a third time, he went back to his followers and said to them, "Are you still sleeping and resting? That's enough. The time has come for the Son of Man to be handed over to sinful people. [42]Get up, we must go. Look, here comes the man who has turned against me."

Jesus Is Arrested

[43]At once, while Jesus was still speaking, Judas, one of the twelve apostles, came up. With him were many people carrying swords and clubs who had been sent from the leading priests, the teachers of the law, and the Jewish elders.

[44]Judas had planned a signal for them, saying, "The man I kiss is Jesus. Arrest him and guard him while you lead him away." [45]So Judas went straight to Jesus and said, "Teacher!" and kissed him. [46]Then the people grabbed Jesus and arrested him. [47]One of his followers standing nearby pulled out his sword and struck the servant of the high priest and cut off his ear.

[48]Then Jesus said, "You came to get me with swords and clubs as if I were a criminal. [49]Every day I was with you teaching in the Temple, and you did not arrest me there. But all these things have happened to make the Scriptures come true." [50]Then all of Jesus' followers left him and ran away.

[51]A young man, wearing only a linen cloth, was following Jesus, and the people also grabbed him. [52]But the cloth he was wearing came off, and he ran away naked.

Jesus Before the Leaders

[53]The people who arrested Jesus led him to the house of the high priest, where all the leading priests, the elders, and the teachers of the law were gathered. [54]Peter followed far behind and entered the courtyard of the high priest's house. There he sat with the guards, warming himself by the fire.

[55]The leading priests and the whole Jewish council tried to find something that Jesus had done wrong so they could kill him. But the council could find no proof of anything. [56]Many people came and told false things about him, but all said different things—none of them agreed.

[57]Then some people stood up and lied about Jesus, saying, [58]"We heard this man say, 'I will destroy this Temple that people made. And three days later, I will build another Temple not made by people.' " [59]But even the things these people said did not agree.

[60]Then the high priest stood before them and asked Jesus, "Aren't you going to answer? Don't you have something to say about their charges against you?" [61]But Jesus said nothing; he did not answer.

The high priest asked Jesus another question: "Are you the Christ, the Son of the blessed God?"

[62]Jesus answered, "I am. And in the future you will see the Son of Man sitting at the right hand of God, the Powerful One, and coming on clouds in the sky."

[63]When the high priest heard this, he tore his clothes and said, "We don't need any more witnesses! [64]You all heard him say these things against God. What do you think?"

They all said that Jesus was guilty and should die. [65]Some of the people there began to spit at Jesus. They blindfolded him and beat him with their fists and said, "Prove you are a prophet!" Then the guards led Jesus away and beat him.

Peter Says He Doesn't Know Jesus

[66]While Peter was in the courtyard, a servant girl of the high priest came there. [67]She saw Peter warming himself at the fire and looked closely at him.

Then she said, "You also were with Jesus, that man from Nazareth."

25% more women than men are currently entering college.

(*Prevention*)

[68]But Peter said that he was never with Jesus. He said, "I don't know or understand what you are talking about." Then Peter left and went toward the entrance of the courtyard. And the rooster crowed.[n]

[69]The servant girl saw Peter there, and again she said to the people who were standing nearby, "This man is one of those who followed Jesus." [70]Again Peter said that it was not true.

A short time later, some people were standing near Peter saying, "Surely you are one of those who followed Jesus, because you are from Galilee, too."

[71]Then Peter began to place a curse on himself and swear, "I don't know this man you're talking about!"

[72]At once, the rooster crowed the second time. Then Peter remembered what Jesus had told him: "Before the rooster crows twice, you will say three times that you don't know me." Then Peter lost control of himself and began to cry.

Pilate Questions Jesus

15 Very early in the morning, the leading priests, the elders, the teachers of the law, and all the Jewish council decided what to do with Jesus. They tied him, led him away, and turned him over to Pilate, the governor.

[2]Pilate asked Jesus, "Are you the king of the Jews?"

Jesus answered, "Those are your words."

[3]The leading priests accused Jesus of many things. [4]So Pilate asked Jesus another question, "You can see that they are accusing you of many things. Aren't you going to answer?"

[5]But Jesus still said nothing, so Pilate was very surprised.

Pilate Tries to Free Jesus

[6]Every year at the time of the Passover the governor would free one prisoner whom the people chose. [7]At that time, there was a man named Barabbas in prison who was a rebel and had committed murder during a riot. [8]The crowd came to Pilate and began to ask him to free a prisoner as he always did.

[9]So Pilate asked them, "Do you want me to free the king of the Jews?" [10]Pilate knew that the leading priests had turned Jesus in to him because they were jealous. [11]But the leading priests had persuaded the people to ask Pilate to free Barabbas, not Jesus.

[12]Then Pilate asked the crowd again, "So what should I do with this man you call the king of the Jews?"

[13]They shouted, "Crucify him!"

[14]Pilate asked, "Why? What wrong has he done?"

But they shouted even louder, "Crucify him!"

[15]Pilate wanted to please the crowd, so he freed Barabbas for them. After having Jesus beaten with whips, he handed Jesus over to the soldiers to be crucified.

[16]The soldiers took Jesus into the governor's palace (called the Praetorium) and called all the other soldiers together. [17]They put a purple robe on Jesus and used thorny branches to make a crown for his head. [18]They began to call out to him, "Hail, King of the Jews!" [19]The soldiers beat Jesus on the head many times with a stick. They spit on him and made fun of him by bowing on their knees and worshiping him. [20]After they finished, the soldiers took off the purple robe and put his own clothes on him again. Then they led him out of the palace to be crucified.

Jesus Is Crucified

[21]A man named Simon from Cyrene, the father of Alexander and Rufus, was coming from the fields to the city. The soldiers forced Simon to carry the cross for Jesus. [22]They led Jesus to the place called Golgotha, which means the Place of the Skull. [23]The soldiers tried to give Jesus wine mixed with myrrh to drink, but he refused. [24]The soldiers crucified Jesus and divided his clothes among themselves, throwing lots to decide what each soldier would get.

[25]It was nine o'clock in the morning when they crucified Jesus. [26]There was a sign with this charge against Jesus written on it: THE KING OF THE JEWS. [27]They also put two robbers on crosses beside Jesus, one on the right, and the other on the left. [[28]And the Scripture came true that says, "They put him with criminals."][n] [29]People walked by and insulted Jesus and shook their heads, saying, "You said you could destroy the Temple and build it again in three days. [30]So save yourself! Come down from that cross!"

[31]The leading priests and the teachers of the law were also making fun of Jesus. They said to each other, "He saved other people, but he can't save himself. [32]If he is really the Christ, the king of Israel, let him come down now from the cross. When we see this, we will believe in him." The robbers who were being crucified beside Jesus also insulted him.

Jesus Dies

[33]At noon the whole country became dark, and the darkness lasted for three hours. [34]At three o'clock Jesus cried in a loud voice, "Eloi, Eloi, lama sabachthani." This means, "My God, my God, why have you abandoned me?"

[35]When some of the people standing there heard this, they said, "Listen! He is calling Elijah."

[36]Someone there ran and got a sponge, filled it with vinegar, tied it to a stick, and gave it to Jesus to drink. He said, "We want to see if Elijah will come to take him down from the cross."

[37]Then Jesus cried in a loud voice and died.

[38]The curtain in the Temple[n] was torn into two pieces, from the top to the bot-

14:68 And the rooster crowed. Some Greek copies do not have this phrase. **15:28 And . . . criminals."** Some Greek copies do not contain the bracketed text, which quotes from Isaiah 53:12. **15:38 curtain in the Temple** A curtain divided the Most Holy Place from the other part of the Temple. That was the special building in Jerusalem where God commanded the Jewish people to worship him.

tom. [39]When the army officer who was standing in front of the cross saw what happened when Jesus died,[n] he said, "This man really was the Son of God!"

[40]Some women were standing at a distance from the cross, watching; among them were Mary Magdalene, Salome, and Mary the mother of James and Joseph. (James was her youngest son.) [41]These women had followed Jesus in Galilee and helped him. Many other women were also there who had come with Jesus to Jerusalem.

Jesus Is Buried

[42]This was Preparation Day. (That means the day before the Sabbath day.) That evening, [43]Joseph from Arimathea was brave enough to go to Pilate and ask for Jesus' body. Joseph, an important member of the Jewish council, was one of the people who was waiting for the kingdom of God to come. [44]Pilate was amazed that Jesus would have already died, so he called the army officer who had guarded Jesus and asked him if Jesus had already died. [45]The officer told Pilate that he was dead, so Pilate told Joseph he could have the body. [46]Joseph bought some linen cloth, took the body down from the cross, and wrapped it in the linen. He put the body in a tomb that was cut out of a wall of rock. Then he rolled a very large stone to block the entrance of the tomb. [47]And Mary Magdalene and Mary the mother of Joseph saw the place where Jesus was laid.

Jesus Rises from the Dead

16 The day after the Sabbath day, Mary Magdalene, Mary the mother of James, and Salome bought some sweet-smelling spices to put on Jesus' body. [2]Very early on that day, the first day of the week, soon after sunrise, the women were on their way to the tomb. [3]They said to each other, "Who will roll away for us the stone that covers the entrance of the tomb?"

[4]Then the women looked and saw that the stone had already been rolled away, even though it was very large. [5]The women entered the tomb and saw a young man wearing a white robe and sitting on the right side, and they were afraid.

[6]But the man said, "Don't be afraid. You are looking for Jesus from Nazareth, who has been crucified. He has risen from the dead; he is not here. Look, here is the place they laid him. [7]Now go and tell his followers and Peter, 'Jesus is going into Galilee ahead of you, and you will see him there as he told you before.' "

[8]The women were confused and shaking with fear, so they left the tomb and ran away. They did not tell anyone about what happened, because they were afraid.

Verses 9–20 are not included in some of the earliest surviving Greek copies of Mark.

Some Followers See Jesus

[[9]After Jesus rose from the dead early on the first day of the week, he showed himself first to Mary Magdalene. One time in the past, he had forced seven demons out of her. [10]After Mary saw Jesus, she went and told his followers, who were very sad and were crying. [11]But Mary told them that Jesus was alive. She said that she had seen him, but the followers did not believe her.

[12]Later, Jesus showed himself to two of his followers while they were walking in the country, but he did not look the same as before. [13]These followers went back to the others and told them what had happened, but again, the followers did not believe them.

Jesus Talks to the Apostles

[14]Later Jesus showed himself to the eleven apostles while they were eating, and he criticized them because they had no faith. They were stubborn and refused to believe those who had seen him after he had risen from the dead.

[15]Jesus said to his followers, "Go everywhere in the world, and tell the Good News to everyone. [16]Anyone who believes and is baptized will be saved, but anyone who does not believe will be punished. [17]And those who believe will be able to do these things as proof: They will use my name to force out demons. They will speak in new languages.[n] [18]They will pick up snakes and drink poison without being hurt. They will touch the sick, and the sick will be healed."

[19]After the Lord Jesus said these things to his followers, he was carried up into heaven, and he sat at the right side of God. [20]The followers went everywhere in the world and told the Good News to people, and the Lord helped them. The Lord proved that the Good News they told was true by giving them power to work miracles.]

15:39 when Jesus died Some Greek copies read "when Jesus cried out and died." . **16:17 languages** This can also be translated "tongues."

the big picture Mark

Good News on the Go

Of the four Gospels, Mark's is the one written for movers and shakers.

Mark was a man of action who wrote his account of Jesus' life, death, and resurrection for the non-Jewish believers in Rome. They didn't have the Old Testament background the Jewish readers had, so Mark focused less on Jewish history and more on Jesus' interactions during his time on earth.

Mark covers Jesus' ministry and miracles quickly and then devotes much of the book to Jesus' last days, his crucifixion, and his resurrection. Jesus' resurrection holds special importance for Mark's audience because it means hope for non-Jewish people who choose to believe Jesus and repent. God's story had been specifically for the Israelites up until Jesus came, but Jesus' victory meant the rest of the world could receive eternal life also. This is the same Good News we've received today—God extends his grace, pulling us out of our sinful, broken state and making us right with himself through Jesus.

Mark focuses on six themes: service, suffering, sin, salvation, Savior, and sharing. Mark details Jesus' life of *service*, his *suffering* for our *sins*, his death that brings us *salvation*, his victory that makes him our *Savior*, and his command to *share* the Good News with a world that needs him.

Will you be a mover and shaker for God?

Get Real

Service is a consistent theme in Mark. Who are you serving? (John 12:26)

Discover a few others who served God. (Luke 1:1–2, 47–48; 2:29; 2 Corinthians 4:5; Colossians 1:7; 4:7; James 1:1; 2 Peter 1:1; Jude 1; Revelation 1:1)

In John 15:12–15, John quotes Jesus as saying that believers aren't called his servants anymore, but his *friends*. Other scriptures refer to Christians as servants of Jesus and of others (Acts 4:29; 1 Peter 4:10). How can you be both servant and friend?

How will God help you share your faith? (Exodus 4:11–12; Acts 1:8)

Mark describes Jesus' sufferings on earth. How did God turn persecution into a way to spread his Good News? (Acts 8:1–4)

notes

luke

If you're the kind of person who just loves to brew some hot tea and curl up with a good book, this is the Gospel for you. Like a well-written novel with perfect narrative structure, Luke's Gospel gathers the details of Jesus' life and compiles them into a very readable story (Luke 1:3–4).

Luke includes a lot more background information than the other Gospels, especially when it comes to Jesus' birth and childhood. Plus, Luke stresses Jesus' compassion toward people who were usually ignored or mistreated in his culture: children, women, the poor, and the disreputable. These people, who many considered to be lower-class citizens, all received specific kindness from Jesus.

Prayer is another big element in this book. Keep an eye out for Jesus' teachings about prayer, examples of his prayers, and descriptions of how he prayed. It's obvious that spending time talking with the Father was extremely important to Jesus.

So break out the hot beverages, settle into your favorite chair, and immerse yourself in this story about Jesus. As you read, pray that God will give you understanding and begin transforming you into someone who loves and prays like Jesus.

Luke Writes About Jesus' Life

1 Many have tried to report on the things that happened among us. [2]They have written the same things that we learned from others—the people who saw those things from the beginning and served God by telling people his message. [3]Since I myself have studied everything carefully from the beginning, most excellent[n] Theophilus, it seemed good for me to write it out for you. I arranged it in order, [4]to help you know that what you have been taught is true.

Zechariah and Elizabeth

[5]During the time Herod ruled Judea, there was a priest named Zechariah who belonged to Abijah's group.[n] Zechariah's wife, Elizabeth, came from the family of Aaron. [6]Zechariah and Elizabeth truly did what God said was good. They did everything the Lord commanded and were without fault in keeping his law. [7]But they had no children, because Elizabeth could not have a baby, and both of them were very old.

[8]One day Zechariah was serving as a priest before God, because his group was on duty. [9]According to the custom of the priests, he was chosen by lot to go into the Temple of the Lord and burn incense. [10]There were a great many people outside praying at the time the incense was offered. [11]Then an angel of the Lord appeared to Zechariah, standing on the right side of the incense table. [12]When he saw the angel, Zechariah was startled and frightened. [13]But the angel said to him, "Zechariah, don't be afraid. God has heard your prayer. Your wife, Elizabeth, will give birth to a son, and you will name him John. [14]He will bring you joy and gladness, and many people will be happy because of his birth. [15]John will be a great man for the Lord. He will never drink wine or beer,

1:3 excellent This word was used to show respect to an important person like a king or ruler. **1:5 Abijah's group** The Jewish priests were divided into twenty-four groups. See 1 Chronicles 24.

Getting Ready

How long does it take you to get ready every morning? There's the major "what-do-I-wear" decision, the shower and shave ritual, hair, makeup, perfume, and accessories—it's quite the process. But it could be worse. Imagine being Queen Esther. She underwent *twelve months* of beauty treatments before meeting the king (Esther 2:12)! Talk about a long preparation process! What about when you meet with *your* King? How long do you take to prepare yourself for him each day? How do you make your life a sweet-smelling fragrance that pleases him? Be sure you are preparing your heart for entering his presence.

and even from birth, he will be filled with the Holy Spirit. [16]He will help many people of Israel return to the Lord their God. [17]He will go before the Lord in spirit and power like Elijah. He will make peace between parents and their children and will bring those who are not obeying God back to the right way of thinking, to make a people ready for the coming of the Lord."

[18]Zechariah said to the angel, "How can I know that what you say is true? I am an old man, and my wife is old, too."

[19]The angel answered him, "I am Gabriel. I stand before God, who sent me to talk to you and to tell you this good news. [20]Now, listen! You will not be able to speak until the day these things happen, because you did not believe what I told you. But they will really happen."

[21]Outside, the people were still waiting for Zechariah and were surprised that he was staying so long in the Temple. [22]When Zechariah came outside, he could not speak to them, and they knew he had seen a vision in the Temple. He could only make signs to them and remained unable to speak. [23]When his time of service at the Temple was finished, he went home.

[24]Later, Zechariah's wife, Elizabeth, became pregnant and did not go out of her house for five months. Elizabeth said, [25]"Look what the Lord has done for me! My people were ashamed[n] of me, but now the Lord has taken away that shame."

An Angel Appears to Mary

[26]During Elizabeth's sixth month of pregnancy, God sent the angel Gabriel to Nazareth, a town in Galilee, [27]to a virgin. She was engaged to marry a man named Joseph from the family of David. Her name was Mary. [28]The angel came to her and said, "Greetings! The Lord has blessed you and is with you."

[29]But Mary was very startled by what the angel said and wondered what this greeting might mean.

[30]The angel said to her, "Don't be afraid, Mary; God has shown you his grace. [31]Listen! You will become pregnant and give birth to a son, and you will name him Jesus. [32]He will be great and will be called the Son of the Most High. The Lord God will give him the throne of King David, his ancestor. [33]He will rule over the people of Jacob forever, and his kingdom will never end."

[34]Mary said to the angel, "How will this happen since I am a virgin?"

[35]The angel said to Mary, "The Holy Spirit will come upon you, and the power of the Most High will cover you. For this reason the baby will be holy and will be called the Son of God. [36]Now Elizabeth, your relative, is also pregnant with a son though she is very old. Everyone thought she could not have a baby, but she has been pregnant for six months. [37]God can do anything!"

[38]Mary said, "I am the servant of the Lord. Let this happen to me as you say!" Then the angel went away.

Mary Visits Elizabeth

[39]Mary got up and went quickly to a town in the hills of Judea. [40]She came to Zechariah's house and greeted Elizabeth. [41]When Elizabeth heard Mary's greeting, the unborn baby inside her jumped, and Elizabeth was filled with the Holy Spirit. [42]She cried out in a loud voice, "God has blessed you more than any other woman, and he has blessed the baby to which you will give birth. [43]Why has this good thing happened to me, that the mother of my Lord comes to me? [44]When I heard your voice, the baby inside me jumped with joy. [45]You are blessed because you believed that what the Lord said to you would really happen."

Mary Praises God

[46]Then Mary said,
"My soul praises the Lord;
[47] my heart rejoices in God my Savior,
[48]because he has shown his concern for his humble servant girl.
From now on, all people will say that I am blessed,
[49] because the Powerful One has done great things for me.
His name is holy.
[50]God will show his mercy forever and ever
to those who worship and serve him.
[51]He has done mighty deeds by his power.
He has scattered the people who are proud
and think great things about themselves.
[52]He has brought down rulers from their thrones
and raised up the humble.
[53]He has filled the hungry with good things
and sent the rich away with nothing.
[54]He has helped his servant, the people of Israel,
remembering to show them mercy

1:25 ashamed The Jewish people thought it was a disgrace for women not to have children.

55as he promised to our ancestors,
to Abraham and to his children
forever."

56Mary stayed with Elizabeth for about three months and then returned home.

The Birth of John

57When it was time for Elizabeth to give birth, she had a boy. 58Her neighbors and relatives heard how good the Lord was to her, and they rejoiced with her.

59When the baby was eight days old, they came to circumcise him. They wanted to name him Zechariah because this was his father's name, 60but his mother said, "No! He will be named John."

61The people said to Elizabeth, "But no one in your family has this name." 62Then they made signs to his father to find out what he would like to name him.

63Zechariah asked for a writing tablet and wrote, "His name is John," and everyone was surprised. 64Immediately Zechariah could talk again, and he began praising God. 65All their neighbors became alarmed, and in all the mountains of Judea people continued talking about all these things. 66The people who heard about them wondered, saying, "What will this child be?" because the Lord was with him.

Zechariah Praises God

67Then Zechariah, John's father, was filled with the Holy Spirit and prophesied:

68"Let us praise the Lord, the God of
Israel,
because he has come to help his
people and has given them
freedom.
69He has given us a powerful Savior
from the family of God's servant
David.
70He said that he would do this
through his holy prophets who
lived long ago:
71He promised he would save us from
our enemies
and from the power of all those
who hate us.
72He said he would give mercy to our
ancestors
and that he would remember his
holy promise.
73God promised Abraham, our
father,
74that he would save us from the
power of our enemies
so we could serve him without
fear,
75being holy and good before God as
long as we live.

76"Now you, child, will be called a
prophet of the Most High
God.
You will go before the Lord to
prepare his way.
77You will make his people know that
they will be saved
by having their sins forgiven.
78With the loving mercy of our
God,
a new day from heaven will dawn
upon us.
79It will shine on those who live in
darkness,
in the shadow of death.
It will guide us into the path of
peace."

80And so the child grew up and became strong in spirit. John lived in the desert until the time when he came out to preach to Israel.

The Birth of Jesus

2 At that time, Augustus Caesar sent an order that all people in the countries under Roman rule must list their names in a register. 2This was the first registration;[n] it was taken while Quirinius was governor of Syria. 3And all went to their own towns to be registered.

4So Joseph left Nazareth, a town in Galilee, and went to the town of Bethlehem in Judea, known as the town of David. Joseph went there because he was from the family of David. 5Joseph registered with Mary, to whom he was engaged[n] and who was now pregnant. 6While they were in Bethlehem, the time came for Mary to have the baby, 7and she gave birth to her first son. Because there were no rooms left in the inn, she wrapped the baby with pieces of cloth and laid him in a feeding trough.

Shepherds Hear About Jesus

8That night, some shepherds were in the fields nearby watching their sheep. 9Then an angel of the Lord stood before them. The glory of the Lord was shining around them, and they became very frightened. 10The angel said to them, "Do not be afraid. I am bringing you good news that will be a great joy to all the people. 11Today your Savior was born in the town of David. He is Christ, the

all about MEN

Tell It to Him Straight

Not-so-news flash: Communication between men and women doesn't always come easily! From church sermons to talk-show topics to bookstore shelves, communication between the sexes has been studied to dizzying degrees! Since no two people are wired the same, we process information and emotions differently. One way to improve our relationships with the guys in our lives is to be upfront about our thoughts and feelings—gently, of course. Tell him straight up what's on your mind so he won't have to resort to guessing games, which often lead to feelings of failure and frustration. Good communication takes practice, but it clears confusion and invites connection. So ask God for wisdom to communicate your heart in the most productive way.

2:2 registration Census. A counting of all the people and the things they own. **2:5 engaged** For the Jewish people, an engagement was a lasting agreement. It could only be broken by divorce.

Luke 2:19

We're surrounded with media messages—commercials, flyers, billboards—on a daily basis. Some of it's bound to go in one ear and out the other, but when it comes to something we really care about, we give it our undivided focus. God's Word deserves our full and ongoing attention, to say the least. More than something we hear at church or glance at occasionally, God intends his Word to be so much more!

Take Mary, for example. She may not have understood everything about Jesus' birth, but she knew God was working in amazing ways. Her response? She quietly tucked away everything in her heart and pondered it. The Bible says she "treasured" what she heard. She mulled over the things God was revealing about himself.

We should do the same today. We should deeply value and meditate on Scripture. When you encounter things you don't fully understand at first glance, contemplate them and ask God for wisdom. Keep dwelling on those verses that grip you. Memorize them. Let them become part of you. Reading Psalm 119 can remind you of all kinds of reasons to saturate your life with God's Word. When it comes to Scripture, we can't afford to ignore it. Make sure it goes in your ears and straight to your heart!

Lord. [12]This is how you will know him: You will find a baby wrapped in pieces of cloth and lying in a feeding box."

[13]Then a very large group of angels from heaven joined the first angel, praising God and saying:

[14]"Give glory to God in heaven,
and on earth let there be peace
among the people who please God."[n]

[15]When the angels left them and went back to heaven, the shepherds said to each other, "Let's go to Bethlehem. Let's see this thing that has happened which the Lord has told us about."

[16]So the shepherds went quickly and found Mary and Joseph and the baby, who was lying in a feeding trough. [17]When they had seen him, they told what the angels had said about this child. [18]Everyone was amazed at what the shepherds said to them. [19]But Mary treasured these things and continued to think about them. [20]Then the shepherds went back to their sheep, praising God and thanking him for everything they had seen and heard. It had been just as the angel had told them.

[21]When the baby was eight days old, he was circumcised and was named Jesus, the name given by the angel before the baby began to grow inside Mary.

Jesus Is Presented in the Temple

[22]When the time came for Mary and Joseph to do what the law of Moses taught about being made pure,[n] they took Jesus to Jerusalem to present him to the Lord. [23](It is written in the law of the Lord: "Every firstborn male shall be given to the Lord.")[n] [24]Mary and Joseph also went to offer a sacrifice, as the law of the Lord says: "You must sacrifice two doves or two young pigeons."[n]

Simeon Sees Jesus

[25]In Jerusalem lived a man named Simeon who was a good man and godly. He was waiting for the time when God would take away Israel's sorrow, and the Holy Spirit was in him. [26]Simeon had been told by the Holy Spirit that he would not die before he saw the Christ promised by the Lord. [27]The Spirit led Simeon to the Temple. When Mary and Joseph brought the baby Jesus to the Temple to do what the law said they must do, [28]Simeon took the baby in his arms and thanked God:

[29]"Now, Lord, you can let me, your servant,
die in peace as you said.
[30]With my own eyes I have seen your salvation,
[31] which you prepared before all people.
[32]It is a light for the non-Jewish people to see
and an honor for your people, the Israelites."

[33]Jesus' father and mother were amazed at what Simeon had said about him. [34]Then Simeon blessed them and said to Mary, "God has chosen this child to cause the fall and rise of many in Israel. He will be a sign from God that many people will not accept [35]so that the thoughts of many will be made known. And the things that will happen will make your heart sad, too."

Anna Sees Jesus

[36]There was a prophetess, Anna, from the family of Phanuel in the tribe of Asher. Anna was very old. She had once been married for seven years. [37]Then her husband died, and she was a widow for eighty-four years. Anna never left the Temple but worshiped God, going without food and praying day and night. [38]Standing there at that time, she thanked God and spoke about Jesus to all who were waiting for God to free Jerusalem.

2:14 and . . . God Some Greek copies read "and on earth let there be peace and goodwill among people." **2:22 pure** The Law of Moses said that forty days after a Jewish woman gave birth to a son, she must be cleansed by a ceremony at the Temple. Read Leviticus 12:2–8. **2:23 "Every . . . Lord."** Quotation from Exodus 13:2. **2:24 "You . . . pigeons."** Quotation from Leviticus 12:8.

Joseph and Mary Return Home

[39]When Joseph and Mary had done everything the law of the Lord commanded, they went home to Nazareth, their own town in Galilee. [40]The little child grew and became strong. He was filled with wisdom, and God's goodness was upon him.

Jesus As a Boy

[41]Every year Jesus' parents went to Jerusalem for the Passover Feast. [42]When he was twelve years old, they went to the feast as they always did. [43]After the feast days were over, they started home. The boy Jesus stayed behind in Jerusalem, but his parents did not know it. [44]Thinking that Jesus was with them in the group, they traveled for a whole day. Then they began to look for him among their family and friends. [45]When they did not find him, they went back to Jerusalem to look for him there. [46]After three days they found Jesus sitting in the Temple with the teachers, listening to them and asking them questions. [47]All who heard him were amazed at his understanding and answers. [48]When Jesus' parents saw him, they were astonished. His mother said to him, "Son, why did you do this to us? Your father and I were very worried about you and have been looking for you."

[49]Jesus said to them, "Why were you looking for me? Didn't you know that I must be in my Father's house?" [50]But they did not understand the meaning of what he said.

[51]Jesus went with them to Nazareth and was obedient to them. But his mother kept in her mind all that had happened. [52]Jesus became wiser and grew physically. People liked him, and he pleased God.

The Preaching of John

3 It was the fifteenth year of the rule of Tiberius Caesar. These men were under Caesar: Pontius Pilate, the ruler of Judea; Herod, the ruler of Galilee; Philip, Herod's brother, the ruler of Iturea and Traconitis; and Lysanias, the ruler of Abilene. [2]Annas and Caiaphas were the high priests. At this time, the word of God came to John son of Zechariah in the desert. [3]He went all over the area around the Jordan River preaching a baptism of changed hearts and lives for the forgiveness of sins. [4]As it is written in the book of Isaiah the prophet:

"This is a voice of one
who calls out in the desert:
'Prepare the way for the Lord.
Make the road straight for him.
[5]Every valley should be filled in,
and every mountain and hill
should be made flat.
Roads with turns should be made
straight,
and rough roads should be made
smooth.
[6]And all people will know about the
salvation of God!' "

Isaiah 40:3–5

[7]To the crowds of people who came to be baptized by John, he said, "You are all snakes! Who warned you to run away from God's coming punishment? [8]Do the things that show you really have changed your hearts and lives. Don't begin to say to yourselves, 'Abraham is our father.' I tell you that God could make children for Abraham from these rocks. [9]The ax is now ready to cut down the trees, and every tree that does not produce good fruit will be cut down and thrown into the fire."[n]

[10]The people asked John, "Then what should we do?"

[11]John answered, "If you have two shirts, share with the person who does not have one. If you have food, share that also."

[12]Even tax collectors came to John to be baptized. They said to him, "Teacher, what should we do?"

[13]John said to them, "Don't take more taxes from people than you have been ordered to take."

[14]The soldiers asked John, "What about us? What should we do?"

John said to them, "Don't force people to give you money, and don't lie about them. Be satisfied with the pay you get."

[15]Since the people were hoping for the Christ to come, they wondered if John might be the one.

[16]John answered everyone, "I baptize you with water, but there is one coming who is greater than I am. I am not good enough to untie his sandals. He will baptize you with the Holy Spirit and fire. [17]He will come ready to clean the grain, separating the good grain from the chaff. He will put the good part of the grain into his barn, but he will burn the chaff with a fire that cannot be put out."[n] [18]And John continued to preach the Good News, saying many other things to encourage the people.

[19]But John spoke against Herod, the governor, because of his sin with Herodias, the wife of Herod's brother, and

Health

Get Motivated and Get Moving

Finding it hard to get off the couch? Here are a few tips for exercise-phobes. **Start small:** You don't need to run a marathon the first day. Depending on your weight, just fifteen minutes of brisk walking can burn off a serving of ice cream. Add time or intensity incrementally. **Set a goal:** You may be training for a 5K, or you may simply want to look good in skinny jeans. Whatever your objective, let it motivate you. (Read 1 Corinthians 9:24–27 for inspiration!) **Cross-train:** Boredom sets in with repetitive exercise, but that's no excuse for quitting. Try mixing it up with kickboxing, a spin class, or even tap dancing. Finally, **track your progress:** Keep your stats (weight loss, miles run, minutes of exercise) in a calendar, PDA, or blog. Celebrate each baby step—but not with food!

3:9 The ax . . . fire. This means that God is ready to punish his people who do not obey him. **3:17 He will . . . out.** This means that Jesus will come to separate good people from bad people, saving the good and punishing the bad.

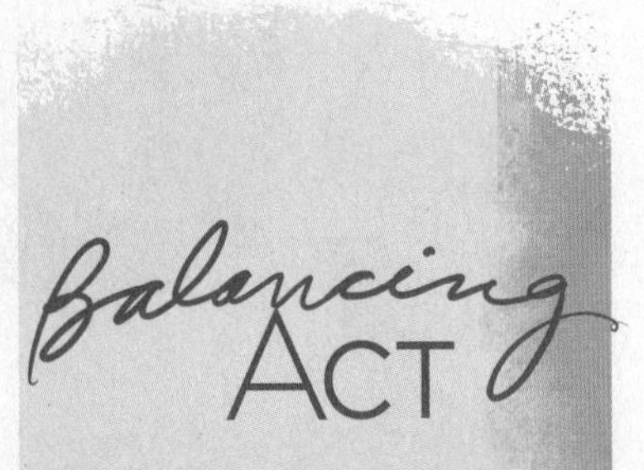

Save Time by Planning

Does the thought of beginning a new project overwhelm you? Perhaps you're not sure where to start or how to reach the desired result. You could hit the ground running and hope for the best—or you could make a plan. Ask yourself: *What am I trying to accomplish? What tools will I need? What specific steps are involved? How much time should be allotted for each step? Is there a more efficient process? How much will it cost?* (See Luke 14:28–30.) Have a plan B in mind if any part of the project falls short of your expectations. Spending a few moments in preparation will alleviate your preproject stress and save you time—precious time you can spend with family or friends!

because of the many other evil things Herod did. [20]So Herod did something even worse: He put John in prison.

Jesus Is Baptized by John

[21]When all the people were being baptized by John, Jesus also was baptized. While Jesus was praying, heaven opened [22]and the Holy Spirit came down on him in the form of a dove. Then a voice came from heaven, saying, "You are my Son, whom I love, and I am very pleased with you."

The Family History of Jesus

[23]When Jesus began his ministry, he was about thirty years old. People thought that Jesus was Joseph's son.

Joseph was the son[n] of Heli.
[24]Heli was the son of Matthat.
Matthat was the son of Levi.
Levi was the son of Melki.
Melki was the son of Jannai.
Jannai was the son of Joseph.
[25]Joseph was the son of Mattathias.
Mattathias was the son of Amos.
Amos was the son of Nahum.
Nahum was the son of Esli.
Esli was the son of Naggai.
[26]Naggai was the son of Maath.
Maath was the son of Mattathias.
Mattathias was the son of Semein.
Semein was the son of Josech.
Josech was the son of Joda.
[27]Joda was the son of Joanan.
Joanan was the son of Rhesa.
Rhesa was the son of Zerubbabel.
Zerubbabel was the grandson of Shealtiel.
Shealtiel was the son of Neri.
[28]Neri was the son of Melki.
Melki was the son of Addi.
Addi was the son of Cosam.
Cosam was the son of Elmadam.
Elmadam was the son of Er.
[29]Er was the son of Joshua.
Joshua was the son of Eliezer.
Eliezer was the son of Jorim.
Jorim was the son of Matthat.
Matthat was the son of Levi.
[30]Levi was the son of Simeon.
Simeon was the son of Judah.
Judah was the son of Joseph.
Joseph was the son of Jonam.
Jonam was the son of Eliakim.
[31]Eliakim was the son of Melea.
Melea was the son of Menna.
Menna was the son of Mattatha.
Mattatha was the son of Nathan.
Nathan was the son of David.
[32]David was the son of Jesse.
Jesse was the son of Obed.
Obed was the son of Boaz.
Boaz was the son of Salmon.[n]
Salmon was the son of Nahshon.
[33]Nahshon was the son of Amminadab.
Amminadab was the son of Admin.
Admin was the son of Arni.
Arni was the son of Hezron.
Hezron was the son of Perez.
Perez was the son of Judah.
[34]Judah was the son of Jacob.
Jacob was the son of Isaac.
Isaac was the son of Abraham.
Abraham was the son of Terah.
Terah was the son of Nahor.
[35]Nahor was the son of Serug.
Serug was the son of Reu.
Reu was the son of Peleg.
Peleg was the son of Eber.
Eber was the son of Shelah.
[36]Shelah was the son of Cainan.
Cainan was the son of Arphaxad.
Arphaxad was the son of Shem.
Shem was the son of Noah.
Noah was the son of Lamech.
[37]Lamech was the son of Methuselah.
Methuselah was the son of Enoch.
Enoch was the son of Jared.
Jared was the son of Mahalalel.
Mahalalel was the son of Kenan.
[38]Kenan was the son of Enosh.
Enosh was the son of Seth.
Seth was the son of Adam.
Adam was the son of God.

Jesus Is Tempted by the Devil

4 Jesus, filled with the Holy Spirit, returned from the Jordan River. The Spirit led Jesus into the desert [2]where the devil tempted Jesus for forty days. Jesus ate nothing during that time, and when those days were ended, he was very hungry.

[3]The devil said to Jesus, "If you are the Son of God, tell this rock to become bread."

[4]Jesus answered, "It is written in the Scriptures: 'A person does not live on bread alone.' "[n]

3:23 son "Son" in Jewish lists of ancestors can sometimes mean grandson or more distant relative. **3:32 Salmon** Some Greek copies read "Sala." **4:4 'A person . . . alone.'** Quotation from Deuteronomy 8:3.

[5]Then the devil took Jesus and showed him all the kingdoms of the world in an instant. [6]The devil said to Jesus, "I will give you all these kingdoms and all their power and glory. It has all been given to me, and I can give it to anyone I wish. [7]If you worship me, then it will all be yours."

[8]Jesus answered, "It is written in the Scriptures: 'You must worship the Lord your God and serve only him.' "[n]

[9]Then the devil led Jesus to Jerusalem and put him on a high place of the Temple. He said to Jesus, "If you are the Son of God, jump down. [10]It is written in the Scriptures:

'He has put his angels in charge of you
to watch over you.' *Psalm 91:11*

[11]It is also written:

'They will catch you in their hands
so that you will not hit your foot on a rock.' " *Psalm 91:12*

[12]Jesus answered, "But it also says in the Scriptures: 'Do not test the Lord your God.' "[n]

[13]After the devil had tempted Jesus in every way, he left him to wait until a better time.

Jesus Teaches the People

[14]Jesus returned to Galilee in the power of the Holy Spirit, and stories about him spread all through the area. [15]He began to teach in their synagogues, and everyone praised him.

[16]Jesus traveled to Nazareth, where he had grown up. On the Sabbath day he went to the synagogue, as he always did, and stood up to read. [17]The book of Isaiah the prophet was given to him. He opened the book and found the place where this is written:

[18]"The Lord has put his Spirit in me,
because he appointed me to tell the Good News to the poor.
He has sent me to tell the captives they are free
and to tell the blind that they can see again. *Isaiah 61:1*
God sent me to free those who have been treated unfairly *Isaiah 58:6*
[19] and to announce the time when the Lord will show his kindness." *Isaiah 61:2*

[20]Jesus closed the book, gave it back to the assistant, and sat down. Everyone in the synagogue was watching Jesus closely. [21]He began to say to them, "While you heard these words just now, they were coming true!"

[22]All the people spoke well of Jesus and were amazed at the words of grace he spoke. They asked, "Isn't this Joseph's son?"

[23]Jesus said to them, "I know that you will tell me the old saying: 'Doctor, heal yourself.' You want to say, 'We heard about the things you did in Capernaum. Do those things here in your own town!' " [24]Then Jesus said, "I tell you the truth, a prophet is not accepted in his hometown. [25]But I tell you the truth, there were many widows in Israel during the time of Elijah. It did not rain in Israel for three and one-half years, and there was no food anywhere in the whole country. [26]But Elijah was sent to none of those widows, only to a widow in Zarephath, a town in Sidon. [27]And there were many with skin diseases living in Israel during the time of the prophet Elisha. But none of them were healed, only Naaman, who was from the country of Syria."

[28]When all the people in the synagogue heard these things, they became very angry. [29]They got up, forced Jesus out of town, and took him to the edge of the cliff on which the town was built. They planned to throw him off the edge, [30]but Jesus walked through the crowd and went on his way.

Jesus Forces Out an Evil Spirit

[31]Jesus went to Capernaum, a city in Galilee, and on the Sabbath day, he taught the people. [32]They were amazed at his teaching, because he spoke with authority. [33]In the synagogue a man who had within him an evil spirit shouted in a loud voice, [34]"Jesus of Nazareth! What do you want with us? Did you come to destroy us? I know who you are—God's Holy One!"

[35]Jesus commanded the evil spirit, "Be quiet! Come out of the man!" The evil spirit threw the man down to the ground before all the people and then left the man without hurting him.

[36]The people were amazed and said to each other, "What does this mean? With authority and power he commands evil spirits, and they come out." [37]And so the news about Jesus spread to every place in the whole area.

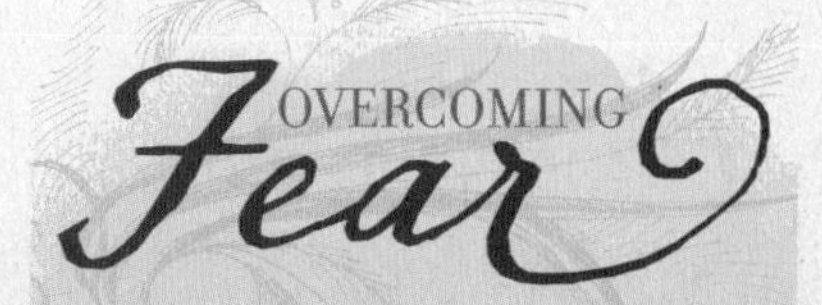

Self-Talk

Do you talk to yourself? Even if you don't speak audibly, your brain is constantly communicating with itself. If your mind is full of worry and ungrounded fear, recognize these thoughts for what they are—irrational and sometimes even destructive. Replace your fearful self-talk with hopeful, uplifting words and scripture-based thoughts. Use any anxiety you feel as a prompt to give your fears to God through prayer. Keep God's Word in your heart and on your lips at all times. Use praise as a spiritual weapon to drive out fear. Instead of being overtaken by fear, let God take over your fear!

Jesus Heals Many People

[38]Jesus left the synagogue and went to the home of Simon.[n] Simon's mother-in-law was sick with a high fever, and they asked Jesus to help her. [39]He came to her side and commanded the fever to leave. It

4:8 'You . . . him.' Quotation from Deuteronomy 6:13. **4:12 'Do . . . God.'** Quotation from Deuteronomy 6:16. **4:38 Simon** Simon's other name was Peter.

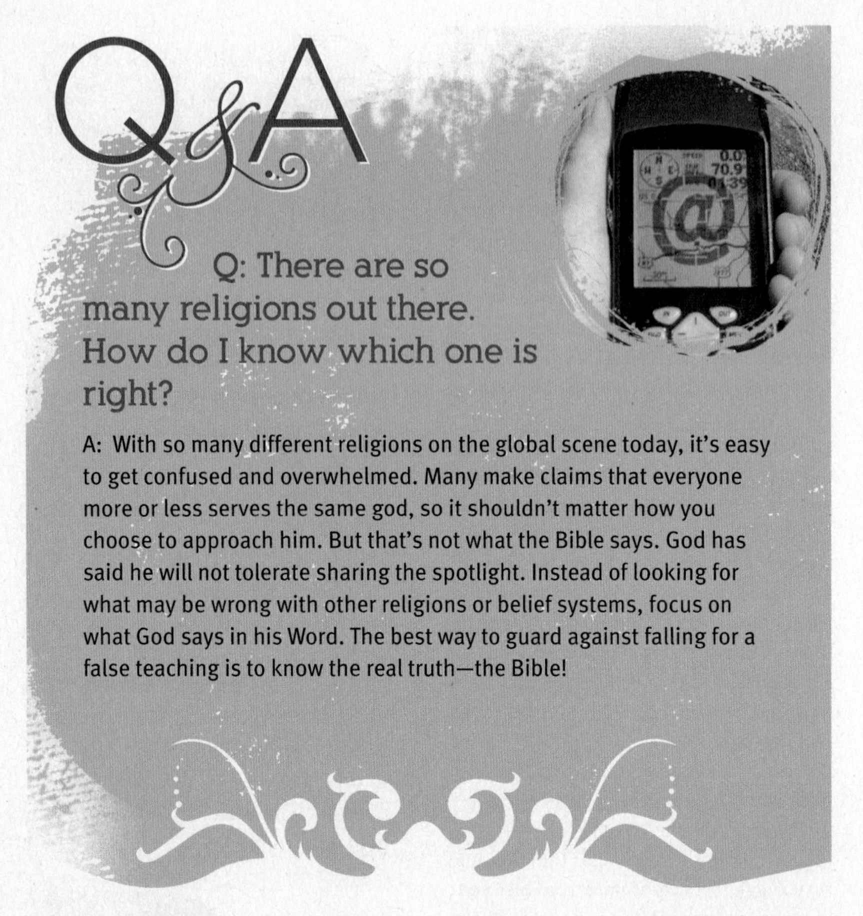

left her, and immediately she got up and began serving them.

[40]When the sun went down, the people brought those who were sick to Jesus. Putting his hands on each sick person, he healed every one of them. [41]Demons came out of many people, shouting, "You are the Son of God." But Jesus commanded the demons and would not allow them to speak, because they knew Jesus was the Christ.

[42]At daybreak, Jesus went to a lonely place, but the people looked for him. When they found him, they tried to keep him from leaving. [43]But Jesus said to them, "I must preach about God's kingdom to other towns, too. This is why I was sent."

[44]Then he kept on preaching in the synagogues of Judea.[n]

Jesus' First Followers

5 One day while Jesus was standing beside Lake Galilee, many people were pressing all around him to hear the word of God. [2]Jesus saw two boats at the shore of the lake. The fishermen had left them and were washing their nets. [3]Jesus got into one of the boats, the one that belonged to Simon,[n] and asked him to push off a little from the land. Then Jesus sat down and continued to teach the people from the boat.

[4]When Jesus had finished speaking, he said to Simon, "Take the boat into deep water, and put your nets in the water to catch some fish."

[5]Simon answered, "Master, we worked hard all night trying to catch fish, and we caught nothing. But you say to put the nets in the water, so I will." [6]When the fishermen did as Jesus told them, they caught so many fish that the nets began to break. [7]They called to their partners in the other boat to come and help them. They came and filled both boats so full that they were almost sinking.

[8]When Simon Peter saw what had happened, he bowed down before Jesus and said, "Go away from me, Lord. I am a sinful man!" [9]He and the other fishermen were amazed at the many fish they caught, as were [10]James and John, the sons of Zebedee, Simon's partners.

Jesus said to Simon, "Don't be afraid. From now on you will fish for people." [11]When the men brought their boats to the shore, they left everything and followed Jesus.

Jesus Heals a Sick Man

[12]When Jesus was in one of the towns, there was a man covered with a skin disease. When he saw Jesus, he bowed before him and begged him, "Lord, you can heal me if you will."

[13]Jesus reached out his hand and touched the man and said, "I will. Be healed!" Immediately the disease disappeared. [14]Then Jesus said, "Don't tell anyone about this, but go and show yourself to the priest[n] and offer a gift for your healing, as Moses commanded.[n] This will show the people what I have done."

[15]But the news about Jesus spread even more. Many people came to hear Jesus and to be healed of their sicknesses, [16]but Jesus often slipped away to be alone so he could pray.

Jesus Heals a Paralyzed Man

[17]One day as Jesus was teaching the people, the Pharisees and teachers of the law from every town in Galilee and Judea and from Jerusalem were there. The Lord was giving Jesus the power to heal people. [18]Just then, some men were carrying on a mat a man who was paralyzed. They tried to bring him in and put him down before Jesus. [19]But because there were so many people there, they could not find a way in. So they went up on the roof and lowered the man on his mat through the ceiling into the middle of the crowd right before Jesus. [20]Seeing their faith, Jesus said, "Friend, your sins are forgiven."

[21]The Jewish teachers of the law and the Pharisees thought to themselves, "Who is this man who is speaking as if he were God? Only God can forgive sins."

[22]But Jesus knew what they were thinking and said, "Why are you thinking these things? [23]Which is easier: to say, 'Your sins are forgiven,' or to say, 'Stand up and walk'? [24]But I will prove to you that the Son of Man has authority on earth to for-

4:44 Judea Some Greek copies read "Galilee." **5:3 Simon** Simon's other name was Peter. **5:14 show . . . priest** The Law of Moses said a priest must say when a Jewish person with a skin disease was well. **5:14 Moses commanded** Read about this in Leviticus 14:1–32.

give sins." So Jesus said to the paralyzed man, "I tell you, stand up, take your mat, and go home."

[25]At once the man stood up before them, picked up his mat, and went home, praising God. [26]All the people were fully amazed and began to praise God. They were filled with much respect and said, "Today we have seen amazing things!"

Levi Follows Jesus

[27]After this, Jesus went out and saw a tax collector named Levi sitting in the tax collector's booth. Jesus said to him, "Follow me!" [28]So Levi got up, left everything, and followed him.

[29]Then Levi gave a big dinner for Jesus at his house. Many tax collectors and other people were eating there, too. [30]But the Pharisees and the men who taught the law for the Pharisees began to complain to Jesus' followers, "Why do you eat and drink with tax collectors and sinners?"

[31]Jesus answered them, "It is not the healthy people who need a doctor, but the sick. [32]I have not come to invite good people but sinners to change their hearts and lives."

Jesus Answers a Question

[33]They said to Jesus, "John's followers often fast[n] for a certain time and pray, just as the Pharisees do. But your followers eat and drink all the time."

[34]Jesus said to them, "You cannot make the friends of the bridegroom fast while he is still with them. [35]But the time will come when the bridegroom will be taken away from them, and then they will fast."

[36]Jesus told them this story: "No one takes cloth off a new coat to cover a hole in an old coat. Otherwise, he ruins the new coat, and the cloth from the new coat will not be the same as the old cloth. [37]Also, no one ever pours new wine into old leather bags. Otherwise, the new wine will break the bags, the wine will spill out, and the leather bags will be ruined. [38]New wine must be put into new leather bags. [39]No one after drinking old wine wants new wine, because he says, 'The old wine is better.' "

Jesus Is Lord over the Sabbath

6 One Sabbath day Jesus was walking through some fields of grain. His followers picked the heads of grain, rubbed them in their hands, and ate them. [2]Some Pharisees said, "Why do you do what is not lawful on the Sabbath day?"

[3]Jesus answered, "Have you not read what David did when he and those with him were hungry? [4]He went into God's house and took and ate the holy bread, which is lawful only for priests to eat. And he gave some to the people who were with him." [5]Then Jesus said to the Pharisees, "The Son of Man is Lord of the Sabbath day."

Jesus Heals a Man's Hand

[6]On another Sabbath day Jesus went into the synagogue and was teaching, and a man with a crippled right hand was there. [7]The teachers of the law and the Pharisees were watching closely to see if Jesus would heal on the Sabbath day so they could accuse him. [8]But he knew what they were thinking, and he said to the man with the crippled hand, "Stand up here in the middle of everyone." The man got up and stood there. [9]Then Jesus said to them, "I ask you, which is lawful on the Sabbath day: to do good or to do evil, to save a life or to destroy it?" [10]Jesus looked around at all of them and said to the man, "Hold out your hand." The man held out his hand, and it was healed.

[11]But the Pharisees and the teachers of the law were very angry and discussed with each other what they could do to Jesus.

Jesus Chooses His Apostles

[12]At that time Jesus went off to a mountain to pray, and he spent the night praying to God. [13]The next morning,

What do you like to do in your spare time?

HE: Fly-fishing and photography

SHE: Hanging out with friends

fun facts

Only 1 out of 16 consumers actually contacts a company to report a bad experience, but almost 33% let their friends and family know about it.

(*Kiplinger's*)

5:33 fast The people would give up eating for a special time of prayer and worship to God. It was also done to show sadness and disappointment.

Jesus called his followers to him and chose twelve of them, whom he named apostles: [14]Simon (Jesus named him Peter), his brother Andrew, James, John, Philip, Bartholomew, [15]Matthew, Thomas, James son of Alphaeus, Simon (called the Zealot), [16]Judas son of James, and Judas Iscariot, who later turned Jesus over to his enemies.

Jesus Teaches and Heals

[17]Jesus and the apostles came down from the mountain, and he stood on level ground. A large group of his followers was there, as well as many people from all around Judea, Jerusalem, and the seacoast cities of Tyre and Sidon. [18]They all came to hear Jesus teach and to be healed of their sicknesses, and he healed those who were troubled by evil spirits. [19]All the people were trying to touch Jesus, because power was coming from him and healing them all.

[20]Jesus looked at his followers and said,

"You people who are poor are blessed,
because the kingdom of God
belongs to you.
[21]You people who are now hungry are
blessed,
because you will be satisfied.
You people who are now crying are
blessed,
because you will laugh with joy.

[22]"People will hate you, shut you out, insult you, and say you are evil because you follow the Son of Man. But when they do, you will be blessed. [23]Be full of joy at that time, because you have a great reward in heaven. Their ancestors did the same things to the prophets.

[24]"But how terrible it will be for you
who are rich,
because you have had your easy
life.
[25]How terrible it will be for you who
are full now,
because you will be hungry.
How terrible it will be for you who
are laughing now,
because you will be sad and cry.

[26]"How terrible when everyone says only good things about you, because their ancestors said the same things about the false prophets.

Love Your Enemies

[27]"But I say to you who are listening, love your enemies. Do good to those who hate you, [28]bless those who curse you, pray for those who are cruel to you. [29]If anyone slaps you on one cheek, offer him the other cheek, too. If someone takes your coat, do not stop him from taking your shirt. [30]Give to everyone who asks you, and when someone takes something that is yours, don't ask for it back. [31]Do to others what you would want them to do to you. [32]If you love only the people who love you, what praise should you get? Even sinners love the people who love them. [33]If you do good only to those who do good to you, what praise should you get? Even sinners do that! [34]If you lend things to people, always hoping to get something back, what praise should you get? Even sinners lend to other sinners so that they can get back the same amount! [35]But love your enemies, do good to them, and lend to them without hoping to get anything back. Then you will have a great reward, and you will be children of the Most High God, because he is kind even to people who are ungrateful and full of sin. [36]Show mercy, just as your Father shows mercy.

Look at Yourselves

[37]"Don't judge others, and you will not be judged. Don't accuse others of being guilty, and you will not be accused of being guilty. Forgive, and you will be forgiven. [38]Give, and you will receive. You will be given much. Pressed down, shaken together, and running over, it will spill into your lap. The way you give to others is the way God will give to you."

[39]Jesus told them this story: "Can a blind person lead another blind person? No! Both of them will fall into a ditch. [40]A student is not better than the teacher, but the student who has been fully trained will be like the teacher.

[41]"Why do you notice the little piece of dust in your friend's eye, but you don't notice the big piece of wood in your own eye? [42]How can you say to your friend, 'Friend, let me take that little piece of dust out of your eye' when you cannot see that big piece of wood in your own eye! You hypocrite! First, take the wood out of your own

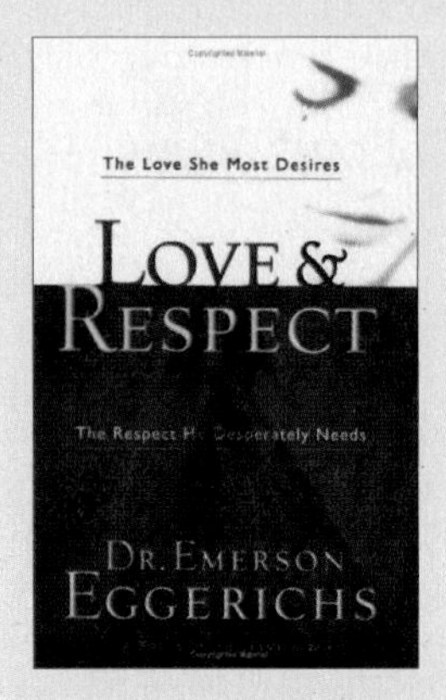

Love & Respect
by Dr. Emerson Eggerichs

Do you want your husband to act more loving? Do you want him to be more sensitive to your needs? No matter how tempting it may be to hint, nag, or lecture him in frustration, none of those approaches will lead to what you need, according to author Dr. Emerson Eggerichs. But you can get your husband's attention and inspire him to express his love for you more frequently if you give him what he needs most: respect. This book will help you learn how to unconditionally respect your husband, which will trigger his love for you and give you both what you desire.

eye. Then you will see clearly to take the dust out of your friend's eye.

Two Kinds of Fruit

[43]"A good tree does not produce bad fruit, nor does a bad tree produce good fruit. [44]Each tree is known by its own fruit. People don't gather figs from thornbushes, and they don't get grapes from bushes. [45]Good people bring good things out of the good they stored in their hearts. But evil people bring evil things out of the evil they stored in their hearts. People speak the things that are in their hearts.

Two Kinds of People

[46]"Why do you call me, 'Lord, Lord,' but do not do what I say? [47]I will show you what everyone is like who comes to me and hears my words and obeys. [48]That person is like a man building a house who dug deep and laid the foundation on rock. When the floods came, the water tried to wash the house away, but it could not shake it, because the house was built well. [49]But the one who hears my words and does not obey is like a man who built his house on the ground without a foundation. When the floods came, the house quickly fell and was completely destroyed."

Jesus Heals a Soldier's Servant

7 When Jesus finished saying all these things to the people, he went to Capernaum. [2]There was an army officer who had a servant who was very important to him. The servant was so sick he was nearly dead. [3]When the officer heard about Jesus, he sent some Jewish elders to him to ask Jesus to come and heal his servant. [4]The men went to Jesus and begged him, saying, "This officer is worthy of your help. [5]He loves our people, and he built us a synagogue."

[6]So Jesus went with the men. He was getting near the officer's house when the officer sent friends to say, "Lord, don't trouble yourself, because I am not worthy to have you come into my house. [7]That is why I did not come to you myself. But you only need to command it, and my servant will be healed. [8]I, too, am a man under the authority of others, and I have soldiers under my command. I tell one soldier, 'Go,' and he goes. I tell another soldier, 'Come,' and he comes. I say to my servant, 'Do this,' and my servant does it."

[9]When Jesus heard this, he was amazed. Turning to the crowd that was following him, he said, "I tell you, this is the greatest faith I have found anywhere, even in Israel."

[10]Those who had been sent to Jesus went back to the house where they found the servant in good health.

Jesus Brings a Man Back to Life

[11]Soon afterwards Jesus went to a town called Nain, and his followers and a large crowd traveled with him. [12]When he came near the town gate, he saw a funeral. A mother, who was a widow, had lost her only son. A large crowd from the town was with the mother while her son was being carried out. [13]When the Lord saw her, he felt very sorry for her and said, "Don't cry." [14]He went up and touched the coffin, and the people who were carrying it stopped. Jesus said, "Young man, I tell you, get up!" [15]And the son sat up and began to talk. Then Jesus gave him back to his mother.

[16]All the people were amazed and began praising God, saying, "A great prophet has come to us! God has come to help his people."

[17]This news about Jesus spread through all Judea and into all the places around there.

John Asks a Question

[18]John's followers told him about all these things. He called for two of his followers [19]and sent them to the Lord to ask, "Are you the One who is to come, or should we wait for someone else?"

[20]When the men came to Jesus, they said, "John the Baptist sent us to you with this question: 'Are you the One who is to come, or should we wait for someone else?' "

[21]At that time, Jesus healed many people of their sicknesses, diseases, and evil spirits, and he gave sight to many blind people. [22]Then Jesus answered John's

---

Be Still & KNOW

Pray Over Life Decisions

Sometimes it seems as if every decision you face is a critical one. Choices about career, relationships, and purpose can bring on major stress in a hurry. When you find yourself at a crossroads, find peace in knowing that the Author of your life already knows the whole story. He will not let you be defeated, and he never sleeps (Psalm 121:3). Your Creator has a good plan for your future (Jeremiah 29:11). You can count on that! And he promises that when you seek after his will with your whole being, you will find him (Deuteronomy 4:29). Bow before him in prayer, asking for direction in your decision making, and you will surely hear his voice directing your way (Isaiah 30:21).

modern**worship**

Beyond Thanks

What's the difference between thanking God and worshiping him? While the two can overlap, worship goes beyond appreciating what God does and aims for the heart of *who God is*. Worship praises his unchanging character, his constant love, his supreme wisdom, and his matchless power. He's worthy of worship because he's the eternal, unconquerable King. He's God of the very big and the very little details of his world. As Creator, Savior, Ruler, and Judge, he knows all and sees all. If circumstances have you feeling less than worshipful, read Genesis 1—2 for a reminder of God as your Creator. Or pray through the psalms that focus on God's holiness. As you read, remember that worship goes beyond God's actions to his identity.

followers, "Go tell John what you saw and heard here. The blind can see, the crippled can walk, and people with skin diseases are healed. The deaf can hear, the dead are raised to life, and the Good News is preached to the poor. [23]Those who do not stumble in their faith because of me are blessed!"

[24]When John's followers left, Jesus began talking to the people about John: "What did you go out into the desert to see? A reed[n] blown by the wind? [25]What did you go out to see? A man dressed in fine clothes? No, people who have fine clothes and much wealth live in kings' palaces. [26]But what did you go out to see? A prophet? Yes, and I tell you, John is more than a prophet. [27]This was written about him:

> 'I will send my messenger ahead of you,
> who will prepare the way for you.'
> *Malachi 3:1*

[28]I tell you, John is greater than any other person ever born, but even the least important person in the kingdom of God is greater than John."

[29](When the people, including the tax collectors, heard this, they all agreed that God's teaching was good, because they had been baptized by John. [30]But the Pharisees and experts on the law refused to accept God's plan for themselves; they did not let John baptize them.)

[31]Then Jesus said, "What shall I say about the people of this time? What are they like? [32]They are like children sitting in the marketplace, calling to one another and saying,

> 'We played music for you, but you did not dance;
> we sang a sad song, but you did not cry.'

[33]John the Baptist came and did not eat bread or drink wine, and you say, 'He has a demon in him.' [34]The Son of Man came eating and drinking, and you say, 'Look at him! He eats too much and drinks too much wine, and he is a friend of tax collectors and sinners!' [35]But wisdom is proved to be right by what it does."

A Woman Washes Jesus' Feet

[36]One of the Pharisees asked Jesus to eat with him, so Jesus went into the Pharisee's house and sat at the table. [37]A sinful woman in the town learned that Jesus was eating at the Pharisee's house. So she brought an alabaster jar of perfume [38]and stood behind Jesus at his feet, crying. She began to wash his feet with her tears, and she dried them with her hair, kissing them many times and rubbing them with the perfume. [39]When the Pharisee who asked Jesus to come to his house saw this, he thought to himself, "If Jesus were a prophet, he would know that the woman touching him is a sinner!"

[40]Jesus said to the Pharisee, "Simon, I have something to say to you."

Simon said, "Teacher, tell me."

[41]Jesus said, "Two people owed money to the same banker. One owed five hundred coins[n] and the other owed fifty. [42]They had no money to pay what they owed, but the banker told both of them they did not have to pay him. Which person will love the banker more?"

[43]Simon, the Pharisee, answered, "I think it would be the one who owed him the most money."

Jesus said to Simon, "You are right." [44]Then Jesus turned toward the woman and said to Simon, "Do you see this woman? When I came into your house, you gave me no water for my feet, but she washed my feet with her tears and dried them with her hair. [45]You gave me no kiss of greeting, but she has been kissing my feet since I came in. [46]You did not put oil on my head, but she poured perfume on my feet. [47]I tell you that her many sins are forgiven, so she showed great love. But the person who is forgiven only a little will love only a little."

[48]Then Jesus said to her, "Your sins are forgiven."

[49]The people sitting at the table began to say among themselves, "Who is this who even forgives sins?"

[50]Jesus said to the woman, "Because you believed, you are saved from your sins. Go in peace."

The Group with Jesus

8 After this, while Jesus was traveling through some cities and small towns, he preached and told the Good News about God's kingdom. The twelve apostles were with him, [2]and also some women who had been healed of sicknesses and evil spirits: Mary, called Magdalene, from whom seven demons had gone out; [3]Joanna, the wife of Cuza (the manager of Herod's house); Susanna; and many others. These women used their own money to help Jesus and his apostles.

A Story About Planting Seed

[4]When a great crowd was gathered, and people were coming to Jesus from every town, he told them this story:

7:24 reed It means that John was not ordinary or weak like grass blown by the wind. **7:41 coins** Roman denarii. One coin was the average pay for one day's work.

[5]"A farmer went out to plant his seed. While he was planting, some seed fell by the road. People walked on the seed, and the birds ate it up. [6]Some seed fell on rock, and when it began to grow, it died because it had no water. [7]Some seed fell among thorny weeds, but the weeds grew up with it and choked the good plants. [8]And some seed fell on good ground and grew and made a hundred times more."

As Jesus finished the story, he called out, "Let those with ears use them and listen!"

[9]Jesus' followers asked him what this story meant.

[10]Jesus said, "You have been chosen to know the secrets about the kingdom of God. But I use stories to speak to other people so that:

'They will look, but they may not see.
They will listen, but they may not understand.' *Isaiah 6:9*

[11]"This is what the story means: The seed is God's message. [12]The seed that fell beside the road is like the people who hear God's teaching, but the devil comes and takes it away from them so they cannot believe it and be saved. [13]The seed that fell on rock is like those who hear God's teaching and accept it gladly, but they don't allow the teaching to go deep into their lives. They believe for a while, but when trouble comes, they give up. [14]The seed that fell among the thorny weeds is like those who hear God's teaching, but they let the worries, riches, and pleasures of this life keep them from growing and producing good fruit. [15]And the seed that fell on the good ground is like those who hear God's teaching with good, honest hearts and obey it and patiently produce good fruit.

Use What You Have

[16]"No one after lighting a lamp covers it with a bowl or hides it under a bed. Instead, the person puts it on a lampstand so those who come in will see the light. [17]Everything that is hidden will become clear, and every secret thing will be made known. [18]So be careful how you listen. Those who have understanding will be given more. But those who do not have understanding, even what they think they have will be taken away from them."

Luke 8:14

Distractions are the archnemesis of productivity. Isn't it frustrating when your entire day revolves around dealing with unimportant issues instead of the goals you made that morning? It's sometimes a battle to avoid getting sidetracked and ruled by interruptions. In this verse, Jesus identifies three big distractions the world can throw into the path of people who hear God's teachings: the worries, riches, and pleasures of this life.

Our culture constantly offers us all three of those distractions. Expensive clothes, new cars, bigger houses, better jobs . . . pursuing those pleasures might bring some temporary happiness, but never true joy or satisfaction. In fact, the pursuit just makes us want more! So we pursue money even harder, which just leads to greater worries. Before long, that's all we live for: money, possessions, and entertainment. Without intending to, we can end up with a complex, busy existence that is devoid of peace or joy.

If you want to follow Christ, be intentional about not letting yourself get drawn into this world's worries, riches, and pleasures. Remember how distractions can choke out your focus on God's truth and rob you of the life Christ offers you. Keep your eyes fixed on him!

Jesus' True Family

[19]Jesus' mother and brothers came to see him, but there was such a crowd they could not get to him. [20]Someone said to Jesus, "Your mother and your brothers are standing outside, wanting to see you."

[21]Jesus answered them, "My mother and my brothers are those who listen to God's teaching and obey it!"

Jesus Calms a Storm

[22]One day Jesus and his followers got into a boat, and he said to them, "Let's go across the lake." And so they started across. [23]While they were sailing, Jesus fell asleep. A very strong wind blew up on the lake, causing the boat to fill with water, and they were in danger.

[24]The followers went to Jesus and woke him, saying, "Master! Master! We will drown!"

Jesus got up and gave a command to the wind and the waves. They stopped, and it became calm. [25]Jesus said to his followers, "Where is your faith?"

The followers were afraid and amazed and said to each other, "Who is this that commands even the wind and the water, and they obey him?"

A Man with Demons Inside Him

[26]Jesus and his followers sailed across the lake from Galilee to the area of the

Women & Men of the BIBLE

Hannah: Desperate Prayers

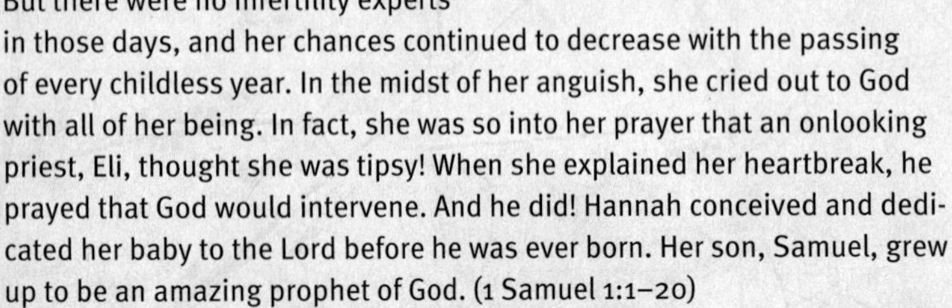

Hannah desperately wanted a baby. But there were no infertility experts in those days, and her chances continued to decrease with the passing of every childless year. In the midst of her anguish, she cried out to God with all of her being. In fact, she was so into her prayer that an onlooking priest, Eli, thought she was tipsy! When she explained her heartbreak, he prayed that God would intervene. And he did! Hannah conceived and dedicated her baby to the Lord before he was ever born. Her son, Samuel, grew up to be an amazing prophet of God. (1 Samuel 1:1–20)

Gerasene[n] people. [27]When Jesus got out on the land, a man from the town who had demons inside him came to Jesus. For a long time he had worn no clothes and had lived in the burial caves, not in a house. [28]When he saw Jesus, he cried out and fell down before him. He said with a loud voice, "What do you want with me, Jesus, Son of the Most High God? I beg you, don't torture me!" [29]He said this because Jesus was commanding the evil spirit to come out of the man. Many times it had taken hold of him. Though he had been kept under guard and chained hand and foot, he had broken his chains and had been forced by the demon out into a lonely place.

[30]Jesus asked him, "What is your name?"

He answered, "Legion,"[n] because many demons were in him. [31]The demons begged Jesus not to send them into eternal darkness.[n] [32]A large herd of pigs was feeding on a hill, and the demons begged Jesus to allow them to go into the pigs. So Jesus allowed them to do this. [33]When the demons came out of the man, they went into the pigs, and the herd ran down the hill into the lake and was drowned.

[34]When the herdsmen saw what had happened, they ran away and told about this in the town and the countryside. [35]And people went to see what had happened. When they came to Jesus, they found the man sitting at Jesus' feet, clothed and in his right mind, because the demons were gone. But the people were frightened. [36]The people who saw this happen told the others how Jesus had made the man well. [37]All the people of the Gerasene country asked Jesus to leave, because they were all very afraid. So Jesus got into the boat and went back to Galilee.

[38]The man whom Jesus had healed begged to go with him, but Jesus sent him away, saying, [39]"Go back home and tell people how much God has done for you." So the man went all over town telling how much Jesus had done for him.

Jesus Gives Life to a Dead Girl and Heals a Sick Woman

[40]When Jesus got back to Galilee, a crowd welcomed him, because everyone was waiting for him. [41]A man named Jairus, a leader of the synagogue, came to Jesus and fell at his feet, begging him to come to his house. [42]Jairus' only daughter, about twelve years old, was dying.

While Jesus was on his way to Jairus' house, the people were crowding all around him. [43]A woman was in the crowd who had been bleeding for twelve years,[n] but no one was able to heal her. [44]She came up behind Jesus and touched the edge of his coat, and instantly her bleeding stopped. [45]Then Jesus said, "Who touched me?"

When all the people said they had not touched him, Peter said, "Master, the people are all around you and are pushing against you."

[46]But Jesus said, "Someone did touch me, because I felt power go out from me." [47]When the woman saw she could not hide, she came forward, shaking, and fell down before Jesus. While all the people listened, she told why she had touched him and how she had been instantly healed. [48]Jesus said to her, "Dear woman, you are made well because you believed. Go in peace."

[49]While Jesus was still speaking, someone came from the house of the synagogue leader and said to him, "Your daughter is dead. Don't bother the teacher anymore."

[50]When Jesus heard this, he said to Jairus, "Don't be afraid. Just believe, and your daughter will be well."

[51]When Jesus went to the house, he let only Peter, John, James, and the girl's father and mother go inside with him. [52]All the people were crying and feeling sad because the girl was dead, but Jesus said, "Stop crying. She is not dead, only asleep."

[53]The people laughed at Jesus because they knew the girl was dead. [54]But Jesus took hold of her hand and called to her, "My child, stand up!" [55]Her spirit came back into her, and she stood up at once. Then Jesus ordered that she be given something to eat. [56]The girl's parents were amazed, but Jesus told them not to tell anyone what had happened.

fun facts

1 out of 4 families headed by people ages 20 to 29 owe more than they own.

(MSN.com)

8:26 Gerasene From Gerasa, an area southeast of Lake Galilee. The exact location is uncertain and some Greek copies read "Gadarene"; others read "Gergesene." **8:30 Legion** Means very many. A legion was about five thousand men in the Roman army. **8:31 eternal darkness** Literally, "the abyss," something like a pit or a hole that has no end. **8:43 years** Some Greek copies continue, "and she had spent all the money she had on doctors."

RELATIONSHIPS

Relationship Punctuation

Ever feel like life is one big run-on sentence with no time for pauses or punctuation stops (a.k.a. downtime)? Unfortunately, schedules that run long on busyness and short on breath-catching moments can take a toll on relationships. Society cheers a task-oriented approach to life—the more you get done the better. How different from Jesus, who prioritized people over his to-do list. He always slowed down, even let himself be sidetracked, to connect with people and listen without sending the message that he had somewhere else to be (Mark 5:21–43; 6:30–44; Luke 10:38–42). Punctuate your schedule with people moments!

Jesus Sends Out the Apostles

9 Jesus called the twelve apostles together and gave them power and authority over all demons and the ability to heal sicknesses. [2]He sent the apostles out to tell about God's kingdom and to heal the sick. [3]He said to them, "Take nothing for your trip, neither a walking stick, bag, bread, money, or extra clothes. [4]When you enter a house, stay there until it is time to leave. [5]If people do not welcome you, shake the dust off of your feet[n] as you leave the town, as a warning to them."

[6]So the apostles went out and traveled through all the towns, preaching the Good News and healing people everywhere.

Herod Is Confused About Jesus

[7]Herod, the governor, heard about all the things that were happening and was confused, because some people said, "John the Baptist has risen from the dead." [8]Others said, "Elijah has come to us." And still others said, "One of the prophets who lived long ago has risen from the dead." [9]Herod said, "I cut off John's head, so who is this man I hear such things about?" And Herod kept trying to see Jesus.

More than Five Thousand Fed

[10]When the apostles returned, they told Jesus everything they had done. Then Jesus took them with him to a town called Bethsaida where they could be alone together. [11]But the people learned where Jesus went and followed him. He welcomed them and talked with them about God's kingdom and healed those who needed to be healed.

[12]Late in the afternoon, the twelve apostles came to Jesus and said, "Send the people away. They need to go to the towns and countryside around here and find places to sleep and something to eat, because no one lives in this place."

[13]But Jesus said to them, "You give them something to eat."

They said, "We have only five loaves of bread and two fish, unless we go buy food for all these people." [14](There were about five thousand men there.)

Jesus said to his followers, "Tell the people to sit in groups of about fifty people."

[15]So the followers did this, and all the people sat down. [16]Then Jesus took the five loaves of bread and two fish, and looking up to heaven, he thanked God for the food. Then he divided the food and gave it to the followers to give to the people. [17]They all ate and were satisfied, and what was left over was gathered up, filling twelve baskets.

Jesus Is the Christ

[18]One time when Jesus was praying alone, his followers were with him, and he asked them, "Who do the people say I am?"

[19]They answered, "Some say you are John the Baptist. Others say you are Elijah.[n] And others say you are one of the prophets from long ago who has come back to life."

[20]Then Jesus asked, "But who do you say I am?"

Peter answered, "You are the Christ from God."

[21]Jesus warned them not to tell anyone, saying, [22]"The Son of Man must suffer many things. He will be rejected by the Jewish elders, the leading priests, and the teachers of the law. He will be killed and after three days will be raised from the dead."

[23]Jesus said to all of them, "If people want to follow me, they must give up the things they want. They must be willing

9:5 shake . . . feet A warning. It showed that they had rejected these people. **9:19 Elijah** A man who spoke for God and who lived hundreds of years before Christ. See 1 Kings 17.

WORLDVIEWS

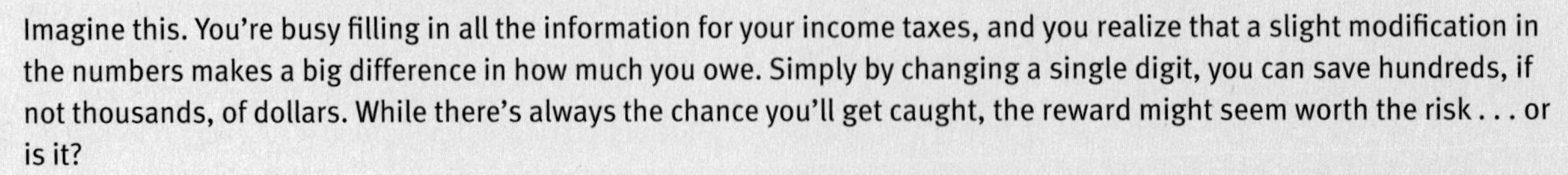

Truth, Right and Wrong, and a God Who Doesn't Change His Mind

Imagine this. You're busy filling in all the information for your income taxes, and you realize that a slight modification in the numbers makes a big difference in how much you owe. Simply by changing a single digit, you can save hundreds, if not thousands, of dollars. While there's always the chance you'll get caught, the reward might seem worth the risk . . . or is it?

It's decision time—and it goes deeper than just obeying the law. After all, who's to say it's actually wrong to cheat? The world seems to think morality depends on the situation or on whether or not you'll get caught. If there's no God, right and wrong are really just matters of opinion, right? Everyone can invent his or her own personal morality. It all depends!

But that's *not* what God says. It doesn't depend on the situation—it depends on him. *He* decides what's right and wrong. God is unchanging . . . and his words don't change either. There's no squirming your way out of it! But it's weird—even though people think they're free when they make their own rules and live however they want, they just end up becoming slaves to sin. Compare that with God's plan. God didn't make rules to ruin our lives. He wants us to love what is right. He offers freedom from the ugliness of sin and the chance to live in the beautiful light of his love and truth.

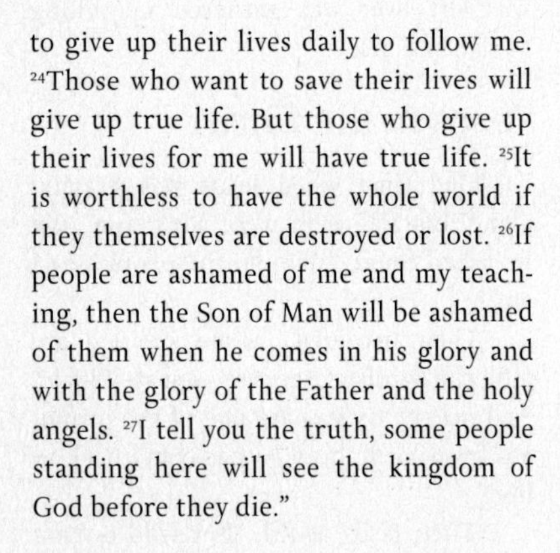

Remember who you are—a follower of Jesus. If you want to be like Christ, obey God. Realize that he's the one who makes the rules, and choose to live by those rules—even when it's not easy or convenient!

to give up their lives daily to follow me. [24]Those who want to save their lives will give up true life. But those who give up their lives for me will have true life. [25]It is worthless to have the whole world if they themselves are destroyed or lost. [26]If people are ashamed of me and my teaching, then the Son of Man will be ashamed of them when he comes in his glory and with the glory of the Father and the holy angels. [27]I tell you the truth, some people standing here will see the kingdom of God before they die."

Jesus Talks with Moses and Elijah

[28]About eight days after Jesus said these things, he took Peter, John, and James and went up on a mountain to pray. [29]While Jesus was praying, the appearance of his face changed, and his clothes became shining white. [30]Then two men, Moses and Elijah,[n] were talking with Jesus. [31]They appeared in heavenly glory, talking about his departure which he would soon bring about in Jerusalem. [32]Peter and the others were very sleepy, but when they awoke fully, they saw the glory of Jesus and the two men standing with him. [33]When Moses and Elijah were about to leave, Peter said to Jesus, "Master, it is good that we are here. Let us make three tents—one for you, one for Moses, and one for Elijah." (Peter did not know what he was talking about.)

[34]While he was saying these things, a cloud came and covered them, and they became afraid as the cloud covered them. [35]A voice came from the cloud, saying, "This is my Son, whom I have chosen. Listen to him!"

[36]When the voice finished speaking, only Jesus was there. Peter, John, and James said nothing and told no one at that time what they had seen.

Jesus Heals a Sick Boy

[37]The next day, when they came down from the mountain, a large crowd met Jesus. [38]A man in the crowd shouted to him, "Teacher, please come and look at my son, because he is my only child. [39]An evil spirit seizes my son, and suddenly he screams. It causes him to lose control of himself and foam at the mouth. The evil spirit keeps on hurting him and almost never leaves him. [40]I begged your followers to force the evil spirit out, but they could not do it."

[41]Jesus answered, "You people have no faith, and your lives are all wrong. How long must I stay with you and put up with you? Bring your son here."

[42]While the boy was coming, the demon threw him on the ground and made him lose control of himself. But Jesus gave a strong command to the evil spirit and healed the boy and gave him back to his father. [43]All the people were amazed at the great power of God.

Jesus Talks About His Death

While everyone was wondering about all that Jesus did, he said to his followers, [44]"Don't forget what I tell you now: The Son of Man will be handed over to people." [45]But the followers did not understand

9:30 Moses and Elijah Two of the most important Jewish leaders in the past. God had given Moses the Law, and Elijah was an important prophet.

what this meant; the meaning was hidden from them so they could not understand. But they were afraid to ask Jesus about it.

Who Is the Greatest?

[46]Jesus' followers began to have an argument about which one of them was the greatest. [47]Jesus knew what they were thinking, so he took a little child and stood the child beside him. [48]Then Jesus said, "Whoever accepts this little child in my name accepts me. And whoever accepts me accepts the One who sent me, because whoever is least among you all is really the greatest."

Anyone Not Against Us Is for Us

[49]John answered, "Master, we saw someone using your name to force demons out of people. We told him to stop, because he does not belong to our group."

[50]But Jesus said to him, "Don't stop him, because whoever is not against you is for you."

A Town Rejects Jesus

[51]When the time was coming near for Jesus to depart, he was determined to go to Jerusalem. [52]He sent some messengers ahead of him, who went into a town in Samaria to make everything ready for him. [53]But the people there would not welcome him, because he was set on going to Jerusalem. [54]When James and John, followers of Jesus, saw this, they said, "Lord, do you want us to call fire down from heaven and destroy those people?"[n]

[55]But Jesus turned and scolded them. [And Jesus said, "You don't know what kind of spirit you belong to. [56]The Son of Man did not come to destroy the souls of people but to save them."][n] Then they went to another town.

Following Jesus

[57]As they were going along the road, someone said to Jesus, "I will follow you any place you go."

[58]Jesus said to them, "The foxes have holes to live in, and the birds have nests, but the Son of Man has no place to rest his head."

[59]Jesus said to another man, "Follow me!"

But he said, "Lord, first let me go and bury my father."

[60]But Jesus said to him, "Let the people who are dead bury their own dead. You must go and tell about the kingdom of God."

[61]Another man said, "I will follow you, Lord, but first let me go and say good-bye to my family."

[62]Jesus said, "Anyone who begins to plow a field but keeps looking back is of no use in the kingdom of God."

Jesus Sends Out the Seventy-Two

10 After this, the Lord chose seventy-two[n] others and sent them out in pairs ahead of him into every town and place where he planned to go. [2]He said to them, "There are a great many people to harvest, but there are only a few workers. So pray to God, who owns the harvest, that he will send more workers to help gather his harvest. [3]Go now, but listen! I am sending you out like sheep among wolves. [4]Don't carry a purse, a bag, or sandals, and don't waste time talking with people on the road. [5]Before you go into a house, say, 'Peace be with this house.' [6]If peace-loving people live there, your blessing of peace will stay with them, but if not, then your blessing will come back to you. [7]Stay in the same house, eating and drinking what the people there give you. A worker should be given his pay. Don't move from house to house. [8]If you go into a town and the people welcome you, eat what they give you. [9]Heal the sick who live there, and tell them, 'The kingdom of God is near you.' [10]But if you go into a town, and the people don't welcome you, then go into the streets and say, [11]'Even the dirt from your town that sticks to our feet we wipe off against you.[n] But remember that the kingdom of God is near.' [12]I tell you, on the Judgment Day it will be better for the people of Sodom[n] than for the people of that town.

Jesus Warns Unbelievers

[13]"How terrible for you, Korazin! How terrible for you, Bethsaida! If the miracles I did in you had happened in Tyre and Sidon,[n] those people would have changed their lives long ago. They would have worn rough cloth and put ashes on themselves to show they had changed. [14]But on the Judgment Day it will be better for Tyre and Sidon than for you. [15]And you, Capernaum,[n] will you be lifted up to heaven? No! You will be thrown down to the depths!

[16]"Whoever listens to you listens to me, and whoever refuses to accept you refuses to accept me. And whoever refuses to accept me refuses to accept the One who sent me."

Satan Falls

[17]When the seventy-two[n] came back, they were very happy and said, "Lord, even the demons obeyed us when we used your name!"

[18]Jesus said, "I saw Satan fall like lightning from heaven. [19]Listen, I have given you power to walk on snakes and scorpions, power that is greater than the enemy has. So nothing will hurt you. [20]But you should not be happy because the spirits obey you but because your names are written in heaven."

Jesus Prays to the Father

[21]Then Jesus rejoiced in the Holy Spirit and said, "I praise you, Father, Lord of

fun facts

There are more than 300 million people living in the United States.

(U.S. Census Bureau)

9:54 people Some Greek copies continue "as Elijah did." **9:55–56 And . . . them."** Some Greek copies do not contain the bracketed text. **10:1, 17 seventy-two** Some Greek copies read "seventy." **10:11 dirt . . . you** A warning. It showed that they had rejected these people. **10:12 Sodom** City that God destroyed because the people were so evil. **10:13 Tyre and Sidon** Towns where wicked people lived. **10:13, 15 Korazin . . . Bethsaida . . . Capernaum** Towns by Lake Galilee where Jesus preached to the people.

HOW HANDY ARE YOU?

1. Yuck! Your toilet is overflowing. What do you do first?

- [] A. Burst into tears
- [] B. Take the top off the tank and jiggle the do-hickey
- [] C. Turn the knob at the base until the water stops gushing
- [] D. Slam the lid down and call 911

2. You find yourself all alone on the side of the road with a flat tire, and—just your luck—there's no cell phone coverage. What do you do?

- [] A. Start rationing out any food you have with you so you'll be sure to survive until help arrives
- [] B. Raise the hood so people know you're having car trouble
- [] C. Pray for the cell phone signal to miraculously reappear
- [] D. Get the jack and spare tire out of the trunk and get busy changing it

3. You're so excited to have a new computer desk. But you find out why the price was so cheap when you get it home and see the million pieces you have to put together. What do you do?

- [] A. Take it back to the store and vow to only buy pre-assembled furniture in the future
- [] B. Immediately start putting it together without even looking at the directions
- [] C. Put on your thinking cap and follow along with the steps for assembly
- [] D. Ask your husband, father, or a guy friend to help you

4. What tools do you have in your toolbox at home?

- [] A. I don't have a toolbox . . . unless you count my makeup bag!
- [] B. The basics—screwdriver, hammer, wrench, and/or pliers
- [] C. The mack daddy—both phillips *and* flatheads, adjustable wrenches, saws, drill bits . . . you name it!
- [] D. Names and numbers for all my plumbers, carpenters, electricians, and guy friends

5. When using jumper cables to start one car battery from another, which color connects with which battery terminal?

- [] A. What are jumper cables, and why would a battery be in a terminal?
- [] B. Red goes to the positive (+); black goes to the negative (-).
- [] C. I'm not 100% sure—but if it sparks, it's wrong.
- [] D. That's why they invented AAA!

Scoring:

1. A=1, B=2, C=3, D=0
2. A=1, B=2, C=0, D=3
3. A=0, B=2, C=3, D=1
4. A=0, B=2, C=3, D=1
5. A=0, B=3, C=2, D=1

If you scored 13 or more, you're one handy mama! You know your way around a tool shed, auto shop, and even the hardware section at your local discount store. You're a strong, independent do-it-yourselfer, knowing without a doubt that you can do all things through Christ.

If you scored 12 or less, you're handy when you have to be. You're no tool and gadget savant, but you can survive around the house. And when you don't know how to do something, you know who to call for help. Just remember, even if you can't imagine yourself ever being very handy, God says that with his power working in us, he can do much more than we could ever ask or imagine (Ephesians 3:20)—even when we tackle handy*woman* projects!

heaven and earth, because you have hidden these things from the people who are wise and smart. But you have shown them to those who are like little children. Yes, Father, this is what you really wanted.

[22]"My Father has given me all things. No one knows who the Son is, except the Father. And no one knows who the Father is, except the Son and those whom the Son chooses to tell."

[23]Then Jesus turned to his followers and said privately, "You are blessed to see what you now see. [24]I tell you, many prophets and kings wanted to see what you now see, but they did not, and they wanted to hear what you now hear, but they did not."

How to Catch His Eye

When a special someone catches your interest, it's only natural to work extra hard at looking your best whenever he's around. Perhaps you spray more perfume, wear your best-fitting jeans, or glam up the makeup. But there are other surefire ways to catch a godly guy's attention. Ruth from the Old Testament is a great example. (See Ruth 2:5–13.) She wowed her dream man without even meaning to. He was captivated not by her trendy outfit or stylish 'do, but by her character. Develop godly character and you will be more and more attractive to the kind of guy you're looking for.

The Good Samaritan

[25]Then an expert on the law stood up to test Jesus, saying, "Teacher, what must I do to get life forever?"

[26]Jesus said, "What is written in the law? What do you read there?"

[27]The man answered, "Love the Lord your God with all your heart, all your soul, all your strength, and all your mind."[n] Also, "Love your neighbor as you love yourself."[n]

[28]Jesus said to him, "Your answer is right. Do this and you will live."

[29]But the man, wanting to show the importance of his question, said to Jesus, "And who is my neighbor?"

[30]Jesus answered, "As a man was going down from Jerusalem to Jericho, some robbers attacked him. They tore off his clothes, beat him, and left him lying there, almost dead. [31]It happened that a priest was going down that road. When he saw the man, he walked by on the other side. [32]Next, a Levite[n] came there, and after he went over and looked at the man, he walked by on the other side of the road. [33]Then a Samaritan[n] traveling down the road came to where the hurt man was. When he saw the man, he felt very sorry for him. [34]The Samaritan went to him, poured olive oil and wine[n] on his wounds, and bandaged them. Then he put the hurt man on his own donkey and took him to an inn where he cared for him. [35]The next day, the Samaritan brought out two coins,[n] gave them to the innkeeper, and said, 'Take care of this man. If you spend more money on him, I will pay it back to you when I come again.' "

[36]Then Jesus said, "Which one of these three men do you think was a neighbor to the man who was attacked by the robbers?"

[37]The expert on the law answered, "The one who showed him mercy."

Jesus said to him, "Then go and do what he did."

Mary and Martha

[38]While Jesus and his followers were traveling, Jesus went into a town. A woman named Martha let Jesus stay at her house. [39]Martha had a sister named Mary, who was sitting at Jesus' feet and listening to him teach. [40]But Martha was busy with all the work to be done. She went in and said, "Lord, don't you care that my sister has left me alone to do all the work? Tell her to help me."

[41]But the Lord answered her, "Martha, Martha, you are worried and upset about many things. [42]Only one thing is important. Mary has chosen the better thing, and it will never be taken away from her."

Jesus Teaches About Prayer

11 One time Jesus was praying in a certain place. When he finished, one of his followers said to him, "Lord, teach us to pray as John taught his followers."

[2]Jesus said to them, "When you pray, say:

'Father, may your name always be
kept holy.
May your kingdom come.
[3]Give us the food we need for each
day.
[4]Forgive us for our sins,
because we forgive everyone who
has done wrong to us.
And do not cause us to be
tempted.' "[n]

Continue to Ask

[5]Then Jesus said to them, "Suppose one of you went to your friend's house at midnight and said to him, 'Friend, loan me three loaves of bread. [6]A friend of mine has come into town to visit me, but I have nothing for him to eat.' [7]Your friend inside the house answers, 'Don't bother me! The door is already locked, and my children and I are in bed. I cannot get up and give you anything.' [8]I tell you, if friendship is not enough to make him get up to give you the bread, your boldness will make him get up and give you whatever you need. [9]So I tell you, ask, and God will give to you. Search, and you will find. Knock, and the door will open for you. [10]Yes, everyone who asks will receive. The one who searches will find. And everyone who knocks will have the door opened. [11]If

10:27 "Love . . . mind." Quotation from Deuteronomy 6:5. **10:27 "Love . . . yourself."** Quotation from Leviticus 19:18. **10:32 Levite** Levites were members of the tribe of Levi who helped the Jewish priests with their work in the Temple. Read 1 Chronicles 23:24–32. **10:33 Samaritan** Samaritans were people from Samaria. These people were part Jewish, but the Jews did not accept them as true Jews. Samaritans and Jews disliked each other. **10:34 olive oil and wine** Oil and wine were used like medicine to soften and clean wounds. **10:35 coins** Roman denarii. One coin was the average pay for one day's work. **11:2–4 'Father . . . tempted.'** Some Greek copies include phrases from Matthew's version of this prayer (Matthew 6:9–13).

Luke 11:11–13

There's nothing like getting a gift that confirms someone really knows and loves you. When it's exactly the perfect color, the right size, or the very thing you were hoping for, it says something important about the person who gave it to you. That's just a glimpse of how God is the best Father and gift giver for each of his children.

Asking God for things can seem sort of tricky. On one hand, Jesus says God will give us what we ask for. Simple enough. But we all know God hasn't granted every single request we've ever made. What's the secret? Well, Jesus also taught that prayer is about lining ourselves up with God's will—wanting what God wants. If he's truly good and promises to give good gifts to his children, how could we want anything other than God's will? Could we possibly have a better idea than what God has planned? Of course not! Instead of seeing God as a genie, we need to focus on sincerely seeking his will.

As you line up with God's plans, you can ask God with complete confidence for each of the blessings he's promised us. Trust him as the perfect gift giver, and know that he'll work everything out for his glory and your good.

your children ask for[n] a fish, which of you would give them a snake instead? [12]Or, if your children ask for an egg, would you give them a scorpion? [13]Even though you are bad, you know how to give good things to your children. How much more your heavenly Father will give the Holy Spirit to those who ask him!"

Jesus' Power Is from God

[14]One time Jesus was sending out a demon who could not talk. When the demon came out, the man who had been unable to speak, then spoke. The people were amazed. [15]But some of them said, "Jesus uses the power of Beelzebul, the ruler of demons, to force demons out of people."

[16]Other people, wanting to test Jesus, asked him to give them a sign from heaven. [17]But knowing their thoughts, he said to them, "Every kingdom that is divided against itself will be destroyed. And a family that is divided against itself will not continue. [18]So if Satan is divided against himself, his kingdom will not continue. You say that I use the power of Beelzebul to force out demons. [19]But if I use the power of Beelzebul to force out demons, what power do your people use to force demons out? So they will be your judges. [20]But if I use the power of God to force out demons, then the kingdom of God has come to you.

[21]"When a strong person with many weapons guards his own house, his possessions are safe. [22]But when someone stronger comes and defeats him, the stronger one will take away the weapons the first man trusted and will give away the possessions.

[23]"Anyone who is not with me is against me, and anyone who does not work with me is working against me.

The Empty Person

[24]"When an evil spirit comes out of a person, it travels through dry places, looking for a place to rest. But when it finds no place, it says, 'I will go back to the house I left.' [25]And when it comes back, it finds that house swept clean and made neat. [26]Then the evil spirit goes out and brings seven other spirits more evil than it is, and they go in and live there. So the person has even more trouble than before."

People Who Are Truly Blessed

[27]As Jesus was saying these things, a woman in the crowd called out to Jesus, "Blessed is the mother who gave birth to you and nursed you."

[28]But Jesus said, "No, blessed are those who hear the teaching of God and obey it."

The People Want a Miracle

[29]As the crowd grew larger, Jesus said, "The people who live today are evil. They want to see a miracle for a sign, but no sign will be given them, except the sign of Jonah.[n] [30]As Jonah was a sign for those people who lived in Nineveh, the Son of Man will be a sign for the people of this time. [31]On the Judgment Day the Queen of the South[n] will stand up with the people who live now. She will show they are guilty, because she came from far away to listen to Solomon's wise teaching. And I tell you that someone greater than Solomon is here. [32]On the Judgment Day the people of Nineveh will stand up with the people who live now, and they will show that you are guilty. When Jonah preached to them, they were sorry and changed their lives. And I tell you that someone greater than Jonah is here.

11:11 for Some Greek copies include the phrase "for bread, which of you would give them a stone, or if they ask for . . ." **11:29 sign of Jonah** Jonah's three days in the fish are like Jesus' three days in the tomb. See Matthew 12:40. **11:31 Queen of the South** The Queen of Sheba. She traveled a thousand miles to learn God's wisdom from Solomon. Read 1 Kings 10:1–3.

Be a Light for the World

[33]"No one lights a lamp and puts it in a secret place or under a bowl, but on a lampstand so the people who come in can see. [34]Your eye is a light for the body. When your eyes are good, your whole body will be full of light. But when your eyes are evil, your whole body will be full of darkness. [35]So be careful not to let the light in you become darkness. [36]If your whole body is full of light, and none of it is dark, then you will shine bright, as when a lamp shines on you."

Jesus Accuses the Pharisees

[37]After Jesus had finished speaking, a Pharisee asked Jesus to eat with him. So Jesus went in and sat at the table. [38]But the Pharisee was surprised when he saw that Jesus did not wash his hands[n] before the meal. [39]The Lord said to him, "You Pharisees clean the outside of the cup and the dish, but inside you are full of greed and evil. [40]You foolish people! The same one who made what is outside also made what is inside. [41]So give what is in your dishes to the poor, and then you will be fully clean. [42]How terrible for you Pharisees! You give God one-tenth of even your mint, your rue, and every other plant in your garden. But you fail to be fair to others and to love God. These are the things you should do while continuing to do those other things. [43]How terrible for you Pharisees, because you love to have the most important seats in the synagogues, and you love to be greeted with respect in the marketplaces. [44]How terrible for you, because you are like hidden graves, which people walk on without knowing."

Jesus Talks to Experts on the Law

[45]One of the experts on the law said to Jesus, "Teacher, when you say these things, you are insulting us, too."

[46]Jesus answered, "How terrible for you, you experts on the law! You make strict rules that are very hard for people to obey, but you yourselves don't even try to follow those rules. [47]How terrible for you, because you build tombs for the prophets whom your ancestors killed! [48]And now you show that you approve of what your ancestors did. They killed the prophets, and you build tombs for them! [49]This is why in his wisdom God said, 'I will send prophets and apostles to them. They will kill some, and they will treat others cruelly.' [50]So you who live now will be punished for the deaths of all the prophets who were killed since the beginning of the world— [51]from the killing of Abel to the killing of Zechariah,[n] who died between the altar and the Temple. Yes, I tell you that you who are alive now will be punished for them all.

[52]"How terrible for you, you experts on the law. You have taken away the key to learning about God. You yourselves would not learn, and you stopped others from learning, too."

[53]When Jesus left, the teachers of the law and the Pharisees began to give him trouble, asking him questions about many things, [54]trying to catch him saying something wrong.

Don't Be Like the Pharisees

12 So many thousands of people had gathered that they were stepping on each other. Jesus spoke first to his followers, saying, "Beware of the

International Justice Mission

The growing industry around the sex-slave trade is one of the most deplorable realities of the modern world. Unspeakable atrocities are committed daily against entire villages of women in faraway places. And women aren't the only victims. It's hard to believe, but slavery still very much exists in many parts of the world. International Justice Mission (IJM) wants to

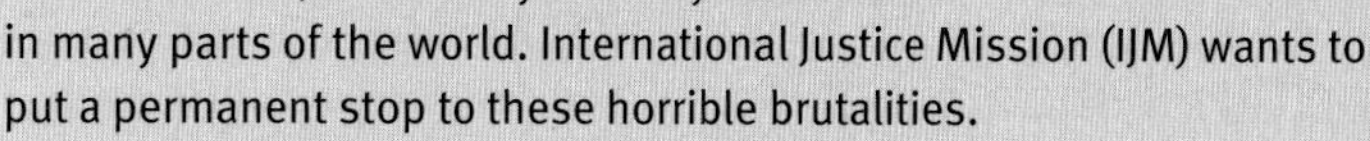

put a permanent stop to these horrible brutalities.

A human rights agency that seeks to aid victims of these types of crimes, IJM is involved in rescuing victims out of violent or oppressive situations and then helping them to heal and recover. But they don't stop with simply helping get the victims out of their situation—they demand justice for the perpetrators as well. IJM also helps educate governments, communities, and other groups about how to reduce or eliminate the atmosphere for such crimes.

You can help put an end to these appalling practices by donating some of your financial resources, time, energy, and heart to IJM. Be part of the solution by funding the work, spreading the word, or inspiring ongoing prayer support among others. Check out www.ijm.org for more details.

11:38 wash his hands This was a Jewish religious custom that the Pharisees thought was very important. **11:51 Abel . . . Zechariah** In the Hebrew Old Testament, the first and last men to be murdered.

What are your favorite foods?

He: Anything Italian

She: Tropical fruits and sorbet

yeast of the Pharisees, because they are hypocrites. [2]Everything that is hidden will be shown, and everything that is secret will be made known. [3]What you have said in the dark will be heard in the light, and what you have whispered in an inner room will be shouted from the housetops.

[4]"I tell you, my friends, don't be afraid of people who can kill the body but after that can do nothing more to hurt you. [5]I will show you the one to fear. Fear the one who has the power to kill you and also to throw you into hell. Yes, this is the one you should fear.

[6]"Five sparrows are sold for only two pennies, and God does not forget any of them. [7]But God even knows how many hairs you have on your head. Don't be afraid. You are worth much more than many sparrows.

Don't Be Ashamed of Jesus

[8]"I tell you, all those who stand before others and say they believe in me, I, the Son of Man, will say before the angels of God that they belong to me. [9]But all who stand before others and say they do not believe in me, I will say before the angels of God that they do not belong to me.

[10]"Anyone who speaks against the Son of Man can be forgiven, but anyone who speaks against the Holy Spirit will not be forgiven.

[11]"When you are brought into the synagogues before the leaders and other powerful people, don't worry about how to defend yourself or what to say. [12]At that time the Holy Spirit will teach you what you must say."

Jesus Warns Against Selfishness

[13]Someone in the crowd said to Jesus, "Teacher, tell my brother to divide with me the property our father left us."

[14]But Jesus said to him, "Who said I should judge or decide between you?" [15]Then Jesus said to them, "Be careful and guard against all kinds of greed. Life is not measured by how much one owns."

[16]Then Jesus told this story: "There was a rich man who had some land, which grew a good crop. [17]He thought to himself, 'What will I do? I have no place to keep all my crops.' [18]Then he said, 'This is what I will do: I will tear down my barns and build bigger ones, and there I will store all my grain and other goods. [19]Then I can say to myself, "I have enough good things stored to last for many years. Rest, eat, drink, and enjoy life!"'

[20]"But God said to him, 'Foolish man! Tonight your life will be taken from you. So who will get those things you have prepared for yourself?'

[21]"This is how it will be for those who store up things for themselves and are not rich toward God."

Don't Worry

[22]Jesus said to his followers, "So I tell you, don't worry about the food you need to live, or about the clothes you need for your body. [23]Life is more than food, and the body is more than clothes. [24]Look at the birds. They don't plant or harvest, they don't have storerooms or barns, but God feeds them. And you are worth much more than birds. [25]You cannot add any time to your life by worrying about it. [26]If you cannot do even the little things, then why worry about the big things? [27]Consider how the lilies grow; they don't work or make clothes for themselves. But I tell you that even Solomon with his riches was not dressed as beautifully as one of these flowers. [28]God clothes the grass in the field, which is alive today but tomorrow is thrown into the fire. So how much more will God clothe you? Don't have so little faith! [29]Don't always think about what you will eat or what you will drink, and don't keep worrying. [30]All the people in the world are trying to get these things, and your Father knows you need them. [31]But seek God's kingdom, and all your other needs will be met as well.

Don't Trust in Money

[32]"Don't fear, little flock, because your Father wants to give you the kingdom. [33]Sell your possessions and give to the poor. Get for yourselves purses that will not wear out, the treasure in heaven that never runs out, where thieves can't steal and moths can't destroy. [34]Your heart will be where your treasure is.

Always Be Ready

[35]"Be dressed, ready for service, and have your lamps shining. [36]Be like servants who are waiting for their master to come home from a wedding party. When he comes and knocks, the servants immediately open the door for him. [37]They will be blessed when their master comes home, because he sees that they were watching for him. I tell you the truth, the master will dress himself to serve and tell the servants to sit at the table, and he will serve them. [38]Those servants will be blessed when he comes in and finds them still waiting, even if it is midnight or later.

[39]"Remember this: If the owner of the house knew what time a thief was coming, he would not allow the thief to enter his house. [40]So you also must be ready, because the Son of Man will come at a time when you don't expect him!"

God has made us what we are. In Christ Jesus, God made us to do good works, which God planned in advance for us to live our lives doing. —*Ephesians 2:10*

march

Go for a walk with someone you want to know better. 1	Switch shampoo and conditioner to revitalize your hair. 2	3	4	It's Women's History Month. Read up on Joan of Arc. 5
Bake brownies for a neighbor. 6	7	8	Daylight Saving Time begins on the 2nd Sunday of March— jump ahead 1 hour! 9	10
11	Add some extra fresh fruit to your diet. 12	13	Become involved! Check out Big Brothers Big Sisters www.bbbsa.org 14	It's March Madness. Enjoy a basketball game on TV with some girlfriends. 15
Pray for your country today. 16	17	Make a list of 3 prayers God has answered recently. 18	19	Read the Book of 1 John. What did you learn about love? 20
Ask yourself: *Am I keeping my New Year's resolutions?* 21	Send a "just because" e-card to 3 friends. 22	23	24	Treat yourself to a manicure or pedicure. 25
26	Join a community volleyball league. 27	28	Look up an old friend you haven't seen in a while. 29	Pray for a person of influence: it's Warren Beatty's birthday. 30
Write a letter to God thanking him for who he is. 31				

Savvy Chef

Buyer Beware!

Do you know what's in the milk you buy? How about poultry? Breakfast meats? If you're not a label reader, now's the time to start this healthful habit. Hormones and antibiotics used on many farms as well as additives like nitrites and other preservatives don't do you any favors. Many brands of milk, meats, and processed foods are loaded with them. However, a well-stocked grocery store likely will carry organic alternatives and other natural varieties of common foods. Remember—you've got only one body and one lifetime to keep it running at its peak.

Who Is the Trusted Servant?

41Peter said, "Lord, did you tell this story to us or to all people?"

42The Lord said, "Who is the wise and trusted servant that the master trusts to give the other servants their food at the right time? 43When the master comes and finds the servant doing his work, the servant will be blessed. 44I tell you the truth, the master will choose that servant to take care of everything he owns. 45But suppose the servant thinks to himself, 'My master will not come back soon,' and he begins to beat the other servants, men and women, and to eat and drink and get drunk. 46The master will come when that servant is not ready and is not expecting him. Then the master will cut him in pieces and send him away to be with the others who don't obey.

47"The servant who knows what his master wants but is not ready, or who does not do what the master wants, will be beaten with many blows! 48But the servant who does not know what his master wants and does things that should be punished will be beaten with few blows. From everyone who has been given much, much will be demanded. And from the one trusted with much, much more will be expected.

Jesus Causes Division

49"I came to set fire to the world, and I wish it were already burning! 50I have a baptism[n] to suffer through, and I feel very troubled until it is over. 51Do you think I came to give peace to the earth? No, I tell you, I came to divide it. 52From now on, a family with five people will be divided, three against two, and two against three. 53They will be divided: father against son and son against father, mother against daughter and daughter against mother, mother-in-law against daughter-in-law and daughter-in-law against mother-in-law."

Understanding the Times

54Then Jesus said to the people, "When you see clouds coming up in the west, you say, 'It's going to rain,' and it happens. 55When you feel the wind begin to blow from the south, you say, 'It will be a hot day,' and it happens. 56Hypocrites! You know how to understand the appearance of the earth and sky. Why don't you understand what is happening now?

Settle Your Problems

57"Why can't you decide for yourselves what is right? 58If your enemy is taking you to court, try hard to settle it on the way. If you don't, your enemy might take you to the judge, and the judge might turn you over to the officer, and the officer might throw you into jail. 59I tell you, you will not get out of there until you have paid everything you owe."

Change Your Hearts

13 At that time some people were there who told Jesus that Pilate[n] had killed some people from Galilee while they were worshiping. He mixed their blood with the blood of the animals they were sacrificing to God. 2Jesus answered, "Do you think this happened to them because they were more sinful than all others from Galilee? 3No, I tell you. But unless you change your hearts and lives, you will be destroyed as they were! 4What about those eighteen people who died when the tower of Siloam fell on them? Do you think they were more sinful than all the others who live in Jerusalem? 5No, I tell you. But unless you change your hearts and lives, you will all be destroyed too!"

The Useless Tree

6Jesus told this story: "A man had a fig tree planted in his vineyard. He came looking for some fruit on the tree, but he found none. 7So the man said to his gardener, 'I have been looking for fruit on this tree for three years, but I never find any. Cut it down. Why should it waste the ground?' 8But the servant answered, 'Master, let the tree have one more year to produce fruit. Let me dig up the dirt around it and put on some fertilizer. 9If the tree produces fruit next year, good. But if not, you can cut it down.' "

Jesus Heals on the Sabbath

10Jesus was teaching in one of the synagogues on the Sabbath day. 11A woman

12:50 I . . . baptism Jesus was talking about the suffering he would soon go through. **13:1 Pilate** Pontius Pilate was the Roman governor of Judea from A.D. 26 to A.D. 36.

was there who, for eighteen years, had an evil spirit in her that made her crippled. Her back was always bent; she could not stand up straight. [12]When Jesus saw her, he called her over and said, "Woman, you are free from your sickness." [13]Jesus put his hands on her, and immediately she was able to stand up straight and began praising God.

[14]The synagogue leader was angry because Jesus healed on the Sabbath day. He said to the people, "There are six days when one has to work. So come to be healed on one of those days, and not on the Sabbath day."

[15]The Lord answered, "You hypocrites! Doesn't each of you untie your work animals and lead them to drink water every day—even on the Sabbath day? [16]This woman that I healed, a daughter of Abraham, has been held by Satan for eighteen years. Surely it is not wrong for her to be freed from her sickness on a Sabbath day!" [17]When Jesus said this, all of those who were criticizing him were ashamed, but the entire crowd rejoiced at all the wonderful things Jesus was doing.

Q&A

Q: Does what I watch on TV matter to God?

A: God cares deeply about all the stuff that goes on in your mind. What concepts and images does your favorite show bring to your thought life? You don't have to wonder what he wants you to be thinking about; he has already provided a list in Philippians 4:8. Do your entertainment choices bring thoughts about things that are "good and worthy of praise"? When the show ends, are you left with images that are "true and honorable and right and pure and beautiful and respected"? If so, then watch away! If not, then consider making wiser decisions about what enters your mind.

Stories of Mustard Seed and Yeast

[18]Then Jesus said, "What is God's kingdom like? What can I compare it with? [19]It is like a mustard seed that a man plants in his garden. The seed grows and becomes a tree, and the wild birds build nests in its branches."

[20]Jesus said again, "What can I compare God's kingdom with? [21]It is like yeast that a woman took and hid in a large tub of flour until it made all the dough rise."

The Narrow Door

[22]Jesus was teaching in every town and village as he traveled toward Jerusalem. [23]Someone said to Jesus, "Lord, will only a few people be saved?"

Jesus said, [24]"Try hard to enter through the narrow door, because many people will try to enter there, but they will not be able. [25]When the owner of the house gets up and closes the door, you can stand outside and knock on the door and say, 'Sir, open the door for us.' But he will answer, 'I don't know you or where you come from.' [26]Then you will say, 'We ate and drank with you, and you taught in the streets of our town.' [27]But he will say to you, 'I don't know you or where you come from. Go away from me, all you who do evil!' [28]You will cry and grind your teeth with pain when you see Abraham, Isaac, Jacob, and all the prophets in God's kingdom, but you yourselves thrown outside. [29]People will come from the east, west, north, and south and will sit down at the table in the kingdom of God. [30]There are those who are last now who will be first in the future. And there are those who are first now who will be last in the future."

Jesus Will Die in Jerusalem

[31]At that time some Pharisees came to Jesus and said, "Go away from here! Herod wants to kill you!"

[32]Jesus said to them, "Go tell that fox Herod, 'Today and tomorrow I am forcing demons out and healing people. Then, on the third day, I will reach my goal.' [33]Yet I must be on my way today and tomorrow and the next day. Surely it cannot be right for a prophet to be killed anywhere except in Jerusalem.

[34]"Jerusalem, Jerusalem! You kill the prophets and stone to death those who are sent to you. Many times I wanted to gather your people as a hen gathers her chicks under her wings, but you would not let me. [35]Now your house is left completely empty. I tell you, you will not see me until that time when you will say, 'God bless the One who comes in the name of the Lord.' "[n]

Healing on the Sabbath

14 On a Sabbath day, when Jesus went to eat at the home of a leading Pharisee, the people were watching Jesus very closely. [2]And in front of him was a man with dropsy.[n] [3]Jesus said to the Pharisees and experts on the law, "Is it right or wrong to heal on the Sabbath day?" [4]But they would not answer his question. So Jesus took the man, healed him, and sent him away. [5]Jesus said to the Pharisees and teachers of the law, "If your child[n] or ox falls into a well on

13:35 'God . . . Lord.' Quotation from Psalm 118:26. **14:2 dropsy** A sickness that causes the body to swell larger and larger. **14:5 child** Some Greek copies read "donkey."

the Sabbath day, will you not pull him out quickly?" [6]And they could not answer him.

Don't Make Yourself Important

[7]When Jesus noticed that some of the guests were choosing the best places to sit, he told this story: [8]"When someone invites you to a wedding feast, don't take the most important seat, because someone more important than you may have been invited. [9]The host, who invited both of you, will come to you and say, 'Give this person your seat.' Then you will be embarrassed and will have to move to the last place. [10]So when you are invited, go sit in a seat that is not important. When the host comes to you, he may say, 'Friend, move up here to a more important place.' Then all the other guests will respect you. [11]All who make themselves great will be made humble, but those who make themselves humble will be made great."

You Will Be Rewarded

[12]Then Jesus said to the man who had invited him, "When you give a lunch or a dinner, don't invite only your friends, your family, your other relatives, and your rich neighbors. At another time they will invite you to eat with them, and you will be repaid. [13]Instead, when you give a feast, invite the poor, the crippled, the lame, and the blind. [14]Then you will be blessed, because they have nothing and cannot pay you back. But you will be repaid when the good people rise from the dead."

A Story About a Big Banquet

[15]One of those at the table with Jesus heard these things and said to him, "Blessed are the people who will share in the meal in God's kingdom."

[16]Jesus said to him, "A man gave a big banquet and invited many people. [17]When it was time to eat, the man sent his servant to tell the guests, 'Come. Everything is ready.'

[18]"But all the guests made excuses. The first one said, 'I have just bought a field, and I must go look at it. Please excuse me.' [19]Another said, 'I have just bought five pairs of oxen; I must go and try them. Please excuse me.' [20]A third person said, 'I just got married; I can't come.' [21]So the servant returned and told his master what had happened. Then the master became angry and said, 'Go at once into the streets and alleys of the town, and bring in the poor, the crippled, the blind, and the lame.' [22]Later the servant said to him, 'Master, I did what you commanded, but we still have room.' [23]The master said to the servant, 'Go out to the roads and country lanes, and urge the people there to come so my house will be full. [24]I tell you, none of those whom I invited first will eat with me.' "

The Cost of Being Jesus' Follower

[25]Large crowds were traveling with Jesus, and he turned and said to them, [26]"If anyone comes to me but loves his father, mother, wife, children, brothers, or sisters—or even life—more than me, he cannot be my follower. [27]Whoever is not willing to carry his cross and follow me cannot be my follower. [28]If you want to build a tower, you first sit down and decide how much it will cost, to see if you have enough money to finish the job. [29]If you don't, you might lay the foundation, but you would not be able to finish. Then all who would see it would make fun of you, [30]saying, 'This person began to build but was not able to finish.'

[31]"If a king is going to fight another king, first he will sit down and plan. He will decide if he and his ten thousand soldiers can defeat the other king who has twenty thousand soldiers. [32]If he can't, then while the other king is still far away, he will send some people to speak to him and ask for peace. [33]In the same way, you must give up everything you have to be my follower.

Don't Lose Your Influence

[34]"Salt is good, but if it loses its salty taste, you cannot make it salty again. [35]It is no good for the soil or for manure; it is thrown away.

"Let those with ears use them and listen."

A Lost Sheep, a Lost Coin

15 The tax collectors and sinners all came to listen to Jesus. [2]But the Pharisees and the teachers of the law began to complain: "Look, this man welcomes sinners and even eats with them."

[3]Then Jesus told them this story: [4]"Suppose one of you has a hundred sheep but loses one of them. Then he will leave the

all about MEN

Avoiding the Savior Syndrome

Do you know a gal who habitually attracts the wrong guy, excusing his bad behavior or claiming he needs her? She probably has some traits of the "savior syndrome," the desire to be the long-awaited heroine who saves her man from his troubled ways. But trying to "fix" another person can lead to disaster. True, God refines us through relationships, but only he is capable of being anyone's all in all. Studying his Word and heeding wise counsel can open our eyes to unhealthy relationship patterns. When we know him as our first love and trust him as our healer and provider, we can attract healthy relationships. A vital connection with Jesus, our only Savior, frees us from mistaking ourselves as anyone else's.

other ninety-nine sheep in the open field and go out and look for the lost sheep until he finds it. [5]And when he finds it, he happily puts it on his shoulders [6]and goes home. He calls to his friends and neighbors and says, 'Be happy with me because I found my lost sheep.' [7]In the same way, I tell you there is more joy in heaven over one sinner who changes his heart and life, than over ninety-nine good people who don't need to change.

[8]"Suppose a woman has ten silver coins,[n] but loses one. She will light a lamp, sweep the house, and look carefully for the coin until she finds it. [9]And when she finds it, she will call her friends and neighbors and say, 'Be happy with me because I have found the coin that I lost.' [10]In the same way, there is joy in the presence of the angels of God when one sinner changes his heart and life."

Luke 15:20

Everyone has something they could feel ashamed about. Maybe you even feel so much shame that you think no one would still love you if you were exposed. Some things just seem too terrible—beyond forgiveness. But the Bible paints a different picture.

Luke 15 gives a portrait of God's love for us. The "prodigal son" breaks his father's heart, wastes his money and life, and hits rock bottom. He finally returns home, a broken and repentant man. The story focuses mostly on the rebellious son, but the real hero is the father. In case you haven't realized it, each of us is like a child that has run away from our heavenly Father. We've rejected him, dishonored him, and taken his blessings for granted. But God's love and grace far outweigh every shameful thing we've ever done. And it's not as if he's sitting up in heaven waiting for us to get our acts together . . . he's on the lookout, ready to run to us with open arms full of forgiveness and love.

Where are you right now? Are you running? Lost and rebellious? Are you far from home, hoping against hope that God might take you back? Be encouraged by this story! God's love and forgiveness, which can erase our shame, is available for everyone who comes home to him.

The Son Who Left Home

[11]Then Jesus said, "A man had two sons. [12]The younger son said to his father, 'Give me my share of the property.' So the father divided the property between his two sons. [13]Then the younger son gathered up all that was his and traveled far away to another country. There he wasted his money in foolish living. [14]After he had spent everything, a time came when there was no food anywhere in the country, and the son was poor and hungry. [15]So he got a job with one of the citizens there who sent the son into the fields to feed pigs. [16]The son was so hungry that he wanted to eat the pods the pigs were eating, but no one gave him anything. [17]When he realized what he was doing, he thought, 'All of my father's servants have plenty of food. But I am here, almost dying with hunger. [18]I will leave and return to my father and say to him, "Father, I have sinned against God and against you. [19]I am no longer worthy to be called your son, but let me be like one of your servants."' [20]So the son left and went to his father.

"While the son was still a long way off, his father saw him and felt sorry for his son. So the father ran to him and hugged and kissed him. [21]The son said, 'Father, I have sinned against God and against you. I am no longer worthy to be called your son.'[n] [22]But the father said to his servants, 'Hurry! Bring the best clothes and put them on him. Also, put a ring on his finger and sandals on his feet. [23]And get our fat calf and kill it so we can have a feast and celebrate. [24]My son was dead, but now he is alive again! He was lost, but now he is found!' So they began to celebrate.

[25]"The older son was in the field, and as he came closer to the house, he heard the sound of music and dancing. [26]So he called to one of the servants and asked what all this meant. [27]The servant said, 'Your brother has come back, and your father killed the fat calf, because your brother came home safely.' [28]The older son was angry and would not go in to the feast. So his father went out and begged him to come in. [29]But the older son said to his father, 'I have served you like a slave for many years and have always obeyed your commands. But you never gave me even a young goat to have at a feast with my friends. [30]But your other son, who wasted all your money on prostitutes, comes home, and you kill the fat calf for him!' [31]The father said to him, 'Son, you are always with me, and all that I have is yours. [32]We had to celebrate and be happy because your brother was dead, but now he is alive. He was lost, but now he is found.'"

True Wealth

16 Jesus also said to his followers, "Once there was a rich man who had a manager to take care of his business. This manager was accused of cheating him. [2]So he called the

15:8 silver coins Roman denarii. One coin was the average pay for one day's work. **15:21 son** Some Greek copies continue, "but let me be like one of your servants" (see verse 19).

Be Still & KNOW

Prayer Tracker

In times of hardship or sorrow, remembering the faithfulness and power God showed in the past can bring great hope. The Israelites practiced this by regularly revisiting the story of their deliverance from Egypt. You can follow their example by keeping a prayer tracker.

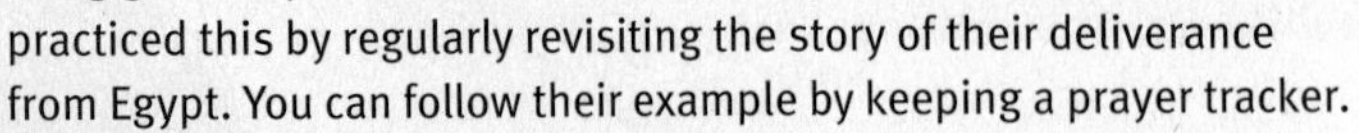

Similar to a prayer list, it's a written collection of requests and concerns that you bring before the Lord. But the tracker goes beyond simply asking to full-on expecting. Leave a space after each entry so you can track updates and answers. Then you can look back and see how faithful God is in responding to your prayers. It just may surprise you, and it's guaranteed to encourage you!

manager in and said to him, 'What is this I hear about you? Give me a report of what you have done with my money, because you can't be my manager any longer.' [3]The manager thought to himself, 'What will I do since my master is taking my job away from me? I am not strong enough to dig ditches, and I am ashamed to beg. [4]I know what I'll do so that when I lose my job people will welcome me into their homes.'

[5]"So the manager called in everyone who owed the master any money. He asked the first one, 'How much do you owe?' [6]He answered, 'Eight hundred gallons of olive oil.' The manager said to him, 'Take your bill, sit down quickly, and write four hundred gallons.' [7]Then the manager asked another one, 'How much do you owe?' He answered, 'One thousand bushels of wheat.' Then the manager said to him, 'Take your bill and write eight hundred bushels.' [8]So, the master praised the dishonest manager for being clever. Yes, worldly people are more clever with their own kind than spiritual people are.

[9]"I tell you, make friends for yourselves using worldly riches so that when those riches are gone, you will be welcomed in those homes that continue forever. [10]Whoever can be trusted with a little can also be trusted with a lot, and whoever is dishonest with a little is dishonest with a lot. [11]If you cannot be trusted with worldly riches, then who will trust you with true riches? [12]And if you cannot be trusted with things that belong to someone else, who will give you things of your own?

[13]"No servant can serve two masters. The servant will hate one master and love the other, or will follow one master and refuse to follow the other. You cannot serve both God and worldly riches."

God's Law Cannot Be Changed

[14]The Pharisees, who loved money, were listening to all these things and made fun of Jesus. [15]He said to them, "You make yourselves look good in front of people, but God knows what is really in your hearts. What is important to people is hateful in God's sight.

[16]"The law of Moses and the writings of the prophets were preached until John[n] came. Since then the Good News about the kingdom of God is being told, and everyone tries to enter it by force. [17]It would be easier for heaven and earth to pass away than for the smallest part of a letter in the law to be changed.

Divorce and Remarriage

[18]"If a man divorces his wife and marries another woman, he is guilty of adultery, and the man who marries a divorced woman is also guilty of adultery."

The Rich Man and Lazarus

[19]Jesus said, "There was a rich man who always dressed in the finest clothes and lived in luxury every day. [20]And a very poor man named Lazarus, whose body was covered with sores, was laid at the rich man's gate. [21]He wanted to eat only the small pieces of food that fell from the rich man's table. And the dogs would come and lick his sores. [22]Later, Lazarus died, and the angels carried him to the arms of Abraham. The rich man died, too, and was buried. [23]In the place of the dead, he was in much pain. The rich man saw Abraham far away with Lazarus at his side. [24]He called, 'Father Abraham, have mercy on me! Send Lazarus to dip his finger in water and cool my tongue, because I am suffering in this fire!' [25]But Abraham said, 'Child, remember when you were alive you had the good things in life, but bad things happened to Lazarus. Now he is comforted here, and you are suffering. [26]Besides, there is a big pit between you and us, so no one can cross over to you, and no one can leave there and come here.' [27]The rich man said, 'Father, then please send Lazarus to my father's house. [28]I have five brothers, and Lazarus could warn them so that they will not come to this place of pain.' [29]But Abraham said, 'They have the law of Moses and the writings of the prophets; let them learn from them.' [30]The rich man said, 'No, father Abraham! If someone goes to them from the dead, they would believe and change their hearts and lives.' [31]But Abraham said to him, 'If they will not listen to Moses and the prophets, they will not listen to someone who comes back from the dead.' "

16:16 John John the Baptist, who preached to people about Christ's coming (Matthew 3, Luke 3).

fun facts

In 2005, *women* held 16.4% of corporate officer positions (those appointed or elected by the board), up from 15.7% in 2002.

(Catalyst.org)

Sin and Forgiveness

17 Jesus said to his followers, "Things that cause people to sin will happen, but how terrible for the person who causes them to happen! [2]It would be better for you to be thrown into the sea with a large stone around your neck than to cause one of these little ones to sin. [3]So be careful!

"If another follower sins, warn him, and if he is sorry and stops sinning, forgive him. [4]If he sins against you seven times in one day and says that he is sorry each time, forgive him."

How Big Is Your Faith?

[5]The apostles said to the Lord, "Give us more faith!"

[6]The Lord said, "If your faith were the size of a mustard seed, you could say to this mulberry tree, 'Dig yourself up and plant yourself in the sea,' and it would obey you.

Be Good Servants

[7]"Suppose one of you has a servant who has been plowing the ground or caring for the sheep. When the servant comes in from working in the field, would you say, 'Come in and sit down to eat'? [8]No, you would say to him, 'Prepare something for me to eat. Then get yourself ready and serve me. After I finish eating and drinking, you can eat.' [9]The servant does not get any special thanks for doing what his master commanded. [10]It is the same with you. When you have done everything you are told to do, you should say, 'We are unworthy servants; we have only done the work we should do.' "

Be Thankful

[11]While Jesus was on his way to Jerusalem, he was going through the area between Samaria and Galilee. [12]As he came into a small town, ten men who had a skin disease met him there. They did not come close to Jesus [13]but called to him, "Jesus! Master! Have mercy on us!"

[14]When Jesus saw the men, he said, "Go and show yourselves to the priests."[n]

As the ten men were going, they were healed. [15]When one of them saw that he was healed, he went back to Jesus, praising God in a loud voice. [16]Then he bowed down at Jesus' feet and thanked him. (And this man was a Samaritan.) [17]Jesus said, "Weren't ten men healed? Where are the other nine? [18]Is this Samaritan the only one who came back to thank God?" [19]Then Jesus said to him, "Stand up and go on your way. You were healed because you believed."

God's Kingdom Is Within You

[20]Some of the Pharisees asked Jesus, "When will the kingdom of God come?"

Jesus answered, "God's kingdom is coming, but not in a way that you will be able to see with your eyes. [21]People will not say, 'Look, here it is!' or, 'There it is!' because God's kingdom is within[n] you."

[22]Then Jesus said to his followers, "The time will come when you will want very much to see one of the days of the Son of Man. But you will not see it. [23]People will say to you, 'Look, there he is!' or, 'Look, here he is!' Stay where you are; don't go away and search.

When Jesus Comes Again

[24]"When the Son of Man comes again, he will shine like lightning, which flashes across the sky and lights it up from one side to the other. [25]But first he must suffer many things and be rejected by the people of this time. [26]When the Son of Man comes again, it will be as it was when Noah lived. [27]People were eating, drinking, marrying, and giving their children to be married until the day Noah entered the boat. Then the flood came and killed them all. [28]It will be the same as during the time of Lot. People were eating, drinking, buying, selling, planting, and building. [29]But the day Lot left Sodom,[n] fire and sulfur rained down from the sky and killed them

LIFEISSUES

History's Legacy

Someday, today will be history. It's interesting to think that one generation's legacy is the next generation's history. Like an endless thread, God connects the past and the future. "Who has controlled history since the beginning? I, the Lord, am the one. I was here at the beginning, and I will be here when all things are finished" (Isaiah 41:4). Like our ancestors before us, our actions today impact the future. Right now we're creating content for future history books and stories around the family table. Will your life's story help others see Christ more clearly?

17:14 show . . . priests The Law of Moses said a priest must say when a person with a skin disease became well. **17:21 within** Or "among." **17:29 Sodom** City that God destroyed because the people were so evil.

RELATIONSHIPS

Competition in Relationships

Healthy competition has its place in life, but it can spell disaster when it runs amuck in relationships. Think about what competition's all about: winning, reaching the top, and being the best. A competitive nature seeks to win for itself, which means that unhealthy competition in a relationship introduces selfishness into the mix. An attitude of one-upping someone doesn't have that person's best—or the relationship's best—at heart. Healthy relationships focus on helping the other person be his or her best and saying "words that will help others become stronger" (Ephesians 4:29). Now that's a winning strategy!

all. [30]This is how it will be when the Son of Man comes again.

[31]"On that day, a person who is on the roof and whose belongings are in the house should not go inside to get them. A person who is in the field should not go back home. [32]Remember Lot's wife.[n] [33]Those who try to keep their lives will lose them. But those who give up their lives will save them. [34]I tell you, on that night two people will be sleeping in one bed; one will be taken and the other will be left. [35]There will be two women grinding grain together; one will be taken, and the other will be left. [[36]Two people will be in the field. One will be taken, and the other will be left.]"[n]

[37]The followers asked Jesus, "Where will this be, Lord?"

Jesus answered, "Where there is a dead body, there the vultures will gather."

God Will Answer His People

18 Then Jesus used this story to teach his followers that they should always pray and never lose hope. [2]"In a certain town there was a judge who did not respect God or care about people. [3]In that same town there was a widow who kept coming to this judge, saying, 'Give me my rights against my enemy.' [4]For a while the judge refused to help her. But afterwards, he thought to himself, 'Even though I don't respect God or care about people, [5]I will see that she gets her rights. Otherwise she will continue to bother me until I am worn out.' "

[6]The Lord said, "Listen to what the unfair judge said. [7]God will always give what is right to his people who cry to him night and day, and he will not be slow to answer them. [8]I tell you, God will help his people quickly. But when the Son of Man comes again, will he find those on earth who believe in him?"

Being Right with God

[9]Jesus told this story to some people who thought they were very good and looked down on everyone else: [10]"A Pharisee and a tax collector both went to the Temple to pray. [11]The Pharisee stood alone and prayed, 'God, I thank you that I am not like other people who steal, cheat, or take part in adultery, or even like this tax collector. [12]I fast[n] twice a week, and I give one-tenth of everything I get!'

[13]"The tax collector, standing at a distance, would not even look up to heaven. But he beat on his chest because he was so sad. He said, 'God, have mercy on me, a sinner.' [14]I tell you, when this man went home, he was right with God, but the Pharisee was not. All who make themselves great will be made humble, but all who make themselves humble will be made great."

Who Will Enter God's Kingdom?

[15]Some people brought even their babies to Jesus so he could touch them. When the followers saw this, they told them to stop. [16]But Jesus called for the children, saying, "Let the little children come to me. Don't stop them, because the kingdom of God belongs to people who are like these children. [17]I tell you the truth, you must accept the kingdom of God as if you were a child, or you will never enter it."

A Rich Man's Question

[18]A certain leader asked Jesus, "Good Teacher, what must I do to have life forever?"

[19]Jesus said to him, "Why do you call me good? Only God is good. [20]You know the commands: 'You must not be guilty of adultery. You must not murder anyone. You must not steal. You must not tell lies about your neighbor. Honor your father and mother.' "[n]

[21]But the leader said, "I have obeyed all these commands since I was a boy."

[22]When Jesus heard this, he said to him,

17:32 Lot's wife A story about what happened to Lot's wife is found in Genesis 19:15–17, 26. **17:36 Two . . . left.** Some Greek copies do not contain the bracketed text. **18:12 fast** The people would give up eating for a special time of prayer and worship to God. It was also done to show sadness and disappointment. **18:20 'You . . . mother.'** Quotation from Exodus 20:12–16; Deuteronomy 5:16–20.

"There is still one more thing you need to do. Sell everything you have and give it to the poor, and you will have treasure in heaven. Then come and follow me." [23]But when the man heard this, he became very sad, because he was very rich.

[24]Jesus looked at him and said, "It is very hard for rich people to enter the kingdom of God. [25]It is easier for a camel to go through the eye of a needle than for a rich person to enter the kingdom of God."

Who Can Be Saved?

[26]When the people heard this, they asked, "Then who can be saved?"

[27]Jesus answered, "The things impossible for people are possible for God."

[28]Peter said, "Look, we have left everything and followed you."

[29]Jesus said, "I tell you the truth, all those who have left houses, wives, brothers, parents, or children for the kingdom of God [30]will get much more in this life. And in the age that is coming, they will have life forever."

Jesus Will Rise from the Dead

[31]Then Jesus took the twelve apostles aside and said to them, "We are going to Jerusalem. Everything the prophets wrote about the Son of Man will happen. [32]He will be turned over to those who are evil. They will laugh at him, insult him, spit on him, [33]beat him with whips, and kill him. But on the third day, he will rise to life again." [34]The apostles did not understand this; the meaning was hidden from them, and they did not realize what was said.

Jesus Heals a Blind Man

[35]As Jesus came near the city of Jericho, a blind man was sitting beside the road, begging. [36]When he heard the people coming down the road, he asked, "What is happening?"

[37]They told him, "Jesus, from Nazareth, is going by."

[38]The blind man cried out, "Jesus, Son of David, have mercy on me!"

[39]The people leading the group warned the blind man to be quiet. But the blind man shouted even more, "Son of David, have mercy on me!"

[40]Jesus stopped and ordered the blind man to be brought to him. When he came near, Jesus asked him, [41]"What do you want me to do for you?"

He said, "Lord, I want to see."

[42]Jesus said to him, "Then see. You are healed because you believed."

[43]At once the man was able to see, and he followed Jesus, thanking God. All the people who saw this praised God.

Zacchaeus Meets Jesus

19 Jesus was going through the city of Jericho. [2]A man was there named Zacchaeus, who was a very important tax collector, and he was wealthy. [3]He wanted to see who Jesus was, but he was not able because he was too short to see above the crowd. [4]He ran ahead to a place where Jesus would come, and he climbed a sycamore tree so he could see him. [5]When Jesus came to that place, he looked up and said to him, "Zacchaeus, hurry and come down! I must stay at your house today."

[6]Zacchaeus came down quickly and welcomed him gladly. [7]All the people saw this and began to complain, "Jesus is staying with a sinner!"

[8]But Zacchaeus stood and said to the Lord, "I will give half of my possessions to the poor. And if I have cheated anyone, I will pay back four times more."

[9]Jesus said to him, "Salvation has come to this house today, because this man also belongs to the family of Abraham. [10]The Son of Man came to find lost people and save them."

A Story About Three Servants

[11]As the people were listening to this, Jesus told them a story because he was near Jerusalem and they thought God's kingdom would appear immediately. [12]He said: "A very important man went to a country far away to be made a king and then to return home. [13]So he called ten of his servants and gave a coin[n] to each servant. He said, 'Do business with this money until I get back.' [14]But the people in the kingdom hated the man. So they sent a group to follow him and say, 'We don't want this man to be our king.'

[15]"But the man became king. When he returned home, he said, 'Call those servants who have my money so I can know how much they earned with it.'

[16]"The first servant came and said, 'Sir, I earned ten coins with the one you gave me.' [17]The king said to the servant, 'Excellent! You are a good servant. Since I can trust you with small things, I will let you rule over ten of my cities.'

[18]"The second servant said, 'Sir, I earned five coins with your one.' [19]The

Brains or Beauty?

If you had to choose just one of the two to ask God for, which would it be? It's an age-old discussion. People have been debating and contemplating it for centuries. King David, for example, probably would've chosen beauty. "No way!" you think. But wait! It's a different aspect of beauty than you may be thinking. He said if he could ask for only one thing, it would be to see the *LORD's beauty* (Psalm 27:4). That's beauty in its purest, most awesome form. Reflecting God's splendor in your life shows you have both brains *and* beauty.

19:13 coin A Greek "mina." One mina was enough money to pay a person for working three months.

Luke 19:10

It's easy to get discouraged by what we see in ourselves. We have a deep desire to be loved, but sometimes it's easy to look in the mirror or peer into our hearts and think, *Who could ever love me?* We have this mistaken impression that we must become "worthy" of love.

But Jesus just doesn't work that way! Luke tells us he "came to find lost people and save them" (Luke 19:10). He wasn't out to find the exceptionally good or beautiful people. He was seeking people who realized how lost and broken they were without him.

This says so much about God's love. First, it doesn't depend on anything we do. The people Jesus loved didn't initially recognize him as the Messiah they needed so desperately. And second, Jesus' love is the reason he saves us. Just like we can't earn his love, we can't earn salvation.

Salvation is the story of God's love for the lost. It's not about flawless people reaching out to God or attractive people earning his attention; it's about God reaching down to ugly sinners and making them into his own beautiful children. What relief and comfort that fact brings! Our relationship with God doesn't depend on our own perfection—it depends on his never-failing love.

king said to this servant, 'You can rule over five cities.'

[20]"Then another servant came in and said to the king, 'Sir, here is your coin which I wrapped in a piece of cloth and hid. [21]I was afraid of you, because you are a hard man. You even take money that you didn't earn and gather food that you didn't plant.' [22]Then the king said to the servant, 'I will condemn you by your own words, you evil servant. You knew that I am a hard man, taking money that I didn't earn and gathering food that I didn't plant. [23]Why then didn't you put my money in the bank? Then when I came back, my money would have earned some interest.'

[24]"The king said to the men who were standing by, 'Take the coin away from this servant and give it to the servant who earned ten coins.' [25]They said, 'But sir, that servant already has ten coins.' [26]The king said, 'Those who have will be given more, but those who do not have anything will have everything taken away from them. [27]Now where are my enemies who didn't want me to be king? Bring them here and kill them before me.' "

Jesus Enters Jerusalem as a King

[28]After Jesus said this, he went on toward Jerusalem. [29]As Jesus came near Bethphage and Bethany, towns near the hill called the Mount of Olives, he sent out two of his followers. [30]He said, "Go to the town you can see there. When you enter it, you will find a colt tied there, which no one has ever ridden. Untie it and bring it here to me. [31]If anyone asks you why you are untying it, say that the Master needs it."

[32]The two followers went into town and found the colt just as Jesus had told them. [33]As they were untying it, its owners came out and asked the followers, "Why are you untying our colt?"

[34]The followers answered, "The Master needs it." [35]So they brought it to Jesus, threw their coats on the colt's back, and put Jesus on it. [36]As Jesus rode toward Jerusalem, others spread their coats on the road before him.

[37]As he was coming close to Jerusalem, on the way down the Mount of Olives, the whole crowd of followers began joyfully shouting praise to God for all the miracles they had seen. [38]They said,

"God bless the king who comes in the
name of the Lord!
Psalm 118:26

There is peace in heaven and
glory to God!"

[39]Some of the Pharisees in the crowd said to Jesus, "Teacher, tell your followers not to say these things."

[40]But Jesus answered, "I tell you, if my followers didn't say these things, then the stones would cry out."

Jesus Cries for Jerusalem

[41]As Jesus came near Jerusalem, he saw the city and cried for it, [42]saying, "I wish you knew today what would bring you peace. But now it is hidden from you. [43]The time is coming when your enemies will build a wall around you and will hold you in on all sides. [44]They will destroy you and all your people, and not one stone will be left on another. All this will happen because you did not recognize the time when God came to save you."

Jesus Goes to the Temple

[45]Jesus went into the Temple and began to throw out the people who were selling things there. [46]He said, "It is written in the Scriptures, 'My Temple will be a house for prayer.'[n] But you have changed it into a 'hideout for robbers'!"[n]

19:46 'My Temple . . . prayer.' Quotation from Isaiah 56:7. **19:46 'hideout for robbers'** Quotation from Jeremiah 7:11.

[47]Jesus taught in the Temple every day. The leading priests, the experts on the law, and some of the leaders of the people wanted to kill Jesus. [48]But they did not know how they could do it, because all the people were listening closely to him.

Jewish Leaders Question Jesus

20 One day Jesus was in the Temple, teaching the people and telling them the Good News. The leading priests, teachers of the law, and elders came up to talk with him, [2]saying, "Tell us what authority you have to do these things? Who gave you this authority?"

[3]Jesus answered, "I will also ask you a question. Tell me: [4]When John baptized people, was that authority from God or just from other people?"

[5]They argued about this, saying, "If we answer, 'John's baptism was from God,' Jesus will say, 'Then why did you not believe him?' [6]But if we say, 'It was from other people,' all the people will stone us to death, because they believe John was a prophet." [7]So they answered that they didn't know where it came from.

[8]Jesus said to them, "Then I won't tell you what authority I have to do these things."

A Story About God's Son

[9]Then Jesus told the people this story: "A man planted a vineyard and leased it to some farmers. Then he went away for a long time. [10]When it was time for the grapes to be picked, he sent a servant to the farmers to get some of the grapes. But they beat the servant and sent him away empty-handed. [11]Then he sent another servant. They beat this servant also, and showed no respect for him, and sent him away empty-handed. [12]So the man sent a third servant. The farmers wounded him and threw him out. [13]The owner of the vineyard said, 'What will I do now? I will send my son whom I love. Maybe they will respect him.' [14]But when the farmers saw the son, they said to each other, 'This son will inherit the vineyard. If we kill him, it will be ours.' [15]So the farmers threw the son out of the vineyard and killed him.

"What will the owner of this vineyard do to them? [16]He will come and kill those farmers and will give the vineyard to other farmers."

When the people heard this story, they said, "Let this never happen!"

[17]But Jesus looked at them and said, "Then what does this verse mean:

'The stone that the builders rejected
became the cornerstone'?

Psalm 118:22

[18]Everyone who falls on that stone will be broken, and the person on whom it falls, that person will be crushed!"

[19]The teachers of the law and the leading priests wanted to arrest Jesus at once, because they knew the story was about them. But they were afraid of what the people would do.

Is It Right to Pay Taxes or Not?

[20]So they watched Jesus and sent some spies who acted as if they were sincere. They wanted to trap Jesus in saying something wrong so they could hand him over to the authority and power of the governor. [21]So the spies asked Jesus, "Teacher, we know that what you say and teach is true. You pay no attention to who people are, and you always teach the truth about God's way. [22]Tell us, is it right for us to pay taxes to Caesar or not?"

[23]But Jesus, knowing they were trying to trick him, said, [24]"Show me a coin. Whose image and name are on it?"

They said, "Caesar's."

[25]Jesus said to them, "Then give to Caesar the things that are Caesar's, and give to God the things that are God's."

[26]So they were not able to trap Jesus in anything he said in the presence of the people. And being amazed at his answer, they became silent.

Some Sadducees Try to Trick Jesus

[27]Some Sadducees, who believed people would not rise from the dead, came to Jesus. [28]They asked, "Teacher, Moses wrote that if a man's brother dies and leaves a wife but no children, then that man must marry the widow and have children for his brother. [29]Once there were seven brothers. The first brother married and died, but had no children. [30]Then the second brother married the widow, and he died. [31]And the third brother married the widow, and he died. The same thing happened with all seven brothers; they died and had no children. [32]Finally, the woman died also. [33]Since all seven brothers had married her, whose wife will she be when people rise from the dead?"

[34]Jesus said to them, "On earth, people marry and are given to someone to marry. [35]But those who will be worthy to be raised from the dead and live again will not marry, nor will they be given to someone to marry. [36]In that life they are like

HE SAID ↙ ↗ SHE SAID

What's your favorite thing about church?

He: Matching up needs with spiritual gifts

She: Learning more about God

virtue BUILDING: Purity

Have you ever thought about what "purity" really means for Christians? The real meaning is actually related to the idea of pure water or pure gold—something that is completely free from all contaminants.

A heart that's purely devoted to God will be free of desires for other things. If you want a pure heart, you can't have any immorality, sinful lusts, hatefulness, or pride thrown into the mix.

Being pure means having one purpose, one desire, and one love—God. Any sin in our lives immediately results in impurity. Having sin in your life is like drinking water that has dirt in it or having "gold" jewelry that's mostly made up of cheap metals—sin makes us filthy and worthless.

Scripture Breakdown
When David was dealing with impurity, he called on God's grace and forgiveness. Psalm 51 is one of his hallmark prayers, and in verse 10 he asks God to create in him a "pure heart." Romans 1:18–32 describes how impurity starts and where it leads. Second Corinthians 6:14—7:1 shows that good and evil can't coexist. If you want to contrast pure and impure living, check out these passages: Ephesians 4:22—5:20 and Colossians 3:1–10.

Build It into Your Life

- Purity is closely related to what you do (and what you don't do), but that's only part of it. You also need to have an inward attitude of purity—a heart that is completely devoted to God. Are you as concerned with having a pure heart as you are with looking pure? (Matthew 23:25–28)
- No matter how good you act, you can never be pure enough on your own to be God's friend and child. But Jesus' blood washes away our sins, and his purity covers us. Are you relying completely on him?
- Are you letting things you know are wrong contaminate your life? Are you trying to follow Jesus but still intentionally flirting with sin? Only a pure heart can be close to God.

angels and cannot die. They are children of God, because they have been raised from the dead. [37]Even Moses clearly showed that the dead are raised to life. When he wrote about the burning bush,[n] he said that the Lord is 'the God of Abraham, the God of Isaac, and the God of Jacob.'[n] [38]God is the God of the living, not the dead, because all people are alive to him."

[39]Some of the teachers of the law said, "Teacher, your answer was good." [40]No one was brave enough to ask him another question.

Is the Christ the Son of David?

[41]Then Jesus said, "Why do people say that the Christ is the Son of David? [42]In the book of Psalms, David himself says:

'The Lord said to my Lord,
"Sit by me at my right side,
[43] until I put your enemies under
your control." '[n] *Psalm 110:1*

[44]David calls the Christ 'Lord,' so how can the Christ be his son?"

Jesus Accuses Some Leaders

[45]While all the people were listening, Jesus said to his followers, [46]"Beware of the teachers of the law. They like to walk around wearing fancy clothes, and they love for people to greet them with respect in the marketplaces. They love to have the most important seats in the synagogues and at feasts. [47]But they cheat widows and steal their houses and then try to make themselves look good by saying long prayers. They will receive a greater punishment."

True Giving

21 As Jesus looked up, he saw some rich people putting their gifts into the Temple money box.[n] [2]Then he saw a poor widow putting two small copper coins into the box. [3]He said, "I tell you the truth, this poor widow gave more than all those rich people. [4]They gave only what they did not need. This woman is very poor, but she gave all she had to live on."

The Temple Will Be Destroyed

[5]Some people were talking about the Temple and how it was decorated with beautiful stones and gifts offered to God.

But Jesus said, [6]"As for these things you are looking at, the time will come when not one stone will be left on another. Every stone will be thrown down."

[7]They asked Jesus, "Teacher, when will these things happen? What will be the sign that they are about to take place?"

[8]Jesus said, "Be careful so you are not fooled. Many people will come in my name, saying, 'I am the One' and, 'The time has come!' But don't follow them. [9]When you hear about wars and riots, don't be afraid, because these things must happen first, but the end will come later."

[10]Then he said to them, "Nations will fight against other nations, and kingdoms against other kingdoms. [11]In various places there will be great earthquakes, sicknesses, and a lack of food. Fearful events and great signs will come from heaven.

[12]"But before all these things happen,

20:37 burning bush Read Exodus 3:1–12 in the Old Testament. **20:37 'the God of . . . Jacob'** These words are taken from Exodus 3:6. **20:43 until . . . control** Literally, "until I make your enemies a footstool for your feet." **21:1 money box** A special box in the Jewish place of worship where people put their gifts to God.

people will arrest you and treat you cruelly. They will judge you in their synagogues and put you in jail and force you to stand before kings and governors, because you follow me. [13]But this will give you an opportunity to tell about me. [14]Make up your minds not to worry ahead of time about what you will say. [15]I will give you the wisdom to say things that none of your enemies will be able to stand against or prove wrong. [16]Even your parents, brothers, relatives, and friends will turn against you, and they will kill some of you. [17]All people will hate you because you follow me. [18]But none of these things can really harm you. [19]By continuing to have faith you will save your lives.

Jerusalem Will Be Destroyed

[20]"When you see armies all around Jerusalem, you will know it will soon be destroyed. [21]At that time, the people in Judea should run away to the mountains. The people in Jerusalem must get out, and those who are near the city should not go in. [22]These are the days of punishment to bring about all that is written in the Scriptures. [23]How terrible it will be for women who are pregnant or have nursing babies! Great trouble will come upon this land, and God will be angry with these people. [24]They will be killed by the sword and taken as prisoners to all nations. Jerusalem will be crushed by non-Jewish people until their time is over.

Don't Fear

[25]"There will be signs in the sun, moon, and stars. On earth, nations will be afraid and confused because of the roar and fury of the sea. [26]People will be so afraid they will faint, wondering what is happening to the world, because the powers of the heavens will be shaken. [27]Then people will see the Son of Man coming in a cloud with power and great glory. [28]When these things begin to happen, look up and hold your heads high, because the time when God will free you is near!"

Jesus' Words Will Live Forever

[29]Then Jesus told this story: "Look at the fig tree and all the other trees. [30]When their leaves appear, you know that summer is near. [31]In the same way, when you see these things happening, you will know that God's kingdom is near.

[32]"I tell you the truth, all these things will happen while the people of this time are still living. [33]Earth and sky will be destroyed, but the words I have spoken will never be destroyed.

Be Ready All the Time

[34]"Be careful not to spend your time feasting, drinking, or worrying about worldly things. If you do, that day might come on you suddenly, [35]like a trap on all people on earth. [36]So be ready all the time. Pray that you will be strong enough to escape all these things that will happen and that you will be able to stand before the Son of Man."

[37]During the day, Jesus taught the people in the Temple, and at night he went out of the city and stayed on the Mount of Olives. [38]Every morning all the people got up early to go to the Temple to listen to him.

Judas Becomes an Enemy of Jesus

22 It was almost time for the Feast of Unleavened Bread, called the Passover Feast. [2]The leading priests and teachers of the law were trying to find a way to kill Jesus, because they were afraid of the people.

[3]Satan entered Judas Iscariot, one of Jesus' twelve apostles. [4]Judas went to the leading priests and some of the soldiers who guarded the Temple and talked to them about a way to hand Jesus over to them. [5]They were pleased and agreed to give Judas money. [6]He agreed and watched for the best time to hand Jesus over to them when he was away from the crowd.

Jesus Eats the Passover Meal

[7]The Day of Unleavened Bread came when the Passover lambs had to be sacrificed. [8]Jesus said to Peter and John, "Go and prepare the Passover meal for us to eat."

[9]They asked, "Where do you want us to prepare it?" [10]Jesus said to them, "After you go into the city, a man carrying a jar of water will meet you. Follow him into the house that he enters, [11]and tell the owner of the house, 'The Teacher says: "Where is the guest room in which I may eat the Passover meal with my followers?"' [12]Then he will show you a large, furnished room upstairs. Prepare the Passover meal there."

Health
Music as Medicine

It turns out that *music*, not laughter, may be the best medicine. Recent studies suggest that patients who crank up the radio after surgery require less pain medication than those who forego the tunes. Here's how it works: music activates pathways in the brain that release endorphins, which inhibit pain transmission. (This gives further credence to the idea that pain is, in fact, all in your head.) Whether you're a little bit country or a little bit rock 'n' roll, the benefits appear to be the same. In other words, the genre of music is not a factor. So instead of reaching for that bottle of aspirin the next time you feel an ache or pain, try popping in a praise CD. As Ephesians instructs, "Speak to each other with psalms, hymns, and spiritual songs, singing and making music in your hearts to the Lord" (5:19).

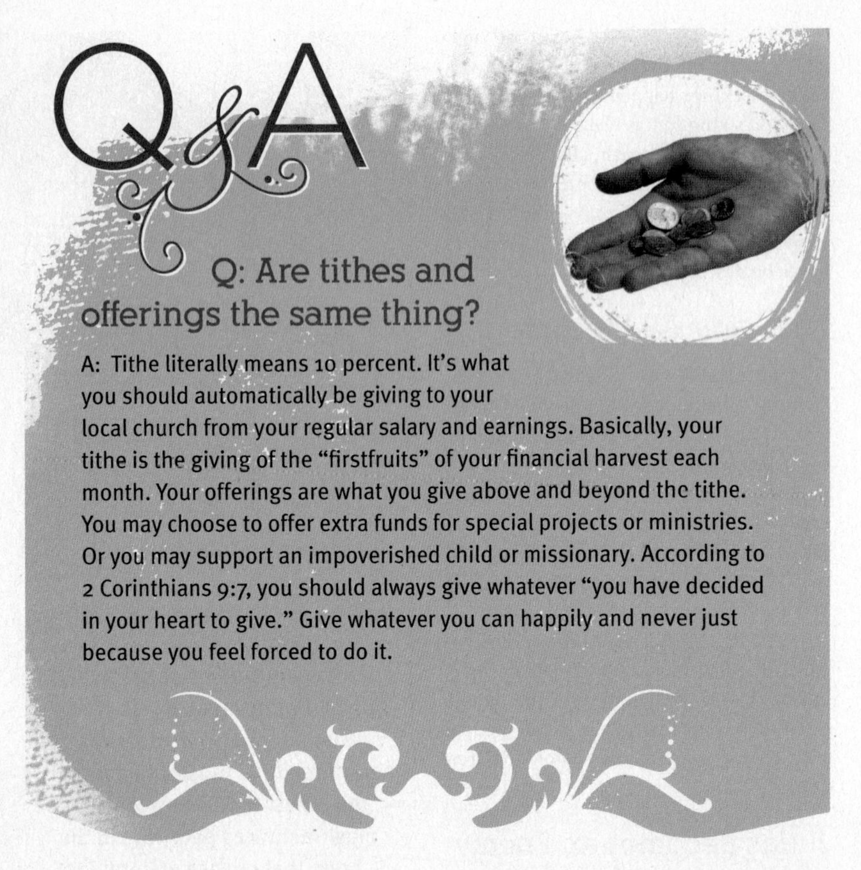

Q: Are tithes and offerings the same thing?

A: Tithe literally means 10 percent. It's what you should automatically be giving to your local church from your regular salary and earnings. Basically, your tithe is the giving of the "firstfruits" of your financial harvest each month. Your offerings are what you give above and beyond the tithe. You may choose to offer extra funds for special projects or ministries. Or you may support an impoverished child or missionary. According to 2 Corinthians 9:7, you should always give whatever "you have decided in your heart to give." Give whatever you can happily and never just because you feel forced to do it.

[13]So Peter and John left and found everything as Jesus had said. And they prepared the Passover meal.

The Lord's Supper

[14]When the time came, Jesus and the apostles were sitting at the table. [15]He said to them, "I wanted very much to eat this Passover meal with you before I suffer. [16]I will not eat another Passover meal until it is given its true meaning in the kingdom of God."

[17]Then Jesus took a cup, gave thanks, and said, "Take this cup and share it among yourselves. [18]I will not drink again from the fruit of the vine[n] until God's kingdom comes."

[19]Then Jesus took some bread, gave thanks, broke it, and gave it to the apostles, saying, "This is my body,[n] which I am giving for you. Do this to remember me." [20]In the same way, after supper, Jesus took the cup and said, "This cup is the new agreement that God makes with his people. This new agreement begins with my blood which is poured out for you.

Who Will Turn Against Jesus?

[21]"But one of you will turn against me, and his hand is with mine on the table. [22]What God has planned for the Son of Man will happen, but how terrible it will be for that one who turns against the Son of Man."

[23]Then the apostles asked each other which one of them would do that.

Be Like a Servant

[24]The apostles also began to argue about which one of them was the most important. [25]But Jesus said to them, "The kings of the non-Jewish people rule over them, and those who have authority over others like to be called 'friends of the people.' [26]But you must not be like that. Instead, the greatest among you should be like the youngest, and the leader should be like the servant. [27]Who is more important: the one sitting at the table or the one serving? You think the one at the table is more important, but I am like a servant among you.

[28]"You have stayed with me through my struggles. [29]Just as my Father has given me a kingdom, I also give you a kingdom [30]so you may eat and drink at my table in my kingdom. And you will sit on thrones, judging the twelve tribes of Israel.

Don't Lose Your Faith!

[31]"Simon, Simon, Satan has asked to test all of you as a farmer sifts his wheat. [32]I have prayed that you will not lose your faith! Help your brothers be stronger when you come back to me."

[33]But Peter said to Jesus, "Lord, I am ready to go with you to prison and even to die with you!"

[34]But Jesus said, "Peter, before the rooster crows this day, you will say three times that you don't know me."

Be Ready for Trouble

[35]Then Jesus said to the apostles, "When I sent you out without a purse, a bag, or sandals, did you need anything?"

They said, "No."

[36]He said to them, "But now if you have a purse or a bag, carry that with you. If you don't have a sword, sell your coat and buy one. [37]The Scripture says, 'He was treated like a criminal,'[n] and I tell you this scripture must have its full meaning. It was written about me, and it is happening now."

[38]His followers said, "Look, Lord, here are two swords."

He said to them, "That is enough."

Jesus Prays Alone

[39]Jesus left the city and went to the Mount of Olives, as he often did, and his followers went with him. [40]When he reached the place, he said to them, "Pray for strength against temptation."

[41]Then Jesus went about a stone's throw away from them. He kneeled down and prayed, [42]"Father, if you are willing, take away this cup[n] of suffering. But do what you want, not what I want." [43]Then an angel from heaven appeared to him to strengthen him. [44]Being full of pain, Jesus prayed even harder. His sweat was like drops of blood falling to the ground. [45]When he finished praying, he went to his followers and found them asleep because of their sadness. [46]Jesus said to them,

22:18 fruit of the vine Product of the grapevine; this may also be translated "wine." **22:19b–20 body** Some Greek copies do not have the rest of verse 19 or verse 20. **22:37 'He . . . criminal.'** Quotation from Isaiah 53:12. **22:42 cup** Jesus is talking about the painful things that will happen to him. Accepting these things will be hard, like drinking a cup of something bitter.

"Why are you sleeping? Get up and pray for strength against temptation."

Jesus Is Arrested

[47]While Jesus was speaking, a crowd came up, and Judas, one of the twelve apostles, was leading them. He came close to Jesus so he could kiss him.

[48]But Jesus said to him, "Judas, are you using the kiss to give the Son of Man to his enemies?"

[49]When those who were standing around him saw what was happening, they said, "Lord, should we strike them with our swords?" [50]And one of them struck the servant of the high priest and cut off his right ear.

[51]Jesus said, "Stop! No more of this." Then he touched the servant's ear and healed him.

[52]Those who came to arrest Jesus were the leading priests, the soldiers who guarded the Temple, and the elders. Jesus said to them, "You came out here with swords and clubs as though I were a criminal. [53]I was with you every day in the Temple, and you didn't arrest me there. But this is your time—the time when darkness rules."

Peter Says He Doesn't Know Jesus

[54]They arrested Jesus, and led him away, and brought him into the house of the high priest. Peter followed far behind them. [55]After the soldiers started a fire in the middle of the courtyard and sat together, Peter sat with them. [56]A servant girl saw Peter sitting there in the firelight, and looking closely at him, she said, "This man was also with him."

[57]But Peter said this was not true; he said, "Woman, I don't know him."

[58]A short time later, another person saw Peter and said, "You are also one of them."

But Peter said, "Man, I am not!"

[59]About an hour later, another man insisted, "Certainly this man was with him, because he is from Galilee, too."

[60]But Peter said, "Man, I don't know what you are talking about!"

At once, while Peter was still speaking, a rooster crowed. [61]Then the Lord turned and looked straight at Peter. And Peter remembered what the Lord had said: "Before the rooster crows this day, you will say three times that you don't know me." [62]Then Peter went outside and cried painfully.

The People Make Fun of Jesus

[63]The men who were guarding Jesus began making fun of him and beating him.

[64]They blindfolded him and said, "Prove that you are a prophet, and tell us who hit you." [65]They said many cruel things to Jesus.

Jesus Before the Leaders

[66]When day came, the council of the elders of the people, both the leading priests and the teachers of the law, came together and led Jesus to their highest court. [67]They said, "If you are the Christ, tell us."

Jesus said to them, "If I tell you, you will not believe me. [68]And if I ask you, you will not answer. [69]But from now on, the Son of Man will sit at the right hand of the powerful God."

[70]They all said, "Then are you the Son of God?"

Jesus said to them, "You say that I am."

[71]They said, "Why do we need witnesses now? We ourselves heard him say this."

Pilate Questions Jesus

23 Then the whole group stood up and led Jesus to Pilate.[n] [2]They began to accuse Jesus, saying, "We caught this man telling things that mislead our people. He says that we should not pay taxes to Caesar, and he calls himself the Christ, a king."

[3]Pilate asked Jesus, "Are you the king of the Jews?"

Jesus answered, "Those are your words."

[4]Pilate said to the leading priests and the people, "I find nothing against this man."

[5]They were insisting, saying, "But Jesus makes trouble with the people, teaching all around Judea. He began in Galilee, and now he is here."

Pilate Sends Jesus to Herod

[6]Pilate heard this and asked if Jesus was from Galilee. [7]Since Jesus was under Herod's authority, Pilate sent Jesus to Herod, who was in Jerusalem at that time. [8]When Herod saw Jesus, he was very glad, because he had heard about Jesus and had wanted to meet him for a long time. He was hoping to see Jesus work a miracle. [9]Herod asked Jesus many questions, but Jesus said nothing. [10]The leading priests and teachers of the law were standing there, strongly accusing Jesus. [11]After Herod and his soldiers had made fun of

Philip: Come and See

Philip did what any true friend would do. When he met Jesus personally, he immediately ran and told his buddy, Nathanael, about the encounter. And when Nathanael questioned the validity of these claims about the Messiah, Philip patiently encouraged him to come along and see for himself. As one of the twelve followers of Jesus, Philip traveled with Jesus throughout his ministry. He saw his miracles, heard his teaching, and watched him be crucified. He later saw the risen Savior with his very own eyes and dedicated the rest of his life to boldly spreading the Good News. (John 1:43–46)

23:1 Pilate Pontius Pilate was the Roman governor of Judea from A.D. 26 to A.D. 36.

Jesus, they dressed him in a kingly robe and sent him back to Pilate. 12In the past, Pilate and Herod had always been enemies, but on that day they became friends.

Jesus Must Die

13Pilate called the people together with the leading priests and the rulers. 14He said to them, "You brought this man to me, saying he makes trouble among the people. But I have questioned him before you all, and I have not found him guilty of what you say. 15Also, Herod found nothing wrong with him; he sent him back to us. Look, he has done nothing for which he should die. 16So, after I punish him, I will let him go free." [17Every year at the Passover Feast, Pilate had to release one prisoner to the people.][n]

18But the people shouted together, "Take this man away! Let Barabbas go free!" 19(Barabbas was a man who was in prison for his part in a riot in the city and for murder.)

20Pilate wanted to let Jesus go free and told this to the crowd. 21But they shouted again, "Crucify him! Crucify him!"

22A third time Pilate said to them, "Why? What wrong has he done? I can find no reason to kill him. So I will have him punished and set him free."

23But they continued to shout, demanding that Jesus be crucified. Their yelling became so loud that 24Pilate decided to give them what they wanted. 25He set free the man who was in jail for rioting and murder, and he handed Jesus over to them to do with him as they wished.

Jesus Is Crucified

26As they led Jesus away, Simon, a man from Cyrene, was coming in from the fields. They forced him to carry Jesus' cross and to walk behind him.

27A large crowd of people was following Jesus, including some women who were sad and crying for him. 28But Jesus turned and said to them, "Women of Jerusalem, don't cry for me. Cry for yourselves and for your children. 29The time is coming when people will say, 'Blessed are the women who cannot have children and who have no babies to nurse.' 30Then people will say to the mountains, 'Fall on us!' And they will say to the hills, 'Cover us!' 31If they act like this now when life is good, what will happen when bad times come?"[n]

32There were also two criminals led out with Jesus to be put to death. 33When they came to a place called the Skull, the soldiers crucified Jesus and the criminals—one on his right and the other on his left. 34Jesus said, "Father, forgive them, because they don't know what they are doing."[n]

The soldiers threw lots to decide who would get his clothes. 35The people stood there watching. And the leaders made fun of Jesus, saying, "He saved others. Let him save himself if he is God's Chosen One, the Christ."

36The soldiers also made fun of him, coming to Jesus and offering him some vinegar. 37They said, "If you are the king of the Jews, save yourself!" 38At the top of the cross these words were written: THIS IS THE KING OF THE JEWS.

39One of the criminals on a cross began to shout insults at Jesus: "Aren't you the Christ? Then save yourself and us."

40But the other criminal stopped him and said, "You should fear God! You are getting the same punishment he is. 41We are punished justly, getting what we deserve for what we did. But this man has done nothing wrong." 42Then he said, "Jesus, remember me when you come into your kingdom."

43Jesus said to him, "I tell you the truth, today you will be with me in paradise."[n]

Jesus Dies

44It was about noon, and the whole land became dark until three o'clock in the afternoon, 45because the sun did not shine. The curtain in the Temple[n] was torn in two. 46Jesus cried out in a loud voice, "Father, I give you my life." After Jesus said this, he died.

47When the army officer there saw what happened, he praised God, saying, "Surely this was a good man!"

48When all the people who had gathered there to watch saw what happened, they returned home, beating their chests because they were so sad. 49But those who were close friends of Jesus, including the women who had followed him from Galilee, stood at a distance and watched.

Joseph Takes Jesus' Body

50There was a good and religious man named Joseph who was a member of the council. 51But he had not agreed to the other leaders' plans and actions against Jesus. He was from the town of Arimathea and was waiting for the kingdom of God to come. 52Joseph went to Pilate to ask for

all about MEN

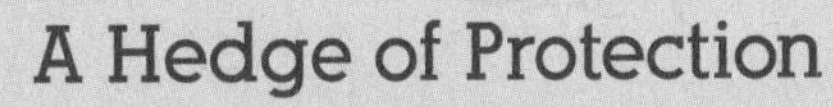

A Hedge of Protection

Whatever relationships you're in with the guys in your life—whether a husband, boyfriend, father, brother, or friend—you can play an important role as a prayer warrior. Men, as well as women, today face enormous challenges, stress, and temptations, and they need every boost of prayer you can send up to God for them. As you pray, imagine a solid wall or a sheltering hedge of protection surrounding the guys you care about. That's what prayer builds. Ask God to fix that strong hedge of protection around their bodies, eyes, minds, and hearts as they say no to the temptations around them. And rest assured that your prayers will not be wasted or unanswered because we know that God will hear our prayers when we ask for anything that aligns with his will (1 John 5:14–15).

23:17 Every . . . people. Some Greek copies do not contain the bracketed text. **23:31 If . . . come?** Literally, "If they do these things in the green tree, what will happen in the dry?" **23:34 Jesus . . . doing."** Some Greek copies do not have this first part of verse 34. **23:43 paradise** Another word for heaven. **23:45 curtain in the Temple** A curtain divided the Most Holy Place from the other part of the Temple, the special building in Jerusalem where God commanded the Jewish people to worship him.

the body of Jesus. [53]He took the body down from the cross, wrapped it in cloth, and put it in a tomb that was cut out of a wall of rock. This tomb had never been used before. [54]This was late on Preparation Day, and when the sun went down, the Sabbath day would begin.

[55]The women who had come from Galilee with Jesus followed Joseph and saw the tomb and how Jesus' body was laid. [56]Then the women left to prepare spices and perfumes.

On the Sabbath day they rested, as the law of Moses commanded.

fun facts

It's estimated that there will be 62,000 new cases of melanoma, the deadliest type of skin cancer, this year.

(American Cancer Society)

Jesus Rises from the Dead

24 Very early on the first day of the week, at dawn, the women came to the tomb, bringing the spices they had prepared. [2]They found the stone rolled away from the entrance of the tomb, [3]but when they went in, they did not find the body of the Lord Jesus. [4]While they were wondering about this, two men in shining clothes suddenly stood beside them. [5]The women were very afraid and bowed their heads to the ground. The men said to them, "Why are you looking for a living person in this place for the dead? [6]He is not here; he has risen from the dead. Do you remember what he told you in Galilee? [7]He said the Son of Man must be handed over to sinful people, be crucified, and rise from the dead on the third day." [8]Then the women remembered what Jesus had said.

[9]The women left the tomb and told all these things to the eleven apostles and the other followers. [10]It was Mary Magdalene, Joanna, Mary the mother of James, and some other women who told the apostles everything that had happened at the tomb. [11]But they did not believe the women, because it sounded like nonsense. [12]But Peter got up and ran to the tomb. Bending down and looking in, he saw only the cloth that Jesus' body had been wrapped in. Peter went away to his home, wondering about what had happened.

Jesus on the Road to Emmaus

[13]That same day two of Jesus' followers were going to a town named Emmaus, about seven miles from Jerusalem. [14]They were talking about everything that had happened. [15]While they were talking and discussing, Jesus himself came near and began walking with them, [16]but they were kept from recognizing him. [17]Then he said, "What are these things you are talking about while you walk?"

The two followers stopped, looking very sad. [18]The one named Cleopas answered, "Are you the only visitor in Jerusalem who does not know what just happened there?"

[19]Jesus said to them, "What are you talking about?"

They said, "About Jesus of Nazareth. He was a prophet who said and did many powerful things before God and all the people. [20]Our leaders and the leading priests handed him over to be sentenced to death, and they crucified him. [21]But we were hoping that he would free Israel. Besides this, it is now the third day since this happened. [22]And today some women among us amazed us. Early this morning they went to the tomb, [23]but they did not find his body there. They came and told us that they had seen a vision of angels who said that Jesus was alive! [24]So some of our group went to the tomb, too. They found it just as the women said, but they did not see Jesus."

[25]Then Jesus said to them, "You are foolish and slow to believe everything the prophets said. [26]They said that the Christ must suffer these things before he enters his glory." [27]Then starting with what Moses and all the prophets had said about him, Jesus began to explain everything that had been written about himself in the Scriptures.

[28]They came near the town of Emmaus, and Jesus acted as if he were going farther. [29]But they begged him, "Stay with us, because it is late; it is almost night." So he went in to stay with them.

[30]When Jesus was at the table with them, he took some bread, gave thanks, divided it, and gave it to them. [31]And then, they were allowed to recognize Jesus. But when they saw who he was, he disappeared. [32]They said to each other, "It felt like a fire burning in us when Jesus talked to us on the road and explained the Scriptures to us."

[33]So the two followers got up at once and went back to Jerusalem. There they found the eleven apostles and others gathered. [34]They were saying, "The Lord really has risen from the dead! He showed himself to Simon."

[35]Then the two followers told what had happened on the road and how they recognized Jesus when he divided the bread.

Jesus Appears to His Followers

[36]While the two followers were telling this, Jesus himself stood right in the middle of them and said, "Peace be with you."

[37]They were fearful and terrified and thought they were seeing a ghost. [38]But Jesus said, "Why are you troubled? Why do you doubt what you see? [39]Look at my hands and my feet. It is I myself! Touch me and see, because a ghost does not have a living body as you see I have."

[40]After Jesus said this, he showed them his hands and feet. [41]While they still could not believe it because they were amazed and happy, Jesus said to them, "Do you have any food here?" [42]They gave him a piece of broiled fish. [43]While the followers watched, Jesus took the fish and ate it.

[44]He said to them, "Remember when I was with you before? I said that everything written about me must happen—everything in the law of Moses, the books of the prophets, and the Psalms."

[45]Then Jesus opened their minds so they could understand the Scriptures. [46]He said to them, "It is written that the Christ would suffer and rise from the dead on the third day [47]and that a change of hearts and lives and forgiveness of sins would be preached in his name to all nations, starting at Jerusalem. [48]You are witnesses of these things. [49]I will send you what my Father has promised, but you must stay in Jerusalem until you have received that power from heaven."

Jesus Goes Back to Heaven

[50]Jesus led his followers as far as Bethany, and he raised his hands and blessed them. [51]While he was blessing them, he was separated from them and carried into heaven. [52]They worshiped him and returned to Jerusalem very happy. [53]They stayed in the Temple all the time, praising God.

Luke

The Whole Story Comes Together

The Gospels are like the climax of God's story. Everything that comes before leads up to the death and resurrection of the Savior. And everything that follows is a result of his victory.

Luke purposefully emphasizes the mix of human history and divine intervention. He traces Jesus' family history all the way back to Adam (Luke 3:23–38) and also describes Jesus' detailed explanation of the scriptures that prophesied his arrival (Luke 24:27, 44–45).

Luke explores the history of humankind: God creates humans. They choose to disobey, and sin enters the world. For thousands of years, people are made right by obeying God's rules and making sacrificial offerings. But the Law isn't enough to unite sinful people with a perfect, holy God. Jesus comes to earth and dies as the ultimate offering, making people right with God when they believe in him. After his resurrection, Jesus explains everything to his followers and commands them to go out and spread the news. He promises to someday return and take his place as Lord and Savior of the entire world. Until then, our main purpose is to cling to him and share his truth through our lives.

Get Real

How did Jesus fulfill the prophecies of the Old Testament? (Psalms 16:10; 22:1; Isaiah 52:14—53:12; Jeremiah 23:5–6; Daniel 9:26; Zechariah 12:10)

Compare Jesus lifted up on the cross with Moses' bronze snake. (Numbers 21:6–8; John 3:14–15)

What "religious" rules do you follow? How can you make your actions more about your relationship with Jesus and less about traditions? (Psalm 51:16–17; Luke 11:46)

Jesus paid special attention to the misfits of society. How can you model your life after his example? (Luke 4:40; 5:27–32; 7:11–17; 10:36–37; 19:5–10)

In what ways are you growing into a well-balanced woman of God? (Luke 2:52)

notes

john

When you and your friends meet on a Saturday to discuss the week over lattes or ice cream, there's no way you'd let each other get away with a basic, factual account of the previous few days. You need details. You want to know how she *felt* and what she *thought*—you want to get to the heart of things!

That's what John does in this Gospel. He had the inside scoop about what happened behind the scenes. Instead of restating the facts about Jesus' public ministry that were already so thoroughly covered in the first three Gospels, John gives us an intimate glimpse into the more private aspects of Jesus' time on earth.

Jesus usually used simple parables and proverbs when he taught the crowds. But John relates some of the more in-depth teachings Jesus shared with his closest followers. We see all kinds of contrasts, like light versus darkness, truth versus lies, and love versus hate. The words reveal Jesus' heart—his deep love for his followers, his commitment to glorifying God, and his desire to show the world how to know God.

Spend an afternoon learning what was going on inside of Jesus' heart. This is your chance to get real with him.

Christ Comes to the World

1 In the beginning there was the Word.[n] The Word was with God, and the Word was God. [2]He was with God in the beginning. [3]All things were made by him, and nothing was made without him. [4]In him there was life, and that life was the light of all people. [5]The Light shines in the darkness, and the darkness has not overpowered[n] it.

[6]There was a man named John[n] who was sent by God. [7]He came to tell people the truth about the Light so that through him all people could hear about the Light and believe. [8]John was not the Light, but he came to tell people the truth about the Light. [9]The true Light that gives light to all was coming into the world!

[10]The Word was in the world, and the world was made by him, but the world did not know him. [11]He came to the world that was his own, but his own people did not accept him. [12]But to all who did accept him and believe in him he gave the right to become children of God. [13]They did not become his children in any human way—by any human parents or human desire. They were born of God.

[14]The Word became a human and lived among us. We saw his glory—the glory that belongs to the only Son of the Father—and he was full of grace and truth. [15]John tells the truth about him and cries out, saying, "This is the One I told you about: 'The One who comes after me is greater than I am, because he was living before me.' "

[16]Because he was full of grace and truth, from him we all received one gift after another. [17]The law was given through Moses, but grace and truth came through Jesus Christ. [18]No one has ever seen God. But God the only Son is very close to the Father,[n] and he has shown us what God is like.

1:1 Word The Greek word is "logos," meaning any kind of communication; it could be translated "message." Here, it means Christ, because Christ was the way God told people about himself. **1:5 overpowered** This can also be translated, "understood." **1:6 John** John the Baptist, who preached to people about Christ's coming (Matthew 3; Luke 3). **1:18 But . . . Father** This could be translated, "But the only God is very close to the Father." Also, some Greek copies read "But the only Son is very close to the Father."

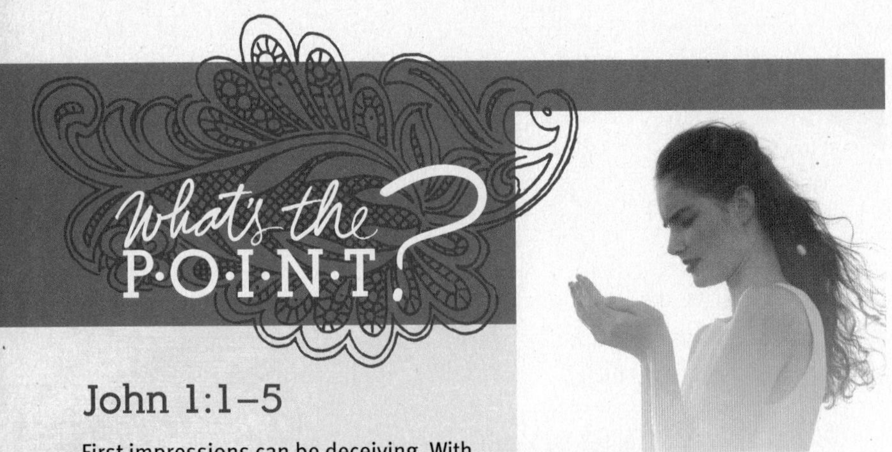

John 1:1–5

First impressions can be deceiving. With some people, your initial glimpse of what they're all about doesn't do justice to who they really are. That's the case with Jesus—despite his humble appearance, he was no ordinary human.

Jesus Christ had the most extraordinary identity of anyone who ever lived—he was human *and* divine. That concept itself has been mind-boggling enough to brew controversy for centuries! But no matter what, Christ's followers have always been certain of this: Jesus Christ *is* God.

Claims have been made that Jesus was just another teacher or religious leader and nothing more. The apostle John faced those lies. He wrote this book to specifically clarify that Jesus' life, actions, and words prove that he's God. The first five verses lay the groundwork. Jesus is identified as the eternal Word of God. From the very beginning, he was *with* God and *was* God.

Profound truth may seem confusing at first glance, but it's not unreachable. God gave us his Word for a reason! Put some time and effort into figuring out who Jesus is by studying the Book of John. Notice what Jesus says about himself, and pay special attention when John talks about the Word, the light, and the truth. Open your heart to knowing who Jesus really is.

John Tells People About Jesus

[19]Here is the truth John[n] told when the leaders in Jerusalem sent priests and Levites to ask him, "Who are you?"

[20]John spoke freely and did not refuse to answer. He said, "I am not the Christ."

[21]So they asked him, "Then who are you? Are you Elijah?"[n]

He answered, "No, I am not."

"Are you the Prophet?"[n] they asked.

He answered, "No."

[22]Then they said, "Who are you? Give us an answer to tell those who sent us. What do you say about yourself?"

[23]John told them in the words of the prophet Isaiah:

"I am the voice of one
calling out in the desert:
'Make the road straight for the Lord.' "

Isaiah 40:3

[24]Some Pharisees who had been sent asked John: [25]"If you are not the Christ or Elijah or the Prophet, why do you baptize people?"

[26]John answered, "I baptize with water, but there is one here with you that you don't know about. [27]He is the One who comes after me. I am not good enough to untie the strings of his sandals."

[28]This all happened at Bethany on the other side of the Jordan River, where John was baptizing people.

[29]The next day John saw Jesus coming toward him. John said, "Look, the Lamb of God,[n] who takes away the sin of the world! [30]This is the One I was talking about when I said, 'A man will come after me, but he is greater than I am, because he was living before me.' [31]Even I did not know who he was, although I came baptizing with water so that the people of Israel would know who he is."

[32-33]Then John said, "I saw the Spirit come down from heaven in the form of a dove and rest on him. Until then I did not know who the Christ was. But the God who sent me to baptize with water told me, 'You will see the Spirit come down and rest on a man; he is the One who will baptize with the Holy Spirit.' [34]I have seen this happen, and I tell you the truth: This man is the Son of God."[n]

The First Followers of Jesus

[35]The next day John[n] was there again with two of his followers. [36]When he saw Jesus walking by, he said, "Look, the Lamb of God!"[n]

[37]The two followers heard John say this, so they followed Jesus. [38]When Jesus turned and saw them following him, he asked, "What are you looking for?"

They said, "Rabbi, where are you staying?" ("Rabbi" means "Teacher.")

[39]He answered, "Come and see." So the two men went with Jesus and saw where he was staying and stayed there with him that day. It was about four o'clock in the afternoon.

[40]One of the two men who followed Jesus after they heard John speak about him was Andrew, Simon Peter's brother. [41]The first thing Andrew did was to find his brother Simon and say to him, "We have found the Messiah." ("Messiah" means "Christ.")

[42]Then Andrew took Simon to Jesus. Jesus looked at him and said, "You are Simon son of John. You will be called Cephas." ("Cephas" means "Peter."[n])

[43]The next day Jesus decided to go to Galilee. He found Philip and said to him, "Follow me."

[44]Philip was from the town of Bethsaida, where Andrew and Peter lived. [45]Philip found Nathanael and told him, "We have found the man that Moses wrote about in the law, and the prophets also wrote about him. He is Jesus, the son of Joseph, from Nazareth."

1:19, 35 John John the Baptist, who preached to people about Christ's coming (Matthew 3, Luke 3). **1:21 Elijah** A prophet who spoke for God. He lived hundreds of years before Christ and was expected to return before Christ (Malachi 4:5–6). **1:21 Prophet** They probably meant the prophet that God told Moses he would send (Deuteronomy 18:15–19). **1:29, 36 Lamb of God** Name for Jesus. Jesus is like the lambs that were offered for a sacrifice to God. **1:34 the Son of God** Some Greek copies read "God's Chosen One." **1:42 Peter** The Greek name "Peter," like the Aramaic name "Cephas," means "rock."

[46]But Nathanael said to Philip, "Can anything good come from Nazareth?"

Philip answered, "Come and see."

[47]As Jesus saw Nathanael coming toward him, he said, "Here is truly an Israelite. There is nothing false in him."

[48]Nathanael asked, "How do you know me?"

Jesus answered, "I saw you when you were under the fig tree, before Philip told you about me."

[49]Then Nathanael said to Jesus, "Teacher, you are the Son of God; you are the King of Israel."

[50]Jesus said to Nathanael, "Do you believe simply because I told you I saw you under the fig tree? You will see greater things than that." [51]And Jesus said to them, "I tell you the truth, you will all see heaven open and 'angels of God going up and coming down'[n] on the Son of Man."

The Wedding at Cana

2 Two days later there was a wedding in the town of Cana in Galilee. Jesus' mother was there, [2]and Jesus and his followers were also invited to the wedding. [3]When all the wine was gone, Jesus' mother said to him, "They have no more wine."

[4]Jesus answered, "Dear woman, why come to me? My time has not yet come."

[5]His mother said to the servants, "Do whatever he tells you to do."

[6]In that place there were six stone water jars that the Jews used in their washing ceremony.[n] Each jar held about twenty or thirty gallons.

[7]Jesus said to the servants, "Fill the jars with water." So they filled the jars to the top.

[8]Then he said to them, "Now take some out and give it to the master of the feast."

So they took the water to the master. [9]When he tasted it, the water had become wine. He did not know where the wine came from, but the servants who had brought the water knew. The master of the wedding called the bridegroom [10]and said to him, "People always serve the best wine first. Later, after the guests have been drinking awhile, they serve the cheaper wine. But you have saved the best wine till now."

[11]So in Cana of Galilee Jesus did his first miracle. There he showed his glory, and his followers believed in him.

Jesus in the Temple

[12]After this, Jesus went to the town of Capernaum with his mother, brothers, and followers. They stayed there for just a few days. [13]When it was almost time for the Jewish Passover Feast, Jesus went to Jerusalem. [14]In the Temple he found people selling cattle, sheep, and doves. He saw others sitting at tables, exchanging different kinds of money. [15]Jesus made a whip out of cords and forced all of them, both the sheep and cattle, to leave the Temple. He turned over the tables and scattered the money of those who were exchanging it. [16]Then he said to those who were selling pigeons, "Take these things out of here! Don't make my Father's house a place for buying and selling!"

[17]When this happened, the followers remembered what was written in the Scriptures: "My strong love for your Temple completely controls me."[n]

[18]Some of his people said to Jesus, "Show us a miracle to prove you have the right to do these things."

[19]Jesus answered them, "Destroy this temple, and I will build it again in three days."

[20]They answered, "It took forty-six

BECOME *Involved*

St. Jude Children's Research Hospital

Few things can touch your heart like a child who is suffering or in pain. That's how the folks at St. Jude Children's Research Hospital feel, too. They can't stand to see a boy or girl afflicted with a painful disease, so they dedicate nearly every waking hour to finding cures, treating little ones, and ministering to their families.

Chances are, you've probably heard of St. Jude before. They're one of the largest charities in the country. And they are a very distinct hospital in that no child is ever turned away just because his or her parents can't afford treatment. Their top-notch doctors and scientists have made great headway in researching common childhood illnesses and cancers.

You can be involved in the very important work of helping sick children. Because St. Jude refuses to turn people away based on money, they are constantly in need of it. And even if you don't have a lot of extra cash lying around, you can help raise funds right where you are. St. Jude even has a program that uses wedding favors to make a difference. Find more ideas for how you can get involved at www.stjude.org.

1:51 'angels . . . down' These words are from Genesis 28:12. **2:6 washing ceremony** The Jewish people washed themselves in special ways before eating, before worshiping in the Temple, and at other special times. **2:17 "My . . . me."** Quotation from Psalm 69:9.

years to build this Temple! Do you really believe you can build it again in three days?"

21(But the temple Jesus meant was his own body. 22After Jesus was raised from the dead, his followers remembered that Jesus had said this. Then they believed the Scripture and the words Jesus had said.)

23When Jesus was in Jerusalem for the Passover Feast, many people believed in him because they saw the miracles he did. 24But Jesus did not believe in them because he knew them all. 25He did not need anyone to tell him about people, because he knew what was in people's minds.

Nicodemus Comes to Jesus

3 There was a man named Nicodemus who was one of the Pharisees and an important Jewish leader. 2One night Nicodemus came to Jesus and said, "Teacher, we know you are a teacher sent from God, because no one can do the miracles you do unless God is with him."

3Jesus answered, "I tell you the truth, unless you are born again, you cannot be in God's kingdom."

4Nicodemus said, "But if a person is already old, how can he be born again? He cannot enter his mother's womb again. So how can a person be born a second time?"

5But Jesus answered, "I tell you the truth, unless you are born from water and the Spirit, you cannot enter God's kingdom. 6Human life comes from human parents, but spiritual life comes from the Spirit. 7Don't be surprised when I tell you, 'You must all be born again.' 8The wind blows where it wants to and you hear the sound of it, but you don't know where the wind comes from or where it is going. It is the same with every person who is born from the Spirit."

9Nicodemus asked, "How can this happen?"

10Jesus said, "You are an important teacher in Israel, and you don't understand these things? 11I tell you the truth, we talk about what we know, and we tell about what we have seen, but you don't accept what we tell you. 12I have told you about things here on earth, and you do not believe me. So you will not believe me if I tell you about things of heaven. 13The only one who has ever gone up to heaven is the One who came down from heaven—the Son of Man.[n]

14"Just as Moses lifted up the snake in the desert,[n] the Son of Man must also be lifted up. 15So that everyone who believes can have eternal life in him.

16"God loved the world so much that he gave his one and only Son so that whoever believes in him may not be lost, but have eternal life. 17God did not send his Son into the world to judge the world guilty, but to save the world through him. 18People who believe in God's Son are not judged guilty. Those who do not believe have already been judged guilty, because they have not believed in God's one and only Son. 19They are judged by this fact: The Light has come into the world, but they did not want light. They wanted darkness, because they were doing evil things. 20All who do evil hate the light and will not come to the light, because it will show all the evil things they do. 21But those who follow the true way come to the light, and it shows that the things they do were done through God."

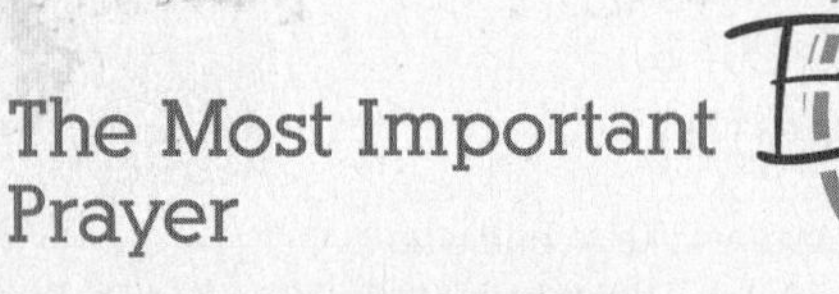

The Most Important Prayer

Be Still & KNOW

Of all the prayers that a believer says, there is one that stands head and shoulders above the rest in eternity—the prayer for salvation. Acts 2:21 says that anyone who calls on the Lord will be saved. This prayer is so important that it literally brings joy to heaven (Luke 15:7). The way to salvation is through a relationship with Jesus (John 3:16), and that relationship begins with a simple prayer of faith asking him to be your Savior. Even if you've never prayed at all, you can lift your voice to him and start an eternal relationship with him today. It's the most important prayer you'll ever pray!

Jesus and John the Baptist

22After this, Jesus and his followers went into the area of Judea, where he stayed with his followers and baptized people. 23John was also baptizing in Aenon, near Salim, because there was plenty of water there. People were going there to be baptized. 24(This was before John was put into prison.)

25Some of John's followers had an argument with a Jew about religious washing.[n] 26So they came to John and said, "Teacher, remember the man who was with you on the other side of the Jordan River, the one you spoke about so much? He is baptizing, and everyone is going to him."

27John answered, "A man can get only what God gives him. 28You yourselves heard me say, 'I am not the Christ, but I am the one sent to prepare the way for him.' 29The bride belongs only to the bridegroom. But the friend who helps

3:13 the Son of Man Some Greek copies continue, "who is in heaven." **3:14 Moses . . . desert** When the Israelites were dying from snake bites, God told Moses to put a bronze snake on a pole. The people who looked at the snake were healed (Numbers 21:4–9). **3:25 religious washing** The Jewish people washed themselves in special ways before eating, before worshiping in the Temple, and at other special times.

the bridegroom stands by and listens to him. He is thrilled that he gets to hear the bridegroom's voice. In the same way, I am really happy. [30]He must become greater, and I must become less important.

The One Who Comes from Heaven

[31]"The One who comes from above is greater than all. The one who is from the earth belongs to the earth and talks about things on the earth. But the One who comes from heaven is greater than all. [32]He tells what he has seen and heard, but no one accepts what he says. [33]Whoever accepts what he says has proven that God is true. [34]The One whom God sent speaks the words of God, because God gives him the Spirit fully. [35]The Father loves the Son and has given him power over everything. [36]Those who believe in the Son have eternal life, but those who do not obey the Son will never have life. God's anger stays on them."

Jesus and a Samaritan Woman

4 The Pharisees heard that Jesus was making and baptizing more followers than John, [2]although Jesus himself did not baptize people, but his followers did. [3]Jesus knew that the Pharisees had heard about him, so he left Judea and went back to Galilee. [4]But on the way he had to go through the country of Samaria.

[5]In Samaria Jesus came to the town called Sychar, which is near the field Jacob gave to his son Joseph. [6]Jacob's well was there. Jesus was tired from his long trip, so he sat down beside the well. It was about twelve o'clock noon. [7]When a Samaritan woman came to the well to get some water, Jesus said to her, "Please give me a drink." [8](This happened while Jesus' followers were in town buying some food.)

[9]The woman said, "I am surprised that you ask me for a drink, since you are a Jewish man and I am a Samaritan woman." (Jewish people are not friends with Samaritans.[n])

[10]Jesus said, "If you only knew the free gift of God and who it is that is asking you for water, you would have asked him, and he would have given you living water."

[11]The woman said, "Sir, where will you get this living water? The well is very deep, and you have nothing to get water with. [12]Are you greater than Jacob, our father, who gave us this well and drank from it himself along with his sons and flocks?"

[13]Jesus answered, "Everyone who drinks this water will be thirsty again, [14]but whoever drinks the water I give will never be thirsty. The water I give will become a spring of water gushing up inside that person, giving eternal life."

[15]The woman said to him, "Sir, give me this water so I will never be thirsty again and will not have to come back here to get more water."

[16]Jesus told her, "Go get your husband and come back here."

[17]The woman answered, "I have no husband."

Jesus said to her, "You are right to say you have no husband. [18]Really you have had five husbands, and the man you live with now is not your husband. You told the truth."

[19]The woman said, "Sir, I can see that you are a prophet. [20]Our ancestors worshiped on this mountain, but you say that Jerusalem is the place where people must worship."

[21]Jesus said, "Believe me, woman. The time is coming when neither in Jerusalem nor on this mountain will you actually worship the Father. [22]You Samaritans worship something you don't understand. We understand what we worship, because salvation comes from the Jews. [23]The time is coming when the true worshipers will worship the Father in spirit and truth, and that time is here already. You see, the Father too is actively seeking such people to worship him. [24]God is spirit, and those who worship him must worship in spirit and truth."

[25]The woman said, "I know that the Messiah is coming." (Messiah is the One called Christ.) "When the Messiah comes, he will explain everything to us."

[26]Then Jesus said, "I am he—I, the one talking to you."

What book, other than the Bible, would you recommend?

He: *A Normal Christian Life* by Watchman Nee

She: *The Pursuit of God* by A.W. Tozer

fun facts

Between 1970 and 2003, the proportion of never-married women between 30 and 34 years old more than tripled, from 6% to 23%.

(U.S. Census Bureau)

4:9 Jewish people . . . Samaritans This can also be translated "Jewish people don't use things that Samaritans have used."

John 4:34

After a long day of back-to-back meetings or a vigorous cardio session at the gym, there's nothing like getting a hot plateful of your favorite food. Finally, some sustenance!

But what about spiritual nourishment? It's easy to forget we need spiritual food just like we need physical food. Jesus said his spiritual food was doing God's work and God's will—pleasing his Father. That's what sustained him and kept him going. He was truly *nourished* by spending time with God and serving him. Interesting food, huh? He was actually more refreshed when he got to spend himself entirely for God!

We should nurture our relationships with God like Christ did. By drawing near to him in Bible study and prayer, we invite him to transform our hearts and minds and show us his will. And just like Jesus, we're also called to invest ourselves in meaningful relationships, teach God's truth, and lovingly serve others.

God designed us to need him. Deuteronomy 8:3 says, "A person does not live on bread alone, but by everything the LORD says." Don't let anything get between you and your time with God. He'll keep you spiritually alive and well.

[27]Just then his followers came back from town and were surprised to see him talking with a woman. But none of them asked, "What do you want?" or "Why are you talking with her?"

[28]Then the woman left her water jar and went back to town. She said to the people, [29]"Come and see a man who told me everything I ever did. Do you think he might be the Christ?" [30]So the people left the town and went to see Jesus.

[31]Meanwhile, his followers were begging him, "Teacher, eat something."

[32]But Jesus answered, "I have food to eat that you know nothing about."

[33]So the followers asked themselves, "Did somebody already bring him food?"

[34]Jesus said, "My food is to do what the One who sent me wants me to do and to finish his work. [35]You have a saying, 'Four more months till harvest.' But I tell you, open your eyes and look at the fields ready for harvest now. [36]Already, the one who harvests is being paid and is gathering crops for eternal life. So the one who plants and the one who harvests celebrate at the same time. [37]Here the saying is true, 'One person plants, and another harvests.' [38]I sent you to harvest a crop that you did not work on. Others did the work, and you get to finish up their work."[n]

[39]Many of the Samaritans in that town believed in Jesus because of what the woman said: "He told me everything I ever did." [40]When the Samaritans came to Jesus, they begged him to stay with them, so he stayed there two more days. [41]And many more believed because of the things he said.

[42]They said to the woman, "First we believed in Jesus because of what you said, but now we believe because we heard him ourselves. We know that this man really is the Savior of the world."

Jesus Heals an Officer's Son

[43]Two days later, Jesus left and went to Galilee. [44](Jesus had said before that a prophet is not respected in his own country.) [45]When Jesus arrived in Galilee, the people there welcomed him. They had seen all the things he did at the Passover Feast in Jerusalem, because they had been there, too.

[46]Jesus went again to visit Cana in Galilee where he had changed the water into wine. One of the king's important officers lived in the city of Capernaum, and his son was sick. [47]When he heard that Jesus had come from Judea to Galilee, he went to Jesus and begged him to come to Capernaum and heal his son, because his son was almost dead. [48]Jesus said to him, "You people must see signs and miracles before you will believe in me."

[49]The officer said, "Sir, come before my child dies."

[50]Jesus answered, "Go. Your son will live."

The man believed what Jesus told him and went home. [51]On the way the man's servants came and met him and told him, "Your son is alive."

[52]The man asked, "What time did my son begin to get well?"

They answered, "Yesterday at one o'clock the fever left him."

[53]The father knew that one o'clock was the exact time that Jesus had said, "Your son will live." So the man and all the people who lived in his house believed in Jesus.

[54]That was the second miracle Jesus did after coming from Judea to Galilee.

Jesus Heals a Man at a Pool

5 Later Jesus went to Jerusalem for a special feast. [2]In Jerusalem there is a pool with five covered porches,

4:38 I . . . their work. As a farmer sends workers to harvest grain, Jesus sends his followers out to bring people to God.

RELATIONSHIPS

Diversify!

Word of the day: "diversify." Do financial investments come to mind? Well, it's good to spread out your relationship wealth, too. Investing in several relationships cuts the risk of draining one person's friendship bank (or being drained yourself!). Limiting all your emotional energy to just one person can lead to depending on that person for all your relationship needs. Consider your friends. One's best for a listening ear, another for a good laugh, right? And they probably value different things about you, too, because God created each of us with unique strengths (1 Corinthians 12:27–30). So diversify—and you'll enjoy better yields from your relationships!

which is called Bethesda[n] in the Hebrew language.[n] This pool is near the Sheep Gate. [3]Many sick people were lying on the porches beside the pool. Some were blind, some were crippled, and some were paralyzed [, and they waited for the water to move. [4]Sometimes an angel of the Lord came down to the pool and stirred up the water. After the angel did this, the first person to go into the pool was healed from any sickness he had].[n] [5]A man was lying there who had been sick for thirty-eight years. [6]When Jesus saw the man and knew that he had been sick for such a long time, Jesus asked him, "Do you want to be well?"

[7]The sick man answered, "Sir, there is no one to help me get into the pool when the water starts moving. While I am coming to the water, someone else always gets in before me."

[8]Then Jesus said, "Stand up. Pick up your mat and walk." [9]And immediately the man was well; he picked up his mat and began to walk.

The day this happened was a Sabbath day. [10]So the Jews said to the man who had been healed, "Today is the Sabbath. It is against our law for you to carry your mat on the Sabbath day."

[11]But he answered, "The man who made me well told me, 'Pick up your mat and walk.' "

[12]Then they asked him, "Who is the man who told you to pick up your mat and walk?"

[13]But the man who had been healed did not know who it was, because there were many people in that place, and Jesus had left.

[14]Later, Jesus found the man at the Temple and said to him, "See, you are well now. Stop sinning so that something worse does not happen to you."

[15]Then the man left and told his people that Jesus was the one who had made him well.

[16]Because Jesus was doing this on the Sabbath day, some evil people began to persecute him. [17]But Jesus said to them, "My Father never stops working, and so I keep working, too."

[18]This made them try still harder to kill him. They said, "First Jesus was breaking the law about the Sabbath day. Now he says that God is his own Father, making himself equal with God!"

Jesus Has God's Authority

[19]But Jesus said, "I tell you the truth, the Son can do nothing alone. The Son does only what he sees the Father doing, because the Son does whatever the Father does. [20]The Father loves the Son and shows the Son all the things he himself does. But the Father will show the Son even greater things than this so that you can all be amazed. [21]Just as the Father raises the dead and gives them life, so also the Son gives life to those he wants to. [22]In fact, the Father judges no one, but he has given the Son power to do all the judging [23]so that all people will honor the Son as much as they honor the Father. Anyone who does not honor the Son does not honor the Father who sent him.

[24]"I tell you the truth, whoever hears what I say and believes in the One who sent me has eternal life. That person will not be judged guilty but has already left death and entered life. [25]I tell you the truth, the time is coming and is already here when the dead will hear the voice of the Son of God, and those who hear will have life. [26]Life comes from the Father himself, and he has allowed the Son to have life in himself as well. [27]And the Father has given the Son the approval to judge, because he is the Son of Man. [28]Don't be surprised at this: A time is coming when all who are dead and in their graves will hear his voice. [29]Then they will come out of their graves. Those who did good will rise and have life forever, but those who did evil will rise to be judged guilty.

5:2 Bethesda Some Greek copies read "Bethzatha" or "Bethsaida," different names for the pool of Bethesda. **5:2 Hebrew language** Or Aramaic, the languages of many people in this region in the first century. **5:3–4 and . . . had** Some Greek copies do not contain all or most of the bracketed text.

QUIZ

HOW GOOD ARE YOU AT CONNECTING WITH OTHERS?

1. When I feel lonely, sad, or overwhelmed, I usually . . .

- [] A. Call a girlfriend or two.
- [] B. Chat online or watch TV.
- [] C. Take a bubble bath or read a book.

2. My best gal pal and I talk either in person, on the phone, or via e-mail on a regular basis. We . . .

- [] A. Have daily or weekly gab sessions.
- [] B. Talk whenever something important happens in her life or my life.
- [] C. Catch up on birthdays and/or major holidays.

3. If I missed Sunday school or my small group Bible study two weeks in a row . . .

- [] A. My friends would be all over my case (unless I had a good reason, of course!).
- [] B. Everyone would wonder what happened to me.
- [] C. I'm not sure anyone would notice.

4. If I could only have one of the following communication aids, it would be . . .

- [] A. My cell phone.
- [] B. E-mail.
- [] C. Text messaging.

5. I know what life issues my friends are struggling with right now because . . .

- [] A. We've talked or prayed about them together.
- [] B. It's obvious from just being around them.
- [] C. I assume they're just dealing with normal stuff that we all face.

Scoring:

If you chose mostly As, you are on your way to becoming a well-connected woman. Even in the midst of your busy life, you make deep friendships a priority. You heed God's command to love others as you invest in their lives. Celebrate the friends you have, for they are a gift from God!

If you chose mostly Bs, you are working toward balance. You already sense the need to connect with others. You know that meaningful friendships are vital and that if you fall, your friends can help you up (Ecclesiastes 4:9–12). Be sure you make connecting with others a priority even when you're busy or tired. You won't be sorry!

If you chose mostly Cs, you are craving connection. Whether by choice or by life circumstances, you might be missing out on some friendships that could enrich your life immensely. Remember, you don't have to go it alone. In fact, it's not good for people to try to do life by themselves (Genesis 2:18). Make the effort to connect more with others. You'll be glad you did!

Jesus Is God's Son

[30]"I can do nothing alone. I judge only the way I am told, so my judgment is fair. I don't try to please myself, but I try to please the One who sent me.

[31]"If only I tell people about myself, what I say is not true. [32]But there is another who tells about me, and I know that the things he says about me are true.

[33]"You have sent people to John, and he has told you the truth. [34]It is not that I need what humans say; I tell you this so you can be saved. [35]John was like a burning and shining lamp, and you were happy to enjoy his light for a while.

[36]"But I have a proof about myself that is greater than that of John. The things I do, which are the things my Father gave me to do, prove that the Father sent me. [37]And the Father himself who sent me has given proof about me. You have never heard his voice or seen what he looks like. [38]His teaching does not live in you, because you don't believe in the One the Father sent. [39]You carefully study the Scriptures because you think they give you eternal life. They do in fact tell about me, [40]but you refuse to come to me to have that life.

[41]"I don't need praise from people. [42]But I know you—I know that you don't have God's love in you. [43]I have come from my Father and speak for him, but you don't accept me. But when another person comes, speaking only for himself, you will accept him. [44]You try to get praise from each other, but you do not try to get the praise that comes from the only God. So how can you believe? [45]Don't think that I will stand before the Father and say you are wrong. The one who says you are wrong is Moses, the one you hoped would save you. [46]If you really believed Moses, you would believe me, because Moses wrote about me. [47]But if you don't believe what Moses wrote, how can you believe what I say?"

More than Five Thousand Fed

6 After this, Jesus went across Lake Galilee (or, Lake Tiberias). [2]Many people followed him because they saw the miracles he did to heal the sick. [3]Jesus went up on a hill and sat down there with his followers. [4]It was almost the time for the Jewish Passover Feast.

[5]When Jesus looked up and saw a large crowd coming toward him, he said to Philip, "Where can we buy enough bread for all these people to eat?" [6](Jesus asked Philip this question to test him, because Jesus already knew what he planned to do.)

[7]Philip answered, "Someone would have to work almost a year to buy enough bread for each person to have only a little piece."

[8]Another one of his followers, Andrew, Simon Peter's brother, said, [9]"Here is a boy with five loaves of barley bread and two little fish, but that is not enough for so many people."

[10]Jesus said, "Tell the people to sit down." There was plenty of grass there, and about five thousand men sat down there. [11]Then Jesus took the loaves of bread, thanked God for them, and gave them to the people who were sitting there. He did the same with the fish, giving as much as the people wanted.

[12]When they had all had enough to eat, Jesus said to his followers, "Gather the leftover pieces of fish and bread so that nothing is wasted." [13]So they gathered up the pieces and filled twelve baskets with the pieces left from the five barley loaves.

[14]When the people saw this miracle that Jesus did, they said, "He must truly be the Prophet[n] who is coming into the world."

[15]Jesus knew that the people planned to come and take him by force and make him their king, so he left and went into the hills alone.

Jesus Walks on the Water

[16]That evening Jesus' followers went down to Lake Galilee. [17]It was dark now, and Jesus had not yet come to them. The followers got into a boat and started across the lake to Capernaum. [18]By now a strong wind was blowing, and the waves on the lake were getting bigger. [19]When they had rowed the boat about three or four miles, they saw Jesus walking on the water, coming toward the boat. The followers were afraid, [20]but Jesus said to them, "It is I. Do not be afraid." [21]Then they were glad to take him into the boat. At once the boat came to land at the place where they wanted to go.

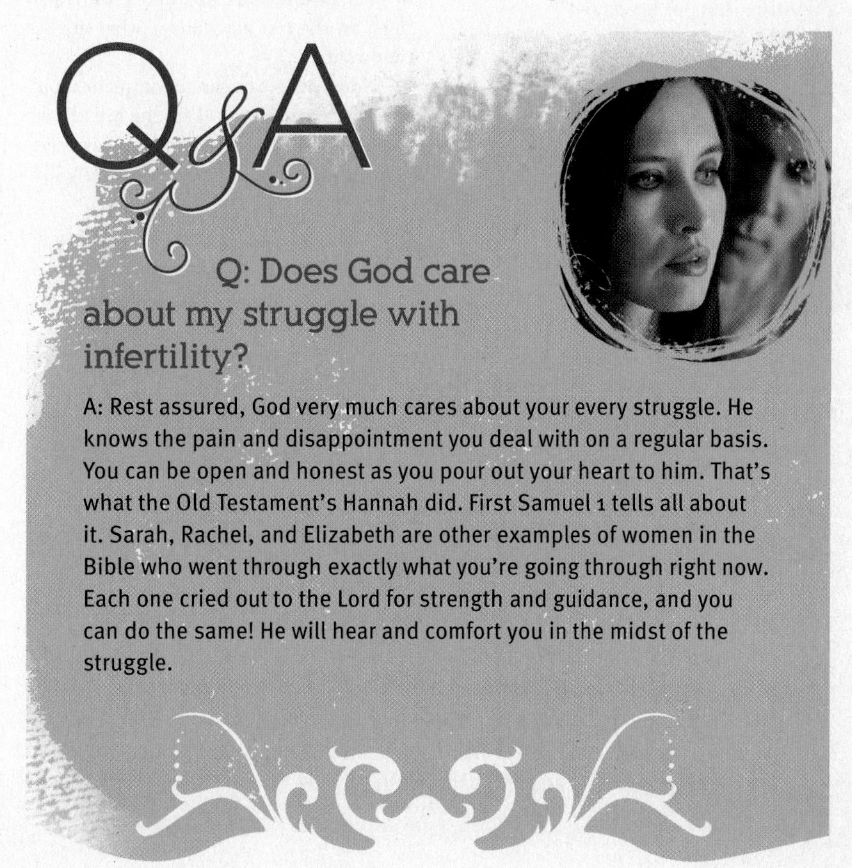

Q&A

Q: Does God care about my struggle with infertility?

A: Rest assured, God very much cares about your every struggle. He knows the pain and disappointment you deal with on a regular basis. You can be open and honest as you pour out your heart to him. That's what the Old Testament's Hannah did. First Samuel 1 tells all about it. Sarah, Rachel, and Elizabeth are other examples of women in the Bible who went through exactly what you're going through right now. Each one cried out to the Lord for strength and guidance, and you can do the same! He will hear and comfort you in the midst of the struggle.

6:14 Prophet They probably meant the prophet that God told Moses he would send (Deuteronomy 18:15–19).

The People Seek Jesus

[22]The next day the people who had stayed on the other side of the lake knew that Jesus had not gone in the boat with his followers but that they had left without him. And they knew that only one boat had been there. [23]But then some boats came from Tiberias and landed near the place where the people had eaten the bread after the Lord had given thanks. [24]When the people saw that Jesus and his followers were not there now, they got into boats and went to Capernaum to find Jesus.

Jesus, the Bread of Life

[25]When the people found Jesus on the other side of the lake, they asked him, "Teacher, when did you come here?"

[26]Jesus answered, "I tell you the truth, you aren't looking for me because you saw me do miracles. You are looking for me because you ate the bread and were satisfied. [27]Don't work for the food that spoils. Work for the food that stays good always and gives eternal life. The Son of Man will give you this food, because on him God the Father has put his power."

[28]The people asked Jesus, "What are the things God wants us to do?"

[29]Jesus answered, "The work God wants you to do is this: Believe the One he sent."

[30]So the people asked, "What miracle will you do? If we see a miracle, we will believe you. What will you do? [31]Our ancestors ate the manna in the desert. This is written in the Scriptures: 'He gave them bread from heaven to eat.' "[n]

[32]Jesus said, "I tell you the truth, it was not Moses who gave you bread from heaven; it is my Father who is giving you the true bread from heaven. [33]God's bread is the One who comes down from heaven and gives life to the world."

[34]The people said, "Sir, give us this bread always."

[35]Then Jesus said, "I am the bread that gives life. Whoever comes to me will never be hungry, and whoever believes in me will never be thirsty. [36]But as I told you before, you have seen me and still don't believe. [37]The Father gives me the people who are mine. Every one of them will come to me, and I will always accept them. [38]I came down from heaven to do what God wants me to do, not what I want to do. [39]Here is what the One who sent me wants me to do: I must not lose even one whom God gave me, but I must raise them all on the last day. [40]Those who see the Son and believe in him have eternal life, and I will raise them on the last day. This is what my Father wants."

[41]Some people began to complain about Jesus because he said, "I am the bread that comes down from heaven." [42]They said, "This is Jesus, the son of Joseph. We know his father and mother. How can he say, 'I came down from heaven'?"

[43]But Jesus answered, "Stop complaining to each other. [44]The Father is the One who sent me. No one can come to me unless the Father draws him to me, and I will raise that person up on the last day. [45]It is written in the prophets, 'They will all be taught by God.'[n] Everyone who listens to the Father and learns from him comes to me. [46]No one has seen the Father except the One who is from God; only he has seen the Father. [47]I tell you the truth, whoever believes has eternal life. [48]I am the bread that gives life. [49]Your ancestors ate the manna in the desert, but still they died. [50]Here is the bread that comes down from heaven. Anyone who eats this bread will never die. [51]I am the living bread that came down from heaven. Anyone who eats this bread will live forever. This bread is my flesh, which I will give up so that the world may have life."

[52]Then the evil people began to argue among themselves, saying, "How can this man give us his flesh to eat?"

[53]Jesus said, "I tell you the truth, you must eat the flesh of the Son of Man and drink his blood. Otherwise, you won't have real life in you. [54]Those who eat my flesh and drink my blood have eternal life, and I will raise them up on the last day. [55]My flesh is true food, and my blood is true drink. [56]Those who eat my flesh and drink my blood live in me, and I live in them. [57]The living Father sent me, and I live because of the Father. So whoever eats me will live because of me. [58]I am not like the bread your ancestors ate. They ate that bread and still died. I am the bread that came down from heaven, and whoever eats this bread will live forever." [59]Jesus said all these things while he was teaching in the synagogue in Capernaum.

The Words of Eternal Life

[60]When the followers of Jesus heard this, many of them said, "This teaching is hard. Who can accept it?"

[61]Knowing that his followers were complaining about this, Jesus said, "Does this teaching bother you? [62]Then will it also bother you to see the Son of Man going back to the place where he came from? [63]It is the Spirit that gives life. The flesh doesn't give life. The words I told you are

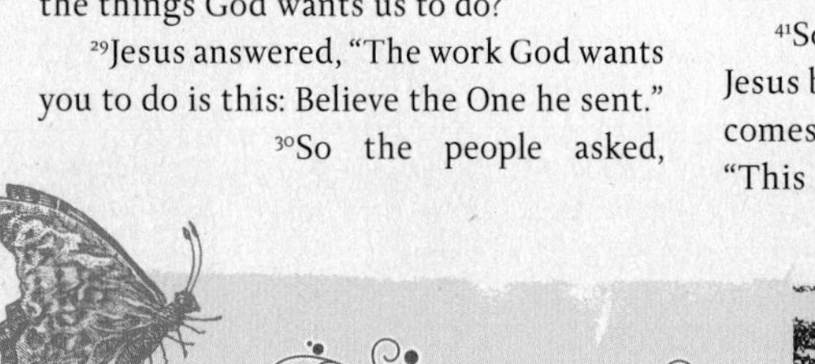

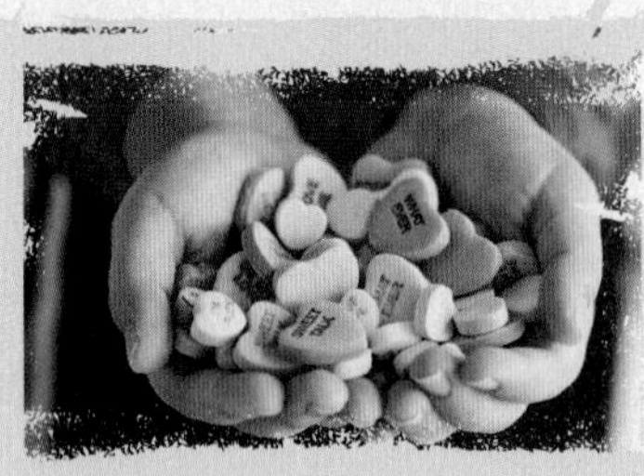

Who's Pretty in the Bible?

Out of all the characters, heroes, and villains in the Bible, only a very few have any mention of their outward appearance. Why? One hint comes from when the Lord was choosing a king for his people. He told the prophet Samuel not to go by the world's standards of appearance because that's not what interests him. "God does not see the same way people see. People look at the outside of a person, but the LORD looks at the heart" (1 Samuel 16:7). If you want to be pretty, prayerfully beautify your heart.

6:31 'He gave . . . eat.' Quotation from Psalm 78:24. **6:45 'They . . . God.'** Quotation from Isaiah 54:13.

spirit, and they give life. [64]But some of you don't believe." (Jesus knew from the beginning who did not believe and who would turn against him.) [65]Jesus said, "That is the reason I said, 'If the Father does not bring a person to me, that one cannot come.' "

[66]After Jesus said this, many of his followers left him and stopped following him.

[67]Jesus asked the twelve followers, "Do you want to leave, too?"

[68]Simon Peter answered him, "Lord, who would we go to? You have the words that give eternal life. [69]We believe and know that you are the Holy One from God."

[70]Then Jesus answered, "I chose all twelve of you, but one of you is a devil."

[71]Jesus was talking about Judas, the son of Simon Iscariot. Judas was one of the twelve, but later he was going to turn against Jesus.

Jesus' Brothers Don't Believe

7 After this, Jesus traveled around Galilee. He did not want to travel in Judea, because some evil people there wanted to kill him. [2]It was time for the Feast of Shelters. [3]So Jesus' brothers said to him, "You should leave here and go to Judea so your followers there can see the miracles you do. [4]Anyone who wants to be well known does not hide what he does. If you are doing these things, show yourself to the world." [5](Even Jesus' brothers did not believe in him.)

[6]Jesus said to his brothers, "The right time for me has not yet come, but any time is right for you. [7]The world cannot hate you, but it hates me, because I tell it the evil things it does. [8]So you go to the feast. I will not go yet[n] to this feast, because the right time for me has not yet come." [9]After saying this, Jesus stayed in Galilee.

[10]But after Jesus' brothers had gone to the feast, Jesus went also. But he did not let people see him. [11]At the feast some people were looking for him and saying, "Where is that man?"

[12]Within the large crowd there, many people were whispering to each other about Jesus. Some said, "He is a good man."

Others said, "No, he fools the people." [13]But no one was brave enough to talk about Jesus openly, because they were afraid of the elders.

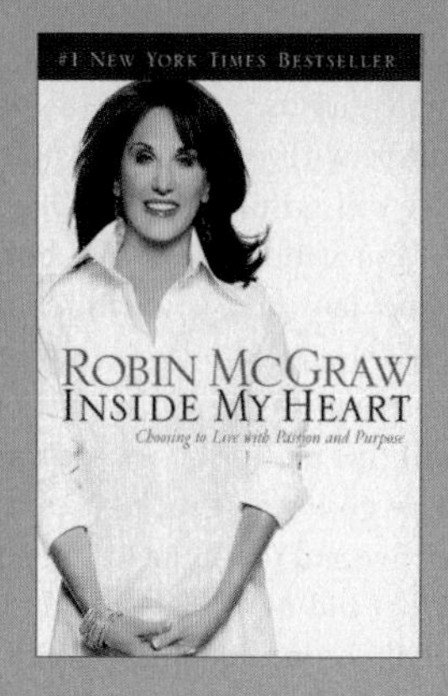

Inside My Heart
by Robin McGraw

Feeling trapped by your circumstances? This book assures you that you have the power to change your life for the better—no matter what. Author Robin McGraw inspires you to rise above simply taking life as it comes and start making deliberate choices for a more meaningful life. She shares her own story with refreshing candor as she helps you consider who you are *now* and who you are meant to become. This book will challenge you to discover the life you were meant to live and equip you to set the priorities and goals to go after it.

Jesus Teaches at the Feast

[14]When the feast was about half over, Jesus went to the Temple and began to teach. [15]The people were amazed and said, "This man has never studied in school. How did he learn so much?"

[16]Jesus answered, "The things I teach are not my own, but they come from him who sent me. [17]If people choose to do what God wants, they will know that my teaching comes from God and not from me. [18]Those who teach their own ideas are trying to get honor for themselves. But those who try to bring honor to the one who sent them speak the truth, and there is nothing false in them. [19]Moses gave you the law,[n] but none of you obeys that law. Why are you trying to kill me?"

[20]The people answered, "A demon has come into you. We are not trying to kill you."

[21]Jesus said to them, "I did one miracle, and you are all amazed. [22]Moses gave you the law about circumcision. (But really Moses did not give you circumcision; it came from our ancestors.) And yet you circumcise a baby boy on a Sabbath day. [23]If a baby boy can be circumcised on a Sabbath day to obey the law of Moses, why are you angry at me for healing a person's whole body on the Sabbath day? [24]Stop judging by the way things look, but judge by what is really right."

Is Jesus the Christ?

[25]Then some of the people who lived in Jerusalem said, "This is the man they are trying to kill. [26]But he is teaching where everyone can see and hear him, and no one is trying to stop him. Maybe the leaders have decided he really is the Christ. [27]But we know where this man is from. Yet when the real Christ comes, no one will know where he comes from."

[28]Jesus, teaching in the Temple, cried out, "Yes, you know me, and you know where I am from. But I have not come by my own authority. I was sent by the One who is true, whom you don't know. [29]But I know him, because I am from him, and he sent me."

[30]When Jesus said this, they tried to

7:8 yet Some Greek copies do not have this word. **7:19 law** Moses gave God's people the Law that God gave him on Mount Sinai (Exodus 34:29–32).

On Good Days and Bad

After a crummy day, worship may be the last thing on your mind. We all have those days, and God knows about them because nothing escapes his notice. But since worship is an offering to him, regardless of our emotions and circumstances, bad days are still a prime time to acknowledge his glory. It's a good thing that worship is all about God, not about us. This means we are welcome in His presence regardless of how we feel.

Jesus spoke plainly regarding this act of reverence in Luke 4:8: "You must worship the Lord your God and serve only him." Our reasons for worshiping God never waver because God's worthiness never wavers. When you take time to honor him despite the day's troubles, you bless him by giving him his rightful place above everything else.

seize him. But no one was able to touch him, because it was not yet the right time. 31But many of the people believed in Jesus. They said, "When the Christ comes, will he do more miracles than this man has done?"

The Leaders Try to Arrest Jesus

32The Pharisees heard the crowd whispering these things about Jesus. So the leading priests and the Pharisees sent some Temple guards to arrest him. 33Jesus said, "I will be with you a little while longer. Then I will go back to the One who sent me. 34You will look for me, but you will not find me. And you cannot come where I am."

35Some people said to each other, "Where will this man go so we cannot find him? Will he go to the Greek cities where our people live and teach the Greek people there? 36What did he mean when he said, 'You will look for me, but you will not find me,' and 'You cannot come where I am'?"

Jesus Talks About the Spirit

37On the last and most important day of the feast Jesus stood up and said in a loud voice, "Let anyone who is thirsty come to me and drink. 38If anyone believes in me, rivers of living water will flow out from that person's heart, as the Scripture says." 39Jesus was talking about the Holy Spirit. The Spirit had not yet been given, because Jesus had not yet been raised to glory. But later, those who believed in Jesus would receive the Spirit.

The People Argue About Jesus

40When the people heard Jesus' words, some of them said, "This man really is the Prophet."[n]

41Others said, "He is the Christ."

Still others said, "The Christ will not come from Galilee. 42The Scripture says that the Christ will come from David's family and from Bethlehem, the town where David lived." 43So the people did not agree with each other about Jesus. 44Some of them wanted to arrest him, but no one was able to touch him.

Some Leaders Won't Believe

45The Temple guards went back to the leading priests and the Pharisees, who asked, "Why didn't you bring Jesus?"

46The guards answered, "The words he says are greater than the words of any other person who has ever spoken!"

47The Pharisees answered, "So Jesus has fooled you also! 48Have any of the leaders or the Pharisees believed in him? No! 49But these people, who know nothing about the law, are under God's curse."

50Nicodemus, who had gone to see Jesus before, was in that group.[n] He said, 51"Our law does not judge a person without hearing him and knowing what he has done."

52They answered, "Are you from Galilee, too? Study the Scriptures, and you will learn that no prophet comes from Galilee."

Some of the earliest surviving Greek copies do not contain 7:53—8:11.

[53And everyone left and went home.

The Woman Caught in Adultery

8 Jesus went to the Mount of Olives. 2But early in the morning he went back to the Temple, and all the people came to him, and he sat and taught them. 3The teachers of the law and the Pharisees brought a woman who had been caught in adultery. They forced her to stand before the people. 4They said to Jesus, "Teacher, this woman was caught having sexual relations with a man who is not her husband. 5The law of Moses commands that we stone to death every woman who does this. What do you say we should do?" 6They were asking this to trick Jesus so that they could have some charge against him.

But Jesus bent over and started writing on the ground with his finger. 7When they continued to ask Jesus their question, he raised up and said, "Anyone here who has never sinned can throw the first stone at her." 8Then Jesus bent over again and wrote on the ground.

9Those who heard Jesus began to leave one by one, first the older men and then the others. Jesus was left there alone with the woman standing before him. 10Jesus raised up again and asked her, "Woman, where are they? Has no one judged you guilty?"

11She answered, "No one, sir."

7:40 Prophet They probably meant the prophet God told Moses he would send (Deuteronomy 18:15–19). **7:50 Nicodemus . . . group.** The story about Nicodemus going and talking to Jesus is in John 3:1–21.

Then Jesus said, "I also don't judge you guilty. You may go now, but don't sin anymore."]

Jesus Is the Light of the World

[12]Later, Jesus talked to the people again, saying, "I am the light of the world. The person who follows me will never live in darkness but will have the light that gives life."

[13]The Pharisees said to Jesus, "When you talk about yourself, you are the only one to say these things are true. We cannot accept what you say."

[14]Jesus answered, "Yes, I am saying these things about myself, but they are true. I know where I came from and where I am going. But you don't know where I came from or where I am going. [15]You judge by human standards. I am not judging anyone. [16]But when I do judge, I judge truthfully, because I am not alone. The Father who sent me is with me. [17]Your own law says that when two witnesses say the same thing, you must accept what they say. [18]I am one of the witnesses who speaks about myself, and the Father who sent me is the other witness."

[19]They asked, "Where is your father?"

Jesus answered, "You don't know me or my Father. If you knew me, you would know my Father, too." [20]Jesus said these things while he was teaching in the Temple, near where the money is kept. But no one arrested him, because the right time for him had not yet come.

John 8:44

If you've ever done something that reminded someone of your mom, you might have heard, "You are your mother's daughter!" Something about you showed how you take after her.

While that remark was probably a kind compliment to you, Jesus offered a similar statement to the Pharisees as a warning. He told them he could see who they were "taking after." When they dismissed Jesus' statements about being the Messiah, they were rejecting truth and embracing a lie—it's not hard to find the instigator there. God cannot ever lie, but Satan is the father of lies. Jesus is the way, the truth, and the life, but the devil steals, kills, and destroys people.

Satan *controlled* the Pharisees with deceit. Do you ever recognize his attempts to do the same thing today? Maybe he tries to convince you that you're not truly loved, forgiven, or freed from sin through Christ. Perhaps he says you can't get anything right or be a part of God's work. Whatever he hurls your way, always remember you have something stronger—God's Word. It will always reveal what's real, so cling to it and live by it! Then you'll be taking after your true Father in heaven.

The People Misunderstand Jesus

[21]Again, Jesus said to the people, "I will leave you, and you will look for me, but you will die in your sins. You cannot come where I am going."

[22]So the Jews asked, "Will he kill himself? Is that why he said, 'You cannot come where I am going'?"

[23]Jesus said, "You people are from here below, but I am from above. You belong to this world, but I don't belong to this world. [24]So I told you that you would die in your sins. Yes, you will die in your sins if you don't believe that I am he."

[25]They asked, "Then who are you?"

Jesus answered, "I am what I have told you from the beginning. [26]I have many things to say and decide about you. But I tell people only the things I have heard from the One who sent me, and he speaks the truth."

[27]The people did not understand that he was talking to them about the Father. [28]So Jesus said to them, "When you lift up the Son of Man, you will know that I am he. You will know that these things I do are not by my own authority but that I say only what the Father has taught me. [29]The One who sent me is with me. I always do what is pleasing to him, so he has not left me alone." [30]While Jesus was saying these things, many people believed in him.

Freedom from Sin

[31]So Jesus said to the Jews who believed in him, "If you continue to obey my teaching, you are truly my followers. [32]Then you will know the truth, and the truth will make you free."

[33]They answered, "We are Abraham's children, and we have never been anyone's slaves. So why do you say we will be free?"

[34]Jesus answered, "I tell you the truth, everyone who lives in sin is a slave to sin. [35]A slave does not stay with a family forever, but a son belongs to the family forever. [36]So if the Son makes you free, you will be truly free. [37]I know you are Abraham's children, but you want to kill me

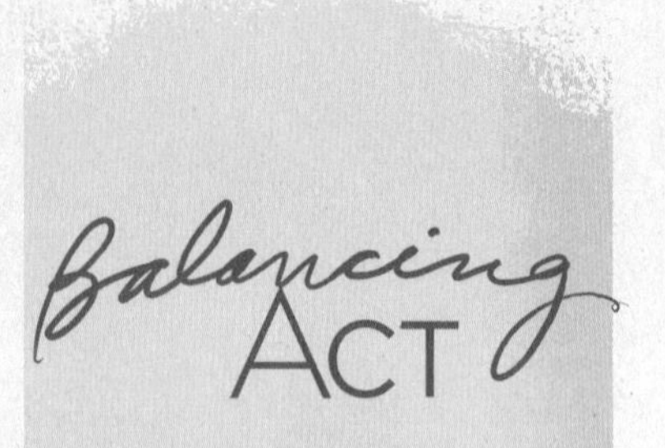

Are You Doing Enough?

An hour of quiet time every morning. Church three times a week. Fellowship group on Saturday night. Bible study on Tuesday morning. Choir rehearsal on Wednesday. When is it ever enough? The answer: never. You can never *do* enough for God because the Christian life isn't about what we do. Studying the Bible is important. And fellowship with other believers encourages us in our faith. But unless you have a personal relationship with the living God, those things are meaningless. Instead of spending so much energy doing things for God, maybe it's time you get to know him better. Prayer—both listening and talking to him—is a great way to start.

because you don't accept my teaching. [38]I am telling you what my Father has shown me, but you do what your father has told you."

[39]They answered, "Our father is Abraham."

Jesus said, "If you were really Abraham's children, you would do[n] the things Abraham did. [40]I am a man who has told you the truth which I heard from God, but you are trying to kill me. Abraham did nothing like that. [41]So you are doing the things your own father did."

But they said, "We are not like children who never knew who their father was. God is our Father; he is the only Father we have."

[42]Jesus said to them, "If God were really your Father, you would love me, because I came from God and now I am here. I did not come by my own authority; God sent me. [43]You don't understand what I say, because you cannot accept my teaching. [44]You belong to your father the devil, and you want to do what he wants. He was a murderer from the beginning and was against the truth, because there is no truth in him. When he tells a lie, he shows what he is really like, because he is a liar and the father of lies. [45]But because I speak the truth, you don't believe me. [46]Can any of you prove that I am guilty of sin? If I am telling the truth, why don't you believe me? [47]The person who belongs to God accepts what God says. But you don't accept what God says, because you don't belong to God."

Jesus Is Greater than Abraham

[48]They answered, "We say you are a Samaritan and have a demon in you. Are we not right?"

[49]Jesus answered, "I have no demon in me. I give honor to my Father, but you dishonor me. [50]I am not trying to get honor for myself. There is One who wants this honor for me, and he is the judge. [51]I tell you the truth, whoever obeys my teaching will never die."

[52]They said to Jesus, "Now we know that you have a demon in you! Even Abraham and the prophets died. But you say, 'Whoever obeys my teaching will never die.' [53]Do you think you are greater than our father Abraham, who died? And the prophets died, too. Who do you think you are?"

[54]Jesus answered, "If I give honor to myself, that honor is worth nothing. The One who gives me honor is my Father, and you say he is your God. [55]You don't really know him, but I know him. If I said I did not know him, I would be a liar like you. But I do know him, and I obey what he says. [56]Your father Abraham was very happy that he would see my day. He saw that day and was glad."

[57]They said to him, "You have never seen Abraham! You are not even fifty years old."

[58]Jesus answered, "I tell you the truth, before Abraham was even born, I am!" [59]When Jesus said this, the people picked up stones to throw at him. But Jesus hid himself, and then he left the Temple.

Jesus Heals a Man Born Blind

9 As Jesus was walking along, he saw a man who had been born blind. [2]His followers asked him, "Teacher, whose sin caused this man to be born blind—his own sin or his parents' sin?"

[3]Jesus answered, "It is not this man's sin or his parents' sin that made him blind. This man was born blind so that God's power could be shown in him. [4]While it is daytime, we must continue doing the work of the One who sent me. Night is coming, when no one can work. [5]While I am in the world, I am the light of the world."

[6]After Jesus said this, he spit on the ground and made some mud with it and put the mud on the man's eyes. [7]Then he told the man, "Go and wash in the Pool of Siloam." (Siloam means Sent.) So the man went, washed, and came back seeing.

[8]The neighbors and some people who had earlier seen this man begging said, "Isn't this the same man who used to sit and beg?"

[9]Some said, "He is the one," but others said, "No, he only looks like him."

The man himself said, "I am the man."

[10]They asked, "How did you get your sight?"

[11]He answered, "The man named Jesus made some mud and put it on my eyes. Then he told me to go to Siloam and wash. So I went and washed, and then I could see."

8:39 "If . . . do Some Greek copies read "If you are really Abraham's children, you will do."

[12]They asked him, "Where is this man?"

"I don't know," he answered.

Pharisees Question the Healing

[13]Then the people took to the Pharisees the man who had been blind. [14]The day Jesus had made mud and healed his eyes was a Sabbath day. [15]So now the Pharisees asked the man, "How did you get your sight?"

He answered, "He put mud on my eyes, I washed, and now I see."

[16]So some of the Pharisees were saying, "This man does not keep the Sabbath day, so he is not from God."

But others said, "A man who is a sinner can't do miracles like these." So they could not agree with each other.

[17]They asked the man again, "What do you say about him since it was your eyes he opened?"

The man answered, "He is a prophet."

[18]These leaders did not believe that he had been blind and could now see again. So they sent for the man's parents [19]and asked them, "Is this your son who you say was born blind? Then how does he now see?"

[20]His parents answered, "We know that this is our son and that he was born blind. [21]But we don't know how he can now see. We don't know who opened his eyes. Ask him. He is old enough to speak for himself." [22]His parents said this because they were afraid of the elders, who had already decided that anyone who said Jesus was the Christ would be avoided. [23]That is why his parents said, "He is old enough. Ask him."

[24]So for the second time, they called the man who had been blind. They said, "You should give God the glory by telling the truth. We know that this man is a sinner."

[25]He answered, "I don't know if he is a sinner. One thing I do know: I was blind, and now I see."

[26]They asked, "What did he do to you? How did he make you see again?"

[27]He answered, "I already told you, and you didn't listen. Why do you want to hear it again? Do you want to become his followers, too?"

[28]Then they insulted him and said, "You are his follower, but we are followers of Moses. [29]We know that God spoke to Moses, but we don't even know where this man comes from."

[30]The man answered, "This is a very strange thing. You don't know where he comes from, and yet he opened my eyes. [31]We all know that God does not listen to sinners, but he listens to anyone who worships and obeys him. [32]Nobody has ever heard of anyone giving sight to a man born blind. [33]If this man were not from God, he could do nothing."

[34]They answered, "You were born full of sin! Are you trying to teach us?" And they threw him out.

Spiritual Blindness

[35]When Jesus heard that they had thrown him out, Jesus found him and said, "Do you believe in the Son of Man?"

[36]He asked, "Who is the Son of Man, sir, so that I can believe in him?"

[37]Jesus said to him, "You have seen him. The Son of Man is the one talking with you."

[38]He said, "Lord, I believe!" Then the man worshiped Jesus.

[39]Jesus said, "I came into this world so that the world could be judged. I came so that the blind[n] would see and so that those who see will become blind."

[40]Some of the Pharisees who were nearby heard Jesus say this and asked, "Are you saying we are blind, too?"

[41]Jesus said, "If you were blind, you would not be guilty of sin. But since you keep saying you see, your guilt remains."

The Shepherd and His Sheep

10 Jesus said, "I tell you the truth, the person who does not enter the sheepfold by the door, but climbs in some other way, is a thief and a robber. [2]The one who enters by the door is the shepherd of the sheep. [3]The one who guards the door opens it for him. And the sheep listen to the voice of the shepherd. He calls his own sheep by name and leads them out. [4]When he brings all his sheep out, he goes ahead of them, and they follow him because they know his voice. [5]But

HE SAID ↙ ↗ SHE SAID

What's the most important quality in a potential spouse?

HE: Loyalty to Jesus

SHE: Kindness

fun facts

90% of the jobs today's kindergartners will be doing when they reach adulthood do not even exist today.

(Academic.org)

9:39 blind Jesus is talking about people who are spiritually blind, not physically blind.

John 10:27–28

We never know what tomorrow will bring. From breast cancer to car accidents to terrorist attacks, there are many tragedies we could potentially be concerned about. And it's smart to exercise caution and wisdom. But do you ever find yourself worrying away like it's your favorite pastime? The almighty God has the entire world in his hands, and he lovingly reminds you that you don't need to lug around the weight of worry. Scripture says, "Give all your worries to him, because he cares about you" (1 Peter 5:7). So don't hold back—offer them up!

Knowing our eternity is secure with God frees us to live with courageous confidence. Jesus is our Good Shepherd, the strongest warrior, and the best caretaker. If we're his, we're perfectly protected for eternity! We shouldn't fear people or circumstances that can only hurt the body; instead, our primary concern should be whether our souls are right with God (Matthew 10:28).

As God's child, you are deeply precious to him. He promises to protect you from eternal harm, and he'll lovingly carry you through this life's difficulties. Take refuge in the King, and instead of worrying, pour your energy into what eternal life is all about: knowing and enjoying the only true God (John 17:3).

they will never follow a stranger. They will run away from him because they don't know his voice." [6]Jesus told the people this story, but they did not understand what it meant.

Jesus Is the Good Shepherd

[7]So Jesus said again, "I tell you the truth, I am the door for the sheep. [8]All the people who came before me were thieves and robbers. The sheep did not listen to them. [9]I am the door, and the person who enters through me will be saved and will be able to come in and go out and find pasture. [10]A thief comes to steal and kill and destroy, but I came to give life—life in all its fullness.

[11]"I am the good shepherd. The good shepherd gives his life for the sheep. [12]The worker who is paid to keep the sheep is different from the shepherd who owns them. When the worker sees a wolf coming, he runs away and leaves the sheep alone. Then the wolf attacks the sheep and scatters them. [13]The man runs away because he is only a paid worker and does not really care about the sheep.

[14]"I am the good shepherd. I know my sheep, and my sheep know me, [15]just as the Father knows me, and I know the Father. I give my life for the sheep. [16]I have other sheep that are not in this flock, and I must bring them also. They will listen to my voice, and there will be one flock and one shepherd. [17]The Father loves me because I give my life so that I can take it back again. [18]No one takes it away from me; I give my own life freely. I have the right to give my life, and I have the right to take it back. This is what my Father commanded me to do."

[19]Again the leaders did not agree with each other because of these words of Jesus. [20]Many of them said, "A demon has come into him and made him crazy. Why listen to him?"

[21]But others said, "A man who is crazy with a demon does not say things like this. Can a demon open the eyes of the blind?"

Jesus Is Rejected

[22]The time came for the Feast of Dedication at Jerusalem. It was winter, [23]and Jesus was walking in the Temple in Solomon's Porch. [24]Some people gathered around him and said, "How long will you make us wonder about you? If you are the Christ, tell us plainly."

[25]Jesus answered, "I told you already, but you did not believe. The miracles I do in my Father's name show who I am. [26]But you don't believe, because you are not my sheep. [27]My sheep listen to my voice; I know them, and they follow me. [28]I give them eternal life, and they will never die, and no one can steal them out of my hand. [29]My Father gave my sheep to me. He is greater than all, and no person can steal my sheep out of my Father's hand. [30]The Father and I are one."

[31]Again some of the people picked up stones to kill Jesus. [32]But he said to them, "I have done many good works from the Father. Which of these good works are you killing me for?"

[33]They answered, "We are not killing you because of any good work you did, but because you speak against God. You are only a human, but you say you are the same as God!"

[34]Jesus answered, "It is written in your law that God said, 'I said, you are gods.'[n] [35]This Scripture called those people gods who received God's message, and Scripture is always true. [36]So why do you say that I speak against God because I said, 'I am God's Son'? I am the one God chose and sent into the world. [37]If I don't do

10:34 'I . . . gods.' Quotation from Psalm 82:6.

what my Father does, then don't believe me. [38]But if I do what my Father does, even though you don't believe in me, believe what I do. Then you will know and understand that the Father is in me and I am in the Father."

[39]They tried to take Jesus again, but he escaped from them.

[40]Then he went back across the Jordan River to the place where John had first baptized. Jesus stayed there, [41]and many people came to him and said, "John never did a miracle, but everything John said about this man is true." [42]And in that place many believed in Jesus.

The Death of Lazarus

11 A man named Lazarus was sick. He lived in the town of Bethany, where Mary and her sister Martha lived. [2]Mary was the woman who later put perfume on the Lord and wiped his feet with her hair. Mary's brother was Lazarus, the man who was now sick. [3]So Mary and Martha sent someone to tell Jesus, "Lord, the one you love is sick."

[4]When Jesus heard this, he said, "This sickness will not end in death. It is for the glory of God, to bring glory to the Son of God." [5]Jesus loved Martha and her sister and Lazarus. [6]But when he heard that Lazarus was sick, he stayed where he was for two more days. [7]Then Jesus said to his followers, "Let's go back to Judea."

[8]The followers said, "But, Teacher, some people there tried to stone you to death only a short time ago. Now you want to go back there?"

[9]Jesus answered, "Are there not twelve hours in the day? If anyone walks in the daylight, he will not stumble, because he can see by this world's light. [10]But if anyone walks at night, he stumbles because there is no light to help him see."

[11]After Jesus said this, he added, "Our friend Lazarus has fallen asleep, but I am going there to wake him."

[12]The followers said, "But, Lord, if he is only asleep, he will be all right."

[13]Jesus meant that Lazarus was dead, but his followers thought he meant Lazarus was really sleeping. [14]So then Jesus said plainly, "Lazarus is dead. [15]And I am glad for your sakes I was not there so that you may believe. But let's go to him now."

[16]Then Thomas (the one called Didymus) said to the other followers, "Let us also go so that we can die with him."

Jesus in Bethany

[17]When Jesus arrived, he learned that Lazarus had already been dead and in the tomb for four days. [18]Bethany was about two miles from Jerusalem. [19]Many of the Jews had come there to comfort Martha and Mary about their brother.

[20]When Martha heard that Jesus was coming, she went out to meet him, but Mary stayed home. [21]Martha said to Jesus, "Lord, if you had been here, my brother would not have died. [22]But I know that even now God will give you anything you ask."

[23]Jesus said, "Your brother will rise and live again."

[24]Martha answered, "I know that he will rise and live again in the resurrection[n] on the last day."

[25]Jesus said to her, "I am the resurrection and the life. Those who believe in me will have life even if they die. [26]And everyone who lives and believes in me will never die. Martha, do you believe this?"

[27]Martha answered, "Yes, Lord. I believe that you are the Christ, the Son of God, the One coming to the world."

Jesus Cries

[28]After Martha said this, she went back and talked to her sister Mary alone. Martha said, "The Teacher is here and he is asking for you." [29]When Mary heard this, she got up quickly and went to Jesus. [30]Jesus had not yet come into the town but was still at the place where Martha had met him. [31]The Jews were with Mary in the house, comforting her. When they saw her stand and leave quickly, they followed her, thinking she was going to the tomb to cry there.

[32]But Mary went to the place where Jesus was. When she saw him, she fell at his feet and said, "Lord, if you had been here, my brother would not have died."

[33]When Jesus saw Mary crying and the Jews who came with her also crying, he was upset and was deeply troubled. [34]He asked, "Where did you bury him?"

"Come and see, Lord," they said.

[35]Jesus cried.

Rational vs. Irrational Fear

There is such a thing as *rational* fear. When you're being chased by a bear in the woods, for example, it's perfectly logical to be afraid. Parachuting out of an airplane is another situation where fear is a legitimate response. Fear can be a healthy, self-preserving response to dangerous situations. But when you walk in fear, day in and day out, it can control your life and your relationships. Second Timothy 1:7 tells us, "God did not give us a spirit that makes us afraid but a spirit of power and love and self-control." God is not the source of irrational fear, so ask him today for discernment between healthy and unhealthy fear in your life.

[36]So the Jews said, "See how much he loved him."

[37]But some of them said, "If Jesus opened the eyes of the blind man, why couldn't he keep Lazarus from dying?"

11:24 resurrection Being raised from the dead to live again.

RELATIONSHIPS

Broadening Your Horizons

Ever feel like life's a bit dull or you could use a new friend? Maybe a good friend moved away and your social calendar lacks a certain pizzazz. If so, why not broaden your horizons? Life is bursting with friendships waiting to happen! Join a book group, take a class, or give manicures at a nursing home. Proverbs 11:25 says, "Those who help others will themselves be helped." When you seek out others, your spirit's sure to get a boost. Step out of your comfort zone, and you'll discover whole new worlds of relationships.

Jesus Raises Lazarus

[38]Again feeling very upset, Jesus came to the tomb. It was a cave with a large stone covering the entrance. [39]Jesus said, "Move the stone away."

Martha, the sister of the dead man, said, "But, Lord, it has been four days since he died. There will be a bad smell."

[40]Then Jesus said to her, "Didn't I tell you that if you believed you would see the glory of God?"

[41]So they moved the stone away from the entrance. Then Jesus looked up and said, "Father, I thank you that you heard me. [42]I know that you always hear me, but I said these things because of the people here around me. I want them to believe that you sent me." [43]After Jesus said this, he cried out in a loud voice, "Lazarus, come out!" [44]The dead man came out, his hands and feet wrapped with pieces of cloth, and a cloth around his face.

Jesus said to them, "Take the cloth off of him and let him go."

The Plan to Kill Jesus

[45]Many of the people, who had come to visit Mary and saw what Jesus did, believed in him. [46]But some of them went to the Pharisees and told them what Jesus had done. [47]Then the leading priests and Pharisees called a meeting of the council. They asked, "What should we do? This man is doing many miracles. [48]If we let him continue doing these things, everyone will believe in him. Then the Romans will come and take away our Temple and our nation."

[49]One of the men there was Caiaphas, the high priest that year. He said, "You people know nothing! [50]You don't realize that it is better for one man to die for the people than for the whole nation to be destroyed."

[51]Caiaphas did not think of this himself. As high priest that year, he was really prophesying that Jesus would die for their nation [52]and for God's scattered children to bring them all together and make them one.

[53]That day they started planning to kill Jesus. [54]So Jesus no longer traveled openly among the people. He left there and went to a place near the desert, to a town called Ephraim and stayed there with his followers.

[55]It was almost time for the Passover Feast. Many from the country went up to Jerusalem before the Passover to do the special things to make themselves pure. [56]The people looked for Jesus and stood in the Temple asking each other, "Is he coming to the Feast? What do you think?" [57]But the leading priests and the Pharisees had given orders that if anyone knew where Jesus was, he must tell them. Then they could arrest him.

Jesus with Friends in Bethany

12 Six days before the Passover Feast, Jesus went to Bethany, where Lazarus lived. (Lazarus is the man Jesus raised from the dead.) [2]There they had a dinner for Jesus. Martha served the food, and Lazarus was one of the people eating with Jesus. [3]Mary brought in a pint of very expensive perfume made from pure nard. She poured the perfume on Jesus' feet, and then she wiped his feet with her hair. And the sweet smell from the perfume filled the whole house.

[4]Judas Iscariot, one of Jesus' followers who would later turn against him, was there. Judas said, [5]"This perfume was worth an entire year's wages. Why wasn't it sold and the money given to the poor?" [6]But Judas did not really care about the poor; he said this because he was a thief. He was the one who kept the money box, and he often stole from it.

[7]Jesus answered, "Leave her alone. It was right for her to save this perfume for today, the day for me to be prepared for

burial. [8]You will always have the poor with you, but you will not always have me."

The Plot Against Lazarus

[9]A large crowd of people heard that Jesus was in Bethany. So they went there to see not only Jesus but Lazarus, whom Jesus raised from the dead. [10]So the leading priests made plans to kill Lazarus, too. [11]Because of Lazarus many of the Jews were leaving them and believing in Jesus.

Jesus Enters Jerusalem

[12]The next day a great crowd who had come to Jerusalem for the Passover Feast heard that Jesus was coming there. [13]So they took branches of palm trees and went out to meet Jesus, shouting,

"Praise[n] God!
God bless the One who comes in the name of the Lord!
God bless the King of Israel!"

Psalm 118:25–26

[14]Jesus found a colt and sat on it. This was as the Scripture says,

[15]"Don't be afraid, people of Jerusalem!
Your king is coming,
sitting on the colt of a donkey."

Zechariah 9:9

[16]The followers of Jesus did not understand this at first. But after Jesus was raised to glory, they remembered that this had been written about him and that they had done these things to him.

People Tell About Jesus

[17]There had been many people with Jesus when he raised Lazarus from the dead and told him to come out of the tomb. Now they were telling others about what Jesus did. [18]Many people went out to meet Jesus, because they had heard about this miracle. [19]So the Pharisees said to each other, "You can see that nothing is going right for us. Look! The whole world is following him."

Jesus Talks About His Death

[20]There were some Greek people, too, who came to Jerusalem to worship at the Passover Feast. [21]They went to Philip, who was from Bethsaida in Galilee, and said, "Sir, we would like to see Jesus." [22]Philip told Andrew, and then Andrew and Philip told Jesus.

[23]Jesus said to them, "The time has come for the Son of Man to receive his glory. [24]I tell you the truth, a grain of wheat must fall to the ground and die to make many seeds. But if it never dies, it remains only a single seed. [25]Those who love their lives will lose them, but those who hate their lives in this world will keep true life forever. [26]Whoever serves me must follow me. Then my servant will be with me everywhere I am. My Father will honor anyone who serves me.

[27]"Now I am very troubled. Should I say, 'Father, save me from this time'? No, I came to this time so I could suffer. [28]Father, bring glory to your name!"

Then a voice came from heaven, "I have brought glory to it, and I will do it again."

[29]The crowd standing there, who heard the voice, said it was thunder.

But others said, "An angel has spoken to him."

[30]Jesus said, "That voice was for your sake, not mine. [31]Now is the time for the world to be judged; now the ruler of this world will be thrown down. [32]If I am lifted up from the earth, I will draw all people toward me." [33]Jesus said this to show how he would die.

[34]The crowd said, "We have heard from the law that the Christ will live forever. So why do you say, 'The Son of Man must be lifted up'? Who is this 'Son of Man'?"

[35]Then Jesus said, "The light will be with you for a little longer, so walk while you have the light. Then the darkness will not catch you. If you walk in the darkness, you will not know where you are going. [36]Believe in the light while you still have it so that you will become children of light." When Jesus had said this, he left and hid himself from them.

Some People Won't Believe in Jesus

[37]Though Jesus had done many miracles in front of the people, they still did not believe in him. [38]This was to bring about what Isaiah the prophet had said:

Be Still & KNOW

Wanted: REST

You lead an incredibly busy life. And the demands placed on you can sometimes seem unmanageable. Apparently being a kind, smart, "together" woman of God isn't always as easy as it looks. In fact, life can be completely overwhelming sometimes, can't it? If only there were somewhere you could go to find instant rest and renewal. Good news! While it may not always be "instant," you can *always* find rest and renewal by spending a little time with your heavenly Father. When you are tired, worn out, and exhausted from the hustle and bustle of life, call on him. In Matthew 11:28 Jesus said that everyone who is tired and under a heavy load can come to him, and he will give rest!

12:13 Praise Literally, "Hosanna," a Hebrew word used at first in praying to God for help, but at this time it was probably a shout of joy used in praising God or his Messiah.

Women & Men of the BIBLE

Mary: Extravagant Love

Mary showed unashamed, extravagant love for Jesus. She sat at his feet every chance she got and hung on his every word. On one occasion, she even poured her most expensive perfume over his feet in a spontaneous act of adoration. Few people understood her over-the-top devotion, however. She caught grief for it on more than one occasion! Jesus' followers and even her own sister didn't get her attitude of reckless abandon. Even so, she never let others deter her from truly worshiping her Savior. No amount of ridicule or personal sacrifice would keep her from loving Jesus! (John 12:1–8)

"Lord, who believed what we told them?
Who saw the Lord's power in this?" *Isaiah 53:1*

[39]This is why the people could not believe: Isaiah also had said,

[40]"He has blinded their eyes,
and he has closed their minds.
Otherwise they would see with their eyes
and understand in their minds
and come back to me and be healed." *Isaiah 6:10*

[41]Isaiah said this because he saw Jesus' glory and spoke about him.

[42]But many believed in Jesus, even many of the leaders. But because of the Pharisees, they did not say they believed in him for fear they would be put out of the synagogue. [43]They loved praise from people more than praise from God.

[44]Then Jesus cried out, "Whoever believes in me is really believing in the One who sent me. [45]Whoever sees me sees the One who sent me. [46]I have come as light into the world so that whoever believes in me would not stay in darkness.

[47]"Anyone who hears my words and does not obey them, I do not judge, because I did not come to judge the world, but to save the world. [48]There is a judge for those who refuse to believe in me and do not accept my words. The word I have taught will be their judge on the last day. [49]The things I taught were not from myself. The Father who sent me told me what to say and what to teach. [50]And I know that eternal life comes from what the Father commands. So whatever I say is what the Father told me to say."

Jesus Washes His Followers' Feet

13 It was almost time for the Passover Feast. Jesus knew that it was time for him to leave this world and go back to the Father. He had always loved those who were his own in the world, and he loved them all the way to the end.

[2]Jesus and his followers were at the evening meal. The devil had already persuaded Judas Iscariot, the son of Simon, to turn against Jesus. [3]Jesus knew that the Father had given him power over everything and that he had come from God and was going back to God. [4]So during the meal Jesus stood up and took off his outer clothing. Taking a towel, he wrapped it around his waist. [5]Then he poured water into a bowl and began to wash the followers' feet, drying them with the towel that was wrapped around him.

[6]Jesus came to Simon Peter, who said to him, "Lord, are you going to wash my feet?"

[7]Jesus answered, "You don't understand now what I am doing, but you will understand later."

[8]Peter said, "No, you will never wash my feet."

Jesus answered, "If I don't wash your feet, you are not one of my people."

[9]Simon Peter answered, "Lord, then wash not only my feet, but wash my hands and my head, too!"

[10]Jesus said, "After a person has had a bath, his whole body is clean. He needs only to wash his feet. And you men are clean, but not all of you." [11]Jesus knew who would turn against him, and that is why he said, "Not all of you are clean."

[12]When he had finished washing their feet, he put on his clothes and sat down again. He asked, "Do you understand what I have just done for you? [13]You call me 'Teacher' and 'Lord,' and you are right, because that is what I am. [14]If I, your Lord and Teacher, have washed your feet, you also should wash each other's feet. [15]I did this as an example so that you should do as I have done for you. [16]I tell you the truth, a servant is not greater than his master. A messenger is not greater than the one who sent him. [17]If you know these things, you will be blessed if you do them.

[18]"I am not talking about all of you. I know those I have chosen. But this is to bring about what the Scripture said: 'The man who ate at my table has turned against me.'[n] [19]I am telling you this now before it happens so that when it happens, you will believe that I am he. [20]I tell you the truth, whoever accepts anyone I send

fun facts

A recent survey found that 8 out of 10 Americans believe they live a simple life.

(Barna.org)

13:18 **'The man . . . me.'** Quotation from Psalm 41:9.

also accepts me. And whoever accepts me also accepts the One who sent me."

Jesus Talks About His Death

[21]After Jesus said this, he was very troubled. He said openly, "I tell you the truth, one of you will turn against me."

[22]The followers all looked at each other, because they did not know whom Jesus was talking about. [23]One of the followers sitting[n] next to Jesus was the follower Jesus loved. [24]Simon Peter motioned to him to ask Jesus whom he was talking about.

[25]That follower leaned closer to Jesus and asked, "Lord, who is it?"

[26]Jesus answered, "I will dip this bread into the dish. The man I give it to is the man who will turn against me." So Jesus took a piece of bread, dipped it, and gave it to Judas Iscariot, the son of Simon. [27]As soon as Judas took the bread, Satan entered him. Jesus said to him, "The thing that you will do—do it quickly." [28]No one at the table understood why Jesus said this to Judas. [29]Since he was the one who kept the money box, some of the followers thought Jesus was telling him to buy what was needed for the feast or to give something to the poor.

[30]Judas took the bread Jesus gave him and immediately went out. It was night.

[31]When Judas was gone, Jesus said, "Now the Son of Man receives his glory, and God receives glory through him. [32]If God receives glory through him,[n] then God will give glory to the Son through himself. And God will give him glory quickly."

[33]Jesus said, "My children, I will be with you only a little longer. You will look for me, and what I told the Jews, I tell you now: Where I am going you cannot come.

[34]"I give you a new command: Love each other. You must love each other as I have loved you. [35]All people will know that you are my followers if you love each other."

Peter Will Say He Doesn't Know Jesus

[36]Simon Peter asked Jesus, "Lord, where are you going?"

Jesus answered, "Where I am going you cannot follow now, but you will follow later."

[37]Peter asked, "Lord, why can't I follow you now? I am ready to die for you!"

[38]Jesus answered, "Are you ready to die for me? I tell you the truth, before the rooster crows, you will say three times that you don't know me."

Jesus Comforts His Followers

14 Jesus said, "Don't let your hearts be troubled. Trust in God, and trust in me. [2]There are many rooms in my Father's house; I would not tell you this if it were not true. I am going there to prepare a place for you. [3]After I go and prepare a place for you, I will come back and take you to be with me so that you may be where I am. [4]You know the way to the place where I am going."[n]

[5]Thomas said to Jesus, "Lord, we don't know where you are going. So how can we know the way?"

[6]Jesus answered, "I am the way, and the truth, and the life. The only way to the Father is through me. [7]If you really knew me, you would know my Father, too. But now you do know him, and you have seen him."

[8]Philip said to him, "Lord, show us the Father. That is all we need."

[9]Jesus answered, "I have been with you a long time now. Do you still not know me, Philip? Whoever has seen me has seen the Father. So why do you say, 'Show us the Father'? [10]Don't you believe that I am in the Father and the Father is in me? The words I say to you don't come from me, but the Father lives in me and does his own work. [11]Believe me when I say that I am in the Father and the Father is in me. Or believe because of the miracles I have done. [12]I tell you the truth, whoever believes in me will do the same things that I do. Those who believe will do even greater things than these, because I am going to the Father. [13]And if you ask for anything in my name, I will do it for you so that the Father's glory will be shown through the Son. [14]If you ask me for anything in my name, I will do it.

The Promise of the Holy Spirit

[15]"If you love me, you will obey my commands. [16]I will ask the Father, and he will give you another Helper[n] to be with you forever— [17]the Spirit of truth. The world cannot accept him, because it does not see him or know him. But you

all about MEN

Team Players for Purity

Our eyes are windows to the world, but they're also windows to the world's temptations. Images that toy with our commitment to purity are prevalent, and guarding godly thoughts and actions is a tough battle that we're not strong enough to win on our own. We need God-sized ammo! Dating or not, it's never too early to ask for God's help in the purity war. But add another strategy: pray that your guy would be committed to pray for *your* purity. God can place that desire on his heart even if you haven't met yet. Purity is a team effort of three—you two and God—and "a rope that is woven of three strings is hard to break" (Ecclesiastes 4:12).

13:23 sitting Literally, "lying." The people of that time ate lying down and leaning on one arm. **13:32 If . . . him** Some Greek copies do not have this phrase. **14:4 You . . . going.** Some Greek copies read "You know where I am going and the way to the place I am going." **14:16 Helper** "Counselor" or "Comforter." Jesus is talking about the Holy Spirit.

know him, because he lives with you and he will be in you.

[18]"I will not leave you all alone like orphans; I will come back to you. [19]In a little while the world will not see me anymore, but you will see me. Because I live, you will live, too. [20]On that day you will know that I am in my Father, and that you are in me and I am in you. [21]Those who know my commands and obey them are the ones who love me, and my Father will love those who love me. I will love them and will show myself to them."

[22]Then Judas (not Judas Iscariot) said, "But, Lord, why do you plan to show yourself to us and not to the rest of the world?"

[23]Jesus answered, "If people love me, they will obey my teaching. My Father will love them, and we will come to them and make our home with them. [24]Those who do not love me do not obey my teaching. This teaching that you hear is not really mine; it is from my Father, who sent me.

[25]"I have told you all these things while I am with you. [26]But the Helper will teach you everything and will cause you to remember all that I told you. This Helper is the Holy Spirit whom the Father will send in my name.

[27]"I leave you peace; my peace I give you. I do not give it to you as the world does. So don't let your hearts be troubled or afraid. [28]You heard me say to you, 'I am going, but I am coming back to you.' If you loved me, you should be happy that I am going back to the Father, because he is greater than I am. [29]I have told you this now, before it happens, so that when it happens, you will believe. [30]I will not talk with you much longer, because the ruler of this world is coming. He has no power over me, [31]but the world must know that I love the Father, so I do exactly what the Father told me to do.

"Come now, let us go.

Jesus Is Like a Vine

15 "I am the true vine; my Father is the gardener. [2]He cuts off every branch of mine that does not produce fruit. And he trims and cleans every branch that produces fruit so that it will produce even more fruit. [3]You are already clean because of the words I have spoken to you. [4]Remain in me, and I will remain in you. A branch cannot produce fruit alone but must remain in the vine. In the same way, you cannot produce fruit alone but must remain in me.

[5]"I am the vine, and you are the branches. If any remain in me and I remain in them, they produce much fruit. But without me they can do nothing. [6]If any do not remain in me, they are like a branch that is thrown away and then dies. People pick up dead branches, throw them into the fire, and burn them. [7]If you remain in me and follow my teachings, you can ask anything you want, and it will be given to you. [8]You should produce much fruit and show that you are my followers, which brings glory to my Father. [9]I loved you as the Father loved me. Now remain in my love. [10]I have obeyed my Father's commands, and I remain in his love. In the same way, if you obey my commands, you will remain in my love. [11]I have told you these things so that you can have the same joy I have and so that your joy will be the fullest possible joy.

[12]"This is my command: Love each other as I have loved you. [13]The greatest love a person can show is to die for his friends. [14]You are my friends if you do what I command you. [15]I no longer call you servants, because a servant does not know what his master is doing. But I call you friends, because I have made known to you everything I heard from my Father. [16]You did not choose me; I chose you. And I gave you this work: to go and produce fruit, fruit that will last. Then

BECOME *Involved*

WorldCrafts

All your what-to-buy-that-friend, gift-shopping woes are gone! WorldCrafts is your one-click stop for beautiful, unique, high-quality gifts that make a real difference to both the recipient and the artisan who made them. A fair trade organization, WorldCrafts works with relief agencies and Christians around the world to import handcrafts from all seven continents. Then they make the products available to you at reasonable and respectable prices.

You (or the friend you're shopping for) get a great purchase at a good price, but you also get the satisfaction of knowing you literally just bought hope for a family in need. You can buy based on country of origin or by type of product. Most of the items are handmade and will amaze you with their beauty and design!

WorldCrafts is looking for people who are willing to host an event or party. They provide you with everything you need and ideas for promotion as well. And to bring home the reality of the partnership with local artisans, the product catalog comes with a prayer guide for the people and countries represented. Find more information and an online store at www.worldcraftsvillage.com. Shop on, sister!

the Father will give you anything you ask for in my name. [17]This is my command: Love each other.

Jesus Warns His Followers

[18]"If the world hates you, remember that it hated me first. [19]If you belonged to the world, it would love you as it loves its own. But I have chosen you out of the world, so you don't belong to it. That is why the world hates you. [20]Remember what I told you: A servant is not greater than his master. If people did wrong to me, they will do wrong to you, too. And if they obeyed my teaching, they will obey yours, too. [21]They will do all this to you on account of me, because they do not know the One who sent me. [22]If I had not come and spoken to them, they would not be guilty of sin, but now they have no excuse for their sin. [23]Whoever hates me also hates my Father. [24]I did works among them that no one else has ever done. If I had not done these works, they would not be guilty of sin. But now they have seen what I have done, and yet they have hated both me and my Father. [25]But this happened so that what is written in their law would be true: 'They hated me for no reason.'[n]

[26]"I will send you the Helper[n] from the Father; he is the Spirit of truth who comes from the Father. When he comes, he will tell about me, [27]and you also must tell people about me, because you have been with me from the beginning.

John 16:33

No one likes to hear, "Get ready to put in extra hours!" when they're assigned a big project at work. Likewise, it would've been nice if Jesus had said, "Once you're mine, you'll never struggle or feel pain again." Instead his message was, "Take up your cross," "the road is narrow," and "in this world you will have trouble." Tough to swallow, right?

But Jesus also promised peace, victory, and eternal life. His is the only path with a good destination and a meaningful relationship along the way. When heartache comes, we won't be alone. Our loving Father never leaves us! His closeness and great power outweigh any earthly pain. When persecution and hardships come, we're not powerless. Our heavenly Father is the King of the world who supplies what's needed to endure anything. Because of Christ, we can see troubles on earth as small and momentary compared to eternity (2 Corinthians 4:17). We have a beautiful future—heaven will be full of God's glory and perfection.

We may rarely find ourselves on the easy road, but the easy road wouldn't let us know and enjoy God. On the narrow road or in the middle of trouble, you'll find the greatest hope there is—Jesus himself.

16 "I have told you these things to keep you from giving up. [2]People will put you out of their synagogues. Yes, the time is coming when those who kill you will think they are offering service to God. [3]They will do this because they have not known the Father and they have not known me. [4]I have told you these things now so that when the time comes you will remember that I warned you.

The Work of the Holy Spirit

"I did not tell you these things at the beginning, because I was with you then. [5]Now I am going back to the One who sent me. But none of you asks me, 'Where are you going?' [6]Your hearts are filled with sadness because I have told you these things. [7]But I tell you the truth, it is better for you that I go away. When I go away, I will send the Helper[n] to you. If I do not go away, the Helper will not come. [8]When the Helper comes, he will prove to the people of the world the truth about sin, about being right with God, and about judgment. [9]He will prove to them that sin is not believing in me. [10]He will prove to them that being right with God comes from my going to the Father and not being seen anymore. [11]And the Helper will prove to them that judgment happened when the ruler of this world was judged.

[12]"I have many more things to say to you, but they are too much for you now. [13]But when the Spirit of truth comes, he will lead you into all truth. He will not speak his own words, but he will speak only what he hears, and he will tell you what is to come. [14]The Spirit of truth will bring glory to me, because he will take what I have to say and tell it to you. [15]All that the Father has is mine. That is why I said that the Spirit will take what I have to say and tell it to you.

Sadness Will Become Happiness

[16]"After a little while you will not see me, and then after a little while you will see me again."

[17]Some of the followers said to each other, "What does Jesus mean when he says, 'After a little while you will not see me, and then after a little while you will see me again'? And what does he mean

15:25 'They . . . reason.' These words could be from Psalm 35:19 or Psalm 69:4. **15:26; 16:7 Helper** "Counselor" or "Comforter." Jesus is talking about the Holy Spirit.

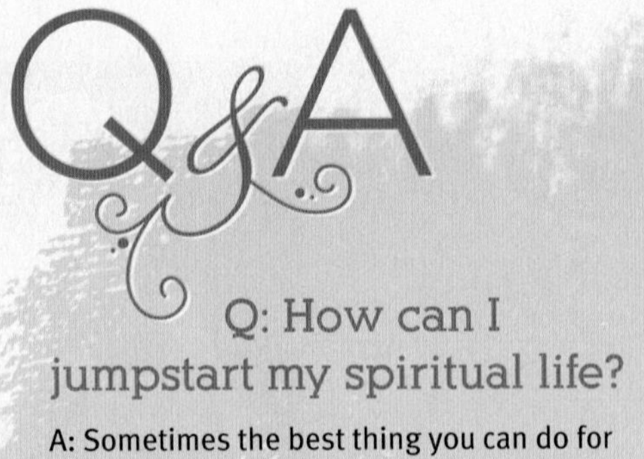

Q: How can I jumpstart my spiritual life?

A: Sometimes the best thing you can do for your spiritual life is to mix it up a little bit. It's very easy to allow godly activities to become so familiar that they lack the impact they once had. If you feel stuck in a rut, try visiting a different church, attending a Christian conference, or participating in a mission trip. Consider spicing up your daily quiet time by adding music, listening to a sermon online, or simply changing locations. Get as creative as you want to be, for you serve a very creative God. You will both enjoy a fun change of pace from time to time!

when he says, 'Because I am going to the Father'?" [18]They also asked, "What does he mean by 'a little while'? We don't understand what he is saying."

[19]Jesus saw that the followers wanted to ask him about this, so he said to them, "Are you asking each other what I meant when I said, 'After a little while you will not see me, and then after a little while you will see me again'? [20]I tell you the truth, you will cry and be sad, but the world will be happy. You will be sad, but your sadness will become joy. [21]When a woman gives birth to a baby, she has pain, because her time has come. But when her baby is born, she forgets the pain, because she is so happy that a child has been born into the world. [22]It is the same with you. Now you are sad, but I will see you again and you will be happy, and no one will take away your joy. [23]In that day you will not ask me for anything. I tell you the truth, my Father will give you anything you ask for in my name. [24]Until now you have not asked for anything in my name. Ask and you will receive, so that your joy will be the fullest possible joy.

Victory over the World

[25]"I have told you these things indirectly in stories. But the time will come when I will not use stories like that to tell you things; I will speak to you in plain words about the Father. [26]In that day you will ask the Father for things in my name. I mean, I will not need to ask the Father for you. [27]The Father himself loves you. He loves you because you loved me and believed that I came from God. [28]I came from the Father into the world. Now I am leaving the world and going back to the Father."

[29]Then the followers of Jesus said, "You are speaking clearly to us now and are not using stories that are hard to understand. [30]We can see now that you know all things. You can answer a person's question even before it is asked. This makes us believe you came from God."

[31]Jesus answered, "So now you believe? [32]Listen to me; a time is coming when you will be scattered, each to your own home. That time is now here. You will leave me alone, but I am never really alone, because the Father is with me.

[33]"I told you these things so that you can have peace in me. In this world you will have trouble, but be brave! I have defeated the world."

Jesus Prays for His Followers

17 After Jesus said these things, he looked toward heaven and prayed, "Father, the time has come. Give glory to your Son so that the Son can give glory to you. [2]You gave the Son power over all people so that the Son could give eternal life to all those you gave him. [3]And this is eternal life: that people know you, the only true God, and that they know Jesus Christ, the One you sent. [4]Having finished the work you gave me to do, I brought you glory on earth. [5]And now, Father, give me glory with you; give me the glory I had with you before the world was made.

[6]"I showed what you are like to those you gave me from the world. They belonged to you, and you gave them to me, and they have obeyed your teaching. [7]Now they know that everything you gave me comes from you. [8]I gave them the teachings you gave me, and they accepted them. They knew that I truly came from you, and they believed that you sent me. [9]I am praying for them. I am not praying for people in the world but for those you gave me, be-

fun facts

The redemption rate for coupons has dropped 25% since 2001.

(Kiplinger's)

cause they are yours. [10]All I have is yours, and all you have is mine. And my glory is shown through them. [11]I am coming to you; I will not stay in the world any longer. But they are still in the world. Holy Father, keep them safe by the power of your name, the name you gave me, so that they will be one, just as you and I are one. [12]While I was with them, I kept them safe by the power of your name, the name you gave me. I protected them, and only one of them, the one worthy of destruction, was lost so that the Scripture would come true.

[13]"I am coming to you now. But I pray these things while I am still in the world so that these followers can have all of my joy in them. [14]I have given them your teaching. And the world has hated them, because they don't belong to the world, just as I don't belong to the world. [15]I am not asking you to take them out of the world but to keep them safe from the Evil One. [16]They don't belong to the world, just as I don't belong to the world. [17]Make them ready for your service through your truth; your teaching is truth. [18]I have sent them into the world, just as you sent me into the world. [19]For their sake, I am making myself ready to serve so that they can be ready for their service of the truth.

[20]"I pray for these followers, but I am also praying for all those who will believe in me because of their teaching. [21]Father, I pray that they can be one. As you are in me and I am in you, I pray that they can also be one in us. Then the world will believe that you sent me. [22]I have given these people the glory that you gave me so that they can be one, just as you and I are one. [23]I will be in them and you will be in me so that they will be completely one. Then the world will know that you sent me and that you loved them just as much as you loved me.

[24]"Father, I want these people that you gave me to be with me where I am. I want them to see my glory, which you gave me because you loved me before the world was made. [25]Father, you are the One who is good. The world does not know you, but I know you, and these people know you sent me. [26]I showed them what you are like, and I will show them again. Then they will have the same love that you have for me, and I will live in them."

Jesus Is Arrested

18 When Jesus finished praying, he went with his followers across the Kidron Valley. On the other side there was a garden, and Jesus and his followers went into it.

[2]Judas knew where this place was, because Jesus met there often with his followers. Judas was the one who turned against Jesus. [3]So Judas came there with a group of soldiers and some guards from the leading priests and the Pharisees. They were carrying torches, lanterns, and weapons.

[4]Knowing everything that would happen to him, Jesus went out and asked, "Who is it you are looking for?"

[5]They answered, "Jesus from Nazareth."

"I am he," Jesus said. (Judas, the one who turned against Jesus, was standing there with them.) [6]When Jesus said, "I am he," they moved back and fell to the ground.

[7]Jesus asked them again, "Who is it you are looking for?"

They said, "Jesus of Nazareth."

[8]"I told you that I am he," Jesus said. "So if you are looking for me, let the others go." [9]This happened so that the words Jesus said before would come true: "I have not lost any of the ones you gave me."

[10]Simon Peter, who had a sword, pulled it out and struck the servant of the high priest, cutting off his right ear. (The servant's name was Malchus.) [11]Jesus said to Peter, "Put your sword back. Shouldn't I drink the cup[n] the Father gave me?"

Jesus Is Brought Before Annas

[12]Then the soldiers with their commander and the guards arrested Jesus. They tied him [13]and led him first to Annas, the father-in-law of Caiaphas, the high priest that year. [14]Caiaphas was the one who told the Jews that it would be better if one man died for all the people.

Peter Says He Doesn't Know Jesus

[15]Simon Peter and another one of Jesus' followers went along after Jesus. This follower knew the high priest, so he went with Jesus into the high priest's courtyard. [16]But Peter waited outside near the door. The follower who knew the high priest came back outside, spoke to the girl at the door, and brought Peter inside. [17]The girl at the door said to Peter, "Aren't you also one of that man's followers?"

Peter answered, "No, I am not!"

[18]It was cold, so the servants and guards had built a fire and were standing around

Health

Is Your Biological Clock Ticking?

It starts in your early twenties as a mellow "tick-tock." By your late thirties, it escalates to a bold "TICK-TOCK." At forty-five, alarm bells are clanging with vigor. For some, the biological clock—a woman's desire and ability to have children—is a frantic race against time. If you're single or childless by choice, maybe you're not worried. But for the woman who really wants a child—but hasn't yet met Mr. Right—the concern is real. A woman's fertility begins to decline at age twenty-five, with a marked decrease after age thirty-five. On the positive side, advances in science are helping women deliver healthy babies in their forties and beyond. And remember, God is not limited by human parameters—he gave Sarah a child in her old age (Romans 4:19). But who says you have to give birth to be a mommy? Adopting or fostering a child is a loving choice.

18:11 cup Jesus is talking about the painful things that will happen to him. Accepting these things will be very hard, like drinking a cup of something bitter.

RELATIONSHIPS

What's Your Love Quality?

Here's a hypothetical question: if someone you love lets you down big-time, would they believe that you still loved them? Sometimes relationships end because of betrayal or other serious hurts. But what if this let-down was a one-time thing? What if the person is genuinely sorry and works hard to repair the damage? Is your love the kind that works through hurts, offering forgiveness and another chance? We're to "love each other deeply, because love will cause people to forgive each other for many sins" (1 Peter 4:8). That quality of love is tough. But then again, that's how God loves us.

it, warming themselves. Peter also was standing with them, warming himself.

The High Priest Questions Jesus

[19]The high priest asked Jesus questions about his followers and his teaching. [20]Jesus answered, "I have spoken openly to everyone. I have always taught in synagogues and in the Temple, where all the Jews come together. I never said anything in secret. [21]So why do you question me? Ask the people who heard my teaching. They know what I said."

[22]When Jesus said this, one of the guards standing there hit him. The guard said, "Is that the way you answer the high priest?"

[23]Jesus answered him, "If I said something wrong, then show what it was. But if what I said is true, why do you hit me?"

[24]Then Annas sent Jesus, who was still tied, to Caiaphas the high priest.

Peter Says Again He Doesn't Know Jesus

[25]As Simon Peter was standing and warming himself, they said to him, "Aren't you one of that man's followers?"

Peter said it was not true; he said, "No, I am not."

[26]One of the servants of the high priest was there. This servant was a relative of the man whose ear Peter had cut off. The servant said, "Didn't I see you with him in the garden?"

[27]Again Peter said it wasn't true. At once a rooster crowed.

Jesus Is Brought Before Pilate

[28]Early in the morning they led Jesus from Caiaphas's house to the Roman governor's palace. They would not go inside the palace, because they did not want to make themselves unclean;[n] they wanted to eat the Passover meal. [29]So Pilate went outside to them and asked, "What charges do you bring against this man?"

[30]They answered, "If he were not a criminal, we wouldn't have brought him to you."

[31]Pilate said to them, "Take him yourselves and judge him by your own law."

"But we are not allowed to put anyone to death," the Jews answered. [32](This happened so that what Jesus said about how he would die would come true.)

[33]Then Pilate went back inside the palace and called Jesus to him and asked, "Are you the king of the Jews?"

[34]Jesus said, "Is that your own question, or did others tell you about me?"

[35]Pilate answered, "I am not one of you. It was your own people and their leading priests who handed you over to me. What have you done wrong?"

[36]Jesus answered, "My kingdom does not belong to this world. If it belonged to this world, my servants would have fought to keep me from being given over to the Jewish leaders. But my kingdom is from another place."

[37]Pilate said, "So you are a king!"

Jesus answered, "You are the one saying I am a king. This is why I was born and came into the world: to tell people the truth. And everyone who belongs to the truth listens to me."

[38]Pilate said, "What is truth?" After he said this, he went out to the crowd again and said to them, "I find nothing against this man. [39]But it is your custom that I free one prisoner to you at Passover time. Do you want me to free the 'king of the Jews'?"

[40]They shouted back, "No, not him! Let Barabbas go free!" (Barabbas was a robber.)

19 Then Pilate ordered that Jesus be taken away and whipped. [2]The soldiers made a crown from some thorny branches and put it on Jesus' head and put a purple robe around him. [3]Then they came to him many times

18:28 unclean Going into the Roman palace would make them unfit to eat the Passover Feast, according to their Law.

Love is patient and kind.
Love is not jealous, it does not brag,
and it is not proud. —1 Corinthians 13:4

April

It's *April Fool's Day.* Pray for someone instead of playing a prank. 1	2	Treat yourself to a massage. 3	The 1st Friday of April is National Walk to Work Day. Take a stroll! 4	5
Check the dates on your canned goods. Throw away anything questionable. 6	7	Read Genesis 1. Thank God for his creation. 8	Spend some time listening to a worship CD today. 9	Make a donation to a homeless shelter. 10
11	12	Pray for local school teachers today. 13	Spend an afternoon deep cleaning your home. 14	It's Tax Day! Be sure to postmark your returns by today. 15
16	Celebrate National Humor Month—laugh out loud with friends! 17	18	Organize a garage sale for the neighborhood. 19	20
Plant an herb garden. 21	Offer to baby-sit for a single mom. 22	It's William Shakespeare's birthday. Read *Romeo & Juliet.* 23	24	Plan a picnic with your family. 25
Check your first aid kit. Make sure you're well stocked for an emergency. 26	27	Schedule a weekend getaway with friends. 28	Pray for a person of influence: it's Michelle Pfeiffer's birthday. 29	30

HE SAID ↙ ↗ SHE SAID

Are you a morning person or a night owl?

HE: Morning

SHE: Night owl

and said, "Hail, King of the Jews!" and hit him in the face.

[4]Again Pilate came out and said to them, "Look, I am bringing Jesus out to you. I want you to know that I find nothing against him." [5]So Jesus came out, wearing the crown of thorns and the purple robe. Pilate said to them, "Here is the man!"

[6]When the leading priests and the guards saw Jesus, they shouted, "Crucify him! Crucify him!"

But Pilate answered, "Crucify him yourselves, because I find nothing against him."

[7]The leaders answered, "We have a law that says he should die, because he said he is the Son of God."

[8]When Pilate heard this, he was even more afraid. [9]He went back inside the palace and asked Jesus, "Where do you come from?" But Jesus did not answer him. [10]Pilate said, "You refuse to speak to me? Don't you know I have power to set you free and power to have you crucified?"

[11]Jesus answered, "The only power you have over me is the power given to you by God. The man who turned me in to you is guilty of a greater sin."

[12]After this, Pilate tried to let Jesus go. But some in the crowd cried out, "Anyone who makes himself king is against Caesar. If you let this man go, you are no friend of Caesar."

[13]When Pilate heard what they were saying, he brought Jesus out and sat down on the judge's seat at the place called The Stone Pavement. (In the Hebrew language[n] the name is Gabbatha.) [14]It was about noon on Preparation Day of Passover week. Pilate said to the crowd, "Here is your king!"

[15]They shouted, "Take him away! Take him away! Crucify him!"

Pilate asked them, "Do you want me to crucify your king?"

The leading priests answered, "The only king we have is Caesar."

[16]So Pilate handed Jesus over to them to be crucified.

LIFE ISSUES

Hunger

Faces hollowed by malnutrition, eyes sunken without hope. Starving people across the globe, hungry ones close by. It's good to feel compassion for those in need. Fortunately you don't need bottomless pockets to make a difference—you only need Jesus' heart. With loose change and gently used donations, you can support thrift stores, food pantries, child sponsorships, refugee services, or countless other ministries. Even if your efforts help only one person, your acts of kindness and generosity will not soon be forgotten—by that individual or by God.

Jesus Is Crucified

The soldiers took charge of Jesus. [17]Carrying his own cross, Jesus went out to a place called The Place of the Skull, which in the Hebrew language[n] is called Golgotha. [18]There they crucified Jesus. They also crucified two other men, one on each side, with Jesus in the middle. [19]Pilate wrote a sign and put it on the cross. It read: JESUS OF NAZARETH, THE KING OF THE JEWS. [20]The sign was written in Hebrew, in Latin, and in Greek. Many of the people read the sign, because the place where Jesus was crucified was near the city. [21]The leading priests said to Pilate, "Don't write, 'The King of the Jews.' But write, 'This man said, "I am the King of the Jews." ' "

[22]Pilate answered, "What I have written, I have written."

[23]After the soldiers crucified Jesus, they took his clothes and divided them into four parts, with each soldier getting one part. They also took his long shirt, which was all one piece of cloth, woven from top to bottom. [24]So the soldiers said to each other, "We should not tear this into parts. Let's throw lots to see who will get it." This happened so that this Scripture would come true:

> "They divided my clothes among
> them,
> and they threw lots for my
> clothing." *Psalm 22:18*

So the soldiers did this.

[25]Standing near his cross were Jesus' mother, his mother's sister, Mary the wife of Clopas, and Mary Magdalene. [26]When Jesus saw his mother and the follower he loved standing nearby, he said to his mother, "Dear woman, here is your son." [27]Then he said to the follower, "Here is your mother." From that time on, the follower took her to live in his home.

19:13, 17 Hebrew language Or Aramaic, the languages of many people in this region in the first century.

Jesus Dies

28After this, Jesus knew that everything had been done. So that the Scripture would come true, he said, "I am thirsty."[n] 29There was a jar full of vinegar there, so the soldiers soaked a sponge in it, put the sponge on a branch of a hyssop plant, and lifted it to Jesus' mouth. 30When Jesus tasted the vinegar, he said, "It is finished." Then he bowed his head and died.

31This day was Preparation Day, and the next day was a special Sabbath day. Since the religious leaders did not want the bodies to stay on the cross on the Sabbath day, they asked Pilate to order that the legs of the men be broken[n] and the bodies be taken away. 32So the soldiers came and broke the legs of the first man on the cross beside Jesus. Then they broke the legs of the man on the other cross beside Jesus. 33But when the soldiers came to Jesus and saw that he was already dead, they did not break his legs. 34But one of the soldiers stuck his spear into Jesus' side, and at once blood and water came out. 35(The one who saw this happen is the one who told us this, and whatever he says is true. And he knows that he tells the truth, and he tells it so that you might believe.) 36These things happened to make the Scripture come true: "Not one of his bones will be broken."[n] 37And another Scripture says, "They will look at the one they stabbed."[n]

Jesus Is Buried

38Later, Joseph from Arimathea asked Pilate if he could take the body of Jesus. (Joseph was a secret follower of Jesus, because he was afraid of some of the leaders.) Pilate gave his permission, so Joseph came and took Jesus' body away. 39Nicodemus, who earlier had come to Jesus at night, went with Joseph. He brought about seventy-five pounds of myrrh and aloes. 40These two men took Jesus' body and wrapped it with the spices in pieces of linen cloth, which is how they bury the dead. 41In the place where Jesus was crucified, there was a garden. In the garden was a new tomb that had never been used before. 42The men laid Jesus in that tomb because it was nearby, and they were preparing to start their Sabbath day.

Butter Pecan Trifle

Here's a sweet-tooth satisfier that holds its own in both casual and elegant gatherings. In a 9x13 pan, bake a butter pecan cake mix according to package directions. While cake is warm, spread 2/3 to 1 cup of caramel or praline ice cream topping evenly on the cake. Cool in the fridge. Meanwhile, toast 1/2 cup of pecans at 375° for 5–7 minutes and beat 1 pint of heavy whipping cream to stiff peaks. Cut cake into 1-inch cubes. In a trifle bowl, layer cake cubes, cream, and nuts 3 times. Then prepare for the wow factor!

Jesus' Tomb Is Empty

20 Early on the first day of the week, Mary Magdalene went to the tomb while it was still dark. When she saw that the large stone had been moved away from the tomb, 2she ran to Simon Peter and the follower whom Jesus loved. Mary said, "They have taken the Lord out of the tomb, and we don't know where they have put him."

3So Peter and the other follower started for the tomb. 4They were both running, but the other follower ran faster than Peter and reached the tomb first. 5He bent down and looked in and saw the strips of linen cloth lying there, but he did not go in. 6Then following him, Simon Peter arrived and went into the tomb and saw the strips of linen lying there. 7He also saw the cloth that had been around Jesus' head, which was folded up and laid in a different place from the strips of linen. 8Then the other follower, who had reached the tomb first, also went in. He saw and believed. 9(They did not yet understand from the Scriptures that Jesus must rise from the dead.)

Jesus Appears to Mary Magdalene

10Then the followers went back home. 11But Mary stood outside the tomb, crying. As she was crying, she bent down and looked inside the tomb. 12She saw two angels dressed in white, sitting where Jesus' body had been, one at the head and one at the feet.

13They asked her, "Woman, why are you crying?"

She answered, "They have taken away my Lord, and I don't know where they have put him." 14When Mary said this, she turned around and saw Jesus standing there, but she did not know it was Jesus.

15Jesus asked her, "Woman, why are you crying? Whom are you looking for?"

Thinking he was the gardener, she said to him, "Did you take him away, sir? Tell me where you put him, and I will get him."

16Jesus said to her, "Mary."

Mary turned toward Jesus and said in the Hebrew language,[n] "Rabboni." (This means "Teacher.")

17Jesus said to her, "Don't hold on to me,

19:28 "I am thirsty." Read Psalms 22:15; 69:21. **19:31 broken** The breaking of their bones would make them die sooner. **19:36 "Not one . . . broken."** Quotation from Psalm 34:20. The idea is from Exodus 12:46; Numbers 9:12. **19:37 "They . . . stabbed."** Quotation from Zechariah 12:10. **20:16 Hebrew language** Or Aramaic, the languages of many people in this region in the first century.

because I have not yet gone up to the Father. But go to my brothers and tell them, 'I am going back to my Father and your Father, to my God and your God.' "

[18]Mary Magdalene went and said to the followers, "I saw the Lord!" And she told them what Jesus had said to her.

Jesus Appears to His Followers

[19]When it was evening on the first day of the week, Jesus' followers were together. The doors were locked, because they were afraid of the elders. Then Jesus came and stood right in the middle of them and said, "Peace be with you." [20]After he said this, he showed them his hands and his side. His followers were thrilled when they saw the Lord.

[21]Then Jesus said again, "Peace be with you. As the Father sent me, I now send you." [22]After he said this, he breathed on them and said, "Receive the Holy Spirit. [23]If you forgive anyone his sins, they are forgiven. If you don't forgive them, they are not forgiven."

Jesus Appears to Thomas

[24]Thomas (called Didymus), who was one of the twelve, was not with them when Jesus came. [25]The other followers kept telling Thomas, "We saw the Lord."

But Thomas said, "I will not believe it until I see the nail marks in his hands and put my finger where the nails were and put my hand into his side."

[26]A week later the followers were in the house again, and Thomas was with them. The doors were locked, but Jesus came in and stood right in the middle of them. He said, "Peace be with you." [27]Then he said to Thomas, "Put your finger here, and look at my hands. Put your hand here in my side. Stop being an unbeliever and believe."

[28]Thomas said to him, "My Lord and my God!"

[29]Then Jesus told him, "You believe because you see me. Those who believe without seeing me will be truly blessed."

Why John Wrote This Book

[30]Jesus did many other miracles in the presence of his followers that are not written in this book. [31]But these are written so that you may believe that Jesus is the Christ, the Son of God. Then, by believing, you may have life through his name.

Jesus Appears to Seven Followers

21 Later, Jesus showed himself to his followers again—this time at Lake Galilee.[n] This is how he showed himself: [2]Some of the followers were together: Simon Peter, Thomas (called Didymus), Nathanael from Cana in Galilee, the two sons of Zebedee, and two other followers. [3]Simon Peter said, "I am going out to fish."

The others said, "We will go with you." So they went out and got into the boat. They fished that night but caught nothing.

[4]Early the next morning Jesus stood on the shore, but the followers did not know it was Jesus. [5]Then he said to them, "Friends, did you catch any fish?"

They answered, "No."

[6]He said, "Throw your net on the right side of the boat, and you will find some." So they did, and they caught so many fish they could not pull the net back into the boat.

[7]The follower whom Jesus loved said to Peter, "It is the Lord!" When Peter heard him say this, he wrapped his coat around himself. (Peter had taken his clothes off.) Then he jumped into the water. [8]The other followers went to shore in the boat, dragging the net full of fish. They were not very far from shore, only about a hundred yards. [9]When the followers stepped out of the boat and onto the shore, they saw a fire of hot coals. There were fish on the fire, and there was bread.

[10]Then Jesus said, "Bring some of the fish you just caught."

[11]Simon Peter went into the boat and pulled the net to the shore. It was full of big fish, one hundred fifty-three in all, but even though there were so many, the net did not tear. [12]Jesus said to them, "Come and eat." None of the followers dared ask him, "Who are you?" because they knew it was the Lord. [13]Jesus came and took the bread and gave it to them, along with the fish.

[14]This was now the third time Jesus showed himself to his followers after he was raised from the dead.

Jesus Talks to Peter

[15]When they finished eating, Jesus said to Simon Peter, "Simon son of John, do you love me more than these?"

He answered, "Yes, Lord, you know that I love you."

Jesus said, "Feed my lambs."

[16]Again Jesus said, "Simon son of John, do you love me?"

Best Beauty Tip

The hottest tip for looking your best is easy to accomplish, extremely affordable, accessible to everyone, super fast, and super simple . . . just SMILE! Your smile is one of your most valuable assets for looking great. Even without the perfect lipstick shade or those perfectly aligned, pearly whites you see in the magazines, your smile can make you attractive, interesting, and approachable. As long as your heart is at peace with Jesus, you can be a happy girl. And being happy on the inside naturally makes you smile (Proverbs 15:13)! So go ahead—say cheese! Even when there's no camera in sight.

21:1 Lake Galilee Literally, "Sea of Tiberias."

He answered, "Yes, Lord, you know that I love you."

Jesus said, "Take care of my sheep."

[17]A third time he said, "Simon son of John, do you love me?"

Peter was hurt because Jesus asked him the third time, "Do you love me?" Peter said, "Lord, you know everything; you know that I love you!"

He said to him, "Feed my sheep. [18]I tell you the truth, when you were younger, you tied your own belt and went where you wanted. But when you are old, you will put out your hands and someone else will tie you and take you where you don't want to go." [19](Jesus said this to show how Peter would die to give glory to God.) Then Jesus said to Peter, "Follow me!"

[20]Peter turned and saw that the follower Jesus loved was walking behind them. (This was the follower who had leaned against Jesus at the supper and had said, "Lord, who will turn against you?") [21]When Peter saw him behind them, he asked Jesus, "Lord, what about him?"

[22]Jesus answered, "If I want him to live until I come back, that is not your business. You follow me."

[23]So a story spread among the followers that this one would not die. But Jesus did not say he would not die. He only said, "If I want him to live until I come back, that is not your business."

[24]That follower is the one who is telling these things and who has now written them down. We know that what he says is true.

[25]There are many other things Jesus did. If every one of them were written down, I suppose the whole world would not be big enough for all the books that would be written.

fun facts

59% of working-age *women* are part of the workforce today.

(U.S. Census Bureau)

John

Jesus Is God!

At first glance, the Book of John appears redundant—*another* Gospel? Why do we need another testimony of Jesus' life? Well, the Gospels of Matthew, Mark, and Luke narrate what Jesus *did*, but John's Gospel reveals who Jesus *is*. Every chapter oozes with proof and declaration of Jesus' divine nature. In fact, John says that's exactly why he wrote this book: "So that you may believe that Jesus is the Christ, the Son of God" (20:31).

Why is it so important that Jesus is truly God? If he was just some nice person that loved people a lot, Christianity couldn't exist. Jesus' perfection as *God*, wrapped in human form, made him an acceptable sacrifice for our sins . . . and that's the only way we can restore a right relationship with our heavenly Father. We're completely wrecked by sin without Jesus Christ as our Savior.

The Book of John is also significant in the way it complements the rest of the Bible. It gives us an intimate portrait of Jesus: his passion, his devotion, his warmth, his intensity, his self-sacrifice, his humanness, and his deity.

For both the believer and the one who is searching for truth, John provides a profound encounter with our Creator and Savior. As you reflect on the rich imagery and vivid word pictures, the reality of Jesus Christ becomes captivating. John's Gospel is a great place to find Jesus and fall in love with him—for the first time or the hundredth.

Get Real

Why did God choose to live on earth? (Romans 5:8; Ephesians 2:4–5)

Did Jesus care about what people thought about him? Should you? (John 5:41; John 12:42–43; Galatians 1:10)

What part does the Holy Spirit play in your life? (John 16:13; Acts 2:17–21; 9:31)

Do you look out for the well-being of others, or do you mainly focus on your own needs and wants? (Romans 12:10; Ephesians 5:1–2; Philippians 2:3–5; 1 John 3:16–18)

Are you independent or dependent when it comes to your relationship with God? (Psalm 63:1; John 15:5; 2 Corinthians 1:8–10)

notes

acts

You know that feeling of anticipation that surrounds the release of a long-awaited sequel to a popular book or movie? It's always exciting to find out what happens to your favorite characters—especially when the last installment ended with a cliffhanger!

That's kind of what's going on with the Book of Acts. It's Luke's sequel to the Gospel he wrote. The Gospel of Luke ties together most of the loose ends, but it leaves you wondering, "What's going to happen next?"

So once again, Luke picks up his pen and writes to his dear friend, Theophilus. This time, he writes about the beginning of the church. It's a story that revolves around the actions of the apostles—the people who were called to be messengers of the Good News. Luke was actually an eyewitness to huge parts of the story, so he's particularly qualified to share this amazing adventure.

The best thing is that the story's not over! The Book of Acts is almost like an introduction to the ongoing story of Christians sharing the Good News with the world. As you read about the transformations of such diverse characters as Peter, Paul, and Stephen from regular, uneducated, scared, or hate-filled people into dedicated and courageous servants of God, ponder what God might want to accomplish through you.

Luke Writes Another Book

1 To Theophilus.

The first book I wrote was about everything Jesus began to do and teach [2]until the day he was taken up into heaven. Before this, with the help of the Holy Spirit, Jesus told the apostles he had chosen what they should do. [3]After his death, he showed himself to them and proved in many ways that he was alive. The apostles saw Jesus during the forty days after he was raised from the dead, and he spoke to them about the kingdom of God. [4]Once when he was eating with them, he told them not to leave Jerusalem. He said, "Wait here to receive the promise from the Father which I told you about. [5]John baptized people with water, but in a few days you will be baptized with the Holy Spirit."

Jesus Is Taken Up into Heaven

[6]When the apostles were all together, they asked Jesus, "Lord, are you now going to give the kingdom back to Israel?"

[7]Jesus said to them, "The Father is the only One who has the authority to decide dates and times. These things are not for you to know. [8]But when the Holy Spirit comes to you, you will receive power. You will be my witnesses—in Jerusalem, in all of Judea, in Samaria, and in every part of the world."

[9]After he said this, as they were watching, he was lifted up, and a cloud hid him from their sight. [10]As he was going, they were looking into the sky. Suddenly, two men wearing white clothes stood beside them. [11]They said, "Men of Galilee, why are you standing here looking into the sky? Jesus, whom you saw taken up from you into heaven, will come back in the same way you saw him go."

A New Apostle Is Chosen

[12]Then they went back to Jerusalem from the Mount of Olives. (This mountain is about half a mile from Jerusalem.) [13]When they entered the city, they went to the upstairs room where they were staying. Peter, John, James, Andrew, Philip, Thomas,

Bartholomew, Matthew, James son of Alphaeus, Simon (known as the Zealot), and Judas son of James were there. [14]They all continued praying together with some women, including Mary the mother of Jesus, and Jesus' brothers.

[15]During this time there was a meeting of the believers (about one hundred twenty of them). Peter stood up and said, [16-17]"Brothers and sisters, in the Scriptures the Holy Spirit said through David something that must happen involving Judas. He was one of our own group and served together with us. He led those who arrested Jesus." [18](Judas bought a field with the money he got for his evil act. But he fell to his death, his body burst open, and all his intestines poured out. [19]Everyone in Jerusalem learned about this so they named this place Akeldama. In their language Akeldama means "Field of Blood.") [20]"In the Book of Psalms," Peter said, "this is written:

'May his place be empty;
leave no one to live in it.'
Psalm 69:25

And it is also written:

'Let another man replace him as
leader.' *Psalm 109:8*

[21-22]"So now a man must become a witness with us of Jesus' being raised from the dead. He must be one of the men who were part of our group during all the time the Lord Jesus was among us—from the time John was baptizing people until the day Jesus was taken up from us to heaven."

[23]They put the names of two men before the group. One was Joseph Barsabbas, who was also called Justus. The other was Matthias. [24-25]The apostles prayed, "Lord, you know the thoughts of everyone. Show us which one of these two you have chosen to do this work. Show us who should be an apostle in place of Judas, who turned away and went where he belongs." [26]Then they used lots to choose between them, and the lots showed that Matthias was the one. So he became an apostle with the other eleven.

The Coming of the Holy Spirit

2 When the day of Pentecost came, they were all together in one place. [2]Suddenly a noise like a strong, blowing wind came from heaven and filled the whole house where they were sitting. [3]They saw something like flames of fire that were separated and stood over each person there. [4]They were all filled with the Holy Spirit, and they began to speak different languages[n] by the power the Holy Spirit was giving them.

[5]There were some religious Jews staying in Jerusalem who were from every country in the world. [6]When they heard this noise, a crowd came together. They were all surprised, because each one heard them speaking in his own language. [7]They were completely amazed at this. They said, "Look! Aren't all these people that we hear speaking from Galilee? [8]Then how is it possible that we each hear them in our own languages? We are from different places: [9]Parthia, Media, Elam, Mesopotamia, Judea, Cappadocia, Pontus, Asia, [10]Phrygia, Pamphylia, Egypt, the areas of Libya near Cyrene, Rome [11](both Jews and those who had become Jews), Crete, and Arabia. But we hear them telling in our own languages about the great things God has done!" [12]They were all amazed and confused, asking each other, "What does this mean?"

[13]But others were making fun of them, saying, "They have had too much wine."

Peter Speaks to the People

[14]But Peter stood up with the eleven apostles, and in a loud voice he spoke to the crowd: "My fellow Jews, and all of you who are in Jerusalem, listen to me. Pay attention to what I have to say. [15]These people are not drunk, as you think; it is only nine o'clock in the morning! [16]But Joel the prophet wrote about what is happening here today:

[17]'God says: In the last days
I will pour out my Spirit on all
kinds of people.
Your sons and daughters will
prophesy.
Your young men will see visions,
and your old men will dream
dreams.

So Many Needs, So Little Time

Be Still & KNOW

There are so many loved ones, family members, and friends to bring before the Lord in prayer. Just keeping up with them can be difficult, much less finding time to really pray through each one thoroughly. But with a little organization and creativity, you can make sure you're lifting up every person consistently. Try making a list of the people in your life that you most want to pray for on a regular basis. Divide them into groups and make each group your focus for the week, day, or month. Let them know what specific time frame belongs to them so they can keep you updated about how to best pray for them!

2:4 languages This can also be translated "tongues."

Acts 2:23–24

Movie scriptwriters and novelists must love letting their imaginations run wild. Anything they say goes in the "world" they create! It's easy to think we're in the same position with our own personal stories—in charge and independently deciding the plotlines of our individual lives.

But we couldn't be more wrong. We're completely dependent creatures. Our very existence relies on God! As the all-powerful Creator of the universe, nothing can foil his plans. Sometimes it's tough to admit we're not in control. But have you ever noticed that when things get really bad, we suddenly *want* God to be in control? When difficult times make us realize how helpless we are, the idea of a sovereign God who actually has the power to save us becomes appealing.

So it's actually a joy to know God's in charge. Everything, from the course of world history to the tiniest details of your life, is in his hands—the wisest and most trustworthy Director. He's powerfully accomplishing his perfect plan, and he promises he'll take care of everyone who loves him. Instead of waiting to recognize and welcome God's providence, why not open yourself to his wonderful plan and loving guidance right now?

18At that time I will pour out my Spirit
also on my male slaves and
female slaves,
and they will prophesy.
19I will show miracles
in the sky and on the earth:
blood, fire, and thick smoke.
20The sun will become dark,
the moon red as blood,
before the overwhelming and
glorious day of the Lord will
come.
21Then anyone who calls on the Lord
will be saved.' *Joel 2:28–32*

22"People of Israel, listen to these words: Jesus from Nazareth was a very special man. God clearly showed this to you by the miracles, wonders, and signs he did through Jesus. You all know this, because it happened right here among you. 23Jesus was given to you, and with the help of those who don't know the law, you put him to death by nailing him to a cross. But this was God's plan which he had made long ago; he knew all this would happen. 24God raised Jesus from the dead and set him free from the pain of death, because death could not hold him. 25For David said this about him:

'I keep the Lord before me always.
Because he is close by my side,
I will not be hurt.
26So I am glad, and I rejoice.
Even my body has hope,
27because you will not leave me in the
grave.
You will not let your Holy One
rot.
28You will teach me how to live a holy
life.
Being with you will fill me with
joy.' *Psalm 16:8–11*

29"Brothers and sisters, I can tell you truly that David, our ancestor, died and was buried. His grave is still here with us today. 30He was a prophet and knew God had promised him that he would make a person from David's family a king just as he was.[n] 31Knowing this before it happened, David talked about the Christ rising from the dead. He said:

'He was not left in the grave.
His body did not rot.'

32So Jesus is the One whom God raised from the dead. And we are all witnesses to this. 33Jesus was lifted up to heaven and is now at God's right side. The Father has given the Holy Spirit to Jesus as he promised. So Jesus has poured out that Spirit, and this is what you now see and hear. 34David was not the one who was lifted up to heaven, but he said:

'The Lord said to my Lord,
"Sit by me at my right side,
35 until I put your enemies under
your control."'[n] *Psalm 110:1*

36"So, all the people of Israel should know this truly: God has made Jesus—the man you nailed to the cross—both Lord and Christ."

37When the people heard this, they felt guilty and asked Peter and the other apostles, "What shall we do?"

38Peter said to them, "Change your hearts and lives and be baptized, each one of you, in the name of Jesus Christ for the forgiveness of your sins. And you will receive the gift of the Holy Spirit. 39This promise is for you, for your children, and for all who are far away. It is for everyone the Lord our God calls to himself."

40Peter warned them with many other words. He begged them, "Save yourselves from the evil of today's people!" 41Then those people who accepted what Peter said were baptized. About three thousand people were added to the number of believers that day. 42They spent their time learning the apostles' teaching, sharing, breaking bread,[n] and praying together.

2:30 God . . . was See 2 Samuel 7:13; Psalm 132:11. **2:35 until . . . control** Literally, "until I make your enemies a footstool for your feet." **2:42 breaking bread** This may mean a meal as in verse 46, or the Lord's Supper, the special meal Jesus told his followers to eat to remember him (Luke 22:14–20).

The Believers Share

43The apostles were doing many miracles and signs, and everyone felt great respect for God. 44All the believers were together and shared everything. 45They would sell their land and the things they owned and then divide the money and give it to anyone who needed it. 46The believers met together in the Temple every day. They ate together in their homes, happy to share their food with joyful hearts. 47They praised God and were liked by all the people. Every day the Lord added those who were being saved to the group of believers.

Peter Heals a Crippled Man

3 One day Peter and John went to the Temple at three o'clock, the time set each day for the afternoon prayer service. 2There, at the Temple gate called Beautiful Gate, was a man who had been crippled all his life. Every day he was carried to this gate to beg for money from the people going into the Temple. 3The man saw Peter and John going into the Temple and asked them for money. 4Peter and John looked straight at him and said, "Look at us!" 5The man looked at them, thinking they were going to give him some money. 6But Peter said, "I don't have any silver or gold, but I do have something else I can give you. By the power of Jesus Christ from Nazareth, stand up and walk!" 7Then Peter took the man's right hand and lifted him up. Immediately the man's feet and ankles became strong. 8He jumped up, stood on his feet, and began to walk. He went into the Temple with them, walking and jumping and praising God. 9-10All the people recognized him as the crippled man who always sat by the Beautiful Gate begging for money. Now they saw this same man walking and praising God, and they were amazed. They wondered how this could happen.

Peter Speaks to the People

11While the man was holding on to Peter and John, all the people were amazed and ran to them at Solomon's Porch. 12When Peter saw this, he said to them, "People of Israel, why are you surprised? You are looking at us as if it were our own power or goodness that made this man walk. 13The God of Abraham, Isaac, and Jacob, the God of our ancestors, gave glory to Jesus, his servant. But you handed him over to be killed. Pilate decided to let him go free, but you told Pilate you did not want Jesus. 14You did not want the One who is holy and good but asked Pilate to give you a murderer[n] instead. 15And so you killed the One who gives life, but God raised him from the dead. We are witnesses to this. 16It was faith in Jesus that made this crippled man well. You can see this man, and you know him. He was made completely well because of trust in Jesus, and you all saw it happen!

17"Brothers and sisters, I know you did those things to Jesus because neither you nor your leaders understood what you were doing. 18God said through the prophets that his Christ would suffer and die. And now God has made these things come true in this way. 19So you must change your hearts and lives! Come back to God, and he will forgive your sins. Then the Lord will send the time of rest. 20And he will send Jesus, the One he chose to be the Christ. 21But Jesus must stay in heaven until the time comes when all things will be made right again. God told about this time long ago when he spoke through his holy prophets. 22Moses said, 'The Lord your God will give you a prophet like me, who is one of your own people. You must listen to everything he tells you. 23Anyone who does not listen to that prophet will die, cut off from God's people.'[n] 24Samuel, and all the other prophets who spoke for God after Samuel, told about this time now. 25You are descendants of the prophets. You have received the agreement God made with your ancestors. He said to your father Abraham, 'Through your descendants all the nations on the earth will be blessed.'[n] 26God has raised up his servant Jesus and sent him to you first to bless you by turning each of you away from doing evil."

Peter and John at the Council

4 While Peter and John were speaking to the people, priests, the captain of the soldiers that guarded the Temple, and Sadducees came up to them. 2They

Uncharted

by Angela Hunt

In this suspenseful tale from novelist Angela Hunt, five estranged friends travel to the Marshall Islands to fulfill the wishes of a sixth friend whose sudden death inspires them to reunite to celebrate his life. But when a shipwreck leaves them stranded on an uncharted island, they discover more than they ever expected. Their delusions give way to reality, shocking them with the truth about themselves—and each other. Hunt's eerie tale will cause you to reflect on the hidden motives of your own heart and embrace God's forgiveness.

3:14 murderer Barabbas, the man the crowd asked Pilate to set free instead of Jesus (Luke 23:18). **3:22–23 'The Lord . . . people.'** Quotation from Deuteronomy 18:15, 19. **3:25 'Through . . . blessed.'** Quotation from Genesis 22:18; 26:4.

were upset because the two apostles were teaching the people and were preaching that people will rise from the dead through the power of Jesus. 3The older leaders grabbed Peter and John and put them in jail. Since it was already night, they kept them in jail until the next day. 4But many of those who had heard Peter and John preach believed the things they said. There were now about five thousand in the group of believers.

5The next day the rulers, the elders, and the teachers of the law met in Jerusalem. 6Annas the high priest, Caiaphas, John, and Alexander were there, as well as everyone from the high priest's family. 7They made Peter and John stand before them and then asked them, "By what power or authority did you do this?"

8Then Peter, filled with the Holy Spirit, said to them, "Rulers of the people and you elders, 9are you questioning us about a good thing that was done to a crippled man? Are you asking us who made him well? 10We want all of you and all the people to know that this man was made well by the power of Jesus Christ from Nazareth. You crucified him, but God raised him from the dead. This man was crippled, but he is now well and able to stand here before you because of the power of Jesus. 11Jesus is

'the stone[n] that you builders rejected,
which has become the
cornerstone.' *Psalm 118:22*

12Jesus is the only One who can save people. No one else in the world is able to save us."

13The leaders saw that Peter and John were not afraid to speak, and they understood that these men had no special training or education. So they were amazed. Then they realized that Peter and John had been with Jesus. 14Because they saw the healed man standing there beside the two apostles, they could say nothing against them. 15After the leaders ordered them to leave the meeting, they began to talk to each other. 16They said, "What shall we do with these men? Everyone in Jerusalem knows they have done a great miracle, and we cannot say it is not true. 17But to keep it from spreading among the people, we must warn them not to talk to people anymore using that name."

18So they called Peter and John in again and told them not to speak or to teach at all in the name of Jesus. 19But Peter and John answered them, "You decide what God would want. Should we obey you or God? 20We cannot keep quiet. We must speak about what we have seen and heard." 21The leaders warned the apostles again and let them go free. They could not find a way to punish them, because all the people were praising God for what had been done. 22The man who received the miracle of healing was more than forty years old.

The Believers Pray

23After Peter and John left the meeting of leaders, they went to their own group and told them everything the leading priests and the elders had said to them. 24When the believers heard this, they prayed to God together, "Lord, you are the One who made the sky, the earth, the sea, and everything in them. 25By the Holy Spirit, through our father David your servant, you said:

'Why are the nations so angry?
Why are the people making
useless plans?
26The kings of the earth prepare to
fight,
and their leaders make plans
together
against the Lord
and his Christ.' *Psalm 2:1–2*

27These things really happened when Herod, Pontius Pilate, and some Jews and non-Jews all came together against Jesus here in Jerusalem. Jesus is your holy servant, the One you made to be the Christ. 28These people made your plan happen because of your power and your will. 29And now, Lord, listen to their threats. Lord, help us, your servants, to speak your word without fear. 30Show us your power to heal. Give proofs and make miracles happen by the power of Jesus, your holy servant."

31After they had prayed, the place where they were meeting was shaken. They were all filled with the Holy Spirit, and they spoke God's word without fear.

The Believers Share

32The group of believers were united in their hearts and spirit. All those in the group acted as though their private

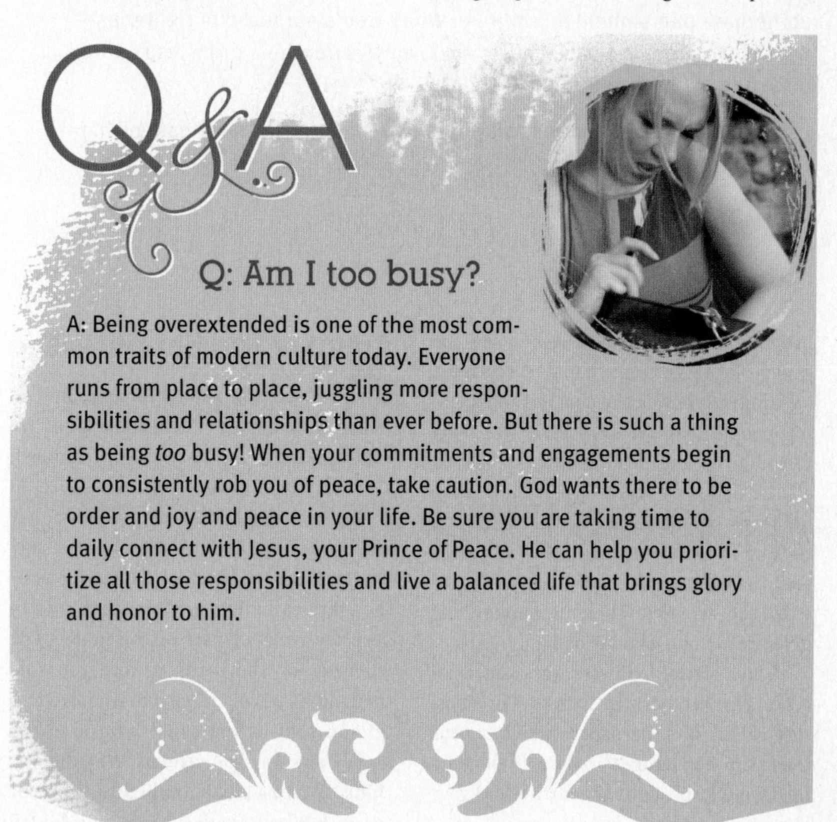

Q&A

Q: Am I too busy?

A: Being overextended is one of the most common traits of modern culture today. Everyone runs from place to place, juggling more responsibilities and relationships than ever before. But there is such a thing as being *too* busy! When your commitments and engagements begin to consistently rob you of peace, take caution. God wants there to be order and joy and peace in your life. Be sure you are taking time to daily connect with Jesus, your Prince of Peace. He can help you prioritize all those responsibilities and live a balanced life that brings glory and honor to him.

4:11 stone A symbol meaning Jesus.

Acts 5:1–10

A "white lie" here, a little stretch of the truth there . . . how bad can a "teeny fib" really be? Much worse than we might realize. Lying is serious, no matter how insignificant we might think it is. Ananias and Sapphira's story gives four reasons why there's no such thing as a small lie.

First, the biggest deal about lying is that we've sinned against a holy God. The fact that Ananias didn't just lie to the community, but to God himself, should make us rethink any urge to twist the truth. Any lie offends God because God is truth. Second, we let Satan rule our thoughts when we lie. Just like Eve in the Garden, we're following the enemy's mindset, questioning if God's ways are right and wondering if pleasing him really matters. Third, we're testing the Holy Spirit when we lie. We're asking, "Will God care if I do this? Is it best to follow his commands?" Fourth, our sin earns death. Ananias and Sapphira received immediate punishment for their lie. When God's standard of righteousness is violated, the payment for sin is always death—a price Jesus paid once and for all for each of his children.

Let these reminders lead you away from sin, including lies—no matter what the size.

property belonged to everyone in the group. In fact, they shared everything. [33]With great power the apostles were telling people that the Lord Jesus was truly raised from the dead. And God blessed all the believers very much. [34]There were no needy people among them. From time to time those who owned fields or houses sold them, brought the money, [35]and gave it to the apostles. Then the money was given to anyone who needed it.

[36]One of the believers was named Joseph, a Levite born in Cyprus. The apostles called him Barnabas (which means "one who encourages"). [37]Joseph owned a field, sold it, brought the money, and gave it to the apostles.

Ananias and Sapphira Die

5 But a man named Ananias and his wife Sapphira sold some land. [2]He kept back part of the money for himself; his wife knew about this and agreed to it. But he brought the rest of the money and gave it to the apostles. [3]Peter said, "Ananias, why did you let Satan rule your thoughts to lie to the Holy Spirit and to keep for yourself part of the money you received for the land? [4]Before you sold the land, it belonged to you. And even after you sold it, you could have used the money any way you wanted. Why did you think of doing this? You lied to God, not to us!" [5-6]When Ananias heard this, he fell down and died. Some young men came in, wrapped up his body, carried it out, and buried it. And everyone who heard about this was filled with fear.

[7]About three hours later his wife came in, but she did not know what had happened. [8]Peter said to her, "Tell me, was the money you got for your field this much?"

Sapphira answered, "Yes, that was the price."

[9]Peter said to her, "Why did you and your husband agree to test the Spirit of the Lord? Look! The men who buried your husband are at the door, and they will carry you out." [10]At that moment Sapphira fell down by his feet and died. When the young men came in and saw that she was dead, they carried her out and buried her beside her husband. [11]The whole church and all the others who heard about these things were filled with fear.

The Apostles Heal Many

[12]The apostles did many signs and miracles among the people. And they would all meet together on Solomon's Porch. [13]None of the others dared to join them, but all the people respected them. [14]More and more men and women believed in the Lord and were added to the group of believers. [15]The people placed their sick on beds and mats in the streets, hoping that when Peter passed by at least his shadow might fall on them. [16]Crowds came from all the towns around Jerusalem, bringing their sick and those who were bothered by evil spirits, and all of them were healed.

Leaders Try to Stop the Apostles

[17]The high priest and all his friends (a group called the Sadducees) became very jealous. [18]They took the apostles and put them in jail. [19]But during the night, an angel of the Lord opened the doors of the jail and led the apostles outside. The angel said, [20]"Go stand in the Temple and tell the people everything about this new life." [21]When the apostles heard this, they obeyed and went into the Temple early in the morning and continued teaching.

When the high priest and his friends arrived, they called a meeting of the leaders and all the important elders. They sent some men to the jail to bring the apostles to them.

[22]But, upon arriving, the officers could not find the apostles. So they went back and reported to the leaders. [23]They said, "The jail was closed and locked, and the guards were standing at the doors. But when we opened the doors, the jail was empty!" [24]Hearing this, the captain of the Temple guards and the leading priests were confused and wondered what was happening.

[25]Then someone came and told them, "Listen! The men you put in jail are standing in the Temple teaching the people." [26]Then the captain and his men went out and brought the apostles back. But the soldiers did not use force, because they were afraid the people would stone them to death.

[27]The soldiers brought the apostles to the meeting and made them stand before the leaders. The high priest questioned them, [28]saying, "We gave you strict orders not to continue teaching in that name. But look, you have filled Jerusalem with your teaching and are trying to make us responsible for this man's death."

[29]Peter and the other apostles answered, "We must obey God, not human authority! [30]You killed Jesus by hanging him on a cross. But God, the God of our ancestors, raised Jesus up from the dead! [31]Jesus is the One whom God raised to be on his right side, as Leader and Savior. Through him, all people could change their hearts and lives and have their sins forgiven. [32]We saw all these things happen. The Holy Spirit, whom God has given to all who obey him, also proves these things are true."

[33]When the leaders heard this, they became angry and wanted to kill them. [34]But a Pharisee named Gamaliel stood up in the meeting. He was a teacher of the law, and all the people respected him. He ordered the apostles to leave the meeting for a little while. [35]Then he said, "People of Israel, be careful what you are planning to do to these men. [36]Remember when Theudas appeared? He said he was a great man, and about four hundred men joined him. But he was killed, and all his followers were scattered; they were able to do nothing. [37]Later, a man named Judas came from Galilee at the time of the registration.[n] He also led a group of followers and was killed, and all his followers were scattered. [38]And so now I tell you: Stay away from these men, and leave them alone. If their plan comes from human authority, it will fail. [39]But if it is from God, you will not be able to stop them. You might even be fighting against God himself!"

The leaders agreed with what Gamaliel said. [40]They called the apostles in, beat them, and told them not to speak in the name of Jesus again. Then they let them go free. [41]The apostles left the meeting full of joy because they were given the honor of suffering disgrace for Jesus. [42]Every day in the Temple and in people's homes they continued teaching the people and telling the Good News—that Jesus is the Christ.

Seven Leaders Are Chosen

6 The number of followers was growing. But during this same time, the Greek-speaking followers had an argument with the other followers. The Greek-speaking widows were not getting their share of the food that was given out every day. [2]The twelve apostles called the whole group of followers together and said, "It is not right for us to stop our work of teaching God's word in order to serve tables. [3]So, brothers and sisters, choose seven of your own men who are good, full of the Spirit and full of wisdom. We will put them in charge of this work. [4]Then we can continue to pray and to teach the word of God."

HE SAID / SHE SAID

Who is your favorite woman in the Bible?

He: The woman caught in adultery because of what her story teaches about God's grace

She: Mary, the mother of Jesus, because of her great faith

Joseph: Faithful in Every Circumstance

Joseph's life had extreme highs and lows. He went from favorite son to unknown slave. But God was with him, and he soon became the most trusted servant of a ruler. Then his boss's wife framed him for something he didn't do, and he was thrown in jail. But God was with him there, too, and he earned his release after years of imprisonment by interpreting some important dreams. He ultimately helped rule Egypt and save his people from starvation. In every circumstance, Joseph remained faithful to God, and God remained faithful to him! (Genesis 37—50)

5:37 registration Census. A counting of all the people and the things they own.

QUIZ

WHICH BIBLE CHARACTER ARE YOU MOST LIKE?

1. WHICH OF THE FOLLOWING GROUPS OF WORDS BEST DESCRIBES YOU?

- [] A. Creative, gregarious, uninhibited
- [] B. Passionate, adventurous, inquisitive
- [] C. Determined, kindhearted, loyal
- [] D. Intense, decisive, bold

2. WHICH WOULD YOU RATHER DO?

- [] A. Go fishing
- [] B. Create something new, like a painting or a song
- [] C. Sing or play a musical instrument
- [] D. Work in your garden or flowerbed

3. IF YOU WERE ON STAFF AT A CHURCH OR MINISTRY, WHICH POSITION WOULD YOU BE MOST LIKELY TO FILL?

- [] A. Sunday school or teaching staff
- [] B. Pastoral Staff
- [] C. Ministry Coordinator
- [] D. Worship Team

4. PRETEND YOU'RE A MILITARY LEADER AND YOU'RE FACING A HUGE ARMY JUST OVER THE HILL. YOU'VE ALREADY TRIED DIPLOMATIC NEGOTIATIONS, BUT THEY WON'T BACK DOWN. WHAT IS MOST LIKELY TO BE YOUR FIRST THOUGHT?

- [] A. We've got to get some allies lined up to help us here.
- [] B. If they would just listen to me, they'd see that we can still resolve this matter peacefully.
- [] C. First of all, don't panic; we're right and we'll win!
- [] D. Let's blow the whole group to smithereens before they can attack us.

5. PRETEND YOU'RE ON A DESERTED ISLAND WITH ONLY FOOD, WATER, A PEN, AND SOME PAPER. WHAT WOULD YOU WRITE TO MAKE YOURSELF FEEL BETTER?

- [] A. Letters to friends and family about your faith
- [] B. A list of all the times God has provided in the past and hopes for how he will do the same here
- [] C. Plans and to-do lists for when you finally get home
- [] D. Prayers or the words to memory verses and songs

SCORING:

1. A=1, B=2, C=3, D=4
2. A=4, B=2, C=1, D=3
3. A=2, B=4, C=3, D=1
4. A=3, B=2, C=1, D=4
5. A=2, B=3, C=4, D=1

IF YOU SCORED MOSTLY 1S, YOU ARE MOST LIKE DAVID. You are a creative, loving, expressive woman of God. Review his story in 1 and 2 Samuel and 1 and 2 Kings to see why he is known as the kind of man God wants (Acts 13:22).

IF YOU SCORED MOSTLY 2S, YOU ARE MOST LIKE PAUL. You are an intelligent, passionate, faithful woman of God. Learn more about Paul's exciting life journey by reading the Book of Acts and the multiple letters he wrote in the New Testament.

IF YOU SCORED MOSTLY 3S, YOU ARE MOST LIKE RUTH. You are a wise, hardworking, loyal woman of God. Check out the Book of Ruth; you'll be inspired by her courage, determination, and faithfulness.

IF YOU SCORED MOSTLY 4S, YOU ARE MOST LIKE PETER. You are a strong, confident, committed woman of God. Reread the Gospels, as well as 1 and 2 Peter, to catch a glimpse of this man Jesus called a rock.

Almost half of online shoppers use the Web to research products but then make their purchase in a retail store.

(*Kiplinger's*)

[5]The whole group liked the idea, so they chose these seven men: Stephen (a man with great faith and full of the Holy Spirit), Philip,[n] Procorus, Nicanor, Timon, Parmenas, and Nicolas (a man from Antioch who had become a follower of the Jewish religion). [6]Then they put these men before the apostles, who prayed and laid their hands[n] on them.

[7]The word of God was continuing to spread. The group of followers in Jerusalem increased, and a great number of the Jewish priests believed and obeyed.

Stephen Is Accused

[8]Stephen was richly blessed by God who gave him the power to do great miracles and signs among the people. [9]But some people were against him. They belonged to the synagogue of Free Men[n] (as it was called), which included people from Cyrene, Alexandria, Cilicia, and Asia. They all came and argued with Stephen.

[10]But the Spirit was helping him to speak with wisdom, and his words were so strong that they could not argue with him. [11]So they secretly urged some men to say, "We heard Stephen speak against Moses and against God."

[12]This upset the people, the elders, and the teachers of the law. They came and grabbed Stephen and brought him to a meeting of the leaders. [13]They brought in some people to tell lies about Stephen, saying, "This man is always speaking against this holy place and the law of Moses. [14]We heard him say that Jesus from Nazareth will destroy this place and that Jesus will change the customs Moses gave us." [15]All the people in the meeting were watching Stephen closely and saw that his face looked like the face of an angel.

Stephen's Speech

7 The high priest said to Stephen, "Are these things true?"

[2]Stephen answered, "Brothers and fathers, listen to me. Our glorious God appeared to Abraham, our ancestor, in Mesopotamia before he lived in Haran. [3]God said to Abraham, 'Leave your country and your relatives, and go to the land I will show you.'[n] [4]So Abraham left the country of Chaldea and went to live in Haran. After Abraham's father died, God sent him to this place where you now live. [5]God did not give Abraham any of this land, not even a foot of it. But God promised that he would give this land to him and his descendants, even before Abraham had a child. [6]This is what God said to him: 'Your descendants will be strangers in a land they don't own. The people there will make them slaves and will mistreat them for four hundred years. [7]But I will punish the nation where they are slaves. Then your descendants will leave that land and will worship me in this place.'[n] [8]God made an agreement with Abraham, the sign of which was circumcision. And so when Abraham had his son Isaac, Abraham circumcised him when he was eight days old. Isaac also circumcised his son Jacob, and Jacob did the same for his sons, the twelve ancestors[n] of our people.

[9]"Jacob's sons became jealous of Joseph and sold him to be a slave in Egypt. But God was with him [10]and saved him from all his troubles. The king of Egypt liked Joseph and respected him because of the wisdom God gave him. The king made him governor of Egypt and put him in charge of all the people in his palace.

[11]"Then all the land of Egypt and Canaan became so dry that nothing would grow, and the people suffered very much. Jacob's sons, our ancestors, could not find anything to eat. [12]But when Jacob heard there was grain in Egypt, he sent his sons there. This was their first trip to Egypt. [13]When they went there a second time, Joseph told his brothers who he was, and the king learned about Joseph's family. [14]Then Joseph sent messengers to invite Jacob, his father, to come to Egypt along with all his relatives (seventy-five persons

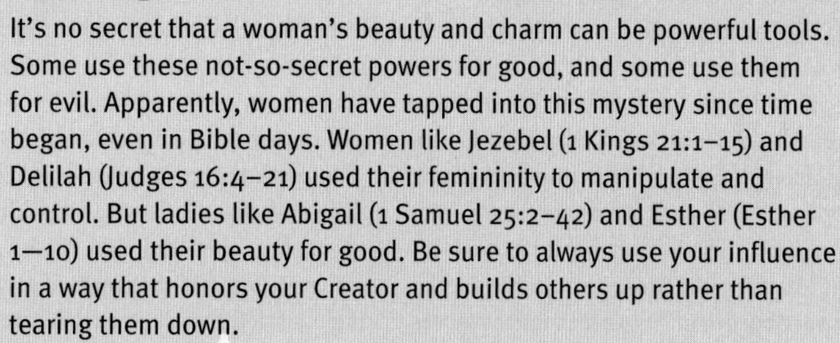

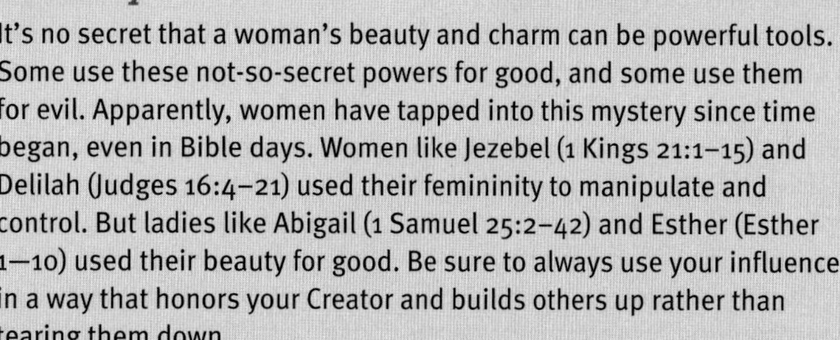

Use Your Beauty Wisely

It's no secret that a woman's beauty and charm can be powerful tools. Some use these not-so-secret powers for good, and some use them for evil. Apparently, women have tapped into this mystery since time began, even in Bible days. Women like Jezebel (1 Kings 21:1–15) and Delilah (Judges 16:4–21) used their femininity to manipulate and control. But ladies like Abigail (1 Samuel 25:2–42) and Esther (Esther 1–10) used their beauty for good. Be sure to always use your influence in a way that honors your Creator and builds others up rather than tearing them down.

6:5 Philip Not the apostle named Philip. **6:6 laid their hands** The laying on of hands had many purposes, including the giving of a blessing, power, or authority. **6:9 Free Men** Jewish people who had been slaves or whose fathers had been slaves, but were now free. **7:3 'Leave . . . you.'** Quotation from Genesis 12:1. **7:6–7 'Your descendants . . . place.'** Quotation from Genesis 15:13–14 and Exodus 3:12. **7:8 twelve ancestors** Important ancestors of the people of Israel; the leaders of the twelve tribes of Israel.

Acts 7:39

Choosing between slavery and freedom isn't exactly a tough call. It probably isn't something you've ever had to deal with, but just imagine your response if you were set free after a lifetime of cruel enslavement. There's no way you'd long for the good old days of slavery . . . you'd cherish every moment of sweet freedom.

But, as ridiculous as it sounds, the Israelites had the exact opposite reaction—constant grumbling, idol worship, and whining pleas to return to Egypt (for its dietary variety) became the norm. They preferred slavery and a guarantee of extra food choices to the adventure of following God and trusting him to provide.

But before we criticize the Israelites, we've got to look at ourselves. Being lost in sin is the deepest and worst kind of slavery imaginable. The fact that Jesus can free us from sin, make us pure and holy, and eventually take us to heaven is a much bigger miracle than freeing Israel from the king of Egypt. But how often do our actions prove that we prefer slavery (sin) to freedom in Christ?

Show your thankfulness by refusing to return to a life of slavery to sin. You're a new woman in Christ—embrace your freedom!

altogether). [15]So Jacob went down to Egypt, where he and his sons died. [16]Later their bodies were moved to Shechem and put in a grave there. (It was the same grave Abraham had bought for a sum of money from the sons of Hamor in Shechem.)

[17]"The promise God made to Abraham was soon to come true, and the number of people in Egypt grew large. [18]Then a new king, who did not know who Joseph was, began to rule Egypt. [19]This king tricked our people and was cruel to our ancestors, forcing them to leave their babies outside to die. [20]At this time Moses was born, and he was very beautiful. For three months Moses was cared for in his father's house. [21]When they put Moses outside, the king's daughter adopted him and raised him as if he were her own son. [22]The Egyptians taught Moses everything they knew, and he was a powerful man in what he said and did.

[23]"When Moses was about forty years old, he thought it would be good to visit his own people, the people of Israel. [24]Moses saw an Egyptian mistreating one of his people, so he defended the Israelite and punished the Egyptian by killing him. [25]Moses thought his own people would understand that God was using him to save them, but they did not. [26]The next day when Moses saw two men of Israel fighting, he tried to make peace between them. He said, 'Men, you are brothers. Why are you hurting each other?' [27]The man who was hurting the other pushed Moses away and said, 'Who made you our ruler and judge? [28]Are you going to kill me as you killed the Egyptian yesterday?'[n] [29]When Moses heard him say this, he left Egypt and went to live in the land of Midian where he was a stranger. While Moses lived in Midian, he had two sons.

[30]"Forty years later an angel appeared to Moses in the flames of a burning bush as he was in the desert near Mount Sinai. [31]When Moses saw this, he was amazed and went near to look closer. Moses heard the Lord's voice say, [32]'I am the God of your ancestors, the God of Abraham, Isaac, and Jacob.'[n] Moses began to shake with fear and was afraid to look. [33]The Lord said to him, 'Take off your sandals, because you are standing on holy ground. [34]I have seen the troubles my people have suffered in Egypt. I have heard their cries and have come down to save them. And now, Moses, I am sending you back to Egypt.'[n]

[35]"This Moses was the same man the two men of Israel rejected, saying, 'Who made you a ruler and judge?'[n] Moses is the same man God sent to be a ruler and savior, with the help of the angel that Moses saw in the burning bush. [36]So Moses led the people out of Egypt. He worked miracles and signs in Egypt, at the Red Sea, and then in the desert for forty years. [37]This is the same Moses that said to the people of Israel, 'God will give you a prophet like me, who is one of your own people.'[n] [38]This is the Moses who was with the gathering of the Israelites in the desert. He was with the angel that spoke to him at Mount Sinai, and he was with our ancestors. He received commands from God that give life, and he gave those commands to us.

[39]"But our ancestors did not want to obey Moses. They rejected him and wanted to go back to Egypt. [40]They said to Aaron, 'Make us gods who will lead us. Moses led us out of Egypt, but we don't know what has happened to him.'[n] [41]So the people made an idol that looked like a calf. Then they brought sacrifices to it and were proud of what they had made with their own hands. [42]But God turned against them and did not try to stop them from worshiping the sun, moon, and stars. This is what is written in the book of the prophets: God says,

7:27–28 'Who . . . yesterday?' Quotation from Exodus 2:14. **7:32 'I am . . . Jacob.'** Quotation from Exodus 3:6. **7:33–34 'Take . . . Egypt.'** Quotation from Exodus 3:5–10. **7:35 'Who . . . judge?'** Quotation from Exodus 2:14. **7:37 'God . . . people.'** Quotation from Deuteronomy 18:15. **7:40 'Make . . . him.'** Quotation from Exodus 32:1.

'People of Israel, you did not bring me
sacrifices and offerings
while you traveled in the desert
for forty years.
43You have carried with you
the tent to worship Molech
and the idols of the star god
Rephan that you made to
worship.
So I will send you away beyond
Babylon.' *Amos 5:25–27*

44"The Holy Tent where God spoke to our ancestors was with them in the desert. God told Moses how to make this Tent, and he made it like the plan God showed him. 45Later, Joshua led our ancestors to capture the lands of the other nations. Our people went in, and God forced the other people out. When our people went into this new land, they took with them this same Tent they had received from their ancestors. They kept it until the time of David, 46who pleased God and asked God to let him build a house for him, the God of Jacob.[n] 47But Solomon was the one who built the Temple.

48"But the Most High does not live in houses that people build with their hands. As the prophet says:

49'Heaven is my throne,
and the earth is my footstool.
So do you think you can build a house
for me? says the Lord.
Do I need a place to rest?
50Remember, my hand made all these
things!'" *Isaiah 66:1–2*

51Stephen continued speaking: "You stubborn people! You have not given your hearts to God, nor will you listen to him! You are always against what the Holy Spirit is trying to tell you, just as your ancestors were. 52Your ancestors tried to hurt every prophet who ever lived. Those prophets said long ago that the One who is good would come, but your ancestors killed them. And now you have turned against and killed the One who is good. 53You received the law of Moses, which God gave you through his angels, but you haven't obeyed it."

Stephen Is Killed

54When the leaders heard this, they became furious. They were so mad they were grinding their teeth at Stephen. 55But Stephen was full of the Holy Spirit. He looked up to heaven and saw the glory of God and Jesus standing at God's right side. 56He said, "Look! I see heaven open and the Son of Man standing at God's right side."

57Then they shouted loudly and covered their ears and all ran at Stephen. 58They took him out of the city and began to throw stones at him to kill him. And those who told lies against Stephen left their coats with a young man named Saul. 59While they were throwing stones, Stephen prayed, "Lord Jesus, receive my spirit." 60He fell on his knees and cried in a loud voice, "Lord, do not hold this sin against them." After Stephen said this, he died.

8 Saul agreed that the killing of Stephen was good.

Troubles for the Believers

On that day the church of Jerusalem began to be persecuted, and all the believers, except the apostles, were scattered throughout Judea and Samaria.

2And some religious people buried Stephen and cried loudly for him. 3Saul was also trying to destroy the church, going from house to house, dragging out men and women and putting them in jail. 4And wherever they were scattered, they told people the Good News.

BECOME *Involved*

Crown Financial Ministries

Many charities ask for your monetary contributions, and some focus on helping those who lack funds. But few teach you how to manage the money you do have. Crown Financial Ministries is one of the latter. A Christian, nonprofit organization, Crown seeks to help people make sound financial decisions so they can honor the Lord as a better manager of his resources . . . and equally important, so they can afford to give more to his kingdom work.

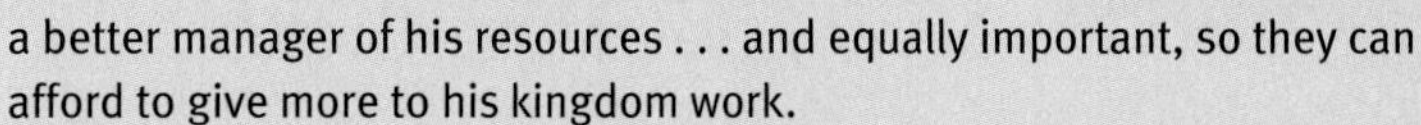

More than anything, Crown is in the education business. They have a great selection of resources to help guide people to sound, godly financial management. They have tools, curriculum, events, and even a network of local people who are willing to help. Crown has assisted countless numbers of families to gain control over debt, make wise investments, and budget for life's expected and unexpected journeys.

Crown needs donations from people who are able to give so they can continue influencing lives. They're also looking for church coordinators and Bible study leaders who are willing to volunteer their time and energy to help reach others. You can find out more about using their resources, volunteering your services, or making a donation at www.crown.org.

7:46 Jacob Some Greek copies read "the house of Jacob." This means the people of Israel.

Philip Preaches in Samaria

[5]Philip went to the city of Samaria and preached about the Christ. [6]When the people there heard Philip and saw the miracles he was doing, they all listened carefully to what he said. [7]Many of these people had evil spirits in them, but Philip made the evil spirits leave. The spirits made a loud noise when they came out. Philip also healed many weak and crippled people there. [8]So the people in that city were very happy.

[9]But there was a man named Simon in that city. Before Philip came there, Simon had practiced magic and amazed all the people of Samaria. He bragged and called himself a great man. [10]All the people—the least important and the most important—paid attention to Simon, saying, "This man has the power of God, called 'the Great Power'!" [11]Simon had amazed them with his magic so long that the people became his followers. [12]But when Philip told them the Good News about the kingdom of God and the power of Jesus Christ, men and women believed Philip and were baptized. [13]Simon himself believed, and after he was baptized, he stayed very close to Philip. When he saw the miracles and the powerful things Philip did, Simon was amazed.

[14]When the apostles who were still in Jerusalem heard that the people of Samaria had accepted the word of God, they sent Peter and John to them. [15]When Peter and John arrived, they prayed that the Samaritan believers might receive the Holy Spirit. [16]These people had been baptized in the name of the Lord Jesus, but the Holy Spirit had not yet come upon any of them. [17]Then, when the two apostles began laying their hands on the people, they received the Holy Spirit.

[18]Simon saw that the Spirit was given to people when the apostles laid their hands on them. So he offered the apostles money, [19]saying, "Give me also this power so that anyone on whom I lay my hands will receive the Holy Spirit."

[20]Peter said to him, "You and your money should both be destroyed, because you thought you could buy God's gift with money. [21]You cannot share with us in this work since your heart is not right before God. [22]Change your heart! Turn away from this evil thing you have done, and pray to the Lord. Maybe he will forgive you for thinking this. [23]I see that you are full of bitter jealousy and ruled by sin."

[24]Simon answered, "Both of you pray for me to the Lord so the things you have said will not happen to me."

[25]After Peter and John told the people what they had seen Jesus do and after they had spoken the message of the Lord, they went back to Jerusalem. On the way, they went through many Samaritan towns and preached the Good News to the people.

Philip Teaches an Ethiopian

[26]An angel of the Lord said to Philip, "Get ready and go south to the road that leads down to Gaza from Jerusalem—the desert road." [27]So Philip got ready and went. On the road he saw a man from Ethiopia, a eunuch. He was an important officer in the service of Candace, the queen of the Ethiopians; he was responsible for taking care of all her money. He had gone to Jerusalem to worship. [28]Now, as he was on his way home, he was sitting in his chariot reading from the Book of Isaiah, the prophet. [29]The Spirit said to Philip, "Go to that chariot and stay near it."

[30]So when Philip ran toward the chariot, he heard the man reading from Isaiah the prophet. Philip asked, "Do you understand what you are reading?"

[31]He answered, "How can I understand unless someone explains it to me?" Then he invited Philip to climb in and sit with him. [32]The portion of Scripture he was reading was this:

"He was like a sheep being led to be killed.
He was quiet, as a lamb is quiet while its wool is being cut;
he never opened his mouth.
[33] He was shamed and was treated unfairly.
He died without children to continue his family.
His life on earth has ended."

Isaiah 53:7–8

[34]The officer said to Philip, "Please tell me, who is the prophet talking about—himself or someone else?" [35]Philip began to speak, and starting with this same Scripture, he told the man the Good News about Jesus.

[36]While they were traveling down the road, they came to some water. The officer said, "Look, here is water. What is stopping me from being baptized?" [[37]Philip answered, "If you believe with all your heart, you can." The officer said, "I believe that Jesus Christ is the Son of God."][n] [38]Then the officer commanded the chariot to stop.

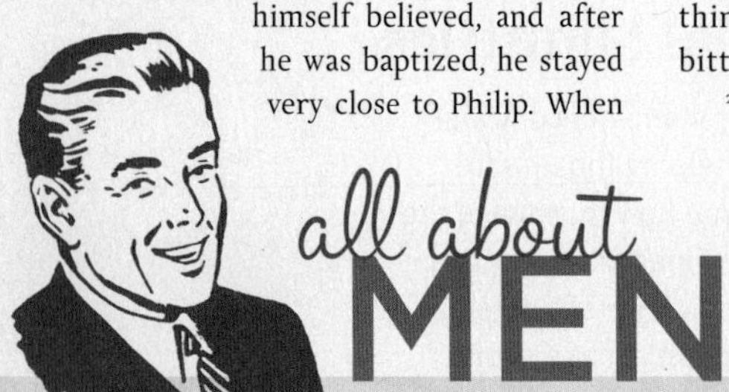

all about MEN

New Life at the Cross

At some point, many couples face a make-it-or-break-it issue together. All relationships have troubles, but if problems start to outweigh love, it's time for big healing. Fortunately, when Jesus died for us on the cross, he defeated death and brought new life to us—and to our relationships. His cross is all about "life that cannot be destroyed" (2 Timothy 1:10)! And when two people look for him at the foot of the cross, they can work through anything with his help. He can heal hurts, change hearts, and transform lives. He can even save a relationship on its last breath. Married or single, plant yourself in Jesus, seek his help, and trust his power to nurture life back into any faltering relationship.

8:37 Philip . . . God." Some Greek copies do not contain the bracketed text.

RELATIONSHIPS

The School of Relationships

They don't require tuition payments, but great relationships do cost time and energy. And they don't involve degrees, but oh, the degrees of blessings they offer! Through other people, we discover strengths that complement our weaknesses, patience with personality quirks, and mercy for our mistakes. We also gain hands-on experience in loving and putting others first. With God as your Guidance Counselor, your relationships can reach their highest potential. He's available 24/7 as Professor Extraordinaire, Tutor of tutors. When you sign up for God's lifelong course in relationships, you'll grow in ways you never imagined.

Both Philip and the officer went down into the water, and Philip baptized him. [39]When they came up out of the water, the Spirit of the Lord took Philip away; the officer never saw him again. And the officer continued on his way home, full of joy. [40]But Philip appeared in a city called Azotus and preached the Good News in all the towns on the way from Azotus to Caesarea.

Saul Is Converted

9 In Jerusalem Saul was still threatening the followers of the Lord by saying he would kill them. So he went to the high priest [2]and asked him to write letters to the synagogues in the city of Damascus. Then if Saul found any followers of Christ's Way, men or women, he would arrest them and bring them back to Jerusalem.

[3]So Saul headed toward Damascus. As he came near the city, a bright light from heaven suddenly flashed around him. [4]Saul fell to the ground and heard a voice saying to him, "Saul, Saul! Why are you persecuting me?"

[5]Saul said, "Who are you, Lord?"

The voice answered, "I am Jesus, whom you are persecuting. [6]Get up now and go into the city. Someone there will tell you what you must do."

[7]The people traveling with Saul stood there but said nothing. They heard the voice, but they saw no one. [8]Saul got up from the ground and opened his eyes, but he could not see. So those with Saul took his hand and led him into Damascus. [9]For three days Saul could not see and did not eat or drink.

[10]There was a follower of Jesus in Damascus named Ananias. The Lord spoke to Ananias in a vision, "Ananias!"

Ananias answered, "Here I am, Lord."

[11]The Lord said to him, "Get up and go to Straight Street. Find the house of Judas,[n] and ask for a man named Saul from the city of Tarsus. He is there now, praying. [12]Saul has seen a vision in which a man named Ananias comes to him and lays his hands on him. Then he is able to see again."

[13]But Ananias answered, "Lord, many people have told me about this man and the terrible things he did to your holy people in Jerusalem. [14]Now he has come here to Damascus, and the leading priests have given him the power to arrest everyone who worships you."

[15]But the Lord said to Ananias, "Go! I have chosen Saul for an important work. He must tell about me to those who are not Jews, to kings, and to the people of Israel. [16]I will show him how much he must suffer for my name."

[17]So Ananias went to the house of Judas. He laid his hands on Saul and said, "Brother Saul, the Lord Jesus sent me. He is the one you saw on the road on your way here. He sent me so that you can see again and be filled with the Holy Spirit." [18]Immediately, something that looked like fish scales fell from Saul's eyes, and he was able to see again! Then Saul got up and was baptized. [19]After he ate some food, his strength returned.

Saul Preaches in Damascus

Saul stayed with the followers of Jesus in Damascus for a few days. [20]Soon he began to preach about Jesus in the synagogues, saying, "Jesus is the Son of God."

[21]All the people who heard him were amazed. They said, "This is the man who was in Jerusalem trying to destroy those who trust in this name! He came here to arrest the followers of Jesus and take them back to the leading priests."

[22]But Saul grew more powerful. His proofs that Jesus is the Christ were so strong that his own people in Damascus could not argue with him.

[23]After many days, they made plans to kill Saul. [24]They were watching the city gates day and night, but Saul learned

9:11 Judas This is not either of the apostles named Judas.

WORLDVIEWS

Love vs. Tolerance

Whenever you walk through your local mall, there's a good chance you'll see some unique people . . . wild hairstyles, metallic hardware embedded in earlobes and eyebrows, crazy clothes . . . the variety ranges from cute to downright bizarre. It's easy to judge people based on those things. But you need to avoid that impulse because outward differences aren't really important. But what about lifestyle choices or religions? Did your best friend move in with her boyfriend? Do you have a friend who is into New Age beliefs? Do you know people who say they're witches? How do you respond?

"Tolerance" is big these days. People seem to think that really loving each other means accepting every kind of lifestyle and religion. It seems reasonable, doesn't it? Isn't it good to get past these silly disagreements and just accept each other?

Sure, if there was no such thing as truth . . . or right and wrong. The fact is, there's more at stake here than just "getting along" and tolerating each other. God's Word is very clear: some lifestyles are just plain wrong. Sin leads away from God. And there's only one way to know God—through Jesus Christ, his Son.

So as a Christian, where should you land on these issues? Consider this: God looks at people's hearts, not at clothes, styles, or skin color (1 Samuel 16:7). Outward things don't matter to him . . . and they shouldn't matter to us either. That's huge! That kind of mindset eliminates racism, gang violence, cliques, and even haughty attitudes. Following Jesus leaves *no* room for those things.

But even though God is loving, he's serious about purity and truth. He loves us but he doesn't accept sin. God is pleased when you follow truth and live a pure life.

View people through God's eyes: love everyone and don't ever judge them based on outward things that don't matter. And be just as careful not to fall for the lie that you should blindly accept immorality or false religions. Ignoring sin and believing lies isn't really love. Sharing God's truth in love is the best way to show that you genuinely care.

about their plan. [25]One night some followers of Saul helped him leave the city by lowering him in a basket through an opening in the city wall.

Saul Preaches in Jerusalem

[26]When Saul went to Jerusalem, he tried to join the group of followers, but they were all afraid of him. They did not believe he was really a follower. [27]But Barnabas accepted Saul and took him to the apostles. Barnabas explained to them that Saul had seen the Lord on the road and the Lord had spoken to Saul. Then he told them how boldly Saul had preached in the name of Jesus in Damascus.

[28]And so Saul stayed with the followers, going everywhere in Jerusalem, preaching boldly in the name of the Lord. [29]He would often talk and argue with the Jewish people who spoke Greek, but they were trying to kill him. [30]When the followers learned about this, they took Saul to Caesarea and from there sent him to Tarsus.

[31]The church everywhere in Judea, Galilee, and Samaria had a time of peace and became stronger. Respecting the Lord by the way they lived, and being encouraged by the Holy Spirit, the group of believers continued to grow.

Peter Heals Aeneas

[32]As Peter was traveling through all the area, he visited God's people who lived in Lydda. [33]There he met a man named Aeneas, who was paralyzed and had not been able to leave his bed for the past eight years. [34]Peter said to him, "Aeneas, Jesus Christ heals you. Stand up and make your bed." Aeneas stood up immediately. [35]All the people living in Lydda and on the Plain of Sharon saw him and turned to the Lord.

Peter Heals Tabitha

[36]In the city of Joppa there was a follower named Tabitha (whose Greek name was Dorcas). She was always doing good deeds and kind acts. [37]While Peter was in Lydda, Tabitha became sick and died. Her body was washed and put in a room upstairs. [38]Since Lydda is near Joppa and the followers in Joppa heard that Peter was in Lydda, they sent two messengers to Peter. They begged him, "Hurry, please come to us!" [39]So Peter got ready and went with them. When he arrived, they took him to the upstairs room where all the widows stood around Peter, crying. They showed

him the shirts and coats Tabitha had made when she was still alive. [40]Peter sent everyone out of the room and kneeled and prayed. Then he turned to the body and said, "Tabitha, stand up." She opened her eyes, and when she saw Peter, she sat up. [41]He gave her his hand and helped her up. Then he called the saints and the widows into the room and showed them that Tabitha was alive. [42]People everywhere in Joppa learned about this, and many believed in the Lord. [43]Peter stayed in Joppa for many days with a man named Simon who was a tanner.

Peter Teaches Cornelius

10 At Caesarea there was a man named Cornelius, an officer in the Italian group of the Roman army. [2]Cornelius was a religious man. He and all the other people who lived in his house worshiped the true God. He gave much of his money to the poor and prayed to God often. [3]One afternoon about three o'clock, Cornelius clearly saw a vision. An angel of God came to him and said, "Cornelius!"

[4]Cornelius stared at the angel. He became afraid and said, "What do you want, Lord?"

The angel said, "God has heard your prayers. He has seen that you give to the poor, and he remembers you. [5]Send some men now to Joppa to bring back a man named Simon who is also called Peter. [6]He is staying with a man, also named Simon, who is a tanner and has a house beside the sea." [7]When the angel who spoke to Cornelius left, Cornelius called two of his servants and a soldier, a religious man who worked for him. [8]Cornelius explained everything to them and sent them to Joppa.

[9]About noon the next day as they came near Joppa, Peter was going up to the roof[n] to pray. [10]He was hungry and wanted to eat, but while the food was being prepared, he had a vision. [11]He saw heaven opened and something coming down that looked like a big sheet being lowered to earth by its four corners. [12]In it were all kinds of animals, reptiles, and birds. [13]Then a voice said to Peter, "Get up, Peter; kill and eat."

[14]But Peter said, "No, Lord! I have never eaten food that is unholy or unclean."

[15]But the voice said to him again, "God has made these things clean, so don't call them 'unholy'!" [16]This happened three times, and at once the sheet was taken back to heaven.

[17]While Peter was wondering what this vision meant, the men Cornelius sent had found Simon's house and were standing at the gate. [18]They asked, "Is Simon Peter staying here?"

[19]While Peter was still thinking about the vision, the Spirit said to him, "Listen, three men are looking for you. [20]Get up and go downstairs. Go with them without doubting, because I have sent them to you."

[21]So Peter went down to the men and said, "I am the one you are looking for. Why did you come here?"

[22]They said, "A holy angel spoke to Cornelius, an army officer and a good man; he worships God. All the people respect him. The angel told Cornelius to ask you to come to his house so that he can hear what you have to say." [23]So Peter asked the men to come in and spend the night.

The next day Peter got ready and went with them, and some of the followers from Joppa joined him. [24]On the following day they came to Caesarea. Cornelius was waiting for them and had called together his relatives and close friends. [25]When Peter entered, Cornelius met him, fell at his feet, and worshiped him. [26]But Peter helped him up, saying, "Stand up. I too am only a human." [27]As he talked with Cornelius, Peter went inside where he saw many people gathered. [28]He said, "You people understand that it is against our law for Jewish people to associate with or visit anyone who is not Jewish. But God has shown me that I should not call any person 'unholy' or 'unclean.' [29]That is why I did not argue when I was asked to come here. Now, please tell me why you sent for me."

[30]Cornelius said, "Four days ago, I was praying in my house at this same time—three o'clock in the afternoon. Suddenly, there was a man standing before me wearing shining clothes. [31]He said, 'Cornelius, God has heard your prayer and has seen that you give to the poor and remembers you. [32]So send some men to Joppa and ask Simon Peter to come. Peter is staying in the house of a man, also named Simon, who is a tanner and has a house beside the sea.' [33]So I sent for you immediately, and it was very good of you to come. Now we are all here before God to hear everything the Lord has commanded you to tell us."

[34]Peter began to speak: "I really understand now that to God every person is the same. [35]In every country God accepts anyone who worships him and does what is right. [36]You know the message that God has sent to the people of Israel is the Good News that peace has come through Jesus Christ. Jesus is the Lord of all people! [37]You know what has happened all over Judea, beginning in Galilee after John[n] preached to the people about

Watering Worship

When your spiritual journey reminds you of a desert trek, it's time to whet your appetite for worship! For starters, refresh the dry ground of restlessness by having your focused time with God at different times of the day. The budding minutes of morning, when the day's unknowns stretch before you, may carry a different worship tune than at night, when you can look back and see how God worked. Next, discover a new oasis for daily worship. Gaze out a window and praise him for nature's colors, the refreshing dew, and the brilliant sunrise. Finally, revitalize your gratitude-attitude by praising him during mundane activities like workouts and meal prep. Nurture worship with these creative juices and you'll soon be overflowing with praise.

10:9 roof In Bible times houses were built with flat roofs. The roof was used for drying things such as flax and fruit. And it was used as an extra room, as a place for worship, and as a cool place to sleep in the summer. **10:37 John** John the Baptist, who preached to people about Christ's coming (Luke 3).

Standing Appointment with God

There's no better way to start a day off right than with some personal time with the one who made it. King David was into this idea; he asked God to tell him about his love and show him what to do each morning (Psalm 143:8). Later, the prophet Jeremiah noted that the Lord's mercies are new every morning (Lamentations 3:22–23). Of course there's nothing wrong with having a personal prayer time with God in the evening if that works best for you. The important thing is that you have a standing appointment with him every day. Tell him about your life. Tell him how great he is. Ask his advice. Take advantage of those new mercies he has for you!

baptism. [38]You know about Jesus from Nazareth, that God gave him the Holy Spirit and power. You know how Jesus went everywhere doing good and healing those who were ruled by the devil, because God was with him. [39]We saw what Jesus did in Judea and in Jerusalem, but the Jews in Jerusalem killed him by hanging him on a cross. [40]Yet, on the third day, God raised Jesus to life and caused him to be seen, [41]not by all the people, but only by the witnesses God had already chosen. And we are those witnesses who ate and drank with him after he was raised from the dead. [42]He told us to preach to the people and to tell them that he is the one whom God chose to be the judge of the living and the dead. [43]All the prophets say it is true that all who believe in Jesus will be forgiven of their sins through Jesus' name."

[44]While Peter was still saying this, the Holy Spirit came down on all those who were listening. [45]The Jewish believers who came with Peter were amazed that the gift of the Holy Spirit had been given even to the nations. [46]These believers heard them speaking in different languages[n] and praising God. Then Peter said, [47]"Can anyone keep these people from being baptized with water? They have received the Holy Spirit just as we did!" [48]So Peter ordered that they be baptized in the name of Jesus Christ. Then they asked Peter to stay with them for a few days.

Peter Returns to Jerusalem

11 The apostles and the believers in Judea heard that some who were not Jewish had accepted God's teaching too. [2]But when Peter came to Jerusalem, some people argued with him. [3]They said, "You went into the homes of people who are not circumcised and ate with them!"

[4]So Peter explained the whole story to them. [5]He said, "I was in the city of Joppa, and while I was praying, I had a vision. I saw something that looked like a big sheet being lowered from heaven by its four corners. It came very close to me. [6]I looked inside it and saw animals, wild beasts, reptiles, and birds. [7]I heard a voice say to me, 'Get up, Peter. Kill and eat.' [8]But I said, 'No, Lord! I have never eaten anything that is unholy or unclean.' [9]But the voice from heaven spoke again, 'God has made these things clean, so don't call them unholy.' [10]This happened three times. Then the whole thing was taken back to heaven. [11]Right then three men who were sent to me from Caesarea came to the house where I was staying. [12]The Spirit told me to go with them without doubting. These six believers here also went with me, and we entered the house of Cornelius. [13]He told us about the angel he saw standing in his house. The angel said to him, 'Send some men to Joppa and invite Simon Peter to come. [14]By the words he will say to you, you and all your family will be saved.' [15]When I began my speech, the Holy Spirit came on them just as he came on us at the beginning. [16]Then I remembered the words of the Lord. He said, 'John baptized with water, but you will be baptized with the Holy Spirit.' [17]Since God gave them the same gift he gave us who believed in the Lord Jesus Christ, how could I stop the work of God?"

[18]When the believers heard this, they stopped arguing. They praised God and said, "So God is allowing even other nations to turn to him and live."

fun facts

9 out of 10 women work for pay at some time during their lives.

(Academic.org)

10:46 languages This can also be translated "tongues."

The Good News Comes to Antioch

[19]Many of the believers were scattered when they were persecuted after Stephen was killed. Some of them went as far as Phoenicia, Cyprus, and Antioch telling the message to others, but only to Jews. [20]Some of these believers were people from Cyprus and Cyrene. When they came to Antioch, they spoke also to Greeks,[n] telling them the Good News about the Lord Jesus. [21]The Lord was helping the believers, and a large group of people believed and turned to the Lord.

[22]The church in Jerusalem heard about all of this, so they sent Barnabas to Antioch. [23-24]Barnabas was a good man, full of the Holy Spirit and full of faith. When he reached Antioch and saw how God had blessed the people, he was glad. He encouraged all the believers in Antioch always to obey the Lord with all their hearts, and many people became followers of the Lord.

[25]Then Barnabas went to the city of Tarsus to look for Saul, [26]and when he found Saul, he brought him to Antioch. For a whole year Saul and Barnabas met with the church and taught many people there. In Antioch the followers were called Christians for the first time.

[27]About that time some prophets came from Jerusalem to Antioch. [28]One of them, named Agabus, stood up and spoke with the help of the Holy Spirit. He said, "A very hard time is coming to the whole world. There will be no food to eat." (This happened when Claudius ruled.) [29]The followers all decided to help the believers who lived in Judea, as much as each one could. [30]They gathered the money and gave it to Barnabas and Saul, who brought it to the elders in Judea.

Acts 12:21–24

You probably lead a relatively simple life. Career, grocery shopping, meeting friends for lunch—your days aren't glamorous, but they're happy. But do you ever hear about a celebrity or wealthy heiress and wonder . . . *What would it be like to have more of what she's got?*

But fame and riches aren't all they're cracked up to be. Herod had everything in a worldly sense. He was wealthy and powerful, with stunning palaces and political pull. Jesus' followers, on the other hand, were an assortment of former fishermen, repentant prostitutes, and peasants—the complete opposite end of the social spectrum from Herod.

While Herod boasted about his own greatness and gladly welcomed praise (the people identified him as a god; apparently he agreed), Jesus' followers were 100 percent dedicated to God's glory. The message of the Good News, besides being full of hope for humanity, is all about God's glory—his perfect love, endless grace, and absolute power in defeating sin and death.

In spite of Herod's worldly advantages and glory, he couldn't escape death. And the message of God, proclaimed by simple fishermen, is undying and continues to this day. Never forget that a life of eternal value is one filled with God's truth and love!

Herod Agrippa Hurts the Church

12 During that same time King Herod began to mistreat some who belonged to the church. [2]He ordered James, the brother of John, to be killed by the sword. [3]Herod saw that some of the people liked this, so he decided to arrest Peter, too. (This happened during the time of the Feast of Unleavened Bread.)

[4]After Herod arrested Peter, he put him in jail and handed him over to be guarded by sixteen soldiers. Herod planned to bring Peter before the people for trial after the Passover Feast. [5]So Peter was kept in jail, but the church prayed earnestly to God for him.

Peter Leaves the Jail

[6]The night before Herod was to bring him to trial, Peter was sleeping between two soldiers, bound with two chains. Other soldiers were guarding the door of the jail. [7]Suddenly, an angel of the Lord stood there, and a light shined in the cell. The angel struck Peter on the side and woke him up. "Hurry! Get up!" the angel said. And the chains fell off Peter's hands. [8]Then the angel told him, "Get dressed and put on your sandals." And Peter did. Then the angel said, "Put on your coat and follow me." [9]So Peter followed him out, but he did not know if what the angel was doing was real; he thought he might be seeing a vision. [10]They went past the first and second guards and came to the iron gate that separated them from the city. The gate opened by itself for them, and they went through it. When they had walked down one street, the angel suddenly left him.

[11]Then Peter realized what had happened. He thought, "Now I know that

11:20 Greeks Some Greek copies read "Hellenists," non-Greeks who spoke Greek.

HE SAID ↙ ↗ SHE SAID

Who is your favorite man in the Bible?

HE: David because he was a man after God's own heart

SHE: Joseph, the son of Jacob, because he is such an inspiration

the Lord really sent his angel to me. He rescued me from Herod and from all the things the people thought would happen."

12When he considered this, he went to the home of Mary, the mother of John Mark. Many people were gathered there, praying. 13Peter knocked on the outside door, and a servant girl named Rhoda came to answer it. 14When she recognized Peter's voice, she was so happy she forgot to open the door. Instead, she ran inside and told the group, "Peter is at the door!"

15They said to her, "You are crazy!" But she kept on saying it was true, so they said, "It must be Peter's angel."

16Peter continued to knock, and when they opened the door, they saw him and were amazed. 17Peter made a sign with his hand to tell them to be quiet. He explained how the Lord led him out of the jail, and he said, "Tell James and the other believers what happened." Then he left to go to another place.

18The next day the soldiers were very upset and wondered what had happened to Peter. 19Herod looked everywhere for him but could not find him. So he questioned the guards and ordered that they be killed.

The Death of Herod Agrippa

Later Herod moved from Judea and went to the city of Caesarea, where he stayed. 20Herod was very angry with the people of Tyre and Sidon, but the people of those cities all came in a group to him. After convincing Blastus, the king's personal servant, to be on their side, they asked Herod for peace, because their country got its food from his country.

21On a chosen day Herod put on his royal robes, sat on his throne, and made a speech to the people. 22They shouted, "This is the voice of a god, not a human!" 23Because Herod did not give the glory to God, an angel of the Lord immediately caused him to become sick, and he was eaten by worms and died.

24God's message continued to spread and reach people.

25After Barnabas and Saul finished their task in Jerusalem, they returned to Antioch, taking John Mark with them.

Barnabas and Saul Are Chosen

13 In the church at Antioch there were these prophets and teachers: Barnabas, Simeon (also called Niger), Lucius (from the city of Cyrene), Manaen (who had grown up with Herod, the ruler), and Saul. 2They were all worshiping the Lord and fasting[n] for a certain time. During this time the Holy Spirit said to them, "Set apart for me Barnabas and Saul to do a special work for which I have chosen them."

3So after they fasted and prayed, they laid their hands on[n] Barnabas and Saul and sent them out.

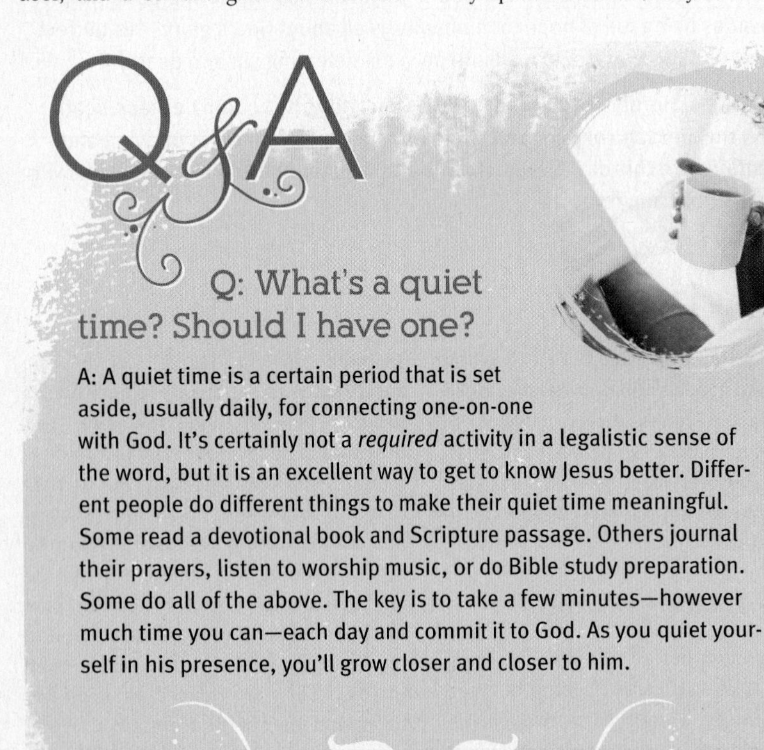

Q&A

Q: What's a quiet time? Should I have one?

A: A quiet time is a certain period that is set aside, usually daily, for connecting one-on-one with God. It's certainly not a *required* activity in a legalistic sense of the word, but it is an excellent way to get to know Jesus better. Different people do different things to make their quiet time meaningful. Some read a devotional book and Scripture passage. Others journal their prayers, listen to worship music, or do Bible study preparation. Some do all of the above. The key is to take a few minutes—however much time you can—each day and commit it to God. As you quiet yourself in his presence, you'll grow closer and closer to him.

13:2 fasting The people would give up eating for a special time of prayer and worship to God. It was also done sometimes to show sadness and disappointment. **13:3 laid their hands on** The laying on of hands had many purposes, including the giving of a blessing, power, or authority.

Barnabas and Saul in Cyprus

[4]Barnabas and Saul, sent out by the Holy Spirit, went to the city of Seleucia. From there they sailed to the island of Cyprus. [5]When they came to Salamis, they preached the Good News of God in the synagogues. John Mark was with them to help.

[6]They went across the whole island to Paphos where they met a magician named Bar-Jesus. He was a false prophet [7]who always stayed close to Sergius Paulus, the governor and a smart man. He asked Barnabas and Saul to come to him, because he wanted to hear the message of God. [8]But Elymas, the magician, was against them. (Elymas is the name for Bar-Jesus in the Greek language.) He tried to stop the governor from believing in Jesus. [9]But Saul, who was also called Paul, was filled with the Holy Spirit. He looked straight at Elymas [10]and said, "You son of the devil! You are an enemy of everything that is right! You are full of evil tricks and lies, always trying to change the Lord's truths into lies. [11]Now the Lord will touch you, and you will be blind. For a time you will not be able to see anything—not even the light from the sun."

Then everything became dark for Elymas, and he walked around, trying to find someone to lead him by the hand. [12]When the governor saw this, he believed because he was amazed at the teaching about the Lord.

Paul and Barnabas Leave Cyprus

[13]Paul and those with him sailed from Paphos and came to Perga, in Pamphylia. There John Mark left them to return to Jerusalem. [14]They continued their trip from Perga and went to Antioch, a city in Pisidia. On the Sabbath day they went into the synagogue and sat down. [15]After the law of Moses and the writings of the prophets were read, the leaders of the synagogue sent a message to Paul and Barnabas: "Brothers, if you have any message that will encourage the people, please speak."

[16]Paul stood up, raised his hand, and said, "You Israelites and you who worship God, please listen! [17]The God of the Israelites chose our ancestors. He made the people great during the time they lived in Egypt, and he brought them out of that country with great power. [18]And he was patient with them[n] for forty years in the desert. [19]God destroyed seven nations in the land of Canaan and gave the land to his people. [20]All this happened in about four hundred fifty years.

"After this, God gave them judges until the time of Samuel the prophet. [21]Then the people asked for a king, so God gave them Saul son of Kish. Saul was from the tribe of Benjamin and was king for forty years. [22]After God took him away, God made David their king. God said about him: 'I have found in David son of Jesse the kind of man I want. He will do all I want him to do.' [23]So God has brought Jesus, one of David's descendants, to Israel to be its Savior, as he promised. [24]Before Jesus came, John[n] preached to all the people of Israel about a baptism of changed hearts and lives. [25]When he was finishing his work, he said, 'Who do you think I am? I am not the Christ. He is coming later, and I am not worthy to untie his sandals.'

[26]"Brothers, sons of the family of Abraham, and others who worship God, listen! The news about this salvation has been sent to us. [27]Those who live in Jerusalem and their leaders did not realize that Jesus was the Savior. They did not understand the words that the prophets wrote, which are read every Sabbath day. But they made them come true when they said Jesus was guilty. [28]They could not find any real reason for Jesus to be put to death, but they asked Pilate to have him killed. [29]When they had done to him all that the Scriptures had said, they took him down from the cross and laid him in a tomb. [30]But God raised him up from the dead! [31]After this, for many days, those who had gone with Jesus from Galilee to Jerusalem saw him. They are now his witnesses to the people. [32]We tell you the Good News about the promise God made to our ancestors. [33]God has made this promise come true for us, his children, by raising Jesus from the dead. We read about this also in Psalm 2:

'You are my Son.
Today I have become your
Father.' *Psalm 2:7*

[34]God raised Jesus from the dead, and he will never go back to the grave and become dust. So God said:

'I will give you the holy and sure
blessings
that I promised to David.'
Isaiah 55:3

[35]But in another place God says:

'You will not let your Holy One
rot.' *Psalm 16:10*

Health

Eat for Your Mood

The three-hour meeting with an angry client accomplished nothing. To top it off, your boss dumps a project on your desk ten minutes before you were planning to go home. When you finally leave the office—two hours later—you need chocolate, *stat*! It's okay to indulge in occasional treats, but a better solution is eating the right nutrients to target your stress. Vitamins B_6 and B_{12} (found in beans and lean meat, respectively) can help banish the blues. Omega-3 fatty acids (in salmon and other sources) diminish frustration. To combat fatigue, eat plenty of iron (in lean meats and spinach). Keeping headaches at bay may be as simple as downing clear liquids. Eat right to fight stress, and turn all your worries over to God (1 Peter 5:7).

13:18 And . . . them Some Greek copies read "And he cared for them." **13:24 John** John the Baptist, who preached to people about Christ's coming (Luke 3).

Sharing Your Faith

How are you known in the workplace? Do people seem to excuse themselves every time the conversation turns toward your faith? Maybe it's your approach. Learning to share your faith with unbelievers is an important skill for all Christians to acquire. We are called to share our faith with others, wherever we go. Try establishing rapport by asking lighter questions about the other person's interests. Lead up to questions about what that person believes and why to open the door for you to share your own beliefs. And always remember to pray—before and after you talk about issues of faith. Remember that God doesn't just go before you, he goes with you and after you, too!

[36]David did God's will during his lifetime. Then he died and was buried beside his ancestors, and his body did rot in the grave. [37]But the One God raised from the dead did not rot in the grave. [38-39]Brothers, understand what we are telling you: You can have forgiveness of your sins through Jesus. The law of Moses could not free you from your sins. But through Jesus everyone who believes is free from all sins. [40]Be careful! Don't let what the prophets said happen to you:

[41]"Listen, you people who doubt!
You can wonder, and then die.
I will do something in your lifetime
that you won't believe even when
you are told about it!' "

Habakkuk 1:5

[42]While Paul and Barnabas were leaving the synagogue, the people asked them to tell them more about these things on the next Sabbath. [43]When the meeting was over, many people with those who had changed to worship God followed Paul and Barnabas from that place. Paul and Barnabas were persuading them to continue trusting in God's grace.

[44]On the next Sabbath day, almost everyone in the city came to hear the word of the Lord. [45]Seeing the crowd, the Jewish people became very jealous and said insulting things and argued against what Paul said. [46]But Paul and Barnabas spoke very boldly, saying, "We must speak the message of God to you first. But you refuse to listen. You are judging yourselves not worthy of having eternal life! So we will now go to the people of other nations. [47]This is what the Lord told us to do, saying:

'I have made you a light for the
nations;
you will show people all over the
world the way to be saved.' "

Isaiah 49:6

[48]When those who were not Jewish heard Paul say this, they were happy and gave honor to the message of the Lord. And the people who were chosen to have life forever believed the message.

[49]So the message of the Lord was spreading through the whole country. [50]But the Jewish people stirred up some of the important religious women and the leaders of the city. They started trouble against Paul and Barnabas and forced them out of their area. [51]So Paul and Barnabas shook the dust off their feet[n] and went to Iconium. [52]But the followers were filled with joy and the Holy Spirit.

Paul and Barnabas in Iconium

14 In Iconium, Paul and Barnabas went as usual to the synagogue. They spoke so well that a great many Jews and Greeks believed. [2]But some people who did not believe excited the others and turned them against the believers. [3]Paul and Barnabas stayed in Iconium a long time and spoke bravely for the Lord. He showed that their message about his grace was true by giving them the power to work miracles and signs. [4]But the city was divided. Some of the people agreed with the Jews, and others believed the apostles.

[5]Some who were not Jews, some Jews, and some of their rulers wanted to mistreat Paul and Barnabas and to stone them to death. [6]When Paul and Barnabas learned about this, they ran away to Lystra and Derbe, cities in Lycaonia, and to the areas around those cities. [7]They announced the Good News there, too.

Paul in Lystra and Derbe

[8]In Lystra there sat a man who had been born crippled; he had never walked. [9]As this man was listening to Paul speak, Paul looked straight at him and saw that he believed God could heal him. [10]So he cried out, "Stand up on your feet!" The man jumped up and began walking around. [11]When the crowds saw what Paul did, they shouted in the Lycaonian language, "The gods have become like humans and have come down to us!" [12]Then the people began to call Barnabas "Zeus"[n] and Paul "Hermes,"[n] because he was the main speaker. [13]The priest in the temple of Zeus, which was near the city, brought some bulls and flowers to the city gates. He and the people wanted to offer a sacrifice to Paul and Barnabas. [14]But when the apostles, Barnabas and Paul, heard about it, they tore their clothes. They ran in among the people, shouting, [15]"Friends, why are you doing these things? We are only human beings like you. We are bringing you the Good News and are telling you to turn away from these worthless things

13:51 shook . . . feet A warning. It showed that they had rejected these people. **14:12 "Zeus"** The Greeks believed in many false gods, of whom Zeus was most important. **14:12 "Hermes"** The Greeks believed he was a messenger for the other gods.

and turn to the living God. He is the One who made the sky, the earth, the sea, and everything in them. [16]In the past, God let all the nations do what they wanted. [17]Yet he proved he is real by showing kindness, by giving you rain from heaven and crops at the right times, by giving you food and filling your hearts with joy." [18]Even with these words, they were barely able to keep the crowd from offering sacrifices to them.

[19]Then some evil people came from Antioch and Iconium and persuaded the people to turn against Paul. So they threw stones at him and dragged him out of town, thinking they had killed him. [20]But the followers gathered around him, and he got up and went back into the town. The next day he and Barnabas left and went to the city of Derbe.

The Return to Antioch in Syria

[21]Paul and Barnabas told the Good News in Derbe, and many became followers. Paul and Barnabas returned to Lystra, Iconium, and Antioch, [22]making the followers of Jesus stronger and helping them stay in the faith. They said, "We must suffer many things to enter God's kingdom." [23]They chose elders for each church, by praying and fasting[n] for a certain time. These elders had trusted the Lord, so Paul and Barnabas put them in the Lord's care.

[24]Then they went through Pisidia and came to Pamphylia. [25]When they had preached the message in Perga, they went down to Attalia. [26]And from there they sailed away to Antioch where the believers had put them into God's care and had sent them out to do this work. Now they had finished.

[27]When they arrived in Antioch, Paul and Barnabas gathered the church together. They told the church all about what God had done with them and how God had made it possible for those who were not Jewish to believe. [28]And they stayed there a long time with the followers.

The Meeting at Jerusalem

15 Then some people came to Antioch from Judea and began teaching the non-Jewish believers: "You cannot be saved if you are not circumcised as Moses taught us." [2]Paul and Barnabas were against this teaching and argued with them about it. So the church decided to send Paul, Barnabas, and some others to Jerusalem where they could talk more about this with the apostles and elders.

[3]The church helped them leave on the trip, and they went through the countries of Phoenicia and Samaria, telling all about how the other nations had turned to God. This made all the believers very happy. [4]When they arrived in Jerusalem, they were welcomed by the apostles, the elders, and the church. Paul, Barnabas, and the others told about everything God had done with them. [5]But some of the believers who belonged to the Pharisee group came forward and said, "The non-Jewish believers must be circumcised. They must be told to obey the law of Moses."

[6]The apostles and the elders gathered to consider this problem. [7]After a long debate, Peter stood up and said to them, "Brothers, you know that in the early days God chose me from among you to preach the Good News to the nations. They heard the Good News from me, and they believed. [8]God, who knows the thoughts of everyone, accepted them. He showed this to us by giving them the Holy Spirit, just as he did to us. [9]To God, those people are not different from us. When they believed,

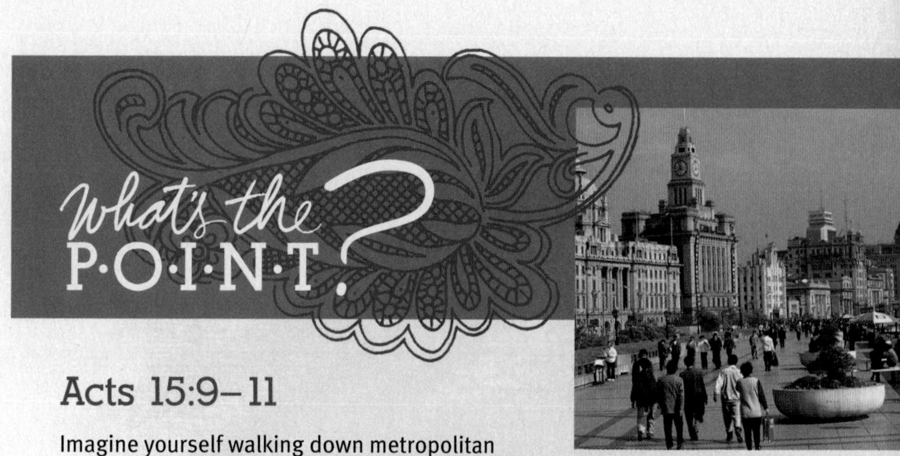

Acts 15:9–11

Imagine yourself walking down metropolitan streets in different cities across the globe. You'd probably notice hundreds of people outrageously different from you. With all those cultural differences, do you find it hard to believe that God sees each of you in the same way?

Early church members dealt with that issue, especially when it came to Jews and non-Jews. Does a Christian need to follow Jewish laws to be right with God? Does a non-Jew need to become a Jew before becoming a Christian? Those were significant questions at the time. Jesus' earliest converts were Jews, and they recognized him as their long-awaited Messiah who fulfilled Jewish prophecy. But before long, Jesus' closest followers realized the Good News wasn't just for Jews—it was for the entire world!

The Jews were used to being God's chosen people, so it was hard for them to realize and accept that God now offered salvation to all people by his amazing grace. What about you? Do you find yourself withholding God's truth from people you're uncomfortable with? To God, those people are no different than you. All of us are sinful people who desperately need God—people who can be made right with him through faith in Christ. So freely share the Good News!

14:23 fasting The people would give up eating for a special time of prayer and worship to God. It was also done sometimes to show sadness and disappointment.

Do the Thing You Fear

People have been hiding from their fears since Adam and Eve hid from God in the Garden of Eden. (Didn't work out too well for them, did it?) Fear of failure—or sometimes even success—keeps us from venturing into new territory and discovering our talents. Some of us even give up things we really enjoy because of paralyzing fear. But facing your fears head-on is the fastest way to snuff them out. Take baby steps to expand your comfort zone, and then celebrate each leg of the journey. You never know what you're capable of until you try. It's confronting your fear—not necessarily success at a task—that boosts courage and increases confidence.

he made their hearts pure. [10]So now why are you testing God by putting a heavy load around the necks of the non-Jewish believers? It is a load that neither we nor our ancestors were able to carry. [11]But we believe that we and they too will be saved by the grace of the Lord Jesus."

[12]Then the whole group became quiet. They listened to Paul and Barnabas tell about all the miracles and signs that God did through them among the people. [13]After they finished speaking, James said, "Brothers, listen to me. [14]Simon has told us how God showed his love for those people. For the first time he is accepting from among them a people to be his own. [15]The words of the prophets agree with this too:

[16]'After these things I will return.
The kingdom of David is like a fallen tent.
But I will rebuild its ruins,
and I will set it up.
[17]Then those people who are left alive may ask the Lord for help,
and the other nations that belong to me,
says the Lord,
who will make it happen.
[18]And these things have been known for a long time.' *Amos 9:11–12*

[19]"So I think we should not bother the other people who are turning to God. [20]Instead, we should write a letter to them telling them these things: Stay away from food that has been offered to idols (which makes it unclean), any kind of sexual sin, eating animals that have been strangled, and blood. [21]They should do these things, because for a long time in every city the law of Moses has been taught. And it is still read in the synagogue every Sabbath day."

Letter to Non-Jewish Believers

[22]The apostles, the elders, and the whole church decided to send some of their men with Paul and Barnabas to Antioch. They chose Judas Barsabbas and Silas, who were respected by the believers. [23]They sent the following letter with them:

From the apostles and elders, your brothers.

To all the non-Jewish believers in Antioch, Syria, and Cilicia:

Greetings!

[24]We have heard that some of our group have come to you and said things that trouble and upset you. But we did not tell them to do this. [25]We have all agreed to choose some messengers and send them to you with our dear friends Barnabas and Paul— [26]people who have given their lives to serve our Lord Jesus Christ. [27]So we are sending Judas and Silas, who will tell you the same things. [28]It has pleased the Holy Spirit that you should not have a heavy load to carry, and we agree. You need to do only these things: [29]Stay away from any food that has been offered to idols, eating any animals that have been strangled, and blood, and any kind of sexual sin. If you stay away from these things, you will do well.

Good-bye.

[30]So they left Jerusalem and went to Antioch where they gathered the church and gave them the letter. [31]When they read it, they were very happy because of the encouraging message. [32]Judas and Silas, who were also prophets, said many things to encourage the believers and make them stronger. [33]After some time Judas and Silas were sent off in peace by the believers, and they went back to those who had sent them [, [34]but Silas decided to remain there].[n]

[35]But Paul and Barnabas stayed in Antioch and, along with many others, preached the Good News and taught the people the message of the Lord.

Paul and Barnabas Separate

[36]After some time, Paul said to Barnabas, "We should go back to all those towns where we preached the message of the Lord. Let's visit the believers and see how they are doing."

[37]Barnabas wanted to take John Mark with them, [38]but he had left them at Pamphylia; he did not continue with them in the work. So Paul did not think it was a good idea to take him. [39]Paul and Barnabas had such a serious argument about this that they separated and went different ways. Barnabas took Mark and sailed to Cyprus, [40]but Paul chose Silas and left. The believers in Antioch put Paul into the Lord's care, [41]and he went through Syria and Cilicia, giving strength to the churches.

Timothy Goes with Paul

16 Paul came to Derbe and Lystra, where a follower named

15:34 but . . . there Some Greek copies do not contain the bracketed text.

Timothy lived. Timothy's mother was Jewish and a believer, but his father was a Greek.

[2]The believers in Lystra and Iconium respected Timothy and said good things about him. [3]Paul wanted Timothy to travel with him, but all the people living in that area knew that Timothy's father was Greek. So Paul circumcised Timothy to please his mother's people. [4]Paul and those with him traveled from town to town and gave the decisions made by the apostles and elders in Jerusalem for the people to obey. [5]So the churches became stronger in the faith and grew larger every day.

Paul Is Called Out of Asia

[6]Paul and those with him went through the areas of Phrygia and Galatia since the Holy Spirit did not let them preach the Good News in Asia. [7]When they came near the country of Mysia, they tried to go into Bithynia, but the Spirit of Jesus did not let them. [8]So they passed by Mysia and went to Troas. [9]That night Paul saw in a vision a man from Macedonia. The man stood and begged, "Come over to Macedonia and help us." [10]After Paul had seen the vision, we immediately prepared to leave for Macedonia, understanding that God had called us to tell the Good News to those people.

Lydia Becomes a Christian

[11]We left Troas and sailed straight to the island of Samothrace. The next day we sailed to Neapolis.[n] [12]Then we went by land to Philippi, a Roman colony[n] and the leading city in that part of Macedonia. We stayed there for several days.

[13]On the Sabbath day we went outside the city gate to the river where we thought we would find a special place for prayer. Some women had gathered there, so we sat down and talked with them. [14]One of the listeners was a woman named Lydia from the city of Thyatira whose job was selling purple cloth. She worshiped God, and he opened her mind to pay attention to what Paul was saying. [15]She and all the people in her house were baptized. Then she invited us to her home, saying, "If you think I am truly a believer in the Lord, then come stay in my house." And she persuaded us to stay with her.

Paul and Silas in Jail

[16]Once, while we were going to the place for prayer, a servant girl met us. She had a special spirit[n] in her, and she earned a lot of money for her owners by telling fortunes. [17]This girl followed Paul and us, shouting, "These men are servants of the Most High God. They are telling you how you can be saved."

[18]She kept this up for many days. This bothered Paul, so he turned and said to the spirit, "By the power of Jesus Christ, I command you to come out of her!" Immediately, the spirit came out.

[19]When the owners of the servant girl saw this, they knew that now they could not use her to make money. So they grabbed Paul and Silas and dragged them before the city rulers in the marketplace. [20]They brought Paul and Silas to the Roman rulers and said, "These men are Jews and are making trouble in our city. [21]They are teaching things that are not right for us as Romans to do."

[22]The crowd joined the attack against

Savvy Chef

Recipe Card Refreshers

Our kitchens are places of comings and goings—the last place we visit before rushing out the door and the first place we dump the cares of a long day. Well, turn your kitchen into a haven of connection with your Creator. Pull out that stash of recipe cards and spend an hour adding a favorite Bible verse, inspirational quote, or song lyric to each one. Before long your kitchen time will serve up recipes for encouragement. Not only will your cards lift your spirit every time you cook—they'll also refresh your friends who ask for copies!

fun facts

There are more than 6.5 million female-owned businesses in the United States.

(U.S. Census Bureau)

16:11 Neapolis City in Macedonia. It was the first city Paul visited on the continent of Europe. **16:12 Roman colony** A town begun by Romans with Roman laws, customs, and privileges. **16:16 spirit** This was a spirit from the devil, which caused her to say she had special knowledge.

HE SAID ↙ ↗ SHE SAID

What do you love most about Jesus?

HE: That he would share his inheritance with us

SHE: That he loved people enough to challenge them

them. The Roman officers tore the clothes of Paul and Silas and had them beaten with rods. [23]Then Paul and Silas were thrown into jail, and the jailer was ordered to guard them carefully. [24]When he heard this order, he put them far inside the jail and pinned their feet down between large blocks of wood.

[25]About midnight Paul and Silas were praying and singing songs to God as the other prisoners listened. [26]Suddenly, there was a strong earthquake that shook the foundation of the jail. Then all the doors of the jail broke open, and all the prisoners were freed from their chains. [27]The jailer woke up and saw that the jail doors were open. Thinking that the prisoners had already escaped, he got his sword and was about to kill himself.[n] [28]But Paul shouted, "Don't hurt yourself! We are all here."

[29]The jailer told someone to bring a light. Then he ran inside and, shaking with fear, fell down before Paul and Silas. [30]He brought them outside and said, "Men, what must I do to be saved?"

[31]They said to him, "Believe in the Lord Jesus and you will be saved—you and all the people in your house." [32]So Paul and Silas told the message of the Lord to the jailer and all the people in his house. [33]At that hour of the night the jailer took Paul and Silas and washed their wounds. Then he and all his people were baptized immediately. [34]After this the jailer took Paul and Silas home and gave them food. He and his family were very happy because they now believed in God.

[35]The next morning, the Roman officers sent the police to tell the jailer, "Let these men go free."

[36]The jailer said to Paul, "The officers have sent an order to let you go free. You can leave now. Go in peace."

[37]But Paul said to the police, "They beat us in public without a trial, even though we are Roman citizens.[n] And they threw us in jail. Now they want to make us go away quietly. No! Let them come themselves and bring us out."

[38]The police told the Roman officers what Paul said. When the officers heard that Paul and Silas were Roman citizens, they were afraid. [39]So they came and told Paul and Silas they were sorry and took them out of jail and asked them to leave the city. [40]So when they came out of the jail, they went to Lydia's house where they saw some of the believers and encouraged them. Then they left.

Paul and Silas in Thessalonica

17 Paul and Silas traveled through Amphipolis and Apollonia and came to Thessalonica where there was a synagogue. [2]Paul went into the synagogue as he always did, and on each Sabbath day for three weeks, he talked with his fellow Jews about the Scriptures. [3]He explained and proved that the Christ must die and then rise from the dead. He said, "This Jesus I am telling you about is the Christ." [4]Some of them were convinced and joined Paul and Silas, along with many of the Greeks who worshiped God and many of the important women.

[5]But some others became jealous. So they got some evil men from the marketplace, formed a mob, and started a riot. They ran to Jason's house, looking for Paul and Silas, wanting to bring them out to

Beautiful People Defined

Ever wonder what God thinks is beautiful? Romans 10:15 solves the mystery! It says that a beautiful person is one who brings the Good News of Christ to others. If you want to be beautiful in his sight, you just have to tell someone about Jesus and what he's done for you. You don't have to follow a specific formula or pretend like you're perfect all the time. You just have to have an intimate friendship with God. The sharing will come naturally as you live out that relationship with your Savior.

16:27 kill himself He thought the leaders would kill him for letting the prisoners escape. **16:37 Roman citizens** Roman law said that Roman citizens must not be beaten before they had a trial.

the people. [6]But when they did not find them, they dragged Jason and some other believers to the leaders of the city. The people were yelling, "These people have made trouble everywhere in the world, and now they have come here too! [7]Jason is keeping them in his house. All of them do things against the laws of Caesar, saying there is another king, called Jesus."

[8]When the people and the leaders of the city heard these things, they became very upset. [9]They made Jason and the others put up a sum of money. Then they let the believers go free.

Paul and Silas Go to Berea

[10]That same night the believers sent Paul and Silas to Berea where they went to the synagogue. [11]These people were more willing to listen than the people in Thessalonica. The Bereans were eager to hear what Paul and Silas said and studied the Scriptures every day to find out if these things were true. [12]So, many of them believed, as well as many important Greek women and men. [13]But the people in Thessalonica learned that Paul was preaching the word of God in Berea, too. So they came there, upsetting the people and making trouble. [14]The believers quickly sent Paul away to the coast, but Silas and Timothy stayed in Berea. [15]The people leading Paul went with him to Athens. Then they carried a message from Paul back to Silas and Timothy for them to come to him as soon as they could.

Paul Preaches in Athens

[16]While Paul was waiting for Silas and Timothy in Athens, he was troubled because he saw that the city was full of idols. [17]In the synagogue, he talked with the Jews and the Greeks who worshiped God. He also talked every day with people in the marketplace.

[18]Some of the Epicurean and Stoic philosophers[n] argued with him, saying, "This man doesn't know what he is talking about. What is he trying to say?" Others said, "He seems to be telling us about some other gods," because Paul was telling them about Jesus and his rising from the dead. [19]They got Paul and took him to a meeting of the Areopagus,[n] where they said, "Please explain to us this new idea you have been teaching. [20]The things you are saying are new to us, and we want to know what this teaching means." [21](All the people of Athens and those from other countries who lived there always used their time to talk about the newest ideas.)

[22]Then Paul stood before the meeting of the Areopagus and said, "People of Athens, I can see you are very religious in all things. [23]As I was going through your city, I saw the objects you worship. I found an altar that had these words written on it: TO A GOD WHO IS NOT KNOWN. You worship a god that you don't know, and this is the God I am telling you about! [24]The God who made the whole world and everything in it is the Lord of the land and the sky. He does not live in temples built by human hands. [25]This God is the One who gives life, breath, and everything else to people. He does not need any help from them; he has everything he needs. [26]God began by making one person, and from him came all the different people who live everywhere in the world. God decided exactly when and where they must live. [27]God wanted them to look for him and perhaps search all around for him and find him, though he is not far from any of us: [28]'By his power we live and move and exist.' Some of your own poets have said: 'For we are his children.' [29]Since we are God's children, you must not think that God is like something that people imagine or make from gold, silver, or rock. [30]In the past, people did not understand God, and he ignored this. But now, God tells all people in the world to change their hearts and lives. [31]God has set a day that he will judge all the world with fairness, by the man he chose long ago. And God has proved this to everyone by raising that man from the dead!"

[32]When the people heard about Jesus being raised from the dead, some of them laughed. But others said, "We will hear more about this from you later." [33]So Paul went away from them. [34]But some of the people believed Paul and joined him. Among those who believed was Dionysius, a member of the Areopagus, a woman named Damaris, and some others.

Paul in Corinth

18 Later Paul left Athens and went to Corinth. [2]Here he met a Jew named Aquila who had been born in the country of Pontus. But Aquila and his wife, Priscilla, had recently moved to Corinth from Italy, because Claudius[n] commanded that all Jews must leave Rome. Paul went to visit Aquila and Priscilla. [3]Because they were tentmakers, just as he was, he stayed with them and worked with them. [4]Every Sabbath day he talked with the Jews and Greeks in the synagogue, trying to persuade them to believe in Jesus.

[5]Silas and Timothy came from Macedonia and joined Paul in Corinth. After this, Paul spent all his time telling people

LIFE ISSUES

Guilt Free

We all know the tug of guilt. While guilt helps us face our sin, God's forgiveness offers freedom from the ongoing kind that keeps us feeling weighed down. He doesn't want you dragged down by past mistakes that you've confessed to him and dealt with. So you have a choice: will you accept forgiveness, let go of the guilt, and move on—or will you crawl back into guilt's trap? We'll deal with sin until heaven, but thanks to forgiveness, God doesn't keep accusing us of wrongs we've already given up to him (Acts 13:38–39). So why should we accuse ourselves? Enjoy your freedom!

17:18 Epicurean and Stoic philosophers Philosophers were those who searched for truth. Epicureans believed that pleasures, especially pleasures of the mind, were the goal of life. Stoics believed that life should be without feelings of joy or grief. **17:19 Areopagus** A council or group of important leaders in Athens. They were like judges. **18:2 Claudius** The emperor (ruler) of Rome, A.D. 41–54.

virtue BUILDING: Wisdom

There are lots of types and definitions of wisdom. By the world's standards, wisdom often refers to philosophical or scientific knowledge. It's about gathering information and knowing facts.

But according to Scripture, wisdom is a lot more than having head knowledge. True wisdom is about *spiritual* understanding. You don't have to necessarily be extremely intelligent or have multiple degrees to have wisdom. There are lots of intelligent and well-educated people who are foolish according to God's standards.

Real wisdom is more than knowledge . . . it's the ability to recognize and understand truth and then apply that truth to your life. And it's something you never get enough of!

Scripture Breakdown

So how do you get real wisdom? True spiritual knowledge starts with "respect for the LORD" (Proverbs 1:7). For a solid introduction to the meaning and benefits of wisdom, read Proverbs 1—4. The opposite of wisdom—foolishness—is caused by disregarding God. Psalm 14:1 says, "Fools say to themselves, 'There is no God.' " James 3:13—4:10 provides a great contrast between foolishness and wisdom. To dig deeper, check out the Book of Proverbs, the Book of Ecclesiastes, 1 Corinthians 1:17—2:16, and James 1:2–8.

Build It into Your Life

- The path to wisdom and the path to foolishness both start with the same question: "How will I view God—will I respect or ignore him?" Your answer will define the rest of your life. How will *you* answer that question?
- What is the "respect for the LORD" that Proverbs 1:7 mentions? If he's really God, doesn't he deserve respect? How should you view yourself in relation to God? Instead of being rebellious ("My way is just as good or better than God's!"), worship and serve God with every breath. That's real wisdom because it reflects the truth about who God is and who we are.
- If you have wisdom, how will you live? (Romans 11:33—12:2; Ephesians 5:15–20)
- How do you get wisdom? (Proverbs 2:1–13; 15:31–33; 17:24, 27; James 1:5)

the Good News, showing them that Jesus is the Christ. [6]But they would not accept Paul's teaching and said some evil things. So he shook off the dust from his clothes[n] and said to them, "If you are not saved, it will be your own fault! I have done all I can do! After this, I will go to other nations." [7]Paul left the synagogue and moved into the home of Titius Justus, next to the synagogue. This man worshiped God. [8]Crispus was the leader of that synagogue, and he and all the people living in his house believed in the Lord. Many others in Corinth also listened to Paul and believed and were baptized.

[9]During the night, the Lord told Paul in a vision: "Don't be afraid. Continue talking to people and don't be quiet. [10]I am with you, and no one will hurt you because many of my people are in this city." [11]Paul stayed there for a year and a half, teaching God's word to the people.

Paul Is Brought Before Gallio

[12]When Gallio was the governor of the country of Southern Greece, some people came together against Paul and took him to the court. [13]They said, "This man is teaching people to worship God in a way that is against our law."

[14]Paul was about to say something, but Gallio spoke, saying, "I would listen to you if you were complaining about a crime or some wrong. [15]But the things you are saying are only questions about words and names—arguments about your own law. So you must solve this problem yourselves. I don't want to be a judge of these things." [16]And Gallio made them leave the court.

[17]Then they all grabbed Sosthenes, the leader of the synagogue, and beat him there before the court. But this did not bother Gallio.

Paul Returns to Antioch

[18]Paul stayed with the believers for many more days. Then he left and sailed for Syria, with Priscilla and Aquila. At Cenchrea Paul cut off his hair,[n] because he had made a promise to God. [19]Then they went to Ephesus, where Paul left Priscilla and Aquila. While Paul was there, he went into the synagogue and talked with the people. [20]When they asked him to stay with them longer, he refused. [21]But as he left, he said, "I will come back to you again if God wants me to." And so he sailed away from Ephesus.

[22]When Paul landed at Caesarea, he went and gave greetings to the church in Jerusalem. After that, Paul went to Antioch. [23]He stayed there for a while and then left and went through the regions of Galatia and Phrygia. He traveled from town to town in these regions, giving strength to all the followers.

Apollos in Ephesus and Corinth

[24]A Jew named Apollos came to Ephesus. He was born in the city of Alexandria and

18:6 shook . . . clothes This was a warning to show that Paul was finished talking to the people in that city. **18:18 cut . . . hair** Jews did this to show that the time of a special promise to God was finished.

RELATIONSHIPS

Clearing the Air

Just like a closed-up room gets stuffy, our relationships need an occasional airing out. It's easy to overlook issues that crop up, but instead of ignoring them, take a little time for some creative air clearing. Trouble spots happen in all relationships, and dealing with a little dust along the way sure beats trying to clean up a problem after it sets in. So freshen the air in your relationships every now and then. Create a safe and healthy environment by talking and praying through habits, hurts, and miscommunication. When you do, you'll both breathe easier!

was a good speaker who knew the Scriptures well. [25]He had been taught about the way of the Lord and was always very excited when he spoke and taught the truth about Jesus. But the only baptism Apollos knew about was the baptism that John[n] taught. [26]Apollos began to speak very boldly in the synagogue, and when Priscilla and Aquila heard him, they took him to their home and helped him better understand the way of God. [27]Now Apollos wanted to go to the country of Southern Greece. So the believers helped him and wrote a letter to the followers there, asking them to accept him. These followers had believed in Jesus because of God's grace, and when Apollos arrived, he helped them very much. [28]He argued very strongly with the Jews before all the people, clearly proving with the Scriptures that Jesus is the Christ.

Paul in Ephesus

19 While Apollos was in Corinth, Paul was visiting some places on the way to Ephesus. There he found some followers [2]and asked them, "Did you receive the Holy Spirit when you believed?"

They said, "We have never even heard of a Holy Spirit."

[3]So he asked, "What kind of baptism did you have?"

They said, "It was the baptism that John taught."

[4]Paul said, "John's baptism was a baptism of changed hearts and lives. He told people to believe in the one who would come after him, and that one is Jesus."

[5]When they heard this, they were baptized in the name of the Lord Jesus. [6]Then Paul laid his hands on them,[n] and the Holy Spirit came upon them. They began speaking different languages[n] and prophesying. [7]There were about twelve people in this group.

[8]Paul went into the synagogue and spoke out boldly for three months. He talked with the people and persuaded them to accept the things he said about the kingdom of God. [9]But some of them became stubborn. They refused to believe and said evil things about the Way of Jesus before all the people. So Paul left them, and taking the followers with him, he went to the school of a man named Tyrannus. There Paul talked with people every day [10]for two years. Because of his work, every Jew and Greek in Asia heard the word of the Lord.

The Sons of Sceva

[11]God used Paul to do some very special miracles. [12]Some people took handkerchiefs and clothes that Paul had used and put them on the sick. When they did this, the sick were healed and evil spirits left them.

[13]But some people also were traveling around and making evil spirits go out of people. They tried to use the name of the Lord Jesus to force the evil spirits out. They would say, "By the same Jesus that Paul talks about, I order you to come out!" [14]Seven sons of Sceva, a leading priest, were doing this.

[15]But one time an evil spirit said to them, "I know Jesus, and I know about Paul, but who are you?"

[16]Then the man who had the evil spirit jumped on them. Because he was so much stronger than all of them, they ran away from the house naked and hurt. [17]All the people in Ephesus—Jews and Greeks—learned about this and were filled with fear and gave great honor to the Lord Jesus. [18]Many of the believers began to confess openly and tell all the evil things they had done. [19]Some of them who had used magic brought their magic books and burned them before everyone. Those books were worth about fifty thousand silver coins.[n]

[20]So in a powerful way the word of the Lord kept spreading and growing.

[21]After these things, Paul decided to

18:25 John John the Baptist, who preached to people about Christ's coming (Luke 3). **19:6 laid his hands on them** The laying on of hands had many purposes, including the giving of a blessing, power, or authority. **19:6 languages** This can also be translated "tongues." **19:19 fifty thousand silver coins** Probably drachmas. One coin was enough to pay a worker for one day's labor.

Women & Men of the BIBLE

Jael: Instrument of God

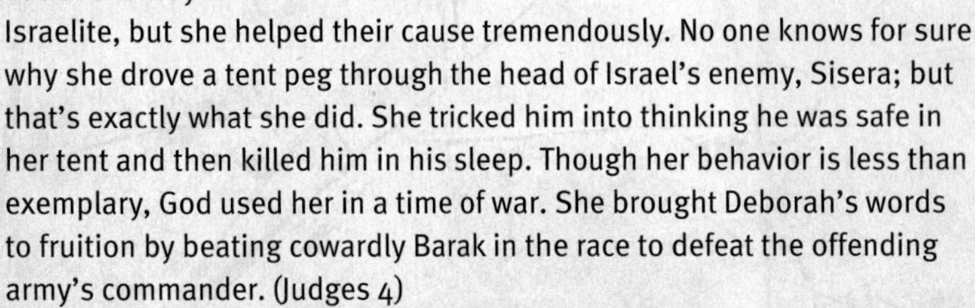

Jael was an obscure woman in an out-of-the-way town. She wasn't an Israelite, but she helped their cause tremendously. No one knows for sure why she drove a tent peg through the head of Israel's enemy, Sisera; but that's exactly what she did. She tricked him into thinking he was safe in her tent and then killed him in his sleep. Though her behavior is less than exemplary, God used her in a time of war. She brought Deborah's words to fruition by beating cowardly Barak in the race to defeat the offending army's commander. (Judges 4)

go to Jerusalem, planning to go through the countries of Macedonia and Southern Greece and then on to Jerusalem. He said, "After I have been to Jerusalem, I must also visit Rome." [22]Paul sent Timothy and Erastus, two of his helpers, ahead to Macedonia, but he himself stayed in Asia for a while.

Trouble in Ephesus

[23]And during that time, there was some serious trouble in Ephesus about the Way of Jesus. [24]A man named Demetrius, who worked with silver, made little silver models that looked like the temple of the goddess Artemis.[n] Those who did this work made much money. [25]Demetrius had a meeting with them and some others who did the same kind of work. He told them, "Men, you know that we make a lot of money from our business. [26]But look at what this man Paul is doing. He has convinced and turned away many people in Ephesus and in almost all of Asia! He says the gods made by human hands are not real. [27]There is a danger that our business will lose its good name, but there is also another danger: People will begin to think that the temple of the great goddess Artemis is not important. Her greatness will be destroyed, and Artemis is the goddess that everyone in Asia and the whole world worships."

[28]When the others heard this, they became very angry and shouted, "Artemis, the goddess of Ephesus, is great!" [29]The whole city became confused. The people grabbed Gaius and Aristarchus, who were from Macedonia and were traveling with Paul, and ran to the theater. [30]Paul wanted to go in and talk to the crowd, but the followers did not let him. [31]Also, some leaders of Asia who were friends of Paul sent him a message, begging him not to go into the theater. [32]Some people were shouting one thing, and some were shouting another. The meeting was completely confused; most of them did not know why they had come together. [33]They put a man named Alexander in front of the people, and some of them told him what to do. Alexander waved his hand so he could explain things to the people. [34]But when they saw that Alexander was a Jew, they all shouted the same thing for two hours: "Great is Artemis of Ephesus!"

[35]Then the city clerk made the crowd be quiet. He said, "People of Ephesus, everyone knows that Ephesus is the city that keeps the temple of the great goddess Artemis and her holy stone[n] that fell from heaven. [36]Since no one can say this is not true, you should be quiet. Stop and think before you do anything. [37]You brought these men here, but they have not said anything evil against our goddess or stolen anything from her temple. [38]If Demetrius and those who work with him have a charge against anyone they should go to the courts and judges where they can argue with each other. [39]If there is something else you want to talk about, it can be decided at the regular town meeting of the people. [40]I say this because some people might see this trouble today and say that we are rioting. We could not explain this, because there is no real reason for this meeting." [41]After the city clerk said these things, he told the people to go home.

Paul in Macedonia and Greece

20 When the trouble stopped, Paul sent for the followers to come to him. After he encouraged them and then told them good-bye, he left and went to the country of Macedonia. [2]He said many things to strengthen the followers in the different places on his way through Macedonia. Then he went to Greece, [3]where he stayed for three months. He was ready to sail for Syria, but some evil people were planning something against him. So Paul decided to go back through Macedonia to Syria. [4]The men who went with him were Sopater son of Pyrrhus, from the city of Berea; Aristarchus and Secundus, from the city of Thessalonica; Gaius, from Derbe; Timothy; and Tychicus and Trophimus, two men from Asia. [5]These men went on ahead and waited for us at Troas. [6]We sailed from Philippi after the Feast of Unleavened Bread. Five days later we met them in Troas, where we stayed for seven days.

Paul's Last Visit to Troas

[7]On the first day of the week,[n] we all met together to break bread,[n] and Paul spoke to the group. Because he was planning to leave the next day, he kept on talking until midnight. [8]We were all together in a room upstairs, and there were many lamps in the room. [9]A young man named Eutychus was sitting in the window. As Paul continued talking, Eutychus was falling into a deep sleep. Finally, he went sound asleep and fell to the ground from the third floor. When they picked him up, he was dead. [10]Paul went down to Eutychus, knelt down, and put his arms around him. He said, "Don't worry. He is alive now." [11]Then Paul went upstairs again, broke bread, and ate. He spoke to them a long time, until it was early morning, and then he left. [12]They took the young man home alive and were greatly comforted.

19:24 Artemis A Greek goddess that the people of Asia Minor worshiped. **19:35 holy stone** Probably a meteorite or stone that the people thought looked like Artemis. **20:7 first day of the week** Sunday, which for Jews began at sunset on our Saturday. But if in this part of Asia a different system of time was used, then the meeting was on our Sunday night. **20:7 break bread** Probably the Lord's Supper, the special meal that Jesus told his followers to eat to remember him (Luke 22:14–20).

Yes, I am sure that neither death, nor life, nor angels, nor ruling spirits, nothing now, nothing in the future,
may
Buy a new pair of sandals for summer. 1
2
Read the Book of John this month and journal what you learn. 3
4
It's Cinco de Mayo. Enjoy fresh Mexican food! 5
Spend an afternoon washing your friend's car. 6
7
Try a new recipe today. Share it with co-workers. 8
Don't forget: Mother's Day is the 2nd Sunday of May. 9
10
11
Replace any burned-out light bulbs in your home. 12
Find out what your phone number spells. www.phonespell.org 13
Plan a backyard picnic with friends. 14
Buy tickets to a local theater performance. 15
Bake fresh bread and share it with a friend. 16
17
It's Older Americans Month. Befriend an elderly person in your neighborhood. 18
It's Skin Cancer Awareness Month. Buy new sunscreen for summer. 19
20
Go bowling. 21
Write a thank-you note to your parents or grandparents. 22
Take a nap this afternoon. 23
24
Visit a public garden. 25
Look for ways to recycle. www.recylenow.com 26
27
28
Organize a bake sale and give the proceeds to charity. 29
30
Pray for a person of influence: Brooke Shields is celebrating a birthday. 31
no powers, nothing above us, nothing below us, nor anything else in the whole world will ever be able to separate us from the love of God that is in Christ Jesus our Lord. —Romans 8:38–39

Acts 20:35

When you exchange Christmas presents with your girlfriends, what brings you the most delight? Is it watching your friends' faces light up? Or are you more excited about the things you get to open? As much fun as it is to receive gifts, there really is something greater about bringing joy to the people around you.

"It is more blessed to give than to receive," Jesus said in this verse. Now, moving beyond the unwrapping-of-gifts scene, think about how you can bless people *daily*. Imagine how your time, money, home, possessions, creativity, talents, and energy can all become a benefit to others. You can probably think of times when even a small thing somebody did made your day or a true sacrifice changed your life. Any effort made with a sincere heart is something God can use to show himself to the world.

As we follow Christ, we're called to love each other deeply with all our hearts (1 Peter 1:22) and to humbly give more honor to others than to ourselves (Philippians 2:3). Lovingly reach out and seek to bless people at your own expense—just like Christ. God will use your life for eternal purposes, and you'll be blessed with bringing joy to others!

The Trip from Troas to Miletus

[13]We went on ahead of Paul and sailed for the city of Assos, where he wanted to join us on the ship. Paul planned it this way because he wanted to go to Assos by land. [14]When he met us there, we took him aboard and went to Mitylene. [15]We sailed from Mitylene and the next day came to a place near Kios. The following day we sailed to Samos, and the next day we reached Miletus. [16]Paul had already decided not to stop at Ephesus, because he did not want to stay too long in Asia. He was hurrying to be in Jerusalem on the day of Pentecost, if that were possible.

The Elders from Ephesus

[17]Now from Miletus Paul sent to Ephesus and called for the elders of the church. [18]When they came to him, he said, "You know about my life from the first day I came to Asia. You know the way I lived all the time I was with you. [19]The evil people made plans against me, which troubled me very much. But you know I always served the Lord unselfishly, and I often cried. [20]You know I preached to you and did not hold back anything that would help you. You know that I taught you in public and in your homes. [21]I warned both Jews and Greeks to change their lives and turn to God and believe in our Lord Jesus. [22]But now I must obey the Holy Spirit and go to Jerusalem. I don't know what will happen to me there. [23]I know only that in every city the Holy Spirit tells me that troubles and even jail wait for me. [24]I don't care about my own life. The most important thing is that I complete my mission, the work that the Lord Jesus gave me—to tell people the Good News about God's grace.

[25]"And now, I know that none of you among whom I was preaching the kingdom of God will ever see me again. [26]So today I tell you that if any of you should be lost, I am not responsible, [27]because I have told you everything God wants you to know. [28]Be careful for yourselves and for all the people the Holy Spirit has given to you to oversee. You must be like shepherds to the church of God,[n] which he bought with the death of his own Son. [29]I know that after I leave, some people will come like wild wolves and try to destroy the flock. [30]Also, some from your own group will rise up and twist the truth and will lead away followers after them. [31]So be careful! Always remember that for three years, day and night, I never stopped warning each of you, and I often cried over you.

[32]"Now I am putting you in the care of God and the message about his grace. It is able to give you strength, and it will give you the blessings God has for all his holy people. [33]When I was with you, I never wanted anyone's money or fine clothes. [34]You know I always worked to take care of my own needs and the needs of those who were with me. [35]I showed you in all things that you should work as I did and help the weak. I taught you to remember the words Jesus said: 'It is more blessed to give than to receive.' "

[36]When Paul had said this, he knelt down with all of them and prayed. [37-38]And they all cried because Paul had said they would never see him again. They put their arms around him and kissed him. Then they went with him to the ship.

Paul Goes to Jerusalem

21 After we all said good-bye to them, we sailed straight to the island of Cos. The next day we reached Rhodes, and from there we went to Patara. [2]There we found a ship going to Phoenicia, so we went aboard and sailed away. [3]We sailed near the island of Cyprus,

20:28 of God Some Greek copies read "of the Lord."

seeing it to the north, but we sailed on to Syria. We stopped at Tyre because the ship needed to unload its cargo there. [4]We found some followers in Tyre and stayed with them for seven days. Through the Holy Spirit they warned Paul not to go to Jerusalem. [5]When we finished our visit, we left and continued our trip. All the followers, even the women and children, came outside the city with us. After we all knelt on the beach and prayed, [6]we said goodbye and got on the ship, and the followers went back home.

[7]We continued our trip from Tyre and arrived at Ptolemais, where we greeted the believers and stayed with them for a day. [8]The next day we left Ptolemais and went to the city of Caesarea. There we went into the home of Philip the preacher, one of the seven helpers,[n] and stayed with him. [9]He had four unmarried daughters who had the gift of prophesying. [10]After we had been there for some time, a prophet named Agabus arrived from Judea. [11]He came to us and borrowed Paul's belt and used it to tie his own hands and feet. He said, "The Holy Spirit says, 'This is how evil people in Jerusalem will tie up the man who wears this belt. Then they will give him to the older leaders.' "

[12]When we all heard this, we and the people there begged Paul not to go to Jerusalem. [13]But he said, "Why are you crying and making me so sad? I am not only ready to be tied up in Jerusalem, I am ready to die for the Lord Jesus!"

[14]We could not persuade him to stay away from Jerusalem. So we stopped begging him and said, "We pray that what the Lord wants will be done."

[15]After this, we got ready and started on our way to Jerusalem. [16]Some of the followers from Caesarea went with us and took us to the home of Mnason, where we would stay. He was from Cyprus and was one of the first followers.

Paul Visits James

[17]In Jerusalem the believers were glad to see us. [18]The next day Paul went with us to visit James, and all the elders were there. [19]Paul greeted them and told them everything God had done among the other nations through him. [20]When they heard this, they praised God. Then they said to Paul, "Brother, you can see that many thousands of our people have become believers. And they think it is very important to obey the law of Moses. [21]They have heard about your teaching, that you tell our people who live among the nations to leave the law of Moses. They have heard that you tell them not to circumcise their children and not to obey customs. [22]What should we do? They will learn that you have come. [23]So we will tell you what to do: Four of our men have made a promise to God. [24]Take these men with you and share in their cleansing ceremony.[n] Pay their expenses so they can shave their heads.[n] Then it will prove to everyone that what they have heard about you is not true and that you follow the law of Moses in your own life. [25]We have already sent a letter to the non-Jewish believers. The letter said: 'Do not eat food that has been offered to idols, or blood, or animals that have been strangled. Do not take part in sexual sin.' "

[26]The next day Paul took the four men and shared in the cleansing ceremony with them. Then he went to the Temple and announced the time when the days of the cleansing ceremony would be finished. On the last day an offering would be given for each of the men.

[27]When the seven days were almost over, some of his people from Asia saw

BECOME Involved

AFS: Intercultural Programs

Many, if not most, high schoolers around the world think that what they see on American TV is the way people generally live in the United States. Wouldn't it be great if you could show them a different side? By hosting an AFS exchange student, you can do just that! Your demonstration of a godly lifestyle could change that student's view—and, more importantly, maybe even his or her heart!

AFS exchanges more than eleven thousand students and teachers each year worldwide. Their intercultural programs have been around for nearly sixty years and include more than fifty countries. Having one of these teenagers in your home could be one of the most rewarding things you ever do. Your family would benefit from learning about life in another culture, and your exchange student would learn valuable lessons about living out your faith.

There are other opportunities for involvement aside from hosting a student. AFS is constantly looking for volunteers who can help students acclimate to their new country or who can help with events and other needs. Check out www.usa.afs.org for more information about how you can be involved in ministering to an international visitor to the United States!

21:8 helpers The seven men chosen for a special work described in Acts 6:1–6. Sometimes they are called "deacons." **21:24 cleansing ceremony** The special things Jews did to end the Nazirite promise. **21:24 shave their heads** Jews did this to show that their promise was finished.

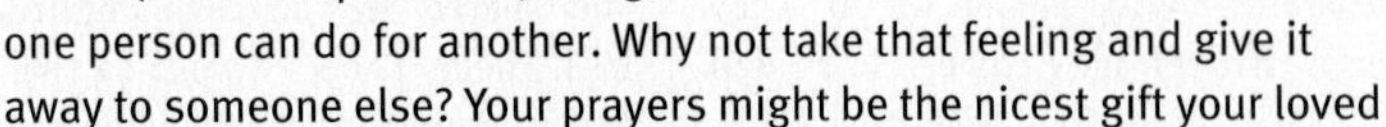

The Gift of Prayer

Be Still & KNOW

Think of how good it makes you feel to know—*really know*—someone has been praying for you. It's one of the nicest (and most powerful!) things one person can do for another. Why not take that feeling and give it away to someone else? Your prayers might be the nicest gift your loved one ever receives. Instead of (or in addition to) a regular birthday gift, consider writing out a heartfelt prayer celebrating that person's life and making specific requests for the future. Or keep a journal of different prayers throughout the year and give it as a Christmas present. The recipient will be touched to see the depth of your love and care as they "listen in" on your prayers!

Paul at the Temple. They caused all the people to be upset and grabbed Paul. [28]They shouted, "People of Israel, help us! This is the man who goes everywhere teaching against the law of Moses, against our people, and against this Temple. Now he has brought some Greeks into the Temple and has made this holy place unclean!" [29](They said this because they had seen Trophimus, a man from Ephesus, with Paul in Jerusalem. They thought that Paul had brought him into the Temple.)

[30]All the people in Jerusalem became upset. Together they ran, took Paul, and dragged him out of the Temple. The Temple doors were closed immediately. [31]While they were trying to kill Paul, the commander of the Roman army in Jerusalem learned that there was trouble in the whole city. [32]Immediately he took some officers and soldiers and ran to the place where the crowd was gathered. When the people saw them, they stopped beating Paul. [33]The commander went to Paul and arrested him. He told his soldiers to tie Paul with two chains. Then he asked who he was and what he had done wrong. [34]Some in the crowd were yelling one thing, and some were yelling another. Because of all this confusion and shouting, the commander could not learn what had happened. So he ordered the soldiers to take Paul to the army building. [35]When Paul came to the steps, the soldiers had to carry him because the people were ready to hurt him. [36]The whole mob was following them, shouting, "Kill him!"

[37]As the soldiers were about to take Paul into the army building, he spoke to the commander, "May I say something to you?"

The commander said, "Do you speak Greek? [38]I thought you were the Egyptian who started some trouble against the government not long ago and led four thousand killers out to the desert."

[39]Paul said, "No, I am a Jew from Tarsus in the country of Cilicia. I am a citizen of that important city. Please, let me speak to the people."

[40]The commander gave permission, so Paul stood on the steps and waved his hand to quiet the people. When there was silence, he spoke to them in the Hebrew language.

Paul Speaks to the People

22 Paul said, "Brothers and fathers, listen to my defense to you." [2]When they heard him speaking the Hebrew language,[n] they became very quiet. Paul said, [3]"I am a Jew, born in Tarsus in the country of Cilicia, but I grew up in this city. I was a student of Gamaliel,[n] who carefully taught me everything about the law of our ancestors. I was very serious about serving God, just as are all of you here today. [4]I persecuted the people who followed the Way of Jesus, and some of them were even killed. I arrested men and women and put them in jail. [5]The high priest and the whole council of elders can tell you this is true. They gave me letters to the brothers in Damascus. So I was going there to arrest these people and bring them back to Jerusalem to be punished.

[6]"About noon when I came near Damascus, a bright light from heaven suddenly flashed all around me. [7]I fell to the ground and heard a voice saying, 'Saul, Saul, why are you persecuting me?' [8]I asked, 'Who are you, Lord?' The voice said, 'I am Jesus from Nazareth whom you are persecuting.' [9]Those who were with me did not understand the voice, but they saw the light. [10]I said, 'What shall I do, Lord?' The Lord answered, 'Get up and go to Damascus. There you will be told about all the things I have planned for you to do.' [11]I could not see, because the bright light had made me blind. So my companions led me into Damascus.

[12]"There a man named Ananias came to me. He was a religious man; he obeyed the law of Moses, and all the Jews who lived there respected him. [13]He stood by me and said, 'Brother Saul, see again!' Immediately I was able to see him. [14]He said, 'The God of our ancestors chose you long ago to know his plan, to see the Righteous One, and to hear words from him. [15]You will be his witness to all people, telling them about what you have seen and heard. [16]Now, why wait any longer? Get up, be baptized, and wash your sins away, trusting in him to save you.'

[17]"Later, when I returned to Jerusalem, I was praying in the Temple, and I

22:2 Hebrew language Or Aramaic, the languages of many people in this region in the first century. **22:3 Gamaliel** A very important teacher of the Pharisees, a Jewish religious group (Acts 5:34).

saw a vision. [18]I saw the Lord saying to me, 'Hurry! Leave Jerusalem now! The people here will not accept the truth about me.' [19]But I said, 'Lord, they know that in every synagogue I put the believers in jail and beat them. [20]They also know I was there when Stephen, your witness, was killed. I stood there agreeing and holding the coats of those who were killing him!' [21]But the Lord said to me, 'Leave now. I will send you far away to the other nations.' "

[22]The crowd listened to Paul until he said this. Then they began shouting, "Get rid of him! He doesn't deserve to live!" [23]They shouted, threw off their coats,[n] and threw dust into the air.[n]

[24]Then the commander ordered the soldiers to take Paul into the army building and beat him. He wanted to make Paul tell why the people were shouting against him like this. [25]But as the soldiers were tying him up, preparing to beat him, Paul said to an officer nearby, "Do you have the right to beat a Roman citizen[n] who has not been proven guilty?"

[26]When the officer heard this, he went to the commander and reported it. The officer said, "Do you know what you are doing? This man is a Roman citizen."

[27]The commander came to Paul and said, "Tell me, are you really a Roman citizen?"

He answered, "Yes."

[28]The commander said, "I paid a lot of money to become a Roman citizen."

But Paul said, "I was born a citizen."

[29]The men who were preparing to question Paul moved away from him immediately. The commander was frightened because he had already tied Paul, and Paul was a Roman citizen.

Paul Speaks to Leaders

[30]The next day the commander decided to learn why the Jews were accusing Paul. So he ordered the leading priests and the council to meet. The commander took Paul's chains off. Then he brought Paul out and stood him before their meeting.

23 Paul looked at the council and said, "Brothers, I have lived my life without guilt feelings before God up to this day." [2]Ananias,[n] the high priest, heard this and told the men who were standing near Paul to hit him on the mouth. [3]Paul said to Ananias, "God will hit you, too! You are like a wall that has been painted white. You sit there and judge me, using the law of Moses, but you are telling them to hit me, and that is against the law."

[4]The men standing near Paul said to him, "You cannot insult God's high priest like that!"

[5]Paul said, "Brothers, I did not know this man was the high priest. It is written in the Scriptures, 'You must not curse a leader of your people.' "[n]

[6]Some of the men in the meeting were Sadducees, and others were Pharisees. Knowing this, Paul shouted to them, "My brothers, I am a Pharisee, and my father was a Pharisee. I am on trial here because I believe that people will rise from the dead."

[7]When Paul said this, there was an argument between the Pharisees and the Sadducees, and the group was divided. [8](The Sadducees do not believe in angels or spirits or that people will rise from the dead. But the Pharisees believe in them all.) [9]So there was a great uproar. Some of the teachers of the law, who were Pharisees, stood up and argued, "We find nothing wrong with this man. Maybe an angel or a spirit did speak to him."

[10]The argument was beginning to turn into such a fight that the commander was afraid some evil people would tear Paul to pieces. So he told the soldiers to go down and take Paul away and put him in the army building.

[11]The next night the Lord came and stood by Paul. He said, "Be brave! You have told people in Jerusalem about me. You must do the same in Rome."

[12]In the morning some evil people made a plan to kill Paul, and they took an oath not to eat or drink anything until they had killed him. [13]There were more than forty men who made this plan. [14]They went to the leading priests and the elders and said, "We have taken an oath not to eat or drink until we have killed Paul. [15]So this is what we want you to do: Send a message to the commander to bring Paul out to you as though you want to ask him more questions. We will be waiting to kill him while he is on the way here."

[16]But Paul's nephew heard about this plan and went to the army building and told Paul. [17]Then Paul called one of the officers and said, "Take this young man to the commander. He has a message for him."

[18]So the officer brought Paul's nephew to the commander and said, "The prisoner, Paul, asked me to bring

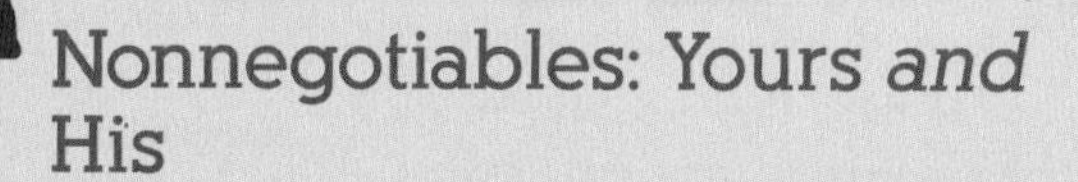

all about MEN

Nonnegotiables: Yours *and* His

What are your nonnegotiables for romantic love? Shared faith and interests? Integrity and respect? A love for children? It's good to know what your main must-haves are—those qualities you won't give up and can't live without in a guy. But here's a twist: whatever your current relationship status is, it's also a great idea to jot down the qualities you want your sweetie to have in a wife! How are you doing at living up to those? It might be a bit unnerving to turn the tables, but don't you want God's best for the man of your dreams? Commit to grow in godly ways that will bless your future husband, and ask God to develop the Proverbs 31:10–31 and Galatians 5:22–25 qualities in you.

22:23 threw off their coats This showed that the people were very angry with Paul. **22:23 threw dust into the air** This showed even greater anger. **22:25 Roman citizen** Roman law said that Roman citizens must not be beaten before they had a trial. **23:2 Ananias** This is not the same man named Ananias in Acts 22:12. **23:5 'You . . . people.'** Quotation from Exodus 22:28.

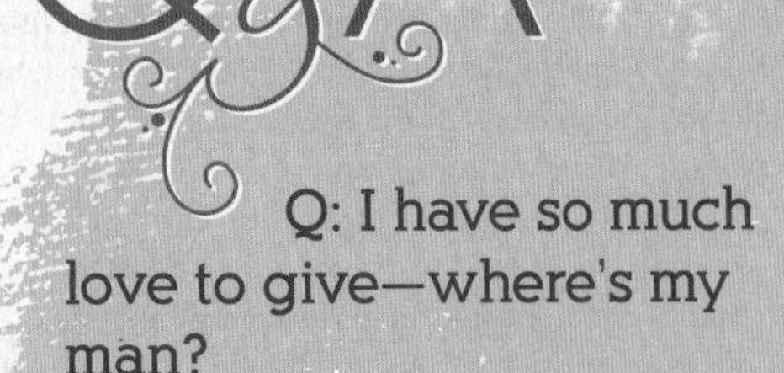

Q: I have so much love to give—where's my man?

A: It's entirely possible that the Lord is preparing you and your mate for each other right now, though only God knows if marriage is in his plans for your future. But one thing is certain: he definitely has plans for you! And if you know Jesus as your Savior, you definitely do have lots of love to give. But you don't have to wait until your special guy comes along to give some of that love away! Find people who need a loving touch and be Jesus to them. They will be blessed—and so will you. Besides, what's more attractive to a godly man than a godly woman showering love on others?

this young man to you. He wants to tell you something."

[19]The commander took the young man's hand and led him to a place where they could be alone. He asked, "What do you want to tell me?"

[20]The young man said, "The Jews have decided to ask you to bring Paul down to their council meeting tomorrow. They want you to think they are going to ask him more questions. [21]But don't believe them! More than forty men are hiding and waiting to kill Paul. They have all taken an oath not to eat or drink until they have killed him. Now they are waiting for you to agree."

[22]The commander sent the young man away, ordering him, "Don't tell anyone that you have told me about their plan."

Paul Is Sent to Caesarea

[23]Then the commander called two officers and said, "I need some men to go to Caesarea. Get two hundred soldiers, seventy horsemen, and two hundred men with spears ready to leave at nine o'clock tonight. [24]Get some horses for Paul to ride so he can be taken to Governor Felix safely." [25]And he wrote a letter that said:

> [26]From Claudius Lysias.
>
> To the Most Excellent Governor Felix:
>
> Greetings.
>
> [27]Some of the Jews had taken this man and planned to kill him. But I learned that he is a Roman citizen, so I went with my soldiers and saved him. [28]I wanted to know why they were accusing him, so I brought him before their council meeting. [29]I learned that these people said Paul did some things that were wrong by their own laws, but no charge was worthy of jail or death. [30]When I was told that some of them were planning to kill Paul, I sent him to you at once. I also told them to tell you what they have against him.

[31]So the soldiers did what they were told and took Paul and brought him to the city of Antipatris that night. [32]The next day the horsemen went with Paul to Caesarea, but the other soldiers went back to the army building in Jerusalem. [33]When the horsemen came to Caesarea and gave the letter to the governor, they turned Paul over to him. [34]The governor read the letter and asked Paul, "What area are you from?" When he learned that Paul was from Cilicia, [35]he said, "I will hear your case when those who are against you come here, too." Then the governor gave orders for Paul to be kept under guard in Herod's palace.

Paul Is Accused

24 Five days later Ananias, the high priest, went to the city of Caesarea with some of the elders and a lawyer named Tertullus. They had come to make charges against Paul before the governor. [2]Paul was called into the meeting, and Tertullus began to accuse him, saying, "Most Excellent Felix! Our people enjoy much peace because of you, and many wrong things in our country are being made right through your wise help. [3]We accept these things always and in every place, and we are thankful for them. [4]But not wanting to take any more of your time, I beg you to be kind and listen to our few words. [5]We have found this man to be a troublemaker, stirring up his people everywhere in the world. He is a leader of the Nazarene group. [6]Also, he was trying to

fun facts

In a recent survey, 73% of pre-retirees said they'd like to develop a strategy to generate income during retirement.

(New York Life's Lifetime Income Survey)

make the Temple unclean, but we stopped him. [And we wanted to judge him by our own law. [7]But the officer Lysias came and used much force to take him from us. [8]And Lysias commanded those who wanted to accuse Paul to come to you.][n] By asking him questions yourself, you can decide if all these things are true." [9]The others agreed and said that all of this was true.

[10]When the governor made a sign for Paul to speak, Paul said, "Governor Felix, I know you have been a judge over this nation for a long time. So I am happy to defend myself before you. [11]You can learn for yourself that I went to worship in Jerusalem only twelve days ago. [12]Those who are accusing me did not find me arguing with anyone in the Temple or stirring up the people in the synagogues or in the city. [13]They cannot prove the things they are saying against me now. [14]But I will tell you this: I worship the God of our ancestors as a follower of the Way of Jesus. The others say that the Way of Jesus is not the right way. But I believe everything that is taught in the law of Moses and that is written in the books of the Prophets. [15]I have the same hope in God that they have—the hope that all people, good and bad, will surely be raised from the dead. [16]This is why I always try to do what I believe is right before God and people.

[17]"After being away from Jerusalem for several years, I went back to bring money to my people and to offer sacrifices. [18]I was doing this when they found me in the Temple. I had finished the cleansing ceremony and had not made any trouble; no people were gathering around me. [19]But there were some people from Asia who should be here, standing before you. If I have really done anything wrong, they are the ones who should accuse me. [20]Or ask these people here if they found any wrong in me when I stood before the council in Jerusalem. [21]But I did shout one thing when I stood before them: 'You are judging me today because I believe that people will rise from the dead!' "

[22]Felix already understood much about the Way of Jesus. He stopped the trial and said, "When commander Lysias comes here, I will decide your case." [23]Felix told the officer to keep Paul guarded but to give him some freedom and to let his friends bring what he needed.

Nothing to Wear?

Everyone does it—you stand in front of a closet full of clothes and still can't find anything to wear. The clock ticks and you have to make a decision and go with it or you'll be late. Regardless of where you'll be going today or what you'll be doing, there are a few things that God says you should always choose to wear: the belt of truth around your waist and the Good News of peace on your feet, for starters. There's a whole list in Ephesians 6:10–18. Check it out.

Paul Speaks to Felix and His Wife

[24]After some days Felix came with his wife, Drusilla, who was Jewish, and asked for Paul to be brought to him. He listened to Paul talk about believing in Christ Jesus. [25]But Felix became afraid when Paul spoke about living right, self-control, and the time when God will judge the world. He said, "Go away now. When I have more time, I will call for you." [26]At the same time Felix hoped that Paul would give him some money, so he often sent for Paul and talked with him.

[27]But after two years, Felix was replaced by Porcius Festus as governor. But Felix had left Paul in prison to please the Jews.

Paul Asks to See Caesar

25 Three days after Festus became governor, he went from Caesarea to Jerusalem. [2]There the leading priests and the important leaders made charges against Paul before Festus. [3]They asked Festus to do them a favor. They wanted him to send Paul back to Jerusalem, because they had a plan to kill him on the way. [4]But Festus answered that Paul would be kept in Caesarea and that he himself was returning there soon. [5]He said, "Some of your leaders should go with me. They can accuse the man there in Caesarea, if he has really done something wrong."

[6]Festus stayed in Jerusalem another eight or ten days and then went back to Caesarea. The next day he told the soldiers to bring Paul before him. Festus was seated on the judge's seat [7]when Paul came into the room. The people who had come from Jerusalem stood around him, making serious charges against him, which they could not prove. [8]This is what Paul said to defend himself: "I have done nothing wrong against the law, against the Temple, or against Caesar."

[9]But Festus wanted to please the people. So he asked Paul, "Do you want to go to Jerusalem for me to judge you there on these charges?"

[10]Paul said, "I am standing at Caesar's judgment seat now, where I should be judged. I have done nothing wrong to them; you know this is true. [11]If I have done something wrong and the law says I must die, I do not ask to be saved from death. But if these charges are not true, then no one can give me to them. I want Caesar to hear my case!"

[12]Festus talked about this with his advisers. Then he said, "You have asked to see Caesar, so you will go to Caesar!"

Paul Before King Agrippa

[13]A few days later King Agrippa and Bernice came to Caesarea to visit Festus. [14]They stayed there for some time, and Festus told the king about Paul's case. Festus said, "There is a man that Felix left in prison. [15]When I went to Jerusalem, the leading priests and the elders there

24:6–8 And . . . you. Some Greek copies do not contain the bracketed text.

QUIZ

YOUR LIFE'S WEATHER FORECAST: ARE YOU HOPEFUL ABOUT YOUR FUTURE?

PLACE AN "X" ALONG THE CONTINUUM TO INDICATE HOW OFTEN YOU AGREE WITH THE FOLLOWING STATEMENTS. BLUE=ALWAYS, GREEN=USUALLY, YELLOW=SOMETIMES, ORANGE=HARDLY EVER.

I am going to make a difference in the world somehow—I just know it!

When I have a lot to do, I tackle one thing at a time until it's all done.

I have a lot to look forward to in the next few months.

Most mornings I wake up refreshed and well-rested.

I do my best to see the glass as half-full instead of half-empty.

When I feel overwhelmed, I am able to relax and regain perspective fairly easily.

In the midst of difficulty or pain, I try to focus on the positives and be thankful that it's not any worse.

When a situation seems hopeless, I rest in the fact that God is more powerful than any circumstance.

I feel fine about growing older; birthdays don't bother me one little bit!

My job is meaningful and satisfying.

I volunteer my time and/or other resources to charities or church ministries.

When I think of dying, I feel more peace than fear.

I have an adequate amount of free time to pursue my hobbies and interests.

I have friends or family members I can call any time I need them.

My retirement plan is aggressive, or at least adequate, for my older years.

SCORING:

IF YOUR ANSWERS WERE MOSTLY IN THE BLUE PART, there are Sunny Skies in store for your future. Your hope is placed in heaven. You can keep moving ahead in confidence because you know that God has very good plans for your life.

IF YOUR ANSWERS WERE MOSTLY IN THE GREEN PART, you have Partly Cloudy skies in your forecast. No need to be concerned, though. God knows what he's planning for you. As long as you stay close to him, the sun will shine through any temporary clouds in your path!

IF YOUR ANSWERS WERE MOSTLY IN THE YELLOW PART, you have a Chance of Rain in the forecast. Things may not look all that great from your perspective right now, but you can rest in the fact that your heavenly Father has plans that will bless you, not hurt you. Turn your future over to him, and he will use the rain to grow lovely grass, trees, and flowers!

IF YOUR ANSWERS WERE MOSTLY IN THE ORANGE PART, you have Storms Brewing on the horizon. But you should know that even if storms do arise, you have a Father who is prepared to handle anything that comes your way. Look to him and he will give you a hope and a future. He will see you through any storm!

Acts 26:24–29

Let's say a foreign woman moves in next door to you. You don't know her native language, so you can't exactly sit down and have a meaningful conversation with her—the words you speak sound like gibberish to her. Even so, that doesn't mean you have to quit trying to communicate with her.

Paul said the truth of Christ will seem like foolishness to the world. It's like an entire language they can't understand unless God opens their minds. But even if people couldn't understand the Cross immediately, Paul said he'd still present the message about Christ crucified in a very bold, straightforward way (1 Corinthians 1:18–31). While he faced the possibility of being beaten, imprisoned, executed, or simply accused of being crazy, his goal remained the same: faithfully share God's truth with others. And he left the results in God's hands. God's powerful enough to resurrect spiritually dead people! Our big responsibility is to communicate truth with clarity and courage.

Whenever you feel like you're speaking a different language when you talk with people about Jesus, remember Paul. Gather your courage, tell them the Good News, and pray that God will use your words. He can miraculously open their minds to understand the language of salvation!

made charges against him, asking me to sentence him to death. [16]But I answered, 'When a man is accused of a crime, Romans do not hand him over until he has been allowed to face his accusers and defend himself against their charges.' [17]So when these people came here to Caesarea for the trial, I did not waste time. The next day I sat on the judge's seat and commanded that the man be brought in. [18]They stood up and accused him, but not of any serious crime as I thought they would. [19]The things they said were about their own religion and about a man named Jesus who died. But Paul said that he is still alive. [20]Not knowing how to find out about these questions, I asked Paul, 'Do you want to go to Jerusalem and be judged there?' [21]But he asked to be kept in Caesarea. He wants a decision from the emperor.[n] So I ordered that he be held until I could send him to Caesar."

[22]Agrippa said to Festus, "I would also like to hear this man myself."

Festus said, "Tomorrow you will hear him."

[23]The next day Agrippa and Bernice appeared with great show, acting like very important people. They went into the judgment room with the army leaders and the important men of Caesarea. Then Festus ordered the soldiers to bring Paul in. [24]Festus said, "King Agrippa and all who are gathered here with us, you see this man. All the people, here and in Jerusalem, have complained to me about him, shouting that he should not live any longer. [25]When I judged him, I found no reason to order his death. But since he asked to be judged by Caesar, I decided to send him. [26]But I have nothing definite to write the emperor about him. So I have brought him before all of you—especially you, King Agrippa. I hope you can question him and give me something to write. [27]I think it is foolish to send a prisoner to Caesar without telling what charges are against him."

Paul Defends Himself

26 Agrippa said to Paul, "You may now speak to defend yourself."

Then Paul raised his hand and began to speak. [2]He said, "King Agrippa, I am very blessed to stand before you and will answer all the charges the evil people make against me. [3]You know so much about all the customs and the things they argue about, so please listen to me patiently.

[4]"All my people know about my whole life, how I lived from the beginning in my own country and later in Jerusalem. [5]They have known me for a long time. If they want to, they can tell you that I was a good Pharisee. And the Pharisees obey the laws of my tradition more carefully than any other group. [6]Now I am on trial because I hope for the promise that God made to our ancestors. [7]This is the promise that the twelve tribes of our people hope to receive as they serve God day and night. My king, they have accused me because I hope for this same promise! [8]Why do any of you people think it is impossible for God to raise people from the dead?

[9]"I, too, thought I ought to do many things against Jesus from Nazareth. [10]And that is what I did in Jerusalem. The leading priests gave me the power to put many of God's people in jail, and when they were being killed, I agreed it was a good thing. [11]In every synagogue, I often punished them and tried to make them speak against Jesus. I was so angry against them I even went to other cities to find them and punish them.

[12]"One time the leading priests gave me permission and the power to go to Damascus. [13]On the way there, at noon, I saw a light from heaven. It was brighter than

25:21 emperor The ruler of the Roman Empire, which was almost all the known world.

Mentors

Who are the women who've taught you most about life? We all benefit from knowing people with more wisdom and life smarts than we currently have. And we can learn a lot about growing as God's daughters by watching women who are walking a step or two ahead of us. The apostle Paul passed along important life lessons to Timothy and Titus, two young leaders he mentored. Ask God to connect you with an older, wiser woman who can help you grow. Then count on opportunities down the road to invest in a younger gal who can learn from you.

the sun and flashed all around me and those who were traveling with me. [14]We all fell to the ground. Then I heard a voice speaking to me in the Hebrew language,[n] saying, 'Saul, Saul, why are you persecuting me? You are only hurting yourself by fighting me.' [15]I said, 'Who are you, Lord?' The Lord said, 'I am Jesus, the one you are persecuting. [16]Stand up! I have chosen you to be my servant and my witness—you will tell people the things that you have seen and the things that I will show you. This is why I have come to you today. [17]I will keep you safe from your own people and also from the others. I am sending you to them [18]to open their eyes so that they may turn away from darkness to the light, away from the power of Satan and to God. Then their sins can be forgiven, and they can have a place with those people who have been made holy by believing in me.'

[19]"King Agrippa, after I had this vision from heaven, I obeyed it. [20]I began telling people that they should change their hearts and lives and turn to God and do things to show they really had changed. I told this first to those in Damascus, then in Jerusalem, and in every part of Judea, and also to the other people. [21]This is why the Jews took me and were trying to kill me in the Temple. [22]But God has helped me, and so I stand here today, telling all people, small and great, what I have seen. But I am saying only what Moses and the prophets said would happen— [23]that the Christ would die, and as the first to rise from the dead, he would bring light to all people."

Paul Tries to Persuade Agrippa

[24]While Paul was saying these things to defend himself, Festus said loudly, "Paul, you are out of your mind! Too much study has driven you crazy!"

[25]Paul said, "Most excellent Festus, I am not crazy. My words are true and sensible. [26]King Agrippa knows about these things, and I can speak freely to him. I know he has heard about all of these things, because they did not happen off in a corner. [27]King Agrippa, do you believe what the prophets wrote? I know you believe."

[28]King Agrippa said to Paul, "Do you think you can persuade me to become a Christian in such a short time?"

[29]Paul said, "Whether it is a short or a long time, I pray to God that not only you but every person listening to me today would be saved and be like me—except for these chains I have."

[30]Then King Agrippa, Governor Festus, Bernice, and all the people sitting with them stood up [31]and left the room. Talking to each other, they said, "There is no reason why this man should die or be put in jail." [32]And Agrippa said to Festus, "We could let this man go free, but he has asked Caesar to hear his case."

Paul Sails for Rome

27 It was decided that we would sail for Italy. An officer named Julius, who served in the emperor's[n] army, guarded Paul and some other prisoners. [2]We got on a ship that was from the city of Adramyttium and was about to sail to different ports in Asia. Aristarchus, a man from the city of Thessalonica in Macedonia, went with us. [3]The next day we came to Sidon. Julius was very good to Paul and gave him freedom to go visit his friends, who took care of his needs. [4]We left Sidon and sailed close to the island of Cyprus, because the wind was blowing against us. [5]We went across the sea by Cilicia and Pamphylia and landed at the city of Myra, in Lycia. [6]There the officer found a ship from Alexandria that was going to Italy, so he put us on it.

[7]We sailed slowly for many days. We had a hard time reaching Cnidus because the wind was blowing against us, and we could not go any farther. So we sailed by the south side of the island of Crete near

26:14 Hebrew language Or Aramaic, the languages of many people in this region in the first century. **27:1 emperor** The ruler of the Roman Empire, which was almost all the known world.

Salmone. [8]Sailing past it was hard. Then we came to a place called Fair Havens, near the city of Lasea.

[9]We had lost much time, and it was now dangerous to sail, because it was already after the Day of Cleansing.[n] So Paul warned them, [10]"Men, I can see there will be a lot of trouble on this trip. The ship, the cargo, and even our lives may be lost." [11]But the captain and the owner of the ship did not agree with Paul, and the officer believed what the captain and owner of the ship said. [12]Since that harbor was not a good place for the ship to stay for the winter, most of the men decided that the ship should leave. They hoped we could go to Phoenix and stay there for the winter. Phoenix, a city on the island of Crete, had a harbor which faced southwest and northwest.

The Storm

[13]When a good wind began to blow from the south, the men on the ship thought, "This is the wind we wanted, and now we have it." So they pulled up the anchor, and we sailed very close to the island of Crete. [14]But then a very strong wind named the "northeaster" came from the island. [15]The ship was caught in it and could not sail against it. So we stopped trying and let the wind carry us. [16]When we went below a small island named Cauda, we were barely able to bring in the lifeboat. [17]After the men took the lifeboat in, they tied ropes around the ship to hold it together. The men were afraid that the ship would hit the sandbanks of Syrtis,[n] so they lowered the sail and let the wind carry the ship. [18]The next day the storm was blowing us so hard that the men threw out some of the cargo. [19]A day later with their own hands they threw out the ship's equipment. [20]When we could not see the sun or the stars for many days, and the storm was very bad, we lost all hope of being saved.

[21]After the men had gone without food for a long time, Paul stood up before them and said, "Men, you should have listened to me. You should not have sailed from Crete. Then you would not have all this trouble and loss. [22]But now I tell you to cheer up because none of you will die. Only the ship will be lost. [23]Last night an angel came to me from the God I belong to and worship. [24]The angel said, 'Paul, do not be afraid. You must stand before Caesar. And God has promised you that he will save the lives of everyone sailing with you.' [25]So men, have courage. I trust in God that everything will happen as his angel told me. [26]But we will crash on an island."

[27]On the fourteenth night we were still being carried around in the Adriatic Sea.[n] About midnight the sailors thought we were close to land, [28]so they lowered a rope with a weight on the end of it into the water. They found that the water was one hundred twenty feet deep. They went a little farther and lowered the rope again. It was ninety feet deep. [29]The sailors were afraid that we would hit the rocks, so they threw four anchors into the water and prayed for daylight to come. [30]Some of the sailors wanted to leave the ship, and they lowered the lifeboat, pretending they were throwing more anchors from the front of the ship. [31]But Paul told the officer and the other soldiers, "If these men do not stay in the ship, your lives cannot be saved." [32]So the soldiers cut the ropes and let the lifeboat fall into the water.

[33]Just before dawn Paul began persuading all the people to eat something. He said, "For the past fourteen days you have been waiting and watching and not eating. [34]Now I beg you to eat something. You need it to stay alive. None of you will lose even one hair off your heads." [35]After he said this, Paul took some bread and thanked God for it before all of them. He broke off a piece and began eating. [36]They all felt better and started eating, too. [37]There were two hundred seventy-six people on the ship. [38]When they had eaten all they wanted, they began making the ship lighter by throwing the grain into the sea.

The Ship Is Destroyed

[39]When daylight came, the sailors saw land. They did not know what land it was, but they saw a bay with a beach and wanted to sail the ship to the beach if they could. [40]So they cut the ropes to the anchors and left the anchors in the sea. At the same time, they untied the ropes that were holding the rudders. Then they raised the front sail into the wind and sailed toward the beach. [41]But the ship hit a sandbank. The front of the ship stuck there and could not move, but the back of the ship began to break up from the big waves.

[42]The soldiers decided to kill the prisoners so none of them could swim away and escape. [43]But Julius, the officer, wanted to let Paul live and did not allow the soldiers to kill the prisoners. Instead he ordered everyone who could swim to jump into the water first and swim to land. [44]The rest were to follow using wooden boards or pieces of the ship. And this is how all the people made it safely to land.

Paul on the Island of Malta

28 When we were safe on land, we learned that the island was called Malta. [2]The people who lived there were very good to us. Because it was raining and very cold, they made a fire and welcomed all of us. [3]Paul gathered a pile of sticks and was putting them on the fire when a poisonous snake came out because of the heat and bit him on the hand. [4]The people living on the island saw the snake hanging from Paul's hand and said to each other, "This man must be a murderer! He did not die in the sea, but Justice[n] does not want him to live." [5]But Paul shook the snake off into the fire and was not hurt.

fun facts

More than 586,000 babies were born to women over age 35 in 2004.

(Centers for Disease Control and Prevention)

27:9 Day of Cleansing An important Jewish holy day in the fall of the year. This was the time of year that bad storms arose on the sea. **27:17 Syrtis** Shallow area in the sea near the Libyan coast. **27:27 Adriatic Sea** The sea between Greece and Italy, including the central Mediterranean. **28:4 Justice** The people thought there was a god named Justice who would punish bad people.

HE SAID / SHE SAID

Why is marrying a Christian so important?

He: Because it gives your relationship a solid foundation

She: Because you can help each other stay on track with God

[6]The people thought that Paul would swell up or fall down dead. They waited and watched him for a long time, but nothing bad happened to him. So they changed their minds and said, "He is a god!"

[7]There were some fields around there owned by Publius, an important man on the island. He welcomed us into his home and was very good to us for three days. [8]Publius' father was sick with a fever and dysentery.[n] Paul went to him, prayed, and put his hands on the man and healed him. [9]After this, all the other sick people on the island came to Paul, and he healed them, too. [10-11]The people on the island gave us many honors. When we were ready to leave, three months later, they gave us the things we needed.

Paul Goes to Rome

We got on a ship from Alexandria that had stayed on the island during the winter. On the front of the ship was the sign of the twin gods.[n] [12]We stopped at Syracuse for three days. [13]From there we sailed to Rhegium. The next day a wind began to blow from the south, and a day later we came to Puteoli. [14]We found some believers there who asked us to stay with them for a week. Finally, we came to Rome. [15]The believers in Rome heard that we were there and came out as far as the Market of Ap-pius[n] and the Three Inns[n] to meet us. When Paul saw them, he was encouraged and thanked God.

Paul in Rome

[16]When we arrived at Rome, Paul was allowed to live alone, with the soldier who guarded him.

[17]Three days later Paul sent for the leaders there. When they came together, he said, "Brothers, I have done nothing against our people or the customs of our ancestors. But I was arrested in Jerusalem and given to the Romans. [18]After they asked me many questions, they could find no reason why I should be killed. They wanted to let me go free, [19]but the evil people there argued against that. So I had to ask to come to Rome to have my trial before Caesar. But I have no charge to bring against my own people. [20]That is why I wanted to see you and talk with you. I am bound with this chain because I believe in the hope of Israel."

[21]They answered Paul, "We have received no letters from Judea about you. None of our Jewish brothers who have come from there brought news or told us anything bad about you. [22]But we want to hear your ideas, because we know that people everywhere are speaking against this religious group."

[23]Paul and the people chose a day for a meeting and on that day many more of the Jews met with Paul at the place he was staying. He spoke to them all day long. Using the law of Moses and the prophets' writings, he explained the kingdom of God, and he tried to persuade them to believe these things about Jesus. [24]Some believed what Paul said, but others did not. [25]So they argued and began leaving after Paul said one more thing to them: "The Holy Spirit spoke the truth to your ancestors through Isaiah the prophet, saying,

[26]'Go to this people and say:
You will listen and listen, but you will
not understand.
You will look and look, but you
will not learn,
[27]because these people have become
stubborn.
They don't hear with their ears,
and they have closed their eyes.
Otherwise, they might really
understand
what they see with their eyes
and hear with their ears.
They might really understand in
their minds
and come back to me and be
healed.' *Isaiah 6:9-10*

[28]"I want you to know that God has also sent his salvation to all nations, and they will listen!" [[29]After Paul said this, the Jews left. They were arguing very much with each other.][n]

[30]Paul stayed two full years in his own rented house and welcomed all people who came to visit him. [31]He boldly preached about the kingdom of God and taught about the Lord Jesus Christ, and no one stopped him.

28:8 dysentery A sickness like diarrhea. **28:10–11 twin gods** Statues of Castor and Pollux, gods in old Greek tales. **28:15 Market of Appius** A town about twenty-seven miles from Rome. **28:15 Three Inns** A town about thirty miles from Rome. **28:29 After . . . other.** Some Greek copies do not contain the bracketed text.

Spreading the News

Jesus is arguably the most famous person who ever lived. Except for a few remote locations in the world, most people have heard of him and his story. Considering he only lived on the earth for thirty-three years and never traveled outside of Israel, it's amazing that, thousands of years later, his renown continues to grow!

How has the message of Jesus' salvation reached the ends of the earth? It's simple: Jesus' first followers obeyed his command. Before he ascended into heaven, Jesus told his followers to spread the Good News. The Book of Acts documents their obedience as the first Christians, empowered by the Holy Spirit, working together—even in the face of persecution—to tell everyone everywhere about the salvation Jesus offers.

To his followers, Jesus' command to share the Good News with *everyone* must have been shocking. Until this point, God had only offered salvation to the Jews, but now he was telling them that it was for every single person on earth. Jesus was reaffirming what his cousin, John the Baptist, had announced: Jesus is the Lamb of God, the perfect sacrifice, who came to take away the sin of the *whole* world (John 1:29).

Because of the first believers' commitment to obey Jesus and speak his truth, the message of salvation traveled. It spread thousands of miles and thousands of years to eventually reach your own ears and heart. And now it's your mission to continue in the tradition of Jesus' followers by making his story and offer of salvation known to the entire earth. Spread the news!

Get Real

What role does the church play in your life? (Romans 12:4–6; Ephesians 4:16)

Why did God send the Holy Spirit? (John 14:16–17, 25–26)

How have you seen the Holy Spirit working in your life? (John 16:7–15; Romans 8:2)

Have you ever experienced persecution because you believe in Jesus? If so, how did you handle it? (Matthew 5:44; 2 Corinthians 4:7–12; 2 Thessalonians 1:4–5)

Like the apostles, do you boldly spread the Good News? If not, why? (Isaiah 44:8; 2 Timothy 4:2)

romans

Everybody wants to leave a legacy—something that they'll be remembered for. Paul was no exception, but unlike most people, he didn't really care whether people remembered him. Instead, he literally poured out his life to make sure that people would remember Jesus Christ and the Good News about God's grace.

If you've read Acts, you know that Paul quickly became a major force in spreading the Good News. He traveled from town to town, leaving a trail of new churches everywhere he went. But circumstances kept Paul from visiting the church in Rome. At the time this letter was written, a trip to Rome was just a hope in Paul's heart. So he wrote this special letter to share the things that were most important—our desperate sinfulness, God's amazing mercy and grace, our renewed relationship with God, and our new life in Christ. From beginning to end, this letter is absolutely packed with everything Paul would've told the Roman church if he'd been able to visit them.

Paul's legacy has lasted because he lived to bring glory to God. Anything that's not done for God's glory will ultimately fade away and be forgotten, but everything done in service to Christ will echo throughout eternity! What will *your* legacy be?

1 From Paul, a servant of Christ Jesus. God called me to be an apostle and chose me to tell the Good News.

[2]God promised this Good News long ago through his prophets, as it is written in the Holy Scriptures. [3-4]The Good News is about God's Son, Jesus Christ our Lord. As a man, he was born from the family of David. But through the Spirit of holiness he was declared to be God's Son with great power by rising from the dead. [5]Through Christ, God gave me the special work of an apostle, which was to lead people of all nations to believe and obey. I do this work for him. [6]And you who are in Rome are also called to belong to Jesus Christ.

[7]To all of you in Rome whom God loves and has called to be his holy people:

Grace and peace to you from God our Father and the Lord Jesus Christ.

A Prayer of Thanks

[8]First I want to say that I thank my God through Jesus Christ for all of you, because people everywhere in the world are talking about your faith. [9]God, whom I serve with my whole heart by telling the Good News about his Son, knows that I always mention you [10]every time I pray. I pray that I will be allowed to come to you, and this will happen if God wants it. [11]I want very much to see you, to give you some spiritual gift to make you strong. [12]I mean that I want us to help each other with the faith we have. Your faith will help me, and my faith will help you. [13]Brothers and sisters, I want you to know that I planned many times to come to you, but this has not been possible. I wanted to come so that I could help you grow spiritually as I have helped the other non-Jewish people.

[14]I have a duty to all people—Greeks and those who are not Greeks, the wise and the foolish. [15]That is why I want so much to preach the Good News to you in Rome.

[16]I am not ashamed of the Good News, because it is the power God uses to save everyone who believes—to save the Jews

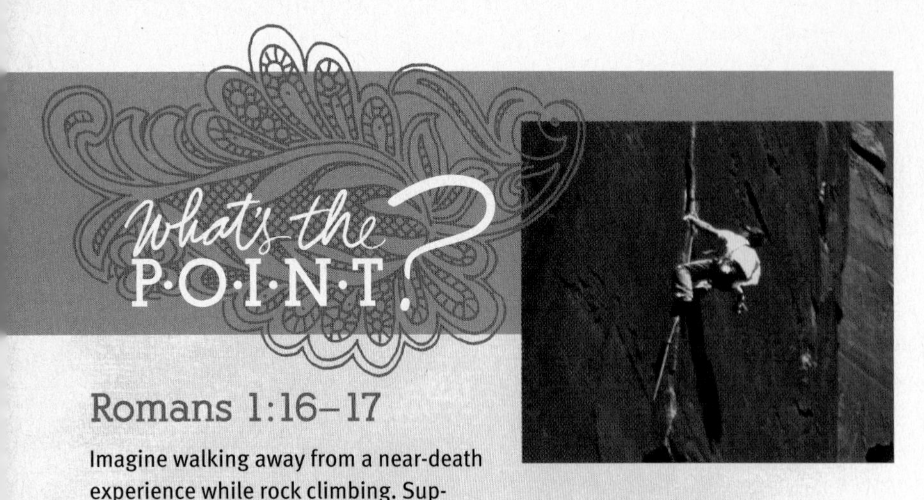

Romans 1:16–17

Imagine walking away from a near-death experience while rock climbing. Suppose the only thing that saved you was a single carabiner (a metal ring that connects ropes and harnesses)! You might not be overly eager for another climb. But you'd probably be quick to recommend that particular brand of carabiner—it saved your life!

Christians know about something powerfully lifesaving: the crucifixion of Christ. God came to earth as a human and lived among people for thirty-three years, teaching, healing, and pouring out love. Then the Creator of the universe was publicly executed in the most brutal way imaginable and suffered all the consequences and punishment for sins he never committed. *God* was crucified (which was an especially shameful way to die) by his own creation, the people he loved. It didn't end there, though! Jesus' death led to his resurrection and his complete victory over sin and death.

Paul said he wasn't ashamed of the Good News—Christ's death brings forgiveness, and his resurrection ensures that everyone who has faith in him will be saved. The message of the Cross is "the power God uses to save everyone who believes" (Romans 1:16). Share that powerful knowledge that glorifies God and saves lives with everyone you can.

first, and then to save non-Jews. [17]The Good News shows how God makes people right with himself—that it begins and ends with faith. As the Scripture says, "But those who are right with God will live by faith."[n]

All People Have Done Wrong

[18]God's anger is shown from heaven against all the evil and wrong things people do. By their own evil lives they hide the truth. [19]God shows his anger because some knowledge of him has been made clear to them. Yes, God has shown himself to them. [20]There are things about him that people cannot see—his eternal power and all the things that make him God. But since the beginning of the world those things have been easy to understand by what God has made. So people have no excuse for the bad things they do. [21]They knew God, but they did not give glory to God or thank him. Their thinking became useless. Their foolish minds were filled with darkness. [22]They said they were wise, but they became fools. [23]They traded the glory of God who lives forever for the worship of idols made to look like earthly people, birds, animals, and snakes.

[24]Because they did these things, God left them and let them go their sinful way, wanting only to do evil. As a result, they became full of sexual sin, using their bodies wrongly with each other. [25]They traded the truth of God for a lie. They worshiped and served what had been created instead of the God who created those things, who should be praised forever. Amen.

[26]Because people did those things, God left them and let them do the shameful things they wanted to do. Women stopped having natural sex and started having sex with other women. [27]In the same way, men stopped having natural sex and began wanting each other. Men did shameful things with other men, and in their bodies they received the punishment for those wrongs.

[28]People did not think it was important to have a true knowledge of God. So God left them and allowed them to have their own worthless thinking and to do things they should not do. [29]They are filled with every kind of sin, evil, selfishness, and hatred. They are full of jealousy, murder, fighting, lying, and thinking the worst about each other. They gossip [30]and say evil things about each other. They hate God. They are rude and conceited and brag about themselves. They invent ways of doing evil. They do not obey their parents. [31]They are foolish, they do not keep their promises, and they show no kindness or mercy to others. [32]They know God's law says that those who live like this should die. But they themselves not only continue to do these evil things, they applaud others who do them.

You People Also Are Sinful

2 If you think you can judge others, you are wrong. When you judge them, you are really judging yourself guilty, because you do the same things they do. [2]God judges those who do wrong things, and we know that his judging is right. [3]You judge those who do wrong, but you do wrong yourselves. Do you think you will be able to escape the judgment of God? [4]He has been very kind and patient, waiting for you to change, but you think nothing of his kindness. Perhaps you do not understand that God is kind to you so you will change your hearts and lives. [5]But you are stubborn and refuse to change, so you are making your own punishment even greater on the day he shows his anger. On that day everyone

1:17 "But those . . . faith." Quotation from Habakkuk 2:4.

will see God's right judgments. [6]God will reward or punish every person for what that person has done. [7]Some people, by always continuing to do good, live for God's glory, for honor, and for life that has no end. God will give them life forever. [8]But other people are selfish. They refuse to follow truth and, instead, follow evil. God will give them his punishment and anger. [9]He will give trouble and suffering to everyone who does evil—to the Jews first and also to those who are not Jews. [10]But he will give glory, honor, and peace to everyone who does good—to the Jews first and also to those who are not Jews. [11]For God judges all people in the same way.

[12]People who do not have the law and who are sinners will be lost, although they do not have the law. And, in the same way, those who have the law and are sinners will be judged by the law. [13]Hearing the law does not make people right with God. It is those who obey the law who will be right with him. [14](Those who are not Jews do not have the law, but when they freely do what the law commands, they are the law for themselves. This is true even though they do not have the law. [15]They show that in their hearts they know what is right and wrong, just as the law commands. And they show this by their consciences. Sometimes their thoughts tell them they did wrong, and sometimes their thoughts tell them they did right.) [16]All these things will happen on the day when God, through Christ Jesus, will judge people's secret thoughts. The Good News that I preach says this.

The Jews and the Law

[17]What about you? You call yourself a Jew. You trust in the law of Moses and brag that you are close to God. [18]You know what he wants you to do and what is important, because you have learned the law. [19]You think you are a guide for the blind and a light for those who are in darkness. [20]You think you can show foolish people what is right and teach those who know nothing. You have the law; so you think you know everything and have all truth. [21]You teach others, so why don't you teach yourself? You tell others not to steal, but you steal. [22]You say that others must not take part in adultery, but you are guilty of that sin. You hate idols, but you steal from temples. [23]You brag about having God's law, but you bring shame to God by breaking his law, [24]just as the Scriptures say: "Those who are not Jews speak against God's name because of you."[n]

[25]If you follow the law, your circumcision has meaning. But if you break the law, it is as if you were never circumcised. [26]People who are not Jews are not circumcised, but if they do what the law says, it is as if they were circumcised. [27]You Jews have the written law and circumcision, but you break the law. So those who are not circumcised in their bodies, but still obey the law, will show that you are guilty. [28]They can do this because a person is not a true Jew if he is only a Jew in his physical body; true circumcision is not only on the outside of the body. [29]A person is a Jew only if he is a Jew inside; true circumcision is done in the heart by the Spirit, not by the written law. Such a person gets praise from God rather than from people.

3 So, do Jews have anything that other people do not have? Is there anything special about being circumcised? [2]Yes, of course, there is in every way. The most important thing is this: God trusted the Jews with his teachings. [3]If some Jews were not faithful to him, will that stop God from doing what he promised? [4]No! God will continue to be true even when every person is false. As the Scriptures say:

> "So you will be shown to be right
> when you speak,
> and you will win your case."
>
> *Psalm 51:4*

[5]When we do wrong, that shows more clearly that God is right. So can we say that God is wrong to punish us? (I am talking as people might talk.) [6]No! If God could not punish us, he could not judge the world.

[7]A person might say, "When I lie, it really gives him glory, because my lie shows God's truth. So why am I judged a sinner?" [8]It would be the same to say, "We should do evil so that good will come." Some people find fault with us and say we teach this, but they are wrong and deserve the punishment they will receive.

All People Are Guilty

[9]So are we Jews better than others? No! We have already said that Jews and those

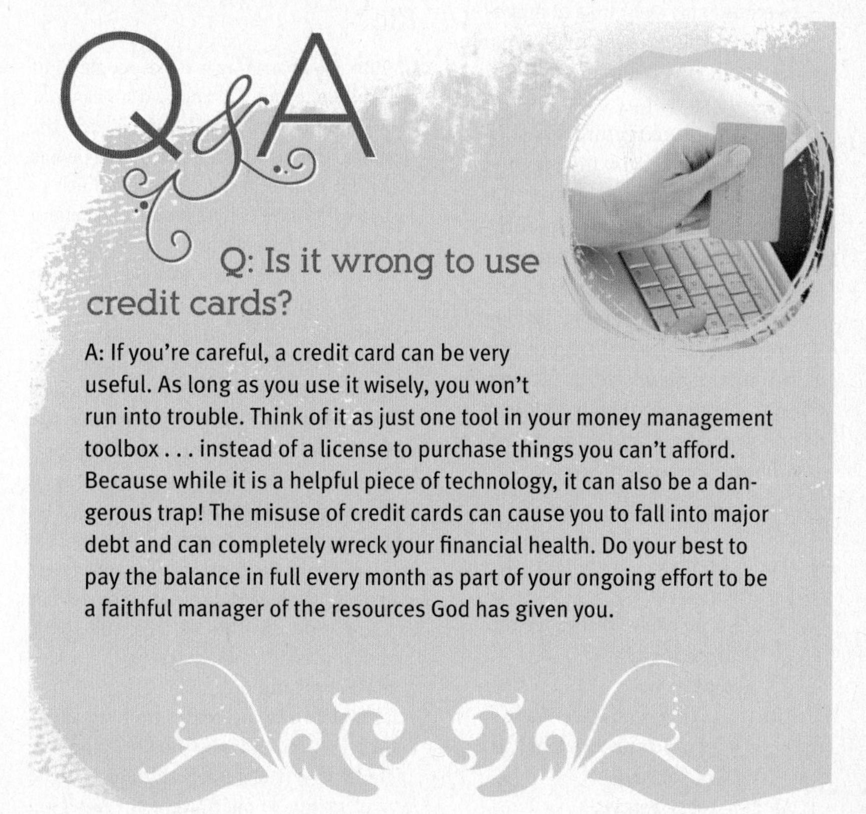

Q: Is it wrong to use credit cards?

A: If you're careful, a credit card can be very useful. As long as you use it wisely, you won't run into trouble. Think of it as just one tool in your money management toolbox . . . instead of a license to purchase things you can't afford. Because while it is a helpful piece of technology, it can also be a dangerous trap! The misuse of credit cards can cause you to fall into major debt and can completely wreck your financial health. Do your best to pay the balance in full every month as part of your ongoing effort to be a faithful manager of the resources God has given you.

2:24 "Those . . . you." Quotation from Isaiah 52:5; Ezekiel 36:20.

Health

Arthritis

We aren't told exactly what the man in Matthew 12:9–13 suffered from, but it might have been a form of arthritis. Today, this degenerative joint disease is the leading cause of disability in the nation. If you think only Granny needs to worry about arthritis, think again. While it's most common in women over fifty, symptoms can begin in your thirties. Here's what happens: cartilage breaks down in inflamed joints leading to stiffness, aching, swelling, and even loss of movement. Risk factors include joint injuries, being overweight, advanced age, and sedentary lifestyle. Your best bet to avoid arthritis is staying active and injury free. If you do encounter symptoms, lessen the effects by maintaining a healthy weight and exercising. Dietary supplements (glucosamine and chondroitin) may rebuild cartilage, while hot and cold therapies and anti-inflammatory drugs (acetaminophen, ibuprofen) help with pain and swelling. Ask your doctor about other treatment options.

who are not Jews are all guilty of sin. [10]As the Scriptures say:

"There is no one who always does
what is right,
not even one.
[11]There is no one who understands.
There is no one who looks to
God for help.
[12]All have turned away.
Together, everyone has become
useless.
There is no one who does anything
good;
there is not even one."
Psalm 14:1–3

[13]"Their throats are like open
graves;
they use their tongues for telling
lies." *Psalm 5:9*
"Their words are like snake poison."
Psalm 140:3
[14] "Their mouths are full of cursing
and hate." *Psalm 10:7*
[15]"They are always ready to kill people.
[16] Everywhere they go they cause
ruin and misery.
[17]They don't know how to live in
peace." *Isaiah 59:7–8*
[18] "They have no fear of God."
Psalm 36:1

[19]We know that the law's commands are for those who have the law. This stops all excuses and brings the whole world under God's judgment, [20]because no one can be made right with God by following the law. The law only shows us our sin.

How God Makes People Right

[21]But God has a way to make people right with him without the law, and he has now shown us that way which the law and the prophets told us about. [22]God makes people right with himself through their faith in Jesus Christ. This is true for all who believe in Christ, because all people are the same: [23]Everyone has sinned and fallen short of God's glorious standard, [24]and all need to be made right with God by his grace, which is a free gift. They need to be made free from sin through Jesus Christ. [25]God sent him to die in our place to take away our sins. We receive forgiveness through faith in the blood of Jesus' death. This showed that God always does what is right and fair, as in the past when he was patient and did not punish people for their sins. [26]And God gave Jesus to show today that he does what is right. God did this so he could judge rightly and so he could make right any person who has faith in Jesus.

[27]So do we have a reason to brag about ourselves? No! And why not? It is the way of faith that stops all bragging, not the way of trying to obey the law. [28]A person is made right with God through faith, not through obeying the law. [29]Is God only the God of the Jews? Is he not also the God of those who are not Jews? [30]Of course he is, because there is only one God. He will make Jews right with him by their faith, and he will also make those who are not Jews right with him through their faith. [31]So do we destroy the law by following the way of faith? No! Faith causes us to be what the law truly wants.

The Example of Abraham

4 So what can we say that Abraham,[n] the father of our people, learned about faith? [2]If Abraham was made right by the things he did, he had a reason to brag. But this is not God's view, [3]because the Scripture says, "Abraham believed God, and God accepted Abraham's faith, and that faith made him right with God."[n]

[4]When people work, their pay is not given as a gift, but as something earned. [5]But people cannot do any work that will make them right with God. So they must trust in him, who makes even evil people right in his sight. Then God accepts their faith, and that makes them right with him. [6]David said the same thing. He said that people are truly blessed when God, without paying attention to their deeds, makes people right with himself.

[7]"Blessed are they
whose sins are forgiven,
whose wrongs are pardoned.
[8]Blessed is the person
whom the Lord does not
consider guilty." *Psalm 32:1–2*

[9]Is this blessing only for those who are circumcised or also for those who are not circumcised? We have already said that God accepted Abraham's faith and that faith made him right with God. [10]So how did this happen? Did God accept Abraham before or after he was circumcised? It was before his circumcision. [11]Abraham was circumcised to show that he was right with God through faith before he was circumcised. So Abraham is the father of all those who believe but are not circumcised; he is the father of all believers who are accepted as being right with God. [12]And Abraham is also the father of those who have been circumcised and who live following the faith that our father Abraham had before he was circumcised.

4:1 Abraham Most respected ancestor of the Jews. Every Jew hoped to see Abraham. **4:3 "Abraham . . . God."** Quotation from Genesis 15:6.

God Keeps His Promise

[13]Abraham[n] and his descendants received the promise that they would get the whole world. He did not receive that promise through the law, but through being right with God by his faith. [14]If people could receive what God promised by following the law, then faith is worthless. And God's promise to Abraham is worthless, [15]because the law can only bring God's anger. But if there is no law, there is nothing to disobey.

[16]So people receive God's promise by having faith. This happens so the promise can be a free gift. Then all of Abraham's children can have that promise. It is not only for those who live under the law of Moses but for anyone who lives with faith like that of Abraham, who is the father of us all. [17]As it is written in the Scriptures: "I am making you a father of many nations."[n] This is true before God, the God Abraham believed, the God who gives life to the dead and who creates something out of nothing.

[18]There was no hope that Abraham would have children. But Abraham believed God and continued hoping, and so he became the father of many nations. As God told him, "Your descendants also will be too many to count."[n] [19]Abraham was almost a hundred years old, much past the age for having children, and Sarah could not have children. Abraham thought about all this, but his faith in God did not become weak. [20]He never doubted that God would keep his promise, and he never stopped believing. He grew stronger in his faith and gave praise to God. [21]Abraham felt sure that God was able to do what he had promised. [22]So, "God accepted Abraham's faith, and that faith made him right with God."[n] [23]Those words ("God accepted Abraham's faith") were written not only for Abraham [24]but also for us. God will accept us also because we believe in the One who raised Jesus our Lord from the dead. [25]Jesus was given to die for our sins, and he was raised from the dead to make us right with God.

Right with God

5 Since we have been made right with God by our faith, we have[n] peace with God. This happened through our Lord Jesus Christ, [2]who through our faith[n] has brought us into that blessing of God's grace that we now enjoy. And we are happy because of the hope we have of sharing God's glory. [3]We also have joy with our troubles, because we know that these troubles produce patience. [4]And patience produces character, and character produces hope. [5]And this hope will never disappoint us, because God has poured out his love to fill our hearts. He gave us his love through the Holy Spirit, whom God has given to us.

[6]When we were unable to help ourselves, at the right time, Christ died for us, although we were living against God. [7]Very few people will die to save the life of someone else. Although perhaps for a good person someone might possibly die. [8]But God shows his great love for us in this way: Christ died for us while we were still sinners.

[9]So through Christ we will surely be saved from God's anger, because we have been made right with God by the blood of Christ's death. [10]While we were God's enemies, he made us his friends through the death of his Son. Surely, now that we are his friends, he will save us through his Son's life. [11]And not only that, but now we are also very happy in God through our Lord Jesus Christ. Through him we are now God's friends again.

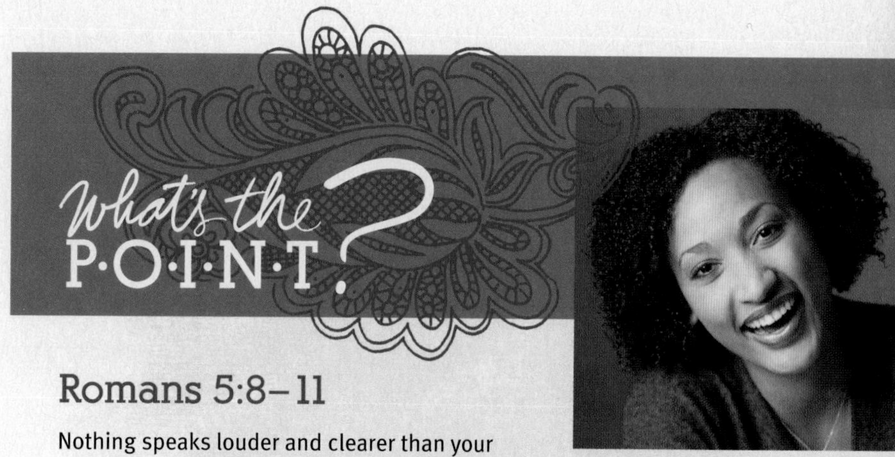

Romans 5:8–11

Nothing speaks louder and clearer than your actions. And some things, like love, can never be sufficiently communicated with mere words. It's easy to say you love someone, but your actions will either prove or disprove the truth.

The Bible has been described as a huge "love letter" from God to us. What an accurate description! And instead of just *saying,* "I love you," God proved it at the Cross. One of the things that makes God's love so remarkable, though, is that we were so far from deserving it. We ignored him, disobeyed him, and rejected him, but he persistently and passionately loved us anyway. Christ died for people whose lives proved they hated him. We were truly God's enemies, but Christ's death made it possible for God to make us his friends—even more than that, his beloved family members.

To be called God's child is an indescribable gift. It's so undeserved and so miraculous, there's really no way we can repay it. How do you view the close relationship God offers and the love he's poured out through Christ? Like Paul, are you "very happy in God through our Lord Jesus Christ" (Romans 5:11)? Let *your* actions display the joy you have in your salvation.

4:13 Abraham Most respected ancestor of the Jews. Every Jew hoped to see Abraham. **4:17 "I . . . nations."** Quotation from Genesis 17:5. **4:18 "Your . . . count."** Quotation from Genesis 15:5. **4:22 "God . . . God."** Quotation from Genesis 15:6. **5:1 we have** Some Greek copies read "let us have." **5:2 through our faith** Some Greek copies do not have this phrase.

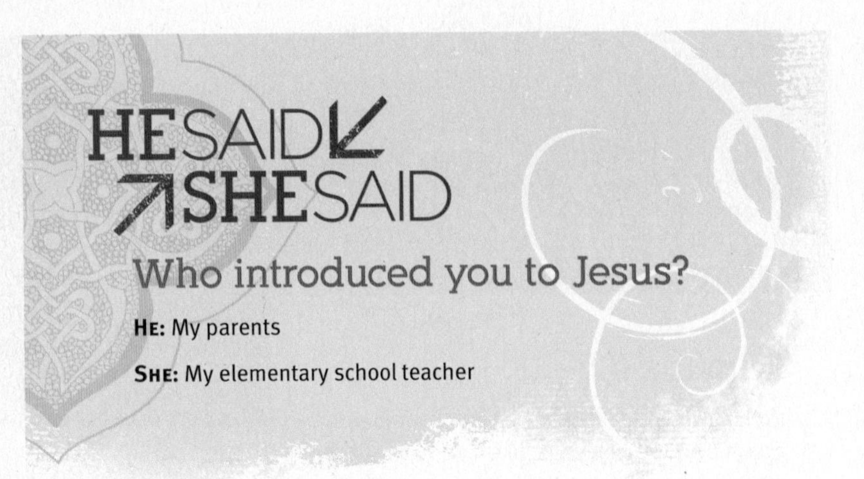

HE SAID ↙ ↗ SHE SAID

Who introduced you to Jesus?

He: My parents

She: My elementary school teacher

Adam and Christ Compared

[12]Sin came into the world because of what one man did, and with sin came death. This is why everyone must die—because everyone sinned. [13]Sin was in the world before the law of Moses, but sin is not counted against us as breaking a command when there is no law. [14]But from the time of Adam to the time of Moses, everyone had to die, even those who had not sinned by breaking a command, as Adam had.

Adam was like the One who was coming in the future. [15]But God's free gift is not like Adam's sin. Many people died because of the sin of that one man. But the grace from God was much greater; many people received God's gift of life by the grace of the one man, Jesus Christ. [16]After Adam sinned once, he was judged guilty. But the gift of God is different. God's free gift came after many sins, and it makes people right with God. [17]One man sinned, and so death ruled all people because of that one man. But now those people who accept God's full grace and the great gift of being made right with him will surely have true life and rule through the one man, Jesus Christ.

[18]So as one sin of Adam brought the punishment of death to all people, one good act that Christ did makes all people right with God. And that brings true life for all. [19]One man disobeyed God, and many became sinners. In the same way, one man obeyed God, and many will be made right. [20]The law came to make sin worse. But when sin grew worse, God's grace increased. [21]Sin once used death to rule us, but God gave people more of his grace so that grace could rule by making people right with him. And this brings life forever through Jesus Christ our Lord.

Dead to Sin but Alive in Christ

6 So do you think we should continue sinning so that God will give us even more grace? [2]No! We died to our old sinful lives, so how can we continue living with sin? [3]Did you forget that all of us became part of Christ when we were baptized? We shared his death in our baptism. [4]When we were baptized, we were buried with Christ and shared his death. So, just as Christ was raised from the dead by the wonderful power of the Father, we also can live a new life.

[5]Christ died, and we have been joined with him by dying too. So we will also be joined with him by rising from the dead as he did. [6]We know that our old life died with Christ on the cross so that our sinful selves would have no power over us and we would not be slaves to sin. [7]Anyone who has died is made free from sin's control.

[8]If we died with Christ, we know we will also live with him. [9]Christ was raised from the dead, and we know that he cannot die again. Death has no power over him now. [10]Yes, when Christ died, he died to de-

Saying Grace

Praying before meals is a beautiful tradition in countless families across the world. Angel-faced little children do it by reciting cute little rhyming verses and songs from the time they learn to say their first words. But thanking God for his provision is more than a cute tradition. It's a way to follow the example Jesus set at the Last Supper when he thanked God for the food before giving it to his followers (Matthew 26:26). Simply acknowledging that the Lord is the one who provides daily bread for you and your family is a lovely gesture of appreciation. And when you pray as a family, even a simple mealtime prayer, you are setting an important example for your children or guests.

feat the power of sin one time—enough for all time. He now has a new life, and his new life is with God. [11]In the same way, you should see yourselves as being dead to the power of sin and alive with God through Christ Jesus.

[12]So, do not let sin control your life here on earth so that you do what your sinful self wants to do. [13]Do not offer the parts of your body to serve sin, as things to be used in doing evil. Instead, offer yourselves to God as people who have died and now live. Offer the parts of your body to God to be used in doing good. [14]Sin will not be your master, because you are not under law but under God's grace.

Be Slaves of Righteousness

[15]So what should we do? Should we sin because we are under grace and not under law? No! [16]Surely you know that when you give yourselves like slaves to obey someone, then you are really slaves of that person. The person you obey is your master. You can follow sin, which brings spiritual death, or you can obey God, which makes you right with him. [17]In the past you were slaves to sin—sin controlled you. But thank God, you fully obeyed the things that you were taught. [18]You were made free from sin, and now you are slaves to goodness. [19]I use this example because this is hard for you to understand. In the past you offered the parts of your body to be slaves to sin and evil; you lived only for evil. In the same way now you must give yourselves to be slaves of goodness. Then you will live only for God.

[20]In the past you were slaves to sin, and goodness did not control you. [21]You did evil things, and now you are ashamed of them. Those things only bring death. [22]But now you are free from sin and have become slaves of God. This brings you a life that is only for God, and this gives you life forever. [23]The payment for sin is death. But God gives us the free gift of life forever in Christ Jesus our Lord.

Time-Saving Tidbits

Today's on-the-go lifestyles leave most of us craving extra time, especially when it comes to kitchen efficiency. Does your kitchen need a boost of time-saving potential? Try these heart-of-the-home helpers. **Dish It Out**—Save minutes unloading the dishwasher by loading similar utensils together: forks together, spoons together, etc. **Spice It Up**—Alphabetize your spice rack. **Keep It Handy**—Reevaluate your cupboard organization for user-friendliness. **Freshen the Fridge**—Thin it out every garbage day to avoid wasting time wading through old items. **Clarify the Clutter**—Don't let your counter space double as a junk drawer! Buy a basket for paper piles.

An Example from Marriage

7 Brothers and sisters, all of you understand the law of Moses. So surely you know that the law rules over people only while they are alive. [2]For example, a woman must stay married to her husband as long as he is alive. But if her husband dies, she is free from the law of marriage. [3]But if she marries another man while her husband is still alive, the law says she is guilty of adultery. But if her husband dies, she is free from the law of marriage. Then if she marries another man, she is not guilty of adultery.

[4]In the same way, my brothers and sisters, your old selves died, and you became free from the law through the body of Christ. This happened so that you might belong to someone else—the One who was raised from the dead—and so that we might be used in service to God. [5]In the past, we were ruled by our sinful selves. The law made us want to do sinful things that controlled our bodies, so the things we did were bringing us death. [6]In the past, the law held us like prisoners, but our old selves died, and we were made free

fun facts

The average American household has $8,650 in credit card debt.

(*Redbook*)

Women & Men of the BIBLE

Peter: Passionate Follower

Peter was an intense, passionate follower of Christ. He was an all-or-nothing kind of guy. It wasn't enough to see Jesus walking on the water—he wanted to do it, too. And when the soldiers came to arrest Jesus, it was Peter who wanted to fight for him. But when he messed up, he did that big, too. He and his buddies slept through Jesus' darkest hour in the garden, and he later denied that he even knew Jesus. Then he got to experience unbelievable forgiveness and passionately followed his Lord the rest of his life. He wasn't perfect, but Peter was a fully devoted follower of Christ and served him wholeheartedly. (The Gospels)

from the law. So now we serve God in a new way with the Spirit, and not in the old way with written rules.

Our Fight Against Sin

[7]You might think I am saying that sin and the law are the same thing. That is not true. But the law was the only way I could learn what sin meant. I would never have known what it means to want to take something belonging to someone else if the law had not said, "You must not want to take your neighbor's things."[n] [8]And sin found a way to use that command and cause me to want all kinds of things I should not want. But without the law, sin has no power. [9]I was alive before I knew the law. But when the law's command came to me, then sin began to live, [10]and I died. The command was meant to bring life, but for me it brought death. [11]Sin found a way to fool me by using the command to make me die.

[12]So the law is holy, and the command is holy and right and good. [13]Does this mean that something that is good brought death to me? No! Sin used something that is good to bring death to me. This happened so that I could see what sin is really like; the command was used to show that sin is very evil.

LIFE ISSUES

Hurt by Church

Churches are amazing places where Jesus' followers worship together and encourage each other. Yet no church is perfect because they're formed by imperfect people who, unfortunately, sometimes hurt each other. If you've been hurt at church—whether from gossip, wrong teaching, or other issues—let yourself grieve. But keep your eyes on Jesus and your faith based on his faithfulness. Ask God for healing attitudes to forgive those who have hurt you, and pray Romans 15:5–6 for that church. God can bring good from the pain. Maybe through your experience, he'll help grow a hurting church.

The War Within Us

[14]We know that the law is spiritual, but I am not spiritual since sin rules me as if I were its slave. [15]I do not understand the things I do. I do not do what I want to do, and I do the things I hate. [16]And if I do not want to do the hated things I do, that means I agree that the law is good. [17]But I am not really the one who is doing these hated things; it is sin living in me that does them. [18]Yes, I know that nothing good lives in me—I mean nothing good lives in the part of me that is earthly and sinful. I want to do the things that are good, but I do not do them. [19]I do not do the good things I want to do, but I do the bad things I do not want to do. [20]So if I do things I do not want to do, then I am not the one doing them. It is sin living in me that does those things.

[21]So I have learned this rule: When I want to do good, evil is there with me. [22]In my mind, I am happy with God's law. [23]But I see another law working in my body, which makes war against the law that my mind accepts. That other law working in my body is the law of sin, and it makes me its prisoner. [24]What a miserable man I am! Who will save me from this body that brings me death? [25]I thank God for saving me through Jesus Christ our Lord!

So in my mind I am a slave to God's law, but in my sinful self I am a slave to the law of sin.

Be Ruled by the Spirit

8 So now, those who are in Christ Jesus are not judged guilty.[n] [2]Through Christ Jesus the law of the Spirit that brings life made you[n] free from the law that brings sin and death. [3]The law was without power, because the law was made weak by our sinful selves. But God did what the law could not do. He sent his own Son to earth with the same human life that others use for sin. By sending his Son to be an offering for sin, God used a human life to destroy sin. [4]He did this so that we could be the kind of people the law correctly wants us to be. Now we do not live following our sinful selves, but we live following the Spirit.

[5]Those who live following their sinful selves think only about things that their sinful selves want. But those who live fol-

7:7 "You . . . things." Quotation from Exodus 20:17. **8:1 guilty** Some Greek copies continue, "those who do not live in the power of their sinful selves, but in the power of the Spirit." **8:2 you** Some Greek copies read "me."

lowing the Spirit are thinking about the things the Spirit wants them to do. [6]If people's thinking is controlled by the sinful self, there is death. But if their thinking is controlled by the Spirit, there is life and peace. [7]When people's thinking is controlled by the sinful self, they are against God, because they refuse to obey God's law and really are not even able to obey God's law. [8]Those people who are ruled by their sinful selves cannot please God.

[9]But you are not ruled by your sinful selves. You are ruled by the Spirit, if that Spirit of God really lives in you. But the person who does not have the Spirit of Christ does not belong to Christ. [10]Your body will always be dead because of sin. But if Christ is in you, then the Spirit gives you life, because Christ made you right with God. [11]God raised Jesus from the dead, and if God's Spirit is living in you, he will also give life to your bodies that die. God is the One who raised Christ from the dead, and he will give life through[n] his Spirit that lives in you.

[12]So, my brothers and sisters, we must not be ruled by our sinful selves or live the way our sinful selves want. [13]If you use your lives to do the wrong things your sinful selves want, you will die spiritually. But if you use the Spirit's help to stop doing the wrong things you do with your body, you will have true life.

[14]The true children of God are those who let God's Spirit lead them. [15]The Spirit we received does not make us slaves again to fear; it makes us children of God. With that Spirit we cry out, "Father."[n] [16]And the Spirit himself joins with our spirits to say we are God's children. [17]If we are God's children, we will receive blessings from God together with Christ. But we must suffer as Christ suffered so that we will have glory as Christ has glory.

Our Future Glory

[18]The sufferings we have now are nothing compared to the great glory that will be shown to us. [19]Everything God made is waiting with excitement for God to show his children's glory completely. [20]Everything God made was changed to become useless, not by its own wish but because God wanted it and because all along there was this hope: [21]that everything God made would be set free from ruin to have the freedom and glory that belong to God's children.

[22]We know that everything God made has been waiting until now in pain, like a woman ready to give birth. [23]Not only the world, but we also have been waiting with pain inside us. We have the Spirit as the first part of God's promise. So we are waiting for God to finish making us his own children, which means our bodies will be made free. [24]We were saved, and we have this hope. If we see what we are waiting for, that is not really hope. People do not hope for something they already have. [25]But we are hoping for something we do not have yet, and we are waiting for it patiently.

[26]Also, the Spirit helps us with our weakness. We do not know how to pray as we should. But the Spirit himself speaks to God for us, even begs God for us with deep feelings that words cannot explain. [27]God can see what is in people's hearts. And he knows what is in the mind of the Spirit, because the Spirit speaks to God for his people in the way God wants.

[28]We know that in everything God works for the good of those who love him.[n] They are the people he called, because that was his plan. [29]God knew them before he made the world, and he chose them to be like his Son so that Jesus would be the firstborn[n] of many brothers and sisters. [30]God planned for them to be like his Son; and

BECOME *Involved*

National Domestic Violence Hotline

The number of domestic violence cases reported in the United States is staggering. Four million women in America are seriously assaulted by a partner during an average year. Yet many are too scared to tell anyone, and even if they wanted to, where could they go for help?

The National Domestic Violence Hotline is a great place to start. They answer more than sixteen thousand calls every month. A clearinghouse for local agencies, the Hotline can connect a battered woman with someone close by who can help her quickly. They also provide information and support for family and friends of the abused and online materials for victims, families, and abusers alike.

The Hotline is always in need of funding to hire more advocates (people who handle the calls) and to upgrade their technology. Your financial donation could help them expand the capacity to help more people. They also have programs for donating cars and phones. Log on to www.ndvh.org for more information about how you can help. Your donation could literally help save the life of an innocent victim of domestic abuse.

8:11 through Some Greek copies read "because of." **8:15 "Father"** Literally, "Abba, Father." Jewish children called their fathers "Abba." **8:28 We . . . him.** Some Greek copies read "We know that everything works together for good for those who love God." **8:29 firstborn** Here this probably means that Christ was the first in God's family to share God's glory.

Romans 9:33

Suppose you find your dream job and eagerly apply for the position. Can you imagine the company responding with, "You're kind of hired. Come in and work . . . or not. Money may or may not be involved." Not a chance! It'd be complete acceptance or rejection, nothing in between.

A relationship with Jesus works in the same all-or-nothing way. From Jesus' descriptions of himself, it's clear he's the dividing line between death and life—people who follow him will be saved, and everyone else will face judgment. (See Matthew 7 and John 14.) Paul quoted Old Testament prophecy in this verse when he described Jesus as a "stone that causes people to stumble, a rock that makes them fall." But he goes on to say, "Anyone who trusts in him will never be disappointed." What's he talking about?

Christ—his birth, life, death, and resurrection—is like a gigantic, unavoidable stone in the middle of the road of life. People who ignore or refuse him will inevitably run into him and fall. Everybody wants to get to heaven, but so many people trip over the fact that Jesus is the one and only way to get there.

Only two options exist when it comes to Christ: full acceptance or complete rejection. What's your response?

those he planned to be like his Son, he also called; and those he called, he also made right with him; and those he made right, he also glorified.

God's Love in Christ Jesus

31So what should we say about this? If God is for us, no one can defeat us. 32He did not spare his own Son but gave him for us all. So with Jesus, God will surely give us all things. 33Who can accuse the people God has chosen? No one, because God is the One who makes them right. 34Who can say God's people are guilty? No one, because Christ Jesus died, but he was also raised from the dead, and now he is on God's right side, appealing to God for us. 35Can anything separate us from the love Christ has for us? Can troubles or problems or sufferings or hunger or nakedness or danger or violent death? 36As it is written in the Scriptures:

"For you we are in danger of death all
the time.
People think we are worth no
more than sheep to be killed."
Psalm 44:22

37But in all these things we are completely victorious through God who showed his love for us. 38Yes, I am sure that neither death, nor life, nor angels, nor ruling spirits, nothing now, nothing in the future, no powers, 39nothing above us, nothing below us, nor anything else in the whole world will ever be able to separate us from the love of God that is in Christ Jesus our Lord.

God and the Jewish People

9 I am in Christ, and I am telling you the truth; I do not lie. My conscience is ruled by the Holy Spirit, and it tells me I am not lying. 2I have great sorrow and always feel much sadness. 3I wish I could help my Jewish brothers and sisters, my people. I would even wish that I were cursed and cut off from Christ if that would help them. 4They are the people of Israel, God's chosen children. They have seen the glory of God, and they have the agreements that God made between himself and his people. God gave them the law of Moses and the right way of worship and his promises. 5They are the descendants of our great ancestors, and they are the earthly family into which Christ was born, who is God over all. Praise him forever![n] Amen.

6It is not that God failed to keep his promise to them. But only some of the people of Israel are truly God's people,[n] 7and only some of Abraham's[n] descendants are true children of Abraham. But God said to Abraham: "The descendants I promised you will be from Isaac."[n] 8This means that not all of Abraham's descendants are God's true children. Abraham's true children are those who become God's children because of the promise God made to Abraham. 9God's promise to Abraham was this: "At the right time I will return, and Sarah will have a son."[n] 10And that is not all. Rebekah's sons had the same father, our father Isaac. 11-12But before the two boys were born, God told Rebekah, "The older will serve the younger."[n] This was before the boys had done anything good or bad. God said this so that the one chosen would be chosen because of God's own plan. He was chosen because he was the one God wanted to call, not because of anything he did. 13As the Scripture says, "I loved Jacob, but I hated Esau."[n]

14So what should we say about this? Is God unfair? In no way. 15God said to Moses, "I will show kindness to anyone to whom I want to show kindness, and I will show mercy to anyone to whom I want to

9:5 born . . . forever! This can also mean "born. May God, who rules over all things, be praised forever!" **9:6 God's people** Literally, "Israel," the people God chose to bring his blessings to the world. **9:7 Abraham** Most respected ancestor of the Jews. Every Jew hoped to see Abraham. **9:7 "The descendants . . . Isaac."** Quotation from Genesis 21:12. **9:9 "At . . . son."** Quotation from Genesis 18:10, 14. **9:11–12 "The older . . . younger."** Quotation from Genesis 25:23. **9:13 "I . . . Esau."** Quotation from Malachi 1:2–3.

Body Basics

Taking good care of your body is not only beneficial to your physical well-being, but it's also an important aspect of your spiritual worship, too. In 1 Corinthians 6:19–20, Paul reminds believers that your body is not really yours anyway. It belongs to God, so the way you treat it should always bring him honor. Getting proper amounts of exercise, sleep, food, and water will not only help you look and feel your best, but you will be honoring your body's real owner in the process. Let your love for God motivate you to pursue a healthy, fit lifestyle.

show mercy."[n] [16]So God will choose the one to whom he decides to show mercy; his choice does not depend on what people want or try to do. [17]The Scripture says to the king of Egypt: "I made you king for this reason: to show my power in you so that my name will be talked about in all the earth."[n] [18]So God shows mercy where he wants to show mercy, and he makes stubborn the people he wants to make stubborn.

[19]So one of you will ask me: "Then why does God blame us for our sins? Who can fight his will?" [20]You are only human, and human beings have no right to question God. An object should not ask the person who made it, "Why did you make me like this?" [21]The potter can make anything he wants to make. He can use the same clay to make one thing for special use and another thing for daily use.

[22]It is the same way with God. He wanted to show his anger and to let people see his power. But he patiently stayed with those people he was angry with—people who were made ready to be destroyed. [23]He waited with patience so that he could make known his rich glory to the people who receive his mercy. He has prepared these people to have his glory, [24]and we are those people whom God called. He called us not from the Jews only but also from those who are not Jews. [25]As the Scripture says in Hosea:

"I will say, 'You are my people'
to those I had called 'not my people.'
And I will show my love
to those people I did not love."
Hosea 2:1, 23

[26]"They were called,
'You are not my people,'
but later they will be called
'children of the living God.' "
Hosea 1:10

[27]And Isaiah cries out about Israel:
"The people of Israel are many,
like the grains of sand by the sea.
But only a few of them will be saved,
[28] because the Lord will quickly
and completely punish the
people on the earth."
Isaiah 10:22–23

[29]It is as Isaiah said:
"The Lord All-Powerful
allowed a few of our descendants
to live.
Otherwise we would have been
completely destroyed
like the cities of Sodom and
Gomorrah."[n] *Isaiah 1:9*

[30]So what does all this mean? Those who are not Jews were not trying to make themselves right with God, but they were made right with God because of their faith. [31]The people of Israel tried to follow a law to make themselves right with God. But they did not succeed, [32]because they tried to make themselves right by the things they did instead of trusting in God to make them right. They stumbled over the stone that causes people to stumble. [33]As it is written in the Scripture:
"I will put in Jerusalem a
stone that causes people
to stumble,

all about MEN

More Than You Imagine

Whether you've read Ephesians 3:14–21 countless times or it's brand new to you, take a minute to check out these eight verses with fresh eyes. What a powerful prayer! Imagine praying this for the man God gives you. Imagine him understanding the Lord's enormous love for him. Imagine what a mighty tool he can be in his Savior's hand! Through your prayers that God will "do much, much more than anything [he] can ask or imagine" (3:20), you can play a vital role as God works in your guy's heart, mind, and character. If God has marriage in store for you, he either has provided or will provide *you* as your soul mate's prayer champion. So why not begin praying these verses over him today?

9:15 "I . . . mercy." Quotation from Exodus 33:19. **9:17 "I . . . earth."** Quotation from Exodus 9:16. **9:29 Sodom and Gomorrah** Two cities that God destroyed because the people were so evil.

a rock that makes them fall.
Anyone who trusts in him will never
be disappointed."
Isaiah 8:14; 28:16

10 Brothers and sisters, the thing I want most is for all the Jews to be saved. That is my prayer to God. [2]I can say this about them: They really try to follow God, but they do not know the right way. [3]Because they did not know the way that God makes people right with him, they tried to make themselves right in their own way. So they did not accept God's way of making people right. [4]Christ ended the law so that everyone who believes in him may be right with God.

[5]Moses writes about being made right by following the law. He says, "A person who obeys these things will live because of them."[n] [6]But this is what the Scripture says about being made right through faith: "Don't say to yourself, 'Who will go up into heaven?' " (That means, "Who will go up to heaven and bring Christ down to earth?") [7]"And do not say, 'Who will go down into the world below?' " (That means, "Who will go down and bring Christ up from the dead?") [8]This is what the Scripture says: "The word is near you; it is in your mouth and in your heart."[n] That is the teaching of faith that we are telling. [9]If you declare with your mouth, "Jesus is Lord," and if you believe in your heart that God raised Jesus from the dead, you will be saved. [10]We believe with our hearts, and so we are made right with God. And we declare with our mouths that we believe, and so we are saved. [11]As the Scripture says, "Anyone who trusts in him will never be disappointed."[n] [12]That Scripture says "anyone" because there is no difference between those who are Jews and those who are not. The same Lord is the Lord of all and gives many blessings to all who trust in him, [13]as the Scripture says, "Anyone who calls on the Lord will be saved."[n]

[14]But before people can ask the Lord for help, they must believe in him; and before they can believe in him, they must hear about him; and for them to hear about the Lord, someone must tell them; [15]and before someone can go and tell them, that person must be sent. It is written, "How beautiful is the person who comes to bring good news."[n] [16]But not all the Jews accepted the good news. Isaiah said, "Lord, who believed what we told them?"[n] [17]So faith comes from hearing the Good News, and people hear the Good News when someone tells them about Christ.

[18]But I ask: Didn't people hear the Good News? Yes, they heard—as the Scripture says:

"Their message went out through all
the world;
their words go everywhere on
earth." *Psalm 19:4*

[19]Again I ask: Didn't the people of Israel understand? Yes, they did understand. First, Moses says:

"I will use those who are not a nation
to make you jealous.

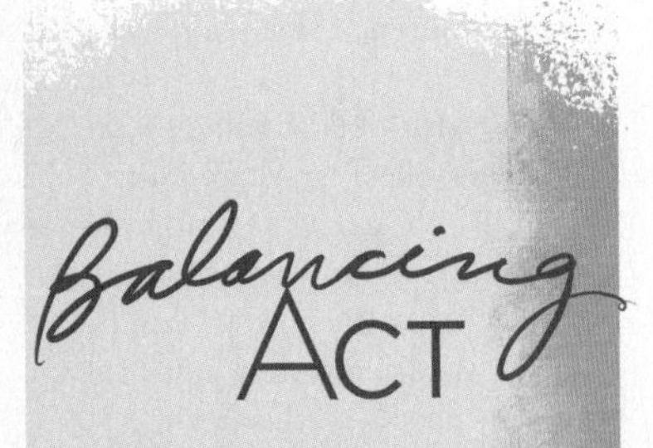

Is He Worthy of Your Time?

You've just met Mr. Right—you're sure of it! Suddenly you find yourself canceling lunch with your friends to see him. You end up at the movies with him, rather than at the gym for that afternoon workout. You even skip church to meet him for brunch. Sounds like you've got a case of "my-new-boyfriend-is-my-everything-itis"—and that's serious! Take a step back and evaluate: *How long have I known this guy? Do we have compatible interests and beliefs? Am I giving up things I love to make him happy?* Even if he's totally worth your attention, you risk "burning out" if you spend too much time together too soon. Time with friends keeps you grounded—their input can help you make good decisions about the relationship, too. And, most importantly, any guy who keeps you from spending time with God is definitely not the guy for you!

Only God

When it comes to worship, God leaves no room for debate—he's it, the only one worthy of receiving glory and praise for being . . . well, just for being himself. His identity as Almighty entitles him to expect our humble reverence and awe. Unlike any other being, he's unmatchable and unconquerable. But what makes him even more worthy of worship is the fact that he is utterly holy, too. God's first commandment has never changed: "You must not have any other gods except me" (Exodus 20:3). His identity as God commands our worship. His holy kindness invites it.

10:5 "A person . . . them." Quotation from Leviticus 18:5. **10:6–8 But . . . heart."** Quotations from Deuteronomy 9:4; 30:12–14; Psalm 107:26. **10:11 "Anyone . . . disappointed."** Quotation from Isaiah 28:16. **10:13 "Anyone . . . saved."** Quotation from Joel 2:32. **10:15 "How . . . news."** Quotation from Isaiah 52:7. **10:16 "Lord, . . . them?"** Quotation from Isaiah 53:1.

RELATIONSHIPS

Defensiveness

Defensiveness is a communication killer! There's no reasoning with someone who feels attacked by the smallest comment and won't consider her part in a problem. So what's the answer? Proverbs 15:1 offers help: "A gentle answer will calm a person's anger, but an unkind answer will cause more anger." Gentleness is a powerful tool for chipping through defenses. No matter how unreasonable someone gets, you always have the option to stay calm—even while holding your ground when necessary. Flying off the handle usually just encourages someone's hostility. Ask God to help you gently chip through walls of defensiveness.

I will use a nation that does
not understand to make you
angry." *Deuteronomy 32:21*

[20]Then Isaiah is bold enough to say:

"I was found by those who were not
asking me for help.
I made myself known to people
who were not looking for me."
Isaiah 65:1

[21]But about Israel God says,

"All day long I stood ready to accept
people who disobey and are
stubborn." *Isaiah 65:2*

God Shows Mercy to All People

11 So I ask: Did God throw out his people? No! I myself am an Israelite from the family of Abraham, from the tribe of Benjamin. [2]God chose the Israelites to be his people before they were born, and he has not thrown his people out. Surely you know what the Scripture says about Elijah, how he prayed to God against the people of Israel. [3]"Lord," he said, "they have killed your prophets, and they have destroyed your altars. I am the only prophet left, and now they are trying to kill me, too."[n] [4]But what answer did God give Elijah? He said, "But I have left seven thousand people in Israel who have never bowed down before Baal."[n] [5]It is the same now. There are a few people that God has chosen by his grace. [6]And if he chose them by grace, it is not for the things they have done. If they could be made God's people by what they did, God's gift of grace would not really be a gift.

[7]So this is what has happened: Although the Israelites tried to be right with God, they did not succeed, but the ones God chose did become right with him. The others were made stubborn and refused to listen to God. [8]As it is written in the Scriptures:

"God gave the people a dull mind so
they could not understand."
Isaiah 29:10

"He closed their eyes so they could
not see
and their ears so they could not
hear.
This continues until today."
Deuteronomy 29:4

[9]And David says:

"Let their own feasts trap them and
cause their ruin;
let their feasts cause them to
stumble and be paid back.
[10]Let their eyes be closed so they
cannot see
and their backs be forever weak
from troubles." *Psalm 69:22–23*

[11]So I ask: When the Jews fell, did that fall destroy them? No! But their failure brought salvation to those who are not Jews, in order to make the Jews jealous. [12]The Jews' failure brought rich blessings for the world, and the Jews' loss brought rich blessings for the non-Jewish people.

fun facts

Cuts and scrapes heal up to 25% faster on people who exercise on a regular basis.

(Journal of Gerontology)

11:3 "they . . . too" Quotation from 1 Kings 19:10, 14. **11:4 "But . . . Baal."** Quotation from 1 Kings 19:18.

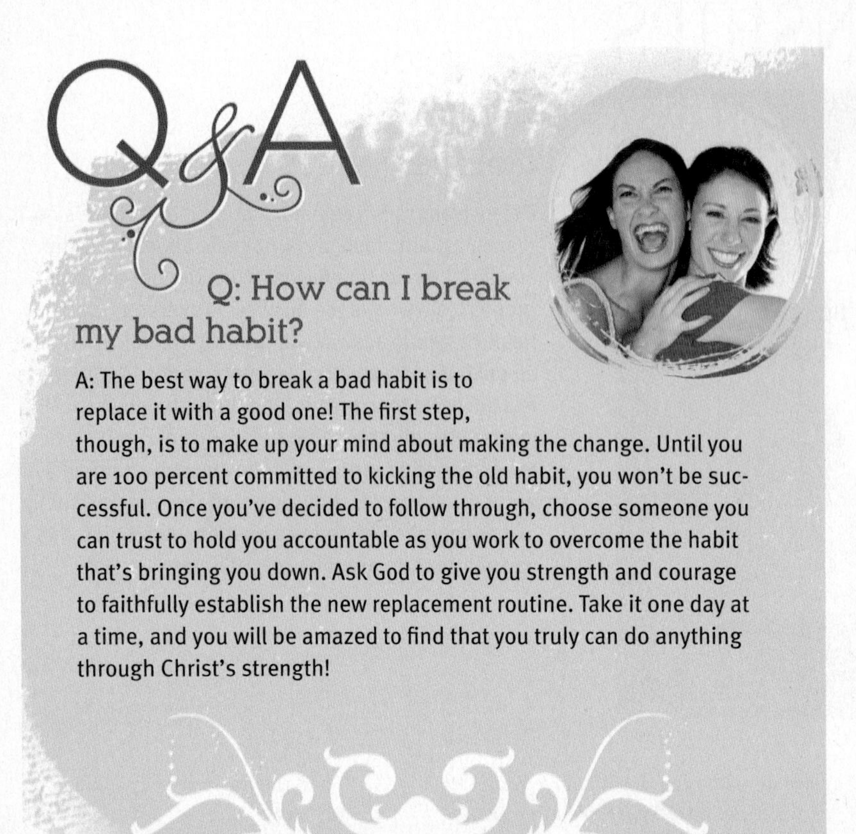

Q&A

Q: How can I break my bad habit?

A: The best way to break a bad habit is to replace it with a good one! The first step, though, is to make up your mind about making the change. Until you are 100 percent committed to kicking the old habit, you won't be successful. Once you've decided to follow through, choose someone you can trust to hold you accountable as you work to overcome the habit that's bringing you down. Ask God to give you strength and courage to faithfully establish the new replacement routine. Take it one day at a time, and you will be amazed to find that you truly can do anything through Christ's strength!

So surely the world will receive much richer blessings when enough Jews become the kind of people God wants.

[13]Now I am speaking to you who are not Jews. I am an apostle to those who are not Jews, and since I have that work, I will make the most of it. [14]I hope I can make my own people jealous and, in that way, help some of them to be saved. [15]When God turned away from the Jews, he became friends with other people in the world. So when God accepts the Jews, surely that will bring them life after death.

[16]If the first piece of bread is offered to God, then the whole loaf is made holy. If the roots of a tree are holy, then the tree's branches are holy too.

[17]It is as if some of the branches from an olive tree have been broken off. You non-Jewish people are like the branch of a wild olive tree that has been joined to that first tree. You now share the strength and life of the first tree, the Jews. [18]So do not brag about those branches that were broken off. If you brag, remember that you do not support the root, but the root supports you. [19]You will say, "Branches were broken off so that I could be joined to their tree." [20]That is true. But those branches were broken off because they did not believe, and you continue to be part of the tree only because you believe. Do not be proud, but be afraid. [21]If God did not let the natural branches of that tree stay, then he will not let you stay if you don't believe.

[22]So you see that God is kind and also very strict. He punishes those who stop following him. But God is kind to you, if you continue following in his kindness. If you do not, you will be cut off from the tree. [23]And if the Jews will believe in God again, he will accept them back. God is able to put them back where they were. [24]It is not natural for a wild branch to be part of a good tree. And you who are not Jews are like a branch cut from a wild olive tree and joined to a good olive tree. But since those Jews are like a branch that grew from the good tree, surely they can be joined to their own tree again.

[25]I want you to understand this secret, brothers and sisters, so you will understand that you do not know everything: Part of Israel has been made stubborn, but that will change when many who are not Jews have come to God. [26]And that is how all Israel will be saved. It is written in the Scriptures:

> "The Savior will come from
> Jerusalem;
> he will take away all evil from
> the family of Jacob.[n]
> [27]And I will make this agreement with
> those people
> when I take away their sins."
> *Isaiah 59:20–21; 27:9*

[28]The Jews refuse to accept the Good News, so they are God's enemies. This has happened to help you who are not Jews. But the Jews are still God's chosen people, and he loves them very much because of the promises he made to their ancestors. [29]God never changes his mind about the people he calls and the things he gives them. [30]At one time you refused to obey God. But now you have received mercy, because those people refused to obey. [31]And now the Jews refuse to obey, because God showed mercy to you. But this happened so that they also can[n] receive mercy from him. [32]God has given all people over to their stubborn ways so that he can show mercy to all.

Praise to God

[33]Yes, God's riches are very great, and his wisdom and knowledge have no end! No one can explain the things God decides or understand his ways. [34]As the Scripture says,

> "Who has known the mind of the
> Lord,
> or who has been able to give him
> advice?" *Isaiah 40:13*
> [35]"No one has ever given God anything
> that he must pay back." *Job 41:11*

[36]Yes, God made all things, and everything continues through him and for him. To him be the glory forever! Amen.

Give Your Lives to God

12 So brothers and sisters, since God has shown us great mercy, I beg you to offer your lives as a living sacrifice to him. Your offering must be only for God and pleasing to him, which is the spiritual way for you

11:26 Jacob Father of the twelve family groups of Israel, the people God chose to be his people. **11:31 can** Some Greek copies read "can now."

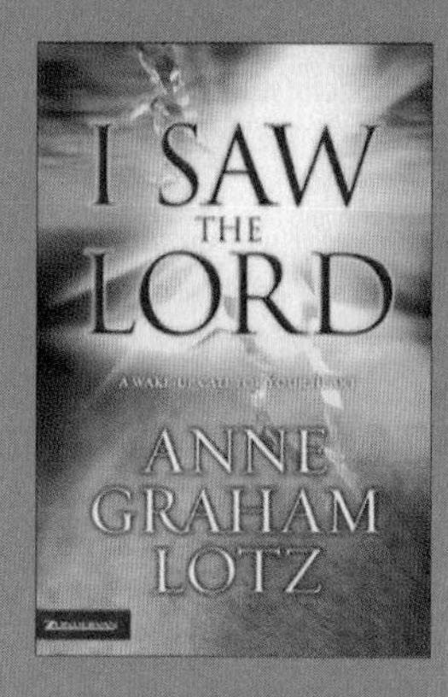

I Saw the Lord
by Anne Graham Lotz

If you've fallen into complacency, this book is a welcome wake-up call. Author Anne Graham Lotz's enthusiasm is contagious as she guides you on a journey to draw closer to Jesus and experience him in all his fullness. She shows how faith is much more than just a religious activity and tenderly motivates readers to seek a closer relationship with God. Lotz urges readers to rise above daily demands and live a passionate life in the midst of a world that desperately needs to see faith in action.

to worship. [2]Do not be shaped by this world; instead be changed within by a new way of thinking. Then you will be able to decide what God wants for you; you will know what is good and pleasing to him and what is perfect. [3]Because God has given me a special gift, I have something to say to everyone among you. Do not think you are better than you are. You must decide what you really are by the amount of faith God has given you. [4]Each one of us has a body with many parts, and these parts all have different uses. [5]In the same way, we are many, but in Christ we are all one body. Each one is a part of that body, and each part belongs to all the other parts. [6]We all have different gifts, each of which came because of the grace God gave us. The person who has the gift of prophecy should use that gift in agreement with the faith. [7]Anyone who has the gift of serving should serve. Anyone who has the gift of teaching should teach. [8]Whoever has the gift of encouraging others should encourage. Whoever has the gift of giving to others should give freely. Anyone who has the gift of being a leader should try hard when he leads. Whoever has the gift of showing mercy to others should do so with joy.

[9]Your love must be real. Hate what is evil, and hold on to what is good. [10]Love each other like brothers and sisters. Give each other more honor than you want for yourselves. [11]Do not be lazy but work hard, serving the Lord with all your heart. [12]Be joyful because you have hope. Be patient when trouble comes, and pray at all times. [13]Share with God's people who need help. Bring strangers in need into your homes.

[14]Wish good for those who harm you; wish them well and do not curse them. [15]Be happy with those who are happy, and be sad with those who are sad. [16]Live in peace with each other. Do not be proud, but make friends with those who seem unimportant. Do not think how smart you are.

[17]If someone does wrong to you, do not pay him back by doing wrong to him. Try to do what everyone thinks is right. [18]Do your best to live in peace with everyone. [19]My friends, do not try to punish others when they wrong you, but wait for God to punish them with his anger. It is written: "I will punish those who do wrong; I will repay them,"[n] says the Lord. [20]But you should do this:

> "If your enemy is hungry, feed him;
> if he is thirsty, give him a drink.
> Doing this will be like pouring
> burning coals on his head."
>
> *Proverbs 25:21–22*

[21]Do not let evil defeat you, but defeat evil by doing good.

Fear of Death

Did you know that the most common fear is speaking in public? Ranked a little lower at number three on the most common fears list is the fear of death—something everyone experiences at one time or another. As followers of Jesus, we can rest assured that this earthly life is not the end. Romans 8:38–39 tells us that death can't separate us from God's love, and the Bible also cautions, "Don't be afraid of people, who can kill the body but cannot kill the soul. The only one you should fear is the one who can destroy the soul and the body in hell" (Matthew 10:28). For those who put their faith in God, death is not to be feared. Heaven is our hope (5:12).

12:19 "I . . . them." Quotation from Deuteronomy 32:35.

Romans 13:8

A massive handbook of rules can be intimidating. If your job involves following countless regulations, trying to measure up probably keeps you pretty busy. A job like that provides a glimpse of what the Old Testament Jews faced. God set up hundreds of detailed rules, and if they broke any of them, they had to go through a ritual or offer a sacrifice. Besides being a heavy burden, it was a constant reminder that God is holy and people simply can't live up to his standards.

But now, because of the Cross, God's children are free from condemnation. That's not to say we're exempt from all rules—Jesus both simplified and deepened the standard of real purity. Instead of just obeying outward laws, Jesus tells us to strive for purity even in our thoughts and motives. He gave a helpful guideline to keep us on the right track: if we love God and each other, we'll be obeying the entire law!

When you're not sure what's right, pray for wisdom, check God's Word, and show love in everything you think, say, and do. Instead of living by a rule list, let love control your actions, and God will guard you from sinning against him or hurting people around you.

Christians Should Obey the Law

13 All of you must yield to the government rulers. No one rules unless God has given him the power to rule, and no one rules now without that power from God. [2]So those who are against the government are really against what God has commanded. And they will bring punishment on themselves. [3]Those who do right do not have to fear the rulers; only those who do wrong fear them. Do you want to be unafraid of the rulers? Then do what is right, and they will praise you. [4]The ruler is God's servant to help you. But if you do wrong, then be afraid. He has the power to punish; he is God's servant to punish those who do wrong. [5]So you must yield to the government, not only because you might be punished, but because you know it is right.

[6]This is also why you pay taxes. Rulers are working for God and give their time to their work. [7]Pay everyone, then, what you owe. If you owe any kind of tax, pay it. Show respect and honor to them all.

Loving Others

[8]Do not owe people anything, except always owe love to each other, because the person who loves others has obeyed all the law. [9]The law says, "You must not be guilty of adultery. You must not murder anyone. You must not steal. You must not want to take your neighbor's things."[n] All these commands and all others are really only one rule: "Love your neighbor as you love yourself."[n] [10]Love never hurts a neighbor, so loving is obeying all the law.

[11]Do this because we live in an important time. It is now time for you to wake up from your sleep, because our salvation is nearer now than when we first believed. [12]The "night"[n] is almost finished, and the "day"[n] is almost here. So we should stop doing things that belong to darkness and take up the weapons used for fighting in the light. [13]Let us live in a right way, like people who belong to the day. We should not have wild parties or get drunk. There should be no sexual sins of any kind, no fighting or jealousy. [14]But clothe yourselves with the Lord Jesus Christ and forget about satisfying your sinful self.

Do Not Criticize Other People

14 Accept into your group someone who is weak in faith, and do not argue about opinions. [2]One person believes it is right to eat all kinds of food.[n] But another, who is weak, believes it is right to eat only vegetables. [3]The one who knows that it is right to eat any kind of food must not reject the one who eats only vegetables. And the person who eats only vegetables must not think that the one who eats all foods is wrong, because God has accepted that person. [4]You cannot judge another person's servant. The master decides if the servant is doing well or not. And the Lord's servant will do well because the Lord helps him do well.

[5]Some think that one day is more important than another, and others think that every day is the same. Let all be sure in their own mind. [6]Those who think one day is more important than other days are doing that for the Lord. And those who eat all kinds of food are doing that for the Lord, and they give thanks to God. Others who refuse to eat some foods do that for the Lord, and they give thanks to God. [7]We do not live or die for ourselves. [8]If we live, we are living for the Lord, and if we die, we are dying for the Lord. So living or dying, we belong to the Lord.

13:9 "You . . . things." Quotation from Exodus 20:13–15, 17. **13:9 "Love . . . yourself."** Quotation from Leviticus 19:18. **13:12 "night"** This is used as a symbol of the sinful world we live in. This world will soon end. **13:12 "day"** This is used as a symbol of the good time that is coming, when we will be with God. **14:2 all . . . food** The Jewish law said there were some foods Jews should not eat. When Jews became Christians, some of them did not understand they could now eat all foods.

Now you who are not Jewish are not foreigners or strangers any longer, but are citizens together with God's holy people. You belong to God's family.
—Ephesians 2:19
june
Plan a camping trip for your own backyard.
1
Read John 15:1–5. How are you doing at remaining in Jesus?
2
3
4
Reorganize the furniture in your living room.
5
6
Enjoy an affordable night on the town.
www.entertainment.com
7
Clean out your closet. Consider donating to www.dressforsuccess.org
8
9
10
Eliminate directory assistance charges by using 1-800-FREE-411.
11
Develop a plan to get out of debt
www.crown.org
12
Don't forget: Father's Day is the 3rd Sunday of June.
13
Plan a neighborhood BBQ.
14
Organize a team to build a float for your town's 4th of July parade.
15
Visit a historical site in your community.
16
Invite someone over for lunch after church.
17
Attend a free summer concert.
18
It's Charles Spurgeon's birthday. Research his life online.
19
20
It's the 1st day of summer! Celebrate with friends.
21
Pray for a person of influence: it's Meryl Streep's birthday.
22
23
Reconnect with your grandparents by asking them about their childhoods.
24
25
Plan an '80s movie marathon with friends.
26
27
Hang a birdfeeder on your porch and enjoy God's creation.
28
Pray for persecuted Christians around the world.
www.opendoorsusa.org
29
Build a fitness routine around your favorite fun activities.
30

HE SAID ↙ ↗ SHE SAID

What fear do you wrestle with most?

He: Rejection

She: Failure

[9]The reason Christ died and rose from the dead to live again was so he would be Lord over both the dead and the living. [10]So why do you judge your brothers or sisters in Christ? And why do you think you are better than they are? We will all stand before God to be judged, [11]because it is written in the Scriptures:

"'As surely as I live,' says the Lord,
'Everyone will bow before me;
everyone will say that I am God.'"
Isaiah 45:23

[12]So each of us will have to answer to God.

Be Still & Know

Pray on the Run

Women are excellent multitaskers by nature. Even before the idea was fashionable, moms, daughters, and sisters handled multiple matters at once. It's just part of the feminine, nurturing DNA that makes the gender fabulous! But did you know that your more-than-one-thing-at-a-time talent that allows you to cook, talk on the phone, listen to the radio, and watch TV all at once can be put to use in your prayer life, too? Next time you're waiting in the drive-thru lane or working out your groove on the treadmill, take a few minutes to check in with God. After all, 1 Thessalonians 5:17 says to pray continually. That means every believer is called to be a multitasking person of prayer!

Do Not Cause Others to Sin

[13]For that reason we should stop judging each other. We must make up our minds not to do anything that will make another Christian sin. [14]I am in the Lord Jesus, and I know that there is no food that is wrong to eat. But if a person believes something is wrong, that thing is wrong for him. [15]If you hurt your brother's or sister's faith because of something you eat, you are not really following the way of love. Do not destroy someone's faith by eating food he thinks is wrong, because Christ died for him. [16]Do not allow what you think is good to become what others say is evil. [17]In the kingdom of God, eating and drinking are not important. The important things are living right with God, peace, and joy in the Holy Spirit. [18]Anyone who serves Christ by living this way is pleasing God and will be accepted by other people.

[19]So let us try to do what makes peace and helps one another. [20]Do not let the eating of food destroy the work of God. All foods are all right to eat, but it is wrong to eat food that causes someone else to sin. [21]It is better not to eat meat or drink wine or do anything that will cause your brother or sister to sin.

[22]Your beliefs about these things should be kept secret between you and God. People are happy if they can do what they think is right without feeling guilty. [23]But those who eat something without being sure it is right are wrong because they did not believe it was right. Anything that is done without believing it is right is a sin.

15 We who are strong in faith should help the weak with their weaknesses, and not please only ourselves. [2]Let each of us please our neighbors for their good, to help them be stronger in faith. [3]Even Christ did not live to please himself. It was as the Scriptures said: "When people insult you, it hurts me."[n] [4]Everything that was written in the past was written to teach us. The Scriptures give us patience and encouragement so that we can have hope. [5]May the patience and encouragement that come from God allow you to live in harmony with each other the way Christ Jesus

15:3 "When . . . me." Quotation from Psalm 69:9.

wants. [6]Then you will all be joined together, and you will give glory to God the Father of our Lord Jesus Christ. [7]Christ accepted you, so you should accept each other, which will bring glory to God. [8]I tell you that Christ became a servant of the Jews to show that God's promises to the Jewish ancestors are true. [9]And he also did this so that those who are not Jews could give glory to God for the mercy he gives to them. It is written in the Scriptures:

"So I will praise you among the
non-Jewish people.
I will sing praises to your name."
Psalm 18:49

[10]The Scripture also says,

"Be happy, you who are not Jews,
together with his people."
Deuteronomy 32:43

[11]Again the Scripture says,

"All you who are not Jews, praise the
Lord.
All you people, sing praises to
him." *Psalm 117:1*

[12]And Isaiah says,

"A new king will come from the
family of Jesse.[n]
He will come to rule over the
non-Jewish people,
and they will have hope because of
him." *Isaiah 11:10*

[13]I pray that the God who gives hope will fill you with much joy and peace while you trust in him. Then your hope will overflow by the power of the Holy Spirit.

Hair Care

You and your stylist are not the only ones who care about your hair. Your heavenly Father cares, too! In fact, he knows more about its condition than you do. While you're shampooing, conditioning, trimming, blow-drying, and styling, he's monitoring exactly how many hairs are on your head (Matthew 10:30). That's just one of many examples of how very important you—and every part of your existence—are to God. He cares about the things you care about. He knows you better than you know yourself. You can trust him to care for all the details in your life.

Paul Talks About His Work

[14]My brothers and sisters, I am sure that you are full of goodness. I know that you have all the knowledge you need and that you are able to teach each other. [15]But I have written to you very openly about some things I wanted you to remember. I did this because God gave me this special gift: [16]to be a minister of Christ Jesus to those who are not Jews. I served God by teaching his Good News, so that the non-Jewish people could be an offering that God would accept—an offering made holy by the Holy Spirit.

[17]So I am proud of what I have done for God in Christ Jesus. [18]I will not talk about anything except what Christ has done through me in leading those who are not Jews to obey God. They have obeyed God because of what I have said and done, [19]because of the power of miracles and the great things they saw, and because of the power of the Holy Spirit. I preached the Good News from Jerusalem all the way around to Illyricum, and so I have finished that part of my work. [20]I always want to preach the Good News in places where people have never heard of Christ, because I do not want to build on the work someone else has already started. [21]But it is written in the Scriptures:

"Those who were not told about him
will see,
and those who have not heard
about him will understand."
Isaiah 52:15

Paul's Plan to Visit Rome

[22]This is the reason I was stopped many times from coming to you. [23]Now I have finished my work here. Since for many years I have wanted to come to you, [24]I hope to visit you on my way to Spain. After I enjoy being with you for a while, I hope you can help me on my trip. [25]Now I am going to Jerusalem to help God's people. [26]The believers in Macedonia and Southern Greece were happy to give their money to help the poor among God's people at Jerusalem. [27]They were happy to do this, and really they owe it to them. These who are not Jews have shared in the Jews' spiritual blessings, so they should use their material possessions to help the Jews. [28]After I am sure the poor in Jerusalem get the money that has been given for them, I will leave for Spain and stop and visit you. [29]I know that when I come to you I will bring Christ's full blessing.

[30]Brothers and sisters, I beg you to help me in my work by praying to God for me. Do this because of our Lord Jesus and the love that the Holy Spirit gives us. [31]Pray that I will be saved from the nonbelievers in Judea and that this help I bring to Jerusalem will please God's people there. [32]Then, if God wants me to, I will come to you with joy, and together you and I will have a time of rest. [33]The God who gives peace be with you all. Amen.

Greetings to the Christians

16 I recommend to you our sister Phoebe, who is a helper[n] in the church in Cenchrea. [2]I ask you to accept her in the Lord in the way God's people should. Help her with anything she needs, because she has helped me and many other people also.

[3]Give my greetings to Priscilla and Aquila, who work together with me in Christ Jesus [4]and who risked their own lives to save my life. I am thankful to them, and all the non-Jewish churches are thankful as well. [5]Also, greet for me the church that meets at their house.

15:12 Jesse Jesse was the father of David, king of Israel. Jesus was from their family. **16:1 helper** Literally, "deaconess." This might mean the same as one of the special women helpers in 1 Timothy 3:11.

Romans 16:17–20

There will always be those who seem to thrive on stirring up trouble, but that's nothing new. Maybe you've encountered people who seem bent on spreading gossip, cutting people down, or promoting themselves. What type of God-honoring mindset can you develop to help you lovingly and effectively counter such harmful attitudes?

Paul was concerned about the exact same issue. He knew that even in the church there were people who had a knack for causing conflict. And it involved more than just hurt feelings. In some cases, all the fighting and false teaching was shaking people's faith. Some people weren't sure how to handle the division.

So Paul gave some advice along with a warning: become wise about good things, and be innocent about evil. In other words, get your heart rooted in truth, love, grace, and faithfulness, and don't leave any room for hatred, jealousy, anger, or bitterness. If we can keep the right heart attitudes, we'll never cause trouble or tear down each other's faith. Plus, our love and unity won't be broken when other people try to stir up fights! So focus on becoming wiser about good things instead of listening to troublemakers. Be an example of Christ's love by spreading unity and peace.

Greetings to my dear friend Epenetus, who was the first person in Asia to follow Christ. [6]Greetings to Mary, who worked very hard for you. [7]Greetings to Andronicus and Junia, my relatives, who were in prison with me. They are very important apostles. They were believers in Christ before I was. [8]Greetings to Ampliatus, my dear friend in the Lord. [9]Greetings to Urbanus, a worker together with me for Christ. And greetings to my dear friend Stachys. [10]Greetings to Apelles, who was tested and proved that he truly loves Christ. Greetings to all those who are in the family of Aristobulus. [11]Greetings to Herodion, my fellow citizen. Greetings to all those in the family of Narcissus who belong to the Lord. [12]Greetings to Tryphena and Tryphosa, women who work very hard for the Lord. Greetings to my dear friend Persis, who also has worked very hard for the Lord. [13]Greetings to Rufus, who is a special person in the Lord, and to his mother, who has been like a mother to me also. [14]Greetings to Asyncritus, Phlegon, Hermes, Patrobas, Hermas, and all the brothers and sisters who are with them. [15]Greetings to Philologus and Julia, Nereus and his sister, and Olympas, and to all God's people with them. [16]Greet each other with a holy kiss. All of Christ's churches send greetings to you.

[17]Brothers and sisters, I ask you to look out for those who cause people to be against each other and who upset other people's faith. They are against the true teaching you learned, so stay away from them. [18]Such people are not serving our Lord Christ but are only doing what pleases themselves. They use fancy talk and fine words to fool the minds of those who do not know about evil. [19]All the believers have heard that you obey, so I am very happy because of you. But I want you to be wise in what is good and innocent in what is evil.

[20]The God who brings peace will soon defeat Satan and give you power over him.

The grace of our Lord Jesus be with you.

[21]Timothy, a worker together with me, sends greetings, as well as Lucius, Jason, and Sosipater, my relatives.

[22]I am Tertius, and I am writing this letter from Paul. I send greetings to you in the Lord.

[23]Gaius is letting me and the whole church here use his home. He also sends greetings to you, as do Erastus, the city treasurer, and our brother Quartus. [[24]The grace of our Lord Jesus Christ be with all of you. Amen.][n]

[25]Glory to God who can make you strong in faith by the Good News that I tell people and by the message about Jesus Christ. The message about Christ is the secret that was hidden for long ages past but is now made known. [26]It has been made clear through the writings of the prophets. And by the command of the eternal God it is made known to all nations that they might believe and obey.

[27]To the only wise God be glory forever through Jesus Christ! Amen.

16:24 The . . . Amen. Some Greek copies do not contain the bracketed text.

The Good News Defined

Ever wonder what Christianity's really about? Romans sums it up perfectly.

Here's the breakdown: We're all sinners. We're hopeless on our own (Romans 3:23). Because of sin, we deserve death. Through Jesus Christ and his life, sacrifice, and resurrection, we are made right with God. He offers eternal life with him. It's an undeserved gift, showing us God's mercy, love, grace, and compassion, as well as his complete purity and justice (Romans 6:23).

How does it work, then? If we deserve death and God is just, how can he give us eternal life? Before Jesus came, sacrifices were required to make people pure in God's eyes. When Jesus lived a perfect life and died on the cross, he became the ultimate, perfect sacrifice for our sins (Romans 5:8). No other sacrifice will ever be needed.

The only way to receive this unbelievably generous gift of God's grace is through faith . . . trusting completely in Jesus Christ's payment for your sins. When you do that, Jesus' righteousness and perfection covers you. You become pure in God's eyes, and you can actually have a relationship with him! As you grow closer to God, you'll truly become freer from sin and start to look more like Jesus as you become set apart from the world.

Romans makes it clear that life is about knowing Jesus. We don't have to look for answers in the world—it's all right here in God's Word. Paul tells us why we really need Jesus, explains salvation, describes Christian living, and shares the hope we have in Christ (Romans 15:13). What a reason to celebrate and live confidently in the truth!

Get Real

What role does the Law play in our salvation? (Romans 3:19–21)

How do we know that salvation from sin through Jesus Christ was always the plan? (Isaiah 52:13—53:12; Joel 2:32)

What does it mean to you that life is now defined by the Cross, keeping in mind that believers in the Old Testament were waiting for Jesus to come? (1 Corinthians 1:18; 2:2)

How has Jesus changed your life? (Luke 9:23; Romans 6:6; 7:14—8:16)

1 corinthians

If you've ever found yourself in the uncomfortable position of confronting a close friend about serious sin in her life, you can sympathize with what Paul must have been feeling as he wrote this difficult letter to the Corinthian church. Even after all the time he'd invested in them, sin and confusion had somehow crept in.

Corinth was a big city with a reputation for immorality, and the Corinthian believers found themselves struggling to maintain their purity and commitment to God in the surrounding chaos.

Although his tone is strong, Paul carefully includes kind encouragement along with the rebukes. He starts out by saying how thankful he is for the Corinthians before firing off a series of instructions aimed at correcting their specific problems. First Corinthians is a great study about our need for the Holy Spirit's illumination as we study Scripture, the importance of purity in the church, the true nature of love, and the proper use of spiritual gifts—info that is just as relevant for the church today.

Sometimes, the most loving thing you can do is be straight with people about sin. Instead of judging people, lovingly draw them into the joy of serving God purely and faithfully. It's an important aspect of being useful members of Christ's body!

1 From Paul. God called me to be an apostle of Christ Jesus because that is what God wanted. Also from Sosthenes, our brother in Christ.

[2]To the church of God in Corinth, to you who have been made holy in Christ Jesus. You were called to be God's holy people with all people everywhere who pray in the name of the Lord Jesus Christ—their Lord and ours:

[3]Grace and peace to you from God our Father and the Lord Jesus Christ.

Paul Gives Thanks to God

[4]I always thank my God for you because of the grace God has given you in Christ Jesus. [5]I thank God because in Christ you have been made rich in every way, in all your speaking and in all your knowledge. [6]Just as our witness about Christ has been guaranteed to you, [7]so you have every gift from God while you wait for our Lord Jesus Christ to come again. [8]Jesus will keep you strong until the end so that there will be no wrong in you on the day our Lord Jesus Christ comes again. [9]God, who has called you into fellowship with his Son, Jesus Christ our Lord, is faithful.

Problems in the Church

[10]I beg you, brothers and sisters, by the name of our Lord Jesus Christ that all of you agree with each other and not be split into groups. I beg that you be completely joined together by having the same kind of thinking and the same purpose. [11]My brothers and sisters, some people from Chloe's family have told me quite plainly that there are quarrels among you. [12]This is what I mean: One of you says, "I follow Paul"; another says, "I follow Apollos"; another says, "I follow Peter"; and another says, "I follow Christ." [13]Christ has been divided up into different groups! Did Paul die on the cross for you? No! Were you baptized in the name of Paul? No! [14]I thank God I did not baptize any of you except Crispus and Gaius [15]so that now no one can say you were baptized

1 Corinthians 1:20–29

You've got to love it when an underdog comes out on top. Who wouldn't love a story where the humble, overlooked assistant works hard, proves her talent, and becomes a confident, savvy leader in her industry? Or how about when the persistent guy with no visible athletic ability overcomes the odds and scores the winning touchdown in the big game? There's just something satisfying about those stories.

In the world's eyes, Jesus wasn't exactly hero material. He was a poor carpenter and died a criminal's death on a cross. Not a likely candidate to become the Savior of the world, right? The world's idea of a hero is an amazing warrior with superpowers, and an extremely wealthy secret identity. But when God came to earth to save us from the worst enemy of all—our own sin—he came as a humble teacher with a servant's heart.

That's the model for Christians to follow. God loves to use normal, everyday people to bring glory to himself. If you feel like an underdog, that's more than okay . . . you're just the kind of woman God can use to do amazing things. Let God's life-changing power work in and through you!

in my name. [16](I also baptized the family of Stephanas, but I do not remember that I baptized anyone else.) [17]Christ did not send me to baptize people but to preach the Good News. And he sent me to preach the Good News without using words of human wisdom so that the cross[n] of Christ would not lose its power.

Christ Is God's Power and Wisdom

[18]The teaching about the cross is foolishness to those who are being lost, but to us who are being saved it is the power of God. [19]It is written in the Scriptures:

"I will cause the wise to lose their
wisdom;
I will make the wise unable to
understand." *Isaiah 29:14*

[20]Where is the wise person? Where is the educated person? Where is the skilled talker of this world? God has made the wisdom of the world foolish. [21]In the wisdom of God the world did not know God through its own wisdom. So God chose to use the message that sounds foolish to save those who believe. [22]The Jews ask for miracles, and the Greeks want wisdom. [23]But we preach a crucified Christ. This causes the Jews to stumble and is foolishness to non-Jews. [24]But Christ is the power of God and the wisdom of God to those people God has called—Jews and Greeks. [25]Even the foolishness of God is wiser than human wisdom, and the weakness of God is stronger than human strength.

[26]Brothers and sisters, look at what you were when God called you. Not many of you were wise in the way the world judges wisdom. Not many of you had great influence. Not many of you came from important families. [27]But God chose the foolish things of the world to shame the wise, and he chose the weak things of the world to shame the strong. [28]He chose what the world thinks is unimportant and what the world looks down on and thinks is nothing in order to destroy what the world thinks is important. [29]God did this so that no one can brag in his presence. [30]Because of God you are in Christ Jesus, who has become for us wisdom from God. In Christ we are put right with God, and have been made holy, and have been set free from sin. [31]So, as the Scripture says, "If people want to brag, they should brag only about the Lord."[n]

The Message of Christ's Death

2 Dear brothers and sisters, when I came to you, I did not come preaching God's secret[n] with fancy words or a show of human wisdom. [2]I decided that while I was with you I would forget about everything except Jesus Christ and his death on the cross. [3]So when I came to you, I was weak and fearful and trembling. [4]My teaching and preaching were not with words of human wisdom that persuade people but with proof of the power that the Spirit gives. [5]This was so that your faith would be in God's power and not in human wisdom.

God's Wisdom

[6]However, I speak a wisdom to those who are mature. But this wisdom is not from this world or from the rulers of this world, who are losing their power. [7]I speak God's secret wisdom, which he has kept hidden. Before the world began, God planned this wisdom for our glory. [8]None of the rulers of this world understood it. If they had, they would not have crucified the Lord of glory. [9]But as it is written in the Scriptures:

"No one has ever seen this,
and no one has ever heard about
it.

1:17 cross Paul uses the cross as a picture of the Good News, the story of Christ's death and rising from the dead for people's sins. The cross, or Christ's death, was God's way to save people. **1:31 "If . . . Lord."** Quotation from Jeremiah 9:24. **2:1 God's secret** Some Greek copies read "God's message."

Women & Men of the BIBLE

Ruth: Trusting God

You never know when love will come. That was certainly the case for Ruth. She was a widow living in a foreign land working hard to provide food and shelter for her mother-in-law and herself. She had trusted the God of Israel as her own Savior, and now she was trusting him to care for her every need. Boaz had already noticed Ruth's dedication and character, so when he found out he was a relative who was supposed to take care of her, he gladly made her his wife! (Ruth 1–4)

No one has ever imagined
what God has prepared for those
who love him." *Isaiah 64:4*

[10]But God has shown us these things through the Spirit.

The Spirit searches out all things, even the deep secrets of God. [11]Who knows the thoughts that another person has? Only a person's spirit that lives within him knows his thoughts. It is the same with God. No one knows the thoughts of God except the Spirit of God. [12]Now we did not receive the spirit of the world, but we received the Spirit that is from God so that we can know all that God has given us. [13]And we speak about these things, not with words taught us by human wisdom but with words taught us by the Spirit. And so we explain spiritual truths to spiritual people. [14]A person who does not have the Spirit does not accept the truths that come from the Spirit of God. That person thinks they are foolish and cannot understand them, because they can only be judged to be true by the Spirit. [15]The spiritual person is able to judge all things, but no one can judge him. The Scripture says:

[16]"Who has known the mind of the
Lord?
Who has been able to teach him?"
Isaiah 40:13

But we have the mind of Christ.

Following People Is Wrong

3 Brothers and sisters, in the past I could not talk to you as I talk to spiritual people. I had to talk to you as I would to people without the Spirit—babies in Christ. [2]The teaching I gave you was like milk, not solid food, because you were not able to take solid food. And even now you are not ready. [3]You are still not spiritual, because there is jealousy and quarreling among you, and this shows that you are not spiritual. You are acting like people of the world. [4]One of you says, "I belong to Paul," and another says, "I belong to Apollos." When you say things like this, you are acting like people of the world.

[5]Is Apollos important? No! Is Paul important? No! We are only servants of God who helped you believe. Each one of us did the work God gave us to do. [6]I planted the seed, and Apollos watered it. But God is the One who made it grow. [7]So the one who plants is not important, and the one who waters is not important. Only God, who makes things grow, is important. [8]The one who plants and the one who waters have the same purpose, and each will be rewarded for his own work. [9]We are God's workers, working together; you are like God's farm, God's house.

[10]Using the gift God gave me, I laid the foundation of that house like an expert builder. Others are building on that foundation, but all people should be careful how they build on it. [11]The foundation that has already been laid is Jesus Christ, and no one can lay down any other foundation. [12]But if people build on that foundation, using gold, silver, jewels, wood, grass, or straw, [13]their work will be clearly seen, because the Day of Judgment[n] will make it visible. That Day will appear with fire, and the fire will test everyone's work to show

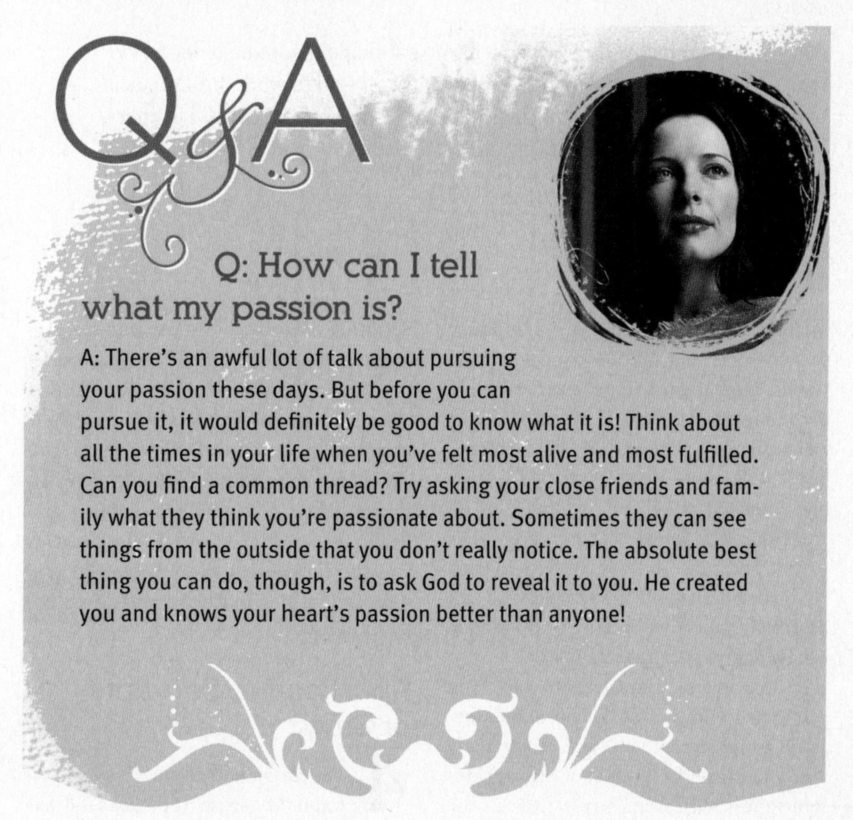

Q&A

Q: How can I tell what my passion is?

A: There's an awful lot of talk about pursuing your passion these days. But before you can pursue it, it would definitely be good to know what it is! Think about all the times in your life when you've felt most alive and most fulfilled. Can you find a common thread? Try asking your close friends and family what they think you're passionate about. Sometimes they can see things from the outside that you don't really notice. The absolute best thing you can do, though, is to ask God to reveal it to you. He created you and knows your heart's passion better than anyone!

3:13 Day of Judgment The day Christ will come to judge all people and take his people home to live with him.

1 Corinthians 3:5–7

You may know the heartbreak of spending years praying for an unsaved friend and never seeing them change. Or maybe you repeatedly share the Good News with a lost family member, but she never seems to embrace it. In your discouragement, you might end up wondering, *What am I doing wrong?*

But there's something extremely critical to remember: people don't save people—God saves people. God reveals himself to humans and leads them to understand his truth. And he uses individuals, like Apollos and Paul, to be his hands and feet that carry the message. For the Corinthians, Paul was the initial voice of the Good News message—that was like planting a seed. Apollos helped new believers take their first steps of growth—that was like watering the plant. But those men weren't responsible for creating the seed or causing the plant's growth; they planted and watered, and God used their efforts.

We're not responsible for evoking a particular response from someone we reach out to. We're called to be faithful and trust God to work through us in the ways he sees fit. We all have different roles to play. Be faithful in your role, whatever it is, and trust God with the results.

what sort of work it was. [14]If the building that has been put on the foundation still stands, the builder will get a reward. [15]But if the building is burned up, the builder will suffer loss. The builder will be saved, but it will be as one who escaped from a fire.

[16]Don't you know that you are God's temple and that God's Spirit lives in you? [17]If anyone destroys God's temple, God will destroy that person, because God's temple is holy and you are that temple.

[18]Do not fool yourselves. If you think you are wise in this world, you should become a fool so that you can become truly wise, [19]because the wisdom of this world is foolishness with God. It is written in the Scriptures, "He catches those who are wise in their own clever traps."[n] [20]It is also written in the Scriptures, "The Lord knows what wise people think. He knows their thoughts are just a puff of wind."[n] [21]So you should not brag about human leaders. All things belong to you: [22]Paul, Apollos, and Peter; the world, life, death, the present, and the future—all these belong to you. [23]And you belong to Christ, and Christ belongs to God.

Apostles Are Servants of Christ

4 People should think of us as servants of Christ, the ones God has trusted with his secrets. [2]Now in this way those who are trusted with something valuable must show they are worthy of that trust. [3]As for myself, I do not care if I am judged by you or by any human court. I do not even judge myself. [4]I know of no wrong I have done, but this does not make me right before the Lord. The Lord is the One who judges me. [5]So do not judge before the right time; wait until the Lord comes. He will bring to light things that are now hidden in darkness, and will make known the secret purposes of people's hearts. Then God will praise each one of them.

[6]Brothers and sisters, I have used Apollos and myself as examples so you could learn through us the meaning of the saying, "Follow only what is written in the Scriptures." Then you will not be more proud of one person than another. [7]Who says you are better than others? What do you have that was not given to you? And if it was given to you, why do you brag as if you did not receive it as a gift?

[8]You think you already have everything you need. You think you are rich. You think you have become kings without us. I wish you really were kings so we could be kings together with you. [9]But it seems to me that God has put us apostles in last place, like those sentenced to die. We are like a show for the whole world to see—angels and people. [10]We are fools for Christ's sake, but you are very wise in Christ. We are weak, but you are strong. You receive honor, but we are shamed. [11]Even to this very hour we do not have enough to eat or drink or to wear. We are often beaten, and we have no homes in which to live. [12]We work hard with our own hands for our food. When people curse us, we bless them. When they hurt us, we put up with it. [13]When they tell evil lies about us, we speak nice words about them. Even today, we are treated as though we were the garbage of the world—the filth of the earth.

[14]I am not trying to make you feel ashamed. I am writing this to give you a warning as my own dear children. [15]For though you may have ten thousand teachers in Christ, you do not have many fathers. Through the Good News I became your father in Christ Jesus, [16]so I beg you, please follow my example. [17]That is why I am sending to you Timothy, my son in the Lord. I love Timothy, and he is faithful.

3:19 "He . . . traps." Quotation from Job 5:13. **3:20 "The Lord . . . wind."** Quotation from Psalm 94:11.

He will help you remember my way of life in Christ Jesus, just as I teach it in all the churches everywhere.

[18]Some of you have become proud, thinking that I will not come to you again. [19]But I will come to you very soon if the Lord wishes. Then I will know what the proud ones do, not what they say, [20]because the kingdom of God is present not in talk but in power. [21]Which do you want: that I come to you with punishment or with love and gentleness?

Wickedness in the Church

5 It is actually being said that there is sexual sin among you. And it is a kind that does not happen even among people who do not know God. A man there has his father's wife. [2]And you are proud! You should have been filled with sadness so that the man who did this should be put out of your group. [3]I am not there with you in person, but I am with you in spirit. And I have already judged the man who did that sin as if I were really there. [4]When you meet together in the name of our Lord Jesus, and I meet with you in spirit with the power of our Lord Jesus, [5]then hand this man over to Satan. So his sinful self[n] will be destroyed, and his spirit will be saved on the day of the Lord.

[6]Your bragging is not good. You know the saying, "Just a little yeast makes the whole batch of dough rise." [7]Take out all the old yeast so that you will be a new batch of dough without yeast, which you really are. For Christ, our Passover lamb, has been sacrificed. [8]So let us celebrate this feast, but not with the bread that has the old yeast—the yeast of sin and wickedness. Let us celebrate this feast with the bread that has no yeast—the bread of goodness and truth.

[9]I wrote you in my earlier letter not to associate with those who sin sexually. [10]But I did not mean you should not associate with those of this world who sin sexually, or with the greedy, or robbers, or those who worship idols. To get away from them you would have to leave this world. [11]I am writing to tell you that you must not associate with those who call themselves believers in Christ but who sin sexually, or are greedy, or worship idols, or abuse others with words, or get drunk, or cheat people. Do not even eat with people like that.

[12-13]It is not my business to judge those who are not part of the church. God will judge them. But you must judge the people who are part of the church. The Scripture says, "You must get rid of the evil person among you."[n]

Judging Problems Among Christians

6 When you have something against another Christian, how can you bring yourself to go before judges who are not right with God? Why do you not let God's people decide who is right? [2]Surely you know that God's people will judge the world. So if you are to judge the world, are you not able to judge small cases as well? [3]You know that in the future we will judge angels, so surely we can judge the ordinary things of this life. [4]If you have ordinary cases that must be judged, are you going to appoint people as judges who mean nothing to the church? [5]I say this to shame you. Surely there is someone among you wise enough to judge a complaint between believers. [6]But now one believer goes to court against another believer—and you do this in front of unbelievers!

Wycliffe Bible Translators

It's so amazing how you can read your Bible many times over, and yet it still speaks to you every time. And if you have a question about how God feels about any certain subject, you can do some in-depth study and find the answer right there in the Scriptures! Unfortunately, not everyone around the world shares these privileges.

Astonishing numbers of people still don't have the Word of God in their own language. According to Wycliffe Bible Translators, more than 270 million people worldwide do not have access to the Bible in their native tongue. Wycliffe missionaries have the laborious task of learning a new language and then faithfully translating the Scriptures so others can enjoy the same transforming power that you do when you study *your* Bible.

Wycliffe has been around for more than seventy years, and so far they have been involved in more than six hundred translations. But there is still much work to be done. Next time you have a special time with God while reading his Word, consider supporting Wycliffe in their efforts to begin translating the Bible into every remaining language by 2025. Find out how to donate at www.wycliffe.org.

5:5 sinful self Literally, "flesh." This could also mean his body. **5:12–13 "You . . . you."** Quotation from Deuteronomy 17:7; 19:19; 22:21, 24; 24:7.

SCRIPTURE SHUFFLE: WHERE DOES IT LIVE?

Match these famous Bible passages with their locations in Scripture by drawing a line from the passage on the left to the appropriate Scripture reference on the right. You will use each reference only once.

1. "In the beginning God created the sky and the earth."
2. The Ten Commandments
3. "The Lord is my shepherd . . . "
4. The Good Wife
5. "Here I am. Send me!"
6. The Birth of Jesus
7. "But when the Holy Spirit comes to you, you will receive power."
8. The Lord's Prayer—"Our Father in heaven, may your name always be kept holy . . . "
9. "God loved the world so much that he gave his one and only Son . . . "
10. "We know that in everything God works for the good of those who love him."
11. "In the beginning there was the Word. The Word was with God, and the Word was God."
12. The Hall of Faith—"It was by faith that . . . "
13. "I am the Alpha and the Omega, the First and the Last, the Beginning and the End."

Luke 2

Psalm 23:1

John 3:16

Proverbs 31:10–31

Revelation 22:13

Romans 8:28

Acts 1:8

Genesis 1:1

John 1:1

Matthew 6:9–13

Isaiah 6:8

Exodus 20:3–17

Hebrews 11

Scoring:

If you made 6–13 correct matches, Word Up! You're familiar with God's Word and have obviously spent some time studying it. That's a total plus when you're in need of a little pick-me-up in life. You know just where to go to find the help and inspiration you need!

If you made 0–5 correct matches, Dive In! There are some amazing passages of Scripture just waiting to be read and cherished. You'll find all you need for life's journey right here in the Word of God! And the passages highlighted in this quiz are a great place to start if you need a little direction.

ANSWER KEY: 1 — Genesis 1:1; 2 — Exodus 20:3–17; 3 — Psalm 23:1; 4 — Proverbs 31:10–31; 5 — Isaiah 6:8; 6 — Luke 2; 7 — Acts 1:8; 8 — Matthew 6:9–13; 9 — John 3:16; 10 — Romans 8:28; 11 — John 1:1; 12 — Hebrews 11; 13 — Revelation 22:13

RELATIONSHIPS

Love Those Imperfections!

Of all the qualities we love about those we care about, most of us wouldn't rank their imperfections very high on the list. Adore your best friend's tardy streak? Mom's habit of worrying? Fido's doggy drool? Fortunately, habits that try our patience can also add character to the relationship . . . and to us. If you let him, God will use frustrating imperfections to raise your acceptance level of others. Romans 15:7 says, "Christ accepted you, so you should accept each other." Good reminder, especially since your inner circle of family and friends love you with all your quirks, too!

[7]The fact that you have lawsuits against each other shows that you are already defeated. Why not let yourselves be wronged? Why not let yourselves be cheated? [8]But you yourselves do wrong and cheat, and you do this to other believers!

[9-10]Surely you know that the people who do wrong will not inherit God's kingdom. Do not be fooled. Those who sin sexually, worship idols, take part in adultery, those who are male prostitutes, or men who have sexual relations with other men, those who steal, are greedy, get drunk, lie about others, or rob—these people will not inherit God's kingdom. [11]In the past, some of you were like that, but you were washed clean. You were made holy, and you were made right with God in the name of the Lord Jesus Christ and in the Spirit of our God.

Use Your Bodies for God's Glory

[12]"I am allowed to do all things," but not all things are good for me to do. "I am allowed to do all things," but I will not let anything make me its slave. [13]"Food is for the stomach, and the stomach for food," but God will destroy them both. The body is not for sexual sin but for the Lord, and the Lord is for the body. [14]By his power God has raised the Lord from the dead and will also raise us from the dead. [15]Surely you know that your bodies are parts of Christ himself. So I must never take the parts of Christ and join them to a prostitute! [16]It is written in the Scriptures, "The two will become one body."[n] So you should know that anyone who joins with a prostitute becomes one body with the prostitute. [17]But the one who joins with the Lord is one spirit with the Lord.

[18]So run away from sexual sin. Every other sin people do is outside their bodies, but those who sin sexually sin against their own bodies. [19]You should know that your body is a temple for the Holy Spirit who is in you. You have received the Holy Spirit from God. So you do not belong to yourselves, [20]because you were bought by God for a price. So honor God with your bodies.

About Marriage

7 Now I will discuss the things you wrote me about. It is good for a man not to have sexual relations with a woman. [2]But because sexual sin is a danger, each man should have his own wife, and each woman should have her own husband. [3]The husband should give his wife all that he owes her as his wife. And the wife should give her husband all that she owes him as her husband. [4]The wife does not have full rights over her own body; her husband shares them. And the husband does not have full rights over his own body; his wife shares them. [5]Do not refuse to give your bodies to each other, unless you both agree to stay away from sexual relations for a time so you can give your time to prayer. Then come together again so Satan cannot tempt you because of a lack of self-control. [6]I say this to give you permission to stay away from sexual relations for a time. It is not a command to do so. [7]I wish that everyone were like me, but each person has his own gift from God. One has one gift, another has another gift.

[8]Now for those who are not married and for the widows I say this: It is good for them to stay unmarried as I am. [9]But if they cannot control themselves, they should marry. It is better to marry than to burn with sexual desire.

[10]Now I give this command for the married people. (The command is not from me; it is from the Lord.) A wife should not leave her husband. [11]But if she does leave, she must not marry again, or she should make up with her husband. Also the husband should not divorce his wife.

[12]For all the others I say this (I am saying this, not the Lord): If a Christian man

6:16 "The two . . . body." Quotation from Genesis 2:24.

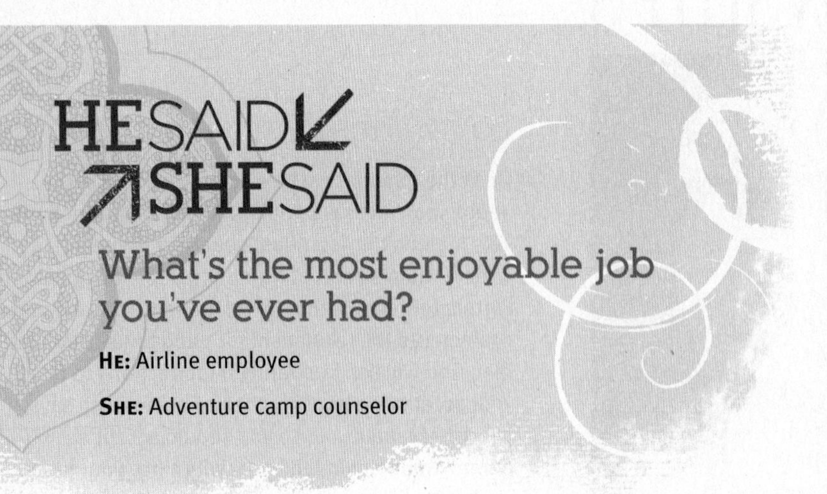

has a wife who is not a believer, and she is happy to live with him, he must not divorce her. [13]And if a Christian woman has a husband who is not a believer, and he is happy to live with her, she must not divorce him. [14]The husband who is not a believer is made holy through his believing wife. And the wife who is not a believer is made holy through her believing husband. If this were not true, your children would not be clean, but now your children are holy.

[15]But if those who are not believers decide to leave, let them leave. When this happens, the Christian man or woman is free. But God called us[n] to live in peace. [16]Wife, you don't know; maybe you will save your husband. And husband, you don't know; maybe you will save your wife.

Live as God Called You

[17]But in any case each one of you should continue to live the way God has given you to live—the way you were when God called you. This is a rule I make in all the churches. [18]If a man was already circumcised when he was called, he should not undo his circumcision. If a man was without circumcision when he was called, he should not be circumcised. [19]It is not important if a man is circumcised or not. The important thing is obeying God's commands. [20]Each one of you should stay the way you were when God called you. [21]If you were a slave when God called you, do not let that bother you. But if you can be free, then make good use of your freedom. [22]Those who were slaves when the Lord called them are free persons who belong to the Lord. In the same way, those who were free when they were called are now Christ's slaves. [23]You all were bought at a great price, so do not become slaves of people. [24]Brothers and sisters, each of you should stay as you were when you were called, and stay there with God.

Questions About Getting Married

[25]Now I write about people who are not married. I have no command from the Lord about this; I give my opinion. But I can be trusted, because the Lord has shown me mercy. [26]The present time is a time of trouble, so I think it is good for you to stay the way you are. [27]If you have a wife, do not try to become free from her. If you are not married, do not try to find a wife. [28]But if you decide to marry, you have not sinned. And if a girl who has never married decides to marry, she has not sinned. But those who marry will have trouble in this life, and I want you to be free from trouble.

[29]Brothers and sisters, this is what I mean: We do not have much time left. So starting now, those who have wives should live as if they had no wives. [30]Those who are crying should live as if they were not crying. Those who are happy should live as if they were not happy. Those who buy things should live as if they own nothing. [31]Those who use the things of the world should live as if they were not using them, because this world in its present form will soon be gone.

[32]I want you to be free from worry. A man who is not married is busy with the Lord's work, trying to please the Lord. [33]But a man who is married is busy with things of the world, trying to please his wife. [34]He must think about two things—pleasing his wife and pleasing the Lord. A woman who is not married or a girl

all about MEN

Take It to God First

"A quarreling [woman] is as bothersome as a continual dripping on a rainy day. Stopping her is like stopping the wind" (Proverbs 27:15–16). Ouch. God knows our womanly natures! We love offering opinions and pointing out areas for a guy to improve, which can sometimes fall into the dangerous habit of *nagging*. But what's a girl to do with an issue her guy either can't or won't see? Take it to God first. Pray and let your heavenly Father work on the man in the way he knows best. Many battles have been avoided (and won!) when entrusted to God's hands.

7:15 **us** Some Greek copies read "you."

who has never married is busy with the Lord's work. She wants to be holy in body and spirit. But a married woman is busy with things of the world, as to how she can please her husband. [35]I am saying this to help you, not to limit you. But I want you to live in the right way, to give yourselves fully to the Lord without concern for other things.

[36]If a man thinks he is not doing the right thing with the girl he is engaged to, if she is almost past the best age to marry and he feels he should marry her, he should do what he wants. They should get married. It is no sin. [37]But if a man is sure in his mind that there is no need for marriage, and has his own desires under control, and has decided not to marry the one to whom he is engaged, he is doing the right thing. [38]So the man who marries his girl does right, but the man who does not marry will do better.

[39]A woman must stay with her husband as long as he lives. But if her husband dies, she is free to marry any man she wants, but she must marry another believer. [40]The woman is happier if she does not marry again. This is my opinion, but I believe I also have God's Spirit.

About Food Offered to Idols

8 Now I will write about meat that is sacrificed to idols. We know that "we all have knowledge." Knowledge puffs you up with pride, but love builds up. [2]If you think you know something, you do not yet know anything as you should. [3]But if any person loves God, that person is known by God.

[4]So this is what I say about eating meat sacrificed to idols: We know that an idol is really nothing in the world, and we know there is only one God. [5]Even though there are things called gods, in heaven or on earth (and there are many "gods" and "lords"), [6]for us there is only one God—our Father. All things came from him, and we live for him. And there is only one Lord—Jesus Christ. All things were made through him, and we also were made through him.

[7]But not all people know this. Some people are still so used to idols that when they eat meat, they still think of it as being sacrificed to an idol. Because their conscience is weak, when they eat it, they feel guilty. [8]But food will not bring us closer to God. Refusing to eat does not make us less pleasing to God, and eating does not make us better in God's sight.

[9]But be careful that your freedom does not cause those who are weak in faith to fall into sin. [10]Suppose one of you who has knowledge eats in an idol's temple.[n] Someone who is weak in faith might see you eating there and be encouraged to eat meat sacrificed to idols while thinking it is wrong to do so. [11]This weak believer for whom Christ died is ruined because of your "knowledge." [12]When you sin against your brothers and sisters in Christ like this and cause them to do what they feel is wrong, you are also sinning against Christ. [13]So if the food I eat causes them to fall into sin, I will never eat meat again so that I will not cause any of them to sin.

Paul Is like the Other Apostles

9 I am a free man. I am an apostle. I have seen Jesus our Lord. You people are all an example of my work in the Lord. [2]If others do not accept me as an apostle, surely you do, because you are proof that I am an apostle in the Lord.

[3]This is the answer I give people who want to judge me: [4]Do we not have the right to eat and drink? [5]Do we not have the right to bring a believing wife with us when we travel as do the other apostles and the Lord's brothers and Peter? [6]Are Barnabas and I the only ones who must work to earn our living? [7]No soldier ever serves in the army and pays his own salary. No one ever plants a vineyard without eating some of the grapes. No person takes care of a flock without drinking some of the milk.

[8]I do not say this by human authority; God's law also says the same thing. [9]It is written in the law of Moses: "When an ox is working in the grain, do not cover its mouth to keep it from eating."[n] When God said this, was he thinking only about oxen? No. [10]He was really talking about us. Yes, that Scripture was written for us, because it goes on to say: "The one who plows and the one who works in the grain should hope to get some of the grain for their work." [11]Since we planted spiritual seed among you, is it too much if we should harvest material things? [12]If others have the right to get something from you, surely we have this right, too. But we do not use it. No, we put up with everything ourselves so that we will not keep anyone from believing the Good News of Christ. [13]Surely you know that those who work at the Temple get their food from the Temple, and those who serve at the altar get part of what is offered at the altar. [14]In the same way, the Lord has commanded that those who tell the Good News should get their living from this work.

Health
Be Proactive

Do you want to be well? It seems like an easy enough question to answer. Of course, we all want to be well. So when Jesus asks it of a man who had been sick for thirty-eight years (John 5:2–9), it seems a little strange. And yet Jesus wasn't taunting the man, but rather engaging him—getting him involved in the process of becoming whole. Regardless of the health issues you're facing, *you*—not your doctor—must play the primary role in your recovery or treatment. Doctors are human and even the best make mistakes or omit information. It's up to the patient to ask questions, do research, and seek other opinions. Don't be afraid to hurt your doctor's feelings. It is your body, and you're the one paying the bills. Don't wait for someone to drag you into the pool (5:7). Dive in!

8:10 idol's temple Building where a god is worshiped. **9:9 "When an ox . . . eating."** Quotation from Deuteronomy 25:4.

WORLDVIEWS

God and Science

Do you ever find yourself flipping through the channels on television and stopping on some sort of scientific show? Maybe the show uses known science to bust popular myths or explore strange weather patterns. Or maybe you're taken with shows about unusual animals from around the world. Well, odds are that if you watch a lot of scientific shows, you'll probably hear some references questioning the creation of the world.

With so much scientific research and so many facts, you may begin to wonder whether or not the idea of Creation—that God created everything—is really true. And it's good to question this carefully. Christianity claims to follow a God of truth. If the Bible was just a bunch of myths, then what would be the point in believing, much less living and dying for it? It's a question you can't afford to ignore . . . especially if you're serious about living for Jesus. We know the Bible is true and that God is the source of all truth, so he can handle all our questions.

Some of the greatest scientific minds in history (including Galileo, Descartes, and Newton) shared a profound belief in God. Instead of leading them to reject God, science constructed a strong conviction that God must be real. So you're in good company if you believe that God is our Creator! You don't have to see science as an enemy of faith. Rather, it can be another place to see and praise God's power and creativity.

Seek out the truth. You'll find that truth (God's truth) has a way of standing up to the most critical inspections. Truth will always come out on top—you don't have to fear that your faith is based on anything less than solid ground.

[15]But I have not used any of these rights. And I am not writing this now to get anything from you. I would rather die than to have my reason for bragging taken away. [16]Telling the Good News does not give me any reason for bragging. Telling the Good News is my duty—something I must do. And how terrible it will be for me if I do not tell the Good News. [17]If I preach because it is my own choice, I have a reward. But if I preach and it is not my choice to do so, I am only doing the duty that was given to me. [18]So what reward do I get? This is my reward: that when I tell the Good News I can offer it freely. I do not use my full rights in my work of preaching the Good News.

[19]I am free and belong to no one. But I make myself a slave to all people to win as many as I can. [20]To the Jews I became like a Jew to win the Jews. I myself am not ruled by the law. But to those who are ruled by the law I became like a person who is ruled by the law. I did this to win those who are ruled by the law. [21]To those who are without the law I became like a person who is without the law. I did this to win those people who are without the law. (But really, I am not without God's law—I am ruled by Christ's law.) [22]To those who are weak, I became weak so I could win the weak. I have become all things to all people so I could save some of them in any way possible. [23]I do all this because of the Good News and so I can share in its blessings.

[24]You know that in a race all the runners run, but only one gets the prize. So run to win! [25]All those who compete in the games use self-control so they can win a crown. That crown is an earthly thing that lasts only a short time, but our crown will never be destroyed. [26]So I do not run without a goal. I fight like a boxer who is hitting something—not just the air. [27]I treat my body hard and make it my slave so that I myself will not be disqualified after I have preached to others.

Warnings from Israel's Past

10 Brothers and sisters, I want you to know what happened to our ancestors who followed Moses. They were all under the cloud and all went through the sea. [2]They were all baptized as followers of Moses in the cloud and in the sea. [3]They all ate the same spiritual food, [4]and all drank the same spiritual drink.

They drank from that spiritual rock that followed them, and that rock was Christ. [5]But God was not pleased with most of them, so they died in the desert.

[6]And these things happened as examples for us, to stop us from wanting evil things as those people did. [7]Do not worship idols, as some of them did. Just as it is written in the Scriptures: "They sat down to eat and drink, and then they got up and sinned sexually."[n] [8]We must not take part in sexual sins, as some of them did. In one day twenty-three thousand of them died because of their sins. [9]We must not test Christ as some of them did; they were killed by snakes. [10]Do not complain as some of them did; they were killed by the angel that destroys.

[11]The things that happened to those people are examples. They were written down to teach us, because we live in a time when all these things of the past have reached their goal. [12]If you think you are strong, you should be careful not to fall. [13]The only temptation that has come to you is that which everyone has. But you can trust God, who will not permit you to be tempted more than you can stand. But when you are tempted, he will also give you a way to escape so that you will be able to stand it.

[14]So, my dear friends, run away from the worship of idols. [15]I am speaking to you as to reasonable people; judge for yourselves what I say. [16]We give thanks for the cup of blessing,[n] which is a sharing in the blood of Christ. And the bread that we break is a sharing in the body of Christ. [17]Because there is one loaf of bread, we who are many are one body, because we all share that one loaf.

[18]Think about the Israelites: Do not those who eat the sacrifices share in the altar? [19]I do not mean that the food sacrificed to an idol is important. I do not mean that an idol is anything at all. [20]But I say that what is sacrificed to idols is offered to demons, not to God. And I do not want you to share anything with demons. [21]You cannot drink the cup of the Lord and the cup of demons also. You cannot share in the Lord's table and the table of demons. [22]Are we trying to make the Lord jealous? We are not stronger than he is, are we?

How to Use Christian Freedom

[23]"We are allowed to do all things," but not all things are good for us to do. "We are allowed to do all things," but not all things help others grow stronger. [24]Do not look out only for yourselves. Look out for the good of others also.

[25]Eat any meat that is sold in the meat market. Do not ask questions about it. [26]You may eat it, "because the earth belongs to the Lord, and everything in it."[n]

[27]Those who are not believers may invite you to eat with them. If you want to go, eat anything that is put before you. Do not ask questions about it. [28]But if anyone says to you, "That food was offered to idols," do not eat it. Do not eat it because of that person who told you and because eating it might be thought to be wrong. [29]I don't mean you think it is wrong, but the other person might. But why, you ask,

Be Still & KNOW

Prayer Positions

Daniel knelt down to pray (Daniel 6:10). Paul said people should pray with their hands lifted up in a holy manner (1 Timothy 2:8). When Jesus was in the garden before his crucifixion, he literally fell to the ground to talk to his Father (Matthew 26:39). And when David was celebrating before the Lord, he all-out danced in the street (2 Samuel 6:14). So many different postures are represented in Scripture. Which one is right? Not surprisingly, *all* of them are right. The truth is, different circumstances call for different methods as you express the inner attitude of your heart!

LIFEISSUES

Haughty Pride, Healthy Pride

Pride gets a bad rap in the Bible . . . and rightly so. God strongly dislikes arrogance of any kind. But is it okay to feel good about our accomplishments? Sure! God loves seeing his people use the talents he gave them for his honor. But keep in mind that everything we do is possible only through God's power. When we're motivated by bringing him glory and loving others, sinful pride doesn't have any room to grow. Take joy in seeing him work through you and others, but steer clear of the temptation to take credit for his successes.

10:7 "They . . . sexually." Quotation from Exodus 32:6. **10:16 cup of blessing** The cup of the fruit of the vine that Christians thank God for and drink at the Lord's Supper. **10:26 "because . . . it"** Quotation from Psalms 24:1; 50:12; 89:11.

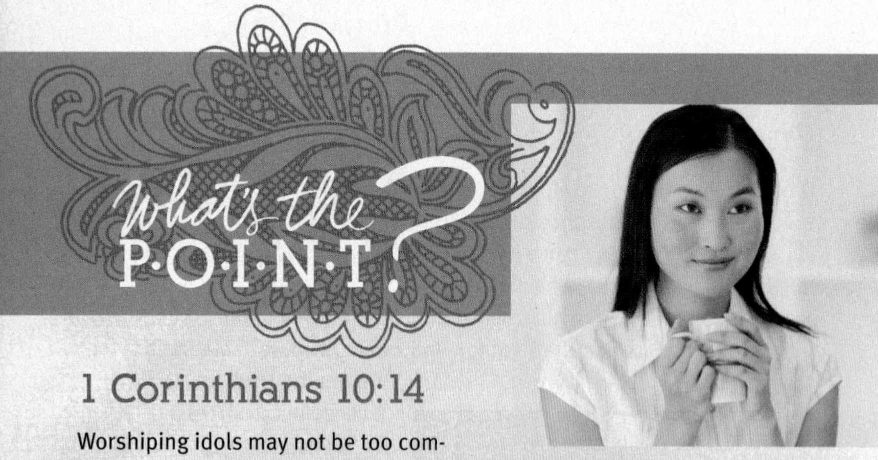

1 Corinthians 10:14

Worshiping idols may not be too common where you live. Or is it? Do you know anyone who seems absolutely consumed with the pursuit of success? Do you know anyone who obsesses over what others think of them? Many of us could be tempted to read 1 Corinthians 10:14 and think, *No problem here . . . I've got that command down!* But worshiping idols goes far beyond just bowing down to a statue.

Jesus always made it clear that sin starts in the heart. That's why he said hating someone is essentially just as bad as murder (Matthew 5:21–22)! It's the same with idol worship. You might not actually pray to a false god, but whenever you love anything more than you love Christ, you're worshiping an idol. It could be power, a job, your reputation, or whatever consumes the bulk of your time and energy. Giving your best to something smaller than God is downright foolish—but it happens all the time.

So God's command to "run away" from idol worship isn't a no-brainer; it's a tough standard! But be encouraged: God can help you. Each morning, tell him you want to put him first, and ask for the strength to follow through. Give him the best of your heart, and seek to love and desire him more than anything else.

should my freedom be judged by someone else's conscience? [30]If I eat the meal with thankfulness, why am I criticized because of something for which I thank God?

[31]The answer is, if you eat or drink, or if you do anything, do it all for the glory of God. [32]Never do anything that might hurt others—Jews, Greeks, or God's church—[33]just as I, also, try to please everybody in every way. I am not trying to do what is good for me but what is good for most people so they can be saved.

11 Follow my example, as I follow the example of Christ.

Being Under Authority

[2]I praise you because you remember me in everything, and you follow closely the teachings just as I gave them to you. [3]But I want you to understand this: The head of every man is Christ, the head of a woman is the man,[n] and the head of Christ is God. [4]Every man who prays or prophesies with his head covered brings shame to his head. [5]But every woman who prays or prophesies with her head uncovered brings shame to her head. She is the same as a woman who has her head shaved. [6]If a woman does not cover her head, she should have her hair cut off. But since it is shameful for a woman to cut off her hair or to shave her head, she should cover her head. [7]But a man should not cover his head, because he is the likeness and glory of God. But woman is man's glory. [8]Man did not come from woman, but woman came from man. [9]And man was not made for woman, but woman was made for man. [10]So that is why a woman should have a symbol of authority on her head, because of the angels.

[11]But in the Lord women are not independent of men, and men are not independent of women. [12]This is true because woman came from man, but also man is born from woman. But everything comes from God. [13]Decide this for yourselves: Is it right for a woman to pray to God with her head uncovered? [14]Even nature itself teaches you that wearing long hair is shameful for a man. [15]But long hair is a woman's glory. Long hair is given to her as a covering. [16]Some people may still want to argue about this, but I would add that neither we nor the churches of God have any other practice.

The Lord's Supper

[17]In the things I tell you now I do not praise you, because when you come together you do more harm than good. [18]First, I hear that when you meet together as a church you are divided, and I believe some of this. [19](It is necessary to have differences among you so that it may be clear which of you really have God's approval.) [20]When you come together, you are not really eating the Lord's Supper.[n] [21]This is because when you eat, each person eats without waiting for the others. Some people do not get enough to eat, while others have too much to drink. [22]You can eat and drink in your own homes! You seem to think God's church is not important, and you embarrass those who are poor. What should I tell you? Should I praise you? I do not praise you for doing this.

[23]The teaching I gave you is the same teaching I received from the Lord: On the night when the Lord Jesus was handed over to be killed, he took bread [24]and gave thanks for it. Then he broke the bread and said, "This is my body; it is[n] for you. Do this to remember me." [25]In the same way, after they ate, Jesus took the cup. He said, "This cup is the new agreement that is sealed with the blood of my death. When you drink this, do it to remember me." [26]Every time you eat this bread and drink this cup you are telling others about the Lord's death until he comes.

[27]So a person who eats the bread or drinks the cup of the Lord in a way that is not worthy of it will be guilty of sin-

11:3 the man This could also mean "her husband." **11:20 Lord's Supper** The meal Jesus told his followers to eat to remember him (Luke 22:14–20). **11:24 it is** Some Greek copies read "it is broken."

ning against the body and the blood of the Lord. [28]Look into your own hearts before you eat the bread and drink the cup, [29]because all who eat the bread and drink the cup without recognizing the body eat and drink judgment against themselves. [30]That is why many in your group are sick and weak, and some of you have died. [31]But if we judged ourselves in the right way, God would not judge us. [32]But when the Lord judges us, he disciplines us so that we will not be destroyed along with the world.

[33]So my brothers and sisters, when you come together to eat, wait for each other. [34]Anyone who is too hungry should eat at home so that in meeting together you will not bring God's judgment on yourselves. I will tell you what to do about the other things when I come.

Beautiful at Any Age

One glance in the mirror and you know you're not the young, teenage kid you once were. It's just a fact of life—every girl on the planet is getting older every day. Don't let it get you down, though. There's no need to fret because age can never diminish true beauty. First Peter 3:4 says that the beauty that comes from within you will never fade. A gentle and quiet spirit is precious to God, and it can never be destroyed. You can walk confidently through life at any age, knowing you are God's precious, beautiful treasure.

Gifts from the Holy Spirit

12 Now, brothers and sisters, I want you to understand about spiritual gifts. [2]You know the way you lived before you were believers. You let yourselves be influenced and led away to worship idols—things that could not speak. [3]So I want you to understand that no one who is speaking with the help of God's Spirit says, "Jesus be cursed." And no one can say, "Jesus is Lord," without the help of the Holy Spirit.

[4]There are different kinds of gifts, but they are all from the same Spirit. [5]There are different ways to serve but the same Lord to serve. [6]And there are different ways that God works through people but the same God. God works in all of us in everything we do. [7]Something from the Spirit can be seen in each person, for the common good. [8]The Spirit gives one person the ability to speak with wisdom, and the same Spirit gives another the ability to speak with knowledge. [9]The same Spirit gives faith to one person. And, to another, that one Spirit gives gifts of healing. [10]The Spirit gives to another person the power to do miracles, to another the ability to prophesy. And he gives to another the ability to know the difference between good and evil spirits. The Spirit gives one person the ability to speak in different kinds of languages[n] and to another the ability to interpret those languages. [11]One Spirit, the same Spirit, does all these things, and the Spirit decides what to give each person.

The Body of Christ Works Together

[12]A person's body is one thing, but it has many parts. Though there are many parts to a body, all those parts make only one body. Christ is like that also. [13]Some of us are Jews, and some are Greeks. Some of us are slaves, and some are free. But we were all baptized into one body through one Spirit. And we were all made to share in the one Spirit.

[14]The human body has many parts. [15]The foot might say, "Because I am not a hand, I am not part of the body." But saying this would not stop the foot from being a part of the body. [16]The ear might say, "Because I am not an eye, I am not part of the body." But saying this would not stop the ear from being a part of the body. [17]If the whole body were an eye, it would not be able to hear. If the whole body were an ear, it would not be able to smell. [18-19]If each part of the body were the same part, there would be no body. But truly God put all the parts, each one of them, in the body as he wanted them. [20]So then there are many parts, but only one body.

[21]The eye cannot say to the hand, "I don't need you!" And the head cannot say to the foot, "I don't need you!" [22]No! Those parts of the body that seem to be the weaker are really necessary. [23]And the parts of the body we think are less deserving are the parts to which we give the most honor. We give special respect to the parts we want to hide. [24]The more respectable parts of our body need no special care. But God put the body together and gave more honor to the parts that need it [25]so our body would not be divided. God wanted

fun facts

The average amount that a parent leaves under a child's pillow for a lost tooth is $1.78.

(Securian Dental)

12:10 languages This can also be translated "tongues."

RELATIONSHIPS

Sense-ational Relationships

Quick—name the five senses! Got them all? Sight, sound, smell, taste, and touch. At the risk of sensory overload, let's add a few more when it comes to relating to other people. In our relationships, a sense of adventure keeps things fresh, a sense of timing helps when broaching tough subjects, a sense of mercy helps forgive mistakes, and a sense of humor keeps us young. Then top those off with sensitivity to others' feelings to add a sense of sweetness to everything. Ask God to grow your extra senses, and you'll enjoy *sense*-ational new blessings in your relationships!

the different parts to care the same for each other. [26]If one part of the body suffers, all the other parts suffer with it. Or if one part of our body is honored, all the other parts share its honor.

[27]Together you are the body of Christ, and each one of you is a part of that body. [28]In the church God has given a place first to apostles, second to prophets, and third to teachers. Then God has given a place to those who do miracles, those who have gifts of healing, those who can help others, those who are able to govern, and those who can speak in different languages.[n] [29]Not all are apostles. Not all are prophets. Not all are teachers. Not all do miracles. [30]Not all have gifts of healing. Not all speak in different languages. Not all interpret those languages. [31]But you should truly want to have the greater gifts.

Love Is the Greatest Gift

And now I will show you the best way of all.

13 I may speak in different languages[n] of people or even angels. But if I do not have love, I am only a noisy bell or a crashing cymbal. [2]I may have the gift of prophecy. I may understand all the secret things of God and have all knowledge, and I may have faith so great I can move mountains. But even with all these things, if I do not have love, then I am nothing. [3]I may give away everything I have, and I may even give my body as an offering to be burned.[n] But I gain nothing if I do not have love.

[4]Love is patient and kind. Love is not jealous, it does not brag, and it is not proud. [5]Love is not rude, is not selfish, and does not get upset with others. Love does not count up wrongs that have been done. [6]Love takes no pleasure in evil but rejoices over the truth. [7]Love patiently accepts all things. It always trusts, always hopes, and always endures.

[8]Love never ends. There are gifts of prophecy, but they will be ended. There are gifts of speaking in different languages, but those gifts will stop. There is the gift of knowledge, but it will come to an end. [9]The reason is that our knowledge and our ability to prophesy are not perfect. [10]But when perfection comes, the things that are not perfect will end. [11]When I was a child, I talked like a child, I thought like a child, I reasoned like a child. When I became a man, I stopped those childish ways. [12]It is the same with us. Now we see a dim reflection, as if we were looking into a mirror, but then we shall see clearly. Now I know only a part, but then I will know fully, as God has known me. [13]So these three things continue forever: faith, hope, and love. And the greatest of these is love.

fun facts

In a recent survey, 81% of Americans described themselves as well informed about current events.

(Barna.org)

Desire Spiritual Gifts

14 You should seek after love, and you should truly want to have the spiritual gifts, especially the gift of prophecy. [2]I will explain why. Those who

12:28; 13:1 languages This can also be translated "tongues." **13:3 give . . . burned** Other Greek copies read "hand over my body in order that I may brag."

have the gift of speaking in different languages[n] are not speaking to people; they are speaking to God. No one understands them; they are speaking secret things through the Spirit. [3]But those who prophesy are speaking to people to give them strength, encouragement, and comfort. [4]The ones who speak in different languages are helping only themselves, but those who prophesy are helping the whole church. [5]I wish all of you had the gift of speaking in different kinds of languages, but more, I wish you would prophesy. Those who prophesy are greater than those who can only speak in different languages—unless someone is there who can explain what is said so that the whole church can be helped.

[6]Brothers and sisters, will it help you if I come to you speaking in different languages? No! It will help you only if I bring you a new truth or some new knowledge, or prophecy, or teaching. [7]It is the same as with lifeless things that make sounds—like a flute or a harp. If they do not make clear musical notes, you will not know what is being played. [8]And in a war, if the trumpet does not give a clear sound, who will prepare for battle? [9]It is the same with you. Unless you speak clearly with your tongue, no one can understand what you are saying. You will be talking into the air! [10]It may be true that there are all kinds of sounds in the world, and none is without meaning. [11]But unless I understand the meaning of what someone says to me, we will be like foreigners to each other. [12]It is the same with you. Since you want spiritual gifts very much, seek most of all to have the gifts that help the church grow stronger.

[13]The one who has the gift of speaking in a different language should pray for the gift to interpret what is spoken. [14]If I pray in a different language, my spirit is praying, but my mind does nothing. [15]So what should I do? I will pray with my spirit, but I will also pray with my mind. I will sing with my spirit, but I will also sing with my mind. [16]If you praise God with your spirit, those persons there without understanding cannot say amen[n] to your prayer of thanks, because they do not know what you are saying. [17]You may be thanking God in a good way, but the other person is not helped.

[18]I thank God that I speak in different kinds of languages more than all of you. [19]But in the church meetings I would rather speak five words I understand in order to teach others than thousands of words in a different language.

[20]Brothers and sisters, do not think like children. In evil things be like babies, but in your thinking you should be like adults. [21]It is written in the Scriptures:

"With people who use strange words
and foreign languages
I will speak to these people.
But even then they will not listen to
me," *Isaiah 28:11–12*

says the Lord.

[22]So the gift of speaking in different kinds of languages is a sign for those who do not believe, not for those who do believe. And prophecy is for people who believe, not for those who do not believe. [23]Suppose the whole church meets together and everyone speaks in different languages. If some people come in who do not understand or do not believe, they will say you are crazy. [24]But suppose everyone is prophesying and some people come in who do not believe or do not understand. If everyone is prophesying, their sin will be shown to them, and they will be judged by all that they hear. [25]The secret things in their hearts will be made known. So they will bow down and worship God saying, "Truly, God is with you."

Meetings Should Help the Church

[26]So, brothers and sisters, what should you do? When you meet together, one person has a song, and another has a teaching. Another has a new truth from God. Another speaks in a different language,[n] and another person interprets that language. The purpose of all these things should be to help the church grow strong. [27]When you meet together, if anyone speaks in a different language, it should be only two, or not more than three, who speak. They should speak one after the other, and someone should interpret. [28]But if there is no interpreter, then those who speak in a different language should be quiet in the church meeting. They should speak only to themselves and to God.

[29]Only two or three prophets should speak, and the others should judge what they say. [30]If a message from God comes to another person who is sitting, the first speaker should stop. [31]You can all prophesy one after the other. In this way all the people can be taught and encouraged. [32]The spirits of prophets are under the control of the prophets themselves. [33]God is not a God of confusion but a God of peace.

As is true in all the churches of God's people, [34]women should keep quiet in the church meetings. They are not allowed to speak, but they must yield to this rule as the law says. [35]If they want to learn something, they should ask their own husbands at home. It is shameful for a woman to speak in the church meeting. [36]Did God's teaching come from you? Or are you the only ones to whom it has come?

[37]Those who think they are prophets

HE SAID / SHE SAID

What amazes you most about God?

HE: All the details he puts into his creation

SHE: How big and beyond our understanding he really is

14:2, 26 languages This can also be translated "tongues." **14:16 amen** To say amen means to agree with the things that were said.

1 Corinthians 15:19–20

We all need some motivation in life. Bill payments and work projects have deadlines for a reason. But one of the best motivations is an exciting goal . . . like when you operate in all-out frugal mode for months so you can afford a vacation. Things you'd normally avoid become a joy when you realize they'll help you reach your goal.

What's your motivation for following Christ? While living this life, don't forget about our hope for the next life. That hope rests on Christ's resurrection. Without it, our religion is worthless, and our expectations of eternity with God are misplaced. But we know that the resurrection is real and our hope is sure!

Far from being selfishly motivated, a Christian's desire for heaven should be driven by deep love for Christ and a burning passion to be with him—something that will be fully realized in heaven. That beautiful hope should motivate us to act like Christ in this life, serving others constantly and pouring out love selflessly. In fact, people should look at your life and think, *She must be crazy! How can she live so unselfishly?* Your answer? You're not living for today—you're focused on eternity!

You can confidently live for Christ today because of the hope you have in his promises!

or spiritual persons should understand that what I am writing to you is the Lord's command. 38Those who ignore this will be ignored by God.[n]

39So my brothers and sisters, you should truly want to prophesy. But do not stop people from using the gift of speaking in different kinds of languages. 40But let everything be done in a right and orderly way.

The Good News About Christ

15 Now, brothers and sisters, I want you to remember the Good News I brought to you. You received this Good News and continue strong in it. 2And you are being saved by it if you continue believing what I told you. If you do not, then you believed for nothing.

3I passed on to you what I received, of which this was most important: that Christ died for our sins, as the Scriptures say; 4that he was buried and was raised to life on the third day as the Scriptures say; 5and that he was seen by Peter and then by the twelve apostles. 6After that, Jesus was seen by more than five hundred of the believers at the same time. Most of them are still living today, but some have died. 7Then he was seen by James and later by all the apostles. 8Last of all he was seen by me—as by a person not born at the normal time. 9All the other apostles are greater than I am. I am not even good enough to be called an apostle, because I persecuted the church of God. 10But God's grace has made me what I am, and his grace to me was not wasted. I worked harder than all the other apostles. (But it was not I really; it was God's grace that was with me.) 11So if I preached to you or the other apostles preached to you, we all preach the same thing, and this is what you believed.

We Will Be Raised from the Dead

12Now since we preached that Christ was raised from the dead, why do some of you say that people will not be raised from the dead? 13If no one is ever raised from the dead, then Christ has not been raised. 14And if Christ has not been raised, then our preaching is worth nothing, and your faith is worth nothing. 15And also, we are guilty of lying about God, because we testified of him that he raised Christ from the dead. But if people are not raised from the dead, then God never raised Christ. 16If the dead are not raised, Christ has not been raised either. 17And if Christ has not been raised, then your faith has nothing to it; you are still guilty of your sins. 18And those in Christ who have already died are lost. 19If our hope in Christ is for this life only, we should be pitied more than anyone else in the world.

20But Christ has truly been raised from the dead—the first one and proof that those who sleep in death will also be raised. 21Death has come because of what one man did, but the rising from death also comes because of one man. 22In Adam all of us die. In the same way, in Christ all of us will be made alive again. 23But everyone will be raised to life in the right order. Christ was first to be raised. When Christ comes again, those who belong to him will be raised to life, 24and then the end will come. At that time Christ will destroy all rulers, authorities, and powers, and he will hand over the kingdom to God the Father. 25Christ must rule until he puts all enemies under his control. 26The last enemy to be destroyed will be death. 27The Scripture says that God put all things under his control.[n] When it says "all things" are under him, it is clear this does not include God himself. God is the One who put ev-

14:38 Those . . . God. Some Greek copies read "Those who are ignorant of this will stay ignorant." **15:27 God put . . . control.** From Psalm 8:6.

erything under his control. [28]After everything has been put under the Son, then he will put himself under God, who had put all things under him. Then God will be the complete ruler over everything.

[29]If the dead are never raised, what will people do who are being baptized for the dead? If the dead are not raised at all, why are people being baptized for them?

[30]And what about us? Why do we put ourselves in danger every hour? [31]I die every day. That is true, brothers and sisters, just as it is true that I brag about you in Christ Jesus our Lord. [32]If I fought wild animals in Ephesus only with human hopes, I have gained nothing. If the dead are not raised, "Let us eat and drink, because tomorrow we will die."[n]

[33]Do not be fooled: "Bad friends will ruin good habits." [34]Come back to your right way of thinking and stop sinning. Some of you do not know God—I say this to shame you.

Q&A

Q: How can I know if it's God's voice I hear?

A: God will never say anything to you that opposes his written Word. If the "voice" you're hearing isn't in line with the Bible, it's not God's! Once you've established with certainty that what your heart hears is in tune with Scripture, check it out with wise, godly friends that you trust. Ask them to pray about it with you. Then take a look at your surrounding circumstances. Is everything falling into place as if by design? Finally, search deep within your heart. Is there a sense of peace and assurance? If all these areas are in sync, then there's a good chance you've heard from God.

What Kind of Body Will We Have?

[35]But someone may ask, "How are the dead raised? What kind of body will they have?" [36]Foolish person! When you sow a seed, it must die in the ground before it can live and grow. [37]And when you sow it, it does not have the same "body" it will have later. What you sow is only a bare seed, maybe wheat or something else. [38]But God gives it a body that he has planned for it, and God gives each kind of seed its own body. [39]All things made of flesh are not the same: People have one kind of flesh, animals have another, birds have another, and fish have another. [40]Also there are heavenly bodies and earthly bodies. But the beauty of the heavenly bodies is one kind, and the beauty of the earthly bodies is another. [41]The sun has one kind of beauty, the moon has another beauty, and the stars have another. And each star is different in its beauty.

[42]It is the same with the dead who are raised to life. The body that is "planted" will ruin and decay, but it is raised to a life that cannot be destroyed. [43]When the body is "planted," it is without honor, but it is raised in glory. When the body is "planted," it is weak, but when it is raised, it is powerful. [44]The body that is "planted" is a physical body. When it is raised, it is a spiritual body.

There is a physical body, and there is also a spiritual body. [45]It is written in the Scriptures: "The first man, Adam, became a living person."[n] But the last Adam became a spirit that gives life. [46]The spiritual did not come first, but the physical and then the spiritual. [47]The first man came from the dust of the earth. The second man came from heaven. [48]People who belong to the earth are like the first man of earth. But those people who belong to heaven are like the man of heaven. [49]Just as we were made like the man of earth, so we will[n] also be made like the man of heaven.

[50]I tell you this, brothers and sisters: Flesh and blood cannot have a part in the kingdom of God. Something that will ruin cannot have a part in something that never ruins. [51]But look! I tell you this secret: We will not all sleep in death, but we will all be changed. [52]It will take only a second—as quickly as an eye blinks—when the last trumpet sounds. The trumpet will sound, and those who have died will be raised to live forever, and we will all be changed. [53]This body that can be destroyed must clothe itself with something that can never be destroyed. And this body that

Nearly 1/3 of Americans have unhealthy cholesterol levels.

(*Glamour*)

15:32 "Let us . . . die." Quotation from Isaiah 22:13; 56:12. **15:45 "The first . . . person."** Quotation from Genesis 2:7. **15:49 so we will** Some Greek copies read "so let us."

Zacchaeus: Unexpected Personal Encounter

Zacchaeus was a very unlikely candidate to host a dinner party for Jesus. But transforming lives for unlikely candidates is one of Jesus' favorite things to do! With the crowds pressing in, short little Zacchaeus climbed a tree in order to get a better look. Imagine his surprise when Jesus walked right up to that tree and invited himself over for dinner! After meeting the Messiah, the tax collector's life was never the same. He repented of his sins and vowed to make amends for cheating his fellow citizens. His personal encounter with Jesus changed him forever! (Luke 19:1–10)

dies must clothe itself with something that can never die. [54]So this body that can be destroyed will clothe itself with that which can never be destroyed, and this body that dies will clothe itself with that which can never die. When this happens, this Scripture will be made true:

"Death is destroyed forever in
victory." *Isaiah 25:8*

[55]"Death, where is your victory?
Death, where is your pain?" *Hosea 13:14*

[56]Death's power to hurt is sin, and the power of sin is the law. [57]But we thank God! He gives us the victory through our Lord Jesus Christ.

[58]So my dear brothers and sisters, stand strong. Do not let anything move you. Always give yourselves fully to the work of the Lord, because you know that your work in the Lord is never wasted.

The Gift for Other Believers

16 Now I will write about the collection of money for God's people. Do the same thing I told the Galatian churches to do: [2]On the first day of every week, each one of you should put aside money as you have been blessed. Save it up so you will not have to collect money after I come. [3]When I arrive, I will send whomever you approve to take your gift to Jerusalem. I will send them with letters of introduction, [4]and if it seems good for me to go also, they will go along with me.

Paul's Plans

[5]I plan to go through Macedonia, so I will come to you after I go through there. [6]Perhaps I will stay with you for a time or even all winter. Then you can help me on my trip, wherever I go. [7]I do not want to see you now just in passing. I hope to stay a longer time with you if the Lord allows it. [8]But I will stay at Ephesus until Pentecost, [9]because a good opportunity for a great and growing work has been given to me now. And there are many people working against me.

[10]If Timothy comes to you, see to it that he has nothing to fear with you, because he is working for the Lord just as I am. [11]So none of you should treat Timothy as unimportant, but help him on his trip in peace so that he can come back to me. I am expecting him to come with the brothers.

[12]Now about our brother Apollos: I strongly encouraged him to visit you with the other brothers. He did not at all want to come now; he will come when he has the opportunity.

Paul Ends His Letter

[13]Be alert. Continue strong in the faith. Have courage, and be strong. [14]Do everything in love.

[15]You know that the family of Stephanas were the first believers in Southern Greece and that they have given themselves to the service of God's people. I ask you, brothers and sisters, [16]to follow the leading of people like these and anyone else who works and serves with them.

[17]I am happy that Stephanas, Fortunatus, and Achaicus have come. You are not here, but they have filled your place. [18]They have refreshed my spirit and yours. You should recognize the value of people like these.

[19]The churches in Asia send greetings to you. Aquila and Priscilla greet you in the Lord, as does the church that meets in their house. [20]All the brothers and sisters here send greetings. Give each other a holy kiss when you meet.

[21]I, Paul, am writing this greeting with my own hand.

[22]If anyone does not love the Lord, let him be separated from God—lost forever!

Come, O Lord!

[23]The grace of the Lord Jesus be with you.

[24]My love be with all of you in Christ Jesus.[n]

16:24 My . . . Jesus. Some Greek copies add "Amen."

the big picture 1 Corinthians

A Lesson on Unity and Diversity

Paul helped start the church at Corinth with his own blood, sweat, and tears. So when he learned of the people's quarreling, he responded promptly. Paul wrote 1 Corinthians to address divisions in the church, answer questions, and challenge some accusations.

Just like most of the New Testament letters, 1 Corinthians provides specific instruction for the church. It addresses specific cultural and societal issues in Corinth, yet there are countless eternal truths woven throughout the pages of this letter that God intended for us to hear, too. Paul presents some challenging teachings that are still debated today (like women's roles in church and spiritual gifts), but he also gives some of the clearest teachings about the things that matter most: true worship, freedom in Christ, pure living, and the supreme importance of love. Chapter 13 gives us the most complete definition of love ever written.

As his followers, God desires that we remain focused on Jesus and not let the little things divide us. He wants us unified in love, using our God-given gifts to build each other up and serve a hurting world around us. Most importantly, 1 Corinthians reminds us of the importance of Christ. Once we meet Jesus and give ourselves over to him completely, our lives are permanently transformed (take a look at Colossians 3). The past, present, future, and even our identity—everything!—pivots on Jesus' life, death, and resurrection. If we make him the priority, everything else falls into place.

Get Real

Why does the Cross keep coming up in Scripture? (Galatians 6:14; Ephesians 2:16; Colossians 2:13–15)

Why does God's wisdom seem so mysterious at times? (Isaiah 55:8–9)

Does God ever use women in powerful ways? (Judges 4—5; Esther 1—10; Romans 16:1–2; Galatians 3:28)

Why is love such a critical issue? (Matthew 22:36–40; 1 John 3:16–18)

Do you wrestle with knowing who you are and where you belong? (Ephesians 1:3–14)

How do you live *in* the world but not live *like* the world? (John 17:16–18; Romans 12:2)

2 corinthians

Imagine this: you pour vast amounts of time, energy, and love into someone, literally wearing yourself out for her benefit . . . and she repays you by rejecting your friendship and saying cruel things about you! If you've experienced even a mild version of this, you know that few things are more hurtful than betrayal.

Paul and the Corinthian church had quite a history. The Corinthian believers had slipped into serious sin, so Paul wrote a letter (1 Corinthians) to correct and encourage them. Since then, there had been a difficult visit and lots of hurt feelings. Some parts of the situation were improving, but the Corinthians had developed a skewed perception of Paul—they attacked his motives, made fun of him, and rejected his love.

In this letter, Paul carefully reminds the Corinthian believers about his God-given authority as a messenger of the Good News. And he consistently points to Christ as the unifying factor for all Christians.

Keep that in mind as you serve others and lovingly share the Good News with them. Even when your efforts are unappreciated and people respond with rejection, take a tip from Paul: continue to love and serve faithfully as you keep your eyes on Christ.

1 From Paul, an apostle of Christ Jesus. I am an apostle because that is what God wanted. Also from Timothy our brother in Christ.

To the church of God in Corinth, and to all of God's people everywhere in Southern Greece:

[2]Grace and peace to you from God our Father and the Lord Jesus Christ.

Paul Gives Thanks to God

[3]Praise be to the God and Father of our Lord Jesus Christ. God is the Father who is full of mercy and all comfort. [4]He comforts us every time we have trouble, so when others have trouble, we can comfort them with the same comfort God gives us. [5]We share in the many sufferings of Christ. In the same way, much comfort comes to us through Christ. [6]If we have troubles, it is for your comfort and salvation, and if we have comfort, you also have comfort. This helps you to accept patiently the same sufferings we have. [7]Our hope for you is strong, knowing that you share in our sufferings and also in the comfort we receive.

[8]Brothers and sisters, we want you to know about the trouble we suffered in Asia. We had great burdens there that were beyond our own strength. We even gave up hope of living. [9]Truly, in our own hearts we believed we would die. But this happened so we would not trust in ourselves but in God, who raises people from the dead. [10]God saved us from these great dangers of death, and he will continue to save us. We have put our hope in him, and he will save us again. [11]And you can help us with your prayers. Then many people will give thanks for us—that God blessed us because of their many prayers.

The Change in Paul's Plans

[12]This is what we are proud of, and I can say it with a clear conscience: In everything we have done in the world, and

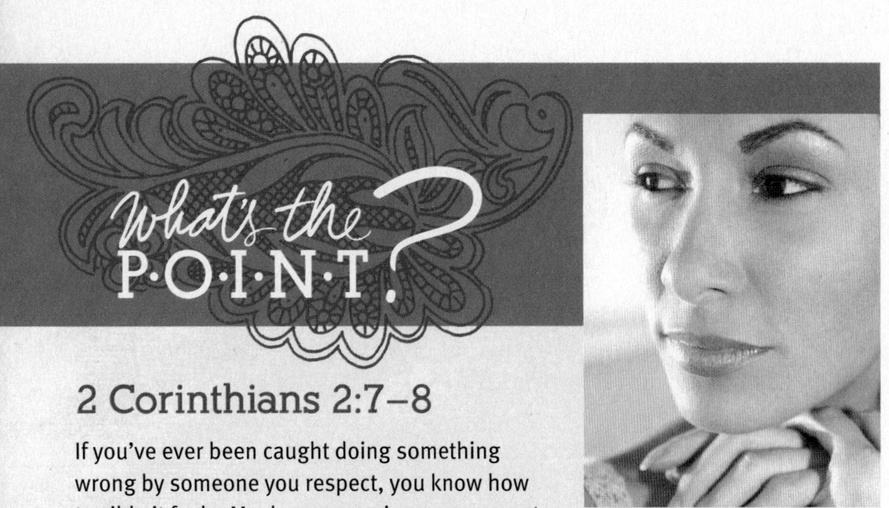

2 Corinthians 2:7–8

If you've ever been caught doing something wrong by someone you respect, you know how terrible it feels. Maybe a supervisor saw you cutting corners at work, a friend caught you being untruthful, or a spiritual mentor heard you laughing at something inappropriate or unkind. What's even worse than actually getting caught is the shame and embarrassment you feel afterward. Nothing's worse than knowing you've disappointed someone important to you.

That's when you really need a little bit of kindness or maybe a hug—something to convince you that you're still loved! When there's no forgiveness, it's likely you'll eventually want to just give up . . . it's too discouraging to feel like your mistake won't ever be erased.

That's why Paul told the Corinthians in this passage to forgive and comfort someone who'd been caught sinning. This person had learned his lesson, and now it was time to move on. Sin always causes pain, and only real forgiveness and love can heal the wounds.

Don't let sin ruin things. Sin is certainly a serious thing, and you shouldn't ever take it lightly. But the love and grace of God is so much stronger! Always remember how he completely erased all of your sin, and always aim to show that same sort of forgiveness to others.

especially with you, we have had an honest[n] and sincere heart from God. We did this by God's grace, not by the kind of wisdom the world has. [13-14]We write to you only what you can read and understand. And I hope that as you have understood some things about us, you may come to know everything about us. Then you can be proud of us, as we will be proud of you on the day our Lord Jesus Christ comes again.

[15]I was so sure of all this that I made plans to visit you first so you could be blessed twice. [16]I planned to visit you on my way to Macedonia and again on my way back. I wanted to get help from you for my trip to Judea. [17]Do you think that I made these plans without really meaning it? Or maybe you think I make plans as the world does, so that I say yes, yes and at the same time no, no.

[18]But since you can believe God, you can believe that what we tell you is never both yes and no. [19]The Son of God, Jesus Christ, that Silas and Timothy and I preached to you, was not yes and no. In Christ it has always been yes. [20]The yes to all of God's promises is in Christ, and through Christ we say yes to the glory of God. [21]Remember, God is the One who makes you and us strong in Christ. God made us his chosen people. [22]He put his mark on us to show that we are his, and he put his Spirit in our hearts to be a guarantee for all he has promised.

[23]I tell you this, and I ask God to be my witness that this is true: The reason I did not come back to Corinth was to keep you from being punished or hurt. [24]We are not trying to control your faith. You are strong in faith. But we are workers with you for your own joy.

2 So I decided that my next visit to you would not be another one to make you sad. [2]If I make you sad, who will make me glad? Only you can make me glad—particularly the person whom I made sad. [3]I wrote you a letter for this reason: that when I came to you I would not be made sad by the people who should make me happy. I felt sure of all of you, that you would share my joy. [4]When I wrote to you before, I was very troubled and unhappy in my heart, and I wrote with many tears. I did not write to make you sad, but to let you know how much I love you.

Forgive the Sinner

[5]Someone there among you has caused sadness, not to me, but to all of you. I mean he caused sadness to all in some way. (I do not want to make it sound worse than it really is.) [6]The punishment that most of you gave him is enough for him. [7]But now you should forgive him and comfort him

fun facts

Americans work almost 200 more hours each year than they did in 1970.

(*Psychology Today*)

1:12 honest Some Greek copies read "holy."

Do not be shaped by this world;
instead be changed within by
a new way of thinking.
july
Go for a walk, hike, or jog with a friend.
1
2
3
It's Independence Day. Enjoy the local parade!
4
5
Read Matthew 6:31–32. Thank God for his provision.
6
7
It's National Tennis Month. Meet a friend on the courts.
8
Fly a kite with kids in the neighborhood.
9
10
11
Make homemade, low-fat ice cream.
12
Put together a get-well basket for a sick friend.
13
14
It's Dental Awareness Day. Don't forget to brush.
15
16
Plan a game night with friends.
17
18
Need free wireless on the go? Check out www.jiwire.com
19
Don't forget to rehydrate. Drink lots of water!
20
Write a long letter to an old friend from elementary school.
21
It's Hammock Day. Enjoy an outdoor siesta.
22
23
Pray for a person of influence: it's Jennifer Lopez's birthday.
24
25
Host a BBQ and water balloon fight with friends.
26
Research your family tree.
27
It's National Blueberry Month! Bake some muffins from scratch.
28
Spend a Saturday at a water park with friends.
29
30
Take a dance lesson. Learn to salsa, waltz, or swing!
31
Then you will be able to decide
what God wants for you;
you will know what is good and pleasing
to him and what is perfect. —Romans 12:2

virtue BUILDING: Patience

In a world that worships instant gratification for every desire, patience is a rare quality. We *want* what we want, and we want it *now*. But patience is vital. It should be a deep-rooted way of life for Christians. As God-followers, we must realize that God is pleased when we patiently wait on him and have patience with other people, just as he is always patient with us (1 Timothy 1:16; 2 Peter 3:8–9).

Patience is the ability to endure anything . . . waiting for God, suffering through trials, resisting temptation, dealing with imperfect situations, and loving people who seem "unlovable."

Scripture Breakdown
Patience comes from the Holy Spirit working in your life (Galatians 5:22)—it certainly doesn't come naturally! Second Corinthians 6:6 says that we show we are servants of God through our patience (among other virtues). Ephesians 4:1–3, Colossians 3:12–17, 1 Timothy 6:11, 2 Timothy 3:10, and Revelation 13:10 clearly teach that patience is an important piece of the puzzle. The quality of patience is essential to living a life that pleases God.

Love requires patience, and hope and faith both include the idea of patiently waiting for God (Romans 12:12; James 5:11). Don't underestimate the importance of being patient!

Build It into Your Life
- Think about the relationship between impatience and other sins. Impatience can lead to cruel words and hurtful treatment of other people. If you wait patiently for God, you won't be easily tempted by the quick (but unfulfilling) satisfaction that sin offers.
- Is your patience stronger than your temper?
- Where do you get patience? (Romans 5:3; 15:5; James 1:3; 2 Peter 1:3–9)
- In what ways is patience an important part of love? Can you really love without having patience? (1 Corinthians 13:4–7)
- If you struggle with impatience, focus on the hope you have in Jesus: eternity in heaven (Romans 15:4; Hebrews 6:12; James 5:7–8). With that as your goal, it will be easier to take a patient approach to the frustrations of life.
- Pray for patience.

to keep him from having too much sadness and giving up completely. [8]So I beg you to show that you love him. [9]I wrote you to test you and to see if you obey in everything. [10]If you forgive someone, I also forgive him. And what I have forgiven—if I had anything to forgive—I forgave it for you, as if Christ were with me. [11]I did this so that Satan would not win anything from us, because we know very well what Satan's plans are.

Paul's Concern in Troas

[12]When I came to Troas to preach the Good News of Christ, the Lord gave me a good opportunity there. [13]But I had no peace, because I did not find my brother Titus. So I said good-bye to them at Troas and went to Macedonia.

Victory Through Christ

[14]But thanks be to God, who always leads us as captives in Christ's victory parade. God uses us to spread his knowledge everywhere like a sweet-smelling perfume. [15]Our offering to God is this: We are the sweet smell of Christ among those who are being saved and among those who are being lost. [16]To those who are lost, we are the smell of death that brings death, but to those who are being saved, we are the smell of life that brings life. So who is able to do this work? [17]We do not sell the word of God for a profit as many other people do. But in Christ we speak the truth before God, as messengers of God.

Servants of the New Agreement

3 Are we starting to brag about ourselves again? Do we need letters of introduction to you or from you, like some other people? [2]You yourselves are our letter, written on our hearts, known and read by everyone. [3]You show that you are a letter from Christ sent through us. This letter is not written with ink but with the Spirit of the living God. It is not written on stone tablets[n] but on human hearts.

[4]We can say this, because through Christ we feel certain before God. [5]We are not saying that we can do this work ourselves. It is God who makes us able to do all that we do. [6]He made us able to be servants of a new agreement from himself to his people. This new agreement is not a written law, but it is of the Spirit. The written law brings death, but the Spirit gives life.

[7]The law that brought death was written in words on stone. It came with God's glory, which made Moses' face so bright that the Israelites could not continue to look at it. But that glory later disappeared. [8]So surely the new way that brings the Spirit has even more glory. [9]If the law that judged people guilty of sin had glory, surely the new way that makes people right with God has much greater glory. [10]That old law had glory, but it really loses

3:3 stone tablets Meaning the Law of Moses that was written on stone tablets (Exodus 24:12; 25:16).

For Women Only
by Shaunti Feldhahn

Have you ever wondered what's going on inside of a guy's mind? Guys can be hard to decipher, but author Shaunti Feldhahn helps you break the code. This enlightening book covers the gamut of issues that perplex women—from why men need respect to why they are so driven to work. She explores topics such as why men care so much about what you look like and what they consider romantic. As you come to understand what men are thinking, you can use that eye-opening information to build closer relationships with your husband, boyfriend, brother, son, or any other man you love.

its glory when it is compared to the much greater glory of this new way. [11]If that law which disappeared came with glory, then this new way which continues forever has much greater glory.

[12]We have this hope, so we are very bold. [13]We are not like Moses, who put a covering over his face so the Israelites would not see it. The glory was disappearing, and Moses did not want them to see it end. [14]But their minds were closed, and even today that same covering hides the meaning when they read the old agreement. That covering is taken away only through Christ. [15]Even today, when they read the law of Moses, there is a covering over their minds. [16]But when a person changes and follows the Lord, that covering is taken away. [17]The Lord is the Spirit, and where the Spirit of the Lord is, there is freedom. [18]Our faces, then, are not covered. We all show the Lord's glory, and we are being changed to be like him. This change in us brings ever greater glory, which comes from the Lord, who is the Spirit.

Preaching the Good News

4 God, with his mercy, gave us this work to do, so we don't give up. [2]But we have turned away from secret and shameful ways. We use no trickery, and we do not change the teaching of God. We teach the truth plainly, showing everyone who we are. Then they can know in their hearts what kind of people we are in God's sight. [3]If the Good News that we preach is hidden, it is hidden only to those who are lost. [4]The devil who rules this world has blinded the minds of those who do not believe. They cannot see the light of the Good News—the Good News about the glory of Christ, who is exactly like God. [5]We do not preach about ourselves, but we preach that Jesus Christ is Lord and that we are your servants for Jesus. [6]God once said, "Let the light shine out of the darkness!" This is the same God who made his light shine in our hearts by letting us know the glory of God that is in the face of Christ.

Spiritual Treasure in Clay Jars

[7]We have this treasure from God, but we are like clay jars that hold the treasure. This shows that the great power is from God, not from us. [8]We have troubles all around us, but we are not defeated. We do not know what to do, but we do not give up the hope of living. [9]We are persecuted, but God does not leave us. We are hurt sometimes, but we are not destroyed. [10]We carry the death of Jesus in our own bodies so that the life of Jesus can also be seen in our bodies. [11]We are alive, but for Jesus we are always in danger of death so that the life of Jesus can be seen in our bodies that die. [12]So death is working in us, but life is working in you.

Glimpses of Eternity

Can you wrap your brain around the concept of eternity? Quite a challenge for our finite, here-and-now minds. We're so wired to run by the clock that the idea of forever often flies over our heads. Try this: in your mind, draw the longest line you can imagine. Haven't reached the end? Keep going . . . and going! Eternity means that we'll *never* reach the end. And as if spending eternity with Jesus weren't enough, his followers will get to *worship* him endlessly—for all of eternity! The heights of worship here on earth can't compare to the joy of seeing Jesus in glory. Let that truth sink in, and worship him now for giving you glimpses of eternity today (Psalm 44:8; 1 Thessalonians 4:17).

2 Corinthians 5:18–19

There's probably no woman in the world who doesn't want peace in her life. But actually having it isn't as easy as wanting it! Whether you're talking about family relationships or the international balance of power, peace is very fragile. Sooner or later, someone makes a cruel remark, does something threatening, or pushes too hard—and peace is broken.

Sin breaks peace with God. When we choose to honor ourselves instead of him, we're essentially declaring war on our own King. Our actions prove that we don't respect, appreciate, or love him. But God still loves us, and he made it possible through Jesus for us to have peace with him.

The Bible is God's message of peace to us, his enemies. Even when we were waging war with him by living for ourselves and ignoring his authority, Jesus gave his life on the cross. By his death and resurrection, he defeated sin and death and paved the way for a new friendship between God and us.

If you think there's no way God would ever want to be your friend, think again. Even if you've spent your whole life apart from him, he's ready to accept you. Give him back his rightful place as King in your life, and make peace with him today.

[13]It is written in the Scriptures, "I believed, so I spoke."[n] Our faith is like this, too. We believe, and so we speak. [14]God raised the Lord Jesus from the dead, and we know that God will also raise us with Jesus. God will bring us together with you, and we will stand before him. [15]All these things are for you. And so the grace of God that is being given to more and more people will bring increasing thanks to God for his glory.

Living by Faith

[16]So we do not give up. Our physical body is becoming older and weaker, but our spirit inside us is made new every day. [17]We have small troubles for a while now, but they are helping us gain an eternal glory that is much greater than the troubles. [18]We set our eyes not on what we see but on what we cannot see. What we see will last only a short time, but what we cannot see will last forever.

5 We know that our body—the tent we live in here on earth—will be destroyed. But when that happens, God will have a house for us. It will not be a house made by human hands; instead, it will be a home in heaven that will last forever. [2]But now we groan in this tent. We want God to give us our heavenly home, [3]because it will clothe us so we will not be naked. [4]While we live in this body, we have burdens, and we groan. We do not want to be naked, but we want to be clothed with our heavenly home. Then this body that dies will be fully covered with life. [5]This is what God made us for, and he has given us the Spirit to be a guarantee for this new life.

[6]So we always have courage. We know that while we live in this body, we are away from the Lord. [7]We live by what we believe, not by what we can see. [8]So I say that we have courage. We really want to be away from this body and be at home with the Lord. [9]Our only goal is to please God whether we live here or there, [10]because we must all stand before Christ to be judged. Each of us will receive what we should get—good or bad—for the things we did in the earthly body.

Becoming Friends with God

[11]Since we know what it means to fear the Lord, we try to help people accept the truth about us. God knows what we really are, and I hope that in your hearts you know, too. [12]We are not trying to prove ourselves to you again, but we are telling you about ourselves so you will be proud

fun facts

The average American checks out 6.9 items from the library each year.

(American Library Association)

4:13 **"I . . . spoke."** Quotation from Psalm 116:10.

of us. Then you will have an answer for those who are proud about things that can be seen rather than what is in the heart. [13]If we are out of our minds, it is for God. If we have our right minds, it is for you. [14]The love of Christ controls us, because we know that One died for all, so all have died. [15]Christ died for all so that those who live would not continue to live for themselves. He died for them and was raised from the dead so that they would live for him.

[16]From this time on we do not think of anyone as the world does. In the past we thought of Christ as the world thinks, but we no longer think of him in that way. [17]If anyone belongs to Christ, there is a new creation. The old things have gone; everything is made new! [18]All this is from God. Through Christ, God made peace between us and himself, and God gave us the work of telling everyone about the peace we can have with him. [19]God was in Christ, making peace between the world and himself. In Christ, God did not hold the world guilty of its sins. And he gave us this message of peace. [20]So we have been sent to speak for Christ. It is as if God is calling to you through us. We speak for Christ when we beg you to be at peace with God. [21]Christ had no sin, but God made him become sin so that in Christ we could become right with God.

6 We are workers together with God, so we beg you: Do not let the grace that you received from God be for nothing. [2]God says,

"At the right time I heard your
prayers.
On the day of salvation I helped
you." *Isaiah 49:8*

I tell you that the "right time" is now, and the "day of salvation" is now.

[3]We do not want anyone to find fault with our work, so nothing we do will be a problem for anyone. [4]But in every way we show we are servants of God: in accepting many hard things, in troubles, in difficulties, and in great problems. [5]We are beaten and thrown into prison. We meet those who become upset with us and start riots. We work hard, and sometimes we get no sleep or food. [6]We show we are servants of God by our pure lives, our understanding, patience, and kindness, by the Holy Spirit, by true love, [7]by speaking the truth, and by God's power. We use our right living to defend ourselves against everything. [8]Some people honor us, but others blame us. Some people say evil things about us, but others say good things. Some people say we are liars, but we speak the truth. [9]We are not known, but we are well known. We seem to be dying, but we continue to live. We are punished, but we are not killed. [10]We have much sadness, but we are always rejoicing. We are poor, but we are making many people rich in faith. We have nothing, but really we have everything.

[11]We have spoken freely to you in Corinth and have opened our hearts to you. [12]Our feelings of love for you have not stopped, but you have stopped your feelings of love for us. [13]I speak to you as if you were my children. Do to us as we have done—open your hearts to us.

Warning About Non-Christians

[14]You are not the same as those who do not believe. So do not join yourselves to them. Good and bad do not belong together. Light and darkness cannot share together. [15]How can Christ and Belial, the devil, have any agreement? What can a believer have together with a nonbeliever? [16]The temple of God cannot have any agreement with idols, and we are the temple of the living God. As God said: "I

BECOME *Involved*

Teen Challenge

Contrary to the name, Teen Challenge is actually not just for "teens." But without a doubt, the "challenge" part is certainly correct. Breaking the addiction to illicit drugs is challenging to say the least. But for those teenagers, men, and women who work through the Teen Challenge program or participate at a resident facility, the task is not insurmountable.

One of the oldest and most successful treatment programs of its kind, Teen Challenge has helped countless individuals reclaim control of their lives. By combining biblical teaching with counselors and volunteers who genuinely care for participants, Teen Challenge is transforming lives all over the United States and beyond.

You can be a part of Teen Challenge by volunteering at one of their centers around the country. If the closest one to you seems too far, you can work with them to start one in your community. Aside from giving of your time, your financial resources are greatly appreciated, as well as your willingness to spread the word about Teen Challenge. You can find out more about volunteering and giving at www.teenchallengeusa.com. When you invest yourself in the recovery of someone's life, you will also be changed. You *can* make a difference!

will live with them and walk with them. And I will be their God, and they will be my people."[n]

[17]"Leave those people,
and be separate, says the Lord.
Touch nothing that is unclean,
and I will accept you."
Isaiah 52:11; Ezekiel 20:34, 41

[18]"I will be your father,
and you will be my sons and daughters,
says the Lord Almighty."
2 Samuel 7:14

7 Dear friends, we have these promises from God, so we should make ourselves pure—free from anything that makes body or soul unclean. We should try to become holy in the way we live, because we respect God.

Paul's Joy

[2]Open your hearts to us. We have not done wrong to anyone, we have not ruined the faith of anyone, and we have not cheated anyone. [3]I do not say this to blame you. I told you before that we love you so much we would live or die with you. [4]I feel very sure of you and am very proud of you. You give me much comfort, and in all of our troubles I have great joy.

[5]When we came into Macedonia, we had no rest. We found trouble all around us. We had fighting on the outside and fear on the inside. [6]But God, who comforts those who are troubled, comforted us when Titus came. [7]We were comforted, not only by his coming but also by the comfort you gave him. Titus told us about your wish to see me and that you are very sorry for what you did. He also told me about your great care for me, and when I heard this, I was much happier.

[8]Even if my letter made you sad, I am not sorry I wrote it. At first I was sorry, because it made you sad, but you were sad only for a short time. [9]Now I am happy, not because you were made sad, but because your sorrow made you change your lives. You became sad in the way God wanted you to, so you were not hurt by us in any way. [10]The kind of sorrow God wants makes people change their hearts and lives. This leads to salvation, and you cannot be sorry for that. But the kind of sorrow the world has brings death. [11]See what this sorrow—the sorrow God wanted you to have—has done to you: It has made you very serious. It made you want to restore yourselves. It made you angry and afraid. It made you want to see me. It made you care. It made you want to do the right thing. In every way you have regained your innocence. [12]I wrote that letter, not because of the one who did the wrong or because of the person who was hurt. I wrote the letter so you could see, before God, the great care you have for us. [13]That is why we were comforted.

Women & Men of the BIBLE

Priscilla: Tentmaker

Priscilla and her husband, Aquila, had just moved to Corinth when Paul arrived. They were tentmakers by trade just like Paul was, so they invited him to stay and work with them while he was in town. They became so close that when he left for Ephesus, they went with him. When Paul moved on from there, they stayed behind to help with the new church. They worked tirelessly among the people, making tents and making converts as they went. Their leadership in the congregation and devoted friendship with Paul left a lasting influence on the early church. (Acts 18)

Keep Asking!

There is a lot of power in persistent praying. If there's a particular person or situation you're lifting up in prayer, don't stop! Pray about it every single day. Talk to God about it as often as it comes to mind. Keep asking him about it until you get your answer. You won't be bugging him—you'll be obeying him. In Luke 18:1–8, Jesus tells a story about a persistent widow who kept on asking a judge for justice. Even though he didn't fear God, he finally gave in just so she wouldn't wear him out with her constant requests. How much faster will God, who always does what is right, answer his children who persistently and patiently ask him for an answer?

6:16 "I . . . people." Quotation from Leviticus 26:11–12; Jeremiah 32:38; Ezekiel 37:27.

Fear of Commitment

"He's afraid to commit." This common lament of girlfriends everywhere isn't just a guy thing. For women, fear of commitment is often tied to fear of intimacy, which is actually rooted in fear of rejection. (Did you get all that?) Basically, we're afraid he won't like us, so we don't get too close and, thus, remain uncommitted. The same scenario can play out in friendships, too. But if we never take the frightening step of sharing our hearts, we'll never know the joy of emotional intimacy with other believers. Committing to walk together in the faith is an important part of our spiritual growth. God created us for fellowship and intimacy with each other, so don't let fear hold you back!

Not only were we very comforted, we were even happier to see that Titus was so happy. All of you made him feel much better. [14]I bragged to Titus about you, and you showed that I was right. Everything we said to you was true, and you have proved that what we bragged about to Titus is true. [15]And his love for you is stronger when he remembers that you were all ready to obey. You welcomed him with respect and fear. [16]I am very happy that I can trust you fully.

Christian Giving

8 And now, brothers and sisters, we want you to know about the grace God gave the churches in Macedonia. [2]They have been tested by great troubles, and they are very poor. But they gave much because of their great joy. [3]I can tell you that they gave as much as they were able and even more than they could afford. No one told them to do it. [4]But they begged and pleaded with us to let them share in this service for God's people. [5]And they gave in a way we did not expect: They first gave themselves to the Lord and to us. This is what God wants. [6]So we asked Titus to help you finish this special work of grace since he is the one who started it. [7]You are rich in everything—in faith, in speaking, in knowledge, in truly wanting to help, and in the love you learned from us.[n] In the same way, be strong also in the grace of giving.

[8]I am not commanding you to give. But I want to see if your love is true by comparing you with others that really want to help. [9]You know the grace of our Lord Jesus Christ. You know that Christ was rich, but for you he became poor so that by his becoming poor you might become rich.

[10]This is what I think you should do: Last year you were the first to want to give, and you were the first who gave. [11]So now finish the work you started. Then your "doing" will be equal to your "wanting to do." Give from what you have. [12]If you want to give, your gift will be accepted. It will be judged by what you have, not by what you do not have. [13]We do not want you to have troubles while other people are at ease, but we want everything to be equal. [14]At this time you have plenty. What you have can help others who are in need. Then later, when they have plenty, they can help you when you are in need, and all will be equal. [15]As it is written in the Scriptures, "The person who gathered more did not have too much, nor did the person who gathered less have too little."[n]

Multitasking

It's a hot buzzword, and studies show that women's brains are designed for multitasking. (Yep, that's right. God made us better at it than men!) But is multitasking—focusing your conscious awareness on more than one task—effective and efficient? Polishing your toenails while watching TV? Definitely. There's not much at stake if you lose concentration. Eating lunch at your desk while answering e-mails? Sure, since eating requires little thought (a "no-brainer"). Driving while catching up on phone calls? No way! It's rude *and* dangerous. Both require alertness; you can't do them well at the same time. Even when tasks can be completed simultaneously, it's not always efficient if you lose momentum while your mind shifts focus. To avoid multitasker's remorse, consider the brainpower required—and what's at stake if you lose your concentration—before deciding if multitasking is the best choice.

8:7 in . . . us Some Greek copies read "in your love for us." **8:15 "The person . . . little."** Quotation from Exodus 16:18.

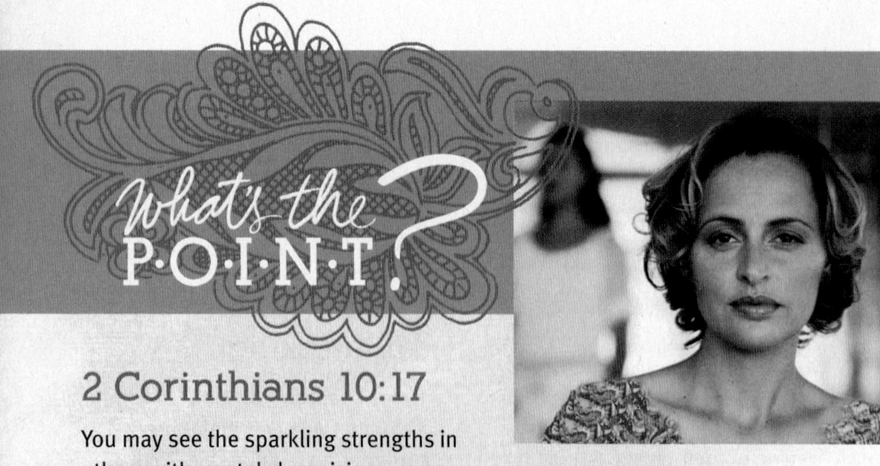

2 Corinthians 10:17

You may see the sparkling strengths in others with crystal clear vision—your sister's successful career, your best friend's striking beauty, or your co-worker's brilliance—but find yourself secretly wondering, *Where are my bragging rights? What have I got to show for myself?*

Paul's resume was impressive, but to him, all of it was like a pile of trash compared to knowing Christ. "The cross of our Lord Jesus Christ is my only reason for bragging," he said (Galatians 6:14). It makes sense . . . what's greater than a holy God lovingly saving sinners who disgrace him and deserve death? No, Paul wouldn't be caught dead glorying in himself.

So life's all about dwelling on God, not ourselves. No accomplishment, talent, wisdom, power, wealth, or even love of humans is bigger than who God is and what he's done. We should spend our energy showing that we know him and want to know him more.

God treasures people who know him deeply and whose lives reflect his justice, righteousness, and love (Jeremiah 9:24). Regardless of your own accomplishments, abilities, or attributes, always come back to valuing and relishing Jesus most. The biggest thing anyone could boast about is knowing the one true God!

Titus and His Companions Help

[16]I thank God because he gave Titus the same love for you that I have. [17]Titus accepted what we asked him to do. He wanted very much to go to you, and this was his own idea. [18]We are sending with him the brother who is praised by all the churches because of his service in preaching the Good News. [19]Also, this brother was chosen by the churches to go with us when we deliver this gift of money. We are doing this service to bring glory to the Lord and to show that we really want to help.

[20]We are being careful so that no one will criticize us for the way we are handling this large gift. [21]We are trying hard to do what the Lord accepts as right and also what people think is right.

[22]Also, we are sending with them our brother, who is always ready to help. He has proved this to us in many ways, and he wants to help even more now, because he has much faith in you.

[23]Now about Titus—he is my partner who is working with me to help you. And about the other brothers—they are sent from the churches, and they bring glory to Christ. [24]So show these men the proof of your love and the reason we are proud of you. Then all the churches can see it.

Help for Fellow Christians

9 I really do not need to write you about this help for God's people. [2]I know you want to help. I have been bragging about this to the people in Macedonia, telling them that you in Southern Greece have been ready to give since last year. And your desire to give has made most of them ready to give also. [3]But I am sending the brothers to you so that our bragging about you in this will not be empty words. I want you to be ready, as I said you would be. [4]If any of the people from Macedonia come with me and find that you are not ready, we will be ashamed that we were so sure of you. (And you will be ashamed, too!) [5]So I thought I should ask these brothers to go to you before we do. They will finish getting in order the generous gift you promised so it will be ready when we come. And it will be a generous gift—not one that you did not want to give.

[6]Remember this: The person who plants a little will have a small harvest, but the person who plants a lot will have a big harvest. [7]Each of you should give as you have decided in your heart to give. You should not be sad when you give, and you should not give because you feel forced to give. God loves the person who gives happily. [8]And God can give you more blessings than you need. Then you will always have plenty of everything—enough to give to every good work. [9]It is written in the Scriptures:

"He gives freely to the poor.
The things he does are right and will continue forever."

Psalm 112:9

[10]God is the One who gives seed to the farmer and bread for food. He will give you all the seed you need and make it grow so there will be a great harvest from your goodness. [11]He will make you rich in every way so that you can always give freely. And your giving through us will cause many to give thanks to God. [12]This service you do not only helps the needs of God's people, it also brings many more thanks to God. [13]It is a proof of your faith. Many people will praise God because you obey the Good News of Christ—the gospel you say you believe—and because you freely share with them and with all others. [14]And when they pray, they will wish they could be

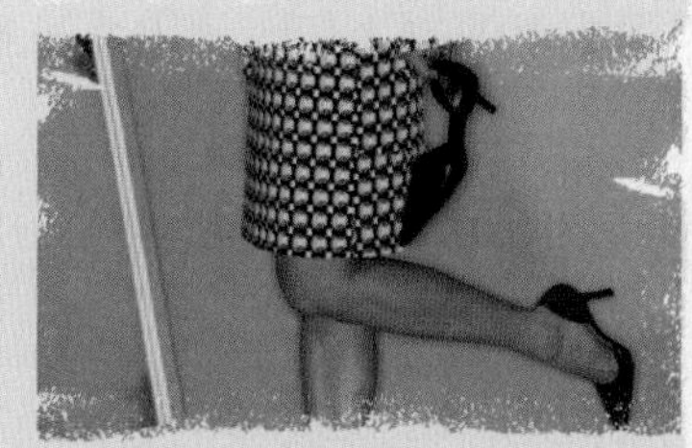

Does It Match?

Let's face it—not all reds are created equal. And those varying shades of black can make it really hard to determine whether your favorite, comfy sweater really matches the new pants you just bought. One false step and you could be the next fashion disaster on some hidden camera TV show! But your clothes aren't the only things that should match. James 3:10 says that even the words you speak should match each other. You should never mix praises and curses in your mouth. It's one or the other—and praises are always the best choice for pleasing, beautiful speech.

with you because of the great grace that God has given you. [15]Thanks be to God for his gift that is too wonderful for words.

Paul Defends His Ministry

10 I, Paul, am begging you with the gentleness and the kindness of Christ. Some people say that I am easy on you when I am with you and bold when I am away. [2]They think we live in a worldly way, and I plan to be very bold with them when I come. I beg you that when I come I will not need to use that same boldness with you. [3]We do live in the world, but we do not fight in the same way the world fights. [4]We fight with weapons that are different from those the world uses. Our weapons have power from God that can destroy the enemy's strong places. We destroy people's arguments [5]and every proud thing that raises itself against the knowledge of God. We capture every thought and make it give up and obey Christ. [6]We are ready to punish anyone there who does not obey, but first we want you to obey fully.

[7]You must look at the facts before you. If you feel sure that you belong to Christ, you must remember that we belong to Christ just as you do. [8]It is true that we brag freely about the authority the Lord gave us. But this authority is to build you up, not to tear you down. So I will not be ashamed. [9]I do not want you to think I am trying to scare you with my letters. [10]Some people say, "Paul's letters are powerful and sound important, but when he is with us, he is weak. And his speaking is nothing." [11]They should know this: We are not there with you now, so we say these things in letters. But when we are there with you, we will show the same authority that we show in our letters.

[12]We do not dare to compare ourselves with those who think they are very important. They use themselves to measure themselves, and they judge themselves by what they themselves are. This shows that they know nothing. [13]But we will not brag about things outside the work that was given us to do. We will limit our bragging to the work that God gave us, and this includes our work with you. [14]We are not bragging too much, as we would be if we had not already come to you. But we have come to you with the Good News of Christ. [15]We limit our bragging to the work that is ours, not what others have done. We hope that as your faith continues to grow, you will help our work to grow much larger. [16]We want to tell the Good News in the areas beyond your city. We do not want to brag about work that has already been done in another person's area. [17]But, "If people want to brag, they should brag only about the Lord."[n] [18]It is not those who say they are good who are accepted but those the Lord thinks are good.

Paul and the False Apostles

11 I wish you would be patient with me even when I am a little foolish, but you are already doing that. [2]I am jealous

all about MEN

The Whole Deal

Ever heard the (eerily true!) statement that married couples start to resemble each other? Adopting someone's expressions or personality traits is understandable in marriage, considering the bond God created by giving Adam's rib to Eve (Genesis 2:21). They truly were part of each other. But how much adapting is healthy while dating? If you habitually change to "fit" your current relationship, you may be giving up too much of yourself. A relationship will be stronger (and more fun!) if you're comfortable with yourself first. Remember, only two whole individuals can make one healthy marriage. God healed the hole in Adam's chest, and he still brings wholeness today. So focus on becoming who God made you to be before becoming "one body" (2:24) with someone else.

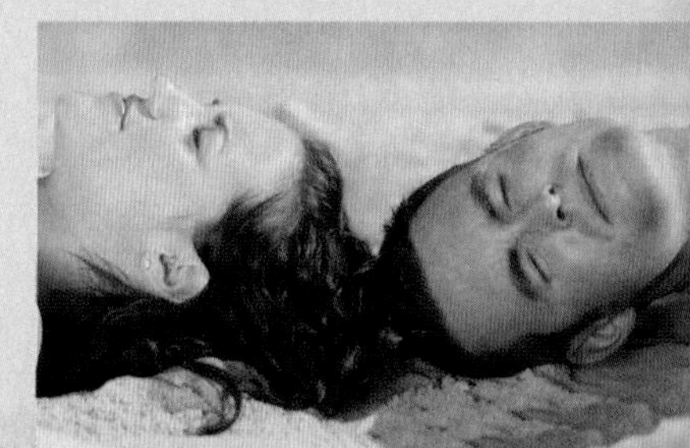

10:17 "If . . . Lord." Quotation from Jeremiah 9:24.

QUIZ

CHECKING ON CHECKUPS: HOW OFTEN SHOULD YOU DO THESE COMMON TASKS?

1. HOW OFTEN SHOULD YOU CHANGE THE OIL IN YOUR CAR?

- [ ] A. Never—that's optional!
- [ ] B. As often as the owner's manual suggests (usually every three thousand miles)
- [ ] C. Only if I'm taking a long road trip

2. HOW OFTEN SHOULD YOU DEFROST YOUR FREEZER?

- [ ] A. Just buy a frost-free freezer, and you won't have to worry about it
- [ ] B. At least once a year
- [ ] C. When the door won't open because it's frozen shut

3. HOW OFTEN SHOULD YOU TRIM YOUR HAIR?

- [ ] A. Whenever it loses its shape and style
- [ ] B. Every six to eight weeks and never longer than three months
- [ ] C. Whenever you start tripping over it because it's so long

4. HOW OFTEN SHOULD YOU SEE A GYNECOLOGIST?

- [ ] A. Never
- [ ] B. About once a year
- [ ] C. Only when you suspect a problem

5. HOW OFTEN SHOULD YOU READ YOUR BIBLE?

- [ ] A. Every Sunday at church
- [ ] B. Every day
- [ ] C. As soon as you encounter a problem

6. HOW OFTEN SHOULD YOU HAVE YOUR EXTERMINATOR DO A PEST INSPECTION?

- [ ] A. Just ignore the bugs—they'll go away!
- [ ] B. At least once a year
- [ ] C. Whenever they start eating more of your food than you do

7. HOW OFTEN SHOULD YOU CHANGE OR CLEAN THE FILTER IN YOUR HEATING/COOLING UNIT OR HEAT PUMP?

- [ ] A. Whenever the air is not hot or cool enough
- [ ] B. As often as the manufacturers recommend—usually about once a month
- [ ] C. Whenever the little thingee on the wall stops working

8. HOW OFTEN SHOULD YOU GIVE YOUR MONETARY TITHE AND OFFERINGS?

- [ ] A. Any time you have some extra cash lying around
- [ ] B. Each time you earn any money
- [ ] C. Whenever you feel charitable

9. HOW OFTEN SHOULD YOU GET A TETANUS SHOT?

- [ ] A. Any time you puncture your skin with something rusty
- [ ] B. Every ten years with a booster every five years
- [ ] C. Never—shots hurt and should be avoided at all cost.

10. HOW OFTEN SHOULD YOU CHANGE YOUR BED SHEETS?

- [ ] A. When they can walk themselves to the laundry room
- [ ] B. About once a week
- [ ] C. When they wear out

SCORING:

IF YOU CHOSE MOSTLY Bs, YOU'RE ONE SMART COOKIE. If you chose mostly As or Cs, you've got a healthy dose of humor on your side.

Everyone has chores to do. It's just a part of life. Some are fun; some not so pleasant. Nevertheless, being a good steward of the resources God's given you is an excellent way to honor him.

over you with a jealousy that comes from God. I promised to give you to Christ, as your only husband. I want to give you as his pure bride. [3]But I am afraid that your minds will be led away from your true and pure following of Christ just as Eve was tricked by the snake with his evil ways. [4]You are very patient with anyone who comes to you and preaches a different Jesus from the one we preached. You are very willing to accept a spirit or gospel that is different from the Spirit and Good News you received from us.

[5]I do not think that those "great apostles" are any better than I am. [6]I may not be a trained speaker, but I do have knowledge. We have shown this to you clearly in every way.

[7]I preached God's Good News to you without pay. I made myself unimportant to make you important. Do you think that was wrong? [8]I accepted pay from other churches, taking their money so I could serve you. [9]If I needed something when I was with you, I did not trouble any of you. The brothers who came from Macedonia gave me all that I needed. I did not allow myself to depend on you in any way, and I will never depend on you. [10]No one in Southern Greece will stop me from bragging about that. I say this with the truth of Christ in me. [11]And why do I not depend on you? Do you think it is because I do not love you? God knows that I love you.

[12]And I will continue doing what I am doing now, because I want to stop those people from having a reason to brag. They would like to say that the work they brag about is the same as ours. [13]Such men are not true apostles but are workers who lie. They change themselves to look like apostles of Christ. [14]This does not surprise us. Even Satan changes himself to look like an angel of light.[n] [15]So it does not surprise us if Satan's servants also make themselves look like servants who work for what is right. But in the end they will be punished for what they do.

Q&A

Q: Am I supposed to keep the Sabbath?

A: When Christ's followers keep the Sabbath, it sends a message to a watching world about our priorities. And our observance also serves as a weekly reminder to our forgetful hearts to rely on God's sustaining power alone—we can and should ask God to provide seven days of results for six days of work! God clearly set forth the precedent for the Sabbath in the Ten Commandments. And although Jesus fulfilled the Law, setting apart one day as holy is still an important aspect of worship. Resting from your work is a significant part of living a balanced, meaningful life. So try keeping the Sabbath, and see what God can do while you rest!

Paul Tells About His Sufferings

[16]I tell you again: No one should think I am a fool. But if you think so, accept me as you would accept a fool. Then I can brag a little, too. [17]When I brag because I feel sure of myself, I am not talking as the Lord would talk but as a fool. [18]Many people are bragging about their lives in the world. So I will brag too. [19]You are wise, so you will gladly be patient with fools! [20]You are even patient with those who order you around, or use you, or trick you, or think they are better than you, or hit you in the face. [21]It is shameful to me to say this, but we were too "weak" to do those things to you!

But if anyone else is brave enough to brag, then I also will be brave and brag. (I am talking as a fool.) [22]Are they Hebrews?[n] So am I. Are they Israelites? So am I. Are they from Abraham's family? So am I. [23]Are they serving Christ? I am serving him more. (I am crazy to talk like this.) I have worked much harder than they. I have been in prison more often. I have been hurt more in beatings. I have been near death many times. [24]Five times the Jews have given me their punishment of thirty-nine lashes with a whip. [25]Three different times I was beaten with rods. One time I was almost stoned to death. Three times I was in ships that wrecked, and one of those times I spent a night and a day in the sea. [26]I have gone

fun facts

$28 billion of merchandise is returned to stores each year because of poor fit.

(National Retail Federation)

11:14 **angel of light** Messenger from God. The devil fools people so that they think he is from God. 11:22 **Hebrews** A name for the Jews that some Jews were very proud of.

RELATIONSHIPS

Speak Up or Keep Quiet?

When someone bad-mouths Christianity, sometimes it's hard to know whether to speak up or keep quiet—especially because Christians are supposed to build relationships, not alienate people who don't know God. We need God's help to know what's best in each situation. The Holy Spirit may nudge you with a response, or he may cause you to hesitate if he wants you to hold your tongue. Ask God for a loving attitude that speaks with or without words. He'll bless your efforts to show his love and your courage to speak up for him.

on many travels and have been in danger from rivers, thieves, my own people, the Jews, and those who are not Jews. I have been in danger in cities, in places where no one lives, and on the sea. And I have been in danger with false Christians. [27]I have done hard and tiring work, and many times I did not sleep. I have been hungry and thirsty, and many times I have been without food. I have been cold and without clothes. [28]Besides all this, there is on me every day the load of my concern for all the churches. [29]I feel weak every time someone is weak, and I feel upset every time someone is led into sin.

[30]If I must brag, I will brag about the things that show I am weak. [31]God knows I am not lying. He is the God and Father of the Lord Jesus Christ, and he is to be praised forever. [32]When I was in Damascus, the governor under King Aretas wanted to arrest me, so he put guards around the city. [33]But my friends lowered me in a basket through a hole in the city wall. So I escaped from the governor.

LIFEISSUES

Hospitality

We all need somewhere to kick back and relax, a place to be ourselves. Oftentimes home is that place, for us and our guests, too. Your home can be a haven of hospitality regardless of space or fine furniture because hospitality starts by making God welcome. When you stay close to him, you'll reflect his grace and make him feel at home there. His Spirit will shine over you and your guests with positively heavenly effects! Ask him to fill your rooms with peace, and your home will be a bit of heaven on earth (Romans 12:13; Revelation 21:3).

A Special Blessing in Paul's Life

12 I must continue to brag. It will do no good, but I will talk now about visions and revelations[n] from the Lord. [2]I know a man in Christ who was taken up to the third heaven fourteen years ago. I do not know whether the man was in his body or out of his body, but God knows. [3-4]And I know that this man was taken up to paradise.[n] I don't know if he was in his body or away from his body, but God knows. He heard things he is not able to explain, things that no human is allowed to tell. [5]I will brag about a man like that, but I will not brag about myself, except about my weaknesses. [6]But if I wanted to brag about myself, I would not be a fool, because I would be telling the truth. But I will not brag about myself. I do not want people to think more of me than what they see me do or hear me say.

[7]So that I would not become too proud of the wonderful things that were shown to me, a painful physical problem[n] was given to me. This problem was a messenger from Satan, sent to beat me and keep me from being too proud. [8]I begged the Lord three times to take this problem away from me. [9]But he said to me, "My grace is enough for you. When you are weak, my power is made

12:1 revelations Revelation is making known a truth that was hidden. **12:3–4 paradise** Another word for heaven. **12:7 painful physical problem** Literally, "thorn in the flesh."

Savvy Chef

Marvelous Marinades

Need some pizzazz for meats and veggies? Sample these flavor-packed marinades: **Balsamic Vinaigrette**—Store-bought dressing is wonderful on anything and couldn't be simpler! **Zesty Apricot**—For chicken, pork, or seafood: Combine equal amounts of apricot preserves and soy sauce. **Sweet & Savory**—For sweet potatoes, salmon, or pork: Combine 2 tablespoons of water, 2 tablespoons of brown sugar, 1 tablespoon of Worcestershire, and 1 tablespoon of soy sauce. **Sensational Steak**—Combine 3 tablespoons of orange juice, 2 tablespoons of lemon juice, 3 minced garlic cloves, 1/2 an onion (chopped), 2 tablespoons of brown sugar, 1/4 cup of Worcestershire, and 1/4 cup of soy sauce.

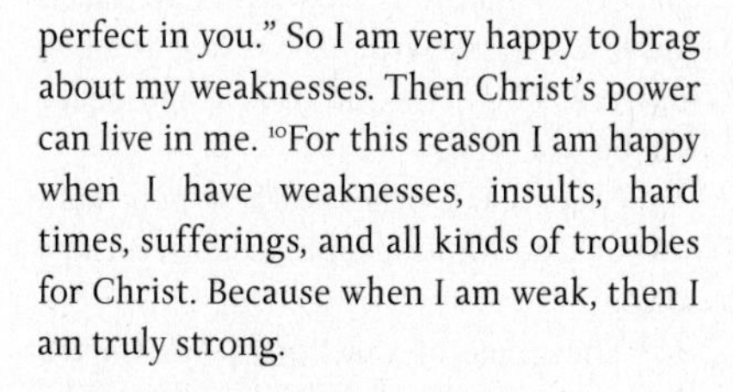

Health

Choosing the Right Doctor

Finding an ob-gyn is one of the hardest—and most important—decisions a woman makes. Let's face it: nobody likes going to *that* doctor, but you should go at least yearly. You'll see this person a lot (especially if you eventually have a baby), so your practitioner should be someone you respect and trust. Ask friends for recommendations. (Co-workers are ideal—they usually have the same insurance as you.) Make sure the doctor is board certified. Decide if you prefer a group practice or individual. (In a group practice, you might see a different doctor each visit.) If you plan to have children, make sure the doctor delivers babies (not all gynecologists do), and be sure you have compatible views on pain management, episiotomy, etc. Above all, your doctor should be someone you're comfortable with. Throughout your search, ask the Great Physician to lead you to your ideal ob-gyn.

perfect in you." So I am very happy to brag about my weaknesses. Then Christ's power can live in me. [10]For this reason I am happy when I have weaknesses, insults, hard times, sufferings, and all kinds of troubles for Christ. Because when I am weak, then I am truly strong.

Paul's Love for the Christians

[11]I have been talking like a fool, but you made me do it. You are the ones who should say good things about me. I am worth nothing, but those "great apostles" are not worth any more than I am!

[12]When I was with you, I patiently did the things that prove I am an apostle—signs, wonders, and miracles. [13]So you received everything that the other churches have received. Only one thing was different: I was not a burden to you. Forgive me for this!

[14]I am now ready to visit you the third time, and I will not be a burden to you. I want nothing from you, except you. Children should not have to save up to give to their parents. Parents should save to give to their children. [15]So I am happy to give everything I have for you, even myself. If I love you more, will you love me less?

[16]It is clear I was not a burden to you, but you think I was tricky and lied to catch you. [17]Did I cheat you by using any of the messengers I sent to you? No, you know I did not. [18]I asked Titus to go to you, and I sent our brother with him. Titus did not cheat you, did he? No, you know that Titus and I did the same thing and with the same spirit.

[19]Do you think we have been defending ourselves to you all this time? We have been speaking in Christ and before God. You are our dear friends, and everything we do is to make you stronger. [20]I am afraid that when I come, you will not be what I want you to be, and I will not be what you want me to be. I am afraid that among you there may be arguing, jealousy, anger, selfish fighting, evil talk, gossip, pride, and confusion. [21]I am afraid that when I come to you again, my God will make me ashamed

2 Corinthians 12:15

Think of someone who's incredibly important to you. Now imagine that person has been diagnosed with a terminal illness. The doctors say it's just a matter of time before the sickness ends your dear friend's life.

But what if a miraculous new procedure could mysteriously extract some "life essence" from a healthy person and share it with a person on death's door? How many years of your own life would you give to bring your friend back to good health?

That's obviously pretty imaginative in terms of realistic medicine . . . but spiritually speaking, it's not that crazy. When it came to people's souls, Paul was willing to literally spend himself—his time, strength, prayers, blood, sweat, and tears—to share the Good News. And even after people accepted Jesus, he worked nonstop to help them grow in their faith. The reason he could live like that was love. His extreme love for God and others drove him to pour out his life as a servant.

So while we probably won't ever have to give away years of our own lives to sick friends, we really should be ready to spend our lives loving and serving the people around us. Are you ready to spend everything you have . . . even yourself?

before you. I may be saddened by many of those who have sinned because they have not changed their hearts or turned from their sexual sins and the shameful things they have done.

Final Warnings and Greetings

13 I will come to you for the third time. "Every case must be proved by two or three witnesses."[n] [2]When I was with you the second time, I gave a warning to those who had sinned. Now I am away from you, and I give a warning to all the others. When I come to you again, I will not be easy with them. [3]You want proof that Christ is speaking through me. My proof is that he is not weak among you, but he is powerful. [4]It is true that he was weak when he was killed on the cross, but he lives now by God's power. It is true that we are weak in Christ, but for you we will be alive in Christ by God's power.

[5]Look closely at yourselves. Test yourselves to see if you are living in the faith. You know that Jesus Christ is in you—unless you fail the test. [6]But I hope you will see that we ourselves have not failed the test. [7]We pray to God that you will not do anything wrong. It is not important to see that we have passed the test, but it is important that you do what is right, even if it seems we have failed. [8]We cannot do anything against the truth, but only for the truth. [9]We are happy to be weak, if you are strong, and we pray that you will become complete. [10]I am writing this while I am away from you so that when I come I will not have to be harsh in my use of authority. The Lord gave me this authority to build you up, not to tear you down.

[11]Now, brothers and sisters, I say goodbye. Live in harmony. Do what I have asked you to do. Agree with each other, and live in peace. Then the God of love and peace will be with you.

[12]Greet each other with a holy kiss. [13]All of God's holy people send greetings to you.

[14]The grace of the Lord Jesus Christ, the love of God, and the fellowship of the Holy Spirit be with you all.

13:1 "Every . . . witnesses." Quotation from Deuteronomy 19:15.

Through Thick and Thin

Talk about loyalty! If Paul was like most people, he would have given up on the Corinthian church long before he wrote 2 Corinthians. They had been a constant source of problems. But because Paul loved them and wanted them to know Christ, he continued to help them. After all he had done for them, it's easy to understand why Paul was hurt to discover they were questioning his authority as an apostle. False teachers were spreading lies about Paul and leading the congregation toward "a different Jesus" than the one Paul had preached (2 Corinthians 11:4). In response to these lies, Paul wrote this letter to the Corinthians to defend himself—and to lead them back toward truth.

Paul probably wasn't surprised to hear that "Satan's servants" were deceiving the Corinthians (2 Corinthians 11:15). Satan has always tried to lead God's people astray: he tempted Adam and Eve (Genesis 3) and put Job's faith on trial by testing him through hardship and loss (Job 1—2). Jesus warned his followers about Satan's false teachers. He said they would come "looking gentle like sheep" but would actually be "dangerous like wolves" (Matthew 7:15).

Satan continues to attempt to mislead God's followers today. Just as Paul's letter helped set the Corinthians straight, we can be sure that God will use the same letter to teach us what it means to know him and walk in truth.

Get Real

What reasons might Paul have had for referring to God as "the Father who is full of mercy" in 2 Corinthians 1:3? (Ephesians 1:3; 1 Peter 1:3)

Based on Jesus' response to Paul in 2 Corinthians 12:9, how does God want us to deal with trials? (Proverbs 3:5)

Why do you think the Corinthians believed the false teachers? (Jeremiah 23:16–17)

How does God want us to give to others? (Luke 6:38; Romans 12:8)

How can you avoid being misled by "false teachers" and remain grounded in the truth? (Ephesians 6:10–18; 2 Timothy 3:16)

galatians

If you ever feel like it's just impossible to be good enough to earn God's favor . . . you're on the right track! God calls us to an incredibly high standard of holiness and purity, and only one person in history ever got it right—Jesus Christ. He's our example. Fortunately, he's also our Savior, and God is full of grace and mercy. By God's grace we can be covered with the righteousness of Jesus. When we come into God's presence, he sees the perfection of his own Son, and we're completely acceptable in his eyes.

The Galatian believers were listening to false teachers who were telling them that certain rituals were required for salvation. These teachers also attacked Paul and the other apostles, saying they didn't really have authority.

This letter from Paul to the Galatians strongly defends the true Good News: salvation is a gift of grace from God, not something we could ever earn. Paul also defends his position as a chosen messenger of God, making it clear that his goal is to please God, not people.

Don't be fooled by any false teaching—only God's grace brings salvation. And remember that it's exclusively through faith in Christ that God's saving grace can be experienced.

1 From Paul, an apostle. I was not chosen to be an apostle by human beings, nor was I sent from human beings. I was made an apostle through Jesus Christ and God the Father who raised Jesus from the dead. [2]This letter is also from all those of God's family[n] who are with me.

To the churches in Galatia:[n]

[3]Grace and peace to you from God our Father and the Lord Jesus Christ. [4]Jesus gave himself for our sins to free us from this evil world we live in, as God the Father planned. [5]The glory belongs to God forever and ever. Amen.

The Only Good News

[6]God, by his grace through Christ, called you to become his people. So I am amazed that you are turning away so quickly and believing something different than the Good News. [7]Really, there is no other Good News. But some people are confusing you; they want to change the Good News of Christ. [8]We preached to you the Good News. So if we ourselves, or even an angel from heaven, should preach to you something different, we should be judged guilty! [9]I said this before, and now I say it again: You have already accepted the Good News. If anyone is preaching something different to you, let that person be judged guilty!

[10]Do you think I am trying to make people accept me? No, God is the One I am trying to please. Am I trying to please people? If I still wanted to please people, I would not be a servant of Christ.

Paul's Authority Is from God

[11]Brothers and sisters, I want you to know that the Good News I preached to you was not made up by human beings. [12]I did not get it from humans, nor did anyone teach it to me, but Jesus Christ showed it to me.

1:2 those . . . family The Greek text says "brothers." **1:2 Galatia** Probably the same country where Paul preached and began churches on his first missionary trip. Read the Book of Acts, chapters 13 and 14.

[13]You have heard about my past life in the Jewish religion. I attacked the church of God and tried to destroy it. [14]I was becoming a leader in the Jewish religion, doing better than most other Jews of my age. I tried harder than anyone else to follow the teachings handed down by our ancestors.

[15]But God had special plans for me and set me apart for his work even before I was born. He called me through his grace [16]and showed his son to me so that I might tell the Good News about him to those who are not Jewish. When God called me, I did not get advice or help from any person. [17]I did not go to Jerusalem to see those who were apostles before I was. But, without waiting, I went away to Arabia and later went back to Damascus.

[18]After three years I went to Jerusalem to meet Peter and stayed with him for fifteen days. [19]I met no other apostles, except James, the brother of the Lord. [20]God knows that these things I write are not lies. [21]Later, I went to the areas of Syria and Cilicia.

[22]In Judea the churches in Christ had never met me. [23]They had only heard it said, "This man who was attacking us is now preaching the same faith that he once tried to destroy." [24]And these believers praised God because of me.

Other Apostles Accepted Paul

2 After fourteen years I went to Jerusalem again, this time with Barnabas. I also took Titus with me. [2]I went because God showed me I should go. I met with the believers there, and in private I told their leaders the Good News that I preach to the non-Jewish people. I did not want my past work and the work I am now doing to be wasted. [3]Titus was with me, but he was not forced to be circumcised, even though he was a Greek. [4]We talked about this problem because some false believers had come into our group secretly. They came in like spies to overturn the freedom we have in Christ Jesus. They wanted to make us slaves. [5]But we did not give in to those false believers for a minute. We wanted the truth of the Good News to continue for you.

[6]Those leaders who seemed to be important did not change the Good News that I preach. (It doesn't matter to me if they were "important" or not. To God everyone is the same.) [7]But these leaders saw that I had been given the work of telling the Good News to those who are not Jewish, just as Peter had the work of telling the Jews. [8]God gave Peter the power to work as an apostle for the Jewish people. But he also gave me the power to work as an apostle for those who are not Jews. [9]James, Peter, and John, who seemed to be the leaders, understood that God had given me this special grace, so they accepted Barnabas and me. They agreed that they would go to the Jewish people and that we should go to those who are not Jewish. [10]The only thing they asked us was to remember to help the poor—something I really wanted to do.

Paul Shows that Peter Was Wrong

[11]When Peter came to Antioch, I challenged him to his face, because he was wrong. [12]Peter ate with the non-Jewish people until some Jewish people sent from James came to Antioch. When they arrived, Peter stopped eating with those who weren't Jewish, and he separated himself from them. He was afraid of the Jews. [13]So Peter was a hypocrite, as were the other Jewish believers who joined with him. Even Barnabas was influenced by what these Jewish believers did. [14]When I saw they were not following the truth of the Good News, I spoke to Peter in front of them all. I said, "Peter, you are a Jew, but

BECOME *Involved*

The P.E.A.C.E. Plan

Rick Warren, pastor of Saddleback Church and best-selling author of *The Purpose-Driven Church* and *The Purpose-Driven Life,* has a new plan for reaching the world. It's called the P.E.A.C.E. Plan, and bringing it to fruition will require unprecedented participation from believers all over the world. Could that include you?

Basically, the P.E.A.C.E. Plan is a massive mobilization effort attempting to unify churches and individuals from all over the world to combat major global issues such as poverty, disease, corruption, lack of education, and spiritual emptiness. Each letter of the plan stands for a different initiative in the fight against these debilitating problems. P.E.A.C.E. is rooted in church-to-church ministry, but the results from ongoing efforts have gained much attention in both the Christian and mainstream communities.

Log on to www.thepeaceplan.com for more detailed information about how you and your church can join the effort. You'll find details about international ministry trips and also learn how to pray for everyone involved on both the giving and receiving ends of P.E.A.C.E. It is an extremely ambitious plan and requires big-time effort and coordination. Join P.E.A.C.E. organizers and volunteers in praying that the *Prince of Peace* will be known in all the earth.

you are not living like a Jew. You are living like those who are not Jewish. So why do you now try to force those who are not Jewish to live like Jews?"

[15]We were not born as non-Jewish "sinners," but as Jews. [16]Yet we know that a person is made right with God not by following the law, but by trusting in Jesus Christ. So we, too, have put our faith in Christ Jesus, that we might be made right with God because we trusted in Christ. It is not because we followed the law, because no one can be made right with God by following the law.

[17]We Jews came to Christ, trying to be made right with God, and it became clear that we are sinners, too. Does this mean that Christ encourages sin? No! [18]But I would really be wrong to begin teaching again those things that I gave up. [19]It was the law that put me to death, and I died to the law so that I can now live for God. [20]I was put to death on the cross with Christ, and I do not live anymore—it is Christ who lives in me. I still live in my body, but I live by faith in the Son of God who loved me and gave himself to save me. [21]By saying these things I am not going against God's grace. Just the opposite, if the law could make us right with God, then Christ's death would be useless.

Blessing Comes Through Faith

3 You people in Galatia were told very clearly about the death of Jesus Christ on the cross. But you were foolish; you let someone trick you. [2]Tell me this one thing: How did you receive the Holy Spirit? Did you receive the Spirit by following the law? No, you received the Spirit because you heard the Good News and believed it. [3]You began your life in Christ by the Spirit. Now are you trying to make it complete by your own power? That is foolish. [4]Were all your experiences wasted? I hope not! [5]Does God give you the Spirit and work miracles among you because you follow the law? No, he does these things because you heard the Good News and believed it.

[6]The Scriptures say the same thing about Abraham: "Abraham believed God, and God accepted Abraham's faith, and that faith made him right with God."[n] [7]So you should know that the true children of Abraham are those who have faith. [8]The Scriptures, telling what would happen in the future, said that God would make the non-Jewish people right through their faith. This Good News was told to Abraham beforehand, as the Scripture says: "All nations will be blessed through you."[n] [9]So all who believe as Abraham believed are blessed just as Abraham was. [10]But those who depend on following the law to make them right are under a curse, because the Scriptures say, "Anyone will be cursed who does not always obey what is written in the Book of the Law."[n] [11]Now it is clear that no one can be made right with God by the law, because the Scriptures say, "Those who are right with God will live by faith."[n] [12]The law is not based on faith. It says, "A person who obeys these things will live because of them."[n] [13]Christ took away the curse the law put on us. He changed places with us and put himself under that curse. It is written in the Scriptures, "Anyone whose body is displayed on a tree[n] is cursed." [14]Christ did this so that God's blessing promised to Abraham might come through Jesus Christ to those who are not Jews. Jesus died so that by our believing we could receive the Spirit that God promised.

The Law and the Promise

[15]Brothers and sisters, let us think in human terms: Even an agreement made

Galatians 3:19–22

Picture what it would be like to start the first week in a very challenging job. It would actually be nice to have a supervisor who's 100 percent upfront about the rules and expectations. In the same way, God has always been clear with his people. Back in Moses' day, he gave them the Law—detailed instructions that left no room for uncertainty. Basically, God said, "You're my people and I'm your God. Just follow my commands." Sounds simple, but it turned out to be easier said than done for them. God's people constantly sinned against him and suffered the consequences.

The Law prepared the way for Jesus. People learned the hard way that it's impossible to meet God's standards. Our inability to measure up makes our sinfulness tough to miss and our need for a Savior blatantly obvious!

Like a straightforward supervisor who lays out exactly what's required of us, God has clearly shown us his expectations for holiness. But unlike any job on earth, we'll *never* be capable of meeting this divine standard of perfection. Only Jesus lived a perfect life. The only way to please God in this life is to have faith that what Jesus did was enough.

3:6 "Abraham . . . God." Quotation from Genesis 15:6. **3:8 "All . . . you."** Quotation from Genesis 12:3 and 18:18. **3:10 "Anyone . . . Law."** Quotation from Deuteronomy 27:26. **3:11 "Those . . . faith."** Quotation from Habakkuk 2:4. **3:12 "A person . . . them."** Quotation from Leviticus 18:5. **3:13 displayed on a tree** Deuteronomy 21:22–23 says that when a person was killed for doing wrong, the body was hung on a tree to show shame. Paul means that the cross of Jesus was like that.

HE SAID / SHE SAID

When do you feel the greatest sense of hope?

He: After worship on Sunday morning

She: After God answers prayer

between two persons is firm. After that agreement is accepted by both people, no one can stop it or add anything to it. [16]God made promises both to Abraham and to his descendant. God did not say, "and to your descendants." That would mean many people. But God said, "and to your descendant." That means only one person; that person is Christ. [17]This is what I mean: God had an agreement with Abraham and promised to keep it. The law, which came four hundred thirty years later, cannot change that agreement and so destroy God's promise to Abraham. [18]If the law could give us Abraham's blessing, then the promise would not be necessary. But that is not possible, because God freely gave his blessings to Abraham through the promise he had made.

[19]So what was the law for? It was given to show that the wrong things people do are against God's will. And it continued until the special descendant, who had been promised, came. The law was given through angels who used Moses for a mediator[n] to give the law to people. [20]But a mediator is not needed when there is only one side, and God is only one.

The Purpose of the Law of Moses

[21]Does this mean that the law is against God's promises? Never! That would be true only if the law could make us right with God. But God did not give a law that can bring life. [22]Instead, the Scriptures showed that the whole world is bound by sin. This was so the promise would be given through faith to people who believe in Jesus Christ.

[23]Before this faith came, we were all held prisoners by the law. We had no freedom until God showed us the way of faith that was coming. [24]In other words, the law was our guardian leading us to Christ so that we could be made right with God through faith. [25]Now the way of faith has come, and we no longer live under a guardian.

[26-27]You were all baptized into Christ, and so you were all clothed with Christ. This means that you are all children of God through faith in Christ Jesus. [28]In Christ, there is no difference between Jew and Greek, slave and free person, male and female. You are all the same in Christ Jesus. [29]You belong to Christ, so you are Abraham's descendants. You will inherit all of God's blessings because of the promise God made to Abraham.

4

I want to tell you this: While those who will inherit their fathers' property are still children, they are no different from slaves. It does not matter that the children own everything. [2]While they are children, they must obey those who are chosen to care for them. But when the children reach the age set by their fathers, they are free. [3]It is the same for us. We were once like children, slaves to the useless rules of this world. [4]But when the

Be Still & Know

Pour Out Your Heart

There's a fine balance between being authentic and real with people and oversharing more than they really want to know. That's especially true with new friends. But there's one friend you never have to worry about oversharing with—Jesus! You can never share more with him than he wants to know. He's interested in your every moment, your every thought, every last thing that's hidden in your heart. In fact, Lamentations 2:19 invites you to pour out your heart to God like water. What a beautiful concept! As his beloved and cherished daughter, you can blab and gab and let down your guard completely. He delights in you and in all the deepest longings and treasures of your heart.

3:19 mediator A person who helps one person talk to or give something to another person.

RELATIONSHIPS

Risking the Truth

Sometimes truth hurts. Like admitting we're sinners. Or that we don't have a perfect personality or Pulitzer Prize potential. The truth can hurt, not just when we face it ourselves but also when we have to share it with others. But being upfront about a harmful habit or lifestyle is far better than letting someone you care about continue down a dangerous path. When we lovingly point out the truth to someone who needs to hear it, even if honesty causes some initial pain, God can use our words to set that person on a path to freedom (John 8:32). Now that's a risk worth taking.

right time came, God sent his Son who was born of a woman and lived under the law. [5]God did this so he could buy freedom for those who were under the law and so we could become his children.

[6]Since you are God's children, God sent the Spirit of his Son into your hearts, and the Spirit cries out, "Father."[n] [7]So now you are not a slave; you are God's child, and God will give you the blessing he promised, because you are his child.

Paul's Love for the Christians

[8]In the past you did not know God. You were slaves to gods that were not real. [9]But now you know the true God. Really, it is God who knows you. So why do you turn back to those weak and useless rules you followed before? Do you want to be slaves to those things again? [10]You still follow teachings about special days, months, seasons, and years. [11]I am afraid for you, that my work for you has been wasted.

[12]Brothers and sisters, I became like you, so I beg you to become like me. You were very good to me before. [13]You remember that it was because of an illness that I came to you the first time, preaching the Good News. [14]Though my sickness was a trouble for you, you did not hate me or make me leave. But you welcomed me as an angel from God, as if I were Jesus Christ himself! [15]You were very happy then, but where is that joy now? I am ready to testify that you would have taken out your eyes and given them to me if that were possible. [16]Now am I your enemy because I tell you the truth?

[17]Those people[n] are working hard to persuade you, but this is not good for you. They want to persuade you to turn against us and follow only them. [18]It is good for people to show interest in you, but only if their purpose is good. This is always true, not just when I am with you. [19]My little children, again I feel the pain of

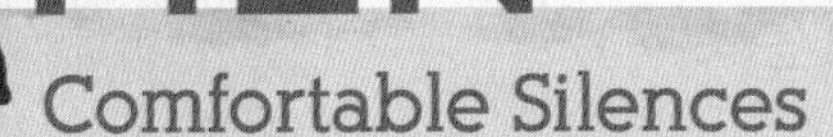

all about MEN

Comfortable Silences

Do you value a comfortable silence? Freed from chatter, some people relax easily, while others think quiet is nerve-wracking. But the ability to sit and just *be* with someone can be a sign of true comfort. As long as a couple has plenty to talk about other times, stillness can be therapeutic and reveal new ways of relating. When you can relax quietly and let the world go by with someone you care about, you enjoy a unique closeness that words can't always express. Why not plan a trip to a park or hike a nature trail and just be together? You never know what insights the quiet might bring out in both of you (Psalm 131:2; Ecclesiastes 3:7; 1 Peter 3:4).

4:6 "Father" Literally, "Abba, Father." Jewish children called their fathers "Abba." **4:17 Those people** They are the false teachers who were bothering the believers in Galatia (Galatians 1:7).

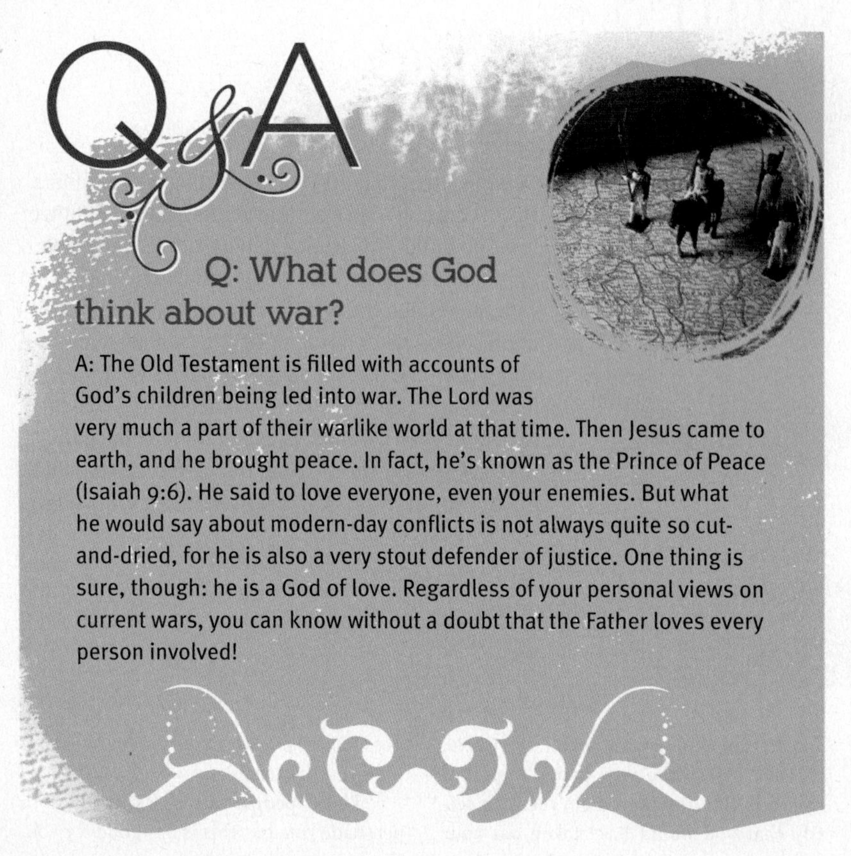

Q&A

Q: What does God think about war?

A: The Old Testament is filled with accounts of God's children being led into war. The Lord was very much a part of their warlike world at that time. Then Jesus came to earth, and he brought peace. In fact, he's known as the Prince of Peace (Isaiah 9:6). He said to love everyone, even your enemies. But what he would say about modern-day conflicts is not always quite so cut-and-dried, for he is also a very stout defender of justice. One thing is sure, though: he is a God of love. Regardless of your personal views on current wars, you can know without a doubt that the Father loves every person involved!

childbirth for you until you truly become like Christ. [20]I wish I could be with you now and could change the way I am talking to you, because I do not know what to think about you.

The Example of Hagar and Sarah

[21]Some of you still want to be under the law. Tell me, do you know what the law says? [22]The Scriptures say that Abraham had two sons. The mother of one son was a slave woman, and the mother of the other son was a free woman. [23]Abraham's son from the slave woman was born in the normal human way. But the son from the free woman was born because of the promise God made to Abraham.

[24]This story teaches something else: The two women are like the two agreements between God and his people. One agreement is the law that God made on Mount Sinai,[n] and the people who are under this agreement are like slaves. The mother named Hagar is like that agreement. [25]She is like Mount Sinai in Arabia and is a picture of the earthly city of Jerusalem. This city and its people are slaves to the law. [26]But the heavenly Jerusalem, which is above, is like the free woman. She is our mother. [27]It is written in the Scriptures:

"Be happy, Jerusalem.
You are like a woman who never gave birth to children.
Start singing and shout for joy.
You never felt the pain of giving birth,
but you will have more children
than the woman who has a husband." *Isaiah 54:1*

[28]My brothers and sisters, you are God's children because of his promise, as Isaac was then. [29]The son who was born in the normal way treated the other son badly. It is the same today. [30]But what does the Scripture say? "Throw out the slave woman and her son. The son of the slave woman should not inherit anything. The son of the free woman should receive it all."[n] [31]So, my brothers and sisters, we are not children of the slave woman, but of the free woman.

Keep Your Freedom

5 We have freedom now, because Christ made us free. So stand strong. Do not change and go back into the slavery of the law. [2]Listen, I Paul tell you that if you go back to the law by being circumcised, Christ does you no good. [3]Again, I warn every man: If you allow yourselves to be circumcised, you must follow all the law. [4]If you try to be made right with God through the law, your life with Christ is over—you have left God's

Fine Pearls

Think of your most treasured piece of jewelry. Is it special because it's really expensive or exquisitely beautiful? Perhaps it's a cherished possession because someone you love gave it to you or because it's been in your family for generations. For whatever reason, it has great worth in your eyes. Jesus said that's what the kingdom of heaven is like—it's the most important, valuable thing a person could ever find (Matthew 13:45–46). If you have a personal relationship with Jesus, guard it like a precious jewel. Give everything you have to keep that relationship strong, vibrant, and healthy.

4:24 Mount Sinai Mountain in Arabia where God gave his Law to Moses (Exodus 19 and 20). **4:30 "Throw . . . all."** Quotation from Genesis 21:10.

grace. [5]But we have the true hope that comes from being made right with God, and by the Spirit we wait eagerly for this hope. [6]When we are in Christ Jesus, it is not important if we are circumcised or not. The important thing is faith—the kind of faith that works through love.

[7]You were running a good race. Who stopped you from following the true way? [8]This change did not come from the One who chose you. [9]Be careful! "Just a little yeast makes the whole batch of dough rise." [10]But I trust in the Lord that you will not believe those different ideas. Whoever is confusing you with such ideas will be punished.

[11]My brothers and sisters, I do not teach that a man must be circumcised. If I teach circumcision, why am I still being attacked? If I still taught circumcision, my preaching about the cross would not be a problem. [12]I wish the people who are bothering you would castrate[n] themselves!

[13]My brothers and sisters, God called you to be free, but do not use your freedom as an excuse to do what pleases your sinful self. Serve each other with love. [14]The whole law is made complete in this one command: "Love your neighbor as you love yourself."[n] [15]If you go on hurting each other and tearing each other apart, be careful, or you will completely destroy each other.

Galatians 6:9–10

It's been one of those days. A large, unexpected bill, a fight with your best friend, a huge mistake at work . . . it just hasn't let up! When you get home, you're worn out and ready to take a break. But then you remember that you promised to help a friend move into her new place.

Chances are your friend would understand your situation and be okay with you not helping her out. But do you find yourself frequently coming up with reasons to avoid doing things you're committed to—especially if those commitments involve serving others?

A significant part of acting like Jesus involves having a servant's heart. Philippians 2 talks about becoming a humble servant like Jesus—putting others' needs ahead of your own. Do you think of other people as more important than yourself? Do you take opportunities to help those around you?

Don't become tired of doing good. If you feel worn out, think of it as a chance to rely more on God's strength instead of your own! Stay focused on eternal things, and show your love for God by being a true servant.

The Spirit and Human Nature

[16]So I tell you: Live by following the Spirit. Then you will not do what your sinful selves want. [17]Our sinful selves want what is against the Spirit, and the Spirit wants what is against our sinful selves. The two are against each other, so you cannot do just what you please. [18]But if the Spirit is leading you, you are not under the law.

[19]The wrong things the sinful self does are clear: being sexually unfaithful, not being pure, taking part in sexual sins, [20]worshiping gods, doing witchcraft, hating, making trouble, being jealous, being angry, being selfish, making people angry with each other, causing divisions among people, [21]feeling envy, being drunk, having wild and wasteful parties, and doing other things like these. I warn you now as I warned you before: Those who do these things will not inherit God's kingdom. [22]But the Spirit produces the fruit of love, joy, peace, patience, kindness, goodness, faithfulness, [23]gentleness, self-control. There is no law that says these things are wrong. [24]Those who belong to Christ Jesus have crucified their own sinful selves. They have given up their old selfish feelings and the evil things they wanted to do. [25]We get our new life from the Spirit, so we should follow the Spirit. [26]We must not be proud or make trouble with each other or be jealous of each other.

Help Each Other

6 Brothers and sisters, if someone in your group does something wrong, you who are spiritual should go to that person and gently help make him right again. But be careful, because you might be tempted to sin, too. [2]By helping each other with your troubles, you truly obey the law of Christ. [3]If anyone thinks he is important when he really is not, he is only fooling himself. [4]Each person should judge his own actions and not compare himself with others. Then he can be proud for what he himself has done. [5]Each person must be responsible for himself.

[6]Anyone who is learning the teaching of God should share all the good things he has with his teacher.

Life Is like Planting a Field

[7]Do not be fooled: You cannot cheat God. People harvest only what they plant.

5:12 castrate To cut off part of the male sex organ. Paul uses this word because it is similar to "circumcision." Paul wanted to show that he is very upset with the false teachers.
5:14 "Love . . . yourself." Quotation from Leviticus 19:18.

[8]If they plant to satisfy their sinful selves, their sinful selves will bring them ruin. But if they plant to please the Spirit, they will receive eternal life from the Spirit. [9]We must not become tired of doing good. We will receive our harvest of eternal life at the right time if we do not give up. [10]When we have the opportunity to help anyone, we should do it. But we should give special attention to those who are in the family of believers.

Paul Ends His Letter

[11]See what large letters I use to write this myself. [12]Some people are trying to force you to be circumcised so the Jews will accept them. They are afraid they will be attacked if they follow only the cross of Christ.[n] [13]Those who are circumcised do not obey the law themselves, but they want you to be circumcised so they can brag about what they forced you to do. [14]I hope I will never brag about things like that. The cross of our Lord Jesus Christ is my only reason for bragging. Through the cross of Jesus my world was crucified, and I died to the world. [15]It is not important if a man is circumcised or uncircumcised. The important thing is being the new people God has made. [16]Peace and mercy to those who follow this rule—and to all of God's people.

[17]So do not give me any more trouble. I have scars on my body that show[n] I belong to Christ Jesus.

[18]My brothers and sisters, the grace of our Lord Jesus Christ be with your spirit. Amen.

6:12 cross of Christ Paul uses the cross as a picture of the Good News, the story of Christ's death and rising from the dead to pay for our sins. The cross, or Christ's death, was God's way to save us. **6:17 that show** Many times Paul was beaten and whipped by people who were against him because he was teaching about Christ. The scars were from these beatings.

Galatians

Free Indeed

Jesus Christ was the perfect sacrifice for sinful, death-deserving people. Grace, through faith in Jesus Christ, is the only way to be saved. Our job is to acknowledge our helplessness—we absolutely cannot pay for our sin—and put complete faith in the Cross. Jesus' sacrifice and resurrection paid for our sin and defeated death once and for all.

We don't deserve salvation. Without Jesus, we deserve hell. Nothing in the world but Jesus' resurrection gives us power over sin. To act like our faith depends on our own good works is an insult to God's plan to make us right with him. As Christians we're united with Christ, and that's the only way we will enter heaven—under his perfection.

The Galatian church knew this was true. They'd studied Christianity under Paul's leadership, and they were strong believers. But some other teachers came in and began to convince them that they had to follow the Jewish law in order to be saved. Paul reminded them that they should know better . . . complete salvation and perfect freedom are given through Christ alone (Galatians 5:1–4). Christ is sufficient!

What an enormous relief it is to know that our salvation isn't dependent upon our ability (Romans 3:20). We're saved only by the grace of God through Jesus Christ. When we follow him, he gives us what we need to live for him. Understanding this leads to complete freedom and fullness (Ephesians 3:19)! We're free from sin, free from the Law, and free to live with the knowledge that Jesus is all we need.

Get Real

How do you define faith? (Hebrews 11:1–3)

What truth can you hold on to when you are confronted with pressure to conform to someone else's philosophy? (Isaiah 55:11; Ephesians 1:13–14)

How can you live a life marked by grace? (Philippians 2:5–7)

How can you show God's truth to others? (Jeremiah 23:28)

What does it mean to be free in Christ? (John 8:31–36; Romans 6:17–18)

notes

ephesians

Everyone loves a good mystery. And although there's definite satisfaction in solving a simple mystery (like guessing the ending of a suspense novel halfway through the book), some things are truly beyond us—things that are almost infinitely mysterious.

The Good News is kind of like that. Anyone can understand and accept God's gift of salvation through Christ. But beyond the surface, the message is riddled with mind-boggling mystery. No matter how much we study, we will never fully understand our infinite God and his phenomenal love for us.

Paul was definitely full of wisdom. His writings make up a huge part of the New Testament! But in this letter to Ephesus, Paul doesn't spend all of his time imparting doctrine or using his powerful mind to persuade his readers. Mixed in with his basic instructions about Christian living, Paul ponders the mystery of the church. He marvels that we are the bride of Christ. He constantly breaks into praises for God's incomprehensible greatness!

Are you amazed by God? If not, take some time to look closer. Even with everything God has shown us, our limited minds can't contain his infinite perfection! As you study God's Word, don't ever lose your sense of awe about the mysterious God who is revealed within its pages.

1 From Paul, an apostle of Christ Jesus. I am an apostle because that is what God wanted.

To God's holy people living in Ephesus,[n] believers in Christ Jesus:

[2]Grace and peace to you from God our Father and the Lord Jesus Christ.

Spiritual Blessings in Christ

[3]Praise be to the God and Father of our Lord Jesus Christ. In Christ, God has given us every spiritual blessing in the heavenly world. [4]That is, in Christ, he chose us before the world was made so that we would be his holy people—people without blame before him. [5]Because of his love, God had already decided to make us his own children through Jesus Christ. That was what he wanted and what pleased him, [6]and it brings praise to God because of his wonderful grace. God gave that grace to us freely, in Christ, the One he loves. [7]In Christ we are set free by the blood of his death, and so we have forgiveness of sins. How rich is God's grace, [8]which he has given to us so fully and freely. God, with full wisdom and understanding, [9]let us know his secret purpose. This was what God wanted, and he planned to do it through Christ. [10]His goal was to carry out his plan, when the right time came, that all things in heaven and on earth would be joined together in Christ as the head.

[11]In Christ we were chosen to be God's people, because from the very beginning God had decided this in keeping with his plan. And he is the One who makes everything agree with what he decides and wants. [12]We are the first people who hoped in Christ, and we were chosen so that we

1:1 in Ephesus Some Greek copies do not have this phrase.

Ephesians 1:7–9

Wouldn't it be frustrating if you continually forgave someone for disappointing you, but she never seemed to appreciate it? Instead of valuing your graciousness and forgiveness, what if that person had a completely casual attitude about the whole situation?

Ephesians 1:8 says God's grace has been "given to us so fully and freely." He offers forgiveness for every sin we've committed and extends incomprehensible love through the death of his precious Son and the gift of the Holy Spirit. He's literally given us everything we need, far surpassing anything we could ever earn or deserve.

And the best part is, you can come to him with any need. Need forgiveness, a fresh start? It's yours. Need relief from shame and the guts to take a step out of the shadows of your past? He's got it.

Consider how you respond to all the goodness God showers on you. Take time each day to meditate on God's grace . . . it'll change the way you live. Think of every moment as a chance to tell God how much you appreciate him!

would bring praise to God's glory. [13]So it is with you. When you heard the true teaching—the Good News about your salvation—you believed in Christ. And in Christ, God put his special mark of ownership on you by giving you the Holy Spirit that he had promised. [14]That Holy Spirit is the guarantee that we will receive what God promised for his people until God gives full freedom to those who are his—to bring praise to God's glory.

Paul's Prayer

[15]That is why since I heard about your faith in the Lord Jesus and your love for all God's people, [16]I have not stopped giving thanks to God for you. I always remember you in my prayers, [17]asking the God of our Lord Jesus Christ, the glorious Father, to give you a spirit of wisdom and revelation so that you will know him better. [18]I pray also that you will have greater understanding in your heart so you will know the hope to which he has called us and that you will know how rich and glorious are the blessings God has promised his holy people. [19]And you will know that God's power is very great for us who believe. That power is the same as the great strength [20]God used to raise Christ from the dead and put him at his right side in the heavenly world. [21]God has put Christ over all rulers, authorities, powers, and kings, not only in this world but also in the next. [22]God put everything under his power and made him the head over everything for the church, [23]which is Christ's body. The church is filled with Christ, and Christ fills everything in every way.

We Now Have Life

2 In the past you were spiritually dead because of your sins and the things you did against God. [2]Yes, in the past you lived the way the world lives, following the ruler of the evil powers that are above the earth. That same spirit is now working in those who refuse to obey God. [3]In the past all of us lived like them, trying to please our sinful selves and doing all the things our bodies and minds wanted. We should have suffered God's anger because we were sinful by nature. We were the same as all other people.

[4]But God's mercy is great, and he loved us very much. [5]Though we were spiritually dead because of the things we did against God, he gave us new life with Christ. You have been saved by God's grace. [6]And he raised us up with Christ and gave us a seat with him in the heavens. He did this for those in Christ Jesus [7]so that for all future time he could show the very great riches of his grace by being kind to us in Christ Jesus. [8]I mean that you have been saved by grace through believing. You did not save yourselves; it was a gift from God. [9]It was not the result of your own efforts, so you cannot brag about it. [10]God has made us what we are. In Christ Jesus, God made us to do good works, which God planned in advance for us to live our lives doing.

One in Christ

[11]You were not born Jewish. You are the people the Jews call "uncircumcised."[n] Those who call you "uncircumcised" call themselves "circumcised." (Their circumcision is only something they themselves do on their bodies.) [12]Remember that in the past you were without Christ. You were not citizens of Israel, and you had no part in the agreements[n] with the promise that God made to his people. You had no hope, and you did not know God. [13]But now in Christ Jesus, you who were far away from God are brought near through the blood of Christ's death. [14]Christ himself is our peace. He made both Jewish people and those who are not Jews one people. They were separated as if there were a wall between them, but Christ broke down that wall of hate by giving his own body. [15]The Jewish law had many commands and rules,

2:11 "uncircumcised" People not having the mark of circumcision as the Jews had. **2:12 agreements** The agreements that God gave to his people in the Old Testament.

book review

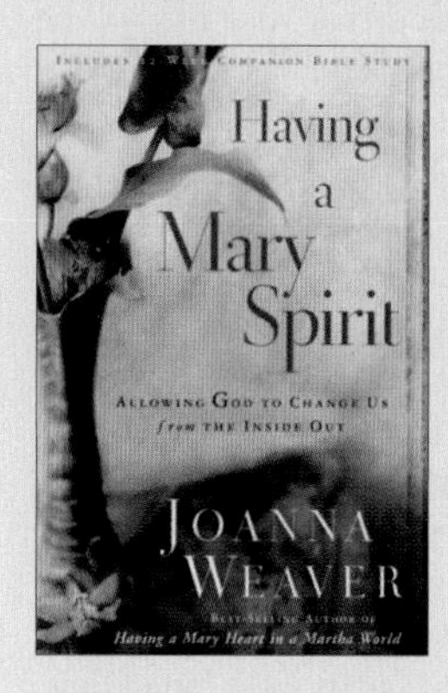

Having a Mary Spirit
by Joanna Weaver

Are you ready for a holy makeover? If your best intentions to change your life for the better seem to result only in frustration, then this book is for you. Author Joanna Weaver encourages you to keep pursuing noble goals and provides tips and insights on how to do so. Whether you want to exercise more, organize your home, or become a more trusting person, Weaver explains how real growth happens. You'll discover that you don't need to keep learning the same lessons over and over if you approach God with a teachable and willing spirit. This book contains rich life lessons that can lead to lasting transformation.

Q&A

Q: What's a Christian's responsibility to the environment?

A: The first job humans ever had was to care for the natural world. Man and woman were created after every other living thing and were given a clear mandate to take custody over all the plants and animals in the garden. So to a certain extent, every person has some responsibility to guard the rest of creation. That's not to say that nature should take precedence over human relationships, but being a good steward of the resources God has provided is part of being a good Christ-follower. Each person should do his or her part to guard creation for future generations.

but Christ ended that law. His purpose was to make the two groups of people become one new people in him and in this way make peace. [16]It was also Christ's purpose to end the hatred between the two groups, to make them into one body, and to bring them back to God. Christ did all this with his death on the cross. [17]Christ came and preached peace to you who were far away from God, and to those who were near to God. [18]Yes, it is through Christ we all have the right to come to the Father in one Spirit.

[19]Now you who are not Jewish are not foreigners or strangers any longer, but are citizens together with God's holy people. You belong to God's family. [20]You are like a building that was built on the foundation of the apostles and prophets. Christ Jesus himself is the most important stone[n] in that building, [21]and that whole building is joined together in Christ. He makes it grow and become a holy temple in the Lord. [22]And in Christ you, too, are being built together with the Jews into a place where God lives through the Spirit.

Paul's Work in Telling the Good News

3 So I, Paul, am a prisoner of Christ Jesus for you who are not Jews. [2]Surely you have heard that God gave me this work to tell you about his grace. [3]He let me know his secret by showing it to me. I have already written a little about this. [4]If you read what I wrote then, you can see that I truly understand the secret about the Christ. [5]People who lived in other times were not told that secret. But now, through the Spirit, God has shown that secret to his holy apostles and prophets. [6]This is that secret: that through the Good News those who are not Jews will share with the Jews in God's blessing. They belong to the same body, and they share together in the promise that God made in Christ Jesus.

[7]By God's special gift of grace given to me through his power, I became a servant to tell that Good News. [8]I am the least important of all God's people, but God gave me this gift—to tell those who are not Jews the Good News about the riches of

2:20 most important stone Literally, "cornerstone." The first and most important stone in a building.

HE SAID ↙ ↗ SHE SAID

What do you appreciate most about your parents?

He: Their commitment to each other

She: Their continued support of me

Christ, which are too great to understand fully. [9]And God gave me the work of telling all people about the plan for his secret, which has been hidden in him since the beginning of time. He is the One who created everything. [10]His purpose was that through the church all the rulers and powers in the heavenly world will now know God's wisdom, which has so many forms. [11]This agrees with the purpose God had since the beginning of time, and he carried out his plan through Christ Jesus our Lord. [12]In Christ we can come before God with freedom and without fear. We can do this through faith in Christ. [13]So I ask you not to become discouraged because of the sufferings I am having for you. My sufferings are for your glory.

Be Still & Know

Difficult Praying

Jesus said to "pray for those who are cruel to you" (Luke 6:28). That can be really difficult sometimes. How do you know what to pray? And how can you sincerely pray for them when you've been so hurt? The key is to realize that Jesus knows your pain. And he knows the heart of the person who hurt you, even if they don't know him. Consider praying for the person's heart. Ask God to be at work there, changing it into a heart that honors him and promotes peace. Pray for your broken relationship to one day be a testimony of his love, power, and reconciliation.

The Love of Christ

[14]So I bow in prayer before the Father [15]from whom every family in heaven and on earth gets its true name. [16]I ask the Father in his great glory to give you the power to be strong inwardly through his Spirit. [17]I pray that Christ will live in your hearts by faith and that your life will be strong in love and be built on love. [18]And I pray that you and all God's holy people will have the power to understand the greatness of Christ's love—how wide and how long and how high and how deep that love is. [19]Christ's love is greater than anyone can ever know, but I pray that you will be able to know that love. Then you can be filled with the fullness of God.

[20]With God's power working in us, God can do much, much more than anything we can ask or imagine. [21]To him be glory in the church and in Christ Jesus for all time, forever and ever. Amen.

The Unity of the Body

4 I am in prison because I belong to the Lord. Therefore I urge you who have been chosen by God to live up to the life to which God called you. [2]Always be humble, gentle, and patient, accepting each other in love. [3]You are joined together with peace through the Spirit, so make every effort to continue together in this way. [4]There is one body and one Spirit, and God called you to have one hope. [5]There is one Lord, one faith, and one baptism. [6]There is one God and Father of everything. He rules everything and is everywhere and is in everything.

[7]Christ gave each one of us the special gift of grace, showing how generous he is. [8]That is why it says in the Scriptures,

> "When he went up to the heights,
> he led a parade of captives,
> and he gave gifts to people."
>
> *Psalm 68:18*

[9]When it says, "He went up," what does it mean? It means that he first came down to the earth. [10]So Jesus came down, and he is the same One who went up above all the heaven. Christ did that to fill everything with his presence. [11]And Christ gave gifts to people—he made some to be apostles, some to be prophets, some to go and tell the Good News,

Brothers and sisters, think about the things that are good and worthy of praise.
August
1
Learn something new: sign up for an art class.
2
Read the Book of 2 John. Share what you learn with a friend.
3
4
5
Pick fresh flowers for a friend.
6
The 1st Sunday in August is National Friendship Day. Reconnect with old friends.
7
8
9
It's National S'mores Day. Enjoy a campfire with friends.
10
Read James 1:19–20. Find ways to put it into practice.
11
Donate your old cell phone to Call to Protect.
www.wirelessfoundation.org
12
13
Spend an evening star-gazing. Praise God for the beauty of creation!
14
Pray for a person of influence: it's Debra Messing's birthday.
15
Make an old family recipe from scratch.
16
Learn about mission opportunities at www.rightnow.org
17
18
19
Look through an old scrapbook and pray for everyone in the photos.
20
August is Romance Awareness Month. Find out how your grandparents met.
21
Host a Mexican fiesta for your neighbors.
22
Introduce yourself to someone new at church.
23
Reorganize your closet.
24
25
Go for a walk at sunset and pray.
26
27
28
Visit a pick-your-own fruit farm.
www.pickyourown.org
29
Pray for a person of influence: Cameron Diaz is celebrating a birthday.
30
31
Think about the things that are true and honorable and right and pure and beautiful and respected.
—Philippians 4:8

Ephesians 4:16

The human brain is truly fascinating. Our mind is like the control center for everything we do daily—walking, eating, thinking, talking, daydreaming, hugging, listening, breathing . . . everything. The rest of our body, from head to toe, behaves according to our brain's direction.

The Bible describes the church as Christ's body, with Christ as the head. That's a perfect metaphor because as parts of his body, we should be acting and moving in unity. The only way to have real love in the church is to keep our common focus on following Christ. We shouldn't pretend we can operate as isolated, self-governing people doing our own thing apart from other believers or apart from God. Instead, we should take care of each other in every way we can, following Christ's leading.

Every morning when you wake up, instead of thinking, *What do I want to do today?* ask God, "What do *you* want me to do today?" Make Christ the head of your life by allowing him to direct your thoughts and actions, and lovingly encourage other Christians to do the same. You'll be amazed at what God will do through the body of Christ when it's working together in obedience!

and some to have the work of caring for and teaching God's people. [12]Christ gave those gifts to prepare God's holy people for the work of serving, to make the body of Christ stronger. [13]This work must continue until we are all joined together in the same faith and in the same knowledge of the Son of God. We must become like a mature person, growing until we become like Christ and have his perfection.

[14]Then we will no longer be babies. We will not be tossed about like a ship that the waves carry one way and then another. We will not be influenced by every new teaching we hear from people who are trying to fool us. They make plans and try any kind of trick to fool people into following the wrong path. [15]No! Speaking the truth with love, we will grow up in every way into Christ, who is the head. [16]The whole body depends on Christ, and all the parts of the body are joined and held together. Each part does its own work to make the whole body grow and be strong with love.

The Way You Should Live

[17]In the Lord's name, I tell you this. Do not continue living like those who do not believe. Their thoughts are worth nothing. [18]They do not understand, and they know nothing, because they refuse to listen. So they cannot have the life that God gives. [19]They have lost all feeling of shame, and they use their lives for doing evil. They continually want to do all kinds of evil. [20]But what you learned in Christ was not like this. [21]I know that you heard about him, and you are in him, so you were taught the truth that is in Jesus. [22]You were taught to leave your old self—to stop living the evil way you lived before. That old self becomes worse, because people are fooled by the evil things they want to do. [23]But you were taught to be made new in your hearts, [24]to become a new person. That new person is made to be like God—made to be truly good and holy.

[25]So you must stop telling lies. Tell each other the truth, because we all belong to each other in the same body.[n] [26]When you are angry, do not sin, and be sure to stop being angry before the end of the day. [27]Do not give the devil a way to defeat you. [28]Those who are stealing must stop stealing and start working. They should earn an honest living for themselves. Then they will have something to share with those who are poor.

[29]When you talk, do not say harmful things, but say what people need—words that will help others become stronger. Then what you say will do good to those who listen to you. [30]And do not make the Holy Spirit sad. The Spirit is God's proof that you belong to him. God gave you the Spirit to show that God will make you free when the final day comes. [31]Do not be bitter or angry or mad. Never shout angrily

fun facts

The U.S. restaurant industry provides more than 70 billion meals and snacks each year.

(National Restaurant Association)

4:25 Tell . . . body. Quotation from Zechariah 8:16.

or say things to hurt others. Never do anything evil. [32]Be kind and loving to each other, and forgive each other just as God forgave you in Christ.

Living in the Light

5 You are God's children whom he loves, so try to be like him. [2]Live a life of love just as Christ loved us and gave himself for us as a sweet-smelling offering and sacrifice to God.

[3]But there must be no sexual sin among you, or any kind of evil or greed. Those things are not right for God's holy people. [4]Also, there must be no evil talk among you, and you must not speak foolishly or tell evil jokes. These things are not right for you. Instead, you should be giving thanks to God. [5]You can be sure of this: No one will have a place in the kingdom of Christ and of God who sins sexually, or does evil things, or is greedy. Anyone who is greedy is serving a false god.

[6]Do not let anyone fool you by telling you things that are not true, because these things will bring God's anger on those who do not obey him. [7]So have nothing to do with them. [8]In the past you were full of darkness, but now you are full of light in the Lord. So live like children who belong to the light. [9]Light brings every kind of goodness, right living, and truth. [10]Try to learn what pleases the Lord. [11]Have nothing to do with the things done in darkness, which are not worth anything. But show that they are wrong. [12]It is shameful even to talk about what those people do in secret. [13]But the light makes all things easy to see, [14]and everything that is made easy to see can become light. This is why it is said:

"Wake up, sleeper!
Rise from death,
and Christ will shine on you."

[15]So be very careful how you live. Do not live like those who are not wise, but live wisely. [16]Use every chance you have for doing good, because these are evil times. [17]So do not be foolish but learn what the Lord wants you to do. [18]Do not be drunk with wine, which will ruin you, but be filled with the Spirit. [19]Speak to each other with psalms, hymns, and spiritual songs, singing and making music in your hearts to the Lord. [20]Always give thanks to God the Father for everything, in the name of our Lord Jesus Christ.

Wives and Husbands

[21]Yield to obey each other as you would to Christ.

[22]Wives, yield to your husbands, as you do to the Lord, [23]because the husband is the head of the wife, as Christ is the head of the church. And he is the Savior of the body, which is the church. [24]As the church yields to Christ, so you wives should yield to your husbands in everything.

[25]Husbands, love your wives as Christ loved the church and gave himself for it [26]to make it belong to God. Christ used the

LIFE ISSUES

Powerful Weakness

What's your greatest weakness? We've all got them. Even the most put-together, spiritually mature woman has something she struggles with. While your first temptation might be to hide your weakness, God takes a very different (and purposeful!) approach. He sees your weaknesses as ways to show his strength to others. If your weaknesses get you down, study 2 Corinthians 12:9–10. Then, like Paul, you can say that "when I am weak, then I am truly strong" because of Christ's power shining through you (12:10). Ask God for firsthand experience of his power—it's life changing!

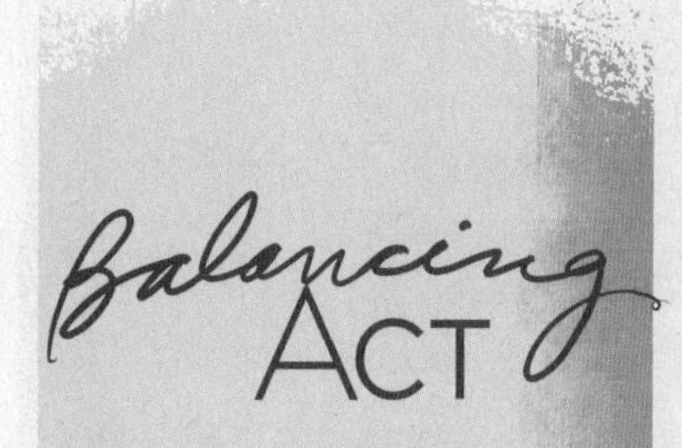

Miser or Good Steward?

Are you the friend who always buys lunch? Maybe you're the moocher (surely not!). Perhaps you're meticulously fair, paying exactly what you owe (with the standard 15 percent tip) and not a penny more or less. God wants us to be balanced in the way we approach money. The Bible is full of references to being generous and caring for those less fortunate! God also warns against wasting money on earthly treasures that bring temporary pleasure (Matthew 6:19). In other words, be generous with others and more conservative when making purchases for yourself. A balanced approach is to hold possessions and money loosely, knowing that ultimately they belong to God.

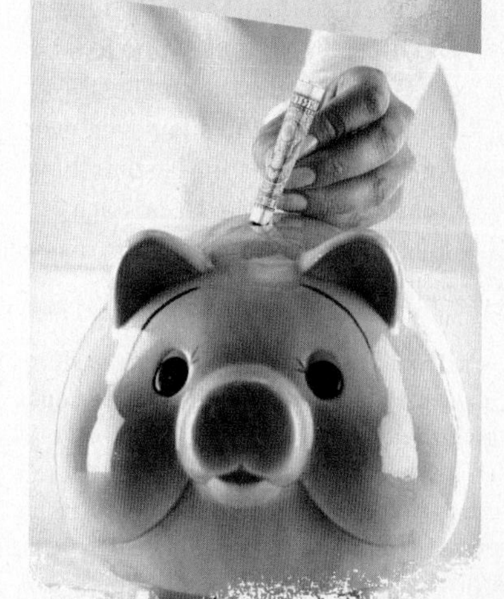

Health

Gluttony

Chances are, you've never heard a sermon on overeating. After all, churches often organize gatherings around a plate of fried chicken or a casserole for fellowship. But the Bible makes it clear that excessive eating, or gluttony, is a sin (Proverbs 23:20–21). We live in a fast-food nation where more than half of all adults are overweight. Carrying just a few extra pounds puts you at higher risk for preventable diseases such as heart disease, high blood pressure, and diabetes. Making healthy food choices is important, but portion control is critical. Most fast-food restaurants offer healthier options than the traditional burger and fries. If you can't say no to greasy fare, order the smallest burger on the menu and never, ever upsize it. If overeating is something you struggle with, ask God each day to help you become more disciplined.

word to make the church clean by washing it with water. [27]He died so that he could give the church to himself like a bride in all her beauty. He died so that the church could be pure and without fault, with no evil or sin or any other wrong thing in it. [28]In the same way, husbands should love their wives as they love their own bodies. The man who loves his wife loves himself. [29]No one ever hates his own body, but feeds and takes care of it. And that is what Christ does for the church, [30]because we are parts of his body. [31]The Scripture says, "So a man will leave his father and mother and be united with his wife, and the two will become one body."[n] [32]That secret is very important—I am talking about Christ and the church. [33]But each one of you must love his wife as he loves himself, and a wife must respect her husband.

Children and Parents

6 Children, obey your parents as the Lord wants, because this is the right thing to do. [2]The command says, "Honor your father and mother."[n] This is the first command that has a promise with it— [3]"Then everything will be well with you, and you will have a long life on the earth."[n]

[4]Fathers, do not make your children angry, but raise them with the training and teaching of the Lord.

Slaves and Masters

[5]Slaves, obey your masters here on earth with fear and respect and from a sincere heart, just as you obey Christ. [6]You must do this not only while they are watching you, to please them. With all your heart you must do what God wants as people who are obeying Christ. [7]Do your work with enthusiasm. Work as if you were serving the Lord, not as if you were serving only men and women. [8]Remember that the Lord will give a reward to everyone, slave or free, for doing good.

[9]Masters, in the same way, be good to your slaves. Do not threaten them. Remember that the One who is your Master and their Master is in heaven, and he treats everyone alike.

Wear the Full Armor of God

[10]Finally, be strong in the Lord and in his great power. [11]Put on the full armor of God so that you can fight against the devil's evil tricks. [12]Our fight is not against people on earth but against the rulers and authorities and the powers of this world's darkness, against the spiritual powers of evil in the heavenly world. [13]That is why you need to put on God's full armor. Then on the day of evil you will be able to stand strong. And when you have finished the whole fight, you will still be standing. [14]So stand strong, with the belt of truth tied around your waist and the protection of

Things That Go Bump in the Night

Whether it's the sound of an old house settling or a deafening clap of thunder, noises that disrupt the calm of night can leave us rattled. Darkness, often used as a metaphor for evil, inhibits our ability to see, compounding the fear. But what we're really afraid of isn't the dark itself, but rather *what's out there*—the "powers of this world's darkness" (Ephesians 6:12). As believers in the Resurrection, we know that our life on earth is temporary, but our spirits are eternal. There's nothing anyone or anything on earth can do to destroy us. When night terror threatens to steal your peace, speak this prayer from God's Word: "I will not be afraid, because the Lord is my helper. People can't do anything to me" (Hebrews 13:6).

5:31 "So . . . body." Quotation from Genesis 2:24. **6:2 "Honor . . . mother."** Quotation from Exodus 20:12; Deuteronomy 5:16. **6:3 "Then . . . earth."** Quotation from Exodus 20:12; Deuteronomy 5:16.

right living on your chest. [15]On your feet wear the Good News of peace to help you stand strong. [16]And also use the shield of faith with which you can stop all the burning arrows of the Evil One. [17]Accept God's salvation as your helmet, and take the sword of the Spirit, which is the word of God. [18]Pray in the Spirit at all times with all kinds of prayers, asking for everything you need. To do this you must always be ready and never give up. Always pray for all God's people.

[19]Also pray for me that when I speak, God will give me words so that I can tell the secret of the Good News without fear. [20]I have been sent to preach this Good News, and I am doing that now, here in prison. Pray that when I preach the Good News I will speak without fear, as I should.

Final Greetings

[21]I am sending to you Tychicus, our brother whom we love and a faithful servant of the Lord's work. He will tell you everything that is happening with me. Then you will know how I am and what I am doing. [22]I am sending him to you for this reason—so that you will know how we are, and he can encourage you.

[23]Peace and love with faith to you brothers and sisters from God the Father and the Lord Jesus Christ. [24]Grace to all of you who love our Lord Jesus Christ with love that never ends.

Carrying Out God's Mission

Did you know that God wants you to play a role in fulfilling his eternal goal for the entire universe? Before the beginning of time, he chose you to help accomplish his plan (Ephesians 1:11). What's God's plan? How can we help to accomplish it? Both questions are answered in the Book of Ephesians.

First, Paul writes that God intends to join all things in heaven and earth together, with Jesus as the head (Ephesians 1:10). God has already been at work achieving this goal. When Adam and Eve sinned, God, who is holy, could no longer have a relationship with humanity. But he loved us and wanted to restore our relationship with him, so he sent Jesus to die so we could be made holy. The first part of God's plan—reconciling his people to himself—was accomplished when Jesus died on the cross.

Not only did Jesus repair the relationship with God and his people, but he also broke down the walls that stood between the people themselves (the second part of his plan to bring everything together). Jesus' death made it possible for everyone to be unified as one family—the church, which is called the body of Christ.

God is now working through us to accomplish his plan by strengthening the church. He wants us to continue the work he started by striving to live in unity with others, seeking him, and growing in him. It's no simple task, but with the Holy Spirit living in us, we can do anything—even play a role in carrying out God's mission for the universe!

Get Real

Why do you think God wants to reconcile his people to himself? (1 John 4:9–10; Revelation 21:3)

What is the purpose of the church? (John 17:20–23)

How does it make you feel to know that God chose you to help fulfill his ultimate purpose? (Romans 8:29–30; 1 Peter 2:9)

Are there any ways that you're hindering the church from being unified? (Romans 12)

How can you play a more effective role in your church? (1 Corinthians 12)

philippians

Too often we think joy will just happen to us when life is easy, fun, and comfortable. Or we think, "If I could just have more [*fill in the blank*], I could have joy." But that's simply not true. How many people do you know who seem to have everything—money, beauty, fame, power—but are totally miserable? If even movie stars, media moguls, glamorous models, and international business tycoons aren't joyful, how can anyone achieve a state of joy?

Paul had the secret. In this affectionate letter to his dear friends in Philippi, Paul says joy is always possible, regardless of the circumstances. The key is to find joy in what God is doing and in *who* God is. Paul expressed joy because of what God was doing in the Philippian believers' lives. He rejoiced in his own difficulties because he knew it was all part of God's plan to spread the Good News. And Paul even counted it a joyful privilege to suffer like Christ suffered because he knew his hardships were making him more like Jesus.

Learn to trust God—take joy in knowing that he is good and that his plans are perfect. He's in control and he loves you, so you can always be joyful when your life belongs to him!

1 From Paul and Timothy, servants of Christ Jesus.

To all of God's holy people in Christ Jesus who live in Philippi, including your overseers and deacons:

[2]Grace and peace to you from God our Father and the Lord Jesus Christ.

Paul's Prayer

[3]I thank my God every time I remember you, [4]always praying with joy for all of you. [5]I thank God for the help you gave me while I preached the Good News—help you gave from the first day you believed until now. [6]God began doing a good work in you, and I am sure he will continue it until it is finished when Jesus Christ comes again.

[7]And I know that I am right to think like this about all of you, because I have you in my heart. All of you share in God's grace with me while I am in prison and while I am defending and proving the truth of the Good News. [8]God knows that I want to see you very much, because I love all of you with the love of Christ Jesus.

[9]This is my prayer for you: that your love will grow more and more; that you will have knowledge and understanding with your love; [10]that you will see the difference between good and bad and will choose the good; that you will be pure and without wrong for the coming of Christ; [11]that you will be filled with the good things produced in your life by Christ to bring glory and praise to God.

Paul's Troubles Help the Work

[12]I want you brothers and sisters to know that what has happened to me has helped to spread the Good News. [13]All the palace guards and everyone else knows

that I am in prison because I am a believer in Christ. [14]Because I am in prison, most of the believers have become more bold in Christ and are not afraid to speak the word of God.

[15]It is true that some preach about Christ because they are jealous and ambitious, but others preach about Christ because they want to help. [16]They preach because they have love, and they know that God gave me the work of defending the Good News. [17]But the others preach about Christ for selfish and wrong reasons, wanting to make trouble for me in prison.

[18]But it doesn't matter. The important thing is that in every way, whether for right or wrong reasons, they are preaching about Christ. So I am happy, and I will continue to be happy. [19]Because you are praying for me and the Spirit of Jesus Christ is helping me, I know this trouble will bring my freedom. [20]I expect and hope that I will not fail Christ in anything but that I will have the courage now, as always, to show the greatness of Christ in my life here on earth, whether I live or die. [21]To me the only important thing about living is Christ, and dying would be profit for me. [22]If I continue living in my body, I will be able to work for the Lord. I do not know what to choose—living or dying. [23]It is hard to choose between the two. I want to leave this life and be with Christ, which is much better, [24]but you need me here in my body. [25]Since I am sure of this, I know I will stay with you to help you grow and have joy in your faith. [26]You will be very happy in Christ Jesus when I am with you again.

[27]Only one thing concerns me: Be sure that you live in a way that brings honor to the Good News of Christ. Then whether I come and visit you or am away from you, I will hear that you are standing strong with one purpose, that you work together as one for the faith of the Good News, [28]and that you are not afraid of those who are against you. All of this is proof that your enemies will be destroyed but that you will be saved by God. [29]God gave you the honor not only of believing in Christ but also of suffering for him, both of which bring glory to Christ. [30]When I was with you, you saw the struggles I had, and you hear about the struggles I am having now. You yourselves are having the same kind of struggles.

2

Does your life in Christ give you strength? Does his love comfort you? Do we share together in the spirit? Do you have mercy and kindness? [2]If so, make me very happy by having the same thoughts, sharing the same love, and having one mind and purpose. [3]When you do things, do not let selfishness or pride be your guide. Instead, be humble and give more honor to others than to yourselves. [4]Do not be interested only in your own

fun facts

A recent survey found that 51% of Americans feel their lives have been greatly transformed by their faith.

(Barna.org)

BECOME Involved

FamilyLife's Hope for Orphans

Firsthand accounts of orphanages around the world highlight deplorable, heart-wrenching stories of mistreatment, neglect, and abandonment. Images of wall-to-wall cribs with multiple children tied or chained so they don't fall out haunt visitors long after they arrive back home. There are so many suffering, though. What can one person do?

The sheer numbers of mother- and fatherless children in the United States and around the world can be overwhelming. Yet caring for orphans is one of the basic tenets of pure religion. It's one duty Christians have that is mentioned over and over again throughout Scripture. FamilyLife's Hope for Orphans is taking that responsibility seriously and helping individuals, families, and churches do the same.

You can do something to aid in rescuing orphans from a loveless life of sorrow. And contrary to initial thoughts, there are many ways to be involved in addition to adopting. You can start or help support a church orphan ministry. You can contribute to FamilyLife. And you can help spread the word and the passion behind Hope for Orphans. Check out www.familylife.com/hopefororphans to find out how you can influence the world—one child at a time.

life, but be interested in the lives of others.

Be Unselfish Like Christ

[5]In your lives you must think and act like Christ Jesus.

[6]Christ himself was like God in everything.
But he did not think that being equal with God was something to be used for his own benefit.
[7]But he gave up his place with God and made himself nothing.
He was born as a man and became like a servant.
[8]And when he was living as a man, he humbled himself and was fully obedient to God,
even when that caused his death—death on a cross.
[9]So God raised him to the highest place.
God made his name greater than every other name
[10]so that every knee will bow to the name of Jesus—
everyone in heaven, on earth, and under the earth.
[11]And everyone will confess that Jesus Christ is Lord
and bring glory to God the Father.

Philippians 2:3–4

The adjectives "selfish" or "proud" may bring to mind particular personalities you've run across in life. Perhaps they were people who spent more time bragging or showing off than they realized. But even if we're not boasting or acting like a know-it-all, we can still have subtle areas of selfishness or pride in our hearts.

Do you ever quietly obsess about your own issues, to the point that you never notice what's going on in other people's lives? Do you have trouble really listening and caring when your friends share their hearts with you? Do you resent giving up your precious time to help meet someone else's needs?

It's so easy to slip unaware into selfish living. We have a natural tendency to focus on ourselves. But total focus on yourself can eventually ruin your ability to love God and other people. Christ's followers are called to give more honor to others than to ourselves and to give the kind of love that Jesus gives to us—that means sacrifice, selflessness, and service.

Whenever you're tempted to be ruled by selfish desires, remember Jesus' example of humility. You'll find new joy in your heart as you pour out love and become transformed into someone who looks more like Jesus every day.

Be the People God Wants You to Be

[12]My dear friends, you have always obeyed God when I was with you. It is even more important that you obey now while I am away from you. Keep on working to complete your salvation with fear and trembling, [13]because God is working in you to help you want to do and be able to do what pleases him.

[14]Do everything without complaining or arguing. [15]Then you will be innocent and without any wrong. You will be God's children without fault. But you are living with crooked and mean people all around you, among whom you shine like stars in the dark world. [16]You offer the teaching that gives life. So when Christ comes again, I can be happy because my work was not wasted. I ran the race and won.

[17]Your faith makes you offer your lives as a sacrifice in serving God. If I have to offer my own blood with your sacrifice, I will be happy and full of joy with all of you. [18]You also should be happy and full of joy with me.

Timothy and Epaphroditus

[19]I hope in the Lord Jesus to send Timothy to you soon. I will be happy to learn how you are. [20]I have no one else like Timothy, who truly cares for you. [21]Other people are interested only in their own lives, not in the work of Jesus Christ. [22]You know the kind of person Timothy is. You know he has served with me in telling the Good News, as a son serves his father. [23]I plan to send him to you quickly when I know what will happen to me. [24]I am sure that the Lord will help me to come to you soon.

[25]Epaphroditus, my brother in Christ, works and serves with me in the army of Christ. When I needed help, you sent him to me. I think now that I must send him back to you, [26]because he wants very much to see all of you. He is worried because you heard that he was sick. [27]Yes, he was sick, and nearly died, but God had mercy on him and me too so that I would not have more sadness. [28]I want very much to send him to you so that when you see him you can be happy, and I can stop worrying about you. [29]Welcome him

QUIZ

WHICH PET IS BEST FOR YOU?

THE FIRST JOB GOD GAVE MANKIND WAS TO CARE FOR THE ANIMALS HE CREATED (GENESIS 2:19). OF COURSE YOU DON'T EXACTLY LIVE IN THE GARDEN OF EDEN, BUT WHY NOT TRY YOUR HAND AT CARING FOR ONE OF GOD'S CREATIONS? CHECK OUT THE QUESTIONS BELOW TO SEE WHICH PET IS RIGHT FOR YOU.

1. HOW MUCH TIME AND ATTENTION DO YOU HAVE TO DEVOTE TO TAKING CARE OF A PET?

- [ ] A. Lots and lots—he or she will be my new BFF!
- [ ] B. A good bit—he or she will be a big part of my life.
- [ ] C. A little—he or she will be fun to have around when I'm bored.
- [ ] D. Hardly any—but I really want a pet anyway.

2. WHICH ONE WORD WOULD YOUR FRIENDS USE TO DESCRIBE YOU?

- [ ] A. Fun
- [ ] B. Kindhearted
- [ ] C. Calm
- [ ] D. Adventurous

3. HOW MUCH FREEDOM WILL YOUR PET HAVE TO ROAM AROUND?

- [ ] A. Whatever his or her little heart desires.
- [ ] B. He or she can have free reign over the whole house or apartment.
- [ ] C. He or she will have to stay contained most of the time.
- [ ] D. They're supposed to roam around? Isn't that why they have cages?

4. HOW OFTEN DO YOU TRAVEL AWAY FROM HOME OVERNIGHT?

- [ ] A. Rarely
- [ ] B. Occasionally
- [ ] C. Frequently
- [ ] D. I'm hardly ever home.

5. WHICH OF THE FOLLOWING DO YOU MOST WANT YOUR PET TO DO FOR YOU?

- [ ] A. Entertain me and give me something to do
- [ ] B. Love me and cuddle with me
- [ ] C. Provide some company for me
- [ ] D. Make me a more interesting person

SCORING:

IF YOU CHOSE MOSTLY AS, YOU SHOULD LOOK FOR AN **UNUSUAL PET.** Consider a potbellied pig, a chinchilla, or a talking bird. Go ahead, girl! You've got the personality to pull it off. You can train your little friend to be the life of the party next time you entertain guests!

IF YOU CHOSE MOSTLY BS, YOU SHOULD LOOK FOR A **TRADITIONAL PET.** A frisky little puppy or a fanciful kitty cat would be ideal for you. Go for it! You can spend time playing together and loving on each other after a hard day at work. Your life will be richer for it!

IF YOU CHOSE MOSTLY CS, YOU SHOULD LOOK FOR AN **OBSERVATIONAL PET.** Why not buy some colorful tropical fish, a little froggy, or a family of hermit crabs? Go ahead! You can enjoy your little critters without having a major time or space commitment. You'll love 'em!

IF YOU CHOSE MOSTLY DS, YOU SHOULD LOOK FOR AN **EXOTIC PET.** Broaden your horizons with a lazy snake or stately iguana. Go for it! Carefully research your choice, and then amaze your friends with your depth and creativity. You can usually leave these little guys alone without major trauma, so no need to feel guilty when you're not spending time with them!

RELATIONSHIPS

The Thank Bank

Need an occasional reminder to thank God for the people he puts in your life? The Thank Bank can do just that! Jot down a list of bright smiles, listening ears, giving natures, and helping hands that perk up your days. Be specific with names—this list is just for you. Add verses and prayers about friendship and love, cut out each item, collect the slips of paper in a jar or box, and put your Thank Bank where you'll see it. Read one each day, and thank God for his gifts! (See 1 Corinthians 1:4 and 1 Thessalonians 1:2.)

in the Lord with much joy. Give honor to people like him, [30]because he almost died for the work of Christ. He risked his life to give me the help you could not give in your service to me.

The Importance of Christ

3 My brothers and sisters, be full of joy in the Lord. It is no trouble for me to write the same things to you again, and it will help you to be more ready. [2]Watch out for those who do evil, who are like dogs, who demand to cut[n] the body. [3]We are the ones who are truly circumcised. We worship God through his Spirit, and our pride is in Christ Jesus. We do not put trust in ourselves or anything we can do, [4]although I might be able to put trust in myself. If anyone thinks he has a reason to trust in himself, he should know that I have greater reason for trusting in myself. [5]I was circumcised eight days after my birth. I am from the people of Israel and the tribe of Benjamin. I am a Hebrew, and my parents were Hebrews. I had a strict view of the law, which is why I became a Pharisee. [6]I was so enthusiastic I tried to hurt the church. No one could find fault with the way I obeyed the law of Moses. [7]Those things were important to me, but now I think they are worth nothing because of Christ. [8]Not only those things, but I think that all things are worth nothing compared with the greatness of knowing Christ Jesus my Lord. Because of him, I have lost all those things, and now I know they are worthless trash. This allows me to have Christ [9]and to belong to him. Now I am right with God, not because I followed the law, but because I believed in Christ. God uses my faith to make me right with him. [10]I want to know Christ and the power that raised him from the dead. I want to share in his sufferings and become like him in his death. [11]Then I have hope that I myself will be raised from the dead.

Continuing Toward Our Goal

[12]I do not mean that I am already as God wants me to be. I have not yet reached that

beauty BECOMES HER

Soften Up!

Lip balm softens the lips. Lotion softens the skin. Moisturizer softens the face, and conditioner softens the hair. But what softens a heart? After all, a heart that is soft and pliable is the kind that Jesus wants. Ask him to make your heart sensitive to the presence and guiding of his Holy Spirit. Be flexible and available to whatever he leads you to do, think, or learn. As you grow closer to him, you will be a tender reflection of his love and beauty. Then your heart will be as soft as the silky, smooth skin you have.

3:2 cut The word in Greek is like the word "circumcise," but it means "to cut completely off."

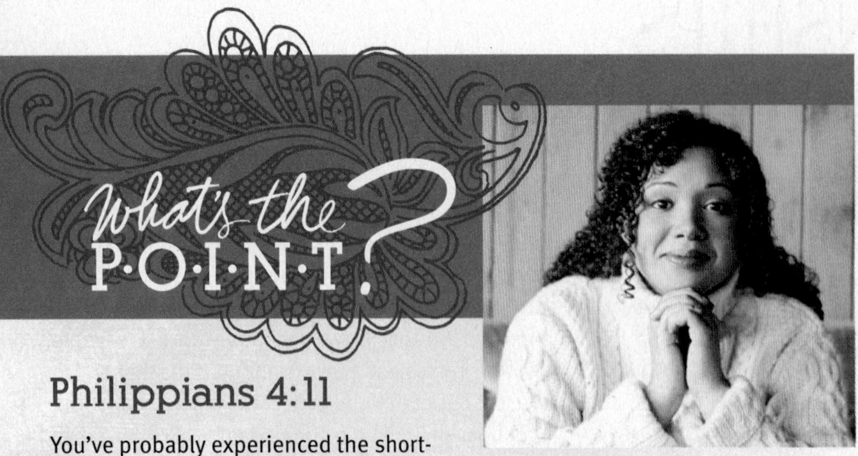

Philippians 4:11

You've probably experienced the short-term satisfaction of reaching a big goal or having a fun experience. Maybe you feel pretty satisfied for a whole day, a week, or even a few months. But eventually, you always get to a point where you realize, *I want more*. No matter what we get from this world, it'll never be enough.

God designed us to need him. His goodness and beauty and love have no end. Only he can fill up our hearts. Anything else will just provide a temporary fix for our emptiness. But when we have Christ, we really have everything! Even when life seems overwhelming, we can be satisfied with the hope God put in our hearts—the hope of an eternity with him!

If you've never had true satisfaction, try switching your focus. Look to Jesus and ask him to help you find all of your delight, joy, and peace in your relationship with him. The more you know him, the more satisfaction you'll have in your heart—no matter what ups and downs you face. Like Paul, you will find that knowing Christ is the "secret of being happy at any time in everything that happens" (Philippians 4:12).

goal, but I continue trying to reach it and to make it mine. Christ wants me to do that, which is the reason he made me his. [13]Brothers and sisters, I know that I have not yet reached that goal, but there is one thing I always do. Forgetting the past and straining toward what is ahead, [14]I keep trying to reach the goal and get the prize for which God called me through Christ to the life above.

[15]All of us who are spiritually mature should think this way, too. And if there are things you do not agree with, God will make them clear to you. [16]But we should continue following the truth we already have.

[17]Brothers and sisters, all of you should try to follow my example and to copy those who live the way we showed you. [18]Many people live like enemies of the cross of Christ. I have often told you about them, and it makes me cry to tell you about them now. [19]In the end, they will be destroyed. They do whatever their bodies want, they are proud of their shameful acts, and they think only about earthly things. [20]But our homeland is in heaven, and we are waiting for our Savior, the Lord Jesus Christ, to come from heaven. [21]By his power to rule all things, he will change our humble bodies and make them like his own glorious body.

What the Christians Are to Do

4 My dear brothers and sisters, I love you and want to see you. You bring me joy and make me proud of you, so stand strong in the Lord as I have told you.

[2]I ask Euodia and Syntyche to agree in the Lord. [3]And I ask you, my faithful friend, to help these women. They served with me in telling the Good News, together with Clement and others who worked with me, whose names are written in the book of life.[n]

[4]Be full of joy in the Lord always. I will say again, be full of joy.

[5]Let everyone see that you are gentle and kind. The Lord is coming soon. [6]Do not worry about anything, but pray and ask

In Spirit and Truth

John 4:19–26 tells of a woman who was confused about worship. Because she didn't know Jesus as Messiah, her Savior, she was missing worship's two key elements: spirit and truth. Jesus clarified that "true worshipers will worship the Father in spirit and truth" (4:23). But what does that mean? It's impossible to understand, or offer, true worship without first understanding the *truth* of who we worship—Jesus, the long-awaited Messiah. And it's impossible to carry the *spirit* of worship in our hearts without a growing relationship with him. Like all of us today, this woman needed a personal encounter with Jesus in order to grasp the full picture of true worship.

➳ **4:3 book of life** God's book that has the names of all God's chosen people (Revelation 3:5; 21:27).

God for everything you need, always giving thanks. [7]And God's peace, which is so great we cannot understand it, will keep your hearts and minds in Christ Jesus.

[8]Brothers and sisters, think about the things that are good and worthy of praise. Think about the things that are true and honorable and right and pure and beautiful and respected. [9]Do what you learned and received from me, what I told you, and what you saw me do. And the God who gives peace will be with you.

Paul Thanks the Christians

[10]I am very happy in the Lord that you have shown your care for me again. You continued to care about me, but there was no way for you to show it. [11]I am not telling you this because I need anything. I have learned to be satisfied with the things I have and with everything that happens. [12]I know how to live when I am poor, and I know how to live when I have plenty. I have learned the secret of being happy at any time in everything that happens, when I have enough to eat and when I go hungry, when I have more than I need and when I do not have enough. [13]I can do all things through Christ, because he gives me strength.

[14]But it was good that you helped me when I needed it. [15]You Philippians remember when I first preached the Good News there. When I left Macedonia, you were the only church that gave me help. [16]Several times you sent me things I needed when I was in Thessalonica. [17]Really, it is not that I want to receive gifts from you, but I want you to have the good that comes from giving. [18]And now I have everything, and more. I have all I need, because Epaphroditus brought your gift to me. It is like a sweet-smelling sacrifice offered to God, who accepts that sacrifice and is pleased with it. [19]My God will use his wonderful riches in Christ Jesus to give you everything you need. [20]Glory to our God and Father forever and ever! Amen.

[21]Greet each of God's people in Christ Jesus. Those who are with me send greetings to you. [22]All of God's people greet you, particularly those from the palace of Caesar.

[23]The grace of the Lord Jesus Christ be with you all.

Philippians
Unending Joy

Despite the fact that Paul wrote this letter from prison, its message is one of pure joy and encouragement. While it contains some of the Bible's greatest teaching on how to be more like Christ, it was also written as a friendly letter of thanks and support to believers from the church Paul established at Philippi.

Some of the Bible's most-quoted sound bites are contained in this little book (Philippians 1:9, 21; 2:14; 3:7–10, 14; 4:4, 6–8, 13). These well-known verses are loaded with truth and have encouraged generations of believers to continue becoming more like Christ.

Paul never wavered from his basic message that a life centered on Christ brings *joy*. He was not referring to *happiness*—which is a temporary emotional state. Paul had experienced highs and lows in his ministry, and he knew that only true joy in Christ could carry him through (Philippians 4:11–13). The way to experience that kind of joy is to become more like Christ (2:1–11).

When we understand sin and our inability to approach God on our own, we can truly find joy in what he's done for us. Discover true satisfaction in knowing Christ. Live joyfully and confidently for him, and be full of hope knowing that someday he will return!

Get Real

How can we rejoice when a Christian dies? (Psalm 116:15; Romans 5:16–21)

What can you do to know Christ better? (Ephesians 1:16–18; 1 John 4:1–3)

Why should we, like Paul, learn to be content with our circumstances? (Proverbs 19:23; Ecclesiastes 4:4–6; 1 Timothy 6:6–9)

Where does real joy come from? (Psalms 16:11; 97:11–12; Ecclesiastes 2:26; John 15:9–11)

How can you encourage friends in the faith? (Romans 12:8; 1 Thessalonians 4:13–18; Hebrews 10:24–25)

colossians

It's fun to mix things up—from creating exciting new treats (like chocolate-mint iced chai) to combining retro accessories with the latest fashions, it's just plain fun to have your own unique take on life.

But when it comes to the Good News, that's one thing you don't want to tamper with. When you add things to the pure message of Christ found in Scripture, the truth about Jesus gets lost along the way.

That's what was happening with the Colossian believers. They began listening to the lies of some false teachers who claimed that in addition to Christ, other religious rituals were necessary. Apparently, it developed into a weird mix of Judaism, ancient pagan practices, and Christianity. They may have even worshiped angels!

Paul doesn't specifically deal with each of the false teachings the Colossians were following. Instead, he combats the lies with the truth: Jesus is enough! Through his death and resurrection our salvation is complete, and we don't need to add anything else.

As you follow Christ in your unique way, make absolutely certain that you stick to Scripture, not some hodgepodge of human ideas. The body of Christ is a wonderful mix of different people, but we all need to be standing firmly on the pure Good News about Jesus Christ!

1 From Paul, an apostle of Christ Jesus. I am an apostle because that is what God wanted. Also from Timothy, our brother.

[2]To the holy and faithful brothers and sisters in Christ that live in Colossae:

Grace and peace to you from God our Father.[n]

[3]In our prayers for you we always thank God, the Father of our Lord Jesus Christ, [4]because we have heard about the faith you have in Christ Jesus and the love you have for all of God's people. [5]You have this faith and love because of your hope, and what you hope for is kept safe for you in heaven. You learned about this hope when you heard the message about the truth, the Good News [6]that was told to you. Everywhere in the world that Good News is bringing blessings and is growing. This has happened with you, too, since you heard the Good News and understood the truth about the grace of God. [7]You learned about God's grace from Epaphras, whom we love. He works together with us and is a faithful servant of Christ for us.[n] [8]He also told us about the love you have from the Holy Spirit.

[9]Because of this, since the day we heard about you, we have continued praying for you, asking God that you will know fully what he wants. We pray that you will also have great wisdom and understanding in spiritual things [10]so that you will live the kind of life that honors and pleases the Lord in every way. You will produce fruit in every good work and grow in the knowledge of God. [11]God will strengthen you with his own great power so that you will not give up when troubles come, but you will be patient. [12]And you will joyfully give thanks to the Father who has made you[n] able to have a share in all that he has prepared for his people in the kingdom of

1:2 Father Some Greek copies continue, "and the Lord Jesus Christ." **1:7 for us** Some Greek copies read "for you." **1:12 you** Some Greek copies read "us."

Colossians 2:6–8

As a Christian, the Bible is your one and only source for discovering God's truth. You wouldn't check a bookstore's secular self-help section for ideas on becoming more Christlike. Praying and reading Scripture is the only way to know God's message to you.

But it's still so easy to let human ideas show us how to live. Instead of getting grounded in God's Word and going to him in prayer every day, we start looking for answers, encouragement, or comfort from other things . . . like friends, books, music, or movies. Sometimes those sources line up with God's truth and sometimes they don't. So we need to carefully compare other influences in our lives to God's Word so we don't get drawn away from him. If you resonate more with a song or sitcom character than with God's Word, you might want to step back and reevaluate your heart.

The psalmist called God's Word "everlasting," "a light for my path," "true," and "a great treasure" (Psalm 119:89, 105, 142, 162). You may receive support and helpful information from other sources, but always rely first and foremost on God's Word and prayer. Nothing can shake you when you're rooted in his truth.

light. [13]God has freed us from the power of darkness, and he brought us into the kingdom of his dear Son. [14]The Son paid for our sins,[n] and in him we have forgiveness.

The Importance of Christ

[15]No one can see God, but Jesus Christ is exactly like him. He ranks higher than everything that has been made. [16]Through his power all things were made—things in heaven and on earth, things seen and unseen, all powers, authorities, lords, and rulers. All things were made through Christ and for Christ. [17]He was there before anything was made, and all things continue because of him. [18]He is the head of the body, which is the church. Everything comes from him. He is the first one who was raised from the dead. So in all things Jesus has first place. [19]God was pleased for all of himself to live in Christ. [20]And through Christ, God has brought all things back to himself again—things on earth and things in heaven. God made peace through the blood of Christ's death on the cross.

[21]At one time you were separated from God. You were his enemies in your minds, and the evil things you did were against God. [22]But now God has made you his friends again. He did this through Christ's death in the body so that he might bring you into God's presence as people who are holy, with no wrong, and with nothing of which God can judge you guilty. [23]This will happen if you continue strong and sure in your faith. You must not be moved away from the hope brought to you by the Good News that you heard. That same Good News has been told to everyone in the world, and I, Paul, help in preaching that Good News.

Paul's Work for the Church

[24]I am happy in my sufferings for you. There are things that Christ must still suffer through his body, the church. I am accepting, in my body, my part of these things that must be suffered. [25]I became a servant of the church because God gave me a special work to do that helps you, and that work is to tell fully the message of God. [26]This message is the secret that was hidden from everyone since the beginning of time, but now it is made known to God's holy people. [27]God decided to let his people know this rich and glorious secret which he has for all people. This secret is Christ himself, who is in you. He is our only hope for glory. [28]So we continue to preach Christ to each person, using all wisdom to warn and to teach everyone, in

fun facts

Nearly 9 in 10 Americans support the idea of donating organs for transplants.

(Transweb.org)

1:14 **sins** Some Greek copies continue, "with his blood."

order to bring each one into God's presence as a mature person in Christ. [29]To do this, I work and struggle, using Christ's great strength that works so powerfully in me.

2 I want you to know how hard I work for you, those in Laodicea, and others who have never seen me. [2]I want them to be strengthened and joined together with love so that they may be rich in their understanding. This leads to their knowing fully God's secret, that is, Christ himself. [3]In him all the treasures of wisdom and knowledge are safely kept.

[4]I say this so that no one can fool you by arguments that seem good, but are false. [5]Though I am absent from you in my body, my heart is with you, and I am happy to see your good lives and your strong faith in Christ.

Continue to Live in Christ

[6]As you received Christ Jesus the Lord, so continue to live in him. [7]Keep your roots deep in him and have your lives built on him. Be strong in the faith, just as you were taught, and always be thankful.

[8]Be sure that no one leads you away with false and empty teaching that is only human, which comes from the ruling spirits of this world, and not from Christ. [9]All of God lives fully in Christ (even when Christ was on earth), [10]and you have a full and true life in Christ, who is ruler over all rulers and powers.

[11]Also in Christ you had a different kind of circumcision, a circumcision not done by hands. It was through Christ's circumcision, that is, his death, that you were made free from the power of your sinful self. [12]When you were baptized, you were buried with Christ, and you were raised up with him through your faith in God's power that was shown when he raised Christ from the dead. [13]When you were spiritually dead because of your sins and because you were not free from the power of your sinful self, God made you alive with Christ, and he forgave all our sins. [14]He canceled the debt, which listed all the rules we failed to follow. He took away that record with its rules and nailed it to the cross. [15]God stripped the spiritual rulers and powers of their authority. With the cross, he won the victory and showed the world that they were powerless.

Don't Follow People's Rules

[16]So do not let anyone make rules for you about eating and drinking or about a religious feast, a New Moon Festival, or a Sabbath day. [17]These things were like a shadow of what was to come. But what is true and real has come and is found in Christ. [18]Do not let anyone disqualify you by making you humiliate yourself and worship angels. Such people enter into visions, which fill them with foolish pride because of their human way of thinking. [19]They do

Q&A

Q: Being a caregiver is wearing me out! What can I do?

A: Caring for the sick and/or elderly can be exhausting physically, mentally, emotionally, and even spiritually. It is completely understandable that you feel "worn out." You need to know, though, that you are not alone. The total burden does not have to rest solely on your shoulders. Your heavenly Father is with you, and he can give you the strength and comfort you need to get through this difficult time. Guard your personal relationship with him carefully so you can minister out of his love and not your own strength. And don't be afraid to ask others for help.

Women & Men of the BIBLE

Elisha: Powerful Prophet

Elisha was chosen to be the successor to the prophet Elijah. He had some big shoes to fill, and he knew it. So before Elijah was taken to heaven, Elisha asked for a double portion of his spirit. And boy, did he ever get it! Elisha did more amazing miracles and had a broader-reaching ministry than his predecessor would have ever dreamed. Long after he was dead and buried, some Israelites hurriedly threw a dead man into Elisha's grave, and when the guy touched the bones in there, he instantly came back to life! Now *that's* a powerful prophet! (2 Kings 2—13)

HE SAID ↙ ↗ SHE SAID

When do you feel the most joy?

He: When my nieces hug me

She: When I sense God is pleased with my life

not hold tightly to Christ, the head. It is from him that all the parts of the body are cared for and held together. So it grows in the way God wants it to grow.

[20]Since you died with Christ and were made free from the ruling spirits of the world, why do you act as if you still belong to this world by following rules like these: [21]"Don't handle this," "Don't taste that," "Don't even touch that thing"? [22]These rules refer to earthly things that are gone as soon as they are used. They are only human commands and teachings. [23]They seem to be wise, but they are only part of a human religion. They make people pretend not to be proud and make them punish their bodies, but they do not really control the evil desires of the sinful self.

Your New Life in Christ

3 Since you were raised from the dead with Christ, aim at what is in heaven, where Christ is sitting at the right hand of God. [2]Think only about the things in heaven, not the things on earth. [3]Your old sinful self has died, and your new life is kept with Christ in God. [4]Christ is your[n] life, and when he comes again, you will share in his glory.

[5]So put all evil things out of your life: sexual sinning, doing evil, letting evil thoughts control you, wanting things that are evil, and greed. This is really serving a false god. [6]These things make God angry.[n] [7]In your past, evil life you also did these things.

[8]But now also put these things out of your life: anger, bad temper, doing or saying things to hurt others, and using evil words when you talk. [9]Do not lie to each other. You have left your old sinful life and the things you did before. [10]You have begun to live the new life, in which you are being made new and are becoming like the One who made you. This new life brings you the true knowledge of God. [11]In the new life there is no difference between Greeks and Jews, those who are circumcised and those who are not circumcised, or people who are foreigners, or Scythians.[n] There is no difference between slaves and free people. But Christ is in all believers, and Christ is all that is important.

[12]God has chosen you and made you his holy people. He loves you. So you should always clothe yourselves with mercy, kindness, humility, gentleness, and patience. [13]Bear with each other, and forgive each other. If someone does wrong to you, forgive that person because the Lord forgave you. [14]Even more than all this, clothe yourself in love. Love is what holds you all together in perfect unity. [15]Let the peace that Christ gives control your thinking, because you were all called together in one body[n] to have peace. Always be thankful. [16]Let the teaching of Christ live in you richly. Use all wisdom to teach and instruct each other by singing psalms, hymns, and spiritual songs with thankfulness in your hearts to God. [17]Everything you do or say should be done to obey Jesus your Lord. And in all you do, give thanks to God the Father through Jesus.

Your New Life with Other People

[18]Wives, yield to the authority of your husbands, because this is the right thing to do in the Lord.

[19]Husbands, love your wives and be gentle with them.

all about MEN

Triangle Growth

Change is one of life's few guarantees, and somehow that isn't very reassuring! As imperfect humans, we're constantly in the process of changing for the good or bad. That reality can make even *considering* a lifetime commitment to one person a frightening concept. Well here's a tip: the way to keep romance vibrant for decades is to structure your relationship like a triangle. The two of you are the bottom points, and God is the third, topmost point. The closer you grow toward God, the closer you grow toward each other. Even during seasons of up and down changes, you're still linked in Christ. Stick to the triangle, and your relationship will "shape" up to be a beautiful picture of godly love.

3:4 your Some Greek copies read "our." **3:6 These . . . angry** Some Greek copies continue, "against the people who do not obey God." **3:11 Scythians** The Scythians were known as very wild and cruel people. **3:15 body** The spiritual body of Christ, meaning the church or his people.

[20]Children, obey your parents in all things, because this pleases the Lord.

[21]Fathers, do not nag your children. If you are too hard to please, they may want to stop trying.

[22]Slaves, obey your masters in all things. Do not obey just when they are watching you, to gain their favor, but serve them honestly, because you respect the Lord. [23]In all the work you are doing, work the best you can. Work as if you were doing it for the Lord, not for people. [24]Remember that you will receive your reward from the Lord, which he promised to his people. You are serving the Lord Christ. [25]But remember that anyone who does wrong will be punished for that wrong, and the Lord treats everyone the same.

4 Masters, give what is good and fair to your slaves. Remember that you have a Master in heaven.

What the Christians Are to Do

[2]Continue praying, keeping alert, and always thanking God. [3]Also pray for us that God will give us an opportunity to tell people his message. Pray that we can preach the secret that God has made known about Christ. This is why I am in prison. [4]Pray that I can speak in a way that will make it clear, as I should.

[5]Be wise in the way you act with people who are not believers, making the most of every opportunity. [6]When you talk, you should always be kind and pleasant so you will be able to answer everyone in the way you should.

Colossians 4:3–6

"I didn't know you're a Christian!" Just imagine how you'd feel if one of your friends said that after seeing an open Bible on your coffee table. Maybe that's never happened to you . . . or if it has, maybe it was a huge wake-up call for you. Either way, no Christian can claim to be a perfect witness for Jesus. All of us have done or said something in front of non-Christians that probably made them think, *Christianity must not be that big of a deal. They're just like the rest of us.*

We're called to be completely different from the world around us. We're supposed to be like candles burning in a dark room or like a big city on a hill—impossible to miss (Matthew 5:14–16)! And the way we live should make people wonder why we're different (in a good way).

Besides our love for God and desire to be more like Jesus, we should be motivated by a burning desire to share the Good News with others. If your actions don't back up your words, people will never listen. But if your life is filled with Christlikeness, people just might start asking you to tell them about Jesus! And no one will ever be surprised to hear you're a Jesus follower.

News About the People with Paul

[7]Tychicus is my dear brother in Christ and a faithful minister and servant with me in the Lord. He will tell you all the things that are happening to me. [8]This is why I am sending him: so you may know how we are[n] and he may encourage you. [9]I send him with Onesimus, a faithful and dear brother in Christ, and one of your group. They will tell you all that has happened here.

[10]Aristarchus, a prisoner with me, and Mark, the cousin of Barnabas, greet you. (I have already told you what to do about Mark. If he comes, welcome him.) [11]Jesus, who is called Justus, also greets you. These are the only Jewish believers who work with me for the kingdom of God, and they have been a comfort to me.

[12]Epaphras, a servant of Jesus Christ, from your group, also greets you. He always prays for you that you will grow to be spiritually mature and have everything God wants for you. [13]I know he has worked hard for you and the people in Laodicea and in Hierapolis. [14]Demas and our dear friend Luke, the doctor, greet you.

[15]Greet the brothers and sisters in Laodicea. And greet Nympha and the church that meets in her house. [16]After this letter is read to you, be sure it is also read to the church in Laodicea. And you read the letter that I wrote to Laodicea. [17]Tell Archippus, "Be sure to finish the work the Lord gave you."

[18]I, Paul, greet you and write this with my own hand. Remember me in prison. Grace be with you.

4:8 so . . . are Some Greek copies read "so he may know how you are."

All You Need Is Christ

When Paul wrote this letter to the Colossian church, he was responding to some deep concerns. Apparently, the Colossian believers were thinking they had to earn their favor with God through their works. Previously, they had been taught that Christ—his death, resurrection, and the grace and mercy that come through that sacrifice—was all they needed. But they had started returning to their old philosophies and pagan rituals. In the process, the Colossian believers were denying that Christ and his work on the cross were sufficient.

Paul wanted to make it clear once and for all: Jesus Christ is all you need!

How often do we make the same mistake today? Have you, as someone who claims to trust in Jesus, thought that you needed something else to make you happy, bring you peace, or satisfy your desires? Do you ever find yourself focusing on something other than Christ to fill you up? Whatever it is, anything you rely on other than Christ will undoubtedly let you down.

The entire Bible tells the story of God's plan for redeeming humans and providing salvation for the lost—for his own glory. And Jesus' sacrifice and resurrection are the most important part of that story—he's what makes it all possible. Colossians shows us that Christ really is everything we need.

Get Real

In what ways is Christ the one you live for? (Philippians 1:20–25; Colossians 3:1–4, 16–17)

Did you know that from the very beginning, God's perfect plan of redemption was all about Jesus' sacrificial death and his defeat of death by his resurrection? (Isaiah 53; Ephesians 1:11; Colossians 1:16–20; 1 Peter 1:10–12)

Are there any people, hopes, dreams, or activities that are replacing Jesus' rightful place in your life? (Galatians 1:6–7; Colossians 1:6–10)

1 thessalonians

Whenever you start a new project, it's nice to get off to a good start—you want to set the right tone for the rest of the endeavor! A bad beginning seems to lead inevitably to a disastrous end.

So it's perfectly understandable that Paul would be concerned about the Thessalonian believers and their ability to stay grounded in their newfound faith. After all, his first visit had been cut short by violent anti-Christian riots, government persecution, and strong opposition from the local Jews. Several brand new Christians were basically kidnapped, taken to the authorities, and falsely accused of stirring up trouble. Within a short time of his arrival, Paul's life was in serious jeopardy, so he was smuggled out of the city in the middle of the night. Talk about a rough start.

But when Paul sent Timothy back to Thessalonica to investigate, the news was unbelievably good! Instead of giving in to the pressures and persecution, the Thessalonians had withstood the challenge. By God's grace, their faith had actually become an amazing testimony in the entire region.

Even if your walk with Christ began under less-than-optimal circumstances, you can be sure that the end result will be perfect—God will complete the good work of salvation that he began in you!

1 From Paul, Silas, and Timothy.

To the church in Thessalonica, the church in God the Father and the Lord Jesus Christ:

Grace and peace to you.

The Faith of the Thessalonians

[2]We always thank God for all of you and mention you when we pray. [3]We continually recall before God our Father the things you have done because of your faith and the work you have done because of your love. And we thank him that you continue to be strong because of your hope in our Lord Jesus Christ.

[4]Brothers and sisters, God loves you, and we know he has chosen you, [5]because the Good News we brought to you came not only with words, but with power, with the Holy Spirit, and with sure knowledge that it is true. Also you know how we lived when we were with you in order to help you. [6]And you became like us and like the Lord. You suffered much, but still you accepted the teaching with the joy that comes from the Holy Spirit. [7]So you became an example to all the believers in Macedonia and Southern Greece. [8]And the Lord's teaching spread from you not only into Macedonia and Southern Greece, but now your faith in God has become known everywhere. So we do not need to say anything about it. [9]People everywhere are telling about the way you accepted us when we were there with you. They tell how you stopped worshiping idols and began serving the living and true God. [10]And you wait for God's Son, whom God raised from the dead, to come from heaven. He is Jesus, who saves us from God's angry judgment that is sure to come.

WORLDVIEWS

Being a Servant Leader

"When I grow up, I want to be a servant!"

What are you . . . crazy? What kind of person's primary goal in life is to become a servant? Well, Jesus Christ for one. And if you call yourself a Christian, servanthood should be your major aspiration, too.

This is opposite from the world's perspective, where it's all about gaining power, prestige, and popularity. This is just one of the ways that a Christian worldview is profoundly different from other worldviews. An attitude of selfless serving and humility will set you apart from those around you. What could possess people to choose that kind of life?

It all started with Jesus. He was God in the flesh—divinity wrapped up in a human body. If anyone on earth had a reason to expect others to serve him, it was Jesus. But instead, he chose to humble himself and serve the people he created. He gave everything he had to help the sick and the poor. And eventually, he gave up his life to save the very people who had turned their backs on him.

Jesus' words and example confirm this conclusion . . . if you want to live out Christianity in a genuine way, you need to look for opportunities to serve and love others. Who is God calling you to reach out to today?

As you're continuing to study God's Word and learning to make Christianity the foundation for your worldview, don't forget this vital element. Become a humble, sincere giver of time and resources to serve God. You'll look a lot like Jesus, and your relationship with God will continue growing deeper and deeper.

Paul's Work in Thessalonica

2 Brothers and sisters, you know our visit to you was not a failure. [2]Before we came to you, we suffered in Philippi. People there insulted us, as you know, and many people were against us. But our God helped us to be brave and to tell you his Good News. [3]Our appeal does not come from lies or wrong reasons, nor were we trying to trick you. [4]But we speak the Good News because God tested us and trusted us to do it. When we speak, we are not trying to please people, but God, who tests our hearts. [5]You know that we never tried to influence you by saying nice things about you. We were not trying to get your money; we had no selfishness to hide from you. God knows that this is true. [6]We were not looking for human praise, from you or anyone else, [7]even though as apostles of Christ we could have used our authority over you.

But we were very gentle with you,[n] like a mother caring for her little children. [8]Because we loved you, we were happy to share not only God's Good News with you, but even our own lives. You had become so dear to us! [9]Brothers and sisters, I know you remember our hard work and difficulties. We worked night and day so we would not burden any of you while we preached God's Good News to you.

[10]When we were with you, we lived in

Comparison Trap

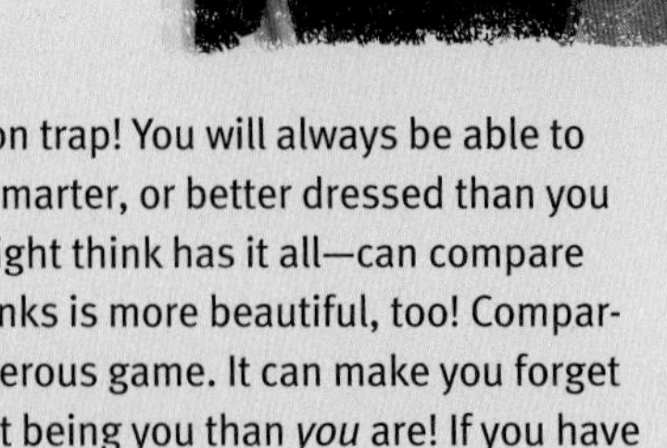

Beware of the dreaded comparison trap! You will always be able to find someone prettier, skinnier, smarter, or better dressed than you are. And that girl—the one you might think has it all—can compare herself and find someone she thinks is more beautiful, too! Comparing yourself with others is a dangerous game. It can make you forget that no one—NO ONE—is better at being you than *you* are! If you have accepted Jesus, you are a beautiful daughter of the King of kings (John 1:12). You don't have to compete with anyone for his love.

2:7 But . . . you Some Greek copies read "But we were like infants among you."

a holy and honest way, without fault. You know this is true, and so does God. [11]You know that we treated each of you as a father treats his own children. [12]We encouraged you, we urged you, and we insisted that you live good lives for God, who calls you to his glorious kingdom.

[13]Also, we always thank God because when you heard his message from us, you accepted it as the word of God, not the words of humans. And it really is God's message which works in you who believe. [14]Brothers and sisters, your experiences have been like those of God's churches in Christ that are in Judea.[n] You suffered from the people of your own country, as they suffered from the Jews [15]who killed both the Lord Jesus and the prophets and forced us to leave that country. They do not please God and are against all people. [16]They try to stop us from teaching those who are not Jews so they may be saved. By doing this, they are increasing their sins to the limit. The anger of God has come to them at last.

Paul Wants to Visit Them Again

[17]Brothers and sisters, though we were separated from you for a short time, our thoughts were still with you. We wanted very much to see you and tried hard to do so. [18]We wanted to come to you. I, Paul, tried to come more than once, but Satan stopped us. [19]You are our hope, our joy, and the crown we will take pride in when our Lord Jesus Christ comes. [20]Truly you are our glory and our joy.

3 When we could not wait any longer, we decided it was best to stay in Athens alone [2]and send Timothy to you. Timothy, our brother, works with us for God and helps us tell people the Good News about Christ. We sent him to strengthen and encourage you in your faith [3]so none of you would be upset by these troubles. You yourselves know that we must face these troubles. [4]Even when we were with you, we told you we all would have to suffer, and you know it has happened. [5]Because of this, when I could wait no longer, I sent Timothy to you so I could learn about your faith. I was afraid the devil had tempted you, and perhaps our hard work would have been wasted.

[6]But Timothy now has come back to us from you and has brought us good news about your faith and love. He told us that you always remember us in a good way and that you want to see us just as much as we want to see you. [7]So, brothers and sisters, while we have much trouble and suffering, we are encouraged about you because of your faith. [8]Our life is really full if you stand strong in the Lord. [9]We have so much joy before our God because of you. We cannot thank him enough for all the joy we feel. [10]Night and day we continue praying with all our heart that we can see

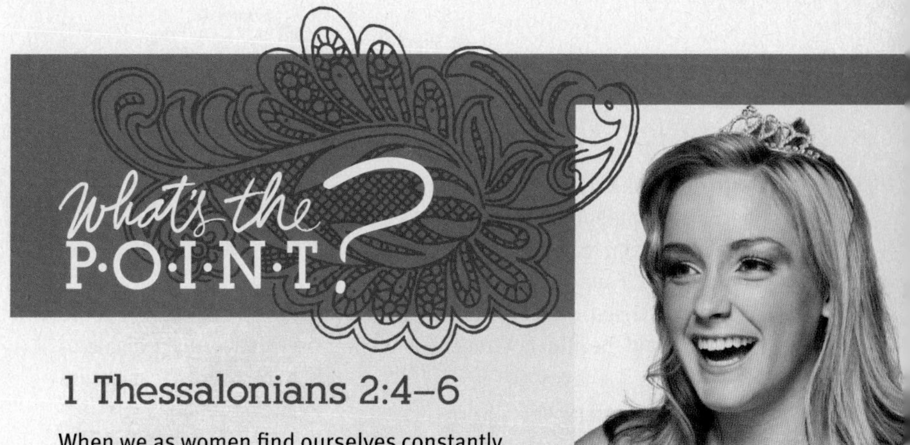

1 Thessalonians 2:4–6

When we as women find ourselves constantly going out of our way to please people, it's good to check ourselves and ask why we're doing it. Perhaps we just want to show people we appreciate or care for them—what a pure, beautiful desire to have! Sometimes we're elated and eager to sincerely tell a friend, "You look fabulous!" But *sometimes* a people-pleasing attitude has selfish motives at the core. Do you ever lavish compliments on people just to make them like you or maybe to get ahead at work? It's easy to slip into people-pleasing mode in order to gain human approval, recognition, or admiration.

Paul wasn't trying to impress the Thessalonians when he taught the message of God's salvation. Rather than offering empty compliments and shallow praise in an effort to please people and win recognition, Paul focused on sharing God's truth. He was motivated by sincere love for his audience and a deep desire to please God.

If you really want to bring joy to people, don't just focus on pleasing them. Instead, become a "God pleaser." Your life will bring him glory, and you'll find the real satisfaction of serving and loving others from a healthy, happy, overflowing heart.

fun facts

More than 7 out of 10 Americans claim to have made a personal commitment to Jesus Christ that is important in their life.

(Barna.org)

2:14 Judea The Jewish land where Jesus lived and taught and where the church first began.

Be Still & KNOW

Pray for Your Land

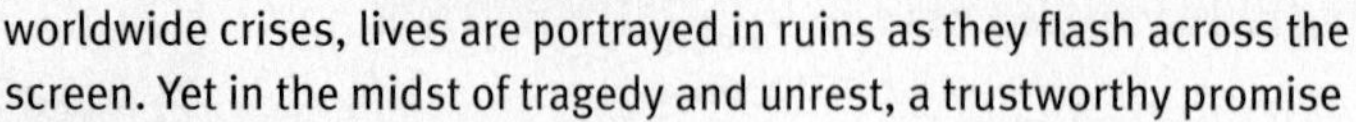

With one look at the evening news, it becomes apparent that there is overwhelming pain, fear, and suffering in our world. From local accidents to worldwide crises, lives are portrayed in ruins as they flash across the screen. Yet in the midst of tragedy and unrest, a trustworthy promise from heaven echoes across the hearts of believers around the globe. God said that if the people who are called by his name will be humble, stop doing evil, and instead pray and seek him, then he will listen to them, forgive them, and heal their land (2 Chronicles 7:14). Next time you see a sad news story, why not stop right there and humbly ask God to heal your land?

you again and give you all the things you need to make your faith strong.

[11]Now may our God and Father himself and our Lord Jesus prepare the way for us to come to you. [12]May the Lord make your love grow more and multiply for each other and for all people so that you will love others as we love you. [13]May your hearts be made strong so that you will be holy and without fault before our God and Father when our Lord Jesus comes with all his holy ones.

A Life that Pleases God

4 Brothers and sisters, we taught you how to live in a way that will please God, and you are living that way. Now we ask and encourage you in the Lord Jesus to live that way even more. [2]You know what we told you to do by the authority of the Lord Jesus. [3]God wants you to be holy and to stay away from sexual sins. [4]He wants each of you to learn to control your own body[n] in a way that is holy and honorable. [5]Don't use your body for sexual sin like the people who do not know God. [6]Also, do not wrong or cheat another Christian in this way. The Lord will punish people who do those things as we have already told you and warned you. [7]God called us to be holy and does not want us to live in sin. [8]So the person who refuses to obey this teaching is disobeying God, not simply a human teaching. And God is the One who gives us his Holy Spirit.

[9]We do not need to write you about having love for your Christian family, because God has already taught you to love each other. [10]And truly you do love the Christians in all of Macedonia. Brothers and sisters, now we encourage you to love them even more.

[11]Do all you can to live a peaceful life. Take care of your own business, and do your own work as we have already told you. [12]If you do, then people who are not believers will respect you, and you will not have to depend on others for what you need.

The Lord's Coming

[13]Brothers and sisters, we want you to know about those Christians who have died so you will not be sad, as others who have no hope. [14]We believe that Jesus died

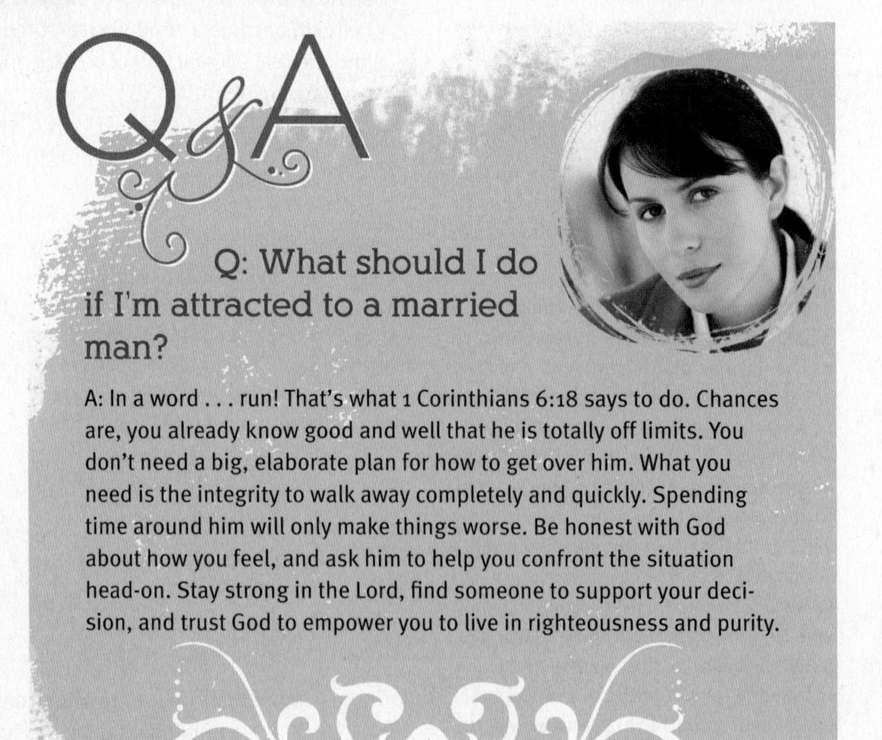

Q&A

Q: What should I do if I'm attracted to a married man?

A: In a word . . . run! That's what 1 Corinthians 6:18 says to do. Chances are, you already know good and well that he is totally off limits. You don't need a big, elaborate plan for how to get over him. What you need is the integrity to walk away completely and quickly. Spending time around him will only make things worse. Be honest with God about how you feel, and ask him to help you confront the situation head-on. Stay strong in the Lord, find someone to support your decision, and trust God to empower you to live in righteousness and purity.

4:4 learn . . . body This might also mean "learn to live with your own wife."

and that he rose again. So, because of him, God will raise with Jesus those who have died. [15]What we tell you now is the Lord's own message. We who are living when the Lord comes again will not go before those who have already died. [16]The Lord himself will come down from heaven with a loud command, with the voice of the archangel,[n] and with the trumpet call of God. And those who have died believing in Christ will rise first. [17]After that, we who are still alive will be gathered up with them in the clouds to meet the Lord in the air. And we will be with the Lord forever. [18]So encourage each other with these words.

Be Ready for the Lord's Coming

5 Now, brothers and sisters, we do not need to write you about times and dates. [2]You know very well that the day the Lord comes again will be a surprise, like a thief that comes in the night. [3]While people are saying, "We have peace and we are safe," they will be destroyed quickly. It is like pains that come quickly to a woman having a baby. Those people will not escape. [4]But you, brothers and sisters, are not living in darkness, and so that day will not surprise you like a thief. [5]You are all people who belong to the light and to the day. We do not belong to the night or to darkness. [6]So we should not be like other people who are sleeping, but we should be alert and have self-control. [7]Those who sleep, sleep at night. Those who get drunk, get drunk at night. [8]But we belong to the day, so we should control ourselves. We should wear faith and love to protect us, and the hope of salvation should be our helmet. [9]God did not choose us to suffer his anger but to have salvation through our Lord Jesus Christ. [10]Jesus died for us so that we can live together with him, whether we are alive or dead when he comes. [11]So encourage each other and give each other strength, just as you are doing now.

Final Instructions and Greetings

[12]Now, brothers and sisters, we ask you to appreciate those who work hard among you, who lead you in the Lord and teach you. [13]Respect them with a very special love because of the work they do.

Live in peace with each other. [14]We ask you, brothers and sisters, to warn those who do not work. Encourage the people who are afraid. Help those who are weak. Be patient with everyone. [15]Be sure that no one pays back wrong for wrong, but always try to do what is good for each other and for all people.

[16]Always be joyful. [17]Pray continually, [18]and give thanks whatever happens. That is what God wants for you in Christ Jesus.

[19]Do not hold back the work of the Holy Spirit. [20]Do not treat prophecy as if it were unimportant. [21]But test everything. Keep what is good, [22]and stay away from everything that is evil.

[23]Now may God himself, the God of peace, make you pure, belonging only to him. May your whole self—spirit, soul, and body—be kept safe and without fault when our Lord Jesus Christ comes. [24]You can trust the One who calls you to do that for you.

[25]Brothers and sisters, pray for us.

[26]Give each other a holy kiss when you meet. [27]I tell you by the authority of the Lord to read this letter to all the believers.

[28]The grace of our Lord Jesus Christ be with you.

1 Thessalonians 5:18

What have your darkest days been like? Maybe they've involved being fired, being abandoned, or being depressed. During those times, it's just plain hard to look at the bright side of things.

But God calls us in this verse to "give thanks whatever happens." It's easy to dwell on what's wrong, but God wants us to always have gratitude going strong in our hearts. It's something we can only do in God's strength.

Through Christ, you can remember that being God's blessed woman doesn't depend on whether you've had a good week. Every breath you've taken, meal you've eaten, bed you've slept in, and person you've loved have all been gifts from God. And the most remarkable thing of all is that God rescued you from the death your sin deserves. He's made you alive in Christ and called you his daughter. You have promises to cling to, a fantastic future to anticipate, and an amazing God to delight in. Picking up your Bible and reading about God's works of love, power, and faithfulness will give you more starting places for thanking him.

Whether your circumstances are pleasing or painful, keep gratitude and joy in your heart. There's always a reason to thank him—he's given us so much to be glad about!

4:16 archangel The leader among God's angels or messengers.

Waiting for Jesus' Return

The Thessalonian church was committed to Christ, they were growing in love for God and each other, and persecution didn't discourage most of them from staying strong in their faith. Paul sent the Thessalonians the gift of encouragement, urging them to stay unified, to hold on to their faith, and to be prepared for Jesus' return.

Naturally, they looked forward to Jesus' return. However, some of the believers were confused about when it would happen. As a result, they didn't always take their faith seriously. Paul told those with shallow faith to commit to a more mature lifestyle of obedience to God. While Paul supported their hope for Jesus' return, he reminded them that there was still work to do in the meantime.

We still have a message to share with the world today—a world that often still hates Christians and who we stand for. The Thessalonian believers' story is just one example of the way God's love transforms our faulty lives. With his power, you can live beyond your own strength and stand victorious and joyful no matter what you go through.

We're a lot closer to Jesus' return than those early believers, but only God knows the perfect time when Jesus will return. So live expectantly!

Get Real

If you've accepted Jesus as your Savior, you can live in the hope of his return. He's coming back to make all things new! (Romans 8:18–37)

What do these psalms tell you about God's presence during trouble? (Psalms 17—18; 46)

Can anything separate you from God's love? (Romans 8:38–39)

Do you want to know more about Jesus' return? Study Matthew 24.

In Matthew 25:1–30, Jesus tells two stories about being prepared for his return. What can you learn from them?

How does Jesus say we should live while we wait for him? (Matthew 25:31–46)

2 thessalonians

We've all experienced it—those moments of panic when you think you've missed something huge (like your mom's birthday or a job interview) followed by a huge sigh of relief when you realize that it's actually happening the next day! That's probably just a fraction of the anxiety the Thessalonian believers felt when they heard rumors that Jesus had already returned. They were scared that they'd missed out.

In this letter, Paul stresses the fact that the exact time of Christ's return is unknown. But he also assures the Thessalonians that there will be unmistakable signs that precede Christ's return—it may be sudden, but no one will accidentally miss it when it happens. It will be impossible to miss!

After relieving their concerns, Paul encourages them to spend their time wisely as they wait for Jesus' return. Some Christians in Thessalonica had a severe lazy streak, so Paul reminded them that there's no excuse for idleness. Christians are called to be diligent workers for God's glory.

So wait eagerly and confidently for Christ's return, and make the most of each day. You don't have to worry about missing the Second Coming, but you still want to be prepared to greet Christ without any shame for the way you've spent your time!

1 From Paul, Silas, and Timothy.

To the church in Thessalonica in God our Father and the Lord Jesus Christ:

[2]Grace and peace to you from God the Father and the Lord Jesus Christ.

Paul Talks About God's Judgment

[3]We must always thank God for you, brothers and sisters. This is only right, because your faith is growing more and more, and the love that every one of you has for each other is increasing. [4]So we brag about you to the other churches of God. We tell them about the way you continue to be strong and have faith even though you are being treated badly and are suffering many troubles.

[5]This is proof that God is right in his judgment. He wants you to be counted worthy of his kingdom for which you are suffering. [6]God will do what is right. He will give trouble to those who trouble you. [7]And he will give rest to you who are troubled and to us also when the Lord Jesus appears with burning fire from heaven with his powerful angels. [8]Then he will punish those who do not know God and who do not obey the Good News about our Lord Jesus Christ. [9]Those people will be punished with a destruction that continues forever. They will be kept away from the Lord and from his great power. [10]This will happen on the day when the Lord Jesus comes to receive glory because of his holy people. And all the people who have believed will be amazed at Jesus. You will be in that group, because you believed what we told you.

[11]That is why we always pray for you, asking our God to help you live the kind of life he called you to live. We pray that with

2 Thessalonians 1:4

Think of people you know who take true, abundant delight in their kids. That's probably most parents you know. From kids' lovable faces to their entertaining behaviors, they can bring so much happiness to their parents' lives.

But beyond the amusement their cuteness can bring, kids can also bring profound honor to their parents. Most moms and dads invest so much time, love, and money to give their kids opportunities for success. You've probably seen proud parents bragging (in a good way) about their children's successes. But, far from any attempt to take credit for their children's achievements, this kind of bragging takes true delight in seeing a child grow into a capable and mature person.

Paul loved to brag about the Thessalonian Christians. Like a proud parent, he wanted to tell everyone about how faithful, brave, and obedient they'd been, even through some extremely tough times. When Christians truly act like Christ, they bring glory to their heavenly Father (2 Thessalonians 1:12). Their behavior is visible proof that God is miraculously transforming sinful people into his own children. And nothing glorifies God more than when his children are like lights in the world.

Is your life bringing that kind of glory to your heavenly Father?

his power God will help you do the good things you want and perform the works that come from your faith. [12]We pray all this so that the name of our Lord Jesus Christ will have glory in you, and you will have glory in him. That glory comes from the grace of our God and the Lord Jesus Christ.

Evil Things Will Happen

2 Brothers and sisters, we have something to say about the coming of our Lord Jesus Christ and the time when we will meet together with him. [2]Do not become easily upset in your thinking or afraid if you hear that the day of the Lord has already come. Someone may have said this in a prophecy or in a message or in a letter as if it came from us. [3]Do not let anyone fool you in any way. That day of the Lord will not come until the turning away[n] from God happens and the Man of Evil,[n] who is on his way to hell, appears. [4]He will be against and put himself above any so-called god or anything that people worship. And that Man of Evil will even go into God's Temple and sit there and say that he is God.

[5]I told you when I was with you that all this would happen. Do you not remember? [6]And now you know what is stopping that Man of Evil so he will appear at the right time. [7]The secret power of evil is already working in the world, but there is one who is stopping that power. And he will continue to stop it until he is taken out of the way. [8]Then that Man of Evil will appear, and the Lord Jesus will kill him with the breath that comes from his mouth and will destroy him with the glory of his coming. [9]The Man of Evil will come by the power of Satan. He will have great power, and he will do many different false miracles, signs, and wonders. [10]He will use every kind of evil to trick those who are lost. They will die, because they refused to love the truth. (If they loved the truth, they would be saved.) [11]For this reason God sends them something powerful that leads them away from the truth so they will believe a lie. [12]So all those will be judged guilty who did not believe the truth, but enjoyed doing evil.

You Are Chosen for Salvation

[13]Brothers and sisters, whom the Lord loves, God chose you from the beginning[n] to be saved. So we must always thank God for you. You are saved by the Spirit that makes you holy and by your faith in the truth. [14]God used the Good News that we preached to call you to be saved so you can share in the glory of our Lord Jesus Christ. [15]So, brothers and sisters, stand strong and

fun facts

15% of couples date long distance.

(Glamour)

2:3 turning away Or "the rebellion." **2:3 Man of Evil** Some Greek copies read "Man of Sin." **2:13 God . . . beginning** Some Greek copies read "God chose you as the firstfruits of the harvest."

RELATIONSHIPS

Make Room for Mercy

Got mercy? We all love receiving it, but *giving* it can be another story. That's because mercy costs us something. It means overlooking a wrong and letting go of the right to hold a grudge. That's not easy if you're feeling hurt! But if no one showed you mercy, you'd always feel judged, never sure of where you stand, and constantly waiting for the hammer to land. Mercy removes those fears (James 2:13). God tells us the mercy we receive ties directly to how much we give. Make room for mercy, and God's mercy will make room for you (Matthew 5:7).

continue to believe the teachings we gave you in our speaking and in our letter.

[16-17]May our Lord Jesus Christ himself and God our Father encourage you and strengthen you in every good thing you do and say. God loved us, and through his grace he gave us a good hope and encouragement that continues forever.

Pray for Us

3 And now, brothers and sisters, pray for us that the Lord's teaching will continue to spread quickly and that people will give honor to that teaching, just as happened with you. [2]And pray that we will be protected from stubborn and evil people, because not all people believe.

[3]But the Lord is faithful and will give you strength and will protect you from the Evil One. [4]The Lord makes us feel sure that you are doing and will continue to do the things we told you. [5]May the Lord lead your hearts into God's love and Christ's patience.

The Duty to Work

[6]Brothers and sisters, by the authority of our Lord Jesus Christ we command you to stay away from any believer who refuses to work and does not follow the teaching we gave you. [7]You yourselves know that you should live as we live. We were not lazy when we were with you. [8]And when we ate another person's food, we always paid for it. We worked very hard night and day so we would not be an expense to any of you. [9]We had the right to ask you to help us, but we worked to take care of ourselves so we would be an example for you to follow. [10]When we were with you, we gave you this rule: "Anyone who refuses to work should not eat."

[11]We hear that some people in your group refuse to work. They do nothing but busy themselves in other people's lives. [12]We command those people and beg them in the Lord Jesus Christ to work quietly and earn their own food. [13]But you, brothers and sisters, never become tired of doing good.

[14]If some people do not obey what we

LIFEISSUES

Eating Disorders

In any neighborhood or social setting, you can find someone—often a young woman—who struggles with unhealthy food issues. Eating disorders are ways of grasping for control, dealing with hurts, or trying to achieve a mixed-up image of perfection. These diseases can be life threatening and long lasting, so if you know someone suffering from an eating disorder, encourage professional help. Most importantly, pray for her. God can heal any hurt and rebuild any self-esteem, but it takes time and lots of care. Pray she'll see herself as God sees her—whole and beautiful simply because he loves her.

tell you in this letter, then take note of them. Have nothing to do with them so they will feel ashamed. [15]But do not treat them as enemies. Warn them as fellow believers.

Final Words

[16]Now may the Lord of peace give you peace at all times and in every way. The Lord be with all of you.

[17]I, Paul, end this letter now in my own handwriting. All my letters have this to show they are from me. This is the way I write.

[18]The grace of our Lord Jesus Christ be with you all.

Saint
by Ted Dekker

This thrilling tale from novelist Ted Dekker will take you on a wild ride through the adventures of a man in search of his true identity. Despite evil efforts to strip his memory and train him as an assassin, this mysterious main character learns that absolutely nothing can take away the truth of who he is in God's eyes. This fast-paced book will keep you intrigued as you try to figure out what's real and what's not. In the end, *Saint* will assure you that even if you forget your faith, your faith will remember you.

BECOME *Involved*

Music Festivals

Next time you're looking for something fun and different to do on a sunny summer weekend, consider attending or volunteering at a Christian music festival. There are quite a few spread out all over the country. For just one ticket price, you get to see anywhere from five to more than a dozen of your favorite bands.

Consider taking a friend and introducing them to new music. Or use it as an outreach opportunity for your small group or circle of friends. Most have speakers and/or workshops along with the concerts, so you can worship, learn, grow, and have fun all at once! The organizers of these music festivals are in great need of volunteers to help staff the event. You can work a T-shirt booth while jamming to the groove or counsel attendees who feel Christ working in their hearts and need someone to talk to. You could make yourself available to serve fellow attendees, staff members, or even the artists themselves.

Some of the most popular annual festivals include Creation (www.creationfest.com), Spirit West Coast (www.spiritwestcoast.org), Ichthus (www.ichthusfestival.org), and Sonshine (www.sonshinefestival.com). However, there are many others around the country, so check your local entertainment calendar for other opportunities.

2 Thessalonians

Clearing the Air

Some believers in Thessalonica were confused. The church wasn't in a huge crisis yet, but Paul felt he needed to address some issues. Some of the believers were discouraged because of their suffering. Others were listening to false teachings. A few were becoming lazy about living a life of faith. They needed guidance.

Paul's gentle rebuke mirrors the way God relates to his children. He is patient and kind, but he doesn't let his followers go uncorrected (Proverbs 3:11–12). And when his loved ones are misled by evil people, he gets angry! One day he'll punish the wicked for their deceitful deeds. In fact, that's one of the major themes of 2 Thessalonians—the coming day of God's judgment.

The only way to avoid destruction on that day is to believe in Jesus and trust him as your Savior. Those who belong to him—people who have been saved from sin through faith in Christ—will share in his glory. And those who don't belong to him will be cast away from him forever.

Knowing the end of the story motivates true believers to share the Good News of Christ with anyone who will listen. Knowing Jesus will return is the antidote to laziness. Who can sit back and relax when they know God is going to come back and judge people who don't know him? And if there's a little suffering involved with serving faithfully and obediently, so be it!

Get Real

How can you protect yourself from the teachings of those who would lead you astray? (Joshua 1:8; 2 Timothy 2:15–16; Hebrews 4:12–13)

Why should you care what happens to unbelievers? (Matthew 18:10–14; 28:19–20; Luke 19:10)

Have you ever been tempted to be lazy? How can you overcome this struggle? (John 15:4; 1 Corinthians 10:31)

How do you respond when you suffer because of your belief in Jesus? (Matthew 5:10–12; John 14:1; Colossians 1:24; 1 Thessalonians 3:3–4; 1 Peter 4:12–16)

1 timothy

Role models—everybody's got one. We tend to latch on to someone with more wisdom and experience, hoping that some of his or her qualities will eventually transfer to us. But what happens when you're suddenly on your own? It's easy to feel lost without a dependable mentor.

Timothy was like a son to Paul. They'd traveled together, endured hardships side by side, and seen God's amazing power at work. But now, Timothy was leading a church by himself. There's a good possibility he felt slightly lost without his mentor. So it's no surprise that Paul wrote Timothy this letter filled with specific directions about the practical side of ministry.

But Paul's biggest emphasis was the importance of being devoted to Scripture. Up to this point, the apostles had been the authority on spiritual matters. But Paul said that long after the apostles were dead and gone, God's Word would always be the ultimate authority for wisdom and guidance. By staying grounded in Scripture, Christians today can know our faith has a firm foundation!

It's great to have human role models—God intends for mature Christians to disciple younger believers—but always remember that God's Word is the final authority and source of truth! Christ is the perfect role model, and the only way to know him is by studying Scripture.

1 From Paul, an apostle of Christ Jesus, by the command of God our Savior and Christ Jesus our hope.

[2]To Timothy, a true child to me because you believe:

Grace, mercy, and peace from God the Father and Christ Jesus our Lord.

Warning Against False Teaching

[3]I asked you to stay longer in Ephesus when I went into Macedonia so you could command some people there to stop teaching false things. [4]Tell them not to spend their time on stories that are not true and on long lists of names in family histories. These things only bring arguments; they do not help God's work, which is done in faith. [5]The purpose of this command is for people to have love, a love that comes from a pure heart and a good conscience and a true faith. [6]Some people have missed these things and turned to useless talk. [7]They want to be teachers of the law, but they do not understand either what they are talking about or what they are sure about.

[8]But we know that the law is good if someone uses it lawfully. [9]We also know that the law is not made for good people

but for those who are against the law and for those who refuse to follow it. It is for people who are against God and are sinful, who are unholy and ungodly, who kill their fathers and mothers, who murder, [10]who take part in sexual sins, who have sexual relations with people of the same sex, who sell slaves, who tell lies, who speak falsely, and who do anything against the true teaching of God. [11]That teaching is part of the Good News of the blessed God that he gave me to tell.

Thanks for God's Mercy

[12]I thank Christ Jesus our Lord, who gave me strength, because he trusted me and gave me this work of serving him. [13]In the past I spoke against Christ and persecuted him and did all kinds of things to hurt him. But God showed me mercy, because I did not know what I was doing. I did not believe. [14]But the grace of our Lord was fully given to me, and with that grace came the faith and love that are in Christ Jesus.

[15]What I say is true, and you should fully accept it: Christ Jesus came into the world to save sinners, of whom I am the worst. [16]But I was given mercy so that in me, the worst of all sinners, Christ Jesus could show that he has patience without limit. His patience with me made me an example for those who would believe in him and have life forever. [17]To the King that rules forever, who will never die, who cannot be seen, the only God, be honor and glory forever and ever. Amen.

[18]Timothy, my child, I am giving you a command that agrees with the prophecies that were given about you in the past. I tell you this so you can follow them and fight the good fight. [19]Continue to have faith and do what you know is right. Some people have rejected this, and their faith has been shipwrecked. [20]Hymenaeus and Alexander have done that, and I have given them to Satan so they will learn not to speak against God.

1 Timothy 2:9

Imagine that you're a member of a royal family, and you're dressing for a special occasion. What would you wear? (Dream up some detailed options here!) What would you want to communicate through your appearance? With each wardrobe choice, you'd probably want to show that you're respectable, noble, and beautiful (of course!).

Our daily life is not much different—our clothing sends a message about who we are. As God's daughter, you belong to a special family that's absolutely pure and worthy of respect. You're like a queen dressing to embody royal dignity every day.

Dressing with respect could include bucking the overexposed Hollywood images by creating your own look—one that leaves lots to the imagination, makes you feel adorable, and makes it clear that you're a lady who loves herself and loves God. Beyond showing respect and self-control in our wardrobe choices, God's daughters should show our beauty through our actions. You can bring people's attention to God's beauty and goodness through acts of humility, service, compassion, forgiveness, and real love.

Remember what a privilege it is to be a daughter of the King! Life is an opportunity to show his purity and beauty of heart to the world in the way you dress and act every day.

fun facts

51% of Americans surveyed listed their family as their top priority.

(Barna.org)

Some Rules for Men and Women

2 First, I tell you to pray for all people, asking God for what they need and being thankful to him. [2]Pray for rulers and for all who have authority so that we can have quiet and peaceful lives full of worship and respect for God. [3]This is good, and it pleases God our Savior, [4]who wants all people to be saved and to know the truth. [5]There is one God and one mediator so that human beings can reach God. That way is through Christ Jesus, who is himself human. [6]He gave himself as a payment to free all people. He is proof that came at the right time. [7]That is why

virtue BUILDING: Honesty

Do you love truth? Or do you avoid complete honesty when the truth is inconvenient? Do you tell "little" lies to make yourself look better? Those are outward expressions of what's in your heart.

The Bible says Satan is a liar, but our God is a God of truth. Jesus even said, "I am . . . the truth" (John 14:6). Truth is wrapped up in God's character, and it's not possible for him to lie (Hebrews 6:18). If you love God, you'll also love truth and be characterized by honesty.

If you desire a close relationship with God, commit to being completely honest regardless of the circumstances. As a Christian, truth should be a priority for you—speak it, live it, and defend it!

Scripture Breakdown
God demands honesty from everyone who claims to follow him, and the Bible commands us to be honest with other people (Ephesians 4:25; Colossians 3:9). Lying to yourself or rationalizing why you should bend one of God's rules isn't a good idea either. Remember—most sins usually start with a lie: *This isn't so bad . . . God won't care. As long as no one finds out, it's okay.*

Honesty is vital to friendship with God, and we can only please him when we live in the truth. Reflect on these verses about truth and honesty: Psalm 25:5; John 8:31–32, 17:17; 2 Thessalonians 2:10–13; and 1 John 1:5–7, 2:20–23.

Build It into Your Life
- How do you think God feels about lies and the people who tell them? (Proverbs 6:16–19; 12:22)
- Do you think you're a good person overall? (1 John 1:8–10)
- Do you know God? (1 John 2:4–6)
- Why does God care about the truth?
- Can you please God if you're a dishonest person? (Exodus 20:16)
- Are "small" lies really that big of a deal? (Revelation 21:8)
- Become someone who *loves* truth—read Scripture daily, be honest with everyone (including God and yourself), and live in a way that demonstrates God's truth.

I was chosen to tell the Good News and to be an apostle. (I am telling the truth; I am not lying.) I was chosen to teach those who are not Jews to believe and to know the truth.

[8]So, I want the men everywhere to pray, lifting up their hands in a holy manner, without anger and arguments.

[9]Also, women should wear proper clothes that show respect and self-control, not using braided hair or gold or pearls or expensive clothes. [10]Instead, they should do good deeds, which is right for women who say they worship God.

[11]Let a woman learn by listening quietly and being ready to cooperate in everything. [12]But I do not allow a woman to teach or to have authority over a man, but to listen quietly, [13]because Adam was formed first and then Eve. [14]And Adam was not tricked, but the woman was tricked and became a sinner. [15]But she will be saved through having children if she continues in faith, love, and holiness, with self-control.

Elders in the Church

3 What I say is true: Anyone wanting to become an overseer desires a good work. [2]An overseer must not give people a reason to criticize him, and he must have only one wife. He must be self-controlled, wise, respected by others, ready to welcome guests, and able to teach. [3]He must not drink too much wine or like to fight, but rather be gentle and peaceable, not loving money. [4]He must be a good family leader, having children who cooperate with full respect. [5](If someone does not know how to lead the family, how can that person take care of God's church?) [6]But an elder must not be a new believer, or he might be too proud of himself and be judged guilty just as the devil was. [7]An elder must also have the respect of people who are not in the church so he will not be criticized by others and caught in the devil's trap.

Deacons in the Church

[8]In the same way, deacons must be respected by others, not saying things they do not mean. They must not drink too much wine or try to get rich by cheating others. [9]With a clear conscience they must follow the secret of the faith that God made known to us. [10]Test them first. Then let them serve as deacons if you find nothing wrong in them. [11]In the same way, women[n] must be respected by others. They must not speak evil of others. They must be self-controlled and trustworthy in everything. [12]Deacons must have only one wife and be good leaders of their children and their own families. [13]Those who serve well as deacons are making an honorable place for themselves, and they will be very bold in their faith in Christ Jesus.

The Secret of Our Life

[14]Although I hope I can come to you soon, I am writing these things to you now. [15]Then, even if I am delayed, you will know how to live in the family of God.

3:11 women This might mean the wives of the deacons, or it might mean women who serve in the same way as deacons.

God did not give us a spirit that makes us afraid but a spirit of power and love and self-control.
—2 Timothy 1:7
september
Labor Day is the 1st Monday of September. Don't forget to rest.
1
2
September is National Piano Month. Sing your favorite hymn.
3
E-mail a message to a missionary you support.
4
Plan a camping adventure with friends.
5
6
7
Share your faith with someone today!
8
Record a fresh voice mail message on your phone.
9
Research the Latino culture online—it's Hispanic Heritage Month!
10
Pray for the families who suffered loss on September 11th, 2001.
11
Enjoy a night of laser tag with friends.
12
13
14
Organize a fondue party.
15
16
17
Invite someone new to your small group or Bible study.
18
19
Plan an appreciation party at work.
20
Consider volunteering with a local Girl Scout troop.
21
22
Spend an evening looking at old photos with your family.
23
Enjoy a latte with a friend.
24
Plant flower bulbs before the first winter freeze.
25
Don't forget to update anti-virus software on your computer.
26
Pray for a person of influence: it's Avril Lavigne's birthday.
27
Pray for a person of influence: Naomi Watts is celebrating a birthday.
28
29
Pray for your co-workers.
30

Health
Aging Gracefully

None of us can stop the aging process, but like fine cheese, we can get better with age (Luke 5:39). It's never too early to start aging gracefully. Besides the obvious—eating well and exercising—there are practical steps you can take to add years to your life. For starters, don't smoke. Apply sunscreen every day, and always wear your seatbelt. Get regular medical exams, including diagnostic tests (pap smear, urinalysis, mammogram, etc.) at intervals recommended by the American Medical Association. When it comes to adding life to your years, attitude is everything! Think positively and maintain close relationships with family and friends. Studies have also shown that those who attend religious services, pray, and have faith in God live longer than those who don't. Read Titus 2:2–8 for a biblical view on aging with purpose and grace.

That family is the church of the living God, the support and foundation of the truth. [16]Without doubt, the secret of our life of worship is great:

> He[n] was shown to us in a human body,
> proved right in spirit,
> and seen by angels.
> He was proclaimed to the nations,
> believed in by the world,
> and taken up in glory.

A Warning About False Teachers

4 Now the Holy Spirit clearly says that in the later times some people will stop believing the faith. They will follow spirits that lie and teachings of demons. [2]Such teachings come from the false words of liars whose consciences are destroyed as if by a hot iron. [3]They forbid people to marry and tell them not to eat certain foods which God created to be eaten with thanks by people who believe and know the truth. [4]Everything God made is good, and nothing should be refused if it is accepted with thanks, [5]because it is made holy by what God has said and by prayer.

Be a Good Servant of Christ

[6]By telling these things to the brothers and sisters, you will be a good servant of Christ Jesus. You will be made strong by the words of the faith and the good teaching which you have been following. [7]But do not follow foolish stories that disagree with God's truth, but train yourself to serve God. [8]Training your body helps you in some ways, but serving God helps you in every way by bringing you blessings in this life and in the future life, too. [9]What I say is true, and you should fully accept it. [10]This is why we work and struggle:[n] We hope in the living God who is the Savior of all people, especially of those who believe.

[11]Command and teach these things. [12]Do not let anyone treat you as if you are unimportant because you are young. Instead, be an example to the believers with your words, your actions, your love, your faith, and your pure life. [13]Until I come, continue to read the Scriptures to the people, strengthen them, and teach them. [14]Use the gift you have, which was given to you through prophecy when the group of elders laid their hands on[n] you. [15]Continue to do those things; give your life to doing them so your progress may be

Be Still & Know
Going Global with Prayer

You can go global without ever leaving your prayer closet! Consider becoming part of the prayer team for a missionary or mission team. They will often provide you with updates from the field and specific needs to lift before the throne. Or go broader by praying for a particular country every day. Operation World (www.operationworld.org) is a great source for systematically praying for the nations. You can also tune into the international news for timely prayer needs across the world. With just a little extra effort, you can be involved in what the Lord is doing all over the globe. Your prayers make a difference!

3:16 He Some Greek copies read "God." **4:10 struggle** Some Greek copies read "suffer." **4:14 laid their hands on** The laying on of hands had many purposes, including the giving of a blessing, power, or authority.

beauty BECOMES HER

High-Quality Perfume

The best-smelling perfume ever is not made of oils, spices, or flowers. It doesn't fit into a bottle, and it isn't dabbed on the neck or wrist. In fact, it's not even liquid at all. It's YOU! To God, you are the sweetest-smelling perfume on the planet! (See 2 Corinthians 2:14–15.) The fragrance of a life lived in complete devotion to Christ is pleasing to him and a wonderful blessing to others. It fills the room wherever you go. Make sure your life is always one that reflects the sweet Spirit of your Savior.

seen by everyone. [16]Be careful in your life and in your teaching. If you continue to live and teach rightly, you will save both yourself and those who listen to you.

Rules for Living with Others

5 Do not speak angrily to an older man, but plead with him as if he were your father. Treat younger men like brothers, [2]older women like mothers, and younger women like sisters. Always treat them in a pure way.

[3]Take care of widows who are truly widows. [4]But if a widow has children or grandchildren, let them first learn to do their duty to their own family and to repay their parents or grandparents. That pleases God. [5]The true widow, who is all alone, puts her hope in God and continues to pray night and day for God's help. [6]But the widow who uses her life to please herself is really dead while she is alive. [7]Tell the believers to do these things so that no one can criticize them. [8]Whoever does not care for his own relatives, especially his own family members, has turned against the faith and is worse than someone who does not believe in God.

[9]To be on the list of widows, a woman must be at least sixty years old. She must have been faithful to her husband. [10]She must be known for her good works—works such as raising her children, welcoming strangers, washing the feet of God's people, helping those in trouble, and giving her life to do all kinds of good deeds.

[11]But do not put younger widows on that list. After they give themselves to Christ, they are pulled away from him by their physical desires, and then they want to marry again. [12]They will be judged for not doing what they first promised to do. [13]Besides that, they learn to waste their time, going from house to house. And they not only waste their time but also begin to gossip and busy themselves with other people's lives, saying things they should not say. [14]So I want the younger widows to marry, have children, and manage their homes. Then no enemy will have any reason to criticize them. [15]But some have already turned away to follow Satan.

[16]If any woman who is a believer has widows in her family, she should care for them herself. The church should not have to care for them. Then it will be able to take care of those who are truly widows.

[17]The elders who lead the church well should receive double honor, especially those who work hard by speaking and teaching, [18]because the Scripture says: "When an ox is working in the grain, do not cover its mouth to keep it from eating,"[n] and "A worker should be given his pay."[n]

[19]Do not listen to someone who accuses an elder, without two or three witnesses. [20]Tell those who continue sinning that they are wrong. Do this in front of the whole church so that the others will have a warning.

[21]Before God and Christ Jesus and the chosen angels, I command you to do these things without showing favor of any kind to anyone.

all about MEN

Checking Your Expectations

Are your romantic expectations realistic? If we believe the media's portrayal of romance, we're likely to cop an attitude if Mr. Right doesn't 1) keep a florist on speed dial, 2) exhibit unparalleled bravery, 3) perfect "tough yet tender," and 4) share all our interests. That dream world is a setup for disappointment with even the godliest man! While it's important not to settle for less than God's best, it's hard to keep a clear head on romance if your information sources are television and drugstore novels. Instead, fill your mind with godly discernment, and ask for God's help in valuing what's important. God's wisdom is filled with good judgment and good sense (Proverbs 8:12), so you'll never be sidetracked by unrealistic expectations again!

5:18 "When . . . eating." Quotation from Deuteronomy 25:4. **5:18 "A worker . . . pay."** Quotation from Luke 10:7.

1 Timothy 6:11–16

What reenergizes you just when you think you're losing steam? Maybe you're in the middle of a pressure-packed month at work, and you're moments from just walking away in frustration. But then you remember how rewarding and meaningful the results of all your hard work will be, and you suddenly get a new burst of energy. The moment you lose sight of your goals is the same moment you start to give up.

Christianity requires the same kind of focus. Living for Christ is serious work, and it's actually impossible without the help of the Holy Spirit. But even when we're taking time to pray and read the Bible, we can get distracted from the real goal and start to lose hope. So what's the secret? What can keep us going when we just feel like giving up? In this letter to Timothy, Paul reminded him about our real goal and our real source of hope: God himself.

When heaven seems like a distant dream and living for Christ feels unrealistic, focus on our all-powerful, never-dying, perfect God (1 Timothy 6:15–16). Each day, remind yourself how good and faithful God is . . . and always has been. He'll give you the strength to make it through another day.

[22]Think carefully before you lay your hands on[n] anyone, and don't share in the sins of others. Keep yourself pure.

[23]Stop drinking only water, but drink a little wine to help your stomach and your frequent sicknesses.

[24]The sins of some people are easy to see even before they are judged, but the sins of others are seen only later. [25]So also good deeds are easy to see, but even those that are not easily seen cannot stay hidden.

6 All who are slaves under a yoke should show full respect to their masters so no one will speak against God's name and our teaching. [2]The slaves whose masters are believers should not show their masters any less respect because they are believers. They should serve their masters even better, because they are helping believers they love.

You must teach and preach these things.

False Teaching and True Riches

[3]Anyone who has a different teaching does not agree with the true teaching of our Lord Jesus Christ and the teaching that shows the true way to serve God. [4]This person is full of pride and understands nothing, but is sick with a love for arguing and fighting about words. This brings jealousy, fighting, speaking against others, evil mistrust, [5]and constant quarrels from those who have evil minds and have lost the truth. They think that serving God is a way to get rich.

[6]Serving God does make us very rich, if we are satisfied with what we have. [7]We brought nothing into the world, so we can take nothing out. [8]But, if we have food and clothes, we will be satisfied with that. [9]Those who want to become rich bring temptation to themselves and are caught in a trap. They want many foolish and harmful things that ruin and destroy people. [10]The love of money causes all kinds of evil. Some people have left the faith, because they wanted to get more money, but they have caused themselves much sorrow.

Some Things to Remember

[11]But you, man of God, run away from all those things. Instead, live in the right way, serve God, have faith, love, patience, and gentleness. [12]Fight the good fight of faith, grabbing hold of the life that continues forever. You were called to have that life when you confessed the good confession before many witnesses. [13]In the sight of God, who gives life to everything, and of Christ Jesus, I give you a command. Christ Jesus made the good confession when he stood before Pontius

fun facts

In a recent survey, 31% of women were experimenting with new hairstyles.

(Redbookmag.com)

5:22 lay your hands on The laying on of hands had many purposes, including the giving of a blessing, power, or authority.

Pilate. [14]Do what you were commanded to do without wrong or blame until our Lord Jesus Christ comes again. [15]God will make that happen at the right time. He is the blessed and only Ruler, the King of all kings and the Lord of all lords. [16]He is the only One who never dies. He lives in light so bright no one can go near it. No one has ever seen God, or can see him. May honor and power belong to God forever. Amen.

[17]Command those who are rich with things of this world not to be proud. Tell them to hope in God, not in their uncertain riches. God richly gives us everything to enjoy. [18]Tell the rich people to do good, to be rich in doing good deeds, to be generous and ready to share. [19]By doing that, they will be saving a treasure for themselves as a strong foundation for the future. Then they will be able to have the life that is true life.

[20]Timothy, guard what God has trusted to you. Stay away from foolish, useless talk and from the arguments of what is falsely called "knowledge." [21]By saying they have that "knowledge," some have missed the true faith.

Grace be with you.

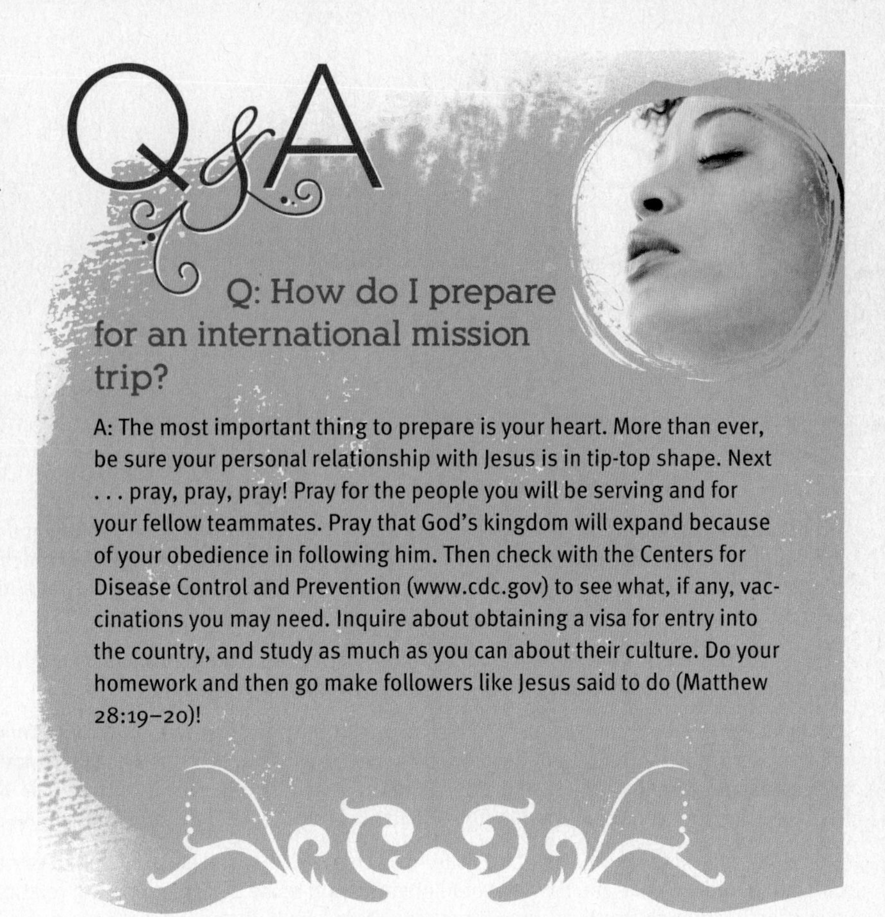

Q: How do I prepare for an international mission trip?

A: The most important thing to prepare is your heart. More than ever, be sure your personal relationship with Jesus is in tip-top shape. Next . . . pray, pray, pray! Pray for the people you will be serving and for your fellow teammates. Pray that God's kingdom will expand because of your obedience in following him. Then check with the Centers for Disease Control and Prevention (www.cdc.gov) to see what, if any, vaccinations you may need. Inquire about obtaining a visa for entry into the country, and study as much as you can about their culture. Do your homework and then go make followers like Jesus said to do (Matthew 28:19–20)!

the big picture

1 Timothy

The Power of a Good Mentor

Timothy was a young pastor of a church that Paul planted on one of his missionary journeys. Paul trusted him to be a leader even though he was young and new to ministry. Paul had led Timothy to the Lord much earlier and spent a lot of time teaching him doctrine and Scripture. Now Paul was writing to help clear up some details about how to organize and run the local church.

These guidelines are still used in churches today, and Paul's warnings against stumbling blocks are very applicable to every believer. The main reason for this letter was to strengthen Timothy's faith.

Paul may have been Timothy's mentor, but he wasn't the only positive influence in Timothy's life. His mother and grandmother were stellar examples of how to walk a godly path, too. Timothy was surrounded by wise, loving mentors who invested in his spiritual growth and aided in his ministry. He humbly welcomed their input and put their words into practice. He knew that the church is meant to function like a body . . . the individual parts need each other.

This letter to Timothy is important for us to read today—Christians always need to remember these teachings about what a church should look like and how it should operate. And those strong mentoring relationships are foundational to any effective church. Through relationships with other people who love and follow God, we can build each other up in real faith and together become a unified body that truly accomplishes God's work.

Get Real

Do you have a humble, teachable spirit? Are you willing to seek out a godly mentor who can walk with you in the faith? (2 Timothy 1:5; Titus 2:3–5)

Are there younger women in your life that you could encourage in the faith? Are you willing to go out of your way to make it happen? (2 Timothy 2:2)

First Timothy 5:22 talks about avoiding negative peer pressure and staying pure. How do you live a pure life? (Psalm 51:10–12; Acts 15:8–9; 1 Peter 1:22–23)

2 timothy

Imagine a marathon runner making that final effort to complete the race. Trembling legs are ready to falter, weary lungs labor to pull in enough air—but the runner never slows the pace. His eyes are fixed on the finish line, and you can see a joyful hope shining through the pain! That's how Paul spent his life. He literally poured all his strength into serving God and spreading the Good News.

As Paul wrote this final letter, the grim prospect of execution loomed before him as he waited in a Roman dungeon. This man who'd boldly proclaimed the Good News for so many years was facing the possibility of being forever silenced. Others had tried to keep him quiet in the past, but they always failed—God's plan couldn't be thwarted. But now his mission was near completion.

Paul's final letter reflects his heart. As he faced death, he had no regrets because he had lived his life for Christ. Like Paul, make your Christian walk a strenuous marathon, not a leisure stroll! Then you, too, can echo Paul's words about a life well lived: "I have fought the good fight, I have finished the race, I have kept the faith" (2 Timothy 4:7).

1 From Paul, an apostle of Christ Jesus by the will of God. God sent me to tell about the promise of life that is in Christ Jesus.

[2]To Timothy, a dear child to me:

Grace, mercy, and peace to you from God the Father and Christ Jesus our Lord.

Encouragement for Timothy

[3]I thank God as I always mention you in my prayers, day and night. I serve him, doing what I know is right as my ancestors did. [4]Remembering that you cried for me, I want very much to see you so I can be filled with joy. [5]I remember your true faith. That faith first lived in your grandmother Lois and in your mother Eunice, and I know you now have that same faith. [6]This is why I remind you to keep using the gift God gave you when I laid my hands on[n] you. Now let it grow, as a small flame grows into a fire. [7]God did not give us a spirit that makes us afraid but a spirit of power and love and self-control.

[8]So do not be ashamed to tell people about our Lord Jesus, and do not be ashamed of me, in prison for the Lord. But suffer with me for the Good News. God, who gives us the strength to do that, [9]saved us and made us his holy people. That was not because of anything we did ourselves but because of God's purpose and grace. That grace was given to us through Christ Jesus before time began, [10]but it is now shown to us by the coming of our Savior Christ Jesus. He

1:6 laid my hands on The laying on of hands had many purposes, including the giving of a blessing, power, or authority.

RELATIONSHIPS

Meeting Again in Heaven

Ever wonder about heaven? What it'll look like, who'll be there, whether you'll recognize anyone? One of the most amazing things about heaven is that Christian relationships will continue forever. Think about that! Good-byes between Jesus' followers on earth are really only see-you-laters. Feeling the hope yet? Keep sight of the fact that connections you're building with believers here on earth will never end. *Never!* Care for them so well now that your joy will be even richer when you see them again someday. And watch for ways to invite others to join you (1 Thessalonians 3:9–13)!

destroyed death, and through the Good News he showed us the way to have life that cannot be destroyed. [11]I was chosen to tell that Good News and to be an apostle and a teacher. [12]I am suffering now because I tell the Good News, but I am not ashamed, because I know Jesus, the One in whom I have believed. And I am sure he is able to protect what he has trusted me with until that day.[n] [13]Follow the pattern of true teachings that you heard from me in faith and love, which are in Christ Jesus. [14]Protect the truth that you were given; protect it with the help of the Holy Spirit who lives in us.

[15]You know that everyone in Asia has left me, even Phygelus and Hermogenes. [16]May the Lord show mercy to the family of Onesiphorus, who has often helped me and was not ashamed that I was in prison. [17]When he came to Rome, he looked eagerly for me until he found me. [18]May the Lord allow him to find mercy from the Lord on that day. You know how many ways he helped me in Ephesus.

Women & Men of the BIBLE

Herodias: Terrible Mother

Herodias was one bad mama. She cheated on her husband with his brother, who happened to be the ruler of Galilee. The prophet John the Baptist had been quite vocal about how wrong it was. Oh, how she hated that man for making waves in her perfect little world of sin! So on her lover's birthday, she had her daughter dance for him. He liked it and promised her anything she wanted. Herodias had her daughter ask for John's head on a platter. Instead of raising a loving, godly child, she used her motherly influence for evil. (Matthew 14:1–11)

A Loyal Soldier of Christ Jesus

2 You then, Timothy, my child, be strong in the grace we have in Christ Jesus. [2]You should teach people whom you can trust the things you and many others have heard me say. Then they will be able to teach others. [3]Share in the troubles we have like a good soldier of Christ Jesus. [4]A soldier wants to please the enlisting officer, so no one serving in the army wastes time with everyday matters. [5]Also an athlete who takes part in a contest must obey all the rules in order to win. [6]The farmer who works hard should be the first person to get some of the food that was grown. [7]Think about what I am saying, because the Lord will give you the ability to understand everything.

[8]Remember Jesus Christ, who was raised from the dead, who is from the family of David. This is the Good News I preach, [9]and I am suffering because of it to the point of being bound with chains like a criminal. But God's teaching is not in chains. [10]So I patiently accept all these troubles so that those whom God has chosen can have the salvation that is in Christ Jesus. With that salvation comes glory that never ends.

[11]This teaching is true:

1:12 day The day Christ will come to judge all people and take his people to live with him.

If we died with him, we will also live
with him.
[12]If we accept suffering, we will also
rule with him.
If we say we don't know him, he will
say he doesn't know us.
[13]If we are not faithful, he will still be
faithful,
because he must be true to who
he is.

A Worker Pleasing to God

[14]Continue teaching these things, warning people in God's presence not to argue about words. It does not help anyone, and it ruins those who listen. [15]Make every effort to give yourself to God as the kind of person he will approve. Be a worker who is not ashamed and who uses the true teaching in the right way. [16]Stay away from foolish, useless talk, because that will lead people further away from God. [17]Their evil teaching will spread like a sickness inside the body. Hymenaeus and Philetus are like that. [18]They have left the true teaching, saying that the rising from the dead has already taken place, and so they are destroying the faith of some people. [19]But God's strong foundation continues to stand. These words are written on the seal: "The Lord knows those who belong to him,"[n] and "Everyone who wants to belong to the Lord must stop doing wrong."

[20]In a large house there are not only things made of gold and silver, but also things made of wood and clay. Some things are used for special purposes, and others are made for ordinary jobs. [21]All who make themselves clean from evil will be used for special purposes. They will be made holy, useful to the Master, ready to do any good work.

[22]But run away from the evil desires of youth. Try hard to live right and to have faith, love, and peace, together with those who trust in the Lord from pure hearts. [23]Stay away from foolish and stupid arguments, because you know they grow into quarrels. [24]And a servant of the Lord must not quarrel but must be kind to everyone, a good teacher, and patient. [25]The Lord's servant must gently teach those who disagree. Then maybe God will let them change their minds so they can accept the truth. [26]And they may wake up and escape from the trap of the devil, who catches them to do what he wants.

The Last Days

3 Remember this! In the last days there will be many troubles, [2]because people will love themselves, love money, brag, and be proud. They will say evil things against others and will not obey their parents or be thankful or be the kind of people God wants. [3]They will not love others, will refuse to forgive, will gossip, and will not control themselves. They will be cruel, will hate what is good, [4]will turn against their friends, and will do foolish things without thinking. They will be conceited, will love pleasure instead of God, [5]and will act as if they serve God but will not have his power. Stay away from those people. [6]Some of them go into homes and get control of silly women who are full of sin and are led by many evil desires. [7]These women are always learning new teachings, but they are never able to understand the truth fully. [8]Just as Jannes and Jambres were against Moses, these people are against the truth. Their thinking has been ruined, and they have failed in trying to follow the faith. [9]But they will not be successful in what they do, because as with Jannes and Jambres, everyone will see that they are foolish.

2 Timothy 2:11–13

Cruel personal attacks, disrespectful judgments, blatant dishonesty—these are *not* the behaviors of loving friends! When someone continually does deeply hurtful things to you, there's a good chance you'll back away from that relationship with gigantic strides. It would probably take a miracle to repair that kind of fall-out.

In 2 Timothy 2:11–12, Paul talks about our friendship with God. If we die to our old, sinful selves, he'll give us true life. If we stay faithful through tough times on earth, we'll reign with Christ in heaven. If we call him our Lord and Savior, he'll call us his children. What an unbelievable friendship—we have everything to gain, and all we have to give up is our worthless life without God!

But verse 13 is the most amazing part: even when we're unfaithful to God—betray him with our words, hurt him with our actions, dishonor him with our thoughts—"he will still be faithful, because he must be true to who he is." What a humbling promise. Because of God's absolute faithfulness, he'll never turn his back on his children.

If you belong to God, are you living as his friend (James 4:4)?

2:19 "The Lord . . . him." Quotation from Numbers 16:5.

Could You Be Approaching Burnout?

1. Do you often have a tough time focusing on the task at hand?

☐ Yes ☐ No

2. Do you often feel overwhelmed at the thought of all you have to do?

☐ Yes ☐ No

3. Do you find yourself feeling cranky and irritable more often than you used to?

☐ Yes ☐ No

4. Are you easily susceptible to the flu bug, colds, and/or viruses?

☐ Yes ☐ No

5. Do you have a hard time telling others no?

☐ Yes ☐ No

6. Are you happy and fulfilled in your job?

☐ Yes ☐ No

7. Does your involvement in church or extra-curricular activities add more stress to your life?

☐ Yes ☐ No

8. Do you often have headaches or feel very tired in the middle of the day?

☐ Yes ☐ No

9. Have you accidentally double-booked yourself in the last six months?

☐ Yes ☐ No

10. Do you feel like you have a clear sense of purpose in life?

☐ Yes ☐ No

11. Do you often participate in or lead groups just because there's no one else to do it or just because people are counting on you?

☐ Yes ☐ No

12. Are you competent and well prepared for all the things you do at work and in your personal life?

☐ Yes ☐ No

13. If you wanted to stop leading or participating in something, would you be able to make that change easily?

☐ Yes ☐ No

14. Have you—or does it feel like you have—been doing the same thing day in and day out for years?

☐ Yes ☐ No

15. Have you forgotten why you first chose to participate in the activities you are now involved in?

☐ Yes ☐ No

Scoring: Give yourself 2 points for every YES and 1 point for every NO. Add your points together and see below.

If you scored 15–20 points, you are avoiding burnout! Way to go! You've got your purposes and priorities in line, and you're moving ahead with grace. It's up to you to look around and help your fellow sisters who are struggling under their loads. You can serve God better by serving them.

If you scored 21–25 points, you are on the brink! Beware! It's time to honestly evaluate what you're involved in and why. Avoiding burnout may be as simple as revisiting your priorities or revamping your schedule. You can serve God better by tackling your tasks with energy and passion.

If you scored 26–30 points, you are burning out fast! Make changes now! You are not doing anyone any favors by being tired and half-present. Ask the Lord to show you how to rearrange your priorities and commitments. Allow yourself to rest in him. You can serve God better by taking care of yourself and then ministering to others.

Obey the Teachings

10But you have followed what I teach, the way I live, my goal, faith, patience, and love. You know I never give up. 11You know how I have been hurt and have suffered, as in Antioch, Iconium, and Lystra. I have suffered, but the Lord saved me from all those troubles. 12Everyone who wants to live as God desires, in Christ Jesus, will be persecuted. 13But people who are evil and cheat others will go from bad to worse. They will fool others, but they will also be fooling themselves.

14But you should continue following the teachings you learned. You know they are true, because you trust those who taught you. 15Since you were a child you have known the Holy Scriptures which are able to make you wise. And that wisdom leads to salvation through faith in Christ Jesus. 16All Scripture is inspired by God and is useful for teaching, for showing people what is wrong in their lives, for correcting faults, and for teaching how to live right. 17Using the Scriptures, the person who serves God will be capable, having all that is needed to do every good work.

4 I give you a command in the presence of God and Christ Jesus, the One who will judge the living and the dead, and by his coming and his kingdom: 2Preach the Good News. Be ready at all times, and tell people what they need to do. Tell them when they are wrong. Encourage them with great patience and careful teaching, 3because the time will come when people will not listen to the true teaching but will find many more teachers who please them by saying the things they want to hear. 4They will stop listening to the truth and will begin to follow false stories. 5But you should control yourself at all times, accept troubles, do the work of telling the Good News, and complete all the duties of a servant of God.

6My life is being given as an offering to God, and the time has come for me to leave this life. 7I have fought the good fight, I have finished the race, I have kept the faith. 8Now, a crown is being held for me—a crown for being right with God. The Lord, the judge who judges rightly, will give the crown to me on that day[n]—not only to me but to all those who have waited with love for him to come again.

Personal Words

9Do your best to come to me as soon as you can, 10because Demas, who loved this world, left me and went to Thessalonica. Crescens went to Galatia, and Titus went to Dalmatia. 11Luke is the only one still with me. Get Mark and bring him with you when you come, because he can help me in my work here. 12I sent Tychicus to Ephesus. 13When I was in Troas, I left my coat there with Carpus. So when you come, bring it to me, along with my books, particularly the ones written on parchment.[n]

14Alexander the metalworker did many harmful things against me. The Lord will punish him for what he did. 15You also should be careful that he does not hurt you, because he fought strongly against our teaching.

16The first time I defended myself, no one helped me; everyone left me. May they be forgiven. 17But the Lord stayed with me and gave me strength so I could fully tell the Good News to all those who are not Jews. So I was saved from the lion's mouth. 18The Lord will save me when anyone tries to hurt me, and he will bring me safely to his heavenly kingdom. Glory forever and ever be the Lord's. Amen.

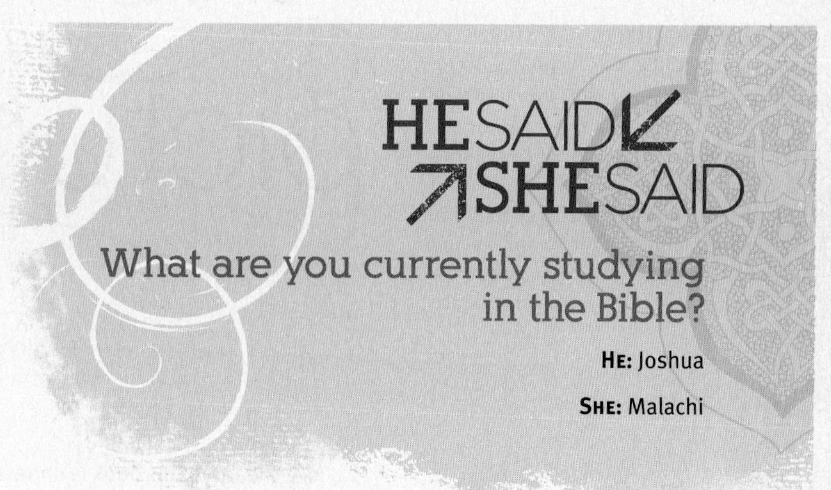

Private and Public

As the most intimate communication with your Savior, worship is a private thing. But there's also a public element to it, which ties into your role in the body of Christ (Hebrews 10:25). When you join in corporate worship, you bless God—that's often obvious by the awesome sense of God's presence in a worship service. But you also help bless his church. Have you felt the Spirit radiate through a room as God's followers lift him up together? Soul-stirring! First Corinthians 12:7 says, "Something from the Spirit can be seen in each person, for the common good." As you glorify him during corporate worship, you also participate in God's work within his church, which only glorifies him even more.

4:8 day The day Christ will come to judge all people and take his people to live with him. **4:13 parchment** A writing paper made from the skins of sheep.

Final Greetings

[19]Greet Priscilla and Aquila and the family of Onesiphorus. [20]Erastus stayed in Corinth, and I left Trophimus sick in Miletus. [21]Try as hard as you can to come to me before winter.

Eubulus sends greetings to you. Also Pudens, Linus, Claudia, and all the brothers and sisters in Christ greet you.

[22]The Lord be with your spirit. Grace be with you.

2 Timothy

Passing the Torch

Every word in this book is understood with deeper emotion and meaning when you consider that it was written by Paul just a short time before his execution. He didn't know if he would ever see Timothy or be able to write to him again.

The style of this letter is hurried, so Paul's instructions don't exactly flow or have smooth transitions. There's no flowery language or "filler" material. In fact, much of it reads like a string of thoughts, warnings, and insights that are only somewhat related.

All the instructions about how to live, lead, and grow in faith came from experience. Paul had accumulated a lot of wisdom since his encounter with God on the way to Damascus (Acts 9:1–22), and he passed that wisdom down and prayed for his beloved friend in this heartfelt letter. The Book of 2 Timothy is filled with practical teachings about the reality of following Jesus wholeheartedly.

Perhaps Paul's biggest piece of advice for Timothy was to always stay true to Scripture. Whenever you don't know what to do or are struggling with what is right and wrong, God's Word is the only 100 percent accurate place you can turn. Every word in the Bible is divinely inspired by God to reveal himself and his plan of salvation to his people (2 Timothy 3:16–17). He used human hands to put his truth down in ink, but it's God's own heart that's written on the pages of Scripture.

Get Real

What spiritual gifts or talents has God given you? Are you developing and using them for his purposes? (Romans 12:6–8; Ephesians 4:12–13; 2 Timothy 1:6)

What do you fear most? Can God be trusted with those frightening feelings? (Psalm 56:11; Luke 1:73–74; Romans 8:15)

If you were writing your last letter to a loved one, what spiritual instructions and insights would you include? (2 Timothy 4:5–7)

titus

If you've ever had to lead a bunch of unmotivated colleagues at work or tried to get an uninspired fifth grader to do his chores and homework, you know there's nothing worse than working with people who won't pay attention or obey!

Titus had his work cut out for him as the new pastor in Crete. These islanders were known as "liars, evil animals, and lazy people who do nothing but eat" (Titus 1:12). Not exactly a choice assignment. But Paul knew Titus was the man for the job—and as a safety measure, he sent Titus this letter with plenty of helpful advice about how to organize a church, avoid false teachings, and live a pure life.

The people of Crete may sound pretty awful, but they actually exemplify some typical human tendencies. And the solution to their issues is the same solution for us today: the life-changing power of God's Word. There's a major connection between sound doctrine (true teachings about God and salvation) and Christian living. Knowledge about God should always lead to action—good works of service and love.

Make your life an example of godliness by being everything that the Cretans weren't—truthful, pure, and hardworking. Get grounded in God's Word, share his truth, and let your life become a labor of love and gratitude for the Savior!

1 From Paul, a servant of God and an apostle of Jesus Christ. I was sent to help the faith of God's chosen people and to help them know the truth that shows people how to serve God. [2]That faith and that knowledge come from the hope for life forever, which God promised to us before time began. And God cannot lie. [3]At the right time God let the world know about that life through preaching. He trusted me with that work, and I preached by the command of God our Savior.

[4]To Titus, my true child in the faith we share:

Grace and peace from God the Father and Christ Jesus our Savior.

Titus' Work in Crete

[5]I left you in Crete so you could finish doing the things that still needed to be done and so you could appoint elders in every town, as I directed you. [6]An elder must not be guilty of doing wrong, must have only one wife, and must have believing children. They must not be known as children who are wild and do not cooperate. [7]As God's managers, overseers must

Titus 1:15–16

Perhaps you or someone you know wears glasses or contacts with a prescription so intense that without them it would be pretty difficult to do even simple things—like recognize friends, read books, or navigate your way through your own home. Just as some of us need some optical help in our day-to-day lives, we all need God's Spirit to help our spiritual eyes see what's right and wrong.

Without Christ, we're spiritually dead. And we have serious trouble identifying what's good and what's bad. Either everything seems bad, or we mistakenly think bad things are good (and vice versa). But when God gives us a brand new, pure conscience, we have no problem understanding what's good, true, and holy. Plus, we're able to avoid evil, because we can see it clearly.

The key to having a trustworthy conscience is a pure heart. When your heart's right with God, you'll be able to make wise decisions about what you should and shouldn't do. If you're having trouble doing what's right, spend some time getting right with God. Fill your heart with his Word, pray constantly, and ask him to give you a pure, reliable conscience to guide you safely through each day.

not be guilty of doing wrong, being selfish, or becoming angry quickly. They must not drink too much wine, like to fight, or try to get rich by cheating others. [8]Overseers must be ready to welcome guests, love what is good, be wise, live right, and be holy and self-controlled. [9]By holding on to the trustworthy word just as we teach it, overseers can help people by using true teaching, and they can show those who are against the true teaching that they are wrong.

[10]There are many people who refuse to cooperate, who talk about worthless things and lead others into the wrong way—mainly those who insist on circumcision to be saved. [11]These people must be stopped, because they are upsetting whole families by teaching things they should not teach, which they do to get rich by cheating people. [12]Even one of their own prophets said, "Cretans are always liars, evil animals, and lazy people who do nothing but eat." [13]The words that prophet said are true. So firmly tell those people they are wrong so they may become strong in the faith, [14]not accepting Jewish false stories and the commands of people who reject the truth. [15]To those who are pure, all things are pure, but to those who are full of sin and do not believe, nothing is pure. Both their minds and their consciences have been ruined. [16]They say they know God, but their actions show they do not accept him. They are hateful people, they refuse to obey, and they are useless for doing anything good.

Following the True Teaching

2 But you must tell everyone what to do to follow the true teaching. [2]Teach older men to be self-controlled, serious, wise, strong in faith, in love, and in patience.

[3]In the same way, teach older women to be holy in their behavior, not speaking against others or enslaved to too much wine, but teaching what is good. [4]Then they can teach the young women to love their husbands, to love their children, [5]to

Grilled Potatoes and Onions

Cut 2 regular or sweet potatoes into 1/4-inch sections, and slice 1 onion into thin strips. While the grill preheats, boil the potatoes until tender, about 15 minutes. Drain water and add minced garlic, salt, and pepper to taste and 2 tablespoons of olive oil, gently tossing to coat potatoes. Wrap potatoes and onions in a large piece of aluminum foil, and place on grill for 15–20 minutes until onions are tender and vegetables are browned, stirring occasionally. Next time, try experimenting with other seasonings. A few suggestions: Cajun, southwest, lemon pepper, dill, or rosemary.

be wise and pure, to be good workers at home, to be kind, and to yield to their husbands. Then no one will be able to criticize the teaching God gave us.

[6]In the same way, encourage young men to be wise. [7]In every way be an example of doing good deeds. When you teach, do it with honesty and seriousness. [8]Speak the truth so that you cannot be criticized. Then those who are against you will be ashamed because there is nothing bad to say about us.

[9]Slaves should yield to their own masters at all times, trying to please them and not arguing with them. [10]They should not steal from them but should show their masters they can be fully trusted so that in everything they do they will make the teaching of God our Savior attractive.

[11]That is the way we should live, because God's grace that can save everyone has come. [12]It teaches us not to live against God nor to do the evil things the world wants to do. Instead, that grace teaches us to live in the present age in a wise and right way and in a way that shows we serve God. [13]We should live like that while we wait for our great hope and the coming of the glory of our great God and Savior Jesus Christ.

[14]He gave himself for us so he might pay the price to free us from all evil and to make us pure people who belong only to him—people who are always wanting to do good deeds.

[15]Say these things and encourage the people and tell them what is wrong in their lives, with all authority. Do not let anyone treat you as if you were unimportant.

The Right Way to Live

3 Remind the believers to yield to the authority of rulers and government leaders, to obey them, to be ready to do good, [2]to speak no evil about anyone, to live in peace, and to be gentle and polite to all people.

[3]In the past we also were foolish. We did not obey, we were wrong, and we were slaves to many things our bodies wanted and enjoyed. We spent our lives doing evil and being jealous. People hated us, and we hated each other. [4]But when the kindness and love of God our Savior was shown, [5]he saved us because of his mercy. It was not because of good deeds we did to be right with him. He saved us through the washing that made us new people through the Holy Spirit. [6]God poured out richly upon us that Holy Spirit through Jesus Christ our Savior. [7]Being made right with God by his grace, we could have the hope of receiving the life that never ends.

Recruit a "You Go, Girl!" Group

Have you ever noticed how one person can cause mayhem in a crowd? A shout of panic here, a seed of worry there, and others join in the fear frenzy. That's why if you're prone to fear and panic, it's especially important to surround yourself with bold, encouraging women. First Thessalonians 5:11 reminds us to "encourage each other and give each other strength." Hang out with positive, gutsy gals, and their courage will rub off on you! Make friends with someone who will broaden your comfort zone. If fear has prevented you from doing something you've always wanted to do, enlist a friend to help you. Everybody needs someone in their corner to shout, "You go, girl!"

Seasonal Insights

The first snowfall's scent, the newness of summer's warmth—ahhh! Both bring a thrill with their freshness. But eventually they become routine. By winter's end you wish for warmer temperatures, and by September you crave relief from sweltering heat. Much like calendar seasons, relationship seasons reveal unique characteristics and hidden surprises. When it comes to romance, there's value in experiencing several seasons together before committing to a lifetime. Can you live with his once-endearing quirks that now try your patience? Have you observed him under high stress? Does he consistently seek God? Ask God to leave nothing hidden that needs to come out, and pursue his guidance and timing. "Everything on earth"—including your love life—"has its special season" (Ecclesiastes 3:1).

[8]This teaching is true, and I want you to be sure the people understand these things. Then those who believe in God will be careful to use their lives for doing good. These things are good and will help everyone.

[9]But stay away from those who have foolish arguments and talk about useless family histories and argue and quarrel about the law. Those things are worth nothing and will not help anyone. [10]After a first and second warning, avoid someone who causes arguments. [11]You can know that such people are evil and sinful; their own sins prove them wrong.

Some Things to Remember

[12]When I send Artemas or Tychicus to you, make every effort to come to me at Nicopolis, because I have decided to stay there this winter. [13]Do all you can to help Zenas the lawyer and Apollos on their journey so that they have everything they need. [14]Our people must learn to use their lives for doing good deeds to provide what is necessary so that their lives will not be useless.

[15]All who are with me greet you. Greet those who love us in the faith.

Grace be with you all.

BECOME Involved

The Father's Ranch

The Father's Ranch is one of the only nonprofit, residential facilities nationwide for the treatment of eating disorders and addictions among young women. Anyone who's between the ages of eighteen and thirty-five and struggling with these life-controlling issues is welcome at The Father's Ranch. And here's the kicker: it's absolutely free!

Girls flock to The Father's Ranch from all over the country. Some arrive at the very end of their rope, desperate for help and void of hope. They stay between six and twelve months during which they experience biblical teaching, counseling, and study. Participants are guided through the recovery and healing process and leave ready to start a new, healthy life wherever they choose to settle.

As a nonprofit, The Father's Ranch is supported through donations. Why not consider helping them financially as they help others? You can also be involved by volunteering in their facility. Service project opportunities abound there, and it's a great summer mission trip for any family or small group. They also need one-year interns to help on a longer-term basis. Find out more at www.thefathersranch.com. Even if you can't give or go, you can still pray for this important ministry.

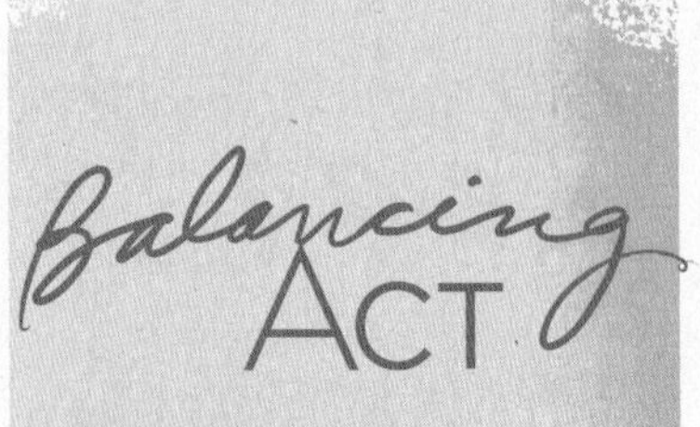

The Big Picture

Have you heard the saying, "The devil is in the details"? Sometimes it seems like the Evil One is lurking behind the tiniest element of any activity, waiting to sabotage! That's why it's important to always have the objective—or the big picture—in mind when tackling a project. Having a clear goal and purpose can prevent meltdown when specific steps in the process are less successful than you had hoped. Combat that "can't-see-the-forest-for-the-trees" mentality by looking back over what you've done and learning from your mistakes and successes. Don't let the details overwhelm you; when something doesn't work, move on to plan B. There are endless different ways to tackle the same problem, so be flexible in the process. And always work toward the goal (Philippians 3:14)!

A Strong Church

Titus may be a short book, but it packs a strong punch. It gives God's instructions for how the church is supposed to stay strong. Those who lead in the church must be pure and grounded in God's Word. Sin or false teachings can't exist in a healthy church. Right living and true teaching can only be based on Scripture. Everyone's roles, interactions, and behavior should grow from being rooted in the Bible.

Paul knew that the church was settling in for the long haul. Before long, Paul and the other apostles' work of laying the foundation for the church would be complete. Then it would be time for the church to start functioning as the body of Christ, fulfilling God's work in the world until Jesus' return. God spoke to the early church through the apostles (Titus 1:3), but church leadership would soon be passed on to other men called elders or overseers (1:5, 7–8). Paul wanted to make sure that Scripture remained the only authority for truth and good teaching. There could be no room for false teachers or people claiming to be new apostles with messages from God.

Paul's message to Titus is clear: God's Word is the source of true teaching (Titus 2:1; 3:8), so choose leaders who teach and live the Scriptures as taught by God through Paul and the other apostles (1:9). Paul also gives some essential information on how all Christians should live and treat each other (chapters 2—3).

The teachings in this book are vital for every Christian, from church leaders to the newest believer. A healthy and true church will constantly live out these important instructions!

Get Real

Are you living the kind of life that builds up your local church? Are you a faithful member of the body of Christ? (1 Corinthians 12:12–27; Ephesians 4; 1 Thessalonians 3:12–13; Titus 3:3–7)

What's so important about the Bible? (2 Timothy 3:14–17; James 1:22–25; 2 Peter 1:20–21)

How should true followers of Jesus live? (Micah 6:8; Romans 12:9–21; Ephesians 4:17–32; Philippians 2:1–5)

philemon

Sometimes a hands-off approach can be very tempting when it comes to delicate, personal situations. Maybe someone you love is about to make a huge mistake . . . but you know that speaking up could ruin the relationship. Nobody wants to rock the boat, but sometimes it's necessary. How do you consistently display love without compromising truth? It can be tricky, but Scripture is clear: truth and love go together. And no matter how difficult it might seem, there's a way to lovingly present even the most difficult-to-hear truths.

This letter to Philemon is a great example of speaking the truth in love. One of Philemon's slaves, Onesimus, had run away, but he became a Christian after meeting Paul. Both the slave and the master are now Christians, but they have serious issues between them!

As Christians we're called to a life of love that transcends social boundaries and personal conflict. So Paul sent Onesimus back to Philemon with this letter. It's an amazing model of giving firm guidance that isn't harsh or argumentative. Without actually demanding that Philemon do anything, Paul points him in the right direction.

People appreciate it when you show you care, even when it means a confrontation. Just remember to be careful and loving no matter what.

[1]From Paul, a prisoner of Christ Jesus, and from Timothy, our brother.

To Philemon, our dear friend and worker with us; [2]to Apphia, our sister; to Archippus, a worker with us; and to the church that meets in your home:

[3]Grace and peace to you from God our Father and the Lord Jesus Christ.

Philemon's Love and Faith

[4]I always thank my God when I mention you in my prayers, [5]because I hear about the love you have for all God's holy people and the faith you have in the Lord Jesus. [6]I pray that the faith you share may make you understand every blessing we have in Christ. [7]I have great joy and comfort, my brother, because the love you have shown to God's people has refreshed them.

Accept Onesimus as a Brother

[8]So, in Christ, I could be bold and order you to do what is right. [9]But because I love you, I am pleading with you instead. I, Paul, an old man now and also a prisoner for Christ Jesus, [10]am pleading with you for my child Onesimus, who became my child while I was in prison. [11]In the past he was useless to you, but now he has become useful for both you and me.

[12]I am sending him back to you, and with him I am sending my own heart. [13]I wanted to keep him with me so that in your place he might help me while I am in prison for the Good News. [14]But I did not want to do anything without asking you first so that any good you do for me will be because you want to do it, not because

I forced you. [15]Maybe Onesimus was separated from you for a short time so you could have him back forever— [16]no longer as a slave, but better than a slave, as a loved brother. I love him very much, but you will love him even more, both as a person and as a believer in the Lord.

[17]So if you consider me your partner, welcome Onesimus as you would welcome me. [18]If he has done anything wrong to you or if he owes you anything, charge that to me. [19]I, Paul, am writing this with my own hand. I will pay it back, and I will say nothing about what you owe me for your own life. [20]So, my brother, I ask that you do this for me in the Lord: Refresh my heart in Christ. [21]I write this letter, knowing that you will do what I ask you and even more.

[22]One more thing—prepare a room for me in which to stay, because I hope God will answer your prayers and I will be able to come to you.

Final Greetings

[23]Epaphras, a prisoner with me for Christ Jesus, sends greetings to you. [24]And also Mark, Aristarchus, Demas, and Luke, workers together with me, send greetings.

[25]The grace of our Lord Jesus Christ be with your spirit.

Philemon

Equality in Christ

This letter to Philemon, a believer in Colosse, may not seem that applicable for us today. More than likely, neither you nor anyone you know is dealing with the issue of an escaped slave! But that doesn't mean there's nothing for us to learn.

First, it's encouraging to see how Paul deals with such a delicate issue: he reminds Philemon about God's grace toward us, tells Philemon he appreciates his good qualities, and then moves into his request about Onesimus.

But it's the case he makes for accepting Onesimus as a brother in Christ, not as a slave (Philemon 16), that's the most relevant reminder for us. Slavery was a major part of Roman society at that time. Most of the labor in the Roman Empire was accomplished by slaves, and slavery was also used as a way to work off debts and pay for crimes.

That's why it's significant when Paul says that slaves and masters, men and women, Jews and non-Jewish people—*all people*—are equal in God's eyes and need the same grace and forgiveness. Paul was committed to making sure that Christian love would always be the highest priority for Christians, regardless of nationality, gender, social standing, or economic status.

The lines of separation in our modern society may look a little different than they did in the early church, but the same principle applies. As Christians, God calls us to a higher standard of love.

Get Real

What does the Bible teach about how God sees us if Christ is in us? (Galatians 3:28; Colossians 3:11)

How are we supposed to treat each other if we have new life in Christ? (Mark 12:29–31; Colossians 3:12–14)

Should we be tolerant of everyone, regardless of how they live? (1 Corinthians 5:9–13; Galatians 5:19–21; 6:1–2; Ephesians 4:17—5:20)

hebrews

"There's got to be a better way!" Have you ever said that to yourself in the middle of a task that seems impossible? Often the solution to the problem isn't found in trying harder or becoming stronger—instead, you find another method, a new approach to the same old problem.

Ever since Adam and Eve first disobeyed God, people have had the same old problem: a broken relationship with God because of sin. But because of his love, God wouldn't let that relationship stay broken. He set up a system for people who wanted to follow him—the old agreement. It involved animal sacrifices, a special group of priests who helped present those sacrifices to God, and a complex system of rituals and laws. This old system was good, but it wasn't the ultimate plan. It was all just preparation for Jesus Christ. He's the better way!

Jesus is the perfect sacrifice. He's the perfect High Priest who speaks to God on our behalf. He's the only way to know God. Because of Jesus' righteousness, we can be friends with God. And by his resurrection, Jesus defeated the power of sin and death.

If you're looking for a better life, you have to recognize that it's all about Christ, and it begins with putting your faith in him.

God Spoke Through His Son

1 In the past God spoke to our ancestors through the prophets many times and in many different ways. [2]But now in these last days God has spoken to us through his Son. God has chosen his Son to own all things, and through him he made the world. [3]The Son reflects the glory of God and shows exactly what God is like. He holds everything together with his powerful word. When the Son made people clean from their sins, he sat down at the right side of God, the Great One in heaven. [4]The Son became much greater than the angels, and God gave him a name that is much greater than theirs.

[5]This is because God never said to any of the angels,

"You are my Son.
Today I have become your Father." *Psalm 2:7*

Nor did God say of any angel,

"I will be his Father,
and he will be my Son." *2 Samuel 7:14*

[6]And when God brings his firstborn Son into the world, he says,

"Let all God's angels worship him."[n] *Psalm 97:7*

[7]This is what God said about the angels:

"God makes his angels become like winds.
He makes his servants become like flames of fire." *Psalm 104:4*

[8]But God said this about his Son:

"God, your throne will last forever and ever.
You will rule your kingdom with fairness.
[9]You love right and hate evil,
so God has chosen you from among your friends;
he has set you apart with much joy." *Psalm 45:6-7*

[10]God also says,

1:6 "Let . . . him." These words are found in Deuteronomy 32:43 in the Septuagint, the Greek version of the Old Testament, and in a Hebrew copy among the Dead Sea Scrolls.

Hebrews 2:17–18

I feel so misunderstood. Has that thought ever run through your mind? Maybe you feel disconnected with people in your life and just wish someone would stop to really listen to you. Someone who could understand, someone who would treat you with kindness, respect, and love.

It may surprise you to know just how understood you truly are right this second. God knows you intensely and perfectly inside and out. He always has. He's completely aware of how you work—he was delighted to create you just the way you are, and his eyes are always on you. He loves you and doesn't want you to walk through life without him.

God knows what you're going through right now—every struggle, every heartache, every fear, and every joy. God himself came to earth as a human and became like us "in every way" (Hebrews 2:17). He lived the perfect human life, meeting the exact same standards he told us to follow. Where we failed, he succeeded. He knows what it's like to be tempted and to deal with suffering.

God deeply loves and understands you. Open your heart to him, drink in his closeness, and depend on his Spirit for all the strength and comfort you need.

"Lord, in the beginning you made the
earth,
and your hands made the skies.
[11]They will be destroyed, but you will
remain.
They will all wear out like
clothes.
[12]You will fold them like a coat.
And, like clothes, you will change
them.
But you never change,
and your life will never end."
Psalm 102:25–27

[13]And God never said this to an angel:
"Sit by me at my right side
until I put your enemies under
your control."[n] *Psalm 110:1*

[14]All the angels are spirits who serve God and are sent to help those who will receive salvation.

Our Salvation Is Great

2 So we must be more careful to follow what we were taught. Then we will not stray away from the truth. [2]The teaching God spoke through angels was shown to be true, and anyone who did not follow it or obey it received the punishment that was earned. [3]So surely we also will be punished if we ignore this great salvation. The Lord himself first told about this salvation, and those who heard him testified it was true. [4]God also testified to the truth of the message by using wonders, great signs, many kinds of miracles, and by giving people gifts through the Holy Spirit, just as he wanted.

Christ Became like Humans

[5]God did not choose angels to be the rulers of the new world that was coming, which is what we have been talking about. [6]It is written in the Scriptures,
"Why are people even important to
you?
Why do you take care of human
beings?
[7]You made them a little lower than
the angels
and crowned them with glory
and honor.[n]
[8]You put all things under their
control." *Psalm 8:4–6*

When God put everything under their control, there was nothing left that they did not rule. Still, we do not yet see them ruling over everything. [9]But we see Jesus, who for a short time was made lower than the angels. And now he is wearing a crown of glory and honor because he suffered and died. And by God's grace, he died for everyone.

[10]God is the One who made all things, and all things are for his glory. He wanted to have many children share his glory, so he made the One who leads people to salvation perfect through suffering.

[11]Jesus, who makes people holy, and those who are made holy are from the same family. So he is not ashamed to call them his brothers and sisters. [12]He says,
"Then, I will tell my brothers and
sisters about you;
I will praise you in the public
meeting." *Psalm 22:22*

[13]He also says,
"I will trust in God." *Isaiah 8:17*

And he also says,
"I am here, and with me are the
children God has given me."
Isaiah 8:18

[14]Since these children are people with physical bodies, Jesus himself became like them. He did this so that, by dying, he could destroy the one who has the power of death—the devil— [15]and free those who were like slaves all their lives because of their fear of death. [16]Clearly,

1:13 until . . . control Literally, "until I make your enemies a footstool for your feet." **2:7 You . . . honor.** Some Greek copies continue, "You put them in charge of everything you made." See Psalm 8:6.

LIFE ISSUES

Workaholism

Even if your career isn't based in a Fortune 500 company, you're one of the fortunate few if you love your job. Enjoying a livelihood that goes beyond paying the bills and actually thrills your heart is a rare treat. But like anything, work can get out of balance. If we prioritize work over relationships with God and others, we miss out on "life in all its fullness" (John 10:10). If you struggle with workaholism, ask God to reveal and heal any misdirected motivations (materialism, pride, avoidance of an issue, unhealthy boundaries) that are out of sync with his desires for you.

it is not angels that Jesus helps, but the people who are from Abraham.[n] [17]For this reason Jesus had to be made like his brothers and sisters in every way so he could be their merciful and faithful high priest in service to God. Then Jesus could die in their place to take away their sins. [18]And now he can help those who are tempted, because he himself suffered and was tempted.

Jesus Is Greater than Moses

3 So all of you holy brothers and sisters, who were called by God, think about Jesus, who was sent to us and is the high priest of our faith. [2]Jesus was faithful to God as Moses was in God's family. [3]Jesus has more honor than Moses, just as the builder of a house has more honor than the house itself. [4]Every house is built by someone, but the builder of everything is God himself. [5]Moses was faithful in God's family as a servant, and he told what God would say in the future. [6]But Christ is faithful as a Son over God's house. And we are God's house if we confidently maintain our hope.

We Must Continue to Follow God

[7]So it is as the Holy Spirit says:
"Today listen to what he says.
[8]Do not be stubborn as in the past
when you turned against God,
when you tested God in the desert.
[9]There your ancestors tried me and tested me
and saw the things I did for forty years.
[10]I was angry with them.
I said, 'They are not loyal to me
and have not understood my ways.'
[11]I was angry and made a promise,
'They will never enter my rest.'"[n]
Psalm 95:7–11

[12]So brothers and sisters, be careful that none of you has an evil, unbelieving heart that will turn you away from the living God. [13]But encourage each other every day while it is "today."[n] Help each other so none of you will become hardened because sin has tricked you. [14]We all share in Christ if we keep till the end the sure faith we had in the beginning. [15]This is what the Scripture says:

"Today listen to what he says.
Do not be stubborn as in the past
when you turned against God."
Psalm 95:7–8

[16]Who heard God's voice and was against him? It was all those people Moses led out of Egypt. [17]And with whom was God angry for forty years? He was angry with those who sinned, who died in the desert.

Be Still & KNOW

Praying in Public

For some, the thought of being called on to pray aloud in public is a scary thing. Sweaty palms and accelerated breathing erupt as the mind instantly draws a blank for appropriate words to say. But for others, the temptation arises to present a dramatic stage play when they get the opportunity to pray in public. Big words abound and theatrics creep in before they even realize what's happened. The most important thing to remember when praying in public is that you're *praying*. That means you're having a conversation with God. Other people may be hearing your words, but the audience is just one—the Lord. Pretend it's just you and him, and he will be honored!

2:16 Abraham Most respected ancestor of the Jews. Every Jew hoped to see Abraham. **3:11 rest** A place of rest God promised to give his people. **3:13 "today"** This word is taken from verse 7. It means that it is important to do these things now.

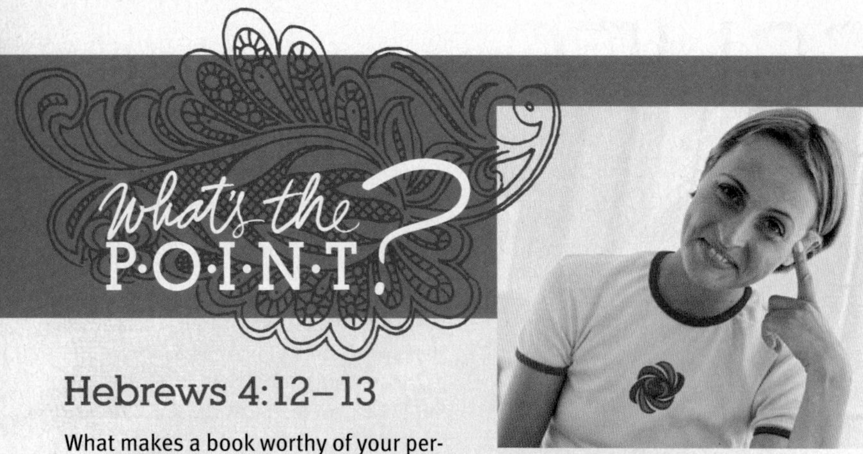

Hebrews 4:12–13

What makes a book worthy of your personal "all-time favorite" list? Perhaps it's the hysterical characters or suspenseful plot, or maybe it's the straight talk about your spiritual, emotional, or physical well-being. Whatever the appeal, a book becomes a favorite because it inspires you to change your outlook, attitude, or thinking.

The Bible's like that, only on a much larger scale. As God's Word, it's no ordinary book, and it's not just inspirational. The Bible is "alive and working" (Hebrews 4:12), and it slices right to the core of our heart issues. When God's Spirit opens your eyes, Scripture's a place where you can meet the living God! It's accounts of how this holy God relates to the imperfect people he loves will pierce your heart. And it'll fill your heart with hope as you read about God's perfect love, grace, and salvation.

Proverbs 2:6 says, "Only the LORD gives wisdom; he gives knowledge and understanding." Let God's Word change you. When you approach Scripture, be prepared to make your life wide open to God. It might be scary at first. But as you trust God more and let him into the deepest parts of your heart, he'll transform you into someone who looks a lot like Jesus.

18 And to whom was God talking when he promised that they would never enter his rest? He was talking to those who did not obey him. 19 So we see they were not allowed to enter and have God's rest, because they did not believe.

4 Now, since God has left us the promise that we may enter his rest, let us be very careful so none of you will fail to enter. 2 The Good News was preached to us just as it was to them. But the teaching they heard did not help them, because they heard it but did not accept it with faith.[n] 3 We who have believed are able to enter and have God's rest. As God has said,

"I was angry and made a
promise,
'They will never enter my rest.'"
Psalm 95:11

But God's work was finished from the time he made the world. 4 In the Scriptures he talked about the seventh day of the week: "And on the seventh day God rested from all his works."[n] 5 And again in the Scripture God said, "They will never enter my rest."

6 It is still true that some people will enter God's rest, but those who first heard the way to be saved did not enter, because they did not obey. 7 So God planned another day, called "today." He spoke about that day through David a long time later in the same Scripture used before:

"Today listen to what he says.
Do not be stubborn." *Psalm 95:7–8*

8 We know that Joshua[n] did not lead the people into that rest, because God spoke later about another day. 9 This shows that the rest[n] for God's people is still coming. 10 Anyone who enters God's rest will rest from his work as God did. 11 Let us try as hard as we can to enter God's rest so that no one will fail by following the example of those who refused to obey.

12 God's word is alive and working and is sharper than a double-edged sword. It cuts all the way into us, where the soul and the spirit are joined, to the center of our joints and bones. And it judges the thoughts and feelings in our hearts. 13 Nothing in all the world can be hidden from God. Everything is clear and lies open before him, and to him we must explain the way we have lived.

Jesus Is Our High Priest

14 Since we have a great high priest, Jesus the Son of God, who has gone into heaven, let us hold on to the faith we have. 15 For our high priest is able to understand our weaknesses. He was tempted in every way that we are, but he did not sin. 16 Let us, then, feel very sure that we can come before God's throne where there is grace. There we can receive mercy and grace to help us when we need it.

5 Every high priest is chosen from among other people. He is given the work of going before God for them to offer gifts and sacrifices for sins. 2 Since he himself is weak, he is able to be gentle with those who do not understand and who are doing wrong things. 3 Because he is weak, the high priest must offer sacrifices for his own sins and also for the sins of the people.

4 To be a high priest is an honor, but no one chooses himself for this work. He must be called by God as Aaron[n] was. 5 So also Christ did not choose himself to have the honor of being a high priest, but God chose him. God said to him,

"You are my Son.
Today I have become your
Father." *Psalm 2:7*

6 And in another Scripture God says,

"You are a priest forever,
a priest like Melchizedek."[n]
Psalm 110:4

4:2 because . . . faith Some Greek copies read "because they did not share the faith of those who heard it." **4:4 "And . . . works."** Quotation from Genesis 2:2. **4:8 Joshua** After Moses died, Joshua became leader of the Jewish people and led them into the land that God promised to give them. **4:9 rest** Literally, "sabbath rest," meaning a sharing in the rest that God began after he created the world. **5:4 Aaron** Moses' brother and the first Jewish high priest. **5:6 Melchizedek** A priest and king who lived in the time of Abraham. (Read Genesis 14:17–24.)

book review

Facing Your Giants
by Max Lucado

What challenges are looming large in your life right now? No matter what "giants" you face—including depression, addiction, financial crisis, divorce, or something else—they don't have to intimidate or overpower you. Author Max Lucado urges you to face down challenges with courage and rely on God's strength to defeat them. Using the biblical story of David and Goliath as a backdrop, Lucado paints a vivid picture of what it looks like to see beyond your struggles. This book will help give you the confidence you need to keep battling your giants until you're victorious.

Q: How can I make friends in a new city?

A: Moving to a new city can be very exciting—and very hard at the same time! Sometimes finding the energy, motivation, and avenue for making new friends can be as hard as finding a place to live or packing up all your belongings. But the effort you put forth will have a very good return on your investment . . . guaranteed. As soon as possible, start visiting local churches. Talk to people at the gym. Join a civic club or volunteer at a charity. Whatever you do, don't just sit around! Get out and explore your new city. You'll have a great new group of friends in no time.

[7]While Jesus lived on earth, he prayed to God and asked God for help. He prayed with loud cries and tears to the One who could save him from death, and his prayer was heard because he trusted God. [8]Even though Jesus was the Son of God, he learned obedience by what he suffered. [9]And because his obedience was perfect, he was able to give eternal salvation to all who obey him. [10]In this way God made Jesus a high priest, a priest like Melchizedek.

Warning Against Falling Away

[11]We have much to say about this, but it is hard to explain because you are so slow to understand. [12]By now you should be teachers, but you need someone to teach you again the first lessons of God's message. You still need the teaching that is like milk. You are not ready for solid food. [13]Anyone who lives on milk is still a baby and knows nothing about right teaching. [14]But solid food is for those who are grown up. They are mature enough to know the difference between good and evil.

6 So let us go on to grown-up teaching. Let us not go back over the beginning lessons we learned about Christ. We should not again start teaching about faith in God and about turning away from those acts that lead to death. [2]We should not return to the teaching about baptisms,[n] about laying on of hands,[n] about the raising of the dead and eternal judgment. [3]And we will go on to grown-up teaching if God allows.

[4]Some people cannot be brought back again to a changed life. They were once in God's light, and enjoyed heaven's gift, and shared in the Holy Spirit. [5]They found out how good God's word is, and they received the powers of his new world. [6]But they fell away from Christ. It is impossible to bring them back to a changed life again, because they are nailing the Son of God to a cross again and are shaming him in front of others.

[7]Some people are like land that gets plenty of rain. The land produces a good crop for those who work it, and it receives God's blessings. [8]Other people are like land that grows thorns and weeds and is worthless. It is about to be cursed by God and will be destroyed by fire.

6:2 baptisms The word here may refer to Christian baptism, or it may refer to the Jewish ceremonial washings. **6:2 laying on of hands** The laying on of hands had many purposes, including the giving of a blessing, power, or authority.

RELATIONSHIPS

Pipe Down and Listen!

Think back to your last argument. You may not remember details—including what started it in the first place!—but you probably recall how heated things got or perhaps even something you said and later regretted. Disagreements aren't bad in and of themselves. The important thing in an argument is *how* two people argue. Hollering and door slamming drown out communication and can destroy any desire to listen. If your next argument becomes a shouting match, take a time-out to chill out and listen (James 1:19–20).

[9]Dear friends, we are saying this to you, but we really expect better things from you that will lead to your salvation. [10]God is fair; he will not forget the work you did and the love you showed for him by helping his people. And he will remember that you are still helping them. [11]We want each of you to go on with the same hard work all your lives so you will surely get what you hope for. [12]We do not want you to become lazy. Be like those who through faith and patience will receive what God has promised.

[13]God made a promise to Abraham. And as there is no one greater than God, he used himself when he swore to Abraham, [14]saying, "I will surely bless you and give you many descendants."[n] [15]Abraham waited patiently for this to happen, and he received what God promised.

[16]People always use the name of someone greater than themselves when they swear. The oath proves that what they say is true, and this ends all arguing. [17]God wanted to prove that his promise was true to those who would get what he promised. And he wanted them to understand clearly that his purposes never change, so he made an oath. [18]These two things cannot change: God cannot lie when he makes a promise, and he cannot lie when he makes an oath. These things encourage us who came to God for safety. They give us strength to hold on to the hope we have been given. [19]We have this hope as an anchor for the soul, sure and strong. It enters behind the curtain in the Most Holy Place in heaven, [20]where Jesus has gone ahead of us and for us. He has become the high priest forever, a priest like Melchizedek.[n]

Women & Men of the BIBLE

David: Bringing Honor to God

From the time he was a precocious little boy, David defended the Lord's honor. He killed a giant named Goliath with a sling and a stone for mocking the Israelites' faith. He remained loyal to his friends even at great personal risk. And throughout his life, he continued to bring honor to God. The feisty little shepherd boy became Israel's greatest king, and from his line came the Messiah. He demonstrated deep, heartfelt worship and gave God credit for all his victories. God said David was just the kind of man he wants! (1 and 2 Samuel; Acts 13:22)

The Priest Melchizedek

7 Melchizedek[n] was the king of Salem and a priest for God Most High. He met Abraham when Abraham was coming back after defeating the kings. When they met, Melchizedek blessed Abraham, [2]and Abraham gave him a tenth of everything he had brought back from the battle. First, Melchizedek's name means "king of goodness," and he is king

6:14 "I . . . descendants." Quotation from Genesis 22:17. **6:20; 7:1 Melchizedek** A priest and king who lived in the time of Abraham. (Read Genesis 14:17–24.)

You also are like living stones,
so let yourselves be used to build
a spiritual temple—
october
Organize a chick flick slumber party. 1
Pray for a person of influence: it's Kelly Ripa's birthday. 2
3
Pray for a person of influence: it's Anne Rice's birthday. 4
It's Pastor Appreciation Month. Let your church staff know you care. 5
6
Columbus Day is the 2nd Monday in October. Learn what happened in 1492. 7
8
Don't forget to schedule your annual checkups before the end of the year. 9
10
Plan a picnic and enjoy the fall colors. 11
12
Experiment with a few "Savvy Chef" recipes in Becoming 2008. 13
14
15
Offer your boss a word of encouragement. 16
17
18
Buy yourself a plant. 19
Check the newspaper for a local fall festival. 20
Research a few of the "Become Involved" organizations listed in Becoming 2008. 21
22
Pray for a person of influence: it's Michael Crichton's birthday. 23
Offer to pray for someone today. Then follow through! 24
It's Pablo Picasso's birthday. Visit a local art gallery. 25
Volunteer on Make a Difference Day www.makeadifferenceday.com 26
Get a jump on the holidays: make your Christmas gift list. 27
28
29
30
Say a prayer today simply thanking God for who he is. 31
to be holy priests who offer spiritual sacrifices to God.
He will accept those sacrifices through Jesus Christ.
—1 Peter 2:5

Health

Germs

While "cleanliness is next to godliness" isn't exactly a biblical truth, there is merit to scrubbing up. Even Old Testament believers understood the importance of keeping clean things separate from unclean things. With food-borne illnesses on the rise and new germ strains exhibiting resistance to antibiotics, we could use a lesson in good, old-fashioned hygiene. It sounds simple, but the best way to prevent germs from spreading is to wash your hands frequently. Keep food-prep surfaces clean with a bleach solution. Store food properly and defrost frozen foods in the refrigerator or the microwave—not on the counter. Use separate cooking utensils for raw meat and cooked meat. Scrub fruits and veggies with a produce spray under running water. Put leftovers away promptly, discarding them after a few days. Not sure how long that pizza has been in the fridge? When in doubt, throw it out.

of Salem, which means "king of peace." [3]No one knows who Melchizedek's father or mother was,[n] where he came from, when he was born, or when he died. Melchizedek is like the Son of God; he continues being a priest forever.

[4]You can see how great Melchizedek was. Abraham, the great father, gave him a tenth of everything that he won in battle. [5]Now the law says that those in the tribe of Levi who become priests must collect a tenth from the people—their own people—even though the priests and the people are from the family of Abraham. [6]Melchizedek was not from the tribe of Levi, but he collected a tenth from Abraham. And he blessed Abraham, the man who had God's promises. [7]Now everyone knows that the more important person blesses the less important person. [8]Priests receive a tenth, even though they are only men who live and then die. But Melchizedek, who received a tenth from Abraham, continues living, as the Scripture says. [9]We might even say that Levi, who receives a tenth, also paid it when Abraham paid Melchizedek a tenth. [10]Levi was not yet born, but he was in the body of his ancestor when Melchizedek met Abraham.

[11]The people were given the law[n] concerning the system of priests from the tribe of Levi, but they could not be made perfect through that system. So there was a need for another priest to come, a priest like Melchizedek, not Aaron. [12]And when a different kind of priest comes, the law must be changed, too. [13]We are saying these things about Christ, who belonged to a different tribe. No one from that tribe ever served as a priest at the altar. [14]It is clear that our Lord came from the tribe of Judah, and Moses said nothing about priests belonging to that tribe.

Jesus Is like Melchizedek

[15]And this becomes even more clear when we see that another priest comes who is like Melchizedek.[n] [16]He was not made a priest by human rules and laws but through the power of his life, which continues forever. [17]It is said about him,

"You are a priest forever,
a priest like Melchizedek."
Psalm 110:4

[18]The old rule is now set aside, because it was weak and useless. [19]The law of Moses could not make anything perfect. But now a better hope has been given to us, and with this hope we can come near to God. [20]It is important that God did this with an oath. Others became priests without an oath, [21]but Christ became a priest with God's oath. God said:

"The Lord has made a promise
and will not change his mind.
'You are a priest forever.'"
Psalm 110:4

[22]This means that Jesus is the guarantee of a better agreement[n] from God to his people.

[23]When one of the other priests died, he could not continue being a priest. So there were many priests. [24]But because Jesus lives forever, he will never stop serving as priest. [25]So he is able always to save those who come to God through him because he always lives, asking God to help them.

[26]Jesus is the kind of high priest we need. He is holy, sinless, pure, not influenced by sinners, and he is raised above the heavens. [27]He is not like the other priests who had to offer sacrifices every day, first for their own sins, and then for the sins of the people. Christ offered his sacrifice only once and for all time when he offered himself. [28]The law chooses high priests who are people with weaknesses, but the word of God's oath came later than the law. It made God's Son to be the high priest, and that Son has been made perfect forever.

Jesus Is Our High Priest

8 Here is the point of what we are saying: We have a high priest who sits on the right side of God's throne in heaven. [2]Our high priest serves in the Most Holy Place, the true place of worship that was made by God, not by humans.

[3]Every high priest has the work of offering gifts and sacrifices to God. So our high priest must also offer something to God. [4]If our high priest were now living on earth, he would not be a priest, because there are already priests here who follow the law by offering gifts to God. [5]The work they do as priests is only a copy and a shadow of what is in heaven. This is why God warned Moses when he was ready to build the Holy Tent: "Be very careful to make everything by the plan I showed you on the mountain."[n] [6]But the priestly work that has been given to Jesus is much greater than the work that was given to the other priests. In the same way, the new agreement that Jesus brought from God to his people is much greater than the old one. And the new agreement is based on promises of better things.

7:3 No . . . was Literally, "Melchizedek was without father, without mother, without genealogy." **7:11 The . . . law** This refers to the people of Israel who were given the Law of Moses. **7:15 Melchizedek** A priest and king who lived in the time of Abraham. (Read Genesis 14:17–24.) **7:22 agreement** God gives a contract or agreement to his people. For the Jews, this agreement was the Law of Moses. But now God has given a better agreement to his people through Christ. **8:5 "Be . . . mountain."** Quotation from Exodus 25:40.

42% of employees ages 25 to 34 don't invest in their 401(k)s.

(Vanguard)

[7]If there had been nothing wrong with the first agreement,[n] there would have been no need for a second agreement. [8]But God found something wrong with his people. He says:[n]

"Look, the time is coming, says the Lord,
when I will make a new agreement
with the people of Israel
and the people of Judah.
[9]It will not be like the agreement
I made with their ancestors
when I took them by the hand
to bring them out of Egypt.
But they broke that agreement,
and I turned away from them,
says the Lord.
[10]This is the agreement I will make
with the people of Israel at that time, says the Lord.
I will put my teachings in their minds
and write them on their hearts.
I will be their God,
and they will be my people.
[11]People will no longer have to teach
their neighbors and relatives
to know the Lord,
because all people will know me,
from the least to the most important.
[12]I will forgive them for the wicked things they did,
and I will not remember their sins anymore."

Jeremiah 31:31–34

[13]God called this a new agreement, so he has made the first agreement old. And anything that is old and worn out is ready to disappear.

The Old Agreement

9 The first agreement[n] had rules for worship and a place on earth for worship. [2]The Holy Tent was set up for this. The first area in the Tent was called the Holy Place. In it were the lamp and the table with the bread that was made holy for God. [3]Behind the second curtain was a room called the Most Holy Place. [4]In it was a golden altar for burning incense and the Ark covered with gold that held the old agreement. Inside this Ark was a golden jar of manna, Aaron's rod that once grew leaves, and the stone tablets of the old agreement. [5]Above the Ark were the creatures that showed God's glory, whose wings reached over the lid. But we cannot tell everything about these things now.

[6]When everything in the Tent was made ready in this way, the priests went into the first room every day to worship. [7]But only the high priest could go into the second room, and he did that only

Save Darfur Coalition

Many people think the idea of genocide—the extermination of an entire race, nation, or political group—went away with Hitler and World War II. Unfortunately, that's not the case. It's hard to believe, but right now an entire group of people are being annihilated in the African country of Sudan. Christians, humanitarians, and good-hearted people everywhere fall into one of two categories. Either they are utterly outraged or simply unaware of what's happening in Darfur, Sudan.

The Save Darfur Coalition is trying to convert the latter group into being "outraged" by raising awareness and lobbying for real change. Communities, congregations, and student groups around the United States are banding together and demanding that the rest of the world stand up and make this atrocity stop immediately. You can help.

You don't have to be some sort of major political activist to help make a difference in policy regarding Darfur. All you need to do is let your voice be heard and help organize others to make theirs ring out as well. The Save Darfur Coalition is a local, grassroots-based idea for seeking change. Log on to www.savedarfur.org to find out how you can help save an entire generation from extinction.

8:7; 9:1 first agreement The contract God gave the Jewish people when he gave them the Law of Moses. **8:8 But . . . says** Some Greek copies read "But God found something wrong and says to his people."

Prayer Retreat Toolbox

Be Still & KNOW

Have you ever had a personal prayer retreat? Whether it's an hour, an afternoon, or a weekend, every woman of faith can greatly benefit from some focused, uninterrupted time with the Lord. When you're ready to retreat for an extended time of conversation with your Father, consider collecting a few tools to take with you. First off, grab your Bible, a pen, and a journal. Add in some Christian music and perhaps a candle to set the mood. Bring along an exhaustive Bible concordance to help you locate passages about specific topics you want to dig into with the Lord. And the most important tool? An open heart that's ready to experience God in a fresh way!

once a year. He could never enter the inner room without taking blood with him, which he offered to God for himself and for sins the people did without knowing they did them. [8]The Holy Spirit uses this to show that the way into the Most Holy Place was not open while the system of the old Holy Tent was still being used. [9]This is an example for the present time. It shows that the gifts and sacrifices offered cannot make the conscience of the worshiper perfect. [10]These gifts and sacrifices were only about food and drink and special washings. They were rules for the body, to be followed until the time of God's new way.

The New Agreement

[11]But when Christ came as the high priest of the good things we now have,[n] he entered the greater and more perfect tent. It is not made by humans and does not belong to this world. [12]Christ entered the Most Holy Place only once—and for all time. He did not take with him the blood of goats and calves. His sacrifice was his own blood, and by it he set us free from sin forever. [13]The blood of goats and bulls and the ashes of a cow are sprinkled on the people who are unclean, and this makes their bodies clean again. [14]How much more is done by the blood of Christ. He offered himself through the eternal Spirit[n] as a perfect sacrifice to God. His blood will make our consciences pure from useless acts so we may serve the living God.

[15]For this reason Christ brings a new agreement from God to his people. Those who are called by God can now receive the blessings he has promised, blessings that will last forever. They can have those things because Christ died so that the people who lived under the first agreement could be set free from sin.

[16]When there is a will,[n] it must be proven that the one who wrote that will is dead. [17]A will means nothing while the person is alive; it can be used only after the person dies. [18]This is why even the first agreement could not begin without blood to show death. [19]First, Moses told all the people every command in the law. Next he took the blood of calves and mixed it with water. Then he used red wool and a branch of the hyssop plant to sprinkle it on the book of the law and on all the people. [20]He said, "This is the blood that begins the Agreement that God commanded you to obey."[n] [21]In the same way, Moses sprinkled the blood on the Holy Tent and over all the things used in worship. [22]The law says that almost everything must be made clean by blood, and sins cannot be forgiven without blood to show death.

Christ's Death Takes Away Sins

[23]So the copies of the real things in heaven had to be made clean by animal sacrifices. But the real things in heaven need much better sacrifices. [24]Christ did not go into the Most Holy Place made by humans, which is only a copy of the real one. He went into heaven itself and is there now before God to help us. [25]The high priest enters the Most Holy Place once every year with blood that is not his own. But Christ did not offer himself many times. [26]Then he would have had to suffer many times since the world was made. But Christ came only once and for all time at just the right time to take away all sin by sacrificing himself. [27]Just as everyone must die once and then be judged, [28]so Christ was offered as a sacrifice one time to take away the sins of many people. And he will come a second time, not to offer himself for sin, but to bring salvation to those who are waiting for him.

10 The law is only an unclear picture of the good things coming in the future; it is not the real thing. The people under the law offer the same sacrifices every year, but these sacrifices can never make perfect those who come near to worship God. [2]If the law could make them perfect, the sacrifices would have already stopped. The worshipers would be made clean, and they would no longer have a sense of sin. [3]But these sacrifices remind them of their sins every year, [4]because it is impossible for the blood of bulls and goats to take away sins.

[5]So when Christ came into the world, he said:

"You do not want sacrifices and
offerings,

9:11 good . . . have Some Greek copies read "good things that are to come." **9:14 Spirit** This refers to the Holy Spirit, to Christ's own spirit, or to the spiritual and eternal nature of his sacrifice. **9:16 will** A legal document that shows how a person's money and property are to be distributed at the time of death. This is the same word in Greek as "agreement" in verse 15. **9:20 "This . . . obey."** Quotation from Exodus 24:8.

but you have prepared a body
for me.
[6]You do not ask for burnt offerings
and offerings to take away sins.
[7]Then I said, 'Look, I have come.
It is written about me in the
book.
God, I have come to do what you
want.'" *Psalm 40:6–8*

[8]In this Scripture he first said, "You do not want sacrifices and offerings. You do not ask for burnt offerings and offerings to take away sins." (These are all sacrifices that the law commands.) [9]Then he said, "Look, I have come to do what you want." God ends the first system of sacrifices so he can set up the new system. [10]And because of this, we are made holy through the sacrifice Christ made in his body once and for all time.

[11]Every day the priests stand and do their religious service, often offering the same sacrifices. Those sacrifices can never take away sins. [12]But after Christ offered one sacrifice for sins, forever, he sat down at the right side of God. [13]And now Christ waits there for his enemies to be put under his power. [14]With one sacrifice he made perfect forever those who are being made holy.

[15]The Holy Spirit also tells us about this. First he says:

[16]"This is the agreement[n] I will
make
with them at that time, says the
Lord.
I will put my teachings in their hearts
and write them on their minds."
Jeremiah 31:33

[17]Then he says:

"Their sins and the evil things they
do—
I will not remember anymore."
Jeremiah 31:34

[18]Now when these have been forgiven, there is no more need for a sacrifice for sins.

Continue to Trust God

[19]So, brothers and sisters, we are completely free to enter the Most Holy Place without fear because of the blood of Jesus' death. [20]We can enter through a new and living way that Jesus opened for us. It leads through the curtain—Christ's body. [21]And since we have a great priest over God's house, [22]let us come near to God with a sincere heart and a sure faith, because we have been made free from a guilty conscience, and our bodies have been washed with pure water. [23]Let us hold firmly to the hope that we have confessed, because we can trust God to do what he promised.

[24]Let us think about each other and help each other to show love and do good deeds. [25]You should not stay away from the church meetings, as some are doing, but you should meet together and encourage each other. Do this even more as you see the day[n] coming.

[26]If we decide to go on sinning after we have learned the truth, there is no longer any sacrifice for sins. [27]There is nothing but fear in waiting for the judgment and the terrible fire that will destroy all those who live against God. [28]Anyone who refused to obey the law of Moses was found guilty from the proof given by two or three witnesses. He was put to death without mercy. [29]So what do you think should be done to those who do not respect the Son of God, who look at the blood of the agreement that made them holy as no different from others' blood, who insult the Spirit of God's grace? Surely they should have a much worse punishment. [30]We know that God said, "I will punish those who do wrong; I will repay them."[n] And he also said, "The Lord will judge his people."[n] [31]It is a terrible thing to fall into the hands of the living God.

[32]Remember those days in the past when you first learned the truth. You had a hard struggle with many sufferings, but you continued strong. [33]Sometimes you were hurt and attacked before crowds of people, and sometimes you shared with those who were being treated that way. [34]You helped the prisoners. You even had joy when all that you owned was taken from you, because you knew you had something better and more lasting.

[35]So do not lose the courage you had in the past, which has a great reward. [36]You must hold on, so you can do what God wants and receive what he has promised. [37]For in a very short time,

"The One who is coming will come
and will not be delayed.
[38]Those who are right with me
will live by faith.
But if they turn back with fear,
I will not be pleased with them."
Habakkuk 2:3–4

[39]But we are not those who turn back and are lost. We are people who have faith and are saved.

all about **MEN**

Encourage His Leadership

How can a woman help a man grow as a godly leader? Two key habits include prayer and encouraging his strengths. It's easy to focus on areas of weakness, but encouraging his abilities carries more power than pointing out what you wish he'd do better. If a guy is uncomfortable praying out loud, talk to God about your desire to see him speak up. But if he's great at showing compassion or helping others, tell him you admire his caring nature or his servant's heart. Leadership shows itself in both outspoken and understated ways. "Encourage [him] with great patience" (2 Timothy 4:2), and ask God to open your eyes to the gifts and potential in the man he chooses for you.

10:16 agreement God gives a contract or agreement to his people. For the Jews, this agreement was the Law of Moses. But now God has given a better agreement to his people through Christ. **10:25 day** The day Christ will come to judge all people and take his people to live with him. **10:30 "I . . . them."** Quotation from Deuteronomy 32:35. **10:30 "The Lord . . . people."** Quotation from Deuteronomy 32:36; Psalm 135:14.

What Is Faith?

11 Faith means being sure of the things we hope for and knowing that something is real even if we do not see it. [2]Faith is the reason we remember great people who lived in the past.

[3]It is by faith we understand that the whole world was made by God's command so what we see was made by something that cannot be seen.

[4]It was by faith that Abel offered God a better sacrifice than Cain did. God said he was pleased with the gifts Abel offered and called Abel a good man because of his faith. Abel died, but through his faith he is still speaking.

[5]It was by faith that Enoch was taken to heaven so he would not die. He could not be found, because God had taken him away. Before he was taken, the Scripture says that he was a man who truly pleased God. [6]Without faith no one can please God. Anyone who comes to God must believe that he is real and that he rewards those who truly want to find him.

[7]It was by faith that Noah heard God's warnings about things he could not yet see. He obeyed God and built a large boat to save his family. By his faith, Noah showed that the world was wrong, and he became one of those who are made right with God through faith.

[8]It was by faith Abraham obeyed God's call to go to another place God promised to give him. He left his own country, not knowing where he was to go. [9]It was by faith that he lived like a foreigner in the country God promised to give him. He lived in tents with Isaac and Jacob, who had received that same promise from God. [10]Abraham was waiting for the city[n] that has real foundations—the city planned and built by God.

[11]He was too old to have children, and Sarah could not have children. It was by faith that Abraham was made able to become a father, because he trusted God to do what he had promised.[n] [12]This man was so old he was almost dead, but from him came as many descendants as there are stars in the sky. Like the sand on the seashore, they could not be counted.

[13]All these great people died in faith. They did not get the things that God promised his people, but they saw them coming far in the future and were glad. They said they were like visitors and strangers on earth. [14]When people say such things, they show they are looking for a country that will be their own. [15]If they had been thinking about the country they had left, they could have gone back. [16]But they were waiting for a better country—a heavenly country. So God is not ashamed to be called their God, because he has prepared a city for them.

[17]It was by faith that Abraham, when God tested him, offered his son Isaac as a sacrifice. God made the promises to Abraham, but Abraham was ready to offer his own son as a sacrifice. [18]God had said, "The descendants I promised you will be from Isaac."[n] [19]Abraham believed that God could raise the dead, and really, it was as if Abraham got Isaac back from death.

[20]It was by faith that Isaac blessed the future of Jacob and Esau. [21]It was by faith that Jacob, as he was dying, blessed each one of Joseph's sons. Then he worshiped as he leaned on the top of his walking stick.

[22]It was by faith that Joseph, while he was dying, spoke about the Israelites leaving Egypt and gave instructions about what to do with his body.

[23]It was by faith that Moses' parents hid him for three months after he was born. They saw that Moses was a beautiful baby, and they were not afraid to disobey the king's order.

[24]It was by faith that Moses, when he grew up, refused to be called the son of the king of Egypt's daughter. [25]He chose to suffer with God's people instead of enjoying sin for a short time. [26]He thought it was better to suffer for the Christ than to have all the treasures of Egypt, because he was looking for God's reward. [27]It was by faith that Moses left Egypt and was not afraid of the king's anger. Moses continued strong as if he could see the God that no one can see. [28]It was by faith that Moses prepared the Passover and spread the blood on the doors so the one who brings death would not kill the firstborn sons of Israel.

[29]It was by faith that the people crossed the Red Sea as if it were dry land. But when the Egyptians tried it, they were drowned.

[30]It was by faith that the walls of Jericho fell after the people had marched around them for seven days.

[31]It was by faith that Rahab, the prostitute, welcomed the spies and was not killed with those who refused to obey God.

[32]Do I need to give more examples? I do not have time to tell you about Gideon, Barak, Samson, Jephthah, David, Samuel, and the prophets. [33]Through their faith they defeated kingdoms. They did what was right, received God's promises, and shut the mouths of lions. [34]They stopped great fires and were saved from being killed with swords. They were weak, and

Everything New

Don't you just love cleaning out your closets and getting a brand-new outfit? And oooh . . . how about that feeling of confidence that comes when you know you've got the look you want? That's exactly how a heart feels when it first begins a personal relationship with Jesus. The old stuff is gone, and everything is made new (2 Corinthians 5:17)—the place has never looked better! There's a great feeling of confidence in knowing that eternity will be spent with God and that from the inside out, you have become an entirely new, wholly beautiful creation in Christ.

11:10 city The spiritual "city" where God's people live with him. Also called "the heavenly Jerusalem." (See Hebrews 12:22.) **11:11 It . . . promised.** Some Greek copies refer to Sarah's faith, rather than Abraham's. **11:18 "The descendants . . . Isaac."** Quotation from Genesis 21:12.

yet were made strong. They were powerful in battle and defeated other armies. [35]Women received their dead relatives raised back to life. Others were tortured and refused to accept their freedom so they could be raised from the dead to a better life. [36]Some were laughed at and beaten. Others were put in chains and thrown into prison. [37]They were stoned to death, they were cut in half,[n] and they were killed with swords. Some wore the skins of sheep and goats. They were poor, abused, and treated badly. [38]The world was not good enough for them! They wandered in deserts and mountains, living in caves and holes in the earth.

[39]All these people are known for their faith, but none of them received what God had promised. [40]God planned to give us something better so that they would be made perfect, but only together with us.

HE SAID / SHE SAID

What's the kindest act you've witnessed?

He: My parents sacrificing for me

She: My great-grandfather caring for my terminally ill great-grandmother

Follow Jesus' Example

12 We are surrounded by a great cloud of people whose lives tell us what faith means. So let us run the race that is before us and never give up. We should remove from our lives anything that would get in the way and the sin that so easily holds us back. [2]Let us look only to Jesus, the One who began our faith and who makes it perfect. He suffered death on the cross. But he accepted the shame as if it were nothing because of the joy that God put before him. And now he is sitting at the right side of God's throne. [3]Think about Jesus' example. He held on while wicked people were doing evil things to him. So do not get tired and stop trying.

God Is like a Father

[4]You are struggling against sin, but your struggles have not yet caused you to be killed. [5]You have forgotten the encouraging words that call you his children:

"My child, don't think the Lord's
discipline is worth nothing,
and don't stop trying when he
corrects you.
[6]The Lord disciplines those he loves,
and he punishes everyone he
accepts as his child."

Proverbs 3:11–12

[7]So hold on through your sufferings, because they are like a father's discipline. God is treating you as children. All children are disciplined by their fathers. [8]If you are never disciplined (and every child must be disciplined), you are not true children. [9]We have all had fathers here on earth who disciplined us, and we respected them. So it is even more important that we accept discipline from the Father of our spirits so we will have life. [10]Our fathers on earth disciplined us for a short time in the way they thought was best. But God disciplines us to help us, so we can become holy as he is. [11]We do not enjoy being disciplined. It is painful at the time, but later, after we have learned from it, we have peace, because we start living in the right way.

Be Careful How You Live

[12]You have become weak, so make yourselves strong again. [13]Keep on the right path, so the weak will not stumble but rather be strengthened.

[14]Try to live in peace with all people, and try to live free from sin. Anyone whose life is not holy will never see the Lord. [15]Be careful that no one fails to receive God's grace and begins to cause trouble among you. A person like that can ruin many of you. [16]Be careful that no one takes part in sexual sin or is like Esau and never thinks about God. As the oldest son, Esau would have received everything from his father, but he sold all that for a single meal. [17]You remember that after Esau did this, he wanted to get his father's blessing, but his father refused. Esau could find no way to change what he had done, even though he wanted the blessing so much that he cried.

[18]You have not come to a mountain that can be touched and that is burning with fire. You have not come to darkness, sadness, and storms. [19]You have not come to the noise of a trumpet or to the sound of a voice like the one the people of Israel heard and begged not to hear another word. [20]They did not want to hear the command: "If anything, even an animal, touches the mountain, it must be put to death with stones."[n] [21]What they saw was so terrible that Moses said, "I am shaking with fear."[n]

[22]But you have come to Mount Zion,[n] to the city of the living God, the heavenly Jerusalem. You have come to thousands of angels gathered together with joy. [23]You have come to the meeting of God's firstborn[n] children whose names are written in heaven. You have come to God, the judge of all people, and to the spirits of good people who have been made perfect. [24]You have come to Jesus, the One who brought the new agreement from God to his people, and you have come to the sprinkled blood[n] that has a better message than the blood of Abel.[n]

[25]So be careful and do not refuse to listen when God speaks. Others refused to listen to him when he warned them on earth, and they did not escape. So it will be worse for us if we refuse to listen to God who warns us from heaven. [26]When

11:37 they were cut in half Some Greek copies also include, "they were tested." **12:20 "If . . . stones."** Quotation from Exodus 19:12–13. **12:21 "I . . . fear."** Quotation from Deuteronomy 9:19. **12:22 Mount Zion** Another name for Jerusalem, here meaning the spiritual city of God's people. **12:23 firstborn** The first son born in a Jewish family was given the most important place in the family and received special blessings. All of God's children are like that. **12:24 sprinkled blood** The blood of Jesus' death. **12:24 Abel** The son of Adam and Eve, who was killed by his brother Cain (Genesis 4:8).

Hebrews 13:3

How do you react when you hear about someone else's problems? Do you feel genuine sadness and hope for positive change . . . but then just move on? Or are you affected to the point of taking action when you hear that someone in your church is sick or that Christians in other countries are being imprisoned for their faith?

In the middle of discussing love and hospitality, the writer of Hebrews drops this bombshell: when you hear about people going through tough times, you should feel as if you're right there with that person, experiencing the same things they are!

How do you live that out? Well, it starts with truly caring for those people. If you have a hard time seeing or remembering what's going on with other people, ask God to fill your heart with Christlike compassion (2 Corinthians 1:3–7). The next step is taking action. Prayer should always come first . . . and in some cases, prayer might be your only option. Other times you'll have chances to serve in additional ways, like reaching out to discouraged friends or donating to charities.

Does your heart break when you see needy people? Put yourself in the same shoes as people who are suffering, and see what you can do to help them!

he spoke before, his voice shook the earth, but now he has promised, "Once again I will shake not only the earth but also the heavens."[n] 27The words "once again" clearly show us that everything that was made—things that can be shaken—will be destroyed. Only the things that cannot be shaken will remain.

28So let us be thankful, because we have a kingdom that cannot be shaken. We should worship God in a way that pleases him with respect and fear, 29because our God is like a fire that burns things up.

13 Keep on loving each other as brothers and sisters. 2Remember to welcome strangers, because some who have done this have welcomed angels without knowing it. 3Remember those who are in prison as if you were in prison with them. Remember those who are suffering as if you were suffering with them.

4Marriage should be honored by everyone, and husband and wife should keep their marriage pure. God will judge as guilty those who take part in sexual sins. 5Keep your lives free from the love of money, and be satisfied with what you have. God has said,

"I will never leave you;
I will never abandon you."
Deuteronomy 31:6

6So we can be sure when we say,

"I will not be afraid, because the Lord is my helper.
People can't do anything to me."
Psalm 118:6

7Remember your leaders who taught God's message to you. Remember how they lived and died, and copy their faith. 8Jesus Christ is the same yesterday, today, and forever.

9Do not let all kinds of strange teachings lead you into the wrong way. Your hearts should be strengthened by God's grace, not by obeying rules about foods, which do not help those who obey them.

10We have a sacrifice, but the priests who serve in the Holy Tent cannot eat from it. 11The high priest carries the blood of animals into the Most Holy Place where he offers this blood for sins. But the bodies of the animals are burned outside the camp. 12So Jesus also suffered outside the city to make his people holy with his own blood. 13So let us go to Jesus outside the camp, holding on as he did when we are abused.

14Here on earth we do not have a city that lasts forever, but we are looking for the city that we will have in the future. 15So through Jesus let us always offer to God our sacrifice of praise, coming from lips that speak his name. 16Do not forget to do good to others, and share with them, because such sacrifices please God.

17Obey your leaders and act under their authority. They are watching over you, because they are responsible for your souls. Obey them so that they will do this work with joy, not sadness. It will not help you to make their work hard.

18Pray for us. We are sure that we have a clear conscience, because we always want to do the right thing. 19I especially beg you to pray so that God will send me back to you soon.

20-21I pray that the God of peace will give you every good thing you need so you can do what he wants. God raised from the dead our Lord Jesus, the Great Shepherd of the sheep, because of the blood of his death. His blood began the eternal agreement that God made with his people. I pray that God will do in us what pleases him, through Jesus Christ, and to him be glory forever and ever. Amen.

22My brothers and sisters, I beg you to listen patiently to this message I have written to encourage you, because it is not very long. 23I want you to know that our brother Timothy has been let out of prison. If he arrives soon, we will both come to see you.

24Greet all your leaders and all of God's people. Those from Italy send greetings to you.

25Grace be with you all.

12:26 "Once . . . heavens." Quotation from Haggai 2:6, 21.

The Only Way to God

If you're wondering if Jesus is really the only way to God, read Hebrews. This book explores the perfect nature, perfect priesthood, perfect sacrifice, and perfect salvation that Jesus embodied in his life, death, and resurrection. There are all kinds of so-called "paths to God," but the only way to truly know God is through Jesus.

Jews in the early church struggled with letting go of the old agreement and wanted to go back to the old system of sacrifices, rituals, and human priests. But the writer of Hebrews makes it clear: Christ has done it all. He's a better priest, a better sacrifice, and a better way to righteousness . . . he's perfect. He's the fulfillment of the old agreement and the foundation for the new agreement. If you want to compare the two agreements, read Exodus, Numbers, and Leviticus. Then read Romans. Those books uncover just how wonderful God's plan of redemption through Christ really is.

The Law showed us that we needed God's grace—grace that is fully expressed in Christ and his work on the Cross. Jesus himself was clear about this: no one can know God unless they know Jesus.

What about you? Are you trying to reach God through your own abilities? Are you thinking that you can really live right on your own? Are you looking at other religions to see if they have something to offer? Don't bother. Jesus is the better way. In fact, he's the only way—and you can get to know him by reading the Bible.

Get Real

Get into the Word. The Bible says you can only please God through faith. We can't be righteous on our own, but by grace through faith, we can have the righteousness of Jesus. (Romans 3:21–31; 5:1–2; Ephesians 2:4–10; 2 Corinthians 5:21; Philippians 3:7–11)

Who do you say Jesus is? (Matthew 16:13–20; John 1:17–18, 29–34; Revelation 5:6–13)

Think of who Jesus is (our God and Savior) and all that he has done. Are you serious about following him? (1 John 2:6; 5:1–12)

james

Everybody needs a little incentive. The real issue is trying to find an incentive that actually motivates people! Because we're such reward-driven creatures, it's hard for us to grasp the fact that our salvation isn't based on anything we do—we simply can't earn it. And that leaves many of us wondering, *If God already views me as perfect because of Christ, why should I bother trying to live a good life?* It's a valid question.

This book was written by James, the half-brother of Jesus. James didn't believe that Jesus was really the Messiah at first, but the Resurrection changed his mind. Imagine witnessing your brother's death, only to see him alive and well just a few days later! James became the pastor of the church in Jerusalem, and he was well known for his devotion to prayer and his pure, godly lifestyle.

James deals with the issue of works in Christianity. Although we're saved by grace through faith, we're not exempt from righteous living!

Be thankful for God's grace and love—and let that motivate you constantly toward a life of good works. Make gratitude and devotion your true incentives!

1 From James, a servant of God and of the Lord Jesus Christ.

To all of God's people who are scattered everywhere in the world:

Greetings.

Faith and Wisdom

[2]My brothers and sisters, when you have many kinds of troubles, you should be full of joy, [3]because you know that these troubles test your faith, and this will give you patience. [4]Let your patience show itself perfectly in what you do. Then you will be perfect and complete and will have everything you need. [5]But if any of you needs wisdom, you should ask God for it. He is generous to everyone and will give you wisdom without criticizing you. [6]But when you ask God, you must believe and not doubt. Anyone who doubts is like a wave in the sea, blown up and down by the wind. [7-8]Such doubters are thinking two different things at the same time, and they cannot decide about anything they do. They should not think they will receive anything from the Lord.

True Riches

[9]Believers who are poor should take pride that God has made them spiritually rich. [10]Those who are rich should take pride that God has shown them that they are spiritually poor. The rich will die like a wild flower in the grass. [11]The sun rises with burning heat and dries up the plants. The flower falls off, and its beauty is gone. In the same way the rich will die while they are still taking care of business.

Temptation Is Not from God

[12]When people are tempted and still continue strong, they should be happy. After they have proved their faith, God will reward them with life forever. God promised

James 2:14

Have you ever heard a preacher make it sound like Christianity is nothing more than a onetime decision? "Say this prayer . . . and that's all there is to it!" On one hand, they're on the right track. Nothing we do can earn a place in heaven. Only faith in Christ can make us right with God. But is Christianity just a single decision—or a lifelong commitment?

When we're first saved, God miraculously forgives all our sins. But it doesn't end there. The next step literally takes a lifetime. From the time you're born again to the day you die, God gradually sets you apart from the world. When you first became a Christian, even though God had changed your heart, you still looked pretty much the same. But over time, God's been transforming you to become more like Jesus.

That's where James is going with this verse. If your faith in Jesus is real, your life will definitely reflect God's transforming power! There will be visible, ongoing results in the way you live.

Instead of letting your Christianity begin and end with a onetime prayer, commit yourself to having a faith that really works. Let your actions show that God has truly changed your heart and mind!

this to all those who love him. [13]When people are tempted, they should not say, "God is tempting me." Evil cannot tempt God, and God himself does not tempt anyone. [14]But people are tempted when their own evil desire leads them away and traps them. [15]This desire leads to sin, and then the sin grows and brings death.

[16]My dear brothers and sisters, do not be fooled about this. [17]Every good action and every perfect gift is from God. These good gifts come down from the Creator of the sun, moon, and stars, who does not change like their shifting shadows. [18]God decided to give us life through the word of truth so we might be the most important of all the things he made.

Listening and Obeying

[19]My dear brothers and sisters, always be willing to listen and slow to speak. Do not become angry easily, [20]because anger will not help you live the right kind of life God wants. [21]So put out of your life every evil thing and every kind of wrong. Then in gentleness accept God's teaching that is planted in your hearts, which can save you.

[22]Do what God's teaching says; when you only listen and do nothing, you are fooling yourselves. [23]Those who hear God's teaching and do nothing are like people who look at themselves in a mirror. [24]They see their faces and then go away and quickly forget what they looked like. [25]But the truly happy people are those who carefully study God's perfect law that makes people free, and they continue to study it. They do not forget what they heard, but they obey what God's teaching says. Those who do this will be made happy.

The True Way to Worship God

[26]People who think they are religious but say things they should not say are just fooling themselves. Their "religion" is worth nothing. [27]Religion that God accepts as pure and without fault is this: caring for orphans or widows who need help, and keeping yourself free from the world's evil influence.

Love All People

2 My dear brothers and sisters, as believers in our glorious Lord Jesus Christ, never think some people are more important than others. [2]Suppose someone comes into your church meeting wearing nice clothes and a gold ring. At the same time a poor person comes in wearing old, dirty clothes. [3]You show special attention to the one wearing nice clothes and say, "Please, sit here in this good seat." But you say to the poor person, "Stand over there," or, "Sit on the floor by my feet." [4]What are you doing? You are making some people more important than others, and with evil thoughts you are deciding that one person is better.

[5]Listen, my dear brothers and sisters! God chose the poor in the world to be rich with faith and to receive the kingdom God promised to those who love him. [6]But you show no respect to the poor. The rich are always trying to control your lives. They are the ones who take you to court. [7]And they are the ones who speak against Jesus, who owns you.

[8]This royal law is found in the Scriptures: "Love your neighbor as you love yourself."[n] If you obey this law, you are doing right. [9]But if you treat one person as being more important than another, you are sinning. You are guilty of breaking God's law. [10]A person who follows all of God's law but fails to obey even one command is guilty of breaking all the commands in that law. [11]The same God who

2:8 "Love . . . yourself." Quotation from Leviticus 19:18.

RELATIONSHIPS

See the Needs

We all need to be seen. Not in a look-at-me-aren't-you-impressed way but in a way that reaffirms that we're valued and appreciated. Unfortunately, it's possible for people to go through life feeling like they don't matter—that they're not important to anyone. How completely sad to God, who formed each cell of their beings and wants them to know his love. God's two greatest commands are to love him first and others second (Matthew 22:36–40). And one of the first steps in loving others is opening our eyes to the needs around us. How can you help someone feel seen (and loved!) today?

said, "You must not be guilty of adultery,"[n] also said, "You must not murder anyone."[n] So if you do not take part in adultery but you murder someone, you are guilty of breaking all of God's law. [12]In everything you say and do, remember that you will be judged by the law that makes people free. [13]So you must show mercy to others, or God will not show mercy to you when he judges you. But the person who shows mercy can stand without fear at the judgment.

Faith and Good Works

[14]My brothers and sisters, if people say they have faith, but do nothing, their faith is worth nothing. Can faith like that save them? [15]A brother or sister in Christ might need clothes or food. [16]If you say to that person, "God be with you! I hope you stay warm and get plenty to eat," but you do not give what that person needs, your words are worth nothing. [17]In the same way, faith by itself—that does nothing—is dead.

[18]Someone might say, "You have faith, but I have deeds." Show me your faith without doing anything, and I will show you my faith by what I do. [19]You believe there is one God. Good! But the demons believe that, too, and they tremble with fear.

[20]You foolish person! Must you be shown that faith that does nothing is worth nothing? [21]Abraham, our ancestor, was made right with God by what he did when he offered his son Isaac on the altar. [22]So you see that Abraham's faith and the things he did worked together. His faith was made perfect by what he did. [23]This shows the full meaning of the Scripture that says: "Abraham believed God, and God accepted Abraham's faith, and that faith made him right with God."[n] And Abraham was called God's friend.[n] [24]So you see that people are made right with God by what they do, not by faith only.

[25]Another example is Rahab, a prostitute, who was made right with God by something she did. She welcomed the spies into her home and helped them escape by a different road.

[26]Just as a person's body that does not

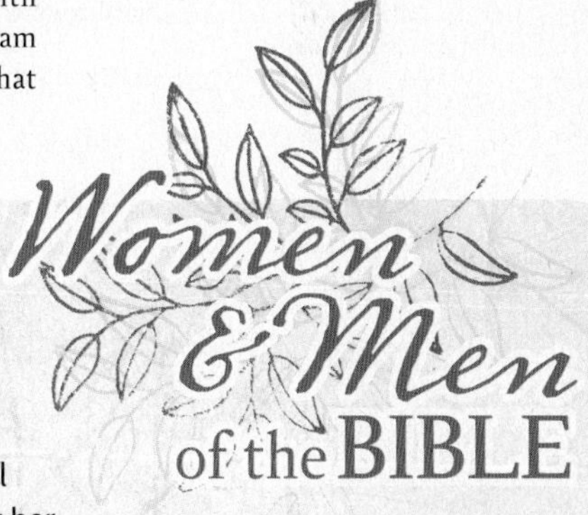

Miriam: #1 Babysitter

Miriam was just a little girl when the king of Egypt declared that all the baby boys of Israel, including her little brother, be killed at birth. Her mother devised a last-ditch plan to try to save her new baby's life. She put him in a basket and floated him along the river. Miriam watched over baby Moses as he bobbled along. She saw God's protection and provision at work when the king's daughter rescued her brother. Later, she would grow up to be a worship leader and prophetess, declaring God's goodness to all who would listen. (Exodus 2:1–10; 15:20–21)

2:11 "You . . . adultery." Quotation from Exodus 20:14 and Deuteronomy 5:18. **2:11 "You . . . anyone."** Quotation from Exodus 20:13 and Deuteronomy 5:17. **2:23 "Abraham . . . God."** Quotation from Genesis 15:6. **2:23 God's friend** These words about Abraham are found in 2 Chronicles 20:7 and Isaiah 41:8.

DO YOU RECOGNIZE HIM FROM THE BIBLE?

SEE IF YOU CAN MATCH THE CRITERIA ON THE LEFT WITH THE ONE MOST APPROPRIATE BIBLE MAN ON THE RIGHT. LOOK UP THE BIBLE PASSAGE IF YOU NEED A LITTLE HINT. YOU WILL ONLY USE EACH ANSWER ONCE.

____ 1. The follower Jesus loved (John 19:26–27)	A. Abraham
____ 2. Heart for missions (1 Corinthians 2:1–5)	B. David
____ 3. Strong (Judges 14:6)	C. Job
____ 4. Handsome (1 Samuel 16:12)	D. Enoch
____ 5. Good kisser (Song of Songs 1:2)	E. Barnabas
____ 6. Able to show his emotions (Jeremiah and Lamentations)	F. Samson
____ 7. Willing to ask the hard questions (John 14:5; 20:24–29)	G. John
____ 8. Good with animals (Genesis 6:19–22)	H. Peter
____ 9. Rich and willing to travel (Genesis 12:1–2)	I. Paul
____ 10. Comes from a godly family (2 Timothy 1:5)	J. Elisha
____ 11. Brave (Joshua 1:6–9)	K. Jacob
____ 12. Physically fit (Daniel 1:15)	L. Noah
____ 13. Willing to give of himself (Genesis 2:21)	M. Solomon
____ 14. Leads others (Exodus 12:31–32)	N. Jonathan
____ 15. Quick to act (Matthew 14:28–29)	O. Daniel
____ 16. Able to cook/good in the kitchen (Genesis 25:29)	P. Thomas
____ 17. Patient (Job 13:15–19)	Q. Moses
____ 18. Understanding (Ruth 2:11–16)	R. Timothy
____ 19. Forgiving (Hosea 3:1)	S. Joseph
____ 20. Good provider (2 Kings 4:2–7)	T. Jeremiah
____ 21. Willing to admit mistakes (Luke 15:21)	U. Joshua
____ 22. Walks with God (Genesis 5:22)	V. Adam
____ 23. Encourages others (Acts 4:36)	W. Boaz
____ 24. Has big dreams (Genesis 37:5–9)	X. Hosea
____ 25. Loyal (1 Samuel 20:1–9)	Y. The Son Who Left Home (Prodigal)

ANSWERS:

1. G–John; 2. I–Paul; 3. F–Samson; 4. B–David; 5. M–Solomon; 6. T–Jeremiah; 7. P–Thomas; 8. L–Noah; 9. A–Abraham; 10. R–Timothy; 11. U–Joshua; 12. O–Daniel; 13. V–Adam; 14. Q–Moses; 15. H–Peter; 16. K–Jacob; 17. C–Job; 18. W–Boaz; 19. X–Hosea; 20. J–Elisha; 21. Y–The Son Who Left Home (Prodigal); 22. D–Enoch; 23. E–Barnabas; 24. S–Joseph; 25. N–Jonathan

Don't Worry

You've probably seen a bumper sticker that makes this simple but powerful statement: "Don't Worry, Be Happy." God agrees! And he doesn't merely suggest that we not worry, he *commands* it: "Do not worry about anything" (Philippians 4:6). The rest of the verse challenges us to pray and ask God for everything we need. Not only that, but we're to be giving thanks as we pray, as if God has already provided it. That's like sending thank-you notes before your birthday party! And yet that's the kind of faith we should have. Faith is the antidote to fear; the two can't exist together. Cultivate your faith . . . and your fear will fade away.

have a spirit is dead, so faith that does nothing is dead!

Controlling the Things We Say

3 My brothers and sisters, not many of you should become teachers, because you know that we who teach will be judged more strictly. [2]We all make many mistakes. If people never said anything wrong, they would be perfect and able to control their entire selves, too. [3]When we put bits into the mouths of horses to make them obey us, we can control their whole bodies. [4]Also a ship is very big, and it is pushed by strong winds. But a very small rudder controls that big ship, making it go wherever the pilot wants. [5]It is the same with the tongue. It is a small part of the body, but it brags about great things.

A big forest fire can be started with only a little flame. [6]And the tongue is like a fire. It is a whole world of evil among the parts of our bodies. The tongue spreads its evil through the whole body. The tongue is set on fire by hell, and it starts a fire that influences all of life. [7]People can tame every kind of wild animal, bird, reptile, and fish, and they have tamed them, [8]but no one can tame the tongue. It is wild and evil and full of deadly poison. [9]We use our tongues to praise our Lord and Father, but then we curse people, whom God made like himself. [10]Praises and curses come from the same mouth! My brothers and sisters, this should not happen. [11]Do good and bad water flow from the same spring? [12]My brothers and sisters, can a fig tree make olives, or can a grapevine make figs? No! And a well full of salty water cannot give good water.

True Wisdom

[13]Are there those among you who are truly wise and understanding? Then they should show it by living right and doing good things with a gentleness that comes from wisdom. [14]But if you are selfish and have bitter jealousy in your hearts, do not brag. Your bragging is a lie that hides the truth. [15]That kind of "wisdom" does not come from God but from the world. It is not spiritual; it is from the devil. [16]Where jealousy and selfishness are, there will be confusion and every kind of evil. [17]But the wisdom that comes from God is first of all pure, then peaceful, gentle, and easy to please. This wisdom is always ready to help those who are troubled and to do good for others. It is always fair and honest. [18]People who work for peace in a peaceful way plant a good crop of right-living.

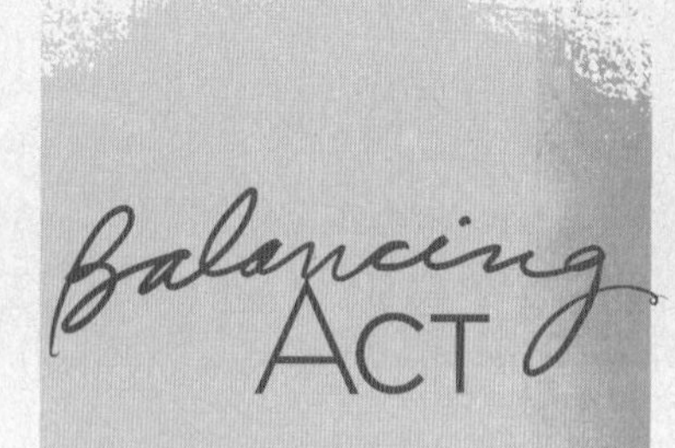

Feminine or Feminist?

Fifty years ago, the responsibilities of men and women were the same in almost every household: he was the breadwinner, and she was the homemaker. But in the twenty-first century, most women have a career outside the home. From administrative assistant to CEO, women are increasingly playing a lead role in corporate America. Additionally, women are taking on leadership positions in society as a whole.

We must understand that God made us unique from men, but he values us no less (1 Corinthians 11:11–12). Even in these new roles, you can still be a lady. We women can accomplish anything we want . . . and we don't have to act like men to do it.

James 5:7–11

It can be easy to develop a complaining attitude if we're not careful. The actions of our co-workers, parents, husband, or friends can sometimes rub us the wrong way. But the bottom line is that we're responsible to maintain a patient and loving heart regardless of how others behave.

So how do we quit grumbling? James offers a clue: he sandwiched this lesson about complaining right in the middle of a discussion about patiently focusing on Christ's return. A mind that's not quick to complain is one that's fixed on Jesus Christ. Steady patience with others *is* possible—it comes from putting hope in the future glory of Christ's return and in the perfect peace that awaits us in heaven!

Disappointments are manageable because God teaches us forgiveness, heals our hurts, and satisfies our hearts. Plus, we follow the example of a humble Servant whose Spirit is alive in us. If we really believe those things, we know we're better off working it out, walking away from bitterness, and asking God to let us see people as he does.

Let God fill your heart with his love that overtakes a grumbling spirit. Then, in the moments you'd normally complain, you can graciously let it go and rest in the satisfying peace of God.

Give Yourselves to God

4 Do you know where your fights and arguments come from? They come from the selfish desires that war within you. [2]You want things, but you do not have them. So you are ready to kill and are jealous of other people, but you still cannot get what you want. So you argue and fight. You do not get what you want, because you do not ask God. [3]Or when you ask, you do not receive because the reason you ask is wrong. You want things so you can use them for your own pleasures.

[4]So, you are not loyal to God! You should know that loving the world is the same as hating God. Anyone who wants to be a friend of the world becomes God's enemy. [5]Do you think the Scripture means nothing that says, "The Spirit that God made to live in us wants us for himself alone"?[n] [6]But God gives us even more grace, as the Scripture says,

"God is against the proud,
but he gives grace to the humble." *Proverbs 3:34*

[7]So give yourselves completely to God. Stand against the devil, and the devil will run from you. [8]Come near to God, and God will come near to you. You sinners, clean sin out of your lives. You who are trying to follow God and the world at the same time, make your thinking pure. [9]Be sad, cry, and weep! Change your laughter into crying and your joy into sadness. [10]Humble yourself in the Lord's presence, and he will honor you.

You Are Not the Judge

[11]Brothers and sisters, do not tell evil lies about each other. If you speak against your fellow believers or judge them, you are judging and speaking against the law they follow. And when you are judging the law, you are no longer a follower of the law. You have become a judge. [12]God is the only Lawmaker and Judge. He is the only One who can save and destroy. So it is not right for you to judge your neighbor.

Let God Plan Your Life

[13]Some of you say, "Today or tomorrow we will go to some city. We will stay there a year, do business, and make money." [14]But you do not know what will happen tomorrow! Your life is like a mist. You can see it for a short time, but then it goes away. [15]So you should say, "If the Lord wants, we will live and do this or that." [16]But now you are proud and you brag. All of this bragging is wrong. [17]Anyone who knows the right thing to do, but does not do it, is sinning.

A Warning to the Rich

5 You rich people, listen! Cry and be very sad because of the troubles that are coming to you. [2]Your riches have rotted, and your clothes have been eaten by moths. [3]Your gold and silver have rusted, and that rust will be a proof that you were wrong. It will eat your bodies like fire. You saved your treasure for the last days. [4]The pay you did not give the workers who mowed your fields cries out against you, and the cries of the workers have been heard by the Lord All-Powerful. [5]Your life on earth was full of rich living and pleasing yourselves with everything you wanted. You made yourselves fat, like an animal ready to be killed. [6]You have judged guilty and then murdered innocent people, who were not against you.

Be Patient

[7]Brothers and sisters, be patient until the Lord comes again. A farmer patiently waits for his valuable crop to grow from the earth and for it to receive the autumn

➤ **4:5 "The Spirit . . . alone."** These words may be from Exodus 20:5.

and spring rains. [8]You, too, must be patient. Do not give up hope, because the Lord is coming soon. [9]Brothers and sisters, do not complain against each other or you will be judged guilty. And the Judge is ready to come! [10]Brothers and sisters, follow the example of the prophets who spoke for the Lord. They suffered many hard things, but they were patient. [11]We say they are happy because they did not give up. You have heard about Job's patience, and you know the Lord's purpose for him in the end. You know the Lord is full of mercy and is kind.

Be Careful What You Say

[12]My brothers and sisters, above all, do not use an oath when you make a promise. Don't use the name of heaven, earth, or anything else to prove what you say. When you mean yes, say only yes, and when you mean no, say only no so you will not be judged guilty.

The Power of Prayer

[13]Anyone who is having troubles should pray. Anyone who is happy should sing praises. [14]Anyone who is sick should call the church's elders. They should pray for and pour oil on the person[n] in the name of the Lord. [15]And the prayer that is said with faith will make the sick person well; the Lord will heal that person. And if the person has sinned, the sins will be forgiven. [16]Confess your sins to each other and pray for each other so God can heal you. When a believing person prays, great things happen. [17]Elijah was a human being just like us. He prayed that it would not rain, and it did not rain on the land for three and a half years! [18]Then Elijah prayed again, and the rain came down from the sky, and the land produced crops again.

Saving a Soul

[19]My brothers and sisters, if one of you wanders away from the truth, and someone helps that person come back, [20]remember this: Anyone who brings a sinner back from the wrong way will save that sinner's soul from death and will cause many sins to be forgiven.

➽ **5:14 pour oil on the person** Oil was used in the name of the Lord as a sign that the person was now set apart for God's special attention and care.

James

Faith That Works

James's letter wasn't written to a specific church or group of believers. Maybe that's why its themes are so universal and still incredibly relevant to believers today. His tone may come across harsh and strict at times, but James's words are highly practical.

The central theme of James has caused debate for centuries, but a careful study of his words can clear up the confusion. James claims that faith that doesn't *do* anything is worthless (James 2:20). Is he saying that we're saved by our actions? Does he believe that we can work our way into heaven? Not at all! Instead, he's pointing out that faith is a life-transforming force. It changes everything about us. If our faith is real and our hearts are truly changed, we'll want to act differently. Contrary to what some people too quickly assume, James's teaching on living out our faith actually goes right along with Paul's teaching on how grace, through faith, makes us right with God (Romans 3–6).

In the rest of his book, James goes on to explain in more detail the behaviors that should flow from our faith in Christ. He teaches about enduring through trials and temptations, using the resources we've been given to help others, being careful of what we say, and making prayer a priority. He uses some unique word pictures (dead flowers and flaming tongues) to get his message across.

Above all, James challenges followers of Christ to live a consistent life that reflects the Savior's heart.

Get Real

How do determination and perseverance help us overcome obstacles in our lives? (Romans 5:3–5; 2 Corinthians 4:8–18)

How *does* James's emphasis on good deeds compare with the teachings of Paul and Peter? (Romans 3:19–31; James 2:14–26; 2 Peter 1:5–11)

Is the childhood "Sticks and Stones" rhyme true? Why or why not? (Job 19:2; Proverbs 12:18)

How should we treat the less fortunate among us? (Exodus 22:21–24; Luke 14:12–14)

1 peter

Suffering is inevitable. The question is, how do you respond—do you lose hope when times get tough? Is there even any room for hope when suffering seems to take over? As Christians, we're guaranteed to face suffering . . . Christianity isn't exactly the key to worldly success and popularity! But the hope of salvation is worth any amount of suffering in this present life.

Peter experienced the depths of hopelessness when he denied knowing Jesus. He spent the next few days in hiding, broken with grief and fear. But Jesus' resurrection began an irreversible change in Peter. On the day of Pentecost, the Holy Spirit transformed him into a courageous, eloquent champion of truth and the Good News. After a rocky beginning, the formerly fearful and brash fisherman learned to trust and obey the one who is the source of all true hope—the risen Christ!

This letter was written to Christians who were beginning to experience suffering. Christians ran the risk of being rejected by their communities, falsely accused of causing trouble, beaten, and thrown in jail—and even worse persecution was just around the corner.

Peter calls Christians to patiently endure suffering. Remain faithful to Christ even when things get tough. Suffering for the sake of Christ is an honor!

1 From Peter, an apostle of Jesus Christ.

To God's chosen people who are away from their homes and are scattered all around Pontus, Galatia, Cappadocia, Asia, and Bithynia. [2]God planned long ago to choose you by making you his holy people, which is the Spirit's work. God wanted you to obey him and to be made clean by the blood of the death of Jesus Christ.

Grace and peace be yours more and more.

We Have a Living Hope

[3]Praise be to the God and Father of our Lord Jesus Christ. In God's great mercy he has caused us to be born again into a living hope, because Jesus Christ rose from the dead. [4]Now we hope for the blessings God has for his children. These blessings, which cannot be destroyed or be spoiled or lose their beauty, are kept in heaven for you. [5]God's power protects you through your faith until salvation is shown to you at the end of time. [6]This makes you very happy, even though now for a short time different kinds of troubles may make you sad. [7]These troubles come to prove that your faith is pure. This purity of faith is worth more than gold, which can be proved to be pure by fire but will ruin. But the purity of your faith will bring you praise and glory and honor when Jesus Christ is shown to you. [8]You have not seen Christ, but still you love him. You cannot see him now, but you believe in him. So you are filled with a joy that cannot be explained, a joy full of glory. [9]And you are receiving the goal of your faith—the salvation of your souls.

[10]The prophets searched carefully and tried to learn about this salvation. They prophesied about the grace that was coming to you. [11]The Spirit of Christ was in the

Savvy Chef

Cook More to Cook Less

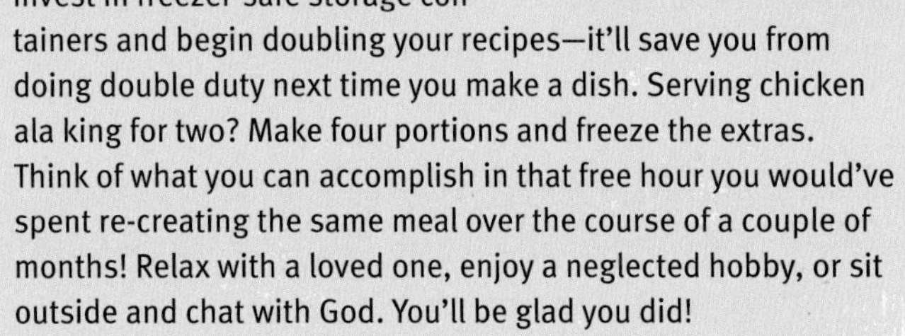

Whether you cook for a crew or specialize in meals for one, make the most of your time in the kitchen. Invest in freezer-safe storage containers and begin doubling your recipes—it'll save you from doing double duty next time you make a dish. Serving chicken ala king for two? Make four portions and freeze the extras. Think of what you can accomplish in that free hour you would've spent re-creating the same meal over the course of a couple of months! Relax with a loved one, enjoy a neglected hobby, or sit outside and chat with God. You'll be glad you did!

prophets, telling in advance about the sufferings of Christ and about the glory that would follow those sufferings. The prophets tried to learn about what the Spirit was showing them, when those things would happen, and what the world would be like at that time. [12]It was shown them that their service was not for themselves but for you, when they told about the truths you have now heard. Those who preached the Good News to you told you those things with the help of the Holy Spirit who was sent from heaven—things into which angels desire to look.

A Call to Holy Living

[13]So prepare your minds for service and have self-control. All your hope should be for the gift of grace that will be yours when Jesus Christ is shown to you. [14]Now that you are obedient children of God do not live as you did in the past. You did not understand, so you did the evil things you wanted. [15]But be holy in all you do, just as God, the One who called you, is holy. [16]It is written in the Scriptures: "You must be holy, because I am holy."[n]

[17]You pray to God and call him Father, and he judges each person's work equally. So while you are here on earth, you should live with respect for God. [18]You know that in the past you were living in a worthless way, a way passed down from the people who lived before you. But you were saved from that useless life. You were bought, not with something that ruins like gold or silver, [19]but with the precious blood of Christ, who was like a pure and perfect lamb. [20]Christ was chosen before the world was made, but he was shown to the world in these last times for your sake. [21]Through Christ you believe in God, who raised Christ from the dead and gave him glory. So your faith and your hope are in God.

[22]Now that your obedience to the truth has purified your souls, you can have true love for your Christian brothers and sisters. So love each other deeply with all your heart.[n] [23]You have been born again, and this new life did not come from something that dies, but from something that cannot die. You were born again through God's living message that continues forever. [24]The Scripture says,

"All people are like the grass,
  and all their glory is like the
    flowers of the field.
The grass dies and the flowers fall,
[25] but the word of the Lord will live
    forever." *Isaiah 40:6–8*

And this is the word that was preached to you.

Jesus Is the Living Stone

2 So then, rid yourselves of all evil, all lying, hypocrisy, jealousy, and

LIFEISSUES

Service and Love

When you love someone, you love showing it! So when you love God, you want to show it by serving him. But it can be easy to confuse the role of service. If you're somehow trying to earn God's affections, you first need to understand his love, namely that you can't earn it. He loves us because he *is* love, not because of anything we do for him. It's easy to think you have to act perfectly to stay on his good side. Not so! His love for us doesn't waver based on our behavior (Ephesians 2:8–10; 1 John 4:10–12, 16).

1:16 "You must be . . . holy." Quotation from Leviticus 11:45; 19:2; 20:7. **1:22 with all your heart** Some Greek copies read "with a pure heart."

evil speech. [2]As newborn babies want milk, you should want the pure and simple teaching. By it you can mature in your salvation, [3]because you have already examined and seen how good the Lord is.

[4]Come to the Lord Jesus, the "stone"[n] that lives. The people of the world did not want this stone, but he was the stone God chose, and he was precious. [5]You also are like living stones, so let yourselves be used to build a spiritual temple—to be holy priests who offer spiritual sacrifices to God. He will accept those sacrifices through Jesus Christ. [6]The Scripture says:

"I will put a stone in the ground in
Jerusalem.
Everything will be built on this
important and precious rock.
Anyone who trusts in him
will never be disappointed."

Isaiah 28:16

[7]This stone is worth much to you who believe. But to the people who do not believe,

"the stone that the builders rejected
has become the cornerstone."

Psalm 118:22

[8]Also, he is

"a stone that causes people to
stumble,
a rock that makes them fall."

Isaiah 8:14

They stumble because they do not obey what God says, which is what God planned to happen to them.

[9]But you are a chosen people, royal priests, a holy nation, a people for God's own possession. You were chosen to tell about the wonderful acts of God, who called you out of darkness into his wonderful light. [10]At one time you were not a people, but now you are God's people. In the past you had never received mercy, but now you have received God's mercy.

Live for God

[11]Dear friends, you are like foreigners and strangers in this world. I beg you to avoid the evil things your bodies want to do that fight against your soul. [12]People who do not believe are living all around you and might say that you are doing wrong. Live such good lives that they will see the good things you do and will give glory to God on the day when Christ comes again.

Yield to Every Human Authority

[13]For the Lord's sake, yield to the people who have authority in this world: the king, who is the highest authority, [14]and the leaders who are sent by him to punish those who do wrong and to praise those who do right. [15]It is God's desire that by doing good you should stop foolish people from saying stupid things about you. [16]Live as free people, but do not use your freedom as an excuse to do evil. Live as servants of God. [17]Show respect for all people: Love the brothers and sisters of God's family, respect God, honor the king.

Follow Christ's Example

[18]Slaves, yield to the authority of your masters with all respect, not only those who are good and kind, but also those who are dishonest. [19]A person might have to suffer even when it is unfair, but if he thinks of God and can stand the pain, God is pleased. [20]If you are beaten for doing wrong, there is no reason to praise you for being patient in your punishment. But if you suffer for doing good, and you are patient, then God is pleased. [21]This is what you were called to do, because Christ suffered for you and gave you an example to follow. So you should do as he did.

BECOME Involved

Susan G. Komen Breast Cancer Foundation

Few women have escaped the broad-reaching effects of breast cancer. With more than two hundred thousand new cases diagnosed each year, countless women have a personal connection to the disease. More than twenty-five years ago, it became very personal for Nancy Goodman Brinker when it took the life of her sister. Out of her grief and a deathbed promise, Nancy started the Susan G. Komen Breast Cancer Foundation.

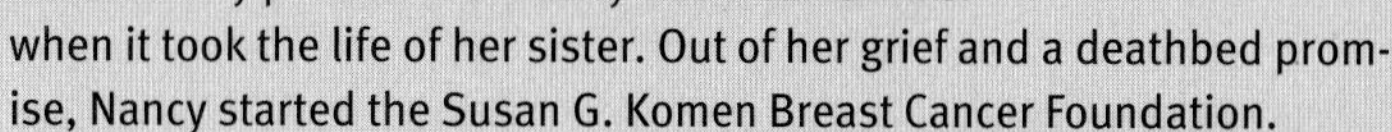

Today, the Komen Foundation has more than seventy-five thousand volunteers. They are most known for their annual Komen Race for the Cure® Series. A large-scale awareness and fund-raising event, Race for the Cure® boasts more than one million participants worldwide. They also facilitate a year-round fund-raising and education program called Passionately Pink for the Cure™. Through these and other efforts, the Komen Foundation says it is "fighting to eradicate breast cancer as a life-threatening disease by funding research grants and supporting education, screening, and treatment projects in communities around the world."

You can help create positive change in women's health worldwide by helping the Komen Foundation. Check out www.komen.org to learn more about volunteering at or participating in your local Komen Race for the Cure®. Your involvement makes a difference!

2:4 **"stone"** The most important stone in God's spiritual temple or house (his people).

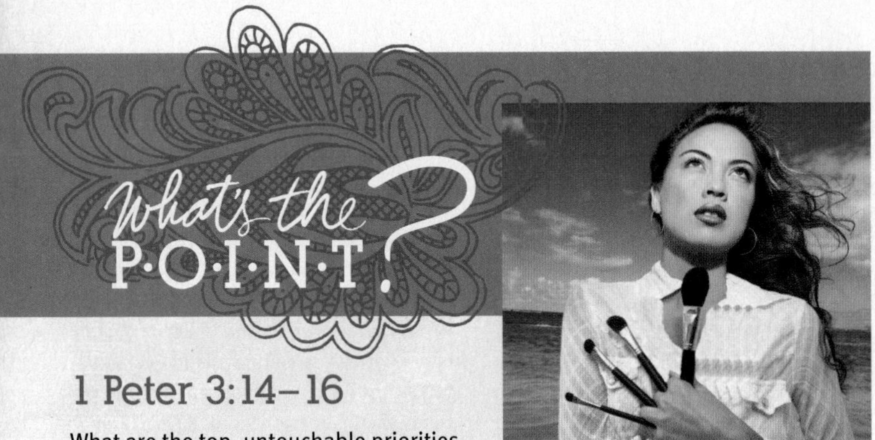

1 Peter 3:14–16

What are the top, untouchable priorities, dreams, or passions in your life? Maybe you dream of having a family or a fabulous job, living on the coast, or maybe you want your painting on display in an art gallery.

Although we as Christians all have different interests and goals individually, we should be defined by our passion to love God and live for him. That should be indisputably recognizable as the most important thing to us. If we're his people, we've got to be *all* his.

Peter told believers to "respect Christ as the holy Lord in your hearts" (1 Peter 3:15). That means setting him apart as the one who controls and directs who you are and how you live. It means deciding that no matter what disappointments, temptations, or insults may come, you will keep Christ the Lord of your life. It means being determined that your life will reflect and please God. And it means maintaining a clear conscience, being forgiving and honest, treating others with gentleness and respect, sharing the hope you have in Christ with others, and suffering for doing good.

Make knowing, serving, and loving God your highest priority. He deserves to be your one defining passion in life!

[22]"He had never sinned,
and he had never lied." *Isaiah 53:9*

[23]People insulted Christ, but he did not insult them in return. Christ suffered, but he did not threaten. He let God, the One who judges rightly, take care of him. [24]Christ carried our sins in his body on the cross so we would stop living for sin and start living for what is right. And you are healed because of his wounds. [25]You were like sheep that wandered away, but now you have come back to the Shepherd and Overseer of your souls.

Wives and Husbands

3 In the same way, you wives should yield to your husbands. Then, if some husbands do not obey God's teaching, they will be persuaded to believe without anyone's saying a word to them. They will be persuaded by the way their wives live. [2]Your husbands will see the pure lives you live with your respect for God. [3]It is not fancy hair, gold jewelry, or fine clothes that should make you beautiful. [4]No, your beauty should come from within you—the beauty of a gentle and quiet spirit that will never be destroyed and is very precious to God. [5]In this same way the holy women who lived long ago and followed God made themselves beautiful, yielding to their own husbands. [6]Sarah obeyed Abraham, her husband, and called him her master. And you women are true children of Sarah if you always do what is right and are not afraid.

[7]In the same way, you husbands should live with your wives in an understanding way, since they are weaker than you. But show them respect, because God gives them the same blessing he gives you—the grace that gives true life. Do this so that nothing will stop your prayers.

Suffering for Doing Right

[8]Finally, all of you should be in agreement, understanding each other, loving each other as family, being kind and humble. [9]Do not do wrong to repay a wrong, and do not insult to repay an insult. But repay with a blessing, because you yourselves were called to do this so that you might receive a blessing. [10]The Scripture says,

"A person must do these things
to enjoy life and have many
happy days.
He must not say evil things,
and he must not tell lies.
[11]He must stop doing evil and do good.
He must look for peace and work
for it.
[12]The Lord sees the good people
and listens to their prayers.
But the Lord is against
those who do evil." *Psalm 34:12–16*

[13]If you are trying hard to do good, no one can really hurt you. [14]But even if you suffer for doing right, you are blessed.

"Don't be afraid of what they fear;
do not dread those things."
Isaiah 8:12–13

[15]But respect Christ as the holy Lord in your hearts. Always be ready to answer everyone who asks you to explain about the hope you have, [16]but answer in a gentle way and with respect. Keep a clear conscience so that those who speak evil of your good life in Christ will be made ashamed. [17]It is better to suffer for doing good than for doing wrong if that is what God wants. [18]Christ himself suffered for sins once. He was not guilty, but he suffered for those who are guilty to bring you to God. His body was killed, but he was made alive in the spirit. [19]And in the spirit he went and preached to the spirits in prison [20]who refused to obey God long ago in the time of Noah. God was waiting patiently for them while Noah was building the boat. Only a

few people—eight in all—were saved by water. [21]And that water is like baptism that now saves you—not the washing of dirt from the body, but the promise made to God from a good conscience. And this is because Jesus Christ was raised from the dead. [22]Now Jesus has gone into heaven and is at God's right side ruling over angels, authorities, and powers.

Change Your Lives

4 Since Christ suffered while he was in his body, strengthen yourselves with the same way of thinking Christ had. The person who has suffered in the body is finished with sin. [2]Strengthen yourselves so that you will live here on earth doing what God wants, not the evil things people want. [3]In the past you wasted too much time doing what nonbelievers enjoy. You were guilty of sexual sins, evil desires, drunkenness, wild and drunken parties, and hateful idol worship. [4]Nonbelievers think it is strange that you do not do the many wild and wasteful things they do, so they insult you. [5]But they will have to explain this to God, who is ready to judge the living and the dead. [6]For this reason the Good News was preached to those who are now dead. Even though they were judged like all people, the Good News was preached to them so they could live in the spirit as God lives.

Use God's Gifts Wisely

[7]The time is near when all things will end. So think clearly and control yourselves so you will be able to pray. [8]Most importantly, love each other deeply, because love will cause people to forgive each other for many sins. [9]Open your homes to each other, without complaining. [10]Each of you has received a gift to use to serve others. Be good servants of God's various gifts of grace. [11]Anyone who speaks should speak words from God. Anyone who serves should serve with the strength God gives so that in everything God will be praised through Jesus Christ. Power and glory belong to him forever and ever. Amen.

Suffering as a Christian

[12]My friends, do not be surprised at the terrible trouble which now comes to test you. Do not think that something strange is happening to you. [13]But be happy that you are sharing in Christ's sufferings so that you will be happy and full of joy when Christ comes again in glory. [14]When people insult you because you follow Christ, you are blessed, because the glorious Spirit, the Spirit of God, is with you. [15]Do not suffer for murder, theft, or any other crime, nor because you trouble other people. [16]But if you suffer because you are a Christian, do not be ashamed. Praise God because you wear that name. [17]It is time for judgment to begin with God's family. And if that judging begins with us, what will

HE SAID ↙ ↗ SHE SAID

What's your favorite thing to do on a Sunday afternoon?

HE: Nap

SHE: Relax with friends

The "I-Don't-Have-It-Together" Prayer

It's ironic that the times of greatest stress, biggest rush, and least available time are the very times that you could most use a moment in the presence of God. But take heart—you don't have to have it all "together" before talking to your Savior! If you're too tired to pray, ask God for energy. If you're too sleepy to stay awake during your morning conversation with the Lord, ask him to help you be alert. If you feel like a big 'ole mess, tell him so! Whatever you're feeling, whatever you're going through, you can be sure of two things: 1) he understands, and 2) he can help you overcome it!

Looking for Beauty

The quest for beauty is a multibillion-dollar industry in the United States. People spend unheard-of amounts of money on cosmetics, hair products, manicures, and even plastic surgery—all in hopes of improving their looks even just a little. And while there's nothing wrong with trying to look your best, it should never be the thing you seek most. Matthew 6:33 says to seek after what God wants first, and then everything else will fall into place. Be sure you focus as much attention on developing your inner character as you do on your outward appearance.

happen to those people who do not obey the Good News of God?

[18]"If it is very hard for a good person to
be saved,
the wicked person and the sinner
will surely be lost!"[n]

[19]So those who suffer as God wants should trust their souls to the faithful Creator as they continue to do what is right.

The Flock of God

5 Now I have something to say to the elders in your group. I also am an elder. I have seen Christ's sufferings, and I will share in the glory that will be shown to us. I beg you to [2]shepherd God's flock, for whom you are responsible. Watch over them because you want to, not because you are forced. That is how God wants it. Do it because you are happy to serve, not because you want money. [3]Do not be like a ruler over people you are responsible for, but be good examples to them. [4]Then when Christ, the Chief Shepherd, comes, you will get a glorious crown that will never lose its beauty.

[5]In the same way, younger people should be willing to be under older people. And all of you should be very humble with each other.

"God is against the proud,
but he gives grace to the
humble." *Proverbs 3:34*

[6]Be humble under God's powerful hand so he will lift you up when the right time comes. [7]Give all your worries to him, because he cares about you.

[8]Control yourselves and be careful! The devil, your enemy, goes around like a roaring lion looking for someone to eat. [9]Refuse to give in to him, by standing strong in your faith. You know that your Christian family all over the world is having the same kinds of suffering.

[10]And after you suffer for a short time, God, who gives all grace, will make everything right. He will make you strong and support you and keep you from falling. He called you to share in his glory in Christ, a glory that will continue forever. [11]All power is his forever and ever. Amen.

Final Greetings

[12]I wrote this short letter with the help of Silas, who I know is a faithful brother in Christ. I wrote to encourage you and to tell you that this is the true grace of God. Stand strong in that grace.

[13]The church in Babylon, who was chosen like you, sends you greetings. Mark, my son in Christ, also greets you. [14]Give each other a kiss of Christian love when you meet.

Peace to all of you who are in Christ.

Worship His Name

Almighty God. Everlasting Father. Alpha and Omega. Worship is all about praising God for who he is, and his various names invoke unique reasons to stand in awe of him. If being *Creator* wasn't already amazing enough, he added *Savior*, *Defender*, *Protector*, *Healer*, and lots of others in between to sketch in the details of his identity. One worship experience might focus you on his holiness, while the next time you might praise him for being such a worthy *Lord* and *King*. In the midst of his majesty, he chose to make himself a humble *Servant*. Contrast that with his unmatchable role as *I Am*, and we're reminded again why only he could ever be our *All in All* and *Emmanuel*, our God who is always with us.

4:18 "If . . . lost!" Quotation from Proverbs 11:31 in the Septuagint, the Greek version of the Old Testament.

Standing Firm

When Peter wrote this book, Jewish and non-Jewish Christians were being persecuted for their faith by people outside the church. They were being thrown in prison, tortured, and even killed because they believed in Jesus Christ. Paul had already been executed, and the number of martyrs was steadily growing. Believers struggled to remain strong in their faith.

Peter had several purposes for writing this letter, and one of the primary reasons was to encourage Christians facing persecution. He challenged them to stand strong and not be defeated spiritually. Peter gave them a perspective beyond their circumstances: Jesus had gracefully endured so much more for them than they would ever face. Furthermore, Christ hadn't abandoned them in the midst of their suffering (1 Peter 3:18; 4:1–2).

Scripture shows us that this world is broken because of sin. The reality is that Christians suffer. In fact, we actually share in Christ's suffering (1 Peter 4:13–14, 16). But anything we endure here on earth is nothing compared to the things God has in store for us (Romans 8:18). Jesus, in his perfection and innocence, went through agony so that we could eventually live in glory.

What do we do in the middle of our trials? Only when Jesus comes again will all things be made right. For now we can know that trials strengthen our faith (James 1:2–4). We can also focus on living in a way that represents Christ well (1 Peter 3:15–16). Finally, we can trust God's promises and hold firmly to the hope we've been given.

Get Real

How can you view suffering for Christ as a blessing? (Matthew 5:10–12)

What should your response be to persecution? (Matthew 5:44; Romans 12:14; 1 Corinthians 4:12–13)

What can you do to help people near you or across the world who are suffering? (Matthew 25:37–46)

2 peter

Whether you struggle with being overly legalistic or tend toward the "judge not" camp, it's no secret that behavior is a big deal in Christian circles. Some Christians are tempted to think that sin's not such a big deal because of Christian liberty, Christ's righteousness covering our sins. Doesn't it stand to reason that we can do whatever we want?

Peter knew that wasn't the case. Even so, some serious heresies were cropping up that basically tried to justify sinful living—all under the guise of Christianity! Some of the newer Christians were still in love with their old sin, and several false teachers exploited that. Their teachings may have been an early version of Gnosticism, a cult that claimed to have secret knowledge from Jesus. Some Gnostics claimed that the physical world and the body were evil and that it was okay to sin with your body since it was separate from the spiritual realm.

But Peter makes a strong case for the connection between our spiritual salvation in Christ and our physical actions in this world. The spiritual reality of our salvation should make a huge impact on how we live! Beware of any church or teacher that doesn't stress holy living. Following Christ always includes living pure lives and avoiding sin!

1 From Simon Peter, a servant and apostle of Jesus Christ.

To you who have received a faith as valuable as ours, because our God and Savior Jesus Christ does what is right.

[2]Grace and peace be given to you more and more, because you truly know God and Jesus our Lord.

God Has Given Us Blessings

[3]Jesus has the power of God, by which he has given us everything we need to live and to serve God. We have these things because we know him. Jesus called us by his glory and goodness. [4]Through these he gave us the very great and precious promises. With these gifts you can share in God's nature, and the world will not ruin you with its evil desires.

[5]Because you have these blessings, do your best to add these things to your lives: to your faith, add goodness; and to your goodness, add knowledge; [6]and to your knowledge, add self-control; and to your self-control, add patience; and to your patience, add service for God; [7]and to your service for God, add kindness for your brothers and sisters in Christ; and to this kindness, add love. [8]If all these things are in you and are growing, they will help you to be useful and productive in your knowledge of our Lord Jesus Christ. [9]But anyone who does not have these things cannot see clearly. He is blind and has forgotten that he was made clean from his past sins.

[10]My brothers and sisters, try hard to be certain that you really are called and chosen by God. If you do all these things, you will never fall. [11]And you will be given a

very great welcome into the eternal kingdom of our Lord and Savior Jesus Christ.

[12]You know these things, and you are very strong in the truth, but I will always help you remember them. [13]I think it is right for me to help you remember as long as I am in this body. [14]I know I must soon leave this body, as our Lord Jesus Christ has shown me. [15]I will try my best so that you may be able to remember these things even after I am gone.

We Saw Christ's Glory

[16]When we told you about the powerful coming of our Lord Jesus Christ, we were not telling just clever stories that someone invented. But we saw the greatness of Jesus with our own eyes. [17]Jesus heard the voice of God, the Greatest Glory, when he received honor and glory from God the Father. The voice said, "This is my Son, whom I love, and I am very pleased with him." [18]We heard that voice from heaven while we were with Jesus on the holy mountain.

[19]This makes us more sure about the message the prophets gave. It is good for you to follow closely what they said as you would follow a light shining in a dark place, until the day begins and the morning star rises in your hearts. [20]Most of all, you must understand this: No prophecy in the Scriptures ever comes from the prophet's own interpretation. [21]No prophecy ever came from what a person wanted to say, but people led by the Holy Spirit spoke words from God.

2 Peter 1:20–21

Words are only as reliable as the people who say them. And the truth is that no human is *completely* reliable. Even the most dependable person can make an honest mistake or forget about a promise she made long ago. While there are so many people we can trust, it's always wise to evaluate what we hear according to the truth of Scripture.

But if there's one person you can trust no matter what, it's God. He will never lie (Titus 1:2), and he never makes mistakes. He's completely faithful to all of his promises, so you can fully rely on him. A big part of relying on God is taking him at his word. This passage makes it clear: prophecy (referring to Scripture) didn't come from human minds. God's Holy Spirit miraculously worked through real people to speak the actual words of God.

Today, spend some time reflecting on God's tremendous faithfulness. You can read about it all throughout the Old Testament. And think about how you can see his promises alive in your own life. As you fill up your heart with the trustworthy words of Scripture, you'll grow in your ability to truly trust God with everything.

False Teachers

2 There used to be false prophets among God's people, just as you will have some false teachers in your group. They will secretly teach things that are wrong—teachings that will cause people to be lost. They will even refuse to accept the Master, Jesus, who bought their freedom. So they will bring quick ruin on themselves. [2]Many will follow their evil ways and say evil things about the way of truth. [3]Those false teachers only want your money, so they will use you by telling you lies. Their judgment spoken against them long ago is still coming, and their ruin is certain.

[4]When angels sinned, God did not let them go free without punishment. He sent them to hell and put them in caves[n] of darkness where they are being held for judgment. [5]And God punished the world long ago when he brought a flood to the world that was full of people who were against him. But God saved Noah, who preached about being right with God, and seven other people with him. [6]And God also destroyed the evil cities of Sodom

fun facts

1 in 4 Americans say they overeat in order to comfort themselves.

(*Psychology Today*)

2:4 caves Some Greek copies read "chains."

HE SAID ↙ ↗ SHE SAID

What's the first thing you notice about the opposite sex?

HE: How she carries herself

SHE: His smile

and Gomorrah[n] by burning them until they were ashes. He made those cities an example of what will happen to those who are against God. [7]But he saved Lot from those cities. Lot, a good man, was troubled because of the filthy lives of evil people. [8](Lot was a good man, but because he lived with evil people every day, his good heart was hurt by the evil things he saw and heard.) [9]So the Lord knows how to save those who serve him when troubles come. He will hold evil people and punish them, while waiting for the Judgment Day. [10]That punishment is especially for those who live by doing the evil things their sinful selves want and who hate authority.

These false teachers are bold and do anything they want. They are not afraid to speak against the angels. [11]But even the angels, who are much stronger and more powerful than false teachers, do not accuse them with insults before[n] the Lord. [12]But these people speak against things they do not understand. They are like animals that act without thinking, animals born to be caught and killed. And, like animals, these false teachers will be destroyed. [13]They have caused many people to suffer, so they themselves will suffer. That is their pay for what they have done. They take pleasure in openly doing evil, so they are like dirty spots and stains among you. They delight in deceiving you while eating meals with you. [14]Every time they look at a woman they want her, and their desire for sin is never satisfied. They lead weak people into the trap of sin, and they have taught their hearts to be greedy. God will punish them! [15]These false teachers left the right road and lost their way, fol-

WORLDVIEWS

Yeah, It *Is* My Fault

"It's not my fault!" you whine. The sound of your voice even grates on your own nerves, but you press on, eager to exonerate yourself. There's an endless supply of excuses, an infinite number of ways to blame everything on anything but yourself. We've all done it at some point. For some of us, passing the blame becomes an ongoing pattern.

Our culture is all about getting rid of individual responsibility and that uncomfortable feeling of guilt that goes along with it. We don't want to admit our own wrongness. Modern philosophers and psychiatrists claim that humans are basically good. We just make bad choices because of pressure from society and compromising situations.

This kind of mass rejection of personal responsibility leads to some serious problems. For one thing, refusing to admit any fault always leads you right back into making poor choices. It doesn't help you change. And trying to ignore or explain away our guilt is extremely unhealthy.

Christianity teaches that all people are sinful. Stepping up to the plate and admitting our mistakes is the first step to really experiencing healing from all the sin and guilt in our lives. Then there's the ultimate Good News: even though we're all sinners, God chooses to show us grace! He offers forgiveness and freedom from sin. But it all starts with facing the music and admitting that we're responsible for the things we do.

If you're serious about living by God's Word, you won't be a whining blame-passer . . . instead, you'll be courageous enough to admit your own shortcomings and learn to deal with them through total reliance on God's grace and forgiveness.

2:6 Sodom and Gomorrah Two cities God destroyed because the people were so evil. **2:11 before** Some Greek copies read "from."

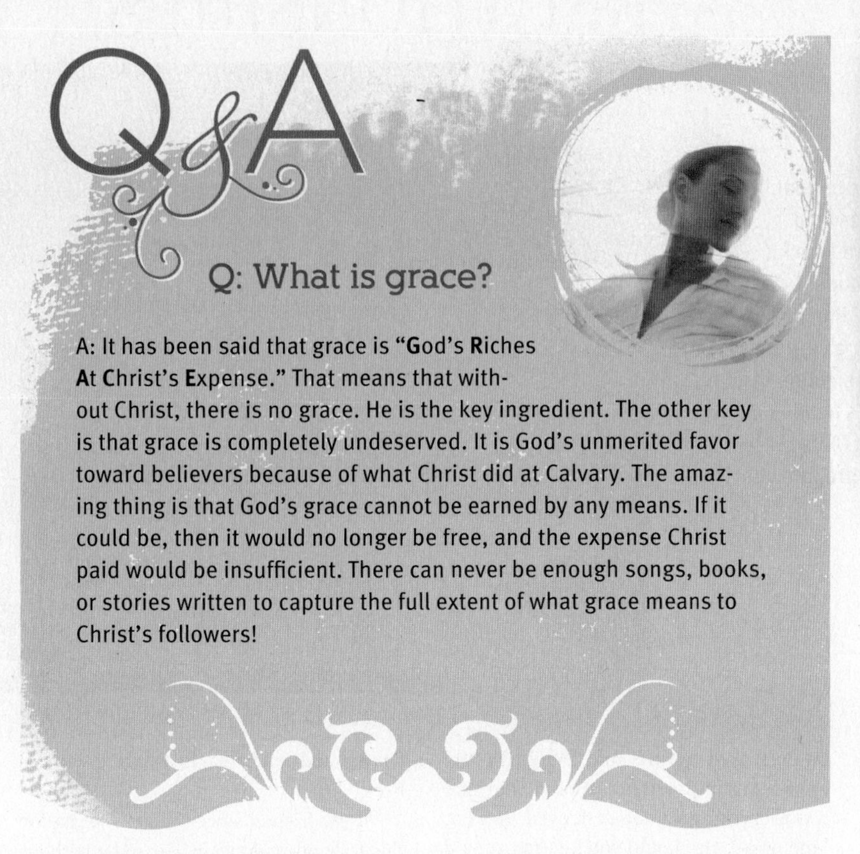

Q: What is grace?

A: It has been said that grace is "**G**od's **R**iches **A**t **C**hrist's **E**xpense." That means that without Christ, there is no grace. He is the key ingredient. The other key is that grace is completely undeserved. It is God's unmerited favor toward believers because of what Christ did at Calvary. The amazing thing is that God's grace cannot be earned by any means. If it could be, then it would no longer be free, and the expense Christ paid would be insufficient. There can never be enough songs, books, or stories written to capture the full extent of what grace means to Christ's followers!

Health

Your Pearly Whites

It's no secret that regular brushing and flossing are the keys to a beautiful smile, but did you know that they're also important to your overall health? Periodontal disease is directly related to diabetes, heart disease, and stroke. So what can you do to maintain good oral health, besides the aforementioned brushing and flossing? See your dental hygienist twice a year to prevent plaque buildup. Wear a protective mouth guard if you grind your teeth while sleeping. (There are nine references to grinding teeth in the New Testament—all associated with pain and anguish!) Follow snacks with a drink of water. Prevent cavities in molars by having dental sealants applied. Finally, scrub away bacteria's breeding ground by using a tongue scraper every time you brush.

lowing the way Balaam went. Balaam was the son of Beor, who loved being paid for doing wrong. [16]But a donkey, which cannot talk, told Balaam he was sinning. It spoke with a man's voice and stopped the prophet's crazy thinking.

[17]Those false teachers are like springs without water and clouds blown by a storm. A place in the blackest darkness has been kept for them. [18]They brag with words that mean nothing. By their evil desires they lead people into the trap of sin—people who are just beginning to escape from others who live in error. [19]They promise them freedom, but they themselves are not free. They are slaves of things that will be destroyed. For people are slaves of anything that controls them. [20]They were made free from the evil in the world by knowing our Lord and Savior Jesus Christ. But if they return to evil things and those things control them, then it is worse for them than it was before. [21]Yes, it would be better for them to have never known the right way than to know it and to turn away from the holy teaching that was given to them. [22]What they did is like this true saying: "A dog goes back to what it has thrown up,"[n] and, "After a pig is washed, it goes back and rolls in the mud."

Jesus Will Come Again

3 My friends, this is the second letter I have written you to help your honest minds remember. [2]I want you to think about the words the holy prophets spoke in the past, and remember the command our Lord and Savior gave us through your apostles. [3]It is most important for you to understand what will happen in the last days. People will laugh at you. They will live doing the evil things they want to do. [4]They will say, "Jesus promised to come again. Where is he? Our fathers have died, but the world continues the way it has been since it was made." [5]But they do not want to remember what happened long ago. By the word of God heaven was made, and the earth was made from water and with water. [6]Then the world was flooded and destroyed with water. [7]And that same word of God is keeping heaven and earth that we now have in order to be destroyed by fire. They are being kept for the Judgment Day and the destruction of all who are against God.

[8]But do not forget this one thing, dear friends: To the Lord one day is as a thousand years, and a thousand years is as one day. [9]The Lord is not slow in doing what he promised—the way some people understand slowness. But God is being patient with you. He does not want anyone to

2:22 "A dog . . . up." Quotation from Proverbs 26:11.

RELATIONSHIPS

Time to Heal

Ecclesiastes 3:3 says, "There is . . . a time to heal." Thank heaven for that! We aren't machines who can bounce back instantly from every hard knock. And sometimes relationships deliver wallops. Even the best ones hurt at times; that's part of life. But if you've really been burned by someone, give your emotions time to recover. Just like a broken bone can heal stronger than it originally was, God's healing can strengthen you in ways you didn't expect (Acts 4:30). In time, he'll rebuild the hurt places and prepare you to reach out again.

be lost, but he wants all people to change their hearts and lives.

[10]But the day of the Lord will come like a thief. The skies will disappear with a loud noise. Everything in them will be destroyed by fire, and the earth and everything in it will be exposed.[n] [11]In that way everything will be destroyed. So what kind of people should you be? You should live holy lives and serve God, [12]as you wait for and look forward to the coming of the day of God. When that day comes, the skies will be destroyed with fire, and everything in them will melt with heat. [13]But God made a promise to us, and we are waiting for a new heaven and a new earth where goodness lives.

[14]Dear friends, since you are waiting for this to happen, do your best to be without sin and without fault. Try to be at peace with God. [15]Remember that we are saved because our Lord is patient. Our dear brother Paul told you the same thing when he wrote to you with the wisdom that God gave him. [16]He writes about this in all his letters. Some things in Paul's letters are hard to understand, and people who are ignorant and weak in faith explain these things falsely. They also falsely explain the other Scriptures, but they are destroying themselves by doing this.

[17]Dear friends, since you already know about this, be careful. Do not let those evil people lead you away by the wrong they do. Be careful so you will not fall from your strong faith. [18]But grow in the grace and knowledge of our Lord and Savior Jesus Christ. Glory be to him now and forever! Amen.

all about MEN

Guy Time

Just like we need our girlfriends (no matter how satisfying romance might be), men need time with each other, too. They process, talk, and act differently than us, and sometimes they need to get away with their own kind! After all, no one understands guys like other guys. Not only do they need time to connect, but some issues of accountability are best dealt with between men. The quality time a man spends with other solid guys can actually enhance your time with him and deepen his appreciation for you. Show him you respect his time with the guys, and pray that his male friendships will be a refining tool in his life. As Proverbs 27:17 says, "As iron sharpens iron, so people can improve each other."

3:10 **and . . . exposed** Some Greek copies read "and everything in it will be burned up."

Be Strong, Be Faithful, Beware

Peter had lived a rich, full, zealous life for Jesus. The time for his martyrdom was now at hand. Just imagine: Peter is hunched over his paper, his weathered hands scrawling out his final letter before he breathes his last breath. The Book of 2 Peter was written to encourage believers to stand up against both complacency and false teaching. It's a message of guidance, caution, and hope.

Short and sweet, 2 Peter can be read cover-to-cover in the time it takes you to put on your makeup in the morning. Yet in its few pages, 2 Peter addresses some vital issues for believers. These issues were certainly not unique to 2 Peter alone. False doctrine, Christ's return, and keeping the faith—all these things are topics covered in various other New Testament letters. Jude, in particular, closely resembles the content and style of 2 Peter's warning against false teachers.

For first-century and twenty-first-century believers alike, the lessons in 2 Peter are both relevant and crucial. Just like the people who originally received this letter, we need to hear this warning to steer clear of deceptive philosophies about God—especially since they seem to be everywhere in our spiritually tolerant culture. We should also take Peter's spiritual advice: don't let your faith get stagnant and boring! By focusing on the task of growing in our love for God and other people, we will avoid slipping into lukewarm living.

Get Real

Does God prefer to show mercy or anger? (Nehemiah 9:16–21; Isaiah 28:21; Romans 2:4–11)

Does God really care that much about being intimately connected with every single soul in this world? (Matthew 10:29–31; Luke 15)

Do you have Jesus' tender heart toward unbelievers? (Mark 6:34; Luke 5:27–31; 10:2; 13:34)

How can you protect yourself from being swayed by false teaching? (Matthew 7:15–20; Acts 17:10–11; 1 Timothy 4:7–8; 2 Timothy 4:3–5)

Are you passionate about getting to know Jesus Christ even more? (Luke 10:38–42; John 15:5–12; Colossians 1:9–14)

1 john

Our culture seems to be obsessed with finding and defining true love! Heartfelt ballads, romance novels, summer movies—we're absolutely saturated with human perspectives on this all-important theme. But behind the sappy sentiments crooned by lovesick balladeers and cheesy confessions of undying love in "romantic" movies, where's the real substance?

John is described as the follower whom Jesus loved. Because of that closeness with the Savior, John knew that Christianity is all about Jesus—knowing him, obeying him, loving him, and living for him.

This letter is a thoughtful meditation on love. John tackles issues like forgiveness, righteousness, and holy living from different angles, but he always returns to the straightforward command to love God and each other. Love should be central to *everything* we do as Christians.

Love is more than a fleeting emotion or a burning passion that randomly flares up and burns out. It's a purposeful, persistent decision to give up everything for the sake of someone else. True love was demonstrated by Christ on the cross. His sacrifice proved that God *is* love!

Don't be fooled by all the counterfeit versions of "love" that permeate our culture. Stick with the real thing. And as you experience more of God's love for you, he'll equip you to truly love those around you.

1 We write you now about what has always existed, which we have heard, we have seen with our own eyes, we have looked at, and we have touched with our hands. We write to you about the Word[n] that gives life. [2]He who gives life was shown to us. We saw him and can give proof about it. And now we announce to you that he has life that continues forever. He was with God the Father and was shown to us. [3]We announce to you what we have seen and heard, because we want you also to have fellowship with us. Our fellowship is with God the Father and with his Son, Jesus Christ. [4]We write this to you so we may be full of joy.[n]

God Forgives Our Sins

[5]Here is the message we have heard from Christ and now announce to you: God is light,[n] and in him there is no darkness at all. [6]So if we say we have fellowship with God, but we continue living in darkness, we are liars and do not follow the truth. [7]But if we live in the light, as God is in the light, we can share fellowship with each other. Then the blood of Jesus, God's Son, cleanses us from every sin.

[8]If we say we have no sin, we are fooling ourselves, and the truth is not in us. [9]But if we confess our sins, he will forgive our sins, because we can trust God to do what is right. He will cleanse us from all the wrongs we have done. [10]If we say we have not sinned, we make God a liar, and we do not accept God's teaching.

Jesus Is Our Helper

2 My dear children, I write this letter to you so you will not sin. But if anyone does sin, we have a helper in the presence of the Father—Jesus Christ, the

1:1 Word The Greek word is "logos," meaning any kind of communication. Here, it means Christ, who was the way God told people about himself. **1:4 so . . . joy** Some Greek copies read "so you may be full of joy." **1:5 light** Here, it is used as a symbol of God's goodness or truth.

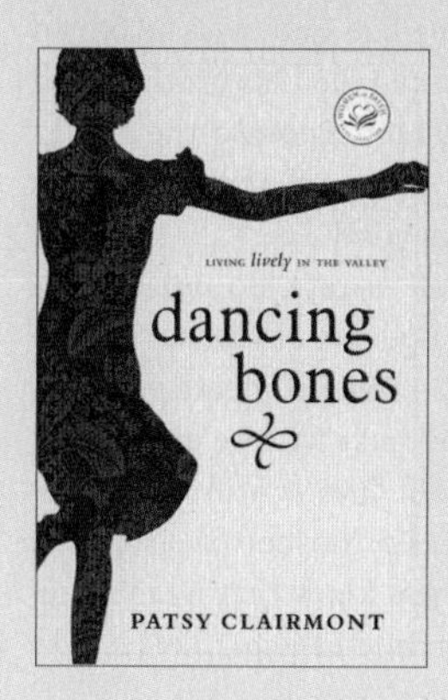

Dancing Bones
by Patsy Clairmont

Sure, it would be great if you could spend life up on the mountaintops. But the reality is that most of life is spent in the valleys—areas of routine and even hardship. Author Patsy Clairmont says that while the view may be better at the top, it's down in the muddle of your everyday life that you can really grow. She motivates you to stop trying to escape challenges and start walking—and even dancing—through them with grace. Even if your faith feels dry and difficult, God is with you and will never leave you!

One who does what is right. [2]He died in our place to take away our sins, and not only our sins but the sins of all people.

[3]We can be sure that we know God if we obey his commands. [4]Anyone who says, "I know God," but does not obey God's commands is a liar, and the truth is not in that person. [5]But if someone obeys God's teaching, then in that person God's love has truly reached its goal. This is how we can be sure we are living in God: [6]Whoever says that he lives in God must live as Jesus lived.

The Command to Love Others

[7]My dear friends, I am not writing a new command to you but an old command you have had from the beginning. It is the teaching you have already heard. [8]But also I am writing a new command to you, and you can see its truth in Jesus and in you, because the darkness is passing away, and the true light is already shining.

[9]Anyone who says, "I am in the light,"[n] but hates a brother or sister, is still in the darkness. [10]Whoever loves a brother or sister lives in the light and will not cause anyone to stumble in his faith. [11]But whoever hates a brother or sister is in darkness, lives in darkness, and does not know where to go, because the darkness has made that person blind.

[12]I write to you, dear children,
because your sins are forgiven
through Christ.
[13]I write to you, fathers,
because you know the One who
existed from the beginning.
I write to you, young people,
because you have defeated the
Evil One.
[14]I write to you, children,
because you know the Father.
I write to you, fathers,
because you know the One who
existed from the beginning.
I write to you, young people,
because you are strong;
the teaching of God lives in you,
and you have defeated the Evil
One.

[15]Do not love the world or the things in the world. If you love the world, the love of the Father is not in you. [16]These are the ways of the world: wanting to please our sinful selves, wanting the sinful things we see, and being too proud of what we have. None of these come from the Father, but all of them come from the world. [17]The world and everything that people want in it are passing away, but the person who does what God wants lives forever.

Reject the Enemies of Christ

[18]My dear children, these are the last days. You have heard that the enemy of Christ is coming, and now many enemies of Christ are already here. This is how we know that these are the last days. [19]These enemies of Christ were in our fellowship, but they left us. They never really belonged to us; if they had been a part of us, they would have stayed with us. But they left, and this shows that none of them really belonged to us.

[20]You have the gift[n] that the Holy One gave you, so you all know the truth.[n] [21]I do not write to you because you do not know the truth but because you do know the truth. And you know that no lie comes from the truth.

[22]Who is the liar? It is the person who does not accept Jesus as the Christ. This is the enemy of Christ: the person who does not accept the Father and his Son. [23]Whoever does not accept the Son does not have the Father. But whoever confesses the Son has the Father, too.

[24]Be sure you continue to follow the teaching you heard from the beginning. If you continue to follow what you heard from the beginning, you will stay in the Son and in the Father. [25]And this is what the Son promised to us—life forever.

[26]I am writing this letter about those people who are trying to lead you the wrong way. [27]Christ gave you a special gift that is still in you, so you do not need any other teacher. His gift teaches you about everything, and it is true, not false. So continue to live in Christ, as his gift taught you.

[28]Yes, my dear children, live in him so that when Christ comes back, we can be without fear and not be ashamed in his presence. [29]Since you know that Christ is righteous, you know that all who do right are God's children.

2:9 light Here, it is used as a symbol of God's goodness or truth. **2:20 gift** This might mean the Holy Spirit, or it might mean teaching or truth as in verse 24. **2:20 you . . . truth** Some Greek copies read "so you know all things."

1 John 3:2–3

Don't you love it when an intense, gripping movie has a particularly powerful ending? Maybe you were shocked at the unveiling of someone's secret identity or touched at how sincerely two of the characters extended selfless love to one another. You can't help but tell your friends all the ways the story delighted you, from the exciting plotline to the fantastic ending, and how watching it was an altogether wonderful experience.

Your life is kind of like a story that God's writing—and you can count on it having the best ending you've ever seen! While we don't have all the specific details, we know that someday, Jesus will return. When he does, we'll finally see him "as he really is" (1 John 3:2). And that's not all. When we see him, we'll actually become like him—pure and holy.

With these kinds of promises to look forward to, there's no question that it'll be more than worth it to spend your life serving Jesus and obeying God. Even if you have trouble seeing the big picture in your life, hold on to the truth that heaven is your destination. With an ending like that, you can be sure that your life story will be perfectly astounding!

We Are God's Children

3 The Father has loved us so much that we are called children of God. And we really are his children. The reason the people in the world do not know us is that they have not known him. [2]Dear friends, now we are children of God, and we have not yet been shown what we will be in the future. But we know that when Christ comes again, we will be like him, because we will see him as he really is. [3]Christ is pure, and all who have this hope in Christ keep themselves pure like Christ.

[4]The person who sins breaks God's law. Yes, sin is living against God's law. [5]You know that Christ came to take away sins and that there is no sin in Christ. [6]So anyone who lives in Christ does not go on sinning. Anyone who goes on sinning has never really understood Christ and has never known him.

[7]Dear children, do not let anyone lead you the wrong way. Christ is righteous. So to be like Christ a person must do what is right. [8]The devil has been sinning since the beginning, so anyone who continues to sin belongs to the devil. The Son of God came for this purpose: to destroy the devil's work.

[9]Those who are God's children do not continue sinning, because the new life from God remains in them. They are not able to go on sinning, because they have become children of God. [10]So we can see who God's children are and who the devil's children are: Those who do not do what is right are not God's children, and those who do not love their brothers and sisters are not God's children.

We Must Love Each Other

[11]This is the teaching you have heard from the beginning: We must love each other. [12]Do not be like Cain who belonged to the Evil One and killed his brother. And why did he kill him? Because the things Cain did were evil, and the things his brother did were good.

[13]Brothers and sisters, do not be surprised when the people of the world hate you. [14]We know we have left death and have come into life because we love each other. Whoever does not love is still dead. [15]Everyone who hates a brother or sister is a murderer,[n] and you know that no murderers have eternal life in them. [16]This is how we know what real love is: Jesus gave his life for us. So we should give our lives for our brothers and sisters. [17]Suppose someone has enough to live and sees a brother or sister in need, but does not help. Then God's love is not living in that person. [18]My children, we should love people not only with words and talk, but by our actions and true caring.

[19-20]This is the way we know that we belong to the way of truth. When our hearts make us feel guilty, we can still have peace before God. God is greater than our hearts, and he knows everything. [21]My dear friends, if our hearts do not make us feel guilty, we can come without fear into God's presence. [22]And God gives us what we ask for because we obey God's commands and do what pleases him. [23]This is what God commands: that we believe in his Son, Jesus Christ, and that we love each other, just as he commanded. [24]The people who obey God's commands live in God, and God lives in them. We know that God lives in us because of the Spirit God gave us.

Warning Against False Teachers

4 My dear friends, many false prophets have gone out into the world. So do not believe every spirit, but test the spirits to see if they are from God. [2]This is how you can know God's Spirit: Every spirit who confesses that Jesus Christ

3:15 Everyone . . . murderer If one person hates a brother or sister, then in the heart that person has killed that brother or sister. Jesus taught about this sin to his followers (Matthew 5:21–26).

Here I am! I stand at the door and knock.
If you hear my voice and open the door,
I will come in and eat with you,
and you will eat with me.
—Revelation 3:20
november
1
Daylight Saving Time ends on the 1st Sunday of November—fall back 1 hour!
2
3
Don't forget to vote—it's Election Day!
4
It's Good Nutrition Month. Add more veggies to your diet.
5
Budget your Christmas shopping so you don't overspend.
6
Read the Book of 3 John this week. Share what you learn with a friend.
7
8
Buy a map as a reference for when you pray for people around the world.
9
Today is Martin Luther's birthday. Read a book about him.
10
It's Veterans' Day. Write a thank-you note to a veteran you know.
11
12
Pull out an old diary to see how much you've grown spiritually!
13
14
Research a place you'd like to visit one day.
15
16
17
Pray for a person of influence: it's Owen Wilson's birthday.
18
Encourage a co-worker this week.
19
Buy yourself fresh flowers today!
20
Sing a song of praise to God.
21
22
Don't forget to bathe your pet before the holidays!
23
24
Volunteer at a local food bank.
25
26
The 4th Thursday of November is Thanksgiving. What are you thankful for?
27
28
29
Toss and replace any old nail polish.
30

Women & Men of the BIBLE

Paul: Missionary Pastor

After Paul saw the light along the road to Damascus, he devoted his life to helping others find Christ, too. He was a missionary, traveling the ancient world telling everyone about Jesus. He started churches all along the way and sent back letters encouraging them to keep growing in their faith. An astute student of God's Word, Paul was a theological genius. His teachings helped define and clarify the unity between the Old and New Testaments and the path to salvation. Above all, Paul loved Christ with all of his heart and his fellow man with godly passion. (Acts; Romans; The Epistles)

came to earth as a human is from God. [3]And every spirit who refuses to say this about Jesus is not from God. It is the spirit of the enemy of Christ, which you have heard is coming, and now he is already in the world.

[4]My dear children, you belong to God and have defeated them; because God's Spirit, who is in you, is greater than the devil, who is in the world. [5]And they belong to the world, so what they say is from the world, and the world listens to them. [6]But we belong to God, and those who know God listen to us. But those who are not from God do not listen to us. That is how we know the Spirit that is true and the spirit that is false.

Love Comes from God

[7]Dear friends, we should love each other, because love comes from God. Everyone who loves has become God's child and knows God. [8]Whoever does not love does not know God, because God is love. [9]This is how God showed his love to us: He sent his one and only Son into the world so that we could have life through him. [10]This is what real love is: It is not our love for God; it is God's love for us. He sent his Son to die in our place to take away our sins.

[11]Dear friends, if God loved us that much we also should love each other. [12]No one has ever seen God, but if we love each other, God lives in us, and his love is made perfect in us.

[13]We know that we live in God and he lives in us, because he gave us his Spirit. [14]We have seen and can testify that the Father sent his Son to be the Savior of the world. [15]Whoever confesses that Jesus is the Son of God has God living inside, and that person lives in God. [16]And so we know the love that God has for us, and we trust that love.

God is love. Those who live in love live in God, and God lives in them. [17]This is how love is made perfect in us: that we can be without fear on the day God judges us, because in this world we are like him. [18]Where God's love is, there is no fear, because God's perfect love drives out fear. It is punishment that makes a person fear, so love is not made perfect in the person who fears.

[19]We love because God first loved us. [20]If people say, "I love God," but hate their brothers or sisters, they are liars. Those who do not love their brothers and sisters, whom they have seen, cannot love God, whom they have never seen. [21]And God gave us this command: Those who love God must also love their brothers and sisters.

Faith in the Son of God

5 Everyone who believes that Jesus is the Christ is God's child, and whoever loves the Father also loves the Father's children. [2]This is how we know we love God's children: when we love God and obey his commands. [3]Loving God means obeying his commands. And God's commands are not too hard for us, [4]because everyone who is a child of God conquers the world. And this is the victory that conquers the world—our faith. [5]So the one who conquers the world is the person who believes that Jesus is the Son of God.

[6]Jesus Christ is the One who came by water[n] and blood.[n] He did not come by

Unique You

Think about your very best feature. Do people tell you how beautiful your eyes are? Do you constantly get compliments about your smile? Now think about your least favorite attribute. Do you wish you had a smaller nose or better hair? No doubt, everyone has some things they like and don't like about themselves. But did you know that before you were ever born, your Creator formed you as a one-of-a-kind, original design? Psalm 139:13–16 says so! He loves your eyes and your nose and your hair...and every little thing about you. He wouldn't change your features for anything.

5:6 water This probably means the water of Jesus' baptism. **5:6 blood** This probably means the blood of Jesus' death.

water only, but by water and blood. And the Spirit says that this is true, because the Spirit is the truth. 7So there are three witnesses:n 8the Spirit, the water, and the blood; and these three witnesses agree. 9We believe people when they say something is true. But what God says is more important, and he has told us the truth about his own Son. 10Anyone who believes in the Son of God has the truth that God told us. Anyone who does not believe makes God a liar, because that person does not believe what God told us about his Son. 11This is what God told us: God has given us eternal life, and this life is in his Son. 12Whoever has the Son has life, but whoever does not have the Son of God does not have life.

We Have Eternal Life Now

13I write this letter to you who believe in the Son of God so you will know you have eternal life. 14And this is the boldness we have in God's presence: that if we ask God for anything that agrees with what he wants, he hears us. 15If we know he hears us every time we ask him, we know we have what we ask from him.

16If anyone sees a brother or sister sinning (sin that does not lead to eternal death), that person should pray, and God will give the sinner life. I am talking about people whose sin does not lead to eternal death. There is sin that leads to death. I do not mean that a person should pray about that sin. 17Doing wrong is always sin, but there is sin that does not lead to eternal death.

18We know that those who are God's children do not continue to sin. The Son of God keeps them safe, and the Evil One cannot touch them. 19We know that we belong to God, but the Evil One controls the whole world. 20We also know that the Son of God has come and has given us understanding so that we can know the True One. And our lives are in the True One and in his Son, Jesus Christ. He is the true God and the eternal life.

21So, dear children, keep yourselves away from false gods.

5:7–8 So . . . witnesses A few very late Greek copies and the Latin Vulgate continue, "in heaven: the Father, the Word, and the Holy Spirit, and these three witnesses agree. 8And there are three witnesses on earth:"

1 John

Living a Life of Love

Love. It's everywhere. Turn on the radio, go to a movie, open a book—it's there. Though our lives are saturated with love, most of us don't really know true love. But John did, and it's not surprising, considering he had observed Jesus at work in the world. He saw him befriend the rejected, heal the sick, sacrifice his own life—the most powerful illustrations of love the world has ever seen. John had a deep, firsthand understanding of Jesus' love for us, and in this letter, he shares the depth of his knowledge.

The purpose of John's letter is to reassure believers that their relationship with God is real. If you know God, John says, you will love God, obey his commands, and love others like Jesus loves you. Love is the distinguishing mark of a true believer—and also of God himself. In fact, God *is* love (1 John 4:16).

Throughout history, God has been proving his love. Because of it, he brought his people out of slavery, sent Jesus, and calls us his children. When Jesus was asked to pinpoint the greatest commandment, he replied that it is to love God and others. So love is vital for believers; if we claim to love God, we *must* love each other.

When we begin to grasp the radical love God has shown us, especially through the sacrifice of Jesus, that same kind of love will naturally flow from our own hearts—unconditionally, sacrificially, and unashamedly.

Get Real

First John 3:16 says that we should love like Jesus loved. How did Jesus love people? (John 15:13; Philippians 2:6–8)

How does it make you feel to know that you are a child of God? (John 1:12; Romans 8:14–17)

Is there any sin in your life that you have not confessed to God? (Micah 7:18–20; Hebrews 10:22–23)

What can you do today to allow the love of God to shine through you? (Matthew 5:13–16)

2 john

Things aren't always what they seem. How often have you totally underestimated someone based on your first impressions? It's easy to do.

Jesus was definitely the most underestimated person in history. He *looked* like a regular guy, but in spite of his humble appearance, he was (and is) God! But some people thought this was nonsense. So John penned this short letter to reaffirm that Jesus was both entirely human and entirely divine. His words combated the false teachers who were actively spreading lies that Jesus only *looked* like a human . . . or that God had just used a human body, like a hand wearing a glove.

God didn't merely "possess" a human body temporarily—he actually *became a human*. The wonderful truth is that Jesus enjoyed the full experience of humanity: he ate, got worn out, fought temptations, felt pain and joy . . . all the things that we experience! Yet he is completely and thoroughly divine, the Lord of lords and King of kings.

Avoid underestimating who Christ is. In fact, you could never *over*estimate his wonderful perfection and beauty! Don't forget to give him the honor and glory that he deserves as our Savior and God. But also remember that you can confidently cling to his merciful grace and kindness—he understands your humanity!

[1]From the Elder.[n]

To the chosen lady[n] and her children:

I love all of you in the truth,[n] and all those who know the truth love you. [2]We love you because of the truth that lives in us and will be with us forever.

[3]Grace, mercy, and peace from God the Father and his Son, Jesus Christ, will be with us in truth and love.

[4]I was very happy to learn that some of your children are following the way of truth, as the Father commanded us. [5]And now, dear lady, this is not a new command but is the same command we have had from the beginning. I ask you that we all love each other. [6]And love means living the way God commanded us to live. As you have heard from the beginning, his command is this: Live a life of love.

[7]Many false teachers are in the world now who do not confess that Jesus Christ came to earth as a human. Anyone who does not confess this is a false teacher and an enemy of Christ. [8]Be careful yourselves that you do not lose everything you[n] have worked for, but that you receive your full reward.

[9]Anyone who goes beyond Christ's teaching and does not continue to follow only his teaching does not have God. But whoever continues to follow the teaching of Christ has both the Father and the Son. [10]If someone comes to you and does not bring this teaching, do not welcome or accept that person into your house. [11]If you welcome such a person, you share in the evil work.

[12]I have many things to write to you, but I do not want to use paper and ink. Instead, I hope to come to you and talk face to face so we can be full of joy. [13]The children of your chosen sister[n] greet you.

1 Elder "Elder" means an older person. It can also mean a special leader in the church (as in Titus 1:5). **1 lady** This might mean a woman, or in this letter it might mean a church. If it is a church, then "her children" would be the people of the church. **1 truth** The truth or "Good News" about Jesus Christ that joins all believers together. **8 you** Some Greek copies read "we." **13 sister** Sister of the "lady" in verse 1. This might be another woman or another church.

Love the Truth, Lose the Liars

The subject of love runs through all of John's writings, and this letter is no exception. He begins by telling the chosen lady and her children of his love for all who walk in the truth of God's salvation. In fact, that truth gives him the ability to love others with God's love.

God commanded us to live a life of love. Loving God means rejecting anything that distorts his truth, which explains John's command about not welcoming false teachers. It might not sound very loving, but John had seen how truth can be twisted very subtly into lies. Those lies are like poison to a person's soul. Christians who don't guard their faith against false teachings are especially vulnerable to Satan's trickery.

The Christian life is a heart commitment and a lifestyle that carries over into eternity. How we live today in a world that needs Christ affects our "full reward" (2 John 8). Do your words and actions draw others to Jesus?

Souls are at stake today, just as they were in John's era, and Christians have a responsibility to guard God's truth for ourselves and others. We need to keep learning God's Word so we don't get pulled away from him.

The strength of your faith will always be directly connected to your close relationship with Jesus. And you can get to know him by being a serious student of the Bible!

Get Real

What do Paul and Peter's words reveal about truth? (1 Corinthians 13:6; Colossians 1:4–6)

What do Jesus' own words tell you about truth? (John 8:31–32; 18:37)

Truth comes from God. Where do lies come from? (John 8:44)

How can you guard yourself against falling away from God's truth? (Galatians 5:7–8; 1 Timothy 6:20)

As other Christians strive to grow in their faith, how do you help or hinder them? (Ephesians 4:13–16; 2 Thessalonians 3:1–2)

3 john

Whether you're a bit of an introvert or a total "people person," you probably appreciate it when someone reaches out to you and invites you over for dinner or coffee. Or better yet, maybe you've discovered the joys of opening your own home to others—nothing's quite as satisfying as taking time to show someone else you care! But being hospitable isn't just about social etiquette. Did you know that sharing your home and food with other people is more than just a nice thing to do—it's actually commanded in Scripture?

In this tiny letter, John commends Gaius for offering hospitality to traveling missionaries. John says that by his hospitality, Gaius was sharing in the work of the missionaries. When you follow Gaius's lead and take care of other Christians' physical needs, you're actually taking part in the spiritual work *they* are doing! The normal, everyday things we do are potential spiritual acts of worship toward God.

Commit yourself to the simple work of hospitality—share your resources with anyone who's in need. And know that these acts of service, in addition to being a great witness for the Good News, are essential aspects of worshiping and honoring God with your life.

[1]From the Elder.[n]

To my dear friend Gaius, whom I love in the truth:[n]

[2]My dear friend, I know your soul is doing fine, and I pray that you are doing well in every way and that your health is good. [3]I was very happy when some brothers and sisters came and told me about the truth in your life and how you are following the way of truth. [4]Nothing gives me greater joy than to hear that my children are following the way of truth.

[5]My dear friend, it is good that you help the brothers and sisters, even those you do not know. [6]They told the church about your love. Please help them to continue their trip in a way worthy of God. [7]They started out in service to Christ, and they have been accepting nothing from nonbelievers. [8]So we should help such people; when we do, we share in their work for the truth.

[9]I wrote something to the church, but Diotrephes, who loves to be their leader, will not listen to us. [10]So if I come, I will talk about what Diotrephes is doing, about how he lies and says evil things about us. But more than that, he refuses to accept the other brothers and sisters; he even stops those who do want to accept them and puts them out of the church.

[11]My dear friend, do not follow what is bad; follow what is good. The one who does good belongs to God. But the one who does evil has never known God.

[12]Everyone says good things about Demetrius, and the truth agrees with what they say. We also speak well of him, and you know what we say is true.

[13]I have many things I want to write you, but I do not want to use pen and ink. [14]I hope to see you soon and talk face to face. [15]Peace to you. The friends here greet you. Please greet each friend there by name.

1 Elder "Elder" means an older person. It can also mean a special leader in the church (as in Titus 1:5). **1 truth** The truth or "Good News" about Jesus Christ that joins all believers together.

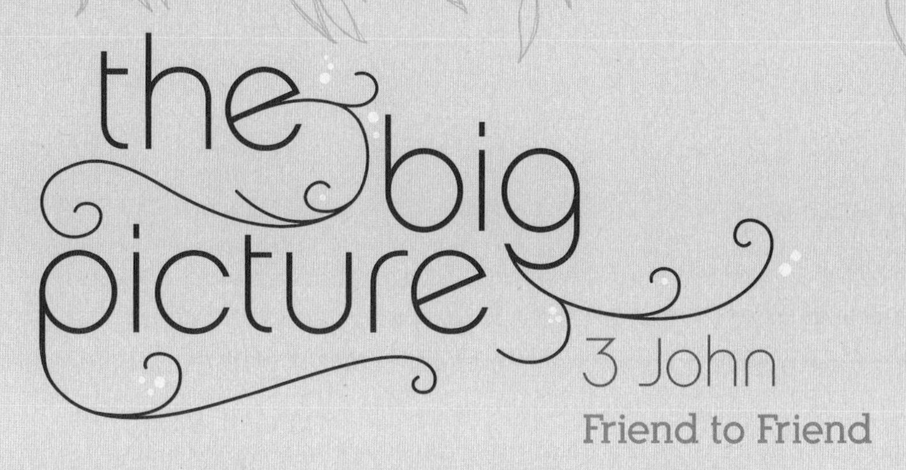

Friend to Friend

John and Gaius shared a strong faith in Jesus that showed in their friendship and in their love for others. In this brief letter, John sent Gaius a word of approval for welcoming and caring for traveling brothers and sisters in Christ.

John also wrote about leadership, warning against prideful leaders, like Diotrephes, who were more concerned about their own power than about serving God. Those leaders hinder the faith of their followers, making themselves into minigods instead of pointing to the real God of love and grace.

The Book of 3 John reminds us that we have a responsibility to care for each other as God's servants. Just as we have each been entrusted with God's Word (1 Timothy 4:6; 6:20–21), we've also been called to be a part of the body of Christ here on earth (Ephesians 4:4–6). We're called to encourage each other and work as a team to spread the Good News. After all, we're united by the same one and only God, and we live to share his love with the world.

This little letter highlights the importance of encouraging others, supporting the church, and practicing wise leadership. Just as the size of this letter doesn't limit its value, each small act of love you do for your Christian brothers and sisters ruins Satan's plans and increases the effectiveness of God's church.

Get Real

What does Romans 15:1–7 say to you about the timelessness of God's Word and about our relationships with other Christians?

Read 1 Corinthians 8:1–3. What's more effective in building up a church–– knowledge or love?

What's your part in caring for Christian brothers and sisters? (Romans 12:4–8; 1 Corinthians 12:12—13:6)

What else can you do to strengthen God's church? (Galatians 5:13–15)

Like John, Paul was a great leader in the early church. What was his attitude about a leader's role? (1 Corinthians 3:1–11)

jude

It's pretty simple, really. We are saved by God's grace through faith in Christ. And once saved, we're called to change our ways. We may have been slaves to sin before, but we've been freed—completely freed from slavery to sin! But false teaching seems to persistently rear its ugly head and bring confusion to this straightforward Good News.

When Jude wrote this letter, false teachers had infiltrated the church and started saying that God's grace removes our responsibility to live pure lives. If we can't earn our salvation and God's grace covers our sin anyway, we can do whatever we want, right? Wrong! Jude wrote this short letter to put a stop to this evil thinking.

Just because God is merciful doesn't mean sin is no big deal to him—he sent his dear Son to pay the penalty for our sin with his own life! The twisted version of the Good News that Jude warns us about treats God's mercy like a rag for wiping our dirty hands. In reality, our salvation is a huge gift of indescribable value. And with this gift comes a new life . . . we're now called to honor God with everything we've got!

Let God's grace motivate you to turn your back on sin and live as his new creation.

[1]From Jude, a servant of Jesus Christ and a brother of James.

To all who have been called by God. God the Father loves you, and you have been kept safe in Jesus Christ:

[2]Mercy, peace, and love be yours richly.

God Will Punish Sinners

[3]Dear friends, I wanted very much to write you about the salvation we all share. But I felt the need to write you about something else: I want to encourage you to fight hard for the faith that was given the holy people of God once and for all time. [4]Some people have secretly entered your group. Long ago the prophets wrote about these people who will be judged guilty. They are against God and have changed the grace of our God into a reason for sexual sin. They also refuse to accept Jesus Christ, our only Master and Lord.

[5]I want to remind you of some things you already know: Remember that the Lord[n] saved his people by bringing them out of the land of Egypt. But later he destroyed all those who did not believe. [6]And remember the angels who did not keep their place of power but left their proper home. The Lord has kept these angels in darkness, bound with everlasting chains, to be judged on the great day. [7]Also remember the cities of Sodom and Gomorrah[n] and the other towns around them. In the same way they were full of sexual sin and people who desired sexual relations that God does not allow. They suffer the punishment of eternal fire, as an example for all to see.

[8]It is the same with these people who have entered your group. They are guided by dreams and make themselves filthy with sin. They reject God's authority and speak against the angels. [9]Not even the archangel[n] Michael, when he argued with the devil about who would have the body of Moses, dared to judge the devil guilty. Instead, he said, "The Lord punish you." [10]But these people speak against things they do not understand. And what they do know, by feeling, as dumb animals know things, are the very things that destroy them. [11]It will be terrible for them. They have followed the way of Cain, and for money they have given themselves to doing the wrong that Balaam did. They have fought against God as Korah

5 the Lord Some Greek copies read "Jesus." **7 Sodom and Gomorrah** Two cities God destroyed because they were so evil. **9 archangel** The leader among God's angels or messengers.

did, and like Korah, they surely will be destroyed. [12]They are like dirty spots in your special Christian meals you share. They eat with you and have no fear, caring only for themselves. They are clouds without rain, which the wind blows around. They are autumn trees without fruit that are pulled out of the ground. So they are twice dead. [13]They are like wild waves of the sea, tossing up their own shameful actions like foam. They are like stars that wander in the sky. A place in the blackest darkness has been kept for them forever.

[14]Enoch, the seventh descendant from Adam, said about these people: "Look, the Lord is coming with many thousands of his holy angels to [15]judge every person. He is coming to punish all who are against God for all the evil they have done against him. And he will punish the sinners who are against God for all the evil they have said against him."

[16]These people complain and blame others, doing the evil things they want to do. They brag about themselves, and they flatter others to get what they want.

A Warning and Things to Do

[17]Dear friends, remember what the apostles of our Lord Jesus Christ said before. [18]They said to you, "In the last times there will be people who laugh about God, following their own evil desires which are against God." [19]These are the people who divide you, people whose thoughts are only of this world, who do not have the Spirit.

[20]But dear friends, use your most holy faith to build yourselves up, praying in the Holy Spirit. [21]Keep yourselves in God's love as you wait for the Lord Jesus Christ with his mercy to give you life forever.

[22]Show mercy to some people who have doubts. [23]Take others out of the fire, and save them. Show mercy mixed with fear to others, hating even their clothes which are dirty from sin.

Praise God

[24]God is strong and can help you not to fall. He can bring you before his glory without any wrong in you and can give you great joy. [25]He is the only God, the One who saves us. To him be glory, greatness, power, and authority through Jesus Christ our Lord for all time past, now, and forever. Amen.

Jude

Making It Real, Making It Last

Once again, God gives us another reminder about staying on guard! Protecting your faith is important. This time the warning is from Jude, James's brother and Jesus' half brother. Jude started to write about salvation and continued to follow the Holy Spirit's promptings to address another critical issue.

Jude knew the people he was writing to were discovering firsthand just what it takes to remain faithful to Jesus. False teachers were an ongoing plague, and many believers were beginning to lose heart, wondering whether their faith was worth all the struggles. Jude sent this letter to encourage them to put their faith into action in every area of life.

If you were to summarize the Book of Jude in a phrase, you might say it's about *authentic faith*. Authentic faith means choosing daily—even hourly—to keep Jesus as your priority, despite confusing circumstances, bitter disappointments, powerful opposition, and endless temptations.

The Christian life isn't easy. Like the early Christians, you're surrounded by distractions that can derail your focus on God.

But . . .

"God is strong and can help you not to fall" (Jude 24). With God's help, you can make it. He's given you his Son to rescue you from sin, his Spirit to guide you, and his Word to equip you. Take Jude to heart as a mighty reminder that your life in Christ is worth everything!

Get Real

What freedoms do Christians have through Jesus? (John 8:34–36; Romans 6:15–23; 8:18–21)

What does *authentic faith* mean to you? (2 Corinthians 13:5–8)

How can troubles actually strengthen your faith? (James 1:2–5)

What do troubles prove about your faith? (1 Peter 1:7)

Read 1 Peter 1:5–6. Does it comfort you to know God protects your faith? How does he help you? (Romans 8:26–27; 2 Thessalonians 3:3)

revelation

Throughout the New Testament we get tiny glimpses of the future. Hints appear here and there about what to expect. We know at least this much: after the trials and pain and joy of serving God in this life, we'll spend eternity with Christ, praising God forever! God will finish the work that was started when we were saved, making us pure and complete. It's a glorious promise, and we can always be filled with life-changing hope because of it!

But John's vision in Revelation is by far the most extensive look at God's big plans for the future. A lot of the book is mysterious and pretty disturbing. Yet beyond its unsettling content, this book is primarily a message of hope and of God's great love for us.

Someday everything wrong will be made right. Sin will be obliterated and righteousness will prevail. Jesus will sit on his rightful throne. Satan will be utterly defeated. All creation will finally give God the glory and recognition he deserves!

As you read and study this book, know that God has a good plan for you and for this world. Take joy in knowing that evil will not last, and put your hope in God's amazing strength and perfect love.

John Tells About This Book

1 This is the revelation[n] of Jesus Christ, which God gave to him, to show his servants what must soon happen. And Jesus sent his angel to show it to his servant John, [2]who has told everything he has seen. It is the word of God; it is the message from Jesus Christ. [3]Blessed is the one who reads the words of God's message, and blessed are the people who hear this message and do what is written in it. The time is near when all of this will happen.

Jesus' Message to the Churches

[4]From John.

To the seven churches in Asia:

Grace and peace to you from the One who is and was and is coming, and from the seven spirits before his throne, [5]and from Jesus Christ. Jesus is the faithful witness, the first among those raised from the dead. He is the ruler of the kings of the earth.

He is the One who loves us, who made us free from our sins with the blood of his death. [6]He made us to be a kingdom of priests who serve God his Father. To Jesus Christ be glory and power forever and ever! Amen.

[7]Look, Jesus is coming with the clouds, and everyone will see him, even those who stabbed him. And all peoples of the earth will cry loudly because of him. Yes, this will happen! Amen.

[8]The Lord God says, "I am the Alpha and the Omega."[n] I am the One who is and was and is coming. I am the Almighty."

[9]I, John, am your brother. All of us share with Christ in suffering, in the kingdom, and in patience to continue. I was on the island of Patmos,[n] because I had preached the word of God and the message about Jesus. [10]On the Lord's day I was in the Spirit, and I heard a loud voice behind me that sounded like a trumpet. [11]The voice said, "Write what you see in a book and send it to the seven churches: to Ephesus, Smyrna,

1:1 revelation Making known truth that has been hidden. **1:8 Alpha and the Omega** The first and last letters of the Greek alphabet. This means "the beginning and the end."
1:9 Patmos A small island in the Aegean Sea, near the coast of Asia Minor (modern Turkey).

Pergamum, Thyatira, Sardis, Philadelphia, and Laodicea."

[12]I turned to see who was talking to me. When I turned, I saw seven golden lampstands [13]and someone among the lampstands who was "like a Son of Man."[n] He was dressed in a long robe and had a gold band around his chest. [14]His head and hair were white like wool, as white as snow, and his eyes were like flames of fire. [15]His feet were like bronze that glows hot in a furnace, and his voice was like the noise of flooding water. [16]He held seven stars in his right hand, and a sharp double-edged sword came out of his mouth. He looked like the sun shining at its brightest time.

[17]When I saw him, I fell down at his feet like a dead man. He put his right hand on me and said, "Do not be afraid. I am the First and the Last. [18]I am the One who lives; I was dead, but look, I am alive forever and ever! And I hold the keys to death and to the place of the dead. [19]So write the things you see, what is now and what will happen later. [20]Here is the secret of the seven stars that you saw in my right hand and the seven golden lampstands: The seven lampstands are the seven churches, and the seven stars are the angels of the seven churches.

To the Church in Ephesus

2 "Write this to the angel of the church in Ephesus:

"The One who holds the seven stars in his right hand and walks among the seven golden lampstands says this: [2]I know what you do, how you work hard and never give up. I know you do not put up with the false teachings of evil people. You have tested those who say they are apostles but really are not, and you found they are liars. [3]You have patience and have suffered troubles for my name and have not given up.

[4]"But I have this against you: You have left the love you had in the beginning. [5]So remember where you were before you fell. Change your hearts and do what you did at first. If you do not change, I will come to you and will take away your lampstand from its place. [6]But there is something you do that is right: You hate what the Nicolaitans[n] do, as much as I.

[7]"Every person who has ears should listen to what the Spirit says to the churches. To those who win the victory I will give the right to eat the fruit from the tree of life, which is in the garden of God.

To the Church in Smyrna

[8]"Write this to the angel of the church in Smyrna:

"The One who is the First and the Last, who died and came to life again, says this: [9]I know your troubles and that you are poor, but really you are rich! I know the bad things some people say about you. They say they are Jews, but they are not true Jews. They are a synagogue that belongs to Satan. [10]Do not be afraid of what you are about to suffer. I tell you, the devil will put some of you in prison to test you, and you will suffer for ten days. But be faithful, even if you have to die, and I will give you the crown of life.

[11]"Everyone who has ears should listen to what the Spirit says to the churches. Those who win the victory will not be hurt by the second death.

To the Church in Pergamum

[12]"Write this to the angel of the church in Pergamum:

"The One who has the sharp, double-edged sword says this: [13]I know where you live. It is where Satan has his throne. But you are true to me. You did not refuse to tell about your faith in me even during the

BECOME *Involved*

Soles4Souls

Are you a shoe girl? You know the type . . . you find an irresistible pair on sale and can't help but buy them—even if you have nothing that matches! You can always build a killer outfit from the bottom up, right? Well, that passion for fashion might just be your ticket to changing the world!

Soles4Souls is a nonprofit organization that facilitates the donation of shoes to impoverished and hurting people worldwide. Originally started as a relief ministry to the Asian Tsunami victims of 2004, Soles4Souls took a step closer to home after Hurricanes Katrina and Rita in 2005. Now they minister to those in need both in the United States and abroad.

Through an extensive network of business relationships, Soles4Souls provides a place for manufacturers and retailers to unload their customer returns, samples, and lightly worn footwear. Individuals and churches donate new and used shoes, too, and the resources are pooled to allow the distribution of hundreds of thousands of shoes every year.

You can put your own best foot forward by helping Soles4Souls collect shoes. Consider organizing a shoe drive at church or among friends. Or help raise money for worldwide shipping. Visit www.soles4souls.org for instructions on how you can put your fashion sense to work!

1:13 "like . . . Man" "Son of Man" is a name Jesus called himself. **2:6 Nicolaitans** This is the name of a religious group that followed false beliefs and ideas.

time of Antipas, my faithful witness who was killed in your city, where Satan lives.

[14]"But I have a few things against you: You have some there who follow the teaching of Balaam. He taught Balak how to cause the people of Israel to sin by eating food offered to idols and by taking part in sexual sins. [15]You also have some who follow the teaching of the Nicolaitans.[n] [16]So change your hearts and lives. If you do not, I will come to you quickly and fight against them with the sword that comes out of my mouth.

[17]"Everyone who has ears should listen to what the Spirit says to the churches.

"I will give some of the hidden manna to everyone who wins the victory. I will also give to each one who wins the victory a white stone with a new name written on it. No one knows this new name except the one who receives it.

To the Church in Thyatira

[18]"Write this to the angel of the church in Thyatira:

"The Son of God, who has eyes that blaze like fire and feet like shining bronze, says this: [19]I know what you do. I know about your love, your faith, your service, and your patience. I know that you are doing more now than you did at first.

[20]"But I have this against you: You let that woman Jezebel spread false teachings. She says she is a prophetess, but by her teaching she leads my people to take part in sexual sins and to eat food that is offered to idols. [21]I have given her time to change her heart and turn away from her sin, but she does not want to change. [22]So I will throw her on a bed of suffering. And all those who take part in adultery with her will suffer greatly if they do not turn away from the wrongs she does. [23]I will also kill her followers. Then all the churches will know I am the One who searches hearts and minds, and I will repay each of you for what you have done.

[24]"But others of you in Thyatira have not followed her teaching and have not learned what some call Satan's deep secrets. I say to you that I will not put any other load on you. [25]Only continue in your loyalty until I come.

[26]"I will give power over the nations to everyone who wins the victory and continues to be obedient to me until the end.

Revelation 3:19

Think of the top five things your parents did throughout your childhood that showed you how much they love you. There's a good chance "punishment" isn't on the list. As a kid, you probably weren't sitting in your room, grounded for a week, thinking what incredibly loving parents you had.

As adults, we all know that good parents will lovingly lay down the law with their children. If you're a parent or guardian, you're responsible to protect and care for that child. So you set up rules to keep him or her away from danger or trouble.

God is our heavenly Father. Like a loving and perfect parent, he's given us rules to guide how we live. And when we stray, he shows his love for us through correction and punishment. He'll use circumstances in our lives to keep us in line, not because he's cruel and bossy but because he loves us.

Even when we didn't appreciate our parents' discipline growing up, they deserved our respect. In the same way, God certainly deserves our trust in his judgment. Instead of resenting discipline from him, ask him to help you learn the deeper lesson. And thank him for loving you enough to keep you on the right track.

[27]'You will rule over them with an iron
rod,
as when pottery is broken into
pieces.' *Psalm 2:9*

[28]This is the same power I received from my Father. I will also give him the morning star. [29]Everyone who has ears should listen to what the Spirit says to the churches.

To the Church in Sardis

3 "Write this to the angel of the church in Sardis:

"The One who has the seven spirits and the seven stars says this: I know what you do. People say that you are alive, but really you are dead. [2]Wake up! Strengthen what you have left before it dies completely. I have found that what you are doing is less than what my God wants. [3]So do not forget what you have received and heard. Obey it, and change your hearts and lives. So you must wake up, or I will come like a thief, and you will not know when I will come to you. [4]But you have a few there in Sardis who have kept their clothes unstained, so they will walk with me and will wear white clothes, because they are worthy. [5]Those who win the victory will be dressed in white clothes like them. And I will not erase their names from the book of life, but I will say they belong to me before my Father and before his angels. [6]Everyone who has ears

2:15 Nicolaitans This is the name of a religious group that followed false beliefs and ideas.

QUIZ WHAT DOES YOUR LIVING SPACE SAY ABOUT YOU?

1. WHEN WAS YOUR BED LAST MADE?

- [] A. This morning of course!
- [] B. Last time I had company coming over
- [] C. I can't remember ever making my bed since I moved out on my own.

2. WHAT TAKES UP THE MOST SPACE ON YOUR DRESSER?

- [] A. Framed pictures
- [] B. Receipts, papers, or books
- [] C. Yesterday's outfit, newspaper, or dinner

3. WHERE DO YOU KEEP YOUR CLOTHES?

- [] A. Either in my closet and drawers or in the laundry hamper
- [] B. On top of the treadmill or some other piece of furniture
- [] C. Either in piles around the room, in the washer or dryer, or on the couch

4. WHAT IS THE PREVAILING COLOR SCHEME AROUND YOUR LIVING SPACE?

- [] A. Light colors or pastels
- [] B. Bright or bold colors
- [] C. Not sure—probably whatever color they were when I moved in

5. WHAT IS ON YOUR SOFA WHEN YOU'RE NOT RELAXING ON IT?

- [] A. Decorative throw pillows
- [] B. My favorite blanket or afghan
- [] C. My backpack, briefcase, purse, or whatever else was in my hand when I came home

SCORING:

Your living space is a reflection of many things—your personality, stage in life, and personal sense of style just to name a few. As you build your living space, remember to make your home a place where God is always honored.

IF YOU SCORED MOSTLY As, YOU ARE ONE ORGANIZED, TOGETHER WOMAN! You're smart, efficient, and meticulous. Try not to take life so seriously that you miss out on unplanned fun. Spontaneity is a spice of life!

IF YOU SCORED MOSTLY Bs, YOU ARE ONE CREATIVE, SASSY CHICK. You're fun, stylish, and adventurous. Try not to pack so much into life that you miss out on the rest you need. Time to relax is important for balance!

IF YOU SCORED MOSTLY Cs, YOU ARE ONE COOL, CRAZY CAT. You're easygoing, loveable, and the life of the party. Try not to be so nonchalant that people mistake you for uninterested. A genuine interest in life around you makes for deeper, more lasting connections!

LIFEISSUES

Contentment

Many women relate to being *mostly* happy, *kind of* joyful, and *sort of* peaceful. But since God promised abundant life, indescribable joy, and peace beyond understanding, why do we struggle with feeling content? How much is enough? If we look for contentment in the wrong places, we only grow more discontent. Nothing satisfies like Jesus because we're created to be truly satisfied only in him. God's Spirit in you is a well of abundance, a truth the apostle Paul discovered. He caps off his journey to contentment in Philippians 4 by saying it's all because of Christ. Some things never change!

should listen to what the Spirit says to the churches.

To the Church in Philadelphia

[7]"Write this to the angel of the church in Philadelphia:

"This is what the One who is holy and true, who holds the key of David, says. When he opens a door, no one can close it. And when he closes it, no one can open it. [8]I know what you do. I have put an open door before you, which no one can close. I know you have little strength, but you have obeyed my teaching and were not afraid to speak my name. [9]Those in the synagogue that belongs to Satan say they are Jews, but they are not true Jews; they are liars. I will make them come before you and bow at your feet, and they will know that I have loved you. [10]You have obeyed my teaching about not giving up your faith. So I will keep you from the time of trouble that will come to the whole world to test those who live on earth.

[11]"I am coming soon. Continue strong in your faith so no one will take away your crown. [12]I will make those who win the victory pillars in the temple of my God, and they will never have to leave it. I will write on them the name of my God and the name of the city of my God, the new Jerusalem,[n] that comes down out of heaven from my God. I will also write on them my new name. [13]Everyone who has ears should listen to what the Spirit says to the churches.

To the Church in Laodicea

[14]"Write this to the angel of the church in Laodicea:

"The Amen,[n] the faithful and true witness, the ruler of all God has made, says this: [15]I know what you do, that you are not hot or cold. I wish that you were hot or cold! [16]But because you are lukewarm—neither hot, nor cold—I am ready to spit you out of my mouth. [17]You say, 'I am rich, and I have become wealthy and do not need anything.' But you do not know that you are really miserable, pitiful, poor, blind, and naked. [18]I advise you to buy from me gold made pure in fire so you can be truly rich. Buy from me white clothes so you can be clothed and so you can cover your shameful nakedness. Buy from me medicine to put on your eyes so you can truly see.

[19]"I correct and punish those whom I love. So be eager to do right, and change your hearts and lives. [20]Here I am! I stand at the door and knock. If you hear my voice and open the door, I will come in and eat with you, and you will eat with me.

[21]"Those who win the victory will sit with me on my throne in the same way that I won the victory and sat down with my Father on his throne. [22]Everyone who has ears should listen to what the Spirit says to the churches."

John Sees Heaven

4 After the vision of these things I looked, and there before me was an open door in heaven. And the same voice that spoke to me before, that sounded like a trumpet, said, "Come up here, and I will show you what must happen after this." [2]Immediately I was in the Spirit, and before me was a throne in heaven, and someone was sitting on

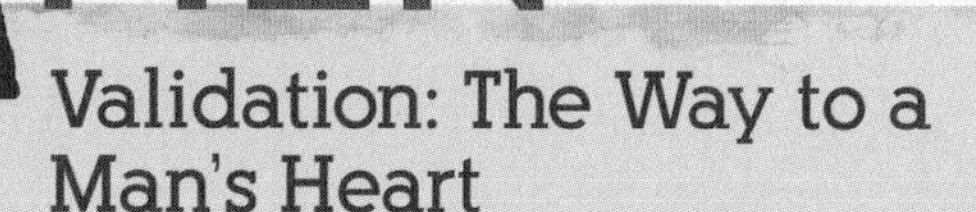

all about MEN

Validation: The Way to a Man's Heart

One of a guy's greatest needs is for validation, whether in his career, friendships, or love. If he doesn't hear positive responses to his efforts or feel valued as a man, he's in danger of emotional depletion. When it comes to romance, a guy needs to know he's capable of earning the respect of the woman he cares about. Saying you admire and appreciate him is good, but how much better to acknowledge his *specific* attributes and strengths! The apostle Paul wrote, "When you talk, do not say harmful things, but say what people need—words that will help others become stronger" (Ephesians 4:29). Is your vocabulary full of words that strengthen and validate your man?

3:12 Jerusalem This name is used to mean the spiritual city God built for his people. See Revelation 21–22. **3:14 Amen** Used here as a name for Jesus; it means to agree fully that something is true.

it. [3]The One who sat on the throne looked like precious stones, like jasper and carnelian. All around the throne was a rainbow the color of an emerald. [4]Around the throne there were twenty-four other thrones with twenty-four elders sitting on them. They were dressed in white and had golden crowns on their heads. [5]Lightning flashes and noises and thunder came from the throne. Before the throne seven lamps were burning, which are the seven spirits of God. [6]Also before the throne there was something that looked like a sea of glass, clear like crystal.

In the center and around the throne were four living creatures with eyes all over them, in front and in back. [7]The first living creature was like a lion. The second was like a calf. The third had a face like a man. The fourth was like a flying eagle. [8]Each of these four living creatures had six wings and was covered all over with eyes, inside and out. Day and night they never stop saying:

"Holy, holy, holy is the Lord God
Almighty.
He was, he is, and he is coming."

[9]These living creatures give glory, honor, and thanks to the One who sits on the throne, who lives forever and ever. [10]Then the twenty-four elders bow down before the One who sits on the throne, and they worship him who lives forever and ever. They put their crowns down before the throne and say:

[11]"You are worthy, our Lord and God,
to receive glory and honor and
power,
because you made all things.
Everything existed and was
made,
because you wanted it."

5

Then I saw a scroll in the right hand of the One sitting on the throne. The scroll had writing on both sides and was kept closed with seven seals. [2]And I saw a powerful angel calling in a loud voice, "Who is worthy to break the seals and open the scroll?" [3]But there was no one in heaven or on earth or under the earth who could open the scroll or look inside it. [4]I cried bitterly because there was no one who was worthy to open the scroll or look inside. [5]But one of the elders said to me, "Do not cry! The Lion[n] from the tribe of Judah, David's descendant, has won the victory so that he is able to open the scroll and its seven seals."

[6]Then I saw a Lamb standing in the center of the throne and in the middle of the four living creatures and the elders. The Lamb looked as if he had been killed. He had seven horns and seven eyes, which are the seven spirits of God that were sent into all the world. [7]The Lamb came and took the scroll from the right hand of the One sitting on the throne. [8]When he took the scroll, the four living creatures and the twenty-four elders bowed down before the Lamb. Each one of them had a harp and golden bowls full of incense, which are the prayers of God's holy people. [9]And they all sang a new song to the Lamb:

"You are worthy to take the scroll
and to open its seals,
because you were killed,
and with the blood of your death
you bought people for God
from every tribe, language,
people, and nation.
[10]You made them to be a kingdom of
priests for our God,
and they will rule on the earth."

[11]Then I looked, and I heard the voices of many angels around the throne, and the four living creatures, and the elders. There were thousands and thousands of angels, [12]saying in a loud voice:

"The Lamb who was killed is worthy
to receive power, wealth, wisdom, and
strength,
honor, glory, and praise!"

[13]Then I heard all creatures in heaven and on earth and under the earth and in the sea saying:

"To the One who sits on the throne
and to the Lamb
be praise and honor and glory and
power
forever and ever."

[14]The four living creatures said, "Amen," and the elders bowed down and worshiped.

6

Then I watched while the Lamb opened the first of the seven seals. I heard one of the four living creatures say with a voice like thunder, "Come!" [2]I looked, and there before me was a white horse. The rider on the horse held a bow, and he was given a crown, and he rode out, determined to win the victory.

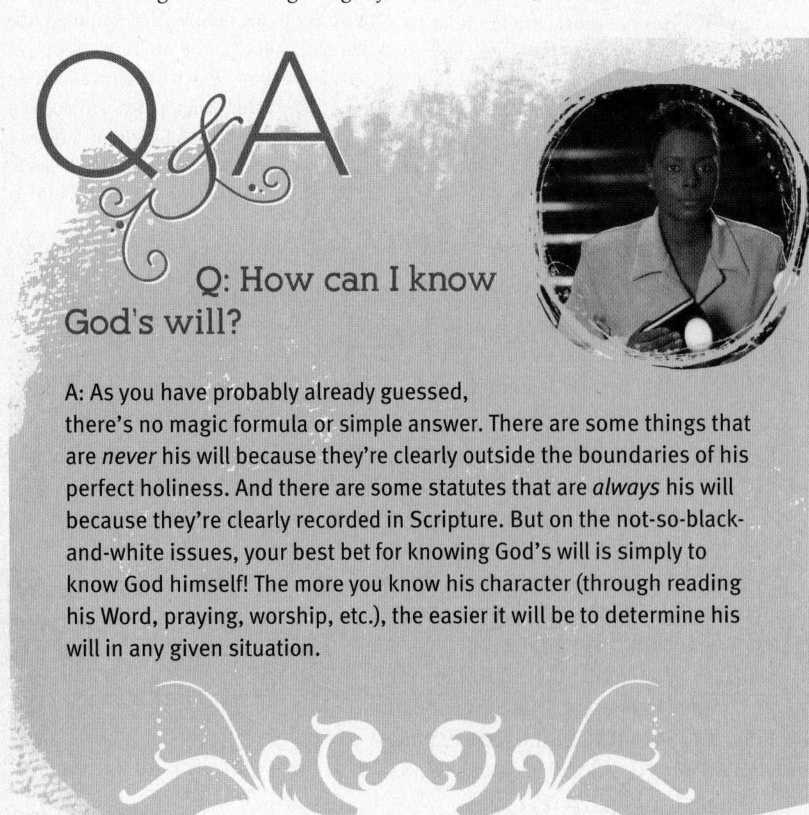

Q: How can I know God's will?

A: As you have probably already guessed, there's no magic formula or simple answer. There are some things that are *never* his will because they're clearly outside the boundaries of his perfect holiness. And there are some statutes that are *always* his will because they're clearly recorded in Scripture. But on the not-so-black-and-white issues, your best bet for knowing God's will is simply to know God himself! The more you know his character (through reading his Word, praying, worship, etc.), the easier it will be to determine his will in any given situation.

5:5 Lion Here refers to Christ.

[3]When the Lamb opened the second seal, I heard the second living creature say, "Come!" [4]Then another horse came out, a red one. Its rider was given power to take away peace from the earth and to make people kill each other, and he was given a big sword.

[5]When the Lamb opened the third seal, I heard the third living creature say, "Come!" I looked, and there before me was a black horse, and its rider held a pair of scales in his hand. [6]Then I heard something that sounded like a voice coming from the middle of the four living creatures. The voice said, "A quart of wheat for a day's pay, and three quarts of barley for a day's pay, and do not damage the olive oil and wine!"

[7]When the Lamb opened the fourth seal, I heard the voice of the fourth living creature say, "Come!" [8]I looked, and there before me was a pale horse. Its rider was named death, and Hades[n] was following close behind him. They were given power over a fourth of the earth to kill people by war, by starvation, by disease, and by the wild animals of the earth.

[9]When the Lamb opened the fifth seal, I saw under the altar the souls of those who had been killed because they were faithful to the word of God and to the message they had received. [10]These souls shouted in a loud voice, "Holy and true Lord, how long until you judge the people of the earth and punish them for killing us?" [11]Then each one of them was given a white robe and was told to wait a short time longer. There were still some of their fellow servants and brothers and sisters in the service of Christ who must be killed as they were. They had to wait until all of this was finished.

[12]Then I watched while the Lamb opened the sixth seal, and there was a great earthquake. The sun became black like rough black cloth, and the whole moon became red like blood. [13]And the stars in the sky fell to the earth like figs falling from a fig tree when the wind blows. [14]The sky disappeared as a scroll when it is rolled up, and every mountain and island was moved from its place.

[15]Then the kings of the earth, the rulers, the generals, the rich people, the powerful people, the slaves, and the free people hid themselves in caves and in the rocks on the mountains. [16]They called to the mountains and the rocks, "Fall on us. Hide us from the face of the One who sits on the throne and from the anger of the Lamb! [17]The great day for their anger has come, and who can stand against it?"

Revelation 6:9–10

Sometimes it seems like there are more injustices in this world than you can even count. It's likely you've heard reports of atrocities taking place across the world—severe poverty, widespread diseases, abandoned orphans, corrupt governments, human trafficking, genocide. The thought of so many people experiencing those things is truly more than we can bear.

In these verses, Christians who've paid the ultimate price to follow Jesus cry out for justice. They ask God, "How long before you deal out proper justice on earth?"

Does your heart ache for that, too? When you hear about innocent people suffering, do you call out to God asking, "How long will this go on?" You can be confident that God will make everything right someday. He is perfectly just. Every sin will be accounted for, and every evil person will pay the price for his or her sin.

But even as you long for justice, make sure you also thank God for his mercy and grace. God's justice requires that every sinner should die, but Christ's death paid our sin's penalty. By accepting that free gift, we're saved by grace from God's just anger over sin. Thank God for his mercy as you look forward to his perfect justice.

The 144,000 People of Israel

7 After the vision of these things I saw four angels standing at the four corners of the earth. The angels were holding the four winds of the earth to keep them from blowing on the land or on the sea or on any tree. [2]Then I saw another angel coming up from the east who had the seal of the living God. And he called out in a loud voice to the four angels to whom God had given power to harm the earth and the sea. [3]He said to them, "Do not harm the land or the sea or the trees until we mark with a sign the foreheads of the people who serve our God." [4]Then I heard how many people were marked with the sign. There were one hundred forty-four thousand from every tribe of the people of Israel.

[5]From the tribe of Judah twelve
thousand were marked with
the sign,
from the tribe of Reuben twelve
thousand,
from the tribe of Gad twelve
thousand,

6:8 **Hades** The unseen world of the dead.

virtue BUILDING: Self-Control

Did you know that apart from God you are a slave to sin? Lots of people resist Christianity because they think they'll have to give up their freedom. But the sad reality is that even though they may not realize it, they're already in bondage.

Self-control doesn't mean you're in charge of your own destiny . . . quite the opposite! Self-control is all about *submitting* control to the Holy Spirit and letting him live through you. When God saves you, you're not a slave to sinful desires anymore—you actually have the ability to do what's right! You can say no to sin and yes to the good things God wants you to do.

Do you have self-control? Or do you constantly give in to the pressures of sin and temptation, even though you wish that you could do what's right? The only way to overcome sin is to rely on God's Spirit to give you self-control.

Scripture Breakdown
Galatians 5:16–26 has great news about every believer's struggle against sin: you can triumph through the Holy Spirit! As these verses explain, self-control is a fruit (or result) of the Spirit working in you. Paul understood how difficult the battle is (Romans 7:14–25), but he also affirmed that if your "thinking is controlled by the Spirit, there is life and peace" (8:6). Romans 8 is an amazing description of a Spirit-filled life. For more thoughts on self-control, read these verses: Proverbs 23:23; 1 Thessalonians 4:1–5, 5:5–11; 2 Timothy 1:7; and 1 Peter 1:13–15.

Build It into Your Life
- How do you think self-control and purity (having a heart that's free from sin) are related?
- Practice discipline to build self-control: study God's Word daily, begin each day with a decision to do what's right, and purposefully make prayer your first—not last—resort.
- Self-control begins in your mind, so think about things that are good and right. If you let your mind wander aimlessly, there's a good chance you'll drift into sinful territory. Control your thoughts!
- Self-control means doing what's right—even (and especially) if you don't feel like it.

[6]from the tribe of Asher twelve
thousand,
from the tribe of Naphtali twelve
thousand,
from the tribe of Manasseh twelve
thousand,
[7]from the tribe of Simeon twelve
thousand,
from the tribe of Levi twelve
thousand,
from the tribe of Issachar twelve
thousand,
[8]from the tribe of Zebulun twelve
thousand,
from the tribe of Joseph twelve
thousand,
and from the tribe of Benjamin
twelve thousand were marked
with the sign.

The Great Crowd Worships God

[9]After the vision of these things I looked, and there was a great number of people, so many that no one could count them. They were from every nation, tribe, people, and language of the earth. They were all standing before the throne and before the Lamb, wearing white robes and holding palm branches in their hands. [10]They were shouting in a loud voice, "Salvation belongs to our God, who sits on the throne, and to the Lamb." [11]All the angels were standing around the throne and the elders and the four living creatures. They all bowed down on their faces before the throne and worshiped God, [12]saying, "Amen! Praise, glory, wisdom, thanks, honor, power, and strength belong to our God forever and ever. Amen!"

[13]Then one of the elders asked me, "Who are these people dressed in white robes? Where did they come from?"

[14]I answered, "You know, sir."

And the elder said to me, "These are the people who have come out of the great distress. They have washed their robes[n] and made them white in the blood of the Lamb. [15]Because of this, they are before the throne of God. They worship him day and night in his temple. And the One who sits on the throne will be present with them. [16]Those people will never be hungry again, and they will never be thirsty again. The sun will not hurt them, and no heat will burn them, [17]because the Lamb at the center of the throne will be their shepherd. He will lead them to springs of water that give life. And God will wipe away every tear from their eyes."

The Seventh Seal

8 When the Lamb opened the seventh seal, there was silence in heaven for about half an hour. [2]And I saw the seven angels who stand before God and to whom were given seven trumpets.

[3]Another angel came and stood at the altar, holding a golden pan for incense. He was given much incense to offer with the prayers of all God's holy people. The angel

7:14 washed their robes This means they believed in Jesus so that their sins could be forgiven by Christ's blood.

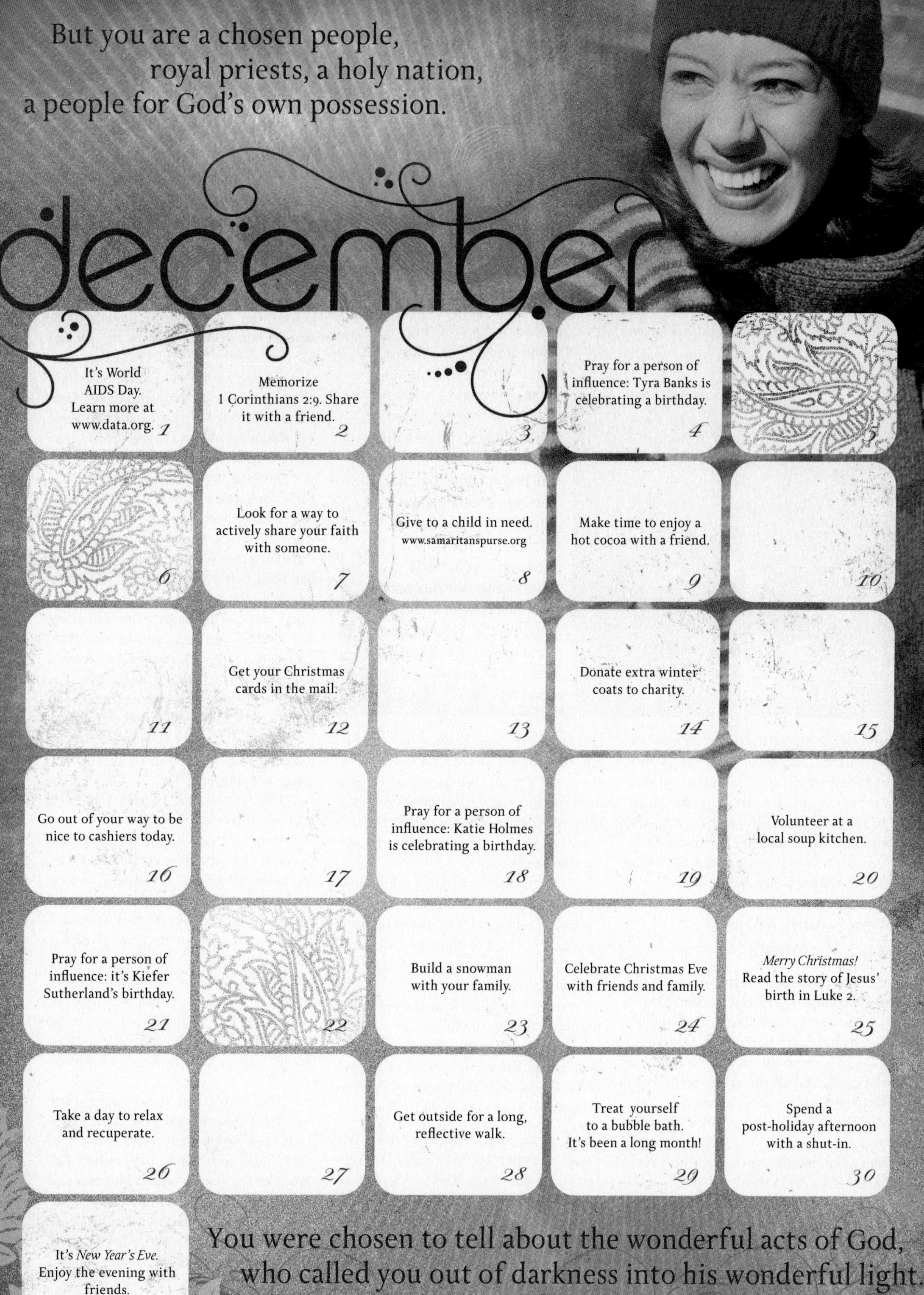

But you are a chosen people,
royal priests, a holy nation,
a people for God's own possession.
december
It's World AIDS Day. Learn more at www.data.org. 1
Memorize 1 Corinthians 2:9. Share it with a friend. 2
3
Pray for a person of influence: Tyra Banks is celebrating a birthday. 4
5
6
Look for a way to actively share your faith with someone. 7
Give to a child in need. www.samaritanspurse.org 8
Make time to enjoy a hot cocoa with a friend. 9
10
11
Get your Christmas cards in the mail. 12
13
Donate extra winter coats to charity. 14
15
Go out of your way to be nice to cashiers today. 16
17
Pray for a person of influence: Katie Holmes is celebrating a birthday. 18
19
Volunteer at a local soup kitchen. 20
Pray for a person of influence: it's Kiefer Sutherland's birthday. 21
22
Build a snowman with your family. 23
Celebrate Christmas Eve with friends and family. 24
Merry Christmas! Read the story of Jesus' birth in Luke 2. 25
Take a day to relax and recuperate. 26
27
Get outside for a long, reflective walk. 28
Treat yourself to a bubble bath. It's been a long month! 29
Spend a post-holiday afternoon with a shut-in. 30
It's New Year's Eve. Enjoy the evening with friends. 31
You were chosen to tell about the wonderful acts of God,
who called you out of darkness into his wonderful light.
—1 Peter 2:9

Answers to Prayer

Be Still & KNOW

God always answers every prayer. Guaranteed. The answer might not always be in the time frame you would like. And it may not be what you necessarily want to hear. But be assured—his answer will always come. Sometimes God will answer with a resounding "yes." Other times, he'll offer a firm "no." But there are times when his answer is simply "wait" or "not yet." Even then, you can be sure that he's hard at work making all things come together for your good (Romans 8:28). There are even times when he chooses to work in your heart and change the desire or request instead of answering directly. Let your heart rejoice that the Father is responding to your every prayer!

put this offering on the golden altar before the throne. [4]The smoke from the incense went up from the angel's hand to God with the prayers of God's people. [5]Then the angel filled the incense pan with fire from the altar and threw it on the earth, and there were flashes of lightning, thunder and loud noises, and an earthquake.

The Seven Angels and Trumpets

[6]Then the seven angels who had the seven trumpets prepared to blow them.

[7]The first angel blew his trumpet, and hail and fire mixed with blood were poured down on the earth. And a third of the earth, and all the green grass, and a third of the trees were burned up.

[8]Then the second angel blew his trumpet, and something that looked like a big mountain, burning with fire, was thrown into the sea. And a third of the sea became blood, [9]a third of the living things in the sea died, and a third of the ships were destroyed.

[10]Then the third angel blew his trumpet, and a large star, burning like a torch, fell from the sky. It fell on a third of the rivers and on the springs of water. [11]The name of the star is Wormwood.[n] And a third of all the water became bitter, and many people died from drinking the water that was bitter.

[12]Then the fourth angel blew his trumpet, and a third of the sun, and a third of the moon, and a third of the stars were struck. So a third of them became dark, and a third of the day was without light, and also the night.

[13]While I watched, I heard an eagle that was flying high in the air cry out in a loud voice, "Trouble! Trouble! Trouble for those who live on the earth because of the remaining sounds of the trumpets that the other three angels are about to blow!"

9 Then the fifth angel blew his trumpet, and I saw a star fall from the sky to the earth. The star was given the key to the deep hole that leads to the bottomless pit. [2]Then it opened up the hole that leads to the bottomless pit, and smoke came up from the hole like smoke from a big furnace. Then the sun and sky became dark because of the smoke from the hole. [3]Then locusts came down to the earth out of the smoke, and they were given the power to sting like scorpions.[n] [4]They were told not to harm the grass on the earth or any plant or tree. They could harm only the people who did not have the sign of God on their foreheads. [5]These locusts were not given the power to kill anyone, but to cause pain to the people for five months. And the pain they felt was like the pain a scorpion gives when it stings someone. [6]During those days people will look for a way to die, but they will not find it. They will want to die, but death will run away from them.

[7]The locusts looked like horses prepared for battle. On their heads they wore what looked like crowns of gold, and their faces looked like human faces. [8]Their hair was like women's hair, and their teeth were like lions' teeth. [9]Their chests looked like iron breastplates, and the sound of their wings was like the noise of many horses and chariots hurrying into battle. [10]The locusts had tails with stingers like scorpions, and in their tails was their power to hurt people for five months. [11]The locusts had a king who was the angel of the bottomless pit. His name in the Hebrew language is Abaddon and in the Greek language is Apollyon.[n]

[12]The first trouble is past; there are still two other troubles that will come.

[13]Then the sixth angel blew his trumpet, and I heard a voice coming from the horns on the golden altar that is before God. [14]The voice said to the sixth angel who had the trumpet, "Free the four angels who are tied at the great river Euphrates." [15]And they let loose the four angels who had been kept ready for this hour and day and month and year so they could kill a third of all people on the earth. [16]I heard how many troops on horses were in their army—two hundred million.

[17]The horses and their riders I saw in the vision looked like this: They had breastplates that were fiery red, dark blue, and yellow like sulfur. The heads of the horses looked like heads of lions, with fire, smoke, and sulfur coming out of their mouths. [18]A third of all the people on earth were killed by these three terrible disasters coming out of

8:11 Wormwood Name of a very bitter plant; used here to give the idea of bitter sorrow. **9:3 scorpions** A scorpion is an insect that stings with a bad poison. **9:11 Abaddon, Apollyon** Both names mean "Destroyer."

the horses' mouths: the fire, the smoke, and the sulfur. [19]The horses' power was in their mouths and in their tails; their tails were like snakes with heads, and with them they hurt people.

[20]The other people who were not killed by these terrible disasters still did not change their hearts and turn away from what they had made with their own hands. They did not stop worshiping demons and idols made of gold, silver, bronze, stone, and wood—things that cannot see or hear or walk. [21]These people did not change their hearts and turn away from murder or evil magic, from their sexual sins or stealing.

The Angel and the Small Scroll

10 Then I saw another powerful angel coming down from heaven dressed in a cloud with a rainbow over his head. His face was like the sun, and his legs were like pillars of fire. [2]The angel was holding a small scroll open in his hand. He put his right foot on the sea and his left foot on the land. [3]Then he shouted loudly like the roaring of a lion. And when he shouted, the voices of seven thunders spoke. [4]When the seven thunders spoke, I started to write. But I heard a voice from heaven say, "Keep hidden what the seven thunders said, and do not write them down."

[5]Then the angel I saw standing on the sea and on the land raised his right hand to heaven, [6]and he made a promise by the power of the One who lives forever and ever. He is the One who made the skies and all that is in them, the earth and all that is in it, and the sea and all that is in it. The angel promised, "There will be no more waiting! [7]In the days when the seventh angel is ready to blow his trumpet, God's secret will be finished. This secret is the Good News God told to his servants, the prophets."

[8]Then I heard the same voice from heaven again, saying to me: "Go and take the open scroll that is in the hand of the angel that is standing on the sea and on the land."

[9]So I went to the angel and told him to give me the small scroll. And he said to me, "Take the scroll and eat it. It will be sour in your stomach, but in your mouth it will be sweet as honey." [10]So I took the small scroll from the angel's hand and ate it. In my mouth it tasted sweet as honey, but after I ate it, it was sour in my stomach. [11]Then I was told, "You must prophesy again about many peoples, nations, languages, and kings."

The Two Witnesses

11 I was given a measuring stick like a rod, and I was told, "Go and measure the temple of God and the altar, and count the people worshiping there. [2]But do not measure the yard outside the temple. Leave it alone, because it has been given to those who are not God's people. And they will trample on the holy city for forty-two months. [3]And I will give power to my two witnesses to prophesy for one thousand two hundred sixty days, and they will be dressed in rough cloth to show their sadness."

[4]These two witnesses are the two olive trees and the two lampstands that stand before the Lord of the earth. [5]And if anyone tries to hurt them, fire comes from their mouths and kills their enemies. And if anyone tries to hurt them in whatever way, in that same way that person will die. [6]These witnesses have the power to stop the sky from raining during the time they are prophesying. And they have power to make the waters become blood, and they have power to send every kind of trouble to the earth as many times as they want.

[7]When the two witnesses have finished telling their message, the beast that comes up from the bottomless pit will fight a war against them. He will defeat them and kill them. [8]The bodies of the two witnesses will lie in the street of the great city where the Lord was killed. This city is named Sodom[n] and Egypt, which has a spiritual meaning. [9]Those from every race of people, tribe, language, and nation will look at the bodies of the two witnesses for three and one-half days, and they will refuse to bury them. [10]People who live on the earth will rejoice and be happy because these two are dead. They will send each other gifts, because these two prophets brought much suffering to those who live on the earth.

[11]But after three and one-half days, God put the breath of life into the two prophets again. They stood on their feet, and everyone who saw them became very afraid. [12]Then the two prophets heard a loud voice from heaven saying, "Come up here!" And they went up into heaven in a cloud as their enemies watched.

[13]In the same hour there was a great earthquake, and a tenth of the city was destroyed. Seven thousand people were killed in the earthquake, and those who did not die were very afraid and gave glory to the God of heaven.

[14]The second trouble is finished. Pay attention: The third trouble is coming soon.

The Seventh Trumpet

[15]Then the seventh angel blew his trumpet. And there were loud voices in heaven, saying:

Health
Moderation

There are all kinds of medical studies to prove that this or that food prevents this or that disease. But for every study promoting the latest "miracle" food, there's an opposing study that presents the negative effects of that same food. For example, we now know that dark chocolate contains antioxidants known to lower blood pressure. But we also know that most chocolate is laced with plenty of sugar, making it high in fat and calories—definitely not a health food. The key is moderation. A balanced diet with a *variety* of healthful foods is the best defense against disease.

11:8 Sodom City that God destroyed because the people were so evil.

RELATIONSHIPS

Right Next Door

Know that old saying, "Good fences make good neighbors"? Well surprise, surprise—Jesus had a different idea! He came to break down walls, not build them up. We all know people who require a wee bit extra grace to deal with. The only thing harder than living with them is living next to them! Sometimes distance is necessary, but if a troublemaking neighbor has you shopping for fencing supplies, consider whether Jesus might use you to break down walls and build unity. Ask him to help you stick to healthy boundaries while living out Luke 10:26–37.

"The power to rule the world now
belongs to our Lord and his Christ,
and he will rule forever and ever."

[16]Then the twenty-four elders, who sit on their thrones before God, bowed down on their faces and worshiped God. [17]They said:

"We give thanks to you, Lord God Almighty,
who is and who was,
because you have used your great power
and have begun to rule!
[18]The people of the world were angry,
but your anger has come.
The time has come to judge the dead,
and to reward your servants the prophets
and your holy people,
all who respect you, great and small.
The time has come to destroy those
who destroy the earth!"

[19]Then God's temple in heaven was opened. The Ark that holds the agreement God gave to his people could be seen in his temple. Then there were flashes of lightning, noises, thunder, an earthquake, and a great hailstorm.

The Woman and the Dragon

12 And then a great wonder appeared in heaven: A woman was clothed with the sun, and the moon was under her feet, and a crown of twelve stars was on her head. [2]She was pregnant and cried out with pain, because she was about to give birth. [3]Then another wonder appeared in heaven: There was a giant red dragon with seven heads and seven crowns on each head. He also had ten horns. [4]His tail swept a third of the stars out of the sky and threw them down to the earth. He stood in front of the woman who was ready to give birth so he could eat her baby as soon as it was born. [5]Then the woman gave birth to a son who will rule all the nations with an iron rod. And her child was taken up to God and to his throne. [6]The woman ran away into the desert to a place God prepared for her where she would be taken care of for one thousand two hundred sixty days.

[7]Then there was a war in heaven. Michael[n] and his angels fought against the dragon, and the dragon and his angels fought back. [8]But the dragon was not strong enough, and he and his angels lost their place in heaven. [9]The giant dragon was thrown down out of heaven. (He is that old snake called the devil or Satan, who tricks the whole world.) The dragon with his angels was thrown down to the earth.

[10]Then I heard a loud voice in heaven saying:

"The salvation and the power and the kingdom of our God
and the authority of his Christ have now come.
The accuser of our brothers and sisters,
who accused them day and night before our God,
has been thrown down.
[11]And our brothers and sisters defeated him
by the blood of the Lamb's death
and by the message they preached.
They did not love their lives so much
that they were afraid of death.
[12]So rejoice, you heavens
and all who live there!
But it will be terrible for the earth and the sea,
because the devil has come down to you!
He is filled with anger,
because he knows he does not have much time."

[13]When the dragon saw he had been thrown down to the earth, he hunted for

12:7 Michael The archangel—leader among God's angels or messengers (Jude 9).

the woman who had given birth to the son. [14]But the woman was given the two wings of a great eagle so she could fly to the place prepared for her in the desert. There she would be taken care of for three and one-half years, away from the snake. [15]Then the snake poured water out of its mouth like a river toward the woman so the flood would carry her away. [16]But the earth helped the woman by opening its mouth and swallowing the river that came from the mouth of the dragon. [17]Then the dragon was very angry at the woman, and he went off to make war against all her other children—those who obey God's commands and who have the message Jesus taught.

[18]And the dragon[n] stood on the seashore.

The Two Beasts

13 Then I saw a beast coming up out of the sea. It had ten horns and seven heads, and there was a crown on each horn. A name against God was written on each head. [2]This beast looked like a leopard, with feet like a bear's feet and a mouth like a lion's mouth. And the dragon gave the beast all of his power and his throne and great authority. [3]One of the heads of the beast looked as if it had been killed by a wound, but this death wound was healed. Then the whole world was amazed and followed the beast. [4]People worshiped the dragon because he had given his power to the beast. And they also worshiped the beast, asking, "Who is like the beast? Who can make war against it?"

[5]The beast was allowed to say proud words and words against God, and it was allowed to use its power for forty-two months. [6]It used its mouth to speak against God, against God's name, against the place where God lives, and against all those who live in heaven. [7]It was given power to make war against God's holy people and to defeat them. It was given power over every tribe, people, language, and nation. [8]And all who live on earth will worship the beast—all the people since the beginning of the world whose names are not written in the Lamb's book of life. The Lamb is the One who was killed.

[9]Anyone who has ears should listen:

[10]If you are to be a prisoner,
then you will be a prisoner.
If you are to be killed with the sword,
then you will be killed with the sword.

This means that God's holy people must have patience and faith.

[11]Then I saw another beast coming up out of the earth. It had two horns like a lamb, but it spoke like a dragon. [12]This beast stands before the first beast and uses the same power the first beast has. By this power it makes everyone living on earth worship the first beast, who had the death wound that was healed. [13]And the second beast does great miracles so that it even makes fire come down from heaven to earth while people are watching. [14]It fools those who live on earth by the miracles it has been given the power to do. It does these miracles to serve the first beast. The second beast orders people to make an idol to honor the first beast, the one that was wounded by the deadly sword but sprang to life again. [15]The second beast was given power to give life to the idol of the first one so that the idol could speak. And the second beast was given power to command all who will not worship the image of the beast to be killed. [16]The second beast also forced all people, small and great, rich and poor, free and slave, to have a mark on their right hand or on their forehead. [17]No one could buy or sell without this mark, which is the name of the beast or the number of its name.

Revelation 12:11

Sometimes criticism is purely constructive, aimed at steering you in the right direction. But some criticisms are meant to tear you down. How can you honestly sort out the legitimate criticism from the malicious accusations? The key is to really know who you are and where you stand.

One of the names the Bible gives to Satan is "the Accuser." It's a good name for him because that's exactly what he does. He loves to antagonize people by throwing out every lie you can imagine. He claims that people will always be worthless sinners who can't ever be close with God.

Like any good liar, Satan mixes his lies with truth. The Bible clearly says that without Jesus, we really are sinners who can never earn God's favor. But when God's grace takes over, everything changes. Jesus gives us his own righteous perfection, brings our dead hearts to life, and turns us into pure children of God!

If Jesus is in your life, his blood and the message of the Good News has already defeated Satan for you. Hold tightly onto God's promises. If you're God's child, standing under the righteousness of Christ, you're completely free from sin and death—no matter what the Accuser says!

12:18 the dragon Some Greek copies read "I."

[18]This takes wisdom. Let the one who has understanding find the meaning of the number, which is the number of a person. Its number is 666.[n]

The Song of the Saved

14 Then I looked, and there before me was the Lamb standing on Mount Zion.[n] With him were one hundred forty-four thousand people who had his name and his Father's name written on their foreheads. [2]And I heard a sound from heaven like the noise of flooding water and like the sound of loud thunder. The sound I heard was like people playing harps. [3]And they sang a new song before the throne and before the four living creatures and the elders. No one could learn the new song except the one hundred forty-four thousand who had been bought from the earth. [4]These are the ones who did not do sinful things with women, because they kept themselves pure. They follow the Lamb every place he goes. These one hundred forty-four thousand were bought from among the people of the earth as people to be offered to God and the Lamb. [5]They were not guilty of telling lies; they are without fault.

The Three Angels

[6]Then I saw another angel flying high in the air. He had the eternal Good News to preach to those who live on earth—to every nation, tribe, language, and people. [7]He preached in a loud voice, "Fear God and give him praise, because the time has come for God to judge all people. So worship God who made the heavens, and the earth, and the sea, and the springs of water."

[8]Then the second angel followed the first angel and said, "Ruined, ruined is the great city of Babylon! She made all the nations drink the wine of the anger of her adultery."

[9]Then a third angel followed the first two angels, saying in a loud voice: "If anyone worships the beast and his idol and gets the beast's mark on the forehead or on the hand, [10]that one also will drink the wine of God's anger, which is prepared with all its strength in the cup of his anger. And that person will be put in pain with burning sulfur before the holy angels and the Lamb. [11]And the smoke from their burning pain will rise forever and ever. There will be no rest, day or night, for those who worship the beast and his idol or who get the mark of his name." [12]This means God's holy people must be patient. They must obey God's commands and keep their faith in Jesus.

[13]Then I heard a voice from heaven saying, "Write this: Blessed are the dead who die from now on in the Lord."

The Spirit says, "Yes, they will rest from their hard work, and the reward of all they have done stays with them."

The Earth Is Harvested

[14]Then I looked, and there before me was a white cloud, and sitting on the white cloud was One who looked like a Son of Man.[n] He had a gold crown on his head and a sharp sickle[n] in his hand. [15]Then another angel came out of the temple and called out in a loud voice to the One who was sitting on the cloud, "Take your sickle and harvest from the earth, because the time to harvest has come, and the fruit of the earth is ripe." [16]So the One who was sitting on the cloud swung his sickle over the earth, and the earth was harvested.

[17]Then another angel came out of the temple in heaven, and he also had a sharp sickle. [18]And then another angel, who has power over the fire, came from the altar. This angel called to the angel with the

BECOME *Involved*

Priority Associates

The transition from school to work can be really hard for young adults. The constant struggle for balance and significance can be exhausting. Oftentimes, people will grapple with these difficult life issues in a vacuum, never realizing how common their plight actually is.

That's where Priority Associates steps in. A ministry of Campus Crusade for Christ, Priority Associates is a "network of creative and corporate professionals seeking to balance their professional, personal, and spiritual lives." They have a presence in dozens of cities nationwide and are constantly looking to expand their horizons with new groups. Their intent is to be a resource for young professionals by "providing opportunities to explore issues of success, personal leadership, and significance in a variety of venues."

Whether you are over the school-to-work hump or are right in the middle of transition, you can benefit by being involved with Priority Associates. A great way to get involved is by volunteering your time and energy to encourage and mentor peers. Perhaps you could even start a new network group in your own city if there is not one already. Log on to www.priorityassociates.org to find out how you can help this talented and passionate generation achieve professional and personal significance.

13:18 666 Some Greek copies read "616." **14:1 Mount Zion** Another name for Jerusalem; here meaning the spiritual city of God's people. **14:14 Son of Man** "Son of Man" is a name Jesus called himself. **14:14 sickle** A farming tool with a curved blade. It was used to harvest grain.

sharp sickle, saying, "Take your sharp sickle and gather the bunches of grapes from the earth's vine, because its grapes are ripe." [19]Then the angel swung his sickle over the earth. He gathered the earth's grapes and threw them into the great winepress of God's anger. [20]They were trampled in the winepress outside the city, and blood flowed out of the winepress as high as horses' bridles for a distance of about one hundred eighty miles.

The Last Troubles

15 Then I saw another wonder in heaven that was great and amazing. There were seven angels bringing seven disasters. These are the last disasters, because after them, God's anger is finished.

[2]I saw what looked like a sea of glass mixed with fire. All of those who had won the victory over the beast and his idol and over the number of his name were standing by the sea of glass. They had harps that God had given them. [3]They sang the song of Moses, the servant of God, and the song of the Lamb:

"You do great and wonderful things, *Psalm 111:2*
Lord God Almighty. *Amos 3:13*
Everything the Lord does is right and true, *Psalm 145:17*
King of the nations.[n]
[4]Everyone will respect you, Lord, *Jeremiah 10:7*
and will honor you.
Only you are holy.
All the nations will come
and worship you, *Psalm 86:9–10*
because the right things you have done
are now made known." *Deuteronomy 32:4*

[5]After this I saw that the temple (the Tent of the Agreement) in heaven was opened. [6]And the seven angels bringing the seven disasters came out of the temple. They were dressed in clean, shining linen and wore golden bands tied around their chests. [7]Then one of the four living creatures gave to the seven angels seven golden bowls filled with the anger of God, who lives forever and ever. [8]The temple was filled with smoke from the glory and the power of God, and no one could enter the temple until the seven disasters of the seven angels were finished.

The Bowls of God's Anger

16 Then I heard a loud voice from the temple saying to the seven angels, "Go and pour out the seven bowls of God's anger on the earth."

[2]The first angel left and poured out his bowl on the land. Then ugly and painful sores came upon all those who had the mark of the beast and who worshiped his idol.

[3]The second angel poured out his bowl on the sea, and it became blood like that of a dead man, and every living thing in the sea died.

[4]The third angel poured out his bowl on the rivers and the springs of water, and they became blood. [5]Then I heard the angel of the waters saying:

"Holy One, you are the One who is
and who was.
You are right to decide to punish
these evil people.
[6]They have poured out the blood of
your holy people and your prophets.
So now you have given them
blood to drink as they deserve."

[7]And I heard a voice coming from the altar saying:

"Yes, Lord God Almighty,
the way you punish evil people is
right and fair."

[8]The fourth angel poured out his bowl on the sun, and he was given power to burn the people with fire. [9]They were burned by the great heat, and they cursed the name of God, who had control over these disasters. But the people refused to change their hearts and lives and give glory to God.

[10]The fifth angel poured out his bowl on the throne of the beast, and darkness covered its kingdom. People gnawed their tongues because of the pain. [11]They also cursed the God of heaven because of their pain and the sores they had, but they refused to change their hearts and turn away from the evil things they did.

[12]The sixth angel poured out his bowl on the great river Euphrates so that the water in the river was dried up to prepare the way for the kings from the east

15:3 King . . . nations Some Greek copies read "King of the ages."

The Woman Who Touched Jesus: Healed by Faith

No one knows her name, but she demonstrated incredible faith. She knew if she could get to Jesus, he could heal her from the terrible bleeding that had plagued her for twelve years. No one else on earth could help; she was out of strength, out of money, and out of options. So in the middle of the street, with a multitude of people crowding all around, she reached out her hand in faith and touched the coat of the Messiah. When Jesus asked who touched him, she knew he was talking to her. She had felt his instant, miraculous healing! (Mark 5:21–34)

to come. [13]Then I saw three evil spirits that looked like frogs coming out of the mouth of the dragon, out of the mouth of the beast, and out of the mouth of the false prophet. [14]These evil spirits are the spirits of demons, which have power to do miracles. They go out to the kings of the whole world to gather them together for the battle on the great day of God Almighty.

[15]"Listen! I will come as a thief comes! Blessed are those who stay awake and keep their clothes on so that they will not walk around naked and have people see their shame."

[16]Then the evil spirits gathered the kings together to the place that is called Armageddon in the Hebrew language.

[17]The seventh angel poured out his bowl into the air. Then a loud voice came out of the temple from the throne, saying, "It is finished!" [18]Then there were flashes of lightning, noises, thunder, and a big earthquake—the worst earthquake that has ever happened since people have been on earth. [19]The great city split into three parts, and the cities of the nations were destroyed. And God remembered the sins of Babylon the Great, so he gave that city the cup filled with the wine of his terrible anger. [20]Then every island ran away, and mountains disappeared. [21]Giant hailstones, each weighing about a hundred pounds, fell from the sky upon people. People cursed God for the disaster of the hail, because this disaster was so terrible.

The Woman on the Animal

17 Then one of the seven angels who had the seven bowls came and spoke to me. He said, "Come, and I will show you the punishment that will be given to the great prostitute, the one sitting over many waters. [2]The kings of the earth sinned sexually with her, and the people of the earth became drunk from the wine of her sexual sin."

[3]Then the angel carried me away by the Spirit to the desert. There I saw a woman sitting on a red beast. It was covered with names against God written on it, and it had seven heads and ten horns. [4]The woman was dressed in purple and red and was shining with the gold, precious jewels, and pearls she was wearing. She had a golden cup in her hand, a cup filled with evil things and the uncleanness of her sexual sin. [5]On her forehead a title was written that was secret. This is what was written:

THE GREAT BABYLON
MOTHER OF PROSTITUTES
AND OF THE EVIL THINGS OF THE EARTH

[6]Then I saw that the woman was drunk with the blood of God's holy people and with the blood of those who were killed because of their faith in Jesus.

When I saw the woman, I was very amazed. [7]Then the angel said to me, "Why are you amazed? I will tell you the secret of this woman and the beast she rides—the one with seven heads and ten horns. [8]The beast you saw was once alive but is not alive now. But soon it will come up out of the bottomless pit and go away to be destroyed. There are people who live on earth whose names have not been written in the book of life since the beginning of the world. They will be amazed when they see the beast, because he was once alive, is not alive now, but will come again.

[9]"You need a wise mind to understand this. The seven heads on the beast are seven mountains where the woman sits. [10]And they are seven kings. Five of the kings have already been destroyed, one of the kings lives now, and another has not yet come. When he comes, he must stay a short time. [11]The beast that was once alive, but is not alive now, is also an eighth king. He belongs to the first seven kings, and he will go away to be destroyed.

[12]"The ten horns you saw are ten kings who have not yet begun to rule, but they will receive power to rule with the beast for one hour. [13]All ten of these kings have the same purpose, and they will give their power and authority to the beast. [14]They will make war against the Lamb, but the Lamb will defeat them, because he is Lord of lords and King of kings. He will defeat them with his called, chosen, and faithful followers."

[15]Then the angel said to me, "The waters that you saw, where the prostitute sits, are peoples, races, nations, and languages. [16]The ten horns and the beast you saw will hate the prostitute. They will take everything she has and leave her naked. They will eat her body and burn her with fire. [17]God made the ten horns want to carry out his purpose by agreeing to give the beast their power to rule, until what God has said comes about. [18]The woman you saw is the great city that rules over the kings of the earth."

Babylon Is Destroyed

18 After the vision of these things, I saw another angel coming down from heaven. This angel had great power, and his glory made the earth bright. [2]He shouted in a powerful voice:

"Ruined, ruined is the great city of
Babylon!
She has become a home for
demons

and a prison for every evil spirit,
and a prison for every unclean bird and unclean beast.

[3]She has been ruined, because all the peoples of the earth
have drunk the wine of the desire of her sexual sin.
She has been ruined also because the kings of the earth
have sinned sexually with her,
and the merchants of the earth
have grown rich from the great wealth of her luxury."

[4]Then I heard another voice from heaven saying:

"Come out of that city, my people,
so that you will not share in her sins,
so that you will not receive the disasters that will come to her.
[5]Her sins have piled up as high as the sky,
and God has not forgotten the wrongs she has done.
[6]Give that city the same as she gave to others.
Pay her back twice as much as she did.
Prepare wine for her that is twice as strong
as the wine she prepared for others.
[7]She gave herself much glory and rich living.
Give her that much suffering and sadness.
She says to herself, 'I am a queen sitting on my throne.
I am not a widow; I will never be sad.'
[8]So these disasters will come to her in one day:
death, and crying, and great hunger,
and she will be destroyed by fire,
because the Lord God who judges her is powerful."

[9]The kings of the earth who sinned sexually with her and shared her wealth will see the smoke from her burning. Then they will cry and be sad because of her death. [10]They will be afraid of her suffering and stand far away and say:

"Terrible! How terrible for you, great city,
powerful city of Babylon,
because your punishment has come in one hour!"

[11]And the merchants of the earth will cry and be sad about her, because now there is no one to buy their cargoes— [12]cargoes of gold, silver, jewels, pearls, fine linen, purple cloth, silk, red cloth; all kinds of citron wood and all kinds of things made from ivory, expensive wood, bronze, iron, and marble; [13]cinnamon, spice, incense, myrrh, frankincense, wine, olive oil, fine flour, wheat, cattle, sheep, horses, carriages, slaves, and human lives.

[14]The merchants will say,

"Babylon, the good things you wanted are gone from you.
All your rich and fancy things have disappeared.
You will never have them again."

[15]The merchants who became rich from selling to her will be afraid of her suffering and will stand far away. They will cry and be sad [16]and say:

"Terrible! How terrible for the great city!
She was dressed in fine linen, purple and red cloth,
and she was shining with gold, precious jewels, and pearls!
[17]All these riches have been destroyed in one hour!"

Every sea captain, every passenger, the sailors, and all those who earn their living from the sea stood far away from Babylon. [18]As they saw the smoke from her burning, they cried out loudly, "There was never a city like this great city!" [19]And they threw dust on their heads and cried out, weeping and being sad. They said:

"Terrible! How terrible for the great city!
All the people who had ships on the sea
became rich because of her wealth!
But she has been destroyed in one hour!
[20]Be happy because of this, heaven!
Be happy, God's holy people and apostles and prophets!
God has punished her because of what she did to you."

[21]Then a powerful angel picked up a large stone, like one used for grinding grain, and threw it into the sea. He said:

"In the same way, the great city of Babylon will be thrown down,
and it will never be found again.
[22]The music of people playing harps
and other instruments, flutes, and trumpets,
will never be heard in you again.
No workman doing any job

all about MEN

Tenderhearted Toughness

From birth, many guys grow up hearing about the importance of physical prowess and power. Little boys love to flex their "big muscles"! God wired them to be protectors and providers, admirable qualities that show up on the playground, in the locker room, on the job, and in the home. But don't mistake tough exteriors as all that goes on inside them. God also instilled men with tenderness, which unfortunately can get buried beneath their day-to-day need to appear strong. When life deals them blows, the hurts are real, so take care of their hearts. Even the toughest tough guy has a tender side. Ask God to empower the men you know with Jesus' strength and compassion (Mark 6:34; Acts 4:10). Now *that's* tenderhearted toughness!

Revelation 19:7

Everyone knows that planning a wedding is an enormous project, full of fun tasks and decisions. What flowers will brilliantly fill the room? What colors will the wedding party wear? What will the bride's dress be like? So much effort goes into every detail to commemorate two people starting a brand new life together. Such an exciting and beautiful thing deserves a grand celebration!

The church has been given the honor of being the bride of Christ. Right now, we're still in the engagement phase, anticipating the great wedding to come. This time between Jesus' life on earth and his Second Coming is meant to prepare us. Slowly but surely, the church is getting ready to be Christ's pure bride! Even the best love stories on earth are just tiny glimpses of the incredible love Jesus has for us.

For Christians, the events in Revelation are the beginning of our grand celebration and "marriage" with Christ! Every sadness will be healed, we'll be reunited with our loved ones, we'll meet Christians from throughout history—and best of all, we'll glorify Jesus face-to-face.

When life starts to get you down, ask God for an eternal perspective. Make every day a miniature celebration of your future hope in Christ!

will ever be found in you again.
The sound of grinding grain
will never be heard in you again.
[23]The light of a lamp
will never shine in you again,
and the voices of a bridegroom and bride
will never be heard in you again.
Your merchants were the world's great people,
and all the nations were tricked by your magic.
[24]You are guilty of the death of the prophets and God's holy people
and all who have been killed on earth."

People in Heaven Praise God

19 After this vision and announcement I heard what sounded like a great many people in heaven saying:

"Hallelujah![n]
Salvation, glory, and power belong to our God,
[2] because his judgments are true and right.
He has punished the prostitute
who made the earth evil with her sexual sin.
He has paid her back for the death of his servants."

[3]Again they said:
"Hallelujah!
She is burning, and her smoke will rise forever and ever."

[4]Then the twenty-four elders and the four living creatures bowed down and worshiped God, who sits on the throne. They said:

"Amen, Hallelujah!"

[5]Then a voice came from the throne, saying:

"Praise our God, all you who serve him
and all you who honor him, both small and great!"

[6]Then I heard what sounded like a great many people, like the noise of flooding water, and like the noise of loud thunder. The people were saying:

"Hallelujah!
Our Lord God, the Almighty, rules.
[7]Let us rejoice and be happy
and give God glory,
because the wedding of the Lamb has come,
and the Lamb's bride has made herself ready.
[8]Fine linen, bright and clean, was given to her to wear."

(The fine linen means the good things done by God's holy people.)

[9]And the angel said to me, "Write this: Blessed are those who have been invited to the wedding meal of the Lamb!" And the angel said, "These are the true words of God."

[10]Then I bowed down at the angel's feet to worship him, but he said to me, "Do not worship me! I am a servant like you and your brothers and sisters who have the message of Jesus. Worship God, because the message about Jesus is the spirit that gives all prophecy."

The Rider on the White Horse

[11]Then I saw heaven opened, and there before me was a white horse. The rider on the horse is called Faithful and True, and he is right when he judges and makes war. [12]His eyes are like burning fire, and on his head are many crowns. He has a name written on him, which no one but himself knows. [13]He is dressed in a robe dipped in blood, and his name is the Word of God.

19:1 Hallelujah This means "praise God!"

[14]The armies of heaven, dressed in fine linen, white and clean, were following him on white horses. [15]Out of the rider's mouth comes a sharp sword that he will use to defeat the nations, and he will rule them with a rod of iron. He will crush out the wine in the winepress of the terrible anger of God the Almighty. [16]On his robe and on his upper leg was written this name: KING OF KINGS AND LORD OF LORDS.

[17]Then I saw an angel standing in the sun, and he called with a loud voice to all the birds flying in the sky: "Come and gather together for the great feast of God [18]so that you can eat the bodies of kings, generals, mighty people, horses and their riders, and the bodies of all people—free, slave, small, and great."

[19]Then I saw the beast and the kings of the earth. Their armies were gathered together to make war against the rider on the horse and his army. [20]But the beast was captured and with him the false prophet who did the miracles for the beast. The false prophet had used these miracles to trick those who had the mark of the beast and worshiped his idol. The false prophet and the beast were thrown alive into the lake of fire that burns with sulfur. [21]And their armies were killed with the sword that came out of the mouth of the rider on the horse, and all the birds ate the bodies until they were full.

The Thousand Years

20 I saw an angel coming down from heaven. He had the key to the bottomless pit and a large chain in his hand. [2]The angel grabbed the dragon, that old snake who is the devil and Satan, and tied him up for a thousand years. [3]Then he threw him into the bottomless pit, closed it, and locked it over him. The angel did this so he could not trick the people of the earth anymore until the thousand years were ended. After a thousand years he must be set free for a short time.

[4]Then I saw some thrones and people sitting on them who had been given the power to judge. And I saw the souls of those who had been killed because they were faithful to the message of Jesus and the message from God. They had not worshiped the beast or his idol, and they had not received the mark of the beast on their foreheads or on their hands. They came back to life and ruled with Christ for a thousand years. [5](The others that were dead did not live again until the thousand years were ended.) This is the first raising of the dead. [6]Blessed and holy are those who share in this first raising of the dead. The second death has no power over them. They will be priests for God and for Christ and will rule with him for a thousand years.

[7]When the thousand years are over, Satan will be set free from his prison. [8]Then he will go out to trick the nations in all the earth—Gog and Magog—to gather them for battle. There are so many people they will be like sand on the seashore. [9]And Satan's army marched across the earth and gathered around the camp of God's people and the city God loves. But fire came down from heaven and burned them up. [10]And Satan, who tricked them, was thrown into the lake of burning sulfur with the beast and the false prophet. There they will be punished day and night forever and ever.

People of the World Are Judged

[11]Then I saw a great white throne and the One who was sitting on it. Earth and sky ran away from him and disappeared. [12]And I saw the dead, great and small, standing before the throne. Then books were opened, and the book of life was opened. The dead were judged by what they had done, which was written in the books. [13]The sea gave up the dead who were in it, and Death and Hades[n] gave up the dead who were in them. Each person was judged by what he had done. [14]And Death and Hades were thrown into the lake of fire. The lake of fire is the second death. [15]And anyone whose name was not found written in the book of life was thrown into the lake of fire.

The New Jerusalem

21 Then I saw a new heaven and a new earth. The first heaven and the first earth had disappeared, and there was no sea anymore. [2]And I saw the holy city, the new Jerusalem,[n] coming down out of heaven from God. It was prepared like a bride dressed for her husband. [3]And I heard a loud voice from the throne, saying, "Now God's presence is with people, and he will live with them, and they will be his people. God himself will be with them and will be their God.[n] [4]He will wipe away every tear from their eyes, and there will be no more death, sadness, crying, or pain, because all the old ways are gone."

[5]The One who was sitting on the throne said, "Look! I am making everything new!" Then he said, "Write this, because these words are true and can be trusted."

[6]The One on the throne said to me, "It

The Praise Family

Have you ever taken a worship stroll through your spiritual history? Worshiping God through his Word can remind you of the spiritual family you're a part of (Hebrews 12:1). Read those ancient writers' praises, and take joy knowing your worship joins theirs. Right now David could be repeating his words from Psalm 66:3–4, this time from heaven, inviting you to "Say to God, 'Your works are amazing! . . . All the earth worships you and sings praises to you.'" Or Peter, who encouraged faraway Christians: "Praise be to the God and Father of our Lord Jesus Christ" (1 Peter 1:3). Just as worship is eternal, God's family shares a forever hope in Christ. (See also 1 Samuel 2:1–10 and Luke 1:46–55.)

20:13 Hades The place of the dead. **21:2 new Jerusalem** The spiritual city where God's people live with him. **21:3 and . . . God** Some Greek copies do not have this phrase.

is finished. I am the Alpha and the Omega,[n] the Beginning and the End. I will give free water from the spring of the water of life to anyone who is thirsty. [7]Those who win the victory will receive this, and I will be their God, and they will be my children. [8]But cowards, those who refuse to believe, who do evil things, who kill, who sin sexually, who do evil magic, who worship idols, and who tell lies—all these will have a place in the lake of burning sulfur. This is the second death."

[9]Then one of the seven angels who had the seven bowls full of the seven last troubles came to me, saying, "Come with me, and I will show you the bride, the wife of the Lamb." [10]And the angel carried me away by the Spirit to a very large and high mountain. He showed me the holy city, Jerusalem, coming down out of heaven from God. [11]It was shining with the glory of God and was bright like a very expensive jewel, like a jasper, clear as crystal. [12]The city had a great high wall with twelve gates with twelve angels at the gates, and on each gate was written the name of one of the twelve tribes of Israel. [13]There were three gates on the east, three on the north, three on the south, and three on the west. [14]The walls of the city were built on twelve foundation stones, and on the stones were written the names of the twelve apostles of the Lamb.

[15]The angel who talked with me had a measuring rod made of gold to measure the city, its gates, and its wall. [16]The city was built in a square, and its length was equal to its width. The angel measured the city with the rod. The city was 1,500 miles long, 1,500 miles wide, and 1,500 miles high. [17]The angel also measured the wall. It was 216 feet high, by human measurements, which the angel was using. [18]The wall was made of jasper, and the city was made of pure gold, as pure as glass. [19]The foundation stones of the city walls were decorated with every kind of jewel. The first foundation was jasper, the second was sapphire, the third was chalcedony, the fourth was emerald, [20]the fifth was onyx, the sixth was carnelian, the seventh was chrysolite, the eighth was beryl, the ninth was topaz, the tenth was chrysoprase, the eleventh was jacinth, and the twelfth was amethyst. [21]The twelve gates were twelve pearls, each gate having been made from a single pearl. And the street of the city was made of pure gold as clear as glass.

[22]I did not see a temple in the city, because the Lord God Almighty and the Lamb are the city's temple. [23]The city does not need the sun or the moon to shine on it, because the glory of God is its light, and the Lamb is the city's lamp. [24]By its light the people of the world will walk, and the kings of the earth will bring their glory into it. [25]The city's gates will never be shut on any day, because there is no night there. [26]The glory and the honor of the nations will be brought into it. [27]Nothing unclean and no one who does shameful things or tells lies will ever go into it. Only those whose names are written in the Lamb's book of life will enter the city.

22

Then the angel showed me the river of the water of life. It was shining like crystal and was flowing from the throne of God and of the Lamb [2]down the middle of the street of the city. The tree of life was on each side of the river. It produces fruit twelve times a year, once each month. The leaves of the tree are for the healing of all the nations. [3]Nothing that God judges guilty will be in that city. The throne of God and of the Lamb will be there, and God's servants will worship him. [4]They will see his face, and his name will be written on their foreheads. [5]There will never be night again. They will not need the light of a lamp or the light of the sun, because the Lord God will give them light. And they will rule as kings forever and ever.

[6]The angel said to me, "These words can be trusted and are true." The Lord, the God of the spirits of the prophets, sent his angel to show his servants the things that must happen soon.

[7]"Listen! I am coming soon! Blessed is the one who obeys the words of prophecy in this book."

[8]I, John, am the one who heard and saw these things. When I heard and

Be Still & KNOW

Letters to God

The Bible has been described as God's love letter to his creation. It's full of his words to mankind and reflects different aspects of his character, emotions, plans, heartbreaks, and victories. Have you ever considered returning the favor? That's what a prayer journal can be—your version of a reply to the love letter God sent you. As you write out your daily prayers, you will reflect different aspects of your character just like he did. Writing your thoughts down on paper can be a great help in expressing what's inside. And it can help you tremendously in staying focused during your personal prayer time, too. Go ahead, give it a try. Begin your reply today!

21:6 Alpha and the Omega The first and last letters of the Greek alphabet. This means "the beginning and the end."

saw them, I bowed down to worship at the feet of the angel who showed these things to me. [9]But the angel said to me, "Do not worship me! I am a servant like you, your brothers the prophets, and all those who obey the words in this book. Worship God!"

[10]Then the angel told me, "Do not keep secret the words of prophecy in this book, because the time is near for all this to happen. [11]Let whoever is doing evil continue to do evil. Let whoever is unclean continue to be unclean. Let whoever is doing right continue to do right. Let whoever is holy continue to be holy."

[12]"Listen! I am coming soon! I will bring my reward with me, and I will repay each one of you for what you have done. [13]I am the Alpha and the Omega,[n] the First and the Last, the Beginning and the End.

[14]"Blessed are those who wash their robes[n] so that they will receive the right to eat the fruit from the tree of life and may go through the gates into the city. [15]Outside the city are the evil people, those who do evil magic, who sin sexually, who murder, who worship idols, and who love lies and tell lies.

[16]"I, Jesus, have sent my angel to tell you these things for the churches. I am the descendant from the family of David, and I am the bright morning star."

[17]The Spirit and the bride say, "Come!" Let the one who hears this say, "Come!" Let whoever is thirsty come; whoever wishes may have the water of life as a free gift.

[18]I warn everyone who hears the words of the prophecy of this book: If anyone adds anything to these words, God will add to that person the disasters written about in this book. [19]And if anyone takes away from the words of this book of prophecy, God will take away that one's share of the tree of life and of the holy city, which are written about in this book.

[20]Jesus, the One who says these things are true, says, "Yes, I am coming soon."

Amen. Come, Lord Jesus!

[21]The grace of the Lord Jesus be with all. Amen.

22:13 Alpha and the Omega The first and last letters of the Greek alphabet. This means "the beginning and the end." **22:14 wash their robes** This means they believed and obeyed Jesus so that their sins could be forgiven by Christ's blood. The "washing" may refer to baptism (Acts 22:16).

Revelation

Holy Is the Lord

It's the final showdown between God and Satan. Simply put, Satan loses; God wins. In his victory message through John, God provides some details about the end and how crucial it is to know and follow Jesus now.

Throughout the Old Testament, God is characterized by his holiness, judgment, and wrath as well as his grace, mercy, and love for his people. In the New Testament, God gives his Son, Jesus Christ, as a sacrifice to defeat sin and restore his children to himself. God promises the glory of heaven to those who call on the name of Jesus. This is all recaptured in the words of Revelation as God pours out destruction on evil in the world and describes the unfathomable beauty of eternity with Jesus. In the end, those who have authentic faith in Jesus Christ will be ushered into the very presence of God. Forever.

John shares a glimpse of heaven in which different creatures "give glory, honor, and thanks to the One who sits on the throne, who lives forever and ever" (Revelation 4:9). They don't ever stop saying the words, "Holy, holy, holy is the Lord God Almighty. He was, he is, and he is coming" (4:8). Then elders bow before the Lord and say he is worthy to receive glory, honor, and power (4:11). They know the Lord and worship him.

In heaven, our lives will be defined by worship—true, unending worship. We will know the fullness and holiness of God. We will be in complete awe. No more sin; only God's glory. This is what awaits believers—for eternity.

Get Real

Why is God worthy of your worship? (Job 36:22—37:24; Revelation 5:9–14)

How do you worship God? (2 Samuel 6:14; Psalms 95; 100; John 4:23–24)

What will heaven be like? (Isaiah 66:1; Revelation 21)

How can you live now with heaven in mind? (Matthew 3:2; 5:1–3, 19–20)

The Miracles of Jesus Christ

Miracle	Matthew	Mark	Luke	John
1. Healing a Man with Skin Disease	8:2	1:40	5:12	
2. Healing an Army Officer's Servant (of paralysis)	8:5		7:1	
3. Healing Peter's Mother-in-law	8:14	1:30	4:38	
4. Healing the Sick at Evening	8:16	1:32	4:40	
5. Calming the Storm	8:23	4:35	8:22	
6. Demons Entering a Herd of Pigs	8:28	5:1	8:26	
7. Healing a Paralyzed Man	9:2	2:3	5:18	
8. Raising the Synagogue Leader's Daughter	9:18, 23	5:22, 35	8:40, 49	
9. Healing the Hemorrhaging Woman	9:20	5:25	8:43	
10. Healing Two Blind Men	9:27			
11. Curing a Demon-possessed, Mute Man	9:32			
12. Healing a Man's Crippled Hand	12:9	3:1	6:6	
13. Curing a Demon-possessed, Blind, and Mute Man	12:22		11:14	
14. Feeding the Five Thousand	14:13	6:30	9:10	6:1
15. Walking on the Lake	14:25	6:48		6:19
16. Healing the Non-Jewish Woman's Daughter	15:21	7:24		
17. Feeding the Four Thousand	15:32	8:1		
18. Healing the Epileptic Boy	17:14	9:17	9:38	
19. Temple Tax in the Fish's Mouth	17:24			
20. Healing Two Blind Men	20:30	10:46	18:35	
21. Drying Up the Fig Tree	21:18	11:12		
22. Casting Out an Evil Spirit		1:23	4:33	
23. Healing a Deaf and Dumb Man		7:31		
24. Healing a Blind Man at Bethsaida		8:22		
25. Escape from the Hostile Multitude			4:30	
26. Catch of Fish			5:1	
27. Raising of a Widow's Son at Nain			7:11	
28. Healing the Infirm, Crippled Woman			13:11	
29. Healing the Man with Dropsy			14:1	
30. Cleansing the Ten Men with Skin Disease			17:11	
31. Restoring a Servant's Ear			22:51	
32. Turning Water into Wine				2:1
33. Healing the Officer's Son				4:46
34. Healing a Sick Man at Bethzatha				5:1
35. Healing a Man Born Blind				9:1
36. Raising of Lazarus				11:43
37. Second Catch of Fish				21:1